The Ecology and Biology

of Mammal-like Reptiles

Nicholas Hotton III, Paul D. MacLean,
Jan J. Roth, and E. Carol Roth
Editors

Smithsonian Institution Press
Washington and London
1986

∞

The paper used in this publication meets the
minimum requirements of the American National
Standard for Permanence of Paper for Printed
Library Materials Z39.48–1984.

Library of Congress Cataloging-in-Publication Data
Main entry under title:

The Ecology and biology of mammal-like reptiles.

　Includes index.
　Supt. of Docs. no.: SI 1.2:R29/4
　1. Synapsida—Congresses.　I. Hotton, Nicholas.
QE862.S8E25　1986　　567.9′3　　85-600207
ISBN 0-87474-524-1
ISBN 0-87474-519-5 (pbk.)

Contents

Dedication   vii

Acknowledgments   viii

Preface   ix

Neurobehavioral significance of the mammal-like reptiles (therapsids),
P. D. MacLean   1

ORIGIN, MORPHOLOGY, AND RELATIONSHIPS   23

The skeletal anatomy and some aspects of the physiology of primitive reptiles,
R. L. Carroll   25

Relationships and ecology of the early therapsids and their predecessors,
E. C. Olson   47

Locomotion and body form in early therapsids (Dinocephalia, Gorgonopsia, and Therocephalia),
H.-D. Sues   61

Dicynodonts and their role as primary consumers,
N. Hotton III   71

An analysis of therapsid relationships,
J. A. Hopson and H. R. Barghusen   83

OF TIME AND PLACE   107

Permian-Triassic paleogeography and paleoclimatology and implications for therapsid distribution,
J. M. Parrish, J. T. Parrish, and A. M. Ziegler   109

Therapsids in Pangaea and their contemporaries and competitors,
E. H. Colbert   133

BIOLOGICAL PROBLEMS AND THERAPSID SOLUTIONS   147

Neurobiology of the therapsid-mammal transition,
P. S. Ulinski   149

The parietal foramen and eye: their function and fate in therapsids,
J. J. Roth, E. C. Roth, and N. Hotton III   173

Body size, homeothermy and the control of heat exchange in mammal-like reptiles,
J. S. Turner and C. R. Tracy   185

A biophysical analysis of possible thermoregulatory adaptations in sailed pelycosaurs,
C. R. Tracy, J. S. Turner, and R. B. Huey   195

The metabolic and thermoregulatory status of therapsids,
A. F. Bennett and J. A. Ruben   207

A new question of pheromones: aspects of possible chemical signaling and reception in the mammal-like reptiles,
D. Duvall   219

The evolution of mammalian reproductive characteristics in therapsid reptiles,
L. J. Guillette, Jr., and N. Hotton III   239

TRANSITION, ADVANCED CYNODONTS TO MAMMALS   251

On the evolutionary origin of the therian tensor veli palatini and tensor tympani muscles,
H. R. Barghausen   253

Changes in mandibular function following the acquisition of a dentary-squamosal jaw articulation,
A. W. Crompton and W. L. Hylander   263

The auditory apparatus of advanced mammal-like reptiles and early mammals,
E. F. Allin   283

Nearctylodon broomi, the first Nearctic tritylodont,
G. E. Lewis   295

SUMMARY   305

Therapsids and their environment, a summary,
J. A. Ruben   307

Commentary on continental drift and therapsid evolution,
David Challinor   313

Index   317

Dedication

We are pleased to dedicate this volume to Dr. John C. Eberhart, who served for two decades as director of the Mental Health Intramural Research Program of the National Institute of Mental Health (NIMH).

John Eberhart would be the first to point out that numerous individuals and organizations contributed to the success of the conference reported herein. But his was a signal contribution. When he assumed directorship of the Intramural Research Program in 1961, Dr. Eberhart was quick to recognize—and champion—the value of the comparative method and ethological approach to research on the brain. He accepted the challenge of establishing an animal research facility that would be devoted to evolutionary studies of the brain. Over the next ten years, Dr. Eberhart met frequently with the scientists, architects, and landscapers for detailed planning of the laboratories and habitats to be located at the National Institute of Health (NIH) Animal Center, already under construction in Poolesville, Maryland near the Potomac River.

The Laboratory of Brain Evolution and Behavior (LBEB) opened in 1971, providing a setting in which biological and behavioral scientists could work collaboratively in the study and observation of animals in a quasi-natural habitat. Over the next decade, the LBEB served as a unique national and international resource for research on brain and behavior, and as a useful and productive forum for multidisciplinary communication aimed at comprehensive understanding of brain development and function.

In 1981, the year in which the conference on *The Ecology and Biology of the Mammal-like Reptiles* was convened, Dr. Eberhart accepted the position of senior advisor to the deputy director for Intramural Research, NIH. Yet the continuity and direction that Dr. Eberhart provided to the NIMH and to the mental health research field extensively during his more than twenty years of able scientific leadership will not soon be forgotten.

It is my privilege, on behalf of my predecessors and colleagues, as well as future generations of scientists at the NIMH, to dedicate this volume to Dr. Eberhart, We do so with respect, affection, and gratitude for his lifelong dedication to science, to the goals of the Institute, and to the joy of learning.

Shervert H. Frazier, M.D.
Director
National Institute of Mental Health

Acknowledgments

It is our pleasant duty to express our thanks to John C. Eberhart, Robert A. Cohen, and Hazel W. Rea of the Intramural Research Program, National Institute of Mental Health (NIMH), who during 1979–81, provided the encouragement and support to organize a small "Conference on the Ecology and Biology of the Mammal-like Reptiles" at the Laboratory of Brain Evolution and Behavior. Since the Laboratory itself would never have come into being without the continued efforts of Dr. Eberhart during the planning phase of the 1960s, it seemed to us that no acknowledgment short of dedicating this volume to him would be sufficient. We thank Hazel Rea for officiating in Dr. Eberhart's place on the opening day of the Conference, and for her gracious introductory remarks.

We thank S. Dillon Ripley, who in 1964, in one of his first acts as Secretary of the Smithsonian Institution, encouraged a consortium of local institutions involved in the investigation of the biology of behavior, and thereby created the spirit conducive to the cosponsorship of the Conference by the Smithsonian Institution. We also thank David Challinor, Assistant Secretary for Science, Smithsonian Institution (SI), not only for endorsing support of the Conference but also for his participation in the meeting.

We express our indebtedness to William C. Atlee and Claire Drullard (Printing and Publications Management Branch, Alcohol, Drug Abuse, and Mental Health Administration) for their help in making the preliminary arrangements for publication of the proceedings of the Conference, and to Felix C. Lowe and Maureen R. Jacoby (Smithsonian Institution Press) for their many helpful consultations and facilitating efforts in our behalf.

We thank the members of our staffs, whose contributions are specified in the articles written by us. Thanks are also due to Teri L. Davis, Alan Carter, and Mary E. Parrish, for their work in editing, design, and illustration, respectively, as well as to Siegfried M. Clemens (Intramural Research Program, NIMH), John R. Ouellette (SI Press), and Joseph H. Shealy (Contracts Office, SI) for their cooperation in making the business arrangements.

Preface

As Broom observed in his monumental work on "The Mammal-like Reptiles of South Africa" (1932), these animals are of great importance because "there is little doubt that among them we have the ancestors of mammals and the remote ancestors of human beings." Accordingly, he said, the remains found in the Karroo beds of South Africa "may be safely regarded as the most important fossil animals ever discovered." Yet despite their immense biological significance, mammal-like reptiles have never achieved the general visibility of more recent reptiles such as dinosaurs, and it is time this was corrected. The present volume, and the conference at which it was generated, are parts of an attempt to disseminate informed opinion about mammal-like reptiles to a more general audience, beyond the confines of paleontological technology.

The mammal-like reptiles belong to the subclass Synapsida, a name alluding to the presence of a single temporal opening. Primitive synapsid reptiles, with a small opening, are known as pelycosaurs, and are found in greatest abundance in the redbeds of Texas, of early Permian age. The body form of pelycosaurs is so lizard-like that one genus is named *Varanosaurus,* after extant monitor lizards. More advanced synapsids are called therapsids because the enlarged temporal opening has a resemblance to that of mammals. The posture of therapsids had acquired mammalian characteristics. Therapsids developed specialized feeding habits, becoming primarily carnivorous or herbivorous. They dominated the land fauna from mid-Permian to mid-Triassic times; their remains have been found on every continent, reflecting their widespread distribution when there was a single landmass, now known as Pangaea.

In the fifty years that have elapsed since the appearance of Broom's monograph, substantive progress has been made in the understanding of the therapsid-mammal transition. The conference accounting for the present volume brought workers in paleontology and biology together, to focus attention almost entirely on synapsid reptiles, reviewing past and recent studies in a search for a more complete picture of their neurobehavioral capacities. Such a review might also serve as an impetus to obtain information about the cerebral development of an extensive range of mammal-like reptiles. At present, there is available only a handful of endocranial casts and other material for obtaining clues about the morphology of the brain in these animals.

It was hoped that the conference might also stimulate further field and laboratory research concerning several biological and behavioral questions. For example, further field studies might turn up evidence as to whether or not mammal-like reptiles laid eggs, and might provide information about possible parental-offspring relationships, as judged by the number and size of individuals found in close proximity. Laboratory studies focusing on musculoskeletal markings and other anatomical details might give clues as to whether or not therapsids engaged in communicative displays.

As reported in the present volume, anatomical studies have supplied considerable detail about the mechanics of the masticatory apparatus of these animals. Analysis of the aural region suggests that the therapsids may have been capable of audiovocal communication.

A clarification of thermoregulation in mammal-like reptiles is basic to inferences regarding their biological and behavioral capacities. It is perhaps in this area that questions can be most profitably addressed at the present time. Papers in this volume discuss evidence regarding the transition from a cold-blooded to a warm-blooded condition in the evolution of mammal-like reptiles. Two contributions pertaining to thermoregulation deal with the controversial question as to whether or not the disappearance of the parietal eye ("third eye") in advanced therapsids reflects the acquisition of endothermy. The parietal eye-pineal complex derives from the epiphysis that forms part of the enigmatic habenulopeduncular system found in all vertebrates. Many species of lizards found in high latitudes have a parietal eye. The finding that excision of the parietal eye in such lizards results in a 2°C elevation of the eccritic temperature suggests that the habenulopeduncular system may be involved in thermoregulation.

The year of the conference marked the tenth anniversary of the opening of the Laboratory of Brain Evolution and Behavior near Poolesville, Maryland. The meetings on the first two days (June 10 and 11, 1981) took place at the Laboratory. The sessions on the last day were held in the Carmichael Auditorium at the National Museum of American History, Smithsonian Institution. It would have been most desirable to have included participants beyond North America, but circumstances dictated otherwise.

PAUL D. MACLEAN
Laboratory of Brain Evolution and Behavior
National Institute of Mental Health
Bethesda, Maryland 20205

Neurobehavioral Significance of the Mammal-like Reptiles (Therapsids)

Introduction

If we except the Pliocene age, . . . there is no period in the world's history so important as that from the Middle Permian to the Upper Trias, as it was during this time that a group of reptiles slowly evolved into more and more mammal-like forms, and ultimately gave rise to primitive but true mammals.

And in the South African Karroo shales we have a nearly continuous history of the land animals of this important period, and the study of the various beds is like examining the pages of a book of history.

Robert Broom, 1932

The mammal-like reptiles (Synapsida) are of great human interest because they are so close to the roots of our family tree. Despite their genealogical significance, these long extinct animals, particularly the forms known as therapsids, have received little attention in books on evolution, and compared with dinosaurs and some other reptilian species, are relatively unknown. In Permian times, long before the dinosaurs (Fig. 1), the mammal-like reptiles populated the world in great numbers. Their remains have turned up on every continent, recalling Alfred Wegener's (1915) original contention that 250 million years ago the earth formed a single land mass, which he called Pangaea. Between 1969 and 1971, fossils of mammal-like reptiles found in Antarctica were the same kind as those in the Karroo beds of South Africa (see Colbert,

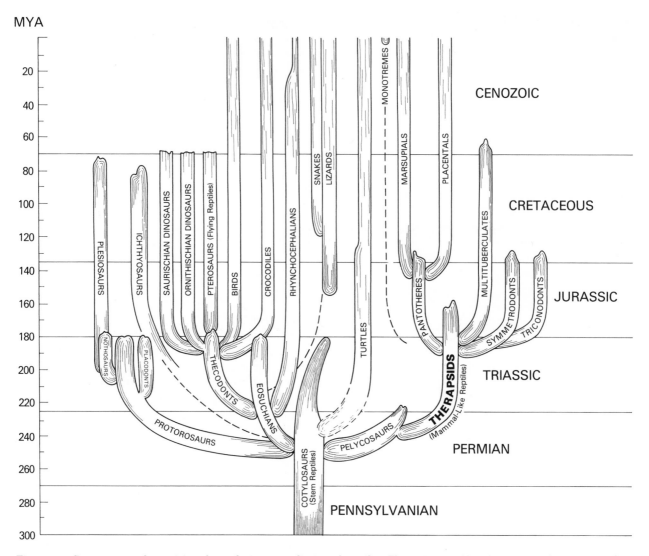

Figure 1. Cactus tree, schematizing the evolutionary radiation of reptiles. The rightmost branch gives emphasis to the therapsid line leading to mammals. Details of the tree are based largely on Romer (1966) and Colbert (1966). The dates for the geological periods are those of Holmes's "final time scale" (see Faul, 1978). MYA, million years ago. (From MacLean, forthcoming.)

1972). Antarctica had been connected to South Africa, forming part of the great southern continent, which Edward Suess (1904) called Gondwanaland because the strata of the untilted table mountains of Africa and South America resembled those of the Gondwana region of India.

In the evolutionary transition from reptiles to mammals, three outstanding behavioral developments were nursing, in conjunction with maternal care, audiovocal communication for maintaining maternal-offspring contact, and playful behavior (MacLean, 1982a, b, 1985). For a further understanding of human evolution, it is of fundamental interest to inquire how these behavioral changes developed. The changes set the stage for a family way of life with its evolving

responsibilities and affiliations that has led to the worldwide acculturation of human beings.

Basically, the behavioral triad in question depended on developments within the brain. In that case, what may one expect to learn from the study of extinct animals, since in fossils, under the best of conditions, nothing remains but the shadow of the brain itself? One answer is that cranial endocasts or reconstructions of the cranial cavity provide information about the form and size of the enclosed brain that may give clues regarding function, as, for example, the evidence of a large olfactory apparatus in some of the mammal-like cynodonts (see below). In the case of the therapsids, there is at the present time only a handful of endocranial casts, and, as far as I know, there are no satisfactory casts of the most advanced forms. Perhaps it was this consideration more than any other that provided the impetus to plan the present conference—the hope being that, directly or indirectly, it might arouse interest in pursuing comparative studies of the endocranial changes occurring in the evolution of therapsids.

There is the related consideration that a further study of other skeletal features of therapsids might help to answer questions that would shed light on their individual and social behavior that in turn might give some indication of their cerebral capabilities. The kinds of questions that arise can be better appreciated after providing background derived from ongoing comparative neurobehavioral studies.

Neurobehavioral Background

Cerebral evolution

The comparative study of brains of extant vertebrates, together with an examination of the fossil record, indicates that the human forebrain has expanded to its great size while retaining features of three basic evolutionary formations that respectively reflect ancestral commonalities with reptiles, early mammals, and late mammals (Fig. 2) (MacLean, 1962, 1970, 1973a). Markedly different in structure and chemistry,

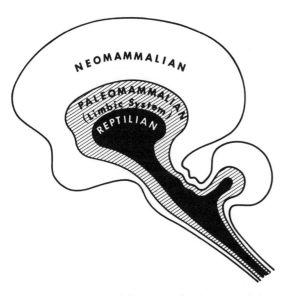

Figure 2. Diagram of the triune development of the evolving mammalian brain. Comparative studies, together with an examination of the fossil record, indicates that in its progressive evolution, the mammalian brain retains the anatomical and chemical features of three basic formations that reflect an ancestral relationship to reptiles, early mammals, and late mammals. (From MacLean, 1967.)

and in an evolutionary sense eons apart, the three formations constitute, so to speak, an amalgamation of three brains in one—a triune brain (MacLean, 1970, 1973a, 1975a). These considerations, together with neurobehavioral findings, attest to marked disparities in the psychological functioning of the three formations. A special complication presents itself in human beings because of evidence that the two evolutionarily older formations do not have the capacity for verbal communication.

In the present context, we are primarily interested in the protoreptilian formation of the forebrain. Embryonically, the structures that comprise this formation in reptiles, birds, and mammals begin to show as two elevations in the ventral and ventrolateral part of the forebrain (Fig. 3). These elevations are not to be confused with an overlying swelling that develops from the "roof area" in reptiles and birds. In the eighteenth century, John Hunter identified in the reptilian brain a ventricular mass that subsequently became known as Hunter's eminence (see Smith, 1901). In 1916, the American comparative neurologist, J. B. Johnston (1916), gave a more detailed description of this mass which, in mountaineer terms, he referred to as the dorsal ventricular ridge (DVR). The DVR in birds is relatively much larger than in reptiles. Some anatomists regard certain ganglia of the DVR as the equivalent of neocortex. As discussed in a later section, some evidence suggests that a structure corresponding to a residual of DVR exists in the mammalian brain.

For many years there was great uncertainty as to what were corresponding parts of basal ventricular swellings in reptiles, birds, and mammals. The first clarification followed Koelle's introduction in 1954 of a method for the histochemical localization of cholinesterase in the brain. Since then it has been demonstrated in all three classes of animals that the Koelle method vividly stains and demarcates telencephalic ganglionic structures that are partly striated in appearance (Karten, 1969; Parent and Olivier, 1970). In reptiles and birds, these ganglia, known as the olfactostriatum (Cairny, 1926) and paleostriatum (Ariëns Kappers, 1908), are separated from the overlying DVR by the dorsal medullary lamina. In mammals, the corresponding ganglia are the olfactostriatum, consisting of the olfactory tubercle and nucleus accumbens, and the part of the corpus striatum comprising the caudate nucleus and putamen. These structures articulate with a pale core of

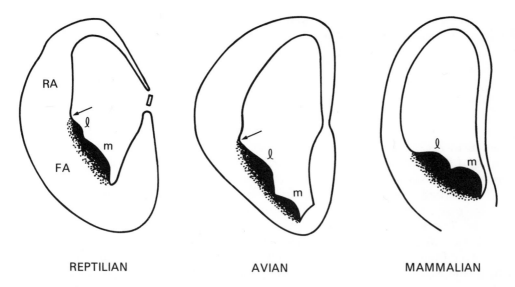

REPTILIAN   AVIAN   MAMMALIAN

Figure 3. Diagram focusing on two elevations (a and b) of the developing striatum in reptilian, avian, and mammalian embryos. In the lefthand drawing of the reptilian embryo, the ventral and dorsal parts of the lateral telencephalic wall are respectively labeled "floor area" (FA) and "roof area" (RA) according to the terminology of Holmgren (1925). These terms have no relevance to the basal and alar plates of the neural tube. Arrow points to boundary between floor and roof areas. The middle and righthand drawings show corresponding picture for avian (sparrow) and human embryos. (Drawings adapted from illustrations in Kallen, 1951; Durward, 1934; and Sidman and Rakic, 1982.)

nerve tissue referred to in mammals as the pallidum. Since there is no term that applies to all of these ganglia and their satellite collections of gray matter, I will refer to the entire group as the striatal complex, or, in a comparative context, as the reptilian complex (R-complex; MacLean, 1973b).

Neurochemically, it has proved to be of great interest that the same structures of the R-complex demarcated by the cholinesterase stain also show a bright green fluorescence because of the presence of dopamine (Juorio and Vogt, 1967), which derives from the ascending axons of dopamine-containing cells in the midbrain. The striatal complex also has other biochemical features of special interest, such as a high content of serotonin (Paasonen and Vogt, 1956; Paasonen, MacLean, and Giarman, 1957), substance P (Amin, Crawford, and Gaddum, 1954), opiate receptors (Pert and Snyder, 1973), and enkephalins (Hong et al., 1977). The pallidal portion of the striatal complex has the highest concentration of iron of any structure in the forebrain (Spatz, 1922). Dr. Joanna Hill (1980) in our laboratory has observed that the pallidal iron in female rats is present in significantly larger amounts than in males and that it undergoes wide fluctuations during the estrous cycle (Hill, 1981a, b) and in pregnancy (Hill, 1982). There is accumulating evidence that iron deficiency specifically affects the function of dopamine (Ashkenazi, Ben-Shachar, and Youdim, 1982).

The question of function

It has been the traditional view in clinical neurology that the striatal complex is primarily part of the motor apparatus under the control of the neocortical motor cortex. This view has prevailed in spite of the recognition that destruction of large parts of the striatal complex may result in no motor deficits and that electrical stimulation may fail to induce any motor responses (see, e.g., review by Jung and Hassler, 1960).

Despite 150 years of experimentation, disappointingly little has been learned about specific functions of the R-complex (Crosby, Humphrey, and Lauer, 1962; Divac and Oberg, 1979). In the past, it has been customary to conduct neurobehavioral studies on animals, living isolated in cages and being subjected to psychological tests in which they manipulate inanimate objects or perform in some apparatus such as a T-maze. Departing from traditional approaches, we have attempted to learn whether or not experiments on animals living under seminatural conditions and interacting with other animals might reveal functions of the R-complex that would otherwise not be apparent. In particular, we have had an interest in investigating the possibility that the R-complex serves to integrate basic forms of species-typical behavior, including that involved in prosematic communication (MacLean, 1975a). Prosematic, meaning rudimentary signaling, applies to any nonverbal signal—vocal, bodily, or chemical—used in communication (MacLean, 1975a).

THE BEHAVIORAL PROFILE

Our experimental approach requires that we become familiar with the entire behavioral profile of different species used in our studies. Apropos of comparative studies on reptiles, it deserves emphasis that none of the extant four orders is phylogenetically in line with the mammal-like reptiles (Fig. 1). In our work, we have focused on lizards because they probably provide the best models of general bodily form for primitive mammal-like reptiles, as illustrated by the pelycosaur Varanosaurus shown in Fig. 5 (see also, MacLean, 1978c). This animal was so-named because of its resemblance to the monitor lizard, of which the Komodo dragon is an outstanding example. In analyzing the behavior of lizards, one can identify more than twenty-five forms of behavior that are also characteristic of mammals (MacLean, 1975a). Notably lacking is the behavioral triad mentioned earlier that comprises nursing in conjunction with maternal care, audiovocal communication for maintaining maternal-offspring contact, and play.

The total of all building blocks of behavior constitutes what ethologists refer to as the ethogram or biogram of an animal. The components of behavior become meaningful when organized into constructs and sequences of constructs (MacLean, 1975a). Exclusive of verbal behavior, one recognizes in all terrestrial vertebrates two main aspects of the behavioral profile that for descriptive purposes might be likened to the profiles of two mountain ranges seen from a distance. Each distinctive behavioral sequence would then represent a mountain peak. In one range are distinctive peaks and subpeaks representing the chain of activities comprising an animal's "daily master routine" and "subroutines." In the other range are four main peaks and subpeaks corresponding to four behavioral patterns, "displays," used in prosematic communication. It is upon these displays that animals, and to a large extent human beings, must rely for obtaining meaning in social communication.

In lizards, the four main types of communicative displays are referred to as *signature, challenge, courtship,* and *submissive displays.* Here I

will focus on the challenge display both because it has a central part in our neurobehavioral work and because it raises questions to be posed in connection with therapsids. Specifically, I will describe the display of the green anolis lizard (*Anolis carolinensis*) in which we have tested the effects of various lesions of the forebrain. Challenge displays are of two types, distant and near, and are used mainly by territorial males in establishing territory, maintaining dominance within a social group, and fending off invaders. The challenge display of the anolis lizard combines the dynamic modifiers of the signature display together with a number of static modifiers. The dynamic components consist of three to five combined head nods and pushups, together with an extension of a crimson throat fan after the second head nod. The static modifiers have the effect of making the animal appear larger in size and involve sagittal expansion and extension of a gular fold, followed by an elevation of a nuchal and dorsal crest and the appearance of a darkly pigmented "eyespot" posterior to the eye.

EXPERIMENTAL FINDINGS

Utilizing an experimental approach that does not interfere with thermoregulation, we have found that partial destruction of the R-complex, but not of other parts of the forebrain, abolishes the challenge display of territorial male lizards (Greenberg, MacLean, and Ferguson, 1979). Similarly, in a study on squirrel monkeys, I found that destruction of the medial pallidal segment of the R-complex (MacLean, 1978a) or its projecting pathways (MacLean, 1975b, 1981) eliminates or alters a particular display that has features in common with the challenge display of this species. In summary, the experiments indicate that in animals as diverse as lizards and primates, the R-complex plays a basic role in the expression of displays used in communication.

Apropos of the other major aspect of the behavioral profile, we have conducted experiments indicating that the R-complex also plays a basic role in integrating the performance of activities making up an animal's daily master routine (Murphy, MacLean, and Hamilton, 1981).

Finally, in concluding this short neurobehavioral overview, it is most significant to mention that an accummulation of findings by others (Stamm, 1955; Slotnick, 1967; Ploog, 1981) and ourselves (Murphy, MacLean, and Hamilton, 1981; MacLean, 1985) has revealed that the behavioral triad that distinguishes the evolutionary transition from reptiles to mammals is represented in the cingulate gyrus, which contains the evolutionarily most recent cortex of the limbic system (see MacLean, 1985). Inclusive of the cingulate gyrus, the limbic system in its totality constitutes a common denominator in the brains of all mammals (MacLean, 1952). Significantly, there appears to be no counterpart of the thalamocingulate structures in the reptilian brain (Clark and Meyer, 1950).

The Mammal-like Reptiles

Before raising questions about the brain and behavior of the mammal-like reptiles, it will be useful to give a brief description of their physical characteristics. As a preliminary, it is necessary to explain skull features that are used to distinguish them from the other main groups of reptiles.

Classificatory features of reptilian skull

According to Osborn (1903), the "tendency to classify the Reptilia by the *structure of the temporal region of the skull*" began in 1867, when Gunther published a description of differences in the "temporal arches" of Rhynchocephalia and Squamata. The classificatory distinctions arrived at over the next seventy-five years applied to the presence or absence of temporal openings and their bony arches. The present terminology can be traced largely to Cope (1892), Osborn (1903), Williston (1925), and Colbert (1945). In the primitive condition, the dermal bony wall of the temporal region forms a solid roof. Cope (1892) seems to have been the first to develop a theory of fenestration to explain how this roof became perforated and provided the site of origin of the temporal muscles participating in the adduction of the jaw. Like Gunther, he referred to the bony arches associated with these fenestrations (openings, fossae). Later, Osborn, who had studied with Cope, introduced the Latin word *apsis* to refer to the arches over the openings, possibly having in mind the architectural meaning of the term as it applies to an arched over niche or alcove.

As illustrated in Fig. 4, there are two connecting bones—the posterior orbital and squamous—which, according to their arched relationship to the openings, provide the key to the taxonomic grouping of reptiles. The stem reptiles that have no temporal fossa and, hence, no temporal arch, are classified as anapsids (Fig. 4A). The same applies to the turtles and tortoises. Osborn (1903)

referred to the mammal-like reptiles "with single or undivided temporal arches" above a single temporal fossa as *synapsids* (Fig. 4C). As opposed to them, he referred to reptiles with two openings as *diapsids* (Fig. 4D). Included in this category are dinosaurs, crocodilians, rhynchocephalians, snakes, and lizards. Finally, an extinct group of reptiles, including aquatic forms known as placodonts, nothosaurs, and plesiosaurs (Fig. 1), are distinguished by a single temporal opening bounded medially by the parietal bone and laterally by a broad cheek plate (Fig. 4B). Colbert (1945) characterized this condition as *euryapsid* because of the underlying broad arch formed by the wide squamous bone and adjoining postorbital.

In advanced synapsids, the temporal fossa undergoes great enlargement, with the result that the arch is so reduced in size as to resemble the zygoma characteristic of mammals. Hence, they are referred to as *therapsids* ("beast arch"), after the Greek word *therion,* signifying *mammal* in zoological nomenclature.

Forms leading to therapsids

In 1880 and 1882, Cope described an order of reptiles that he called Cotylosauria because he regarded them as "stem" reptiles (see also Carroll, this volume). The oldest known reptile, *Hylonomus* (belonging to the suborder Captorhinomorpha), was found in the Coal Measures of Nova Scotia. As already noted, the stem reptiles are characterized as anapsid because of the absence of a temporal fossa.

The synapsids, as Romer (1966) has explained, can be broadly subdivided into primitive forms belonging to the order Pelycosauria and advanced types comprising the order Therapsida. The pelycosaur *Varanosaurus,* mentioned earlier, had a small temporal fossa, and as Romer (1966) notes, its proportions "were not unlike those of many lizards" (Fig. 5). A more advanced form of pelycosaurs is typified by the sphenacodonts best known by the genus *Dimetrodon* with a long-spined "sail" rising from the back. There were other sphenacodonts without the sail, and it is probably from this stock that the therapsids evolved.

Romer (1966) characterizes the phthinosuchids, mainly found in the Permian beds of Russia, as the "most primitive of therapsids." They had a larger temporal opening than the pelycosaurs and possessed a lower canine tooth matched by an upper canine. In these respects, the features of the skull merit their classification as therapsids.

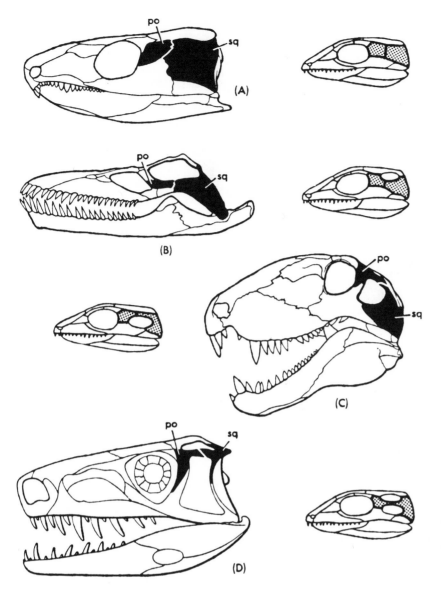

Figure 4. Distinctive skull features used in the classification of reptiles. The two main distinctions pertain to (1) the number of temporal openings (fossae, fenestrae) and (2) the relationship of the openings to the postorbital (po) and squamous bones (sq). In the cranial diagrams, the two key bones are shown in stipple surrounded by heavy lines. Osborn (1903) used the term *apse* to apply to the bony arch forming the roof of a fossa. He referred to the mammal-like reptiles (C) with a single arch above one opening (fossa) as *synapsids*.

A. The anapsid condition (absence of arched fossa) characterizes the stem reptiles and turtles. B, Colbert (1945) referred to an extinct group of reptiles (typified by marine forms) as *euryapsids* because of a wide cheek plate formed by the squamous bone and adjoining postorbital below the opening. D, the diapsid condition is exemplified by dinosaurs and lizards. (Slighly modified after Colbert, 1969.)

Therapsids

The therapsid suborders Theriodontia and the Anomodontia (lawless-teeth) were the predominant terrestrial vertebrates during the late Permian and earliest Triassic times (Fig. 6). It gives one a feeling for their numbers to recall Robert Broom's (1932) calculation that there still lie hidden in the Karroo beds of South Africa the remains of more than 800 billion of these and other mammal-like reptiles.

The Theriodontia were carnivores, while the Anomodontia were predominantly herbivores. Since the mammals are believed to have been derived from the carnivorous variety, particularly the group known as cynodonts, the following discussion will be focused on the types of Theriodontia shown on the left-hand side of Figure 6.

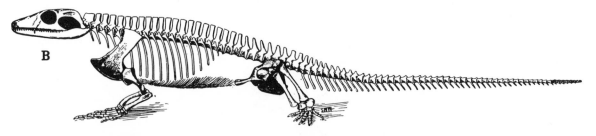

Figure 5. Williston's (1925) conception of the lizardlike appearance of *Varanosaurus* (A), an early mammal-like reptile. The reconstructed skeleton is shown underneath (B). Describing the earlier stem reptiles, Carroll (1964) has repeatedly commented upon the similarity of various bony structures to those of present-day lizards. In view of these and other considerations, it would seem that, of extant reptiles, lizards would come closest to resembling the early mammal-like reptiles. Accordingly, lizards have been chosen for the neurobehavioral work under consideration. (From Williston, 1925.)

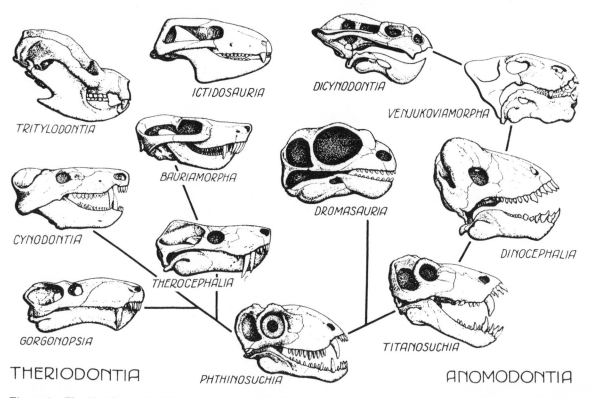

Figure 6. The "family tree" of therapsids. Romer regards the Phthinosuchia as the parent stock leading to "two great groups" characterized, respectively, as being predominantly carnivorous and herbivorous. Therapsids of the carnivorous type leading to mammals are shown on the left. The progressive changes of the skull, teeth, and jaw toward the mammalian condition are described in the text. (Adapted from Romer, 1966.)

P. D. MacLean

Key Changes Toward the Mammalian Condition

As a generalization, paleontologists point out that successive therapsids became progressively more mammal-like with respect to their locomotor skeleton, skull, teeth, jaw joint, and middle ear (Broom, 1932; Romer, 1966; Colbert, 1969). This is not to say that the changes were necessarily gradual and coordinated.

The successive types of therapsids and their development towards the mammalian condition are seen in marvelous parade in the successive zones of the Karroo Beds of South Africa. Table 1 gives the names of the various types found in successive formations laid down in the Middle and Upper Permian and in the Triassic. The successive carnivorous therapsids illustrated on the left-hand side of Figure 6 are the therocephalians, gorgonopsians, cynodonts, bauriomorphs, and ictidosaurs together with the tritylodonts (Broom, 1932).

Table 1.—Theriodonts in successive formations of the Karroo Beds[1]

Period	Beds or zones	Theriodonts	Series
Upper Triassic	Cave Sandstone / Red Beds / Molteno Beds	ICTIDOSAURS and TRITYLODONTS	Stromberg
Middle Triassic			
Lower Triassic	Cynognathus (Procolophon)	BAURIAMORPHS CYNODONTS (numerous)	Upper Beaufort
	Lystrosaurus	SMALL CYNODONTS	
Upper Permian	Cistecephalus	GORGONOPSIANS (many) THEROCEPHALIANS (few)	Lower Beaufort
	Endothiodon	THEROCEPHALIANS (few)	
Middle Permian	Tapinocephalus	GORGONOPSIANS THEROCEPHALIANS	
	Ecca Beds		

[1]Based on Broom (1932) and Colbert (1966). Except for *Cynognathus,* all zones are named for an anomodont. The *Tapinocephalus* zone is about 1,000 feet in thickness; the spacing given for the other zones and beds is roughly proportional.

The body skeleton

In contrast to the wide stance of earlier reptiles, the therapsids assumed a more upright posture, with the limbs supporting from underneath; the elbows were directed backwards and the knees forward. These features, together with the less heavy structure of their bones, indicate that some, at least, were capable of rapid and, perhaps sustained, locomotion. The relative slenderness of the long bones in some of the later therocephalians and of the gorgonopsians are suggestive of a canid alacrity. Most therapsids, however, had a heavyset bony structure that would have given them a robust body build reminiscent of bears or badgers (Hotton, this volume). The therapsid assumption of a more upright posture was accompanied by a change in the phalangeal formula. The therocephalians appear to be the first to have acquired the 2-3-3-3-3 mammalian phalangeal formula familiarly illustrated by our fingers and toes.

Changes in skull

The therocephalians also demonstrate another particular advancement towards the mammalian condition—namely, an increase in the size of the temporal fossa along with a reduction of the postorbitosquamosal arch (Fig. 6). The mammalian likeness is further enhanced in the bauriamorphs in which the loss of the postorbital bar results in a continuation of the temporal fossa with the space for the eye (Fig. 6). This is essentially the mammalian condition. In the bauriamorphs and ictidosaurs other cranial changes included the complete loss of the parietal foramen (Broom, 1932) that houses the parietal, or so-called third eye (see below).

Dentition

Most early reptiles, like many existing forms, had teeth of conical shape that throughout life were alternately shed and replaced (polyphyodonty). In therapsids, there was a change in this pattern in that various teeth became specialized. In therocephalians and gorgonopsians the front teeth became enlarged, whereas the back teeth were either reduced in size or lost. In the cynodonts and bauriamorphs, the teeth are differentiated into incisors for nipping or seizing; canines for tearing; and postcanine, molarlike teeth, for shearing and crushing. In tritylodonts (Lewis, this volume) and ictidosaurs (Fig. 6), the crowns of the molar teeth were comparable to those of some mammals. It seems however, that no therapsids developed the diphyodont condition of mammals (deciduous and permanent dentitions).

Secondary palate

Both the early therocephalians and gorgonopsians demonstrate a notable primitive feature in that they do not have a secondary palate. The later therocephalins may have had a membranous palate. The aquisition by the cynodonts and bauriamorphs of a bony secondary palate represents an important innovation because the partition allowed the animal to chew up food into small pieces and to breathe at the same time without danger of aspiration. Reptiles without such a palate typically cease to breathe while they swallow their food in large chunks. Food chewed into small pieces has the physiological advantage that it can be more easily broken down by digestion and, hence, become a more ready source of energy (for an alternative view, see Bennett and Ruben, this volume).

The jaw joint

Broom (1932, p. 325) has commented that the "ictidosaurians are so near to mammals that the only distinguishing character appears to be that they still retain the articular-quadrate hinge of the jaw." In all reptiles the lower component of the jaw joint consists of an articular bone that hinges with the quadrate in the upper jaw. In mammals, on the contrary, the large dentary bone of the lower jaw articulates directly with the squamosal bone of the skull. In cynodonts the quadrate and articular bone become smaller and smaller until, with the ictidosaurs, they practically disappear. An ictidosaur that approaches the dividing line between reptiles and mammals was called *Diarthrognathus,* because of the double articulation of the jaw—namely, a close contact between the dentary and squamosal bone, as well as the reptilian hinging of the articular and quadrate bones (Crompton, 1963); Crompton and Hylander, this volume).

Some Key Questions

In regard to changes in physiology and behavior during the evolutionary transition from therapsids to mammals, I will limit consideration to five key questions: Were the therapsids warm or cold-blooded? Were they capable of communicative displays? What was the maternal role? Were the therapsids able to hear and to vocalize? What was the size and form of the brain?

Cold-blooded or warm-blooded?

Extant reptiles are said to be "cold-blooded" because if they stay in one place without moving, their body temperature approaches that of the external environment. Because of their poikilothermic condition, they must engage in behavioral thermoregulation, moving between warm and cold places in order to gain or lose heat. Birds and mammals, on the contrary, are en-

dothermic, maintaining physiologically the body temperature within a narrow range without resorting to behavioral thermoregulation. The question of whether or not the therapsids were ectothermic or endothermic is of signal importance because of the primary role of thermoregulation in metabolic processes underlying all aspects of an animal's biological functions and activities.

Since fossils of some advanced mammal-like reptiles have been discovered at high latitudes where they were potentially subject to cold conditions, some workers have proposed that they were protected by a coat of fur (Bakker, 1975). Based on skull markings indicative of foramina around the nasal orifice and mouth, Brink (1956) has suggested that therapsids may have had sweat glands and vibrissae. The presence of such features would be indicative of a hairy integument. The fossil evidence of the existence of nasal turbinate bones has been regarded as another indication of endothermy, since such structures would have served to warm or cool inspired air (see Bennett and Rubin, this volume).

The type of vascularization of bone affords inferences regarding the nature of thermoregulation in extinct forms. In a recent symposium entitled *A Cold-blooded Look at the Warm-blooded Dinosaurs* (Thomas and Olson, eds., 1980), some authors advanced the argument that the dinosaurs were endothermic because the pattern of the haversian canals seen in cross sections of their bones is similar to that of birds and mammals. Bouvier (1977), however, has pointed out that there is great variation in the degree of vascularization of bone in reptiles, birds, and mammals, and that many species of birds and mammals do not have the haversian replacement. In extensive comparative studies, Enlow and Brown (1957) found two types of vascularized bone in therapsid reptiles, one being comparable to haversian bone seen in many mammals.

Finally, the question arises as to the significance of the presence or absence of the parietal eye ("third eye") with respect to thermoregulation. The eye owes its name to its midline location between the two parietal bones. A foramen in the skull leads from the eye to the pineal gland *(epiphysis cerebri),* which in turn is connected to the habenula in the diencephalon. Since it has been found in lizards that destruction of either the parietal eye (Roth and Ralph, 1976) or the pineal body (Roth and Roth, 1980) resets the thermostat for temperature regulation about two degrees higher, it has been argued that animals possessing a parietal eye engage in behavioral thermoregulation. Hence, it has been suggested that the disappearance of the parietal eye in advanced mammal-like reptiles (see above) may have reflected changes toward an endothermic condition (Roth and Roth, 1980). This argument, however, is somewhat tempered by the recognition that there has been a loss of the parietal eye in many ectotherms that have survived into present times.

The question of displays

It is one of the intriguing aspects of neurobehavioral evolution that a number of postures and autonomic changes seen in thermoregulation acquire symbolic significance in animal communication. For example, the piloerection and ruffing of feathers that serves, respectively, in mammals and birds to insulate against the cold, may also serve to enhance the animal's size in aggressive or defensive encounters. Greenberg (1978, p. 220) has cited references to four species of lizards that "use a similar kind of posture in thermoregulation as in a show of aggression." The question arises as to whether or not a detailed study of muscular insertions in therapsids would indicate a capability to engage in communicative displays involving, for example, extension of a gular fold, sagittal expansion, or tiptoe extension of the limbs seen in displays of lizards.

The question of maternal-offspring biology and behavior

Romer (1967) has referred to the amniote egg as "the most marvelous 'invention' in vertebrate history," regarding it as such because it could be deposited on land and mature to the adult form without passing through the risky aquatic larval stage. It may, however, set the stage for one unexpected hazard: since the mother lays eggs and goes off and leaves them, the hatchlings may later be looked upon as foreign and fair prey. Hatchlings of the giant Komodo lizard must take to the trees for the first year of life to avoid parental cannibalism (Auffenberg, 1978). For the same reason, young rainbow lizards must hide in the deep underbrush (Harris, 1964). Female skink lizards, however, may brood their eggs and pay some attention to the hatchlings. Llewellyn Evans (1959) observed that females of the species *Eumeces obsoletus* would regularly turn and clean their eggs with their tongues and on some occasions would move them to a more suitable site. As the young were hatching, the mother would help to express them from their shells. If the young disappeared, she would go searching for them, and upon finding them, would momentarily lick their vents. As documented by motion pictures, such behavior persisted for ten days.

Although the fossil record provides no evidence, it is generally assumed that the mammal-like reptiles were oviparous. The judgment is partly owing to the inference that the therapsids were ancestral to the egg-laying monotremes. Although fossils of the monotremes cannot be traced back beyond the Pleistocene, Romer (1966) argues that it is highly probable that these animals "represent a line of descent from the mammal-like reptiles entirely separate from that of other living forms."

Fitch (1970) suggests that brooding may be an alternative for viviparity and that propinquity to eggs and to hatchlings may be a precondition of maternal interest and care. Under inclement conditions, some oviparous lizards will retain their eggs until the time of hatching (Fitch, 1970). In the case of therapsids, it might be imagined that under periodic cold or arid conditions, some of the smaller ones might have sought underground cover and developed viviparity. Retention of eggs in the oviducts may result in the formation of membranes for the transfer of nutrients and waste material (Fitch, 1970), a process that suggests a mechanism leading to placentation.

The foregoing considerations suggest how maternal interest and placentation might have developed in therapsids. As illustrated by monotremes, however, placentation is not a necessary antecedent to nursing. How might nursing have evolved? Since the last century, it has been generally presumed that milk glands are derived from sweat or sebaceous glands (see Long, 1969), for review). As stated above, the more advanced therapsids may have developed sweat glands and vibrissae, and with them a hairy integument. Evidence adduced for vibrissae also suggests the presence of a muscular lip (not present in extant reptiles) that make it possible for the young to suckle. It has been proposed that the young staying near the mother for warmth might have been drawn to nuzzle around the ventral side (possible brood patch) and thereby happened upon nourishment from glandular secretions (see Guillette and Hotton, this volume; Duvall, this volume).

In regard to the question of parental care, there is one bit of evidence that has suggested the possibility of close parental association. While examining a block of fossils discovered by J. W. Kitching in the "old brickfield Donga" east of Harrismith, Orange Free State, South Africa, Brink (1955) found the skull of a tiny, immature cynodont *(Thrinaxodon liorhinus)* next to that of an adult. Explaining why the adult was probably a female, he conjectured that it "could possibly be the mother of the tiny specimen." Additional findings of this kind would be invaluable for assessing relationships between adult and immature therapsids (see Lewis, this volume).

The question of audiovocal communication

It is commonly assumed that the tiny mammals with affinity to cynodonts survived the onslaught of predatory dinosaurs by living in the dark floor of the forest. They may also have been nocturnal (Crompton and Jenkins, 1979). Under such conditions, audiovocal communication would have been an invaluable asset in maintaining maternal-offspring contact. On the basis of accumulating data, it seems that separation calls (alias isolation or distress calls) are typical of most, if not all, infant mammals (see Newman and MacLean, 1982).

Could the therapsids vocalize, or were they mute like most extant lizards? How well could they hear? Ernest G. Wever (1965, p. 332), who has conducted extensive comparative studies on mechanisms of hearing, has commented, "The lizard ear is of particular interest in relation to the problem of hearing in vertebrates, for this group of reptiles probably is more like the stem reptiles than any others now in existence." He points out that despite electrophysiological evidence of hearing in lizards, "attempts to obtain behavioral indications of hearing have so far been unproductive" (Wever, 1974, p. 163). Some authorities have contended that the primitive mammal-like reptiles (pelycosaurs) were unable to hear; but Hotton (1959) has demonstrated by the use of models that these animals must have had auditory perception in the low range of frequencies. Allin (1975) arrived at similar conclusions (also Allin, this volume). Since the articular and quadrate bones, which become the malleus and incus, respectively, of the mammalian middle ear, were still part of the jaw joint in the advanced therapsids, it is probable that their perception of sound was confined to the low range of frequencies. If so, it is possible that, as in the case of lizards, vocalization did not play a significant role in their communication. This comment, however, must be weighed in the light of Westoll's suggestion that the *recessus mandibularis* of cynodonts functioned not only as a detector of air-borne sound, but also as a vocal resonating amplifier (Westoll 1943, 1945; also Allin, this volume).

The question of brain form and size

In view of the pivotal position of the mammal-like reptiles in our ancestral past, it is disappointing that there exist so few cranial endocasts and reconstructions to give information about the size and form of the brain in these animals. Olson (1944) has described reconstructions of several fossil specimens, but satisfactory endocasts are so rare that reference has been made principally to one pictured seventy years ago by D. M. S. Watson (1913). G. G. Simpson (1927) used Watson's specimen from an intermediate cynodont for comparison with an endocast from an early mammal. The two are depicted in Figure 7. The cynodont endocast on the left reveals that, relative to their length, the cerebral hemispheres were quite narrow, being reminiscent of the shape of the amphibian brain. In a review of available material, Jerison (1973) concluded that the brains of mammal-like reptiles were more reptilian than mammalian in appearance (see Quiroga, 1979, 1980, for contrary view). Apropos of the question of incipient maternal care, it should also be noted that the cynodont endocast reveals that the olfactory bulbs were large and broad (Fig. 7). Fitch (1970) has pointed out that

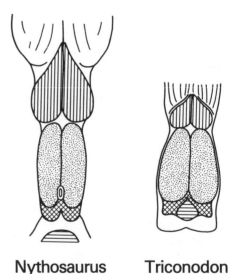

Nythosaurus   Triconodon

Figure 7. Drawings of cranial endocasts, comparing the size and form of the brain of a cynodont mammal-like reptile (*Nythosaurus*) and a primitive mammal (*Triconodon*). The cerebral hemispheres are shown in stipple, while the olfactory bulbs and midbrain are indicated, respectively, by longitudinal shading and cross-hatch. The forebrain in each case is about 1.3 cm long. See text regarding possible structural changes accounting for the wider hemispheres in the primitive mammal. The endocast of *Nythosaurus* indicated the presence of a pineal body. (Redrawn after Simpson, 1927.)

all brooding types of lizards are "secretive," and that olfaction plays an important role in maintaining the female's interest in her eggs.

The Question of Encephalization

The cranial endocast of the triconodont shown on the right in Figure 7, is clearly suggestive that the brain of this primitive mammal was wider than that of a cynodont. What structure or structures might have accounted for this enlargement? There can be no satisfactory answer because there are no extant mammals identified with either triconodonts or their Middle Mesozoic contemporaries. Judging by the so-called living fossils, which resemble their Late Cretaceous relatives, one might be tempted to attribute the widening of the brain to the development of neocortex. After considering two living fossils, however, I will suggest an alternative hypothesis based on experimental micrencephaly.

"Living Fossils"

The marsupials (Metatheria) were once thought to be transitional placental mammals (Eutheria), but the fossil record indicates that both groups branched off from the pantotheres about the same time in the Late Jurassic (Fig. 1). The skull of the common opossum, *Didelphis virginiana,* is almost a perfect match in size and shape for the dawn opossum, *Eodelphis* (Gregory, 1967, p. 48, Fig. 27). As Colbert (1969, p. 267) has commented, it is no figure of speech to refer to the opossum as a *living fossil* because it "has changed very little during the long lapse of time from the Cretaceous period to the present." Gregory (1967, p. 48) points out that the skull of a modern opossum "is at first sight strangely similar to that of one of the mammal-like reptiles of the far-off Triassic." It is of parallel neurobehavioral interest that Evans (1958) has noted that the threat posture and manner of attack of an opossum are typically reptilian, entailing, respectively, an uptilted snout with widely opened mouth and a downward slashing of the teeth.

Until 1924, the opossum was the only living fossil for giving a clue regarding the evolutionary development of the brain in primitive animals. In that year, tiny skulls of true mammals turned up in the Cretaceous beds of Mongolia. Based on a reconstruction of these skulls and other data, Gregory (1967, p. 52) concluded, "All the evidence . . . indicates that the remote ancestors of the line leading to all higher mammals, including man, were small, long-snouted mammals, of insectivorous habits and not unlike

some of the smaller opossums and insectivores in the general appearance of the head." Of existing placental mammals, the English hedgehog and the Madagascar tenrec would perhaps best fit the term *living fossil* (Stephan and Andy, 1964). As illustrated in Figure 8, the incipient neocortex of a basal insectivore, as well as of a basal marsupial, is of small dimensions compared with the evolutionarily old cortex, giving the brain somewhat the appearance of a blunted pyramid.

Origin and use of some cortical terms

Recently, Quiroga (1980) has published the description of an endocast from a relatively ad-

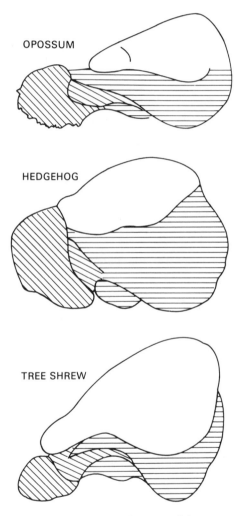

Figure 8. Relative development of the cortex above and below the rhinal sulcus in a basal marsupial, basal insectivore, and in an animal transitional between insectivores and primates. Horizontal shading identifies the prepiriform and piriform areas in an opossum *(Didelphis virginiana),* hedgehog *(Erinaceus europaeus),* and tree shrew *(Tupaia glis).* The shading slanted at 45° identifies the olfactory bulb, while that at an intermediate angle delineates the lateral olfactory tract. Note bulge of tubercle below. The suprarhinal cortex is shown in white. (From MacLean, forthcoming.)

vanced South American therapsid, *Probainognathus jenseni.* The shape of the endocast reminded me of the cerebral hemispheres of rodents in cases of experimental micrencephaly in which neocortical development is particularly affected. Before further comment on this matter, it is necessary to explain the origin of certain terms for different types of pallium (mantle) not explained in standard texts. According to Elliot Smith (1901), Reichert introduced the word "pallium" in 1859 for the purpose of distinguishing the covering of the cerebral hemispheres from underlying structures of the brainstem. The term *pallium,* rather than *cortex,* is usually applied to the outer cerebral gray matter in reptiles and birds in which layering of cellular elements is either lacking or only rudimentary. The diagram of the reptilian forebrain in Figure 9 focuses on three pallial areas. The labels *pir* and *hip* refer to the piriform area and the hippocampal area. The names for these areas in reptiles are taken from nomenclature for convolutions in mammals. The area in between is designated as *general pallium.* Thanks to an influential paper Elliot Smith published in 1901, the general pallium has tended to become regarded as the anlage of the neocortex. Proposing a "natural subdivision of the cerebral hemispheres," Smith referred to the "pyriform" (original spelling) and hippocampal areas as the *old pallium,* whereas he suggested the term *neopallium* for the rest of the cerebral mantle. Here in this paper we find not only the origin of the term *neopallium* (alias,

neocortex), but also the precedent for including too much of the cerebral mantle under this designation (see below).

Sometime later, Edinger, the well-known German neurologist and anatomist, translated Smith's expression *old pallium* as *archipallium,* implying that it represented the first form of cortex (see Smith, 1910). This explains the origin of the term *archipallium* and its synonym, *archicortex.* Smith (1910) was so incensed by Edinger's rendition that he replied with a paper entitled "The term 'archipallium,' a disclaimer." In the meantime Ariëns Kappers (1909) had introduced the word *paleopallium* to refer to the piriform cortex. Later still, Raymond Dart (1934), a former student of Smith, described the identification of two kinds of neopallium in the reptilian brain, one of which he called *parapyriform* and the other *parahippocampal.* Thanks to this chain of naming, the term *neocortex* carried over for the characterization of cortical areas in mammals that, according to such authorities as Ariëns Kappers, Huber, and Crosby (1936, p. 1479), "are really transitional areas between neocortex and the archicortex." In particular, they had in mind limbic areas of the cingulate gyrus that Campbell (1905), Rose (1927), Rose and Woolsey (1948), von Economo (1929), Yakovlev (1948), and others have shown to be distinctive from neocortex. Because of the transitional features of such cortex, M. Rose (1927) had originally referred to it as *mesocortex;* he regarded it as essentially five-layered. Sanides (1969) has used the term *proisocortex* to refer to cingulate and other limbic cortical areas that are transitional with neocortex (isocortex).

Experimental micrencephaly

Given this background, it is of interest to compare the distribution of different cortical areas in the experimentally induced micrencephalic brain with that of the prototypical pallial areas of the reptilian brain shown in Figure 9. In rats, micrencephaly—primarily due to the massive reduction of neocortex—can be produced by injecting a pregnant female with a single dose (20 mg/kg) of the alkylating agent methylazoxymethanol (MAM) on the fifteenth day of gestation (Spatz and Laqueur, 1968; see also Johnston and Coyle, 1979). MAM is the active compound of cycasin, the toxic ingredient of cycad seeds. MAM is converted in vivo to diazomethane, which kills dividing cells by alkylating the purine and pyrimidine bases in their nucleic acids. During the two- to twenty-four-hour effective pe-

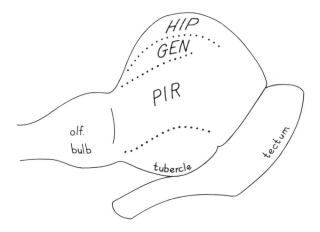

Figure 9. Diagram of the main pallial areas in reptiles, based on brain of the green turtle *(Chelone mydas).* The piriform (PIR) and hippocampal (HIP) areas are regarded as rudimentary forms of the like-named areas of mammals. See text for significance of the intermediate "general" (GEN) pallium. The olfactory tubercle comprises the rest of the cerebral mantle in reptiles. Other labels: **olf. bulb,** olfactory bulb; **tectum** refers to optic tectum. (Redrawn after Papez, 1929.)

riod of the drug, rapidly dividing neuroblasts in the cortical matrix of the fetus are destroyed.

There is a far greater diminution of the cortex and disruption of the cortical layers in the posterior half than in the frontal half of the brain (personal observations). The distribution of the cytoarchitecturally distinctive cortical areas corresponds roughly to the pattern shown in the diagram of Figure 9. A large part of the hippocampal formation is preserved, with the dorsal portion showing, as in the diagram, on the superior part of the hemisphere and the ventral portion adjacent to the piriform area. The greatly diminished limbic cingulate mesocortex occupies a position next to the dorsal hippocampus comparable to Dart's "parahippocampal neocortex," while the location of the diminished limbic entorhinal area is approximately that of "parapyriform area." The entorhinal cortex (Brodmann's area 28), which occupies the posterior part of the hippocampal gyrus in the mammalian brain, is the major source of afferents to the hippocampus (Ramon ý Cajal, 1955). Together, the cingulate and entorhinal areas would occupy a position corresponding to the posterior general pallium. The greatly reduced frontal neocortex would lie in the rostral part.

Given this picture, the possibility is suggested that the widening of the brain seen in the therapsid mammalian transition (Fig. 7) reflects the development of limbic parahippocampal cingulate and entorhinal cortex, rather than of the neocortex. Such an interpretation would harmonize with the hypothesis that the cingulate cortex evolves *pari passu* with the mammalian development of parental care and other aspects of familial behavior. It would also be compatible with the principle of "circumferential differentiation" in the evolution of cortex as implicit in Dart's thesis (1934) and descriptively elaborated upon by Abbie (1940) and by Sanides (1969). It would not conform, however, with what Quiroga (1980) has recently suggested regarding the location of "neocortex" in *Probainognathus*.

A MAMMALIAN COUNTERPART OF THE DVR?

The brains of reptiles and birds are characterized by the development of that part of the DVR located above the dorsal medullary lamina. Is there any structure in the mammalian brain corresponding to this part of the DVR? The evolution of the brain's vasculature offers a possible clue. Elliot Smith (1918–19) called attention to vessels found at the same locus in the brains of reptiles, birds, and mammals that penetrate the brain at a point just medial to the lateral olfactory tract where it adjoins the piriform cortex. At this site in reptiles and birds, there arises a main vessel that courses through the dorsal medullary lamina separating the paleostriatum from the overlying DVR. Smith called it the *lateral striate artery* and depicted it as supplying the DVR (Fig. 10). Based on the study of arterial injections, Shellshear (a student of Smith) concluded that the corresponding vessel in mammals supplies the claustrum (Shellshear, 1920–21), and that Smith had thus wrongly interpreted it as being homologous in all three classes of animals. At the same time, he pointed out that Smith regarded the claustrum as *homologous* to DVR! If the claustral interpretation were correct, the mammalian external capsule would compare to the dorsal medullary lamina.

In the past, the claustrum has been variously interpreted as: one of the basal ganglia closely associated with the corpus striatum (Landau, 1919); the deep layers of the insular cortex (Holmgren, 1925); a continuation of the lateral amygdala (O. C. Smith, 1930); and a structure independent of the cortex and the striatum (de Vries, 1910). It seems that it can be excluded as part of the corpus striatum because it does not show a positive reaction with respect to cholin-

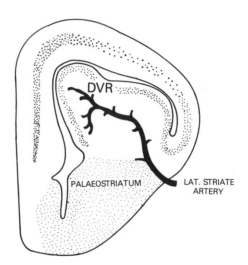

Figure 10. Diagram of section through left hemisphere of a reptilian brain, showing the vascular supply to the dorsal ventricular ridge (DVR). Smith (1918–19) pointed out that the lateral "striate artery" enters the brain in a similar location in reptiles, birds, and mammals. Here, as in both reptiles and birds, the vessel follows a course within dorsal medullary lamina between the paleostriatum and DVR, before distributing to the DVR. Based on vascular findings in mammals (see text), it is suggested that the claustrum may correspond to part of the DVR. (Modified after Elliot Smith's drawing of the brain of the tuatara, 1918–19.)

esterase or dopamine (MacLean, 1972). Certain aspects of its anatomical and functional connectivity that cannot be discussed here, invite further interest in its possible correspondence to a reduced form of DVR.

Some Transcending Questions

The two most primitive types of mammals known to date were found in Wales and are referred to as *Morganucodon* and *Kuehneotherium*. According to Crompton and Jenkins (1973), there seems to be general agreement that members of the Morganucodontidae were ancestral to nontherian mammals (including tricondodonts, multituberculates, and modern monotremes) while the Kuehneotheriidae were the original stock for all Theria (including the symmetrodonts, pantotheres, marsupials, and placentals). In mammals stemming from these two lines, there was incorporation of the quadrate and articular bones into the middle ear.

Directional evolution

It is remarkable that "the incorporation of the quadrate and articular into the middle ear must have occurred independently in therian and nontherian lines" (Crompton and Jenkins, 1973). Olson (1959) has commented, "The most striking feature of the history of the mammal-like reptiles is the independent acquisition of mammal-like characters by the various therapsid lines with the resultant continuing increase of mammalian habitus." He lists many examples, including the development of a secondary palate, broadening of the basal part of the brain, the formation of a double occipital condyle, and reduction of phalangeal formula. Olson points out the difficulty of reconciling "directional evolution" with current genetic-selective concepts of evolution. Where do we stand, he asks, "with respect to the apparent dualism in the therapsids? *Are we dealing with two kinds of systems, one for now and one for the future?*" (Olson, 1959, p. 267, italics added).

The late Harley Shands (1977) remarked that the invention of a written language has made it possible for a society to "invent the future." In a like vein, the evolutionary changes that have just been considered, as well as such mammalian developments as endothermy, placentation, and nursing, could be regarded as inventions. Given the invention, it need not be the "natural selection" of a particular trait or mutation that leads

to survival. Rather, the new invention may provide many species the "natural selection" of several different avenues to survival that previously did not exist.

Summarizing Comment

In the light of current neurobehavioral observations, it has been the purpose of the present overview to present a brief summary of what is known about the therapsids and then to focus on questions that further research might help to clarify regarding cerebral and behavioral changes in lines leading to mammals.

The successive zones of the Karroo beds of South Africa provide incontrovertible evidence of progressive changes of these animals towards the mammalian condition, of which the following are particularly notable:

With respect to the cranium, there is evidence of progressive widening of the temporal fossa, with eventual loss of the postorbital bar; disappearance of the pineal foramen; acquisition of a secondary palate; changes in dentition, including possession of incisors, canines, and molariform teeth (without, however, the development of diphyodonty); and formation of a dentary-squamosal articulation of the jaw but retention of a residual, typically reptilian, quadrate and articular joint. Some skull markings are suggestive of the existence of vibrissae and sweat glands, the presence of which would be indicative of a hairy integument.

In regard to the locomotor system, the most striking changes were the assumption of a mammal-like posture, with the legs supporting the body from underneath, and the acquisition of the mammalian phalangeal formula.

Modifications of the masticatory apparatus would have afforded a more complete comminution of food required for rapid digestion and a quick source of energy, while the changes in the locomotor skeleton would have allowed greater suppleness and alacrity. Altogether, there are indications that the therapsids were approaching the warm-blooded condition of mammals.

Aside from the basic matter of endothermy, there are questions pertaining to the social and procreative behavior of therapsids that further study might help to answer. In regard to social communication, for example, it is suggested that a more detailed examination of fossil remains might yield clues as to whether or not the skeletomuscular system would have lent itself to the kinds of displays seen in extant reptiles. With respect to the behavioral triad characterizing the transition from reptiles to mammals, it would be particularly relevant to search for more examples of associations between adult and immature therapsids.

Finally, there is the need to obtain a far greater assortment of cranial endocasts for obtaining an assessment of encephalization in therapsids and early mammals. The points mentioned with respect to experimental micrencephaly illustrate the nature of questions that arise in connection with cerebral evolution.

The potential for acquiring needed fossil material is best summed up by Robert Broom (1866–1951), who is known for his monumental work on the mammal-like reptiles. Broom, who moved on from Australia to South Africa for the specific purpose of obtaining more information about the evolution of reptiles, encountered such an inexhaustible, movable feast that he never returned home. With typical optimism, he wrote:

> If any intensive collecting is done in the next 20 or 50 years . . . we may then not only be able to trace the lines of evolution, but perhaps be able to see what has been the guiding or compelling force behind it all. America has given the world much of the evolutionary history of the horses; . . . but South Africa will yet give a far fuller account of the evolution of the mammal-like reptiles, and clearly show every step that has led to the warm-blooded mammals. (Broom, 1932, p. 309)

He went on to say:

> Hundreds of thousands of pounds are spent investigating the mysteries of the milky way and the far distant nebulae, but a small fraction of this wealth spent in the further study of the Karroo Book of the Permian and Triassic History would probably yield results quite as important. (Broom, 1932, p. 309)

Broom's projected fifty years have now gone by, but the challenge is more alive and promising than ever, waiting for the young at heart.

Acknowledgments

I am grateful to Robert Gelhard for helping to prepare the illustrations and to Katherine V. Compton and Etta M. Zoerb for typing the manuscript.

I thank Dr. James L. Hill for additional brains I examined in connection with experimental micrencephaly.

In acknowledging the helpful criticisms of colleagues who read the manuscript, I wish to express special appreciation to Nicholas Hotton III, for helping to clarify questions regarding the mammal-like reptiles.

References

Abbie, A. A.
1940. Cortical lamination in the Monotremata. *J. Comp. Neurol.* 72:428–67.

Allin, E. F.
1975. Evolution of the mammalian middle ear. *J. Morph.* 147:403–38.

Amin, A. H.; Crawford, T. B. B.; and Gaddum, J. H.
1954. The distribution of substance P and 5-hydroxytryptamine in the central nervous system of the dog. *J. Physiol. (Lond)* 126:596–618.

Ariëns Kappers, C. U.
1908. Weitere Mitteilungen über die Phylogenese des Corpus striatum und des Thalamus. *Anat. Anz.* 33:321–36.
1909. The phylogenesis of the palaeo-cortex and archi-cortex compared with the evolution of the visual neo-cortex. *Arch. Neurol. Psychiat.* 4:161–73.

Ariëns Kappers, C. U.; Huber, G. C.; and Crosby, E. C.
1936. *The Comparative Anatomy of the Nervous System of Vertebrates, Including Man,* 2 vols, New York: The Macmillan Co.

Ashkenazi, R.; Ben-Shachar, D.; and Youdim, M. B. H.
1982. Iron deficiency and neurotransmitters receptor sensitivity in rat brain. In *The Biochemistry and Physiology of Iron,* ed. P. Saltman and J. Hegenauer, pp. 575–82. Amsterdam: Elsevier North-Holland, Inc.

Auffenberg, W.
1978. Social and feeding behavior in *Varanus komodoensis.* In *The Behavior and Neurology of Lizards,* ed. N. Greenberg and P. D. MacLean, pp. 301–31. Washington, D.C.: U.S. Government Printing Office, DHEW Publications, No. (ADM) 77-491.

Bakker, R. T.
1975. Dinosaur renaissance. *Sci. Amer.* 232:58–78.

Bouvier, M.
1977. Dinosaur Haversian bone and endothermy. *Evolution* 31:449–50.

Brink, A. S.
1955. Note on a very tiny specimen of *Thrinaxodon liorhinus. Palaeont. Afr.* 3:73–76.

1956. Speculations on some advanced mammalian characteristics in the higher mammal-like reptiles. *Palaeont. Afr.* 6:77–95.

Broom, R.
1932. *The Mammal-like Reptiles of South Africa and the Origin of Mammals.* London: H. F. and G. Witherby.

Cairny, J.
1926. A general survey of the forebrain of *Sphenodon punctatum. J. Comp. Neurol.* 42:255–348.

Campbell, A. W.
1905. *Histological Studies on the Localization of Cerebral Functions.* Cambridge: Cambridge University Press.

Carroll, R. L.
1964. The earliest reptiles. *J. Linn. Soc. London (Zool.)* 45:61–83.

Clark, W. E. Le Gros, and Meyer, M.
1950. Anatomical relationships between the cerebral cortex and the hypothalamus. *Brit. Med. Bull.* 6:341–45.

Colbert, E. H.
1945. *The Dinosaur Book: The Ruling Reptiles and Their Relatives.* New York: The American Museum of Natural History.
1966. *The Age of Reptiles.* New York: W. W. Norton & Co., Inc.
1969. *Evolution of the Vertebrates.* New York: John Wiley & Sons, Inc.
1972. Antarctic fossils and the reconstruction of Gondwanaland. *Natural History* 81:66–73.

Cope, E. D.
1880. The skull of empedocles. *Amer. Nat.* 14:382–83.
1882. Third contribution to the history of vertebrata of the Permian formation of Texas. *Proc. Amer. Philos. Soc.* 20:447–61.
1892. On the homologies of the posterior cranial arches in the reptilia. *Trans. Amer. Philos. Soc.* 27.

Crompton, A. W.
1963. On the lower jaw of *Diarthrognathus* and the origin of mammalian lower jaw. *Proc. Zool. Soc. (Lond)* 140:697–750.

Crompton, A. W., and Jenkins, F. A.
1973. Mammals from reptiles: a review of mammalian origins. *Ann. Rev. Earth Plan. Sci.* 1:131–55.
1979. Origin of mammals. In *Mesosoic Mammals,* ed. J. A. Lillegraven, Z. Kielan-Jaworowska, and W. A. Clemens, pp. 59–73. Berkeley: University of California Press.

Crosby, E. C.; Humphrey, T.; and Lauer, E. W.
1962. *Correlative Anatomy of the Nervous System.* New York: The Macmillan Co.

Dart, R. A.
1934. The dual structure of the neopallium: its history and significance. *J. Anat. (British)* 69:3–19.

Divac, I., and Öberg, R. G. E.
1979. Current conceptions of neostriatal functions: history and an evaluation. In *The Neostriatum,* ed. I. Divac and R. G. E. Oberg, pp. 215–30. New York: Pergamon Press.

Durward, A.
1934. Some observations on the development of the corpus striatum of birds, with special reference to certain stages in the common sparrow *(Passer domesticus). J. Anat.* 68:492–99.

Economo, C. von
1929. *The Cytoarchitectonics of the Human Cerebral Cortex.* London: H. Milford, Oxford University Press.

Enlow, D. H., and Brown, S. O.
1957. A comparative study of fossil and recent bone tissue. Part II. Reptiles and birds. *Texas J. Sci.* 9:186–214.

Evans, L. T.
1958. Fighting in young and mature opossums. *Anat. Rec.* 131:549.
1959. A motion picture study of maternal behavior of the lizard, *Eumeces obsoletus* Baird and Girard. *Copeia* 1959 No. 2, 103–10.

Faul, H.
1978. A history of geologic time. *Am. Sci.* 66:159–75.

Fitch, H. S.
1970. Viviparity *versus* oviparity. In F. B. Cross, *Reproductive Cycles in Lizards and Snakes,* ed., F. B. Cross, P. S. Humphrey, R. M. Mengel, and E. H. Taylor, pp. 214–20. Lawrence: The University of Kansas Printing Service.

Greenberg, N.
1978. Ethological considerations in the experimental study of lizard behavior. In *The Behavior and Neurology of Lizards,* ed. N. Greenberg and P. D. MacLean, pp. 203–24. Washington, D.C.: U.S. Government Printing Office, DHEW No. (ADM) 77-491.

Greenberg, N.; MacLean, P. D.; and Ferguson, J. L.
1979. Role of the paleostriatum in species-typical display behavior of the lizard *(Anolis carolinensis). Brain Res.* 172:229–41.

Gregory, W. K.
1967. *Our Face from Fish to Man.* New York: Hafner Publishing Co.

Gunther, A. C.
1867. Contribution to the anatomy of *Hatteria (Rhynchocephalus* Owen). *Philos. Trans. Roy. Soc. (Lond)* 157:595–629.

Harris, V. A.
1964. *The Life of the Rainbow Lizard.* London: W. I. Hutchinson & Co.

Hill, J.
1980. Sex difference in brain iron. *Neurosci. Abst.* 6:131.
1981a. Changes in brain iron during the estrous cycle. *Neurosci. Abst.* 7:219.
1981b. Brain iron in the rat: distribution, sex differences, and effects of sex hormones. Ph.D. dissertation, Michigan State University.
1982. Brain Iron: Sex difference and changes during the estrous cycle and pregnancy. In *The Biochemistry and Physiology of Iron,* ed. P. Saltman and J. Hegenauer, pp. 559–601. Amsterdam: Elsevier North-Holland, Inc.

Holmgren, N.
1925. Points of view concerning forebrain morphology in higher vertebrates. *Acta Zool.* 6:414–77.

Hong, J. S.; Yang, H.-Y. T.; Fratta, W.; and Costa, E.
1977. Determination of methione enkephalin in discrete regions of the rat brain. *Brain Res.* 134:383–86.

Hotton, N.
1959. The pelycosaur tympanum and early evolution of the middle ear. *Evolution* 13:99–121.

Jerison, H. J.
1973. *Evolution of the Brain and Intelligence.* New York: Academic Press, Inc.

Johnston, J. B.
1916. The development of the dorsal ventricular ridge in turtles. *J. Comp. Neurol.* 26:481–505.

Johnston, M. V., and Coyle, J. T.
1979. Histological and neurochemical effects of fetal treatment with methylazoxymethanol on rat neocortex in adulthood. *Brain Res.* 170:135–55.

Jung, R., and Hassler, R.
1960. The extrapyramidal motor system. In *Handbook of Physiology,* ed. F. Field, H. W. Magoun, and V. E. Hall, pp. 863–927. Washington, D. C.: American Physiological Society.

Juorio, A. V., and Vogt, M.
1967. Monoamines and their metabolites in the avian brain. *J. Physiol. (Lond)* 189:489–518.

Kallen, B.
1951. On the ontogeny of the reptilian forebrain. Nuclear structures and ventricular sulci. *J. Comp. Neurol.* 95:307–47.

Karten, H. J.
1969. The organization of the avian telencephalon and some speculations on the phylogeny of the amniote telencephalon. *Ann. N. Y. Acad. Sci.* 167:164–79.

Koelle, G. B.
1954. The histochemical localization of cholinesterases in the central nervous system of the rat. *J. Comp. Neurol.* 100:211–28.

Landau, E.
1919. The comparative anatomy of the nucleus amygdalae, the claustrum and the insular cortex. *J. Anat. (Lond.)* 53:351–60.

Long, C. A.
1969. The origin and evolution of mammary glands. *Bio. Sci.* 19:519–23.

MacLean, P. D.
1952. Some psychiatric implications of physiological studies on frontotemporal portion of limbic system (visceral brain). *Electroenceph. Clin. Neurophysiol.* 4:407–18.
1962. New findings relevant to the evolution of psychosexual functions of the brain. *J. Nerv. Ment. Dis.* 135:289–301.
1967. The brain in relation to empathy and medical education. *J. Nerv. Ment. Dis.* 144:374–82.
1970. The triune brain, emotion, and scientific bias. In *The Neurosciences Second Study Program,* ed. F. O. Schmitt, pp. 336–49. New York: The Rockefeller University Press.
1972. Cerebral evolution and emotional processes: new findings on the striatal complex. *Ann. N.Y. Acad. Sci.* 193:137–49.
1973a. A triune concept of the brain and behavior. In *The Hincks Memorial Lectures,* ed. T. Boag and D. Campbell, pp. 6–66. Toronto: University of Toronto Press.
1973b. The brain's generation gap: Some human implictions. *Zygon J. Relig. Sci.* 8:113–27.
1975a. On the evolution of three mentalities. *Man-Environment Systems* 5: 213–24.
Reprinted 1977 in *New Dimensions in Psychiatry; a World View,* Vol. 2, ed. S. Arieti and G. Chrzanowski, pp. 305–28. New York: John Wiley and Sons.
Reprinted 1978 in *Human Evolution, Biosocial Perspectives (Perspectives on Human Evolution,* Vol. 4), ed. S. L. Washburn and E. R. McCown, pp. 32–57. Menlo Park, California: Benjamin/Cummings Publishing Company.
1975b. Role of pallidal projections in species-typical display behavior of squirrel monkeys. *Trans. Amer. Neurol. Assoc.* 100: 29–32.
1978a. Effects of lesions of globus pallidus on species-typical display behavior of squirrel monkeys. *Brain Res.* 149:175–96.
1978b. A mind of three minds: educating the triune brain. *Seventy-seventh Yearbook of the National Society for the Study of Education,* pp. 308–42. Chicago: The University of Chicago Press.
1978c. Why brain research on lizards? In *The Behavior and Neurology of Lizards,* ed. N. Greenberg

and P. D. MacLean, pp. 1–10. Washington, D.C.: U.S. Government Printing Office, DHEW Publication, No. (ADM) 77-491.

1981. Role of transhypothalamic pathways in social communication. In *Handbook of the Hypothalamus,* vol. 3, ed. P. Morgane and J. Panksepp, pp. 259–87. New York: Marcel Dekker, Inc.

1982a. On the origin and progressive evolution of the triune brain. In *Primate Brain Evolution,* ed. E. Armstrong and D. Falk, pp. 291–316. New York/London: Plenum Press. For another version see also: Evolution of the psychencephalon. *Zygon J. Relig. Sci.* 17(1982): 187–211.

1982b. The co-evolution of the brain and family. *Anthroquest,* (L. S. B. Leakey Foundation News, Pasadena, Calif.) No. 24(Winter, 1982): 1 and 14–15.

1985. Brain evolution relating to family, play, and the separation call. *Arch. Gen. Psychiatry* 42:405–17.

Murphy, M. R.; MacLean, P. D.; Hamilton, S. C.
1981. Species-typical behavior of hamsters deprived from birth of the neocortex. *Science* 213:459–61.

Newman, J. D., and MacLean, P. D.
1982. Effects of tegmental lesions on the isolation call of squirrel monkeys. *Brain Res.* 232:317–29.

Olson, E. C.
1944. Origin of mammals based upon cranial morphology of the therapsid suborders. *Geol. Soc. Am.* 55: 1–136.

1959. The evolution of mammalian characters. *Evolution* 13:344–53.

Osborn, H. F.
1903. The reptilian subclasses Diapsida and Synapsida and the early history of the Diaptosauria. *Memoirs of the American Museum of Natural History* 1, part 8, 451–519.

Paasonen, M. K., and Vogt, M.
1956. The effect of drugs on the amounts of substance P and 5-hydroxytryptamine in mammalian brain. *J. Physiol.* 131: 617–26.

Paasonen, M. K., MacLean, P. D.; and Giarman, N. J.
1957. 5-Hydroxytryptamine (serotonin, enteramine) content of structures of the limbic system. *J. Neurochem.* 1:326–33.

Papez, J. W.
1929. *Comparative Neurology.* New York: Thomas Y. Crowell Co.

Parent, A., and Olivier, A.
1970. Comparative histochemical study of the corpus striatum. *J. Hirnforsch.* 12:75–81.

Pert, C. B., and Synder, S. H.
1973. Opiate receptor: demonstration in nervous tissue. *Science* 179:1011–14.

Ploog, D.
1981. Neurobiology of primate audio-vocal behavior. *Brain Research Reviews* 3:35–61.

Quiroga, J. C.
1979 The brain of two mammal-like reptiles (Cyndontia-Therapsida). *J. Hirnforsch.* 20:341–50.

1980. The brain of the mammal-like reptile *Probainognathus jenseni* (Therapsida, Cynodontia). A correlative paleo-neoneurological approach to the neocortex at the reptile-mammal transition. *J. Hirnforsch.* 21:299–336.

Ramon ý Cajal
1955. *Studies on the Cerebral Cortex (Limbic Structures),* Trans. from the Spanish by L. M. Kraft. London: Lloyd-Luke Ltd.; Chicago: The Year Book Publishers, Inc.

Romer, A. S.
1966. *Vertebrate Paleontology.* Chicago: The University of Chicago Press.

1967. Major steps in vertebrate evolution. *Science* 158:1629–37.

Rose, J. E., and Woolsey, C. N.
1948. Structure and relations of limbic cortex and anterior thalamic nuclei in rabbit and cat. *J. Comp. Neurol.* 89:279–348.

Rose, M.
1912. Histologische Lokalisation der Grosshirnrinde bei kleinen Saügetieren (Rodentia, Insectivora, Chiroptera). *J. Psychol. u. Neurol.* 19:389.

1927. Gyrus limbicus anterior and Regio retrosplenialis. (Cortex holoprotoptychus quinquestratificatus). Vergleichende Architektonik bei Tier und Mensch. *J. Psychol. u. Neurol.* 35:65–173.

Roth, J. J., and Ralph, C. L.
1976. Body temperature of the lizard *(Anolis carolinensis):* effect of parietalectomy. *J. Exp. Zool.* 198:17–28.

Roth, J. J., and Roth, E. C.
1980. The parietal-pineal complex among paleovertebrates: evidence for temperature regulation. In *A Cold Look at the Warm-blooded Dinosaurs,* ed. R. D. K. Thomas and E. C. Olson, pp. 189–231. Boulder, Colo.: West View Press.

Sanides, F.
1969. Comparative architectonics of the neocortex of mammals and their evolutionary interpretation. *Ann. N. Y. Acad. Sci.* 16:404–23.

Shands, H. C.
1977. Science, linguistic science, and the invention of the future. *Semiotica* 19:85–102.

Shellshear, J. L.
1920–21. The basal arteries of the forebrain and their functional significance. *J. Anat. (Lond.)* 55:27–35.

Sidman, R. L., and Rakic, P.
1982. Development of the human central nervous system. In *Histology and Histopathology of the Nervous System,* vol. I, ed. W. Haymaker and R. D. Adams, pp. 3–145. Springfield: Charles C Thomas.

Simpson, G. G.
1927. Mesozoic mammalia. IX. The brain of Jurassic mammals. *Am. J. Sci.* 214: 259–68.

Slotnick, B. M.
1967. Disturbances of maternal behavior in the rat following lesions of the cingulate cortex. *Behavior* 24:204–36.

Smith, G. E.
1901. Notes upon the natural subdivision of the cerebral hemisphere. *J.Anat. Physiol.* 35:431–54.
1910. The term "archipallium," a disclaimer. *Anat. Anz. Jena* 35:429.
1918–19. A preliminary note on the morphology of the corpus striatum and the origin of the neopallium. *J. Anat. (Lond.)* 53:271–91.

Smith, O. C.
1930. The corpus striatum, amygdala, and stria terminalis of Tamandua tetradactyla. *J. Comp. Neurol.* 51:65–127.

Spatz, H.
1922. Uber den Eisennachweis im Gehirn, besonders in Zentren des Extrapyramidal-motorischen Systems. *Z.f.d.g. Neur. U. Psych.* 77:261–390.

Spatz, M., and Laqueur, G. L.
1968. Transplacental chemical induction of microencephaly in two strains of rats. I. (33404). *Proc. Soc. Exptl. Biol. Med.* 129:705–10.

Stamm, J. S.
1955. The function of the median cerebral cortex in maternal behavior of rats. *J. Comp. Physiol. Psychol.* 48:347–56.

Stephan, H., and Andy, O. J.
1964. Quantitative comparisons of brain structures from insectivores to primates. *Am. Zool.* 4: 59–74.

Suess, E.
1904–06. *The Face of the Earth (Das Antlitz der Erde).* Trans. H. B. C. Sollas. Oxford: Clarendon Press.

Thomas, R. D. K., and Olson, E. C., eds.
1980. *A Cold Look at the Warm-Blooded Dinosaurs.* Boulder, Colo.: West View Press.

Vries, H. de
1910. Bemerkungen zur Ontogenie und vergleichenden Anatomie des Claustrums. *Folia neuro-biologica.* 4:481–513.

Watson, D. M. S.
1913. Further notes on the skull, brain, and organs of special sense of *Diademodon. Ann. Mag. Nat. Hist.* 12:217–28.

Wegener, A. L.
1915. *Die Entstehung der Kontinente und Ozeane.* Braunschweig: F. Vieweg.

Westoll, T. S.
1943. The hyomandibular of *Eusthenopteron* and the tetrapod middle ear. *Proc. Roy. Soc. (Lond)* B 131:393–414.
1945. The mammalian middle ear. *Nature (Lond.)* 155:114–15.

Wever, E. G.
1965. Structure and function of the lizard ear. *J. Aud. Res.* 5:331–71.
1974. The lizard ear: Gekkonidae. *J. Morph.* 143:121–66.

Williston, S. W.
1925. *The Osteology of the Reptiles.* Cambridge, Mass.: Harvard University Press.

Yakovlev, P. I.
1948. Motility, behavior and the brain. Stereodynamic organization and neural coordinates of behavior. *J. Nerv. Ment. Dis.* 107:313–35.

ORIGIN, MORPHOLOGY, AND RELATIONSHIPS

ROBERT L. CARROLL
Redpath Museum, McGill University
859 Sherbrooke Street West
Montreal, Quebec H3A 2K6
Canada

The Skeletal Anatomy and Some Aspects of the Physiology of Primitive Reptiles

Introduction

This paper is an analysis of the skeletal anatomy of the early synapsid (mammal-like) reptiles, demonstrating the features that differentiate early synapsids from other primitive amniotes. These features in turn provide a basis for considering the subsequent elaboration of mammalian characteristics.

The relationships of mammal-like reptiles to other amniotes are treated briefly to show the relative time at which each of the major groups differentiated, as well as the phylogenetic position of the living reptilian orders (Fig. 1).

Amniote Relationships

Reptilian phylogeny

No fossils are yet known of the amphibian group immediately ancestral to reptiles, nor of the primitive reptilian stock prior to its initial diversification. The oldest fossil reptiles come from the early Pennsylvanian Period locality of Joggins, Nova Scotia. This fauna includes representatives of two major lineages, the protorothyrid (romeriid) captorhinomorphs and the first of the mammal-like reptiles.

Captorhinomorphs are commonly regarded as the most primitive known reptiles because of their small body size and generally primitive skeleton. They gave rise to the diapsids, which include the majority of reptilian groups, both fossil and living, before the end of the Pennsylvanian Period. The lepidosaurs (including the ancestors of lizards, snakes, and sphenodontids) and the archosaurs differentiated by the end of

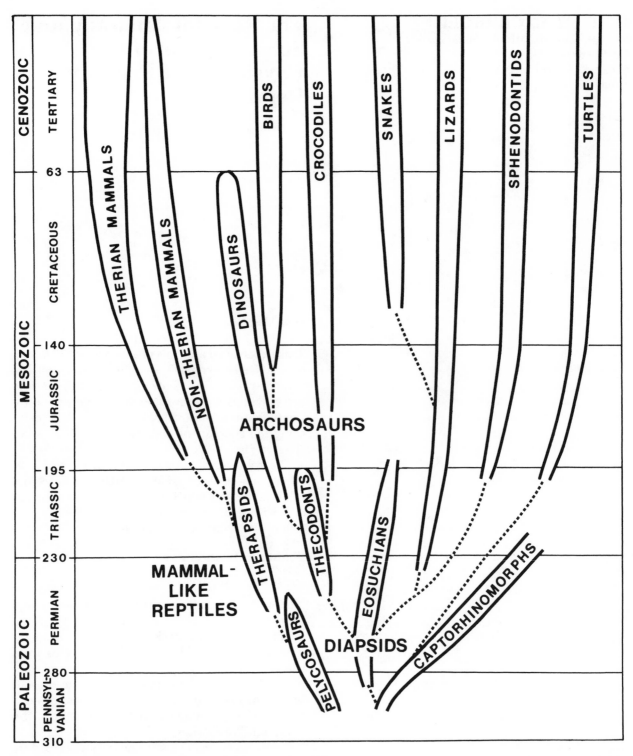

Figure 1. Simplified phylogeny of the amniotes, showing the approximate time of divergence of the major groups, and relationships of the living orders of reptiles. Ages indicated in millions of years.

the Permian Period. Among the archosaurs, the crocodilians diverged from the ancestors of dinosaurs and birds by the early Triassic Period. Crocodiles hence share a more recent common ancestry with the dinosaurs and birds than they do with any of the other living reptiles.

Turtles do not appear in the fossil record until late in the Triassic. Their specific origin has not

R. L. CARROLL

yet been established, although they probably arose from captorhinomorphs or other primitive reptiles that had not yet developed temporal openings. Turtles are frequently considered the most primitive of modern reptiles (principally because they lack temporal openings), but were apparently the last of the major groups to have diverged from the primitive captorhinomorph stock (Gaffney and McKenna, 1979; Carroll, 1982).

The problem of amniote origins

Major features that distinguish all living amniotes from amphibians and fish are two: an egg in which the formation of extraembryonic membranes obviates the necessity of an aquatic larval stage; and an effective system of stretch receptors located in the axial as well as the appendicular muscles (Baker, Hunt, and McIntyre 1974). Their universality in living amniotes suggests that these features had evolved before the differentiation of captorhinomorphs and pelycosaurs. Their establishment was probably decisive in the dominance of Late Paleozoic reptiles over their amphibian antecedents.

Similarity of skeletal anatomy suggests that primitive captorhinomorphs and pelycosaurs shared a common ancestry not much earlier than the time of their first appearance in the fossil record. Differences show initial stages in the separation of mammal-like reptiles from all other amniotes (Fig. 1).

In determining which of these skeletal features are likely to have been present in the common ancestors of all amniotes, and which are specializations of the early mammal-like reptiles, we are handicapped by the absence of any recognized fossils of the amphibian group immediately ancestral to reptiles. Although much has been written concerning the derivation of reptiles from anthracosaurs (Carroll, 1969b, 1970a, 1970b), it is becoming increasingly clear that this relationship, if it is significant at all, is very distant, and none of the known anthracosaurs provide an adequate basis for outgroup comparison of any but the most general reptilian features. In particular, there is no recognized fossil evidence regarding the specific pattern of the skull, which was possessed by the group immediately ancestral to pelycosaurs and protorothyrids.

Other outgroup comparisons are of dubious value since we cannot state with any assurance which of the other known groups of Paleozoic tetrapods are the plesiomorphic sister group of the amniotes.

The families Limnoscelidae, Tseajaiidae, and Diadectidae, united in the Diadectomorpha by Heaton (1980), share some characteristics with early amniotes that suggest their derivation from a common ancestor, independent of other Paleozoic tetrapods. These features include the pattern of the atlas-axis complex, together with a large, platelike supraoccipital bone. Limnoscelids and tseajaiids also share with early amniotes a clearly defined transverse flange of the pterygoid, which, in the diadectids, appears to have been secondarily lost. Other features of limnoscelids and tseajaiids are more primitive than those of early reptiles; and some characteristics, particularly evident in diadectids, are far more specialized. Specialization of the postcranial skeleton in all three families may be attributed primarily to their large body size, compared with that of early amniotes. No adequately known members of these families occur prior to the Late Pennsylvanian, well after the first appearance of the amniotes.

Skeletal characteristics of primitive amniotes

Although the Diadectomorpha as defined by Heaton may represent the sister group of amniotes, their known members are too late in time and too distinct in general anatomy to form a trustworthy basis for evaluating the polarity of features that distinguish captorhinomorphs and pelycosaurs. Evaluation must therefore be based on character states and polarities within the early amniotes themselves, especially the pelycosaurs, captorhinomorphs, and early diapsids (Reisz, 1981). Few of the skeletal features of these animals are unique to the early amniotes. Several are shared with one or more of the families included by Heaton in the Diadectomorpha, while others were achieved convergently within this or other taxonomic groups. Still other traits represent primitive character states, in which other early tetrapods have achieved a more specialized condition. In combination, however, the skeletal features shared by early amniotes serve to distinguish them from all other early tetrapods.

The following features characterize the earliest known captorhinomorphs, and appear to represent the pattern from which pelycosaurs evolved:

1. Supratemporal, tabular, and postparietal bones retained as small, paired elements, ex-

posed largely on the occipital surface. Intertemporal not present as a distinct center of ossification, but appears to have been displaced by lateral margin of parietal, separating postorbital and supratemporal. Squamosal underlies parietal.

2. Transverse flange of pterygoid, associated with elaboration of pterygoideus muscle: flange present in *Tseajaia* and *Limnoscelis* perhaps synapomorphic for "diadectomorphs" and amniotes, secondarily lost in diadectids.

3. Supraoccipital large, platelike, suturally attached to the exoccipital and opisthotic ventrally, and movably articulated with the postparietals and parietals dorsally. Limited contact with tabular. Posttemporal fenestra relatively large: This pattern is probably primitive, relative to that of "diadectomorphs," in which the supraoccipital is solidly integrated with the skull roof and tabular, and the posttemporal fossa is closed. *Desmatodon,* the earliest diadectid for which the occiput is known (Vaughn, 1972), shows the most primitive, captorhinomorphlike pattern of this group. Pelycosaurs secondarily develop a more platelike occiput, with reduction of the size of the posttemporal fossa.

5. Dorsal portion of quadrate thin, triangular in lateral view, covered posteriorly by squamosal: primitive, relative to the condition in tseajaiids and diadectids, in which the quadrate extends dorsally and is exposed posteriorly.

6. Stapes with large footplate, dorsal process, and short stem; directed ventrolaterally toward quadrate. Primitively supports braincase against quadrate: may be primitive to the pattern of *Tseajaia* and *Diadectes.*

7. No evidence for tympanum or impedance-matching middle ear.

8. Atlas-axis complex multipartite. Separate proatlas; paired atlas arch not fused to centrum. Atlas pleurocentrum cylindrical but incompletely ossified dorsally. Axis arch large and in adults fused to large cylindrical pleurocentrum; atlas and axis intercentra separate, crescentic elements. Atlas intercentrum and arches form a loose ring, surrounding the knoblike occipital condyle: present in "diadectomorphs" and is approached in the anthracosaurs *Gephyrostegus* and *Protorogyrinus.*

9. Neural arches of vertebrae narrow, with zygapophyses close to the midline: primitive for tetrapods, but expansion of the neural arches and zygapophyses has occurred separately in several amphibian groups and among several families of early reptiles.

10. Two proximal tarsals; intermedium, proximal centrale and tibiale fused to form an astragalus: approached in the anthracosaur *Gephyrostegus,* and achieved convergently in the microsaurs *Pantylus* and *Tuditanus. Diadectes* is the only "diadectomorph" known to possess an astragalus.

A further feature of critical importance to the biology of ancestral amniotes is their small body size. It is probable that the evolution of extraembryonic membranes occurred via an intermediate stage in which small, anamniotic eggs were laid on land (Carroll, 1970b). If the size of modern plethodontid salamanders is used as a scale, the maximum body size for animals practicing this reproductive strategy would have been no more than about 100 mm in snout-vent length. This is approximately the size of the early captorhinomorph reptiles. The earliest known pelycosaurs are poorly known, but were probably not a great deal larger.

The known "diadectomorphs" are all of much larger size, and there is currently no way to determine whether their immediate ancestors were large or small.

Distinguishing features of early pelycosaurs

The pelycosaurs are a diverse group, ranging from the Middle Pennsylvanian of North America to the Middle Permian of Russia. Three or four major groups are recognized (Reisz, 1980). The suborder Ophiacodontia includes both the most primitive known pelycosaurs and the large, specialized ophiacodontids of the Lower Permian. From the standpoint of the origin of mammals, the most important group is the Sphenacodontia, including large carnivorous genera that diverged from the early pelycosaurs within the Pennsylvanian and gave rise to the therapsids sometime in the Permian. The caseids and edaphosaurs are herbivorous groups that diverged markedly from the primitive pelycosaur stock.

Cranial features

The skulls of pelycosaurs (Fig. 3A, C, E, F; Figs 4 and 5) differ from those of other primitive amniotes (Figs. 2 and 3B, D) in several respects. The presence of a lateral temporal opening is traditionally considered the most important difference. In addition, the supratemporal and postorbital meet above the opening, separating the squamosal and parietal superficially. The postparietals, paired in other primitive tetrapods, comprise a single, median element. In most gen-

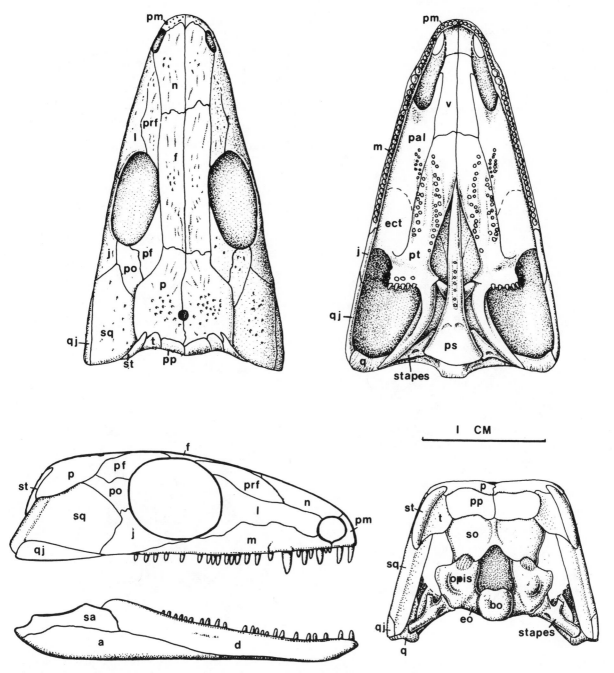

Figure 2. Restoration of the skull of *Paleothyris,* the oldest adequately known captorhinomorph reptile. (From Carroll and Baird, 1972.)

Key to abbreviations used in this and other figures: **a,** angular; **art,** articular; **bo,** basioccipital; **ca,** anterior coronoid; **co,** coronoid; **d,** dentary; **dp,** dorsal process; **ect,** ectopterygoid; **eo,** exoccipital; **f,** frontal; **fp,** footplate of stapes; **fpa,** facet for proatlas; **j,** jugal; **l,** lacrimal; **m,** maxilla; **n,** nasal; **opis,** opisthotic (may include exoccipital); **p,** parietal; **pal,** palatine; **par,** paroccipital process of opisthotic; **pf,** postfrontal; **pm,** premaxilla; **po,** postorbital; **pp,** postparietal; **pra,** prearticular; **prf,** prefontal; **ps,** parasphenoid; **pt,** pterygoid; **pft,** posttemporal fenestra; **q,** quadrate; **qj,** quadratojugal; **sa,** surangular; **sf,** stapedial foramen; **sm,** septomaxilla; **so,** supraoccipital; **sp,** splenial; **sq,** squamosal; **st,** supratemporal; **sta,** stapes; **t,** tabular; **v,** vomer.

era, the occiput is platelike, with the supraoccipital tightly integrated with the skull roof, tabular, and enlarged opisthotic. The posttemporal fenestrae are small. The dorsal margin of the occiput is angled forward, contrasting with the more nearly vertical occiput of captorhinomorphs and early diapsids.

The skulls of pelycosaurs also differ from those

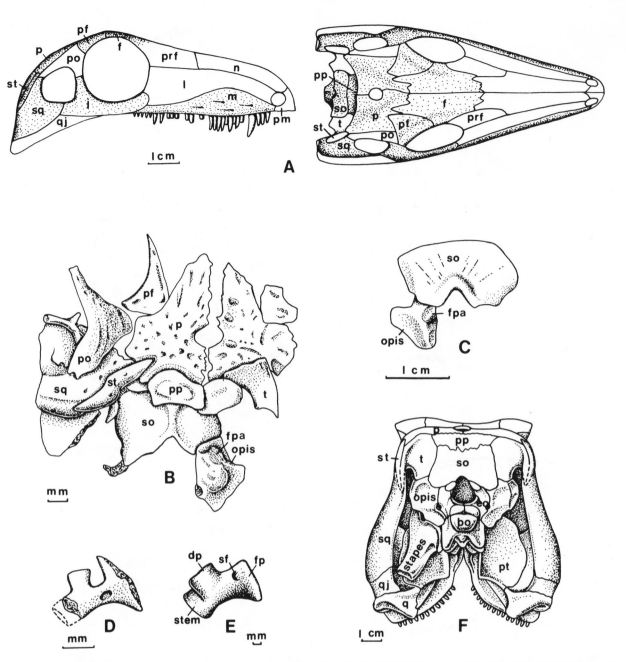

Figure 3. Captorhinomorphs and primitive pelycosaurs. A, *Archaeothyris*, a primitive pelycosaur from the Middle Pennsylvanian. Unshaded bones are restored on the basis of other pelycosaurs. B, *Paleothyris*, detail of back of skull and occiput to show nature of supraoccipital and opisthotic. The latter bone may include part of the exoccipital. C, Supraoccipital and opisthotic of *Archaeothyris*. D, Stapes of *Paleothyris*. E, Stapes of *Archaeothyris*. F, The Lower Permian pelycosaur *Ophiacodon*, showing an early stage in the elaboration of a platelike occiput. Note also the exceedingly massive stapes. (A, C, and E, from Reisz, 1972; B, and D, from Carroll, 1969a; F, from Romer and Price, 1940.) Abbreviations as in Figure 2.

of early captorhinomorphs and diapsids in their proportions, with the postorbital portion of the skull notably shorter than the antorbital.

The presence of a temporal opening and the median postparietal are unquestionably derived features of pelycosaurs, but it is more difficult to establish whether the pattern of the occiput, and the contact between the postorbital and supra-temporal are primitive or derived, since these features appear to resemble those seen in other early tetrapods such as limnoscelids.

Although the skull is not very well preserved in any of the Pennsylvanian pelycosaurs, enough is known to establish the polarity of occipital characteristics. In *Archaeothyris* (Reisz, 1972) from the Upper Pennsylvanian, the configura-

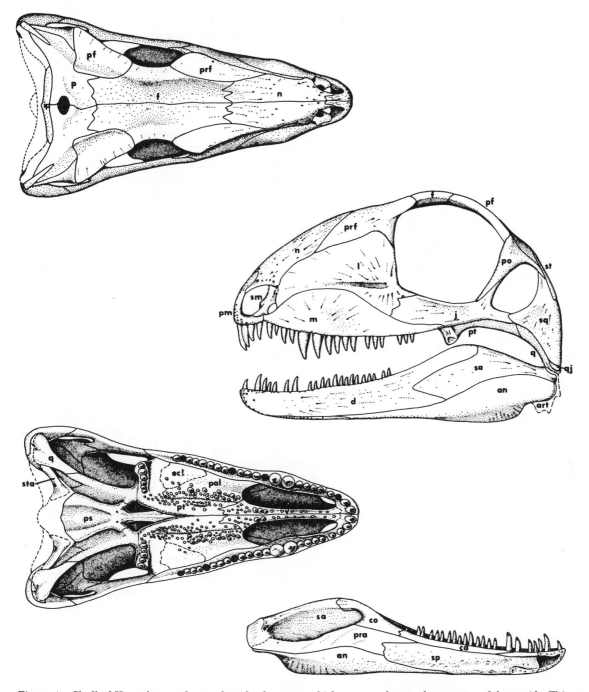

Figure 4. Skull of *Haptodus,* a sphenacodontid pelycosaur, which appears close to the ancestry of therapsids. This genus ranges from the Upper Pennsylvanian into the Lower Permian. (From Currie, 1979.) Abbreviations as in Figure 2.

tion of the supraoccipital and adjacent exoccipital and opisthotic (Fig. 3C) are nearly identical with those in the protorothyrid *Paleothyris* (Fig. 3B) from the same locality. The supraoccipital is a broad plate of bone, apparently only weakly integrated with the rest of the occiput, a condition also encountered in the early diapsid *Petrolacosaurus.* The opisthotic is small and does not reach the cheek. The bone previously identified

as the exoccipital in *Archaeothyris* and *Paleothyris* (Carroll, 1969a) apparently includes at least part of the opisthotic. The close integration of these bones may be a common feature of all early amniotes.

Ophiacodon (Fig. 3F) and the sphenacodontids (Fig. 5A) show successive stages in the elaboration of the occipital plate. In this sequence, the tabular increases in size and grows down to at-

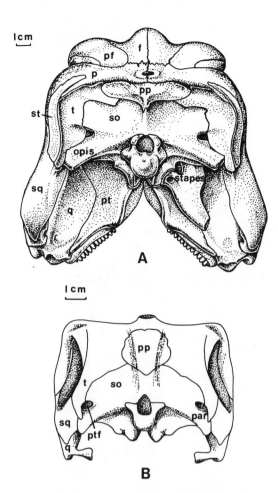

Figure 5. Occiputs of primitive reptiles. A, The advanced pelycosaur *Dimetrodon;* B, The primitive therapsid *Biarmosuchus tener,* showing the further elaboration of a platelike occiput and the ventral shift of the foramen magnum. (A, from Romer and Price, 1940; B, from Sigogneau and Tchudinov, 1972.) Abbreviations as in Figure 2.

tach to the more extensive lateral portion of the opisthotic, reducing, but never completely closing, the posttemporal fenestrae. For the pelycosaurian elaboration of the occipital plate—and its close integration with skull roof, tabular, and cheek—the arrangement of primitive protorothyrids is a better antecedent condition than that of *Limnoscelis,* the latter as suggested by Kemp (1980).

The platelike occiput characteristic of sphenacodont pelycosaurs is further elaborated in the therapsids (Fig. 5B), and forms the back of the bulbous braincase in mammals.

The changes in the occiput and cheek in early reptiles may be a continuation of trends initated in much earlier tetrapods, towards a coalescence of the skull from the loose-knit condition of rhipidistian fish (Carroll, 1980). In the fish, the skull

table, cheek, and braincase are loosely attached to one another. The reduction in the relative size of the otic capsule in early tetrapods results in a weak association between the back of the braincase and skull roof, which is variably strengthened in different groups of early tetrapods. The diadectomorphs and amniotes appear unique among Paleozoic tetrapods in the development of a large supraoccipital between the postparietals and the otic capsule and exoccipitals. In protorothyrids, the opisthotic is not extensively ossified, and primitively does not reach either the cheek or the skull roof. The supraoccipital is ony loosely attached dorsally, and the skull roof and cheek are not strongly attached to one another. Such loose association was presumably possible in this group because of the small size of the skull.

Pelycosaurs, captorhinids (Lower Permian descendants of the protorothyrids) and the diapsids illustrate three strategies in the solidification of the cheek and occiput.

Captorhinids have retained a solid cheek, with a very strong attachment between the squamosal and the parietal. The bones of the occiput tend to be reduced. The tabular is lost as is, later, the supratemporal. The supraoccipital is narrow dorsally but strongly attached to the skull roof. Extremely large posttemporal fenestrae are developoed in late captorhinids and their possible descendants, the turtles. In the latter group, the opisthotic extends to the cheek, above the enlarged quadrates.

In early diapsids and their descendants, the lizards, the supraoccipital remains loosely attached dorsally, but, as in turtles, the opisthotic extends laterally to reach the cheek and so strengthens the attachment of the back of the braincase.

In pelycosaurs, the supraoccipital becomes solidly attached to the skull roof and cheek as a result of the elaboration of the tabular and opisthotic. The great elaboration of the occiput in this group may have been necessary because of the much larger size of the skull and the reduction in the areas of contact of the skull roof and cheek resulting from the development of the temporal opening.

The stapes in both captorhinomorphs and pelycosaurs is robust, with a broad footplate and a stout stem (Fig. 3D, F). Primitively, it served as a strut, supporting the back of the braincase against the quadrate (Heaton, 1978). Its supportive role would have precluded reduction in its mass, initially preventing its function in an impedance matching system. Once the paroccipital process of the opisthotic became expanded in early archosaurs, lizards, and turtles, the stapes was reduced to a light rod, while the quadrate was modified to support a tympanum. If, as seems likely, this complex evolved several times among other reptiles, it is surprising that it did not in pelycosaurs, for they developed a strong attachment between the opisthotic and the cheek before the early Permian. Their descendants eventually evolved an entirely different type of middle ear structure (Allin, 1975).

Kemp (1980) proposed that the large size of the supratemporal and its contact with the postorbital were primitive features of pelycosaurs, shared with limnoscelids. This is difficult to evaluate directly since the supratemporal is not known in primitive Pennsylvanian pelycosaurs. The relationships of surrounding bones led Reisz (1972) and Currie (1977) to reconstruct the supratemporal as a small element. The supratemporal is certainly superficial, and Reisz indicates that the parietal and squamosal met beneath it in *Archaeothyris* as in protorothyrids. The postorbital is much longer in pelycosaurs than in protorothyrids, and may have grown back to strengthen the dorsal margin of the cheek in relationship to the development of a temporal opening.

There is no evidence that the arrangement of the postorbital, supratemporal, parietal, and squamosal in ancestral pelycosaurs was significantly different from the pattern in early captorhinomorphs, and certainly no evidence that it was fundamentally similar to that of limnoscelids.

On the other hand, the skull proportions of early pelycosaurs and their immediate ancestors may well have differed from those of the protorothyrids. Genera such as *Eothyris* and *Oedaleops* (Langston, 1965) have, except for the presence of a small temporal opening, a skull shape superficially resembling that of protorothyrids. They are also considered relatively primitive pelycosaurs. They are, however, advanced in that they have a solidly attached occiput and, like all other short-faced pelycosaurs, are known only in the Permian. Skull proportions of these genera, though protorothyrid-like, may reflect specialization within the pelycosaurs.

Taking the greater age of the Pennsylvanian genus *Archaeothyris* at face value, we may conclude that the distinctive features of its skull are primitive for pelycosaurs. These include the shortness of the postorbital region and its rather

marked flexion downward, relative to the face (Fig. 3A).

The condition of *Archaeothyris* may reflect a difference from the protorothyrid pattern with respect to jaw mechanics. Barghusen (1972) suggests that the difference in jaw musculature between later sphenacodonts and more primitive reptiles reflects adaptation to a more strictly carnivorous diet. He attributes the change to a reorganization of the jaw mechanism that would accommodate forces generated by the struggles of larger prey animals. Barghusen thinks that the temporal opening is of relatively little significance to the pattern of jaw musculature at this stage. His analysis rests primarily on advanced sphenacodontines, but may be extended with no difficulty to earlier Pennsylvanian haptodontine sphenacodontids and, with less assurance, to earlier Pennsylvanian genera such as *Archaeothyris,* which may represent the pattern from which all pelycosaurs evolved.

A further distinguishing feature of the skull of pelycosaurs is its large size. That of the earliest adequately known genus, *Archaeothyris,* is approximately twice the length of that of contemporary protorothyrids. This difference may also be associated with their feeding upon much larger prey. Skull size increased disproportionately in early pelycosaurs, from 34 percent to 64 percent of the trunk length in a series of species in which the snout-vent length increased from 20 cm to 120 cm (Reisz, 1972).

Postcranial skeleton

In the structure of their postcranial skeletons, the early pelycosaurs are very similar to the ancestors of nonsynapsid reptiles. In nearly all aspects, the Carboniferous protorothyrids, *Hylonomus* (Fig. 6A), *Paleothyris,* and *Brouffia,* apear as excellent models for the ancestors of pelycosaurs (Fig. 6B).

Differences are largely proportional and may be associated with the larger body size achieved by all but the most primitive pelycosaurs. The degree of size increase is indicated by Reisz (1972). The humerus, whose size can be compared throughout much of the Pennsylvanian, increased in length from 35 mm to 120 mm. The nearly 350 percent increase in this linear dimension suggests a forty-fold increase in body volume.

The vertebrae are basically similar in early pelycosaurs and protorothyrids, with stout, cylindrical centra fused to the neural arches in adults, but remaining distinct in juveniles. Prim-

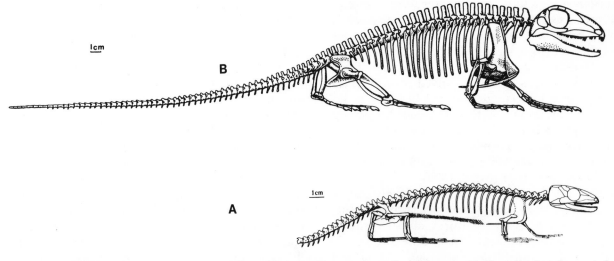

Figure 6. Skeletons of primitive reptiles. A, The earliest captorhinomorph reptile, *Hylonomus*. B, *Haptodus*, based on a skeleton from the Upper Pennsylvanian. (A, from Carroll and Baird, 1972; B, from Currie, 1977.)

itively, the neural arch contributes to the articular surface of the dorsal margin of the centrum in both pelycosaurs (Reisz, 1972) and captorhinomorphs (Carroll and Baird, 1972). The zygapophyses are close to the midline and somewhat angled from the horizontal. Between primitive pelycosaurs and sphenacodontids, the angulation increases from approximately 30 to 45 degrees in the trunk vertebrae. The neural spines are primitively rounded or triangular in lateral view in protorothyrids, but become square or rectangular in later members of this family and in early pelycosaurs. Advanced members of the two groups show divergent specializations. Many pelycosaurs develop much longer spines, while several families that evolved from the protorothyrids tend to have neural arches that are wider and extend the zygapophyses laterally.

The atlas-axis complex of *Ophiacodon* (Fig. 7C) provides a good example of the pattern common to pelycosaurs and serves as a basis for derivation of the therapsid and mammalian patterns (Jenkins, 1971). The atlas has not been described in Pennsylvanian pelycosaurs, but the axis is preserved in *Archaeothyris* (Fig. 7B). It differs from that of later pelycosaurs by having deep vertical grooves on either side of the posterior margin of the neural spine. This feature is shared with Pennsylvanian protorothyrids. The atlas of the earliest known protorothyrid, *Hylonomus* (Fig. 7A), broadly resembles that of *Ophiacodon*. Among both protorothyrids and pelycosaurs, there is a tendency for the axis

intercentrum to become fused to the atlas pleurocentrum. These elements remain separate in sphenacodontids but fuse in therapsids.

Trunk vertebrae of pelycosaurs of the middle and late Pennsylvanian age are distinguished from those of protorothyrids in that they have fairly wide transverse processes, primitively supported by a broad web of bone reaching down to the centra (Fig. 7D, E). This webbing is lost in advanced pelycosaurs (Fig. 7F), so that the transverse processes stand out even more distinctly. Articulation with the tubercular head of the rib is well lateral to the centrum.

The progressive increase in the length of the transverse processes within pelycosaurs probably indicates reorganization of the axial musculature as body size increased over all. Weight increases by the cube of linear dimension, and the increased span of the vertebral column between the piers formed by the girdles would have exacerbated the effect of its load on the unsupported middle. Simple enlargement of undifferentiated axial musculature would have interfered with the lateral undulation, which was vital to the locomotion of primitive tetrapods—pelycosaurs included—and was manifest even in therapsids (Jenkins, 1971). But by rearrangement of the axial musculature above and below the now well-defined transverse processes, pelycosaurs were able to accommodate the mechanical stresses of their increasing size without compromising their basic mode of locomotion. Elongation of the transverse processes probably

R. L. CARROLL

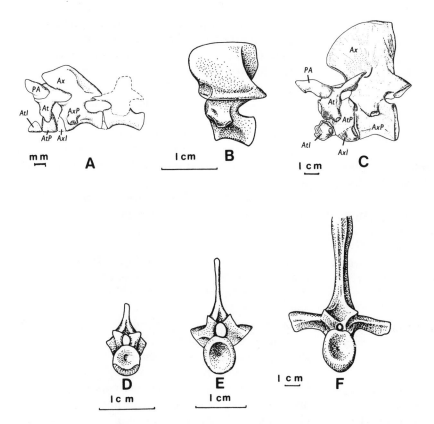

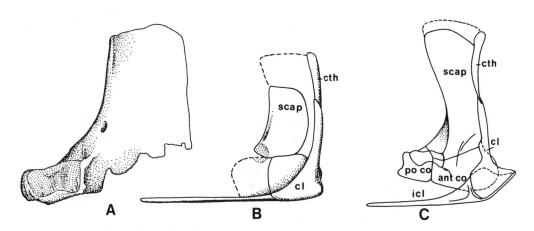

Figure 7. Vertebrae of primitive reptiles. A, Atlas-axis complex of *Hylonomus*. B, Axis of the Middle Pennsylvanian pelycosaur *Archaeothyris*. C, Atlas-axis complex of the Lower Permian pelycosaur *Ophiacodon*. D–F, end-on views of trunk vertebrae of a succession of pelycosaurs, showing elongation of transverse processes: D, The earliest known pelycosaur *Protoclepsydrops*; E, *Archaeothyris*; F, *Dimetrodon*. (A and C, from Carroll, 1969b; B and D , from Reisz, 1972; E, from Carroll et al., 1972; F, form Romer and Price, 1940.)

Key: **At,** atlas arch; **AtI,** atlas intercentrum; **AtP,** atlas pleurocentrum; **Ax,** axis arch; **AxI,** axis intercentrum; **AxP,** axis pleurocentrum; **PA,** proatlas.

Figure 8. Shoulder girdle. A, Mature scapulocoracoid of the protorothyrid *Paleothyris,* showing ossification as a single unit. B, Immature specimen of *Cephalerpeton,* showing separation into three areas of ossification. C, The pelycosaur *Dimetrodon* in which the three centers of ossification remain distinct even in mature individuals. (A, from Carroll, 1969a; B, from Carroll and Baird, 1972; C, from Romer and Price, 1940.)

Key: **ant co,** anterior coracoid; **cl,** clavicle; **cth,** cleithrum; **icl,** interclavicle; **po co,** posterior coracoid; **scap,** scapula.

indicates a more dynamic support of the column on the girdles than is the case in captorhinomorphs.

The general similarity of the limbs and girdles in protorothyrids and pelycosaurs suggests a basic similarity in posture and a primitive pattern of locomotion, in which side-to-side sinusoidal movement of the trunk played an important role.

The dermal shoulder girdle is somewhat variable among pelycosaurs, and there is some question as to what pattern is primitive. The anterior plate of the interclavicle and the ventral portion of the clavicles, which are fairly wide in *Hylonomus,* are not well preserved in the earliest pelycosaurs. The anterior portion of the interclavicle is narrow in ophiacodonts and primitive sphenacodonts, but becomes more broadly expanded in later sphenacodonts.

In pelycosaurs, three centers of ossification can be identified in the scapulocoracoid (Fig. 8C). Protorothyrids typically ossify the scapulocoracoid without a trace of subdivision (Fig. 8A), but there are apparently three distinct elements in young individuals (e.g., Fig. 8B) of several Pennsylvanian genera (Carroll and Baird, 1972). Coossification appears to be progresively delayed in pelycosaurs so that sutures are evident between the elements in more mature specimens. The blade of the scapula appears consistently longer in pelycosaurs, but it is not known in the earliest genera.

The pelycosaur humerus is distinctive in the great expansion of the extremities relative to the short shaft (Fig. 9C). There is a well-developed supinator process and a strong ridge above the ectepicondyle. These features led to the identification of the very incomplete material from Joggins as pelycosaurian (Fig. 9B). All are evident in a less well developed state in early protorothyrids (Fig. 9A). Sphenacodonts show a somewhat less extreme elaboration of the processes than do the ophiacodonts.

Differences in proportions are evident in the structure of the remainder of the forelimb in protorothyrids and pelycosaurs, but few features not associated with the larger size of the early mammal-like reptiles appear significant in distinguishing the two groups (Fig. 10). In both groups the wrist is formed from a complex of elements rather than having a simple hinge as in modern lizards.

Jenkins (1971) and Holmes (1977) have recently discussed the structure and function of the forelimb and girdle in pelycosaurs and captorhinomorphs. In all primitive tetrapods, the glenoid and proximal end of the humerus form a complex joint that mechanically constrains the movement of the forelimb. The distal end of the humerus could not be depressed below the level of the glenoid, and anterior-posterior movement would have been very limited.

Rotation of the humerus around its long axis was important in controlling the position of the more distal limb elements. The great expansion of the distal end of the humerus is related to the importance of the flexors and extensors of the lower limb in supporting the body, as well as for propulsion.

Although the pelvis is not well known in Pennsylvanian pelycosaurs, the differences from that of early protorothyrids seem to be limited to the greater prominence of the lateral public tubercle (Fig. 11). This structure is lost, however, in later pelycosaurs. A prominent pubic tubercle also appears in the earliest known diapsids (Reisz, 1981), only to be lost in later genera. The ilium, which is narrow and posteriorly oriented in early pelycosaurs, becomes expanded anteriorly in sphenacodonts and edaphosaurs in association with the incorporation of one or more additional pairs of sacral ribs.

The basic structure of the femur seems comparable in pelycosaurs and protorothyrids, except for proportional changes that may be attributed to the great bulk of pelycosaurs (Fig. 12). The shaft is straight, and the head is terminal. The tibia and fibula appear similar, except for the prominence of the cnemial crest in pelycosaurs. In both groups, the distal end of the tibia is expanded in the earliest genera; it becomes much narrower in later protorothyrids and decreases somewhat in width in sphenacodont pelycosaurs.

Little systematic difference can be noted in the structure of the tarsus and foot, beyond those attributable to the greater size of pelycosaurs. There is some question as to whether a medial centrale is retained in protorothyrids, as it is in pelycosaurs, or whether it has become integrated into the lateral centrale. The length of the metatarsals and digits increases among the protorothyrids, and markedly decreases among the pelycosaurs.

The function of the hind limb in primitive reptiles has recently been analyzed by Brinkman (1980 and 1981), and that of pelycosaurs and therapsids by Jenkins (1971). As in the forelimb, the mechanisms are similar in captorhinomorphs and pelycosaurs. The femur is held essentially

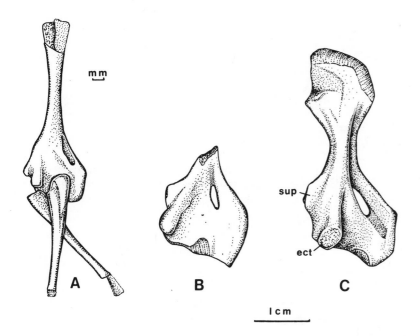

Figure 9. Humeri. A, The captorhino-morph, *Paleothyris*. B, The earliest known pelycosaur, *Protoclepsydrops*. C, The Middle Pennsylvanian pelycosaur, *Archaeothyris*. (A, from Carroll, 1969a; B, from Carroll, 1964; C, from Reisz, 1972.)

Key: **sup,** supinator process; **ect,** ectepicondylar ridge.

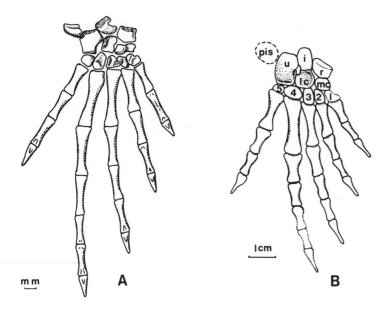

Figure 10. Carpus and manus. A, *Paleothyris*, in ventral view. B, *Haptodus*, in dorsal view. (A, from Carroll, 1969a; B, from Currie, 1977.)

Key: **i,** intermedium; **lc,** lateral centrale; **mc,** medial centrale; **p,** pisiform; **r,** radiale; **u,** ulnare; **1–5,** distal carpals.

horizontal. Rotation about the axis of the shaft is an important component of locomotion. As in modern lizards, the foot is rotated through a broad arc and the digits face nearly laterally during the power stroke.

In comparison with that of living lizards and *Sphenodon,* the tarsus of primitive reptiles is a mosaic of bones, without an effective joint. The posture is digitigrade, and the ankle is passively rolled off the substrate. In contrast, most modern reptiles and mammals have separately evolved an effective ankle joint, in which better fulcra al-low increased leverage provided by either the calcaneum (crocodiles and mammals) or by the hooked fifth metatarsal (lizards and sphenodon-tids). In these groups, the foot functions as an additional propulsive unit of the hind limb. There is no evidence for even the incipient development of such a feature in pelycosaurs.

In nearly all aspects of the postcranial skeleton, for which comparable material is available, the early pelycosaurs and protorothyrids converge on a common pattern near the beginning of the Pennsylvanian. The few features in which

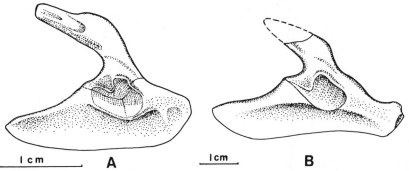

Figure 11. Pelvic girdle. A, *Hylonomus;* B, *Archaothyris.* (B, from Reisz, 1972.)

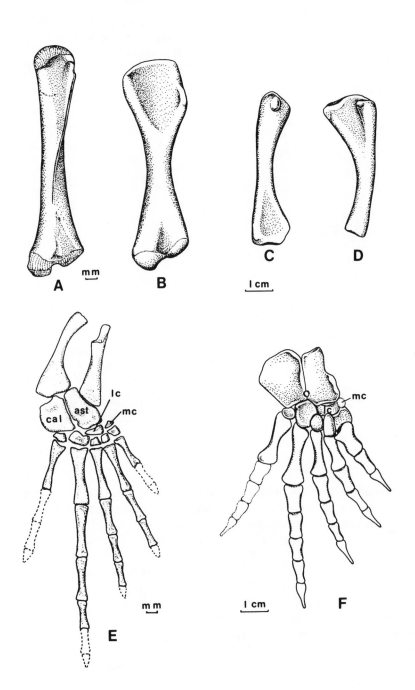

Figure 12. Elements of hind limb of captorhinomorphs and a sphenacodontine pelycosaur. A, Ventral view of the femur of *Paleothyris.* B, Ventral view of femur of *Haptodus.* C and D, Fibula and tibia of *Haptodus.* E, Lower limb elements of *Hylonomus.* F, Tarsus and pes of *Haptodus.* Metatarsals and phalanges become increasingly elongated in protorothyrids and progressively shortened in pelycosaurs. (A, from Carroll, 1969a; B–D and F, from Currie, 1977; E, from Carroll, 1969b.)

Key: **ast,** astragalus; **cal,** calcaneum; **lc,** lateral centrale; **mc,** medial centrale.

R. L. CARROLL

later pelycosaurs differ (such as the presence of a pubic tubercle, a prominent cnemial crest, and elaboration of processes on the humerus) can be attributed to a single factor—increase in body size. The lateral extension of the transverse processes is one possible exception, which may presage the modification of the axial musculature characteristic of therapsids and mammals.

From the late Pennsylvanian to the end of the Lower Permian, there is relatively little change among the sphenacodontid pelycosaurs. The postcranial skeleton shows few significant advances, and the posture, as well as it can be judged, retains the strictly sprawling pattern of the earliest reptiles. This constancy is particularly striking when viewed in contrast to the earliest adequately known therapsids.

The Gap between Pelycosaurs and Therapsids

Postcranial elements of the earliest adequately known therapsids contrast markedly with those of pelycosaurs. The bones illustrated in Figures 13, 14B, and 15 are from the Ezhovo locality in Russia, which Sigogneau and Tchudinov (1972) indicate is upper Kazanian in age. All the elements are clearly advanced over the pattern in the latest adquately known sphenacodontid pelycosaurs. The glenoid and acetabulum are restructured to permit the distal ends of the humerus and femur to be lowered below the horizontal. The change in the femur is perhaps most striking, with the head inflected posteriorly and dorsally, and the shaft curved sigmoidally. The distal condyles are nearly symmetrical. Kemp (1978), in his discussion of the femur of a therocephalian, notes the similarity of this pattern to that of modern crocodiles and suggests that it represents an intermediate stage in the development of a more upright posture in advanced cynodonts and mammals.

The structure of the foot is also significantly advanced, with reduction in the length of the digits and their more symmetrical arrangement. This suggests that the digits were directed more or less anteriorly throughout the stride, rather than being rotated as in primitive reptiles. The astragalus is strikingly modified from the primitive platelike configuration seen in pelycosaurs, indicating a marked advance toward the achievement of the plantigrade posture of advanced therapsids.

Although there is continuing debate over relative dating, these therapsids may be no more than about ten million years younger than the typical pelycosaurs of the Vale and Choza of Texas (Olson, 1954). Almost no evidence is available to suggest any tendency toward these advanced features among sphenacodont pelycosaurs.

Olson (1962, 1974) has described remains from the latest beds of the Texas and Oklahoma Permian sequence, which he believes represent the earliest therapsids. It is unfortunate that most of this material is incomplete, poorly preserved, and provides little anatomical evidence of intermediate stages in the achievement of therapsid features. One possible exception is the femur designated as the type of *Eosyodon*. In its sigmoidal curvature, it resembles the pattern of primitive therapsids from Russia and South Africa. It is uncertain from the illustration and description whether the head is terminal or inflected.

Watongia, from the Upper Permian Chickasha Formation, described by Olson (1974) as a sphenacodontlike gorganospid, lacks the femur or rear foot, which would show very clearly the differences between pelycosaurs and therapsids, but the well preserved elements of the forelimb appear completely pelycosaurian in their configuration.

On the basis of currently available material, there seems to be a very significant gap in skeletal anatomy between pelycosaurs and therapsids.

There is, at present, no evidence to establish whether therapsids evolved rapidly near the end of the Early Permian, or over a long period of time beginning in the late Pennsylvanian. Sigogneau and Tchudinov (1972), Olson (1974), and Currie (1979) have all pointed to the genus *Haptodus* (Figs. 4 and 6B) as the pelycosaur most appropriate as a therapsid ancestor. Recent descriptions of this genus by Currie (1977, 1979) indicate that it remained essentially unchanged for a period of approximately twenty-five million years. Assuming that *Haptodus* actually did give rise to the ancestors of the known therapsids, the transition might have required no more than fifteen million years, or as much as forty million years (Fig. 16).

Aspects of the Soft Anatomy and Physiology of Primitive Reptiles

The high degree of skeletal similarity of early pelycosaurs and primitive captorhinomorph reptiles suggests that the soft anatomy and physi-

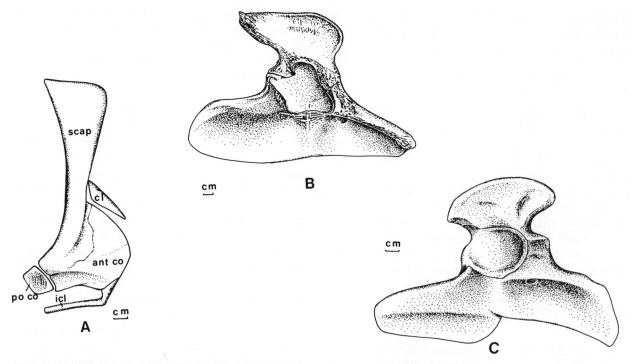

Figure 13. A, Shoulder girdle of the primitive therapsid, *Biarmosuchus tener* (cf. Figure 8C). B, Pelvis of *Dimetrodon,* C, Pelvis of *Biarmosuchus tener,* note anterior expansion of iliac blade. (A and C, from Sigogneau and Tchudinov, 1972; B, from Romer and Price, 1940.) Abbreviations as in Figure 8.

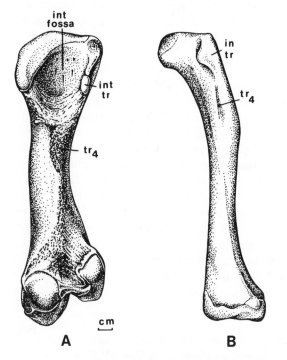

Figure 14. Femora. A, *Dimetrodon.* B, Biarmosuchidae, gen. indet. (no scale given in original). (A, from Romer and Price, 1940; B, from Sigogneau and Tchudinov, 1972.)

Key: **int fossa,** interrochanteric fossa; **int tr,** internal trochanter; **tr₄,** fourth trochanter.

ology of early mammal-like reptiles were also similar to those of the ancestors of lizards, turtles, and crocodiles.

Most aspects of the soft anatomy and physiology of modern reptiles are being reviewed in the multivolume series, *The Biology of the Reptilia* (Gans, 1969 and continuing). To a variable extent, these findings can be applied to the earliest known reptiles. I shall comment on only a few aspects that are associated, by other authors in this volume, with more advanced mammal-like reptiles and early mammals.

More than 300 million years of subsequent evolution separate the ancestors of mammals from other groups of living amniotes. While some systems may have remained relatively conservative, others have diverged greatly from the ancestral condition. One primitive condition that modern lizards, *Sphenodon,* crocodiles, and most turtles almost certainly retain is their low metabolic rate and ectothermy.

Like that of most modern lizards, the small body size of early reptiles would have given them the potential for rapid gain and loss of heat. The larger size of the sphenacodont pelycosaurs, on the other hand, would have rendered them effec-

R. L. CARROLL

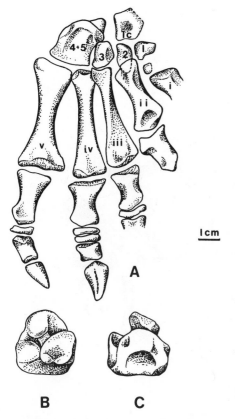

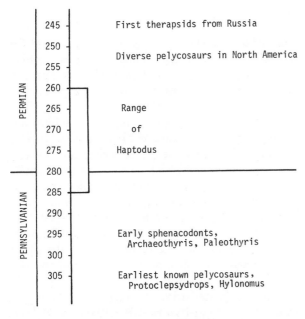

Figure 15. Tarsals and pes of primitive therapsid, Biarmosuchidae, gen. indet. A, Distal tarsals and pes. B and C, Two views of astragalus identified as dorsal and ventral views by Sigogneau and Tchudinov, but comparable to medial and lateral views of Kemp (1978). (From Sigogneau and Tchudinov, 1978.)

Key; lc, lateral centrale; 1–5, distal tarsals; i–v, metatarsals.

Figure 16. Geological range and ages of genera mentioned in text. Ages are from van Eysinga (1970).

tive homeotherms since their temperatures would change very slowly.

The high rate of oxygen consumption and food intake associated with an increased metabolic level in mammals are reflected in the nature of the palate and dentition, as well as in the relative size of the brain and possibly in their bone histology. These changes are all evident among the therapsids, but there is no evidence for their inception among the pelycosaurs.

Brain

Although the general configuration of the brain may be represented in fossils as a mold of the internal surface of the bony braincase, this provides little information in early reptiles. Only the posterior portion of the braincase, up to the level of the pineal opening, is ossified. Anterior to the otic capsules, the side walls of the braincase were largely cartilaginous. Furthermore, among modern reptiles, the brain occupies only about half the space within the braincase, so that surface features of the brain are only vaguely represented in an endocast, and the volume can only be approximated.

No endocasts of captorhinomorph reptiles have been described. The most primitive endocast known to provide any information on the structure of the brain in early reptiles is that of *Diadectes* (Fig. 17A, B), whose phylogenetic relationship with captorhinomorphs is still debated. An endocast of the sphenacodont *Dimetrodon* (Fig. 17 C) is also known; both have recently been discussed by Hopson (1979).

The brains of modern reptiles may be used to interpret the visible structures, but the endocasts provide little independent information regarding the structure of the primitive reptilian brain, except for the extraordinary narrowness of the cerebral and midbrain regions. Both of the known endocasts exhibit conspicuous flexure posteriorly, and the flocculus may be represented by a swelling posterior to the fifth nerve in the pelycosaur.

The general configuration of the brain is relatively uniform among modern reptiles, and the size of the brain relative to body weight is fairly constant (Fig. 18). At this very general level one can reconstruct the expected pattern in Paleozoic reptiles, including the early pelycosaurs.

Reproduction

If we are correct in thinking that the common ancestor of all amniotes had developed extraembryonic membranes and laid eggs on land, we

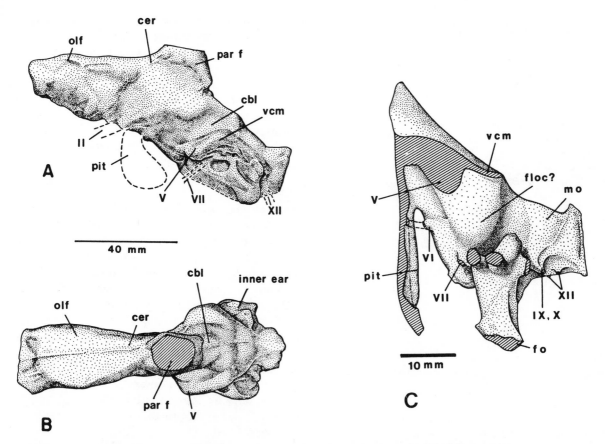

Figure 17.   Endocasts of primitive tetrapods. A and B, Lateral and dorsal views of an endocast of *Diadectes*. Restored portions are indicated by broken lines. C, Lateral view of an endocast of the advanced pelycosaur *Dimetrodon*. (From Hopson, 1979.)

Key: **cbl,** cerebellar region; **cer,** cerebral region; **floc?,** possible flocculus; **fo,** fenestra ovalis; **mo,** medulla oblongata; **ol f,** olfactory bulb; **par f,** parietal foramen; **pit,** pituitary fossa; **vcm,** ridge marking the course of the middle cerebral vein; **II,** optic nerve; **V,** trigeminal foramen; **VI,** canal for the abducens nerve; **VII,** facial nerve; **IX,** foramen foglossaphanygeal nerve; **X,** foramen for vagus nerves; **XII,** hypoglossal nerve.

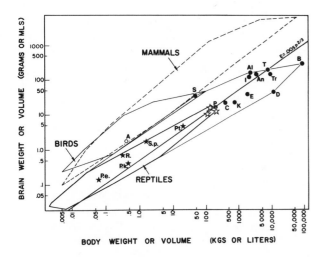

Figure 18.   Brain to body-size relations in modern and fossil reptiles compared with birds and mammals. Line with 2/3 slope passes through the approximate center of a cluster of points for living crocodilians (open stars). Letters identify archosaurs. (From Hopson, 1977.)

must also assume that it practiced internal fertilization and probably lacked copulatory organs, which—being absent in *Sphenodon*—apparently evolved separately in the ancestors of modern archosaurs and squamates.

Szarski (1968) suggests that the earliest amniotes, like many modern lizards and turtles, had only a membraneous covering for the egg, and not a calcified shell. Such eggs are capable of doubling their initial weight by absorbing water from damp ground into the allantois.

Romer and Price (1939) described what they thought was a primitive reptilian egg from the Lower Permian of Texas. Because of the specimen's large size (59 mm in length) and the predominance of pelycosaur bones in these beds, the authors suggested that the egg might belong to an early mammal-like reptile. Hirsch (1979) cast doubt on the likelihood that the object was a calcareous egg, but he did not rule out the possibil-

R. L. CARROLL

ity that it was a reptile egg with a membranous shell.

Hearing

The nature of the middle ear and its sensitivity to air-borne vibrations have often been discussed in relationship to early reptiles. Watson (1953, 1954) attempted to show that the ancestors of diapsids had a tympanum and a middle-ear function comparable to that in most living reptiles and that the pelycosaurs lacked a tympanum and were essentially deaf. Hotton (1959) argued that the pelycosaur stapes was capable of transmitting sound and suggested that they possessed a tympanum and were sensitive to air-born vibrations.

Within the last fifteen years, extensive work by Wever (1978), on the structure and function of the ear in modern reptiles, has provided a model by which the possible function of the middle ear in early reptiles can be evaluated. He has demonstrated that the tympanum and middle-ear ossicles serve as an impedance-matching mechanism that magnifies the force of the air that impinges on the tympanum to compensate for the much greater density of the fluid of the inner ear. This is accomplished by the much greater area of the tympanum, compared with that of the head of the stapes, and—in modern reptiles—by a leverlike arrangement between the columella and extrastapes. The tympanum of modern reptiles may have an area approximately twenty times that of the head of the stapes, and the lever may provide an additional doubling of the force that is applied at the fenestra ovalis. The stapes of extant reptiles is very light and is oriented at right angles to the tympanum.

Examination of the stapes in early pelycosaurs and captorhinomorphs shows that it is a massive bone, with a particularly large head, and may have been held in place by the bones surrounding the fenestra ovalis. Such a stapes might be activated by an enormous tympanum, but it is much more likely that this ear structure functioned in an entirely different manner than the impedance-matching ear of modern reptiles and mammals.

This does not imply that early reptiles were insensitive to air-borne sounds. Many modern reptiles lack a tympanum and middle-ear cavity, and the stapes may be heavy or attached to other elements. Yet they are sensitive to air-borne sounds, although typically in a lower frequency range than reptiles having a tympanum. Snakes commonly are sensitive in the range of 200–400 Hz: *Sphenodon*, from 100–800 Hz; and amphisbaenids, from 200–1,500 Hz. In constrast, lizards with a tympanum may be sensitive to much higher frequencies: *Varanus*, from 400–2,000 Hz, and *Gekko gecko*, up to 4,000 Hz. The Mississippi alligator is sensitive to sounds ranging from 50–3,000 Hz.

The structure of the stapes and surrounding area of the middle ear in captorhinomorphs and early pelycosaurs are sufficiently similar to suggest that their sensitivity to air-born sound was probably equivalent to that of modern reptiles that lack a tympanum. Judged by this standard, their sensitivity to air-born sounds probably did not reach 1,000 Hz. A lightweight stapes and specialized support for the tympanum evolved in turtles, and in several other lines of anapsid and diapsid reptiles, in the late Permian and early Triassic. Presumably, selection also acted to increase the sensitivity of the ears in synapsids.

Summary

The synapsid order Pelycosauria, which includes the remotest ancestors of mammals, is identifiable among the oldest and most primitive reptiles of record. The earliest pelycosaurs are consistently larger than primitive captorhinomorphs, with a skull in which the postorbital region is proportionately shorter and the back of the table is flexed downward. Pelycosaurs and their derivatives, the therapsids, also differ profoundly from all except the most primitive amniotes in the structure and function of the middle ear. In pelycosaurs, as in all primitive reptiles, configuration of the articular surface of limbs and girdles indicates a sprawling posture, with laterally sinusoidal movement of the flexible trunk being an important component of locomotion.

Their generally primitive skeletal structure suggests that early pelycosaurs were no more advanced in their soft anatomy and physiology than the most conservative of living reptiles. In such features as basal metabolic rate, size and configuration of the brain, and reproduction, pelycosaurs in general probably resembled *Sphenodon* and living lizards. Cranial differences between early forms and the most primitive captorhinomorphs may reflect the taking of proportionately larger prey by pelycosaurs.

Subsequent changes, such as the development of a platelike occiput and of long transverse processes on the vertebrae, may be related to the dramatic increase in size that pelycosaurs underwent during the Pennsylvanian. Long transverse processes suggest elaboration of the axial muscles of the transversospinalis group and a more effective suspension of the vertebral column above the girdles. The transition from pelycosaurs of therapsids is poorly known, but its most conspicuous consequence involves locomotion. The presacral column and tail are shortened; the pelvis is more extensively articulated with the column; and posture changes from the sprawled pose of pelycosaurs to one in which at least the hind limbs are more vertically oriented.

Acknowledgments

I wish to thank Dr. Malcolm Heaton and Dr. Robert Reisz, Erindale Campus, University of Toronto, for permission to cite unpublished studies, and for discussion on various aspects of the structure and functional anatomy of early reptiles. Many of the illustrations were redrawn by Mrs. Pamela Gaskill. This work was supported by grants from the National Science and Engineering Research Council of Canada.

References

Allin, E. F.
1975. Evolution of the mammalian middle ear. *Jour. Morph.* 147(4):403–38.

Baker, D; Hunt, D. C; and McIntyre, A. K.
1974. Muscle receptors. In *Handbook of Sensory Physiology,* ed. C. C. Hunt, vol. 3, pt. 2, pp. 1–299. Berlin: Springer-Verlag; New York: Heidelberg.

Barghusen, H. R.
1972. The origin of the mammalian jaw apparatus. In *Morphology of the Maxillomandibular Apparatus,* ed. G. H. Schumacher, pp. 26–32. Leipzig: VEB Georg. Thieme.

Brinkman, D.
1980. The hind limb step cycle of *Caiman sclerops* and the mechanics of the crocodile tarsus and metatarsus. *Can. Jour. Zool.* 58(12):2187–2200.

1981. The hind limb step cycle of *Iguana* and primitive reptiles. *Jour. Zool. Lond.,* 181:91–103.

Carroll, R. L.
1969a. A Middle Pennsylvanian captorhinomorph, and the interrelationships of primitive reptiles. *Jour. Paleon.* 43:151–70.
1969b. Problems of the origin of reptiles. *Biol. Rev. Camb. Phil. Soc.* 44:393–432.

1970a. The ancestry of reptiles. *Phil. Trans. Roy. Soc. Lond.* 257(814):267–308.
1970b. Quantitative aspects of the amphibian-reptilian transition. *Forma et Functio* 3:165–78.
1980. The hyomandibular as a supporting element in the skull of primitive tetrapods. In *The Terrestrial Environment and the Origin of Land* Vertebrates, ed. A. L. Panchen, pp. 293–317. *Systematics Association Special Volume* No. 15. London and New York: Academic Press.
1982. Early evolution of reptiles. *Ann. Rev. Ecol. & Syst.* 13:87–109.

Carroll, R. L., and Baird, D.
1972. Carboniferous stem-reptiles of the family Romeriidae. *Bull. Mus. Comp. Zool.* 143(5):321–63.

Carroll, R. L; Belt, E. S; Dineley, D. L; Baird, D.; and McGregor, D. C.
1972. *Vertebrate Paleonotology of Eastern Canada.* Twenty-fourth International Geological Congress, Montreal. Field Excursion A 59, Twenty-fourth Session.

Currie, P. J.
1977. A new haptodontine sphenacodont (Reptilia, Pelycosauria) from the Upper Pennsylvanian of North America. *Jour. Paleon.* 51(5):927–42.
1979. The osteology of haptodontine sphenacodont (Reptilia: Pelycosauria). *Palaeontographica* 163:130–68.

Gaffney, E. S., and McKenna, M. C.
1979. A later Permian captorhinid from Rhodesia. *Amer. Mus. Nov.* 2688:1–15.

Ganz, C., ed.
1969. *Biology of the Reptilia.* New York and London: Academic Press.

Heaton, M. J.
1978. "Cranial soft anatomy and functional morphology of a primitive captorhinid reptile." Ph.D dissertation, Department of Biology, McGill University.
1980. The Cotylosauria: A reconstruction of a group of archaic tetrapods. In *The Terrestrial Environment and the Origin of Land Vertebrates,* ed. A. L. Panchen, pp. 497–551. *Sys. Assoc. Spec. Vol.* No. 15. New York: Academic Press.

Hirsch, K. F.
1979. The oldest vertebrate egg? *Jour. Paleon.* 53(5):1068–84.

Holmes, R.
1977. The osteology and musculature of the pectoral limb of small captorhinids. *Jour. Morph.* 152(1):101–40.

Hopson, J. A.
1977. Relative brain size and behavior in archosaurian reptiles. *Ann. Rev. Ecol. Syst.* 8:429–48.

1979. Paleoneurology. In *Biology of the Reptila,* ed. C. Gans, vol. 9. New York: Academic Press.

Hotton, N.
1959. The pelycosaur tympanum and early evolution of the middle ear. *Evolution* 13:99–121.

Jenkins, F., Jr.
1971. The postcranial skeleton of African cynodonts. *Bull. Peabody Mus. Nat. Hist.* 36:1–201.

Kemp, T. S.
1978. Stance and gait in the hindlimb of a therocephalian mammalian-like reptile. *Jour. Zool. Lond.* 186:143–61.
1980. Origin of the mammal-like reptiles. *Nature* 283:378–80.

Langston, W., Jr.
1965. *Oedaleops campi* (Reptilia: Pelycosauria): A new genus and species from the Lower Permian of New Mexico and the family Eothyrididae. *Bull. Tex. Mem. Mus.* 9:5–47.

Northcutt, R. G.
1969. Discussion of the preceding paper. In *Comparative and Evolutionary Aspects of the Vertebrate Central Nervous System. Anns. N. Y. Acad. Soc.* 167:1–513. 1969.

Olson, E. C.
1954. Fauna of the Vale and Choza: 8 Pelycosauria: *Dimetrodon. Fieldiana Geol.* 10(18):205–10.
1962. Later Permian terrestrial vertebrates, U.S.A. and U.S.S.R. *Trans. Amer. Phil. Soc.* 52(2):1–197.
1974. On the source of therapsids. *Ann. S. Afr. Mus.* 64:27–46.

Reisz, R.
1972. Pelycosaurian reptiles from the Middle Pennsylvanian of North America. *Bull. Mus. Comp. Zool.* 144(2):26–60.

1980. The pelycosauria: A review of phylogenetic relationships. In *The Terrestrial Environment and the Origin of Land Vertebrates,* ed. A. L. Panchen, pp. 553–92. *Sys. Assoc. Spec. Vol.* No. 15.
1981. A diapsid reptile from the Pennsylvanian of Kansas. *Mus. Nat. His. Spec. Pub.* 7:1–74.

Romer, A. S., and Price, L. I.
1939. The oldest vertebrate egg. *Am. Jour. Sci.* 237:826–29.
1940. Review of the Pelycosauria. *Geol. Soc. Am. Spec. Pap.* No. 28:1–538.

Sigogneau, D., and Tchudinov, P. J.
1972. Reflections on some Russian eotheriodonts (Reptilia, Synapsida, Therapsida). *Palaeovertebrata* 5:79–109.

Szarski, H.
1968. The origin of vertebrate foetal membrane. *Evolution* 22:211–14.

van Eysinga, F. W. B.
1970. *Geological Time Table,* 1st Edition. Amsterdam: Elsevier.

Vaughn, P. P.
1972. More vertebrates, including a new microsaur, from the Upper Pennsylvanian of Central Colorado. *Los Ang. Cty. Mus. Contr. Sci.* 223:1–30.

Watson, D. M. S.
1953. The evolution of the mammalian ear. *Evolution* 7(2):159–77.
1954. On *Bolosaurus* and the origin and classification of reptiles. *Bull. Mus. Comp. Zool.* 3(9):299–444.

Wever, E. G.
1978. *The Reptile Ear.* Princeton, New Jersey: Princeton University Press.

EVERETT C. OLSON
Department of Biology
University of California
Los Angeles, California 90024

Relationships and Ecology of the Early Therapsids and Their Predecessors

Introduction

The principal questions about therapsids, including morphology, function, behavior, and physiology, have centered about the therapsid role in the origin of mammals. The establishment of well-defined therapsid groups—gorgonopsians, therocephalians, cynodonts, dicynodonts, and dinocephalians—set the stage for a massive Upper Permian and Triassic radiation. Although an immense variety of organisms was involved in this branching out, all were linked by a common morphological ground plan upon which was superimposed a mosaic of similar features that developed, in parallel, in different major phyla (Olson, 1944). This mosaic of characters appeared in full array only in the mammals proper, but was displayed at a near-mammalian grade in several lines. An explanation for the parallelism has been sought in functional anatomy, genetic resemblances and parallel continuity, behavior, and physiology. The last, with reference to incipient endothermy, was suggested as an integrating factor around which similar changes developed adaptively in the several phyla (Olson, 1959).

The evolutionary history of the Therapsida is well known only for the interval following establishment of the major subdivisions of the order, but is vague prior to this stage. A relationship of pelycosaurs to therapsids was first recognized by Cope (1878) and, throughout a long and complex history of changing concepts and classification has not been seriously challenged. As long as the knowledge of synapsid evolution came largely from North America and South Africa, a significant morphological, temporal, and geographic hiatus existed between pelycosaurs and therapsids. Sphenacodont pelycosaurs and gorgonopsians clearly were similar, but the general resemblances were insufficient to infer subfamilial, genus-to-genus, evolutionary relationships.

Discoveries of the last thirty years have altered this situation. Two have been particularly important: the Ocher (Ezhovo) locality in the very early Kazanian (Guadalupian) of the Soviet Union (Chudinov, 1959, 1960, 1965; Efremov and Vjushkov, 1955; Olson, 1957, 1962); and the San Angelo locality of Texas (Olson and Beerbower, 1953; Olson, 1962). The stratigraphic relationships are shown in Figure 1. The only other therapsids from Zone I (early Kazanian) of the Soviet Union are *Phthinosuchus* and *Phreatosuchus* from the Santagulov mine in Bashkir, USSR. *Watongia*, tentatively placed as a therapsid, is the only genus yet found in the United States outside of the San Angelo locality. It comes from the Chickasha Formation of west central Oklahoma (Olson, 1974).

The therapsids of these early Guadalupian sites are of interest for their relationship to the more advanced therapsids on the one hand, and to pelycosaurs on the other (Figs. 2 and 3). In these relationships, they give some evidence of the course of transition between the two groups, though data are limited and leave many questions unanswered. This paper includes a summation of the data and the conclusions of the principal studies made during the last thirty years. New interpretations of relationships and ecologies are also presented. The principal works in which more extensive treatment of the early therapsids can be found, along with their phylogenetic and ecological relationships to the pelycosaurs are as follows: Barghusen, 1968, 1973, 1976; Chudinov, 1959, 1960, 1965; Efremov, 1954; Efremov and Vjushkov, 1955; Lewis and Vaughn, 1965; Olson, 1944, 1952, 1957, 1962, 1971, 1974, 1975a and b, 1979; Olson and Vaughn, 1970; Sigogneau, 1970; Sigogneau and Chudinov, 1972; Vaughn, 1969a and b.

The Early Therapsids

Definitions and groups

The early therapsids are termed "eotherapsids" in this paper, to distinguish them collectively from definitive dinocephalians, dicynodonts, gorgonopsians, therocephalians, and cynodonts, which may be called "eutherapsids". The eotherapsids comprise eighteen genera (Table 1), of which all except *Watongia* were treated earlier

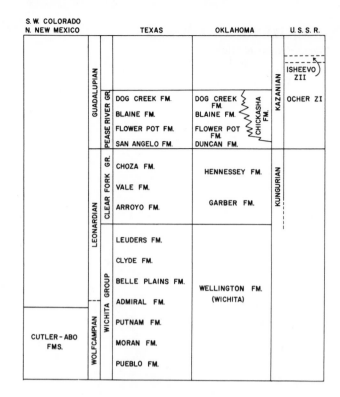

Figure 1. A stratigraphic chart for North America and the Soviet Union.

by the writer (Olson, 1962). Particular aspects of some eotherapsid genera have been elaborated since then by Barghusen, Chudinov and Sigogneau, and Chudinov, as cited above. General references are also to be found in Rozhdestvenskii and Tatarinov (1964), Romer (1966), and Olson (1971).

Eotherapsids are still known only from the Soviet Union and the United States (Table 1). All but one genus are from Efremov's Zone I, the exception being *Phthinosaurus*, from the Belebei-Cotylosaur Complex, assigned to Zone II, but of somewhat uncertain stratigraphic position. All North American genera are from the San Angelo and Chickasha Formations of early Guadalupian age. The samples are small, and the geographic scope is limited.

The systematics of the eotherapsids pose many problems, both within groups and in relationships of the eotherapsids to pelycosaurs and eutherapsids. Within the eotherapsids, familial assignments of the genera are given (Table 1), and the genera and families are grouped into three informal sets in lieu of various more formal classifications which have been used (Olson, 1962; Sigogneau and Chudinov, 1972). Group I includes eleven genera representing what will

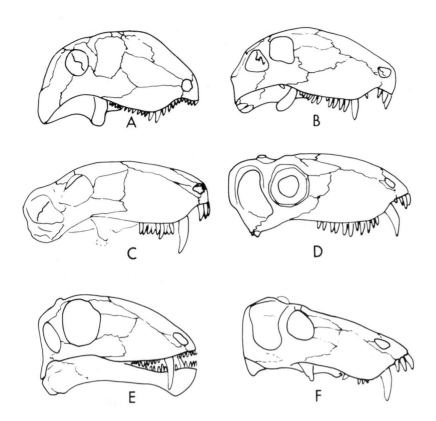

Figure 2. Skulls of pelycosaurs, eotheriodonts, and a brithopodan in lateral aspect: **A,** *Haptodus;* **B,** *Dimetrodon;* **C,** *Eotitanops;* **D,** *Phthinosuchus;* **E,** *Biarmosuchus;* **F,** *Titanosuchus.* (A and B, after Romer and Price, 1940; C–E, after Olson, 1962, based on Chudinov, 1960; F, after Orlov, 1958.) Not to scale.

be called here "eotheriodonts." Group II consists of five genera designated "eodinocephalians." Group III has but two genera, here styled "eodicynodonts." Relationships to pelycosaurs and eutherapsids are detailed later.

Characters of the groups

Ten cranial and mandibular characters are listed in Table 2. One or more of these characters is present in eight of the eotherapsid genera (*Phthinosuchus, Eotitanops, Estemmenosuchus, Biarmosuchus, Archaeosyodon, Eosyodon, Dimacrodon* and *Otsheria*). Associations of these eight genera are also based on less definitive characters of the skulls, jaws, dentitions, and postcrania. Other genera (*Phthinosaurus, Steppesaurus, Knoxosaurus, Gorgodon,* and *Watongia*) are assigned to the eotherapsids only on the basis of less-definitive features. Five genera (*Chthomaloporus, Driveria, Phreatosuchus, Mastersonia* and *Tappenosaurus*) have been considered to be eotherapsids primarily on the basis of postcranial features; however, for *Driveria,* a fragment of skull is preserved. *Chthomaloporus* is placed with the eotheriodonts, and the other four are placed with the eodinocephalians. In *Estemmenosuchus,* placement has been based on the skull, jaw, and postcranial structures. *Dimacrodon* and *Otsheria,* being known only from skulls

and lower jaws, are associated by characters of these parts.

GROUP I, EOTHERIODONTS

Ten of the eleven genera are considered to be carnivores on the basis of their dentitions. The morphology of the best-known skulls and dentitions are illustrated in Figure 4. *Chthomaloporus* has been assigned to the brithopodans by the form of its pelvis (Chudinov, 1965). In several members of this group, the maxillary and dentary teeth are conic, ranging from sharp to blunt, and include one or two large caniniform teeth. Palatal teeth tend to be grouped into patches (three genera). The interpterygoidal vacuity is moderate to small (two genera). The temporal fenestra is large in *Phthinosuchus* and *Eotitanops* but relatively small in *Biarmosuchus.* The angle of the posterior margin of the skull to the vertical axis is "positive" (Figure 5). How widely these features were destributed throughout the group cannot, of course, be determined, but it is assumed that they are representative. Postcranial structures are known in *Watongia, Biarmosuchus* and *Eosyodon,* (Figs. 6 and 7). In *Watongia* the structures are pelycosaurlike, whereas in *Biarmosuchus* and *Eosyodon* they differ significantly from those of any known pelycosaurs and suggest gorgonopsian and brithopodan features,

Table 1.—Systematic assignments, parts preserved, localities, sediments of preservation, and group assignments of eotherapsids

Family–genus	Parts preserved	Locality	Sediment	Group[1]
Phthinosuchidae				
Phthinosuchus	Part skull	Santagulov Mine, USSR, Zone I	Copper Sandstone	I
Phthinosaurus	Part l. jaws	Biik Tay, Belebei, USSR, Zone II	Copper sandstone	I
Eotitanops	Skull	Ocher, USSR, Zone I	Sandstone lens	I
Steppesaurus	Maxilla	San Angelo, USA	Red shale	I
Knoxosaurus	Frag. skull, l. jaw	San Angelo, KQ, USA	Sandy shale	I
Gorgodon	Pt. skull, pt. max.	San Angelo, KQ, USA	Sandy shale	I
Gorgonopsidae				
Watongia	Pt. skull, pt. skeleton	Chickasha, Okla. USA	Red shale	I
Biarmosuchidae				
Biarmosuchus	Skulls, postcranial	Ocher, USSR, Zone I	Sandstone lens	I
Brithopodidae				
Archaeosyodon	Pt. skull	Ocher, USSR, Zone I	Sandstone lens	I
Chthomaloporus	Pelvic girdle	Ocher, USSR, Zone I	Sandstone lens	I
Eosyodon	Pt. jaw, pt. skull, femur, vert.	San Angelo, USA, loc. KQ	Sandy shale, sandstone	I
Phreatosuchidae				
Phreatosuchus	5 femora, pt. ulna	Santagulov mine, USSR, Zone I	Copper sandstone	II
Estemmenosuchidae	Skulls, jaws, and pt.			
Estemmenosuchus	skeletons	Ocher, USSR, Zone I	Sandstone lens	II
Tappenosauridae				
Tappenosaurus	Pt. skeleton	San Angelo, USA	Sandy shale	II
Family Driveriidae	Pt. skeleton, frag.			
Driveria	skull	San Angelo, USA	Sandy shale	II
Family Mastersoniidae				
Mastersonia	Vertebrae, ribs	San Angelo, USA	Gray, sandy shale	II
Family Venjukoviidae				
Dimacrodon	Pt. jaw, pt. skull	San Angelo, USA	Sandy shale	III
Otsheria	Skull	Ocher, USSR	Sandstone lens	III

1. Groups I, II, and III denote informal associations as explained in text: **I**, eotheriodonts; **II**, eodincephalians; **III**, eodicynodonts.

respectively (Olson, 1962); Sigogneau and Chudinov, 1972).

GROUP II, EODINOCEPHALIANS

Five genera form this heterogeneous assemblage. Four (*Estemmenosuchus, Tappenosaurus, Driveria,* and *Mastersonia*) are large, heavy-boned, and are matched in size among their contemporaries only by the largest caseid, *Cotylorhynchus hancocki.* The skull of *Estemmenosuchus,* which is the only well known one in the group, is shown in Figure 8. The fifth genus, *Phreatosuchus,* whose position is uncertain, was smaller and is based upon a series of femora. The postcranial structures of all of the genera differ in many particulars from comparable structures in the pelycosaurs. Two genera, *Tappenosaurus* and *Phreatosuchus,* however, are less distinct than the others from the edaphosaurians.

GROUP III, EODICYNODONTS

Dimacrodon and *Otsheria* are the only two genera assignable to this group (Fig. 9). The former is known from a partial pair of lower jaws and a poorly preserved skull and jaws. *Otsheria* is known from a single, moderately well preserved

Table 2.—Cranial and lower jaw characters of pelycosaurs, the three groups of eotherapsids, and the eutherapsids

	1	2	3	4	5	6	7	8	9	10
Pelycosaurs										
Haptodus	A	A	A	A	A	P$_2$	A	A	A	A
Dimetrodon	A	A	A	A	A	P$_2$	A	P$_2$	A	P$_1$
Edaphosaurus	A	P$_1$	A	A	A	P$_2$	A	A	P$_1$	P$_1$
I. Eotheriodonts										
Phthinosuchus	P$_2$	P$_1$	P$_1$	P$_2$	P$_2$	P$_1$	P$_1$	X	P$_2$	P$_2$
Phthinosaurus	X	X	X	X	X	X	X	P$_1$	X	X
Eotitanops	P$_2$	X	X	P$_1$	P$_2$	A	P$_1$	X	P$_2$	P$_2$
Steppesaurus	X	X	X	X	X	X	X	X	X	X
Knoxosaurus	X	X	X	X	X	X	X	X	X	X
Gorgodon	X	P$_1$	X	X	X	X	X	X	X	X
Watongia	X	X	X	X	X	X	X	X	X	X
Biarmosuchus	A	A	X	P$_1$	A	X	P$_1$	P$_1$	P$_2$	P$_1$
Archaeosyodon	P$_1$	X	X	X	P$_1$	P$_1$	P$_2$	X	X	X
Chthomaloporus	X	X	X	X	X	X	X	X	X	X
Eosyodon	X	X	X	X	X	X	P$_2$	X	X	X
II. Eodinocephalians										
Phreatosuchus	X	X	X	X	X	X	X	X	X	X
Estemmenosuchus	P$_2$	P$_2$	X	P$_2$	P$_2$	P$_1$	A	X	P$_2$	P$_2$
Tappenosaurus	X	X	X	X	X	X	X	X	X	X
Driveria	X	X	X	X	X	X	X	X	X	X
Mastersonia	X	X	X	X	X	X	X	X	X	X
III. Eodicynodonts										
Dimacrodon	X	P$_2$	X	X	X	X	X	X	X	X
Otsheria	P$_2$	P$_2$	P$_1$	P$_2$	P$_2$	P$_1$	A	P$_1$	P$_2$	P$_2$
Eutherapsids										
Gorgonopsian	P$_2$	P$_2$	P$_1$	P$_2$	P$_2$	P$_1$	P$_2$	P$_2$	P$_2$	P$_2$
Brithopodan	P$_2$	P$_2$	P$_2$	P$_2$	P$_2$	P$_1$	P$_2$	P$_2$	P$_2$	P$_2$
Dicynodont	P$_2$	P$_2$	P$_2$	P$_2$	P$_2$	A	A	P$_2$	A	P$_2$

Key characters:
1. Zygomatic arch displaced dorsally.
2. Adductor fossa (temporal opening) large.
3. Adductor ridge in temporal fossa.
4. Akinetic pterygo-quadrate joint.
5. Quadrate process of pterygoid closely associated with basicranium.
6. Interpterygoidal vacuity present.
7. Palatal teeth grouped into small clusters on pterygoid and palatine.
8. Angular flange of angular bone present.
9. Large parietal foramen: P$_1$—present; P$_2$—cratered.
10. Positive angle between slope of posterior margin of skull and vertical (see figure 5): A—angle negative; P$_1$—angle < 15°; P$_2$—angle > 15°. A, absent; P$_1$, present weak; P$_2$, present strong, or as specified in particular instances as indicated in explanation of character numbers; P$_x$, probably present. X, condition unknown.

skull. The dentitions and temporal regions suggest that the two genera are related to each other but sharply separated from the members of groups I and II.

Relationships of eotherapsids and eutherapsids

The broad relationships of each of the three groups to the eutherapsids and to subdivisions of the eutherapsids are moderately clear. They were treated by the writer earlier (Olson, 1962) and have been made somewhat more explicit by subsequent investigators, in particular, Sigogneau and Chudinov (1972).

The various eotheriodonts possess some gorgonopsian and some brithopodan characteristics (Table 2). Most of the characters entered in the

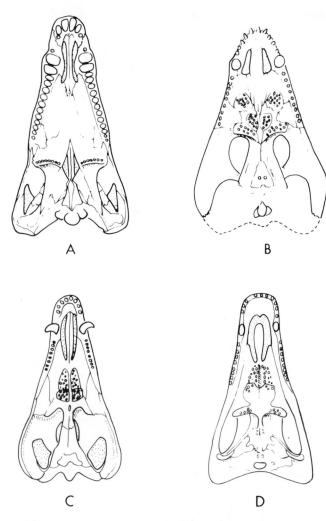

Figure 3. Palatal aspects of sphenacodonts and eotheriodonts: **A,** *Dimetrodon;* **B,** *Archaeosyodon,* a brithopodan; **C,** *Eotitanops;* **D,** *Biarmosuchus.* (A, after Romer and Price, 1940; B and C, after Chudinov, 1960; D, after Sigogneau and Chudinov, 1972. Not to scale.)

table, however, are those of primitive eutherapsids as well. The dental characteristics in particular suggest relationships of each genus to one or another group of eutheriodonts. The best-known genera, *Phthinosuchus, Eotitanops,* and *Biarmosuchus,* are gorgonopsian in skull proportions. On the basis of temporal specializations and the orbits, Sigogneau and Chudinov (1972) have indicated that *Biarmosuchus* appears to be excluded from close relationships to gorgonopsians and to show greater resemblance to ictidorhinids. *Archaeosyodon* (Fig. 3B) resembles brithopodans in the presence of fairly numerous maxillary teeth, strong transverse processes of the pterygoid, and a moderately well-developed interpterygoidal vacuity (Chudinov, 1960). *Eosyodon* also possesses stout palatal teeth, blunt

maxillary teeth, and a large "canine." The lower jaw, as well, is similar to that of the brithopodan *Syodon* (Fig. 4C–G), but the most definitive resemblances to brithopodans are in the femur, (Fig. 6F), which is very similar to that of the brithopodans detailed by Orlov (1958).

The dichotomy within the eotheriodonts, indicated by the gorgonopsianlike and brithopodan forms, had developed before the first appearance of eotheriodonts in the record. It is found both in North America and in the Soviet Union. *Knoxosaurus,* (Fig. 4B), from the San Angelo Formation, appears to have gorgonopsian affinities on the basis of its upper dentition. *Gorgodon* (Fig. 4A)—with its strong canine and moderately well developed, somewhat blunt, postcanine teeth— may well be brithopodan rather than phthinosuchid; the relationship is indicated in Table 1 and earlier, by the writer (Olson, 1962); *Watongia* is very pelycosaurlike. On the basis of the presence of a preparietal bone, this genus was associated with the gorgonopsids by the writer (Olson, 1974); but much better skull material is needed to confirm or deny the placement. *Steppesaurus* (Fig. 4H)—also difficult to place, being known from a maxilla and associated partial lower jaw–appears to belong with the phthinosuchids, but it also attests to the variety of the animals, many known from single individuals, which compose our small sample.

Members of Group II show affinities with the dinocephalians, both the titanosuchids and tapinocephalids. Data are insufficient to make a distinction. The category Dinocephalia poses a problem in classification. Two major subgroups, superfamilies Titanosuchoidea and Tapinocephaloidea (Romer, 1966), are usually recognized. Brithopodans are commonly considered to be titanosuchids, but *Estemmenosuchus,* which is very different from the brithopodans, resembles such South African titanosuchids as *Anteosaurus* and *Jonkeria.* Here, to avoid this problem and its phylogenetic consequences, brithopodans are placed with the eutherapsids rather than dinocephalians.

Among the genera assigned to Group II, only *Estemmenosuchus* can be shown to resemble South African dinocephalians at all closely. The skull is bizarre (Fig. 8). The postcranium is massive, and the pelvis is characterized by a very thick, massive supra-acetabular process (Chudinov, 1965). A similarly massive supra-acetabular process occurs in *Driveria,* but the vertebrae of this genus are deeply amphicoelous and somewhat more primitive than those of *Estemmeno-*

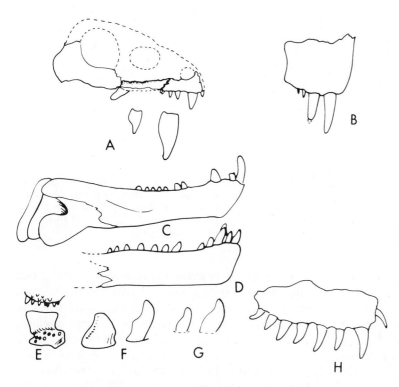

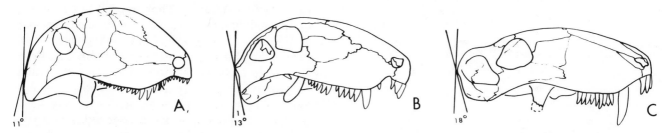

Figure 4. Various eotheriodonts and an advanced brithopodan representing genera known primarily from fragmentary materials: **A,** *Gorgodon;* **B,** *Knoxosaurus;* **C,** *Syodon;* **D,** *Eosyodon,* partial lower jaw; **E,** *Eosyodon,* palatal teeth; **F,** *Syodon,* dentary teeth; **G,** *Eosyodon,* dentary teeth; **H,** *Steppesaurus.* (A, B, D, E, G, and H, after Olson, 1962; C and F, after Orlov, 1958. Not to scale.)

Figure 5. Skulls of pelycosaurs showing angle of posterior slope of the skull relative to the vertical: **A,** *Haptodus;* **B,** *Dimetrodon;* **C,** *Eotitanops.* (After Sigogneau, 1970. Not to scale.)

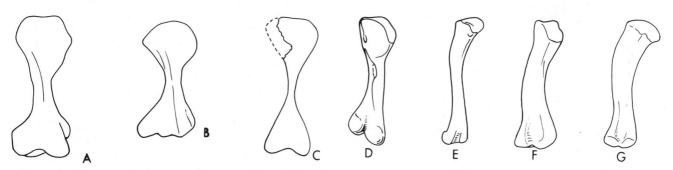

Figure 6. Femur and humerus of pelycosaur eotheriodonts and brithopodans: **A,** humerus of *Dimetrodon;* **B,** humerus of *Watongia;* **C,** humerus of *Biarmosuchus;* **D,** femur of *Dimetrodon;* **E,** femur of *Biarmosuchus;* **F,** femur of *Eosyodon;* **G,** femur of *Titanophoneus.* (A and D, after Romer and Price, 1940; B, after Olson, 1974; C and F, after Olson, 1962; E, after Sigogneau and Chudinov, 1972; G, after Orlov, 1958. Not to scale.)

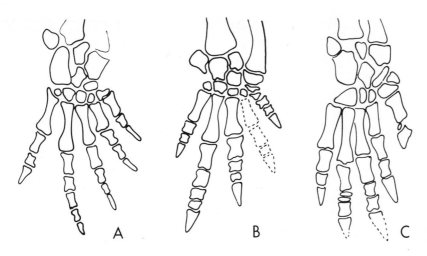

Figure 7. Forefeet of: **A,** *Dimetrodon;* **B,** *Watongia;* **C,** *Biarmosuchus.* (A, after Romer and Price, 1940; B, after Olson, 1974; C, after Sigogneau and Chudinov, 1972. Not to scale.)

suchus and the later Eastern European and South African dinocephalians. *Tappenosaurus* is comparable to *Estemmenosuchus* in size, but in many respects resembles the very large caseid *Cotylorhynchus hancocki,* and doubts of its assignment to the eotherapsids are certainly justified, as discussed earlier (Olson, 1962).

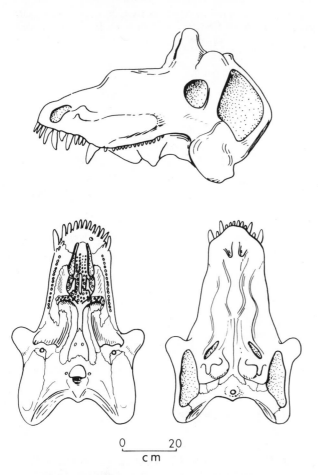

Figure 8. Three views of the skull of *Estemmenosuchus.* (After Chudinov, 1960, 1965; Olson, 1962.)

Mastersonia is known only from vertebrae and ribs. The vertebrae most closely resemble those of the large dicynodont *Placerias,* from the late Triassic, but are somewhat more amphicoelous. The chances of close relationships between these two, on the basis of stratigraphic data alone, seem remote. The femora of *Phreatosuchus* are from animals smaller than the others in the group, but their form suggests a relationship, while also showing resemblances to the femora of edaphosaurians.

The two genera of Group III (Fig. 9) are distinctive and notably different from the genera of the other two groups. They appear to be related to dicynodonts. *Otsheria* is a possible predecessor of *Venjukovia,* which has many dicynodont features (Barghusen, 1976). *Dimacrodon* has been related to *Otsheria* on the basis of its dentition and temporal opening. Not many characters are available for analysis, inasmuch as the ony specimens of *Dimacrodon* are a poor skull and jaw and a pair of partial lower jaws.

Relationships of eotherapsids and pelycosaurs

Relationships between eotherapsids and pelycosaurs remain highly speculative, for all eotherapsids except *Watongia* show major differences from any known pelycosaurs. That a general relationship exists cannot be doubted, the usual interpretation being that the therapsids arose from the sphenacodonts, perhaps from the haptodontines (Olson, 1962; Sigogneau and Chudinov, 1972). This is based on general resemblances of some of the eotheriodonts to sphenacodonts, and the sharing of the angular flange among sphenacodonts and all three groups of eotherapsids. The eotheriodonts, both gorgonopsianlike forms and brithopodans, could well have arisen from the sphenacodonts.

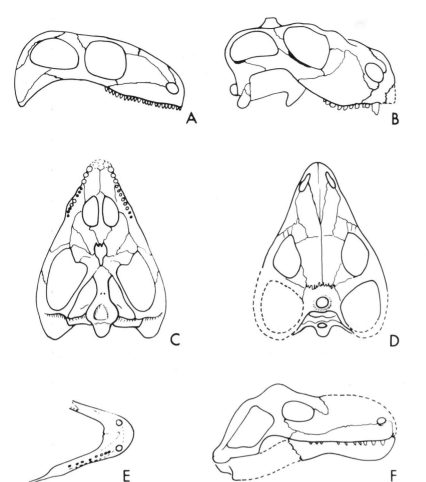

Figure 9. *Edaphosaurus* and eodicynodonts: **A,** skull of *Edaphosaurus* in lateral aspect; **B, C,** and **D,** skull of *Otsheria;* **E,** lower jaw of *Dimacrodon;* **F,** partial skull of *Dimacrodon.* (A, after Romer and Price, 1940; B–D, after Chudinov 1960, also Olson, 1962; E, after Olson, 1962.)

Dimacrodon and *Otsheria* may have arisen from the same base. Barghusen (1976) considered the question of dicynodont ancestry in a study of modification of skulls and jaws, using *Dimetrodon* as the beginning of a morphological series. He concluded that the therapsid ancestry of *Venjukovia,* a putative dicynodont forerunner, is an open question. *Venjukovia* would have been separated from pelycosaurs by a large gap, which, however, may have been filled in part by *Otsheria* (and *Dimacrodon?*). The postcranium, being unknown in eodicynodonts, is of little direct help. Derived characters of the vertebral column in such sphenacodonts as *Dimetrodon* and *Sphenacodon* are not present in dicynodonts. Thus, if in fact *Otsheria* and *Venjukovia* do lie on the line to dicynodonts, it may be inferred that they also lacked these features and were not derived from this type of sphenacodont.

The relationship of members of Group II to the pelycosaurs is even more confusing. First, of course, is the problem that Group II may be synthetic. In any event, we must deal almost

exclusively with postcranial features, except for *Estemennosuchus* (Fig. 8). The lower jaw of *Estemennosuchus* has an angular flange similar to that found in members of Group I and *Venjukovia,* but the skull is quite unlike that known in any pelycosaurs. Only the angular flange and common trends in structures related to feeding suggest pelycosaurian ancestry in common with members of groups I and III. If the flange is a convergent feature, as discussed by Olson (1962), the case for common sphenacodont ancestry is seriously weakened.

Postcranial features of members of Group II show general resemblances to those of the large *Cotylorhynchus* (Caseidae). Detailed comparisons are at best equivocal. *Tappenosaurus* has many caseid features, including fusion of the first four presacral ribs to the transverse processes of the vertebrae. Except for what appears to be a sphenacodontlike basicranial fragment and the presence of a large pubo-ichiadic fossa in the pelvis, this genus could be considered to be an aberrant caseid. Neither *Mastersonia* nor *Driveria* show close resemblances to the caseids, the former differing in the massiveness of the vertebrae and the form of the proximal ends of the ribs, and the latter differing in the presence of the massive supra-acetabular boss. The femora and prepodial elements of *Driveria* are somewhat caseid in proportions, but the resemblances are those to be expected in large, reptilian herbivores of this general type. The postcrania of *Estemmenosuchus* and *Phreatosuchus,* to the extent they are known, suggest affinities to *Mastersonia* and *Driveria,* but again resemblances are only approximate.

Much of the evidence needed to provide a solution to the pelycosaur-eotherapsid relationships is missing. It is impossible at present to go beyond what has been said in the preceding paragraphs. The adaptive aspects of the changes and the taphonomic and ecological circumstances of the pelycosaurs and therapsids, however, provide added insights into what was behind the observed modifications.

The adaptive nature of eotherapsid characters

The basic therapsid characters that occur among the eotherapsids are present in the eutherapsids as well (Table 3), but are augmented by a suite of additional characters, each of which appears and develops independently within the phyla (Olson, 1944). Two of the characters listed in the table need special note. Number 14—the presence of a large, cratered parietal opening—is found among some gorgonopsians and dinocephalians and is weakly developed in some dicynodonts. It is reduced or totally absent in advanced lines of the eutherapsids. Number 15—differentiated, heterodont dentitions—is characteristic of various lines, both eotherapsid and eutherapsid, but in all, the modifications are characteristic of subgroups rather than major categories as a whole.

All characters in Table 3, except number 13, pertain to skulls, lower jaws, and dentitions. Number 13 pertains to the tendency to reduce phalanges (see Fig. 7). Characters 1 to 5 all pertain to structures involved in the procurement, mastication, and ingestion of food. Each represents a modification from the general sphenacodont condition, involving increase in size and efficiency of the jaw musculature (adductors and pterygoids), reduction of the kinetics of the skull, differentiation of the marginal and palatal teeth, and some increase in the relative size of the dentary bone. An important inference developed below is that the initial shift from the pelycosaurian to the therapsid condition was related to feeding habits.

The adaptive features of the postcrania are more difficult to evaluate. The vertebrae of *Watongia* resemble those of sphenacodonts, but are unlike those of any described genus. The limb elements (Figs. 6 and 7) have departed slightly from the sphenacodont condition. Some reduction of phalangeal elements has occurred. *Watongia*

Table 3.—Fifteen characters of eotherapsids and eutherapsids compared on the basis of character states

Characters	A	B	c	d	e	f	g
1. Enlarged adductor fossa	X	X	X	X	X	X	X
2. Pterygoid close to basicranium	X_T	X	X	X	X	X	X
3. Pterygo-quadrate joint akinetic	X	X	X	X	X	X	X
4. Parasphenoidal rostrum reduced or absent	X_T	X_T	X_T	X_T	X_T	X_T	X_T
5. Dentary relatively enlarged	X_i	X_T	X_i	X_i	X_i	X_T	X
6. Quadrate and articular reduced	U	X_T	U	U	X_T	X_T	X
7. Stapes reduced	U	C_T	U	U	U	X_T	X_T
8. Secondary palate present	U	X_T	U	X_i	U	X_T	X
9. Deep floccular fossa	U	X_T	U	X_T	X_T	X_T	X
10. Double occipital condyle	U	X_T	U	U	U	X_T	X
11. Small sella turcica	U	X_T	U	X	U	X_T	X
12. Expanded epipterygoid	U	X_T	X_T	U	X_T	X_{iT}	U
13. Some phalangeal reduction	X_i	X_T	X_T	X_T	X_i	X_T	X_T
14. Large, cratered parietal foramen	X	X_{T1}	X	X_{T1}	X_{T1}	U	U
15. Differentiated dentition	X_v	X_v	X_v	X_v	X_v	X_v	X_v

Key: **A,** Eotherapsids; **B,** Eutherpasids; c–g, subgroups of eutherapsids: **c,** Dinocephalians; **d,** Dicynodonts; **e,** Gorgonopsians; **f,** Therocephalians; **g,** Cynodonts. U, not developed; X, present; X_T, tendency to develop in at least some groups; X_i, incipient; X_{T1}, tendency to lose; X_v, present but in different states in different groups.

E. C. OLSON

was a lightly built animal, probably more active than any pelycosaur (Fig. 6B), and its habits probably were much like those of more advanced and better known brithopodans (Orlov, 1958). The postcranium of *Biarmosuchus* is generally gorgonopsianlike, with gracile limb elements (Fig. 6C, E). It undoubtedly was an active animal. Though eotheriodonts seem to show a trend toward increased activity, eodinocephalians do not. The principal features of the postcrania are related to large size. Eodinocephalians were not highly active, fast-running animals and their habits and behavior were probably similar to those of large eudinocephalians.

Therapsid Characters and Ecology

Two types of trophic systems can be detected in the terrestrial communities of the late Carboniferous and Permian. In one system, the food base is provided primarily by aquatic plants (see Olson, 1971, for brief summary), and, in the other, the base lay in terrestrial plants. The first type is found in the well-known Permo-Carboniferous chronofauna, which—with geographic and ecological variations—stretched along the equatorial regions from the western United States, to the Ural Mountains in Europe. It is from this system that nearly all of the information on ophiacodont and sphenacodont evolution has come.

The second type of trophic system is found in scattered sites in the Leonardian of Texas and Oklahoma, with less clear earlier samples from the late Carboniferous of Colorado and the Wolfcampian Permian of New Mexico and Colorado (Lewis and Vaughn, 1965; Vaughn, 1969 a, b; Olson and Vaughn, 1970). It occurs as well in the early Guadalupian of North America and the Soviet Union. In the United States, this sytem has been called the Caseid Chronofauna and, in its last known occurrence in the Guadalupian, it includes both pelycosaurs and eotherapsids. The principal site at which it is known in the Soviet Union is near the town of Ocher.

The evolution of the pelycosaurs and early therapsids took place in these two types of trophic systems. The second type, with its terrestrial-plant base, presumably diverged from the aquatically based type, but when this took place is uncertain. It is presumed that divergence occurred during the Carboniferous, but it may have occurred earlier (Fig. 10). If therapsids originated from the haptodontine sphenacodont line and evolved in a system having its trophic

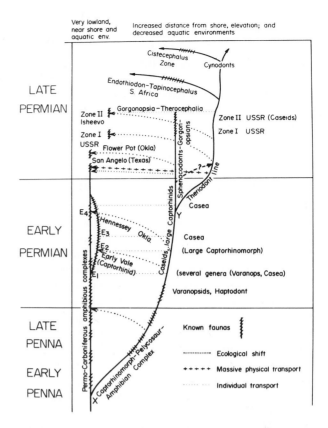

Figure 10. Diagram of a possible ecological "phylogeny" of the chronofaunas of the Permo-Carboniferous. (From Olson, 1975.)

base in terrestrial plants, then separation of eotherapsids from pelycosaurs was clearly no later than the late Carboniferous.

If the sphenacodont ancestry of therapsids is accepted, the morphology of sphenacodonts can be used as a basis for comparison with the therapsids, and therapsid characters can be considered modifications of the sphenacodont base. This is the traditional practice, and *Dimetrodon* has usually been the model, primarily because its morphology is extremely well known. *Dimetrodon,* however, was not ancestral to therapsids, if for no other reason than it had elongate neural spines. It seems, in fact, to have been adapted to the ecology of the Permo-Carboniferous Chronofauna, and its morphology is presumed to reflect its role in the aquatically based communities of this complex.

Dimetrodon, as the top predator during the Wichita phase of its existence (Wolfcampian and early Leonardian), fed on aquatic and semiaquatic animals, likely including such large genera as *Eryops, Diadectes,* and *Ophiacodon.* During this time, however, it was the most abundant of the large animals and must also have found food sources among smaller fishes, amphibians, and reptiles. During the later parts of its existence, *Dimetrodon* was almost the only large animal in the system and, because of its abundant number, must have fed primarily on many fish and small aquatic amphibians and such small terrestrial reptiles as *Captorhinus*. Adaptation to feeding on large animals, as inferred by Barghusen (1973) on the basis of jaw mechanics, was probably attained during the earlier parts of *Dimetrodon's* history, but was retained little modified when the community composition changed. *Sphenacodon,* in which the skull and jaws are very similar to those of *Dimetrodon,* most likely developed in a similar way, but is not known after the Wichita time of the early Permian.

If theriodont therapsids arose before the Permian from a base common to them and sphenacodonts, it follows that at least some of the similarities of cranial and jaw structure developed in parallel in the two lines. For theriodonts, such parallels were adaptive to a stable chronofauna. These circumstances would have permitted the adaptation to predation on large animals to continue, in theriodonts, beyond the level at which it ceased in the water-tied sphenacodonts. It may be inferred that, within the terrestrial system, the more "progressive" eotheriodonts evolved, sphenacodontlike, but with "progressive" modifications in structures related to food procurement, preparation, and ingestion.

Under just what specific circumstances the eotheriodonts actually evolved remains highly speculative. In their earliest occurrence—in the San Angelo and Chickasha Formations of North America—they are associated with members of the Caseid Chronofauna. Herbivores greatly outnumber pelycosaur and eotheriodont predators. The great majority of herbivores, however, are large caseids, *Cotylorhynchus* and *Angelosaurus.* Eodinocephalians are few, although of several types, and poorly preserved. If the sample is even remotely reliable, they, along with the eotheriodonts, formed a small part of the food available to predators. This interpretation, of course, is based on the supposition that the group from the San Angelo and Chickasha Formations has been drawn from a single ecological system.

An eotherapsid assemblage, lacking caseids, has been obtained from the Ocher site in the Soviet Union. Caseids are known from the Soviet Union (Efremov, 1956; Olson, 1962, 1968) and from Central France (Sigogneau-Russell and Russell, 1974), but in neither case are they as-

sociated with eotherapsids. The contrasts in constitution of the samples in North America and Europe may be the result of inadequate sampling. More likely, however, the differences indicate that the grouping in the San Angelo Formation, and perhaps the Chickasha Formation, has been drawn from more than one community. The majority of specimens were washed in, and deposited on, what Smith (1975) has termed "sandy and muddy tidal flats." The most extensive samples are from stream channel deposits; however, there is evidence that some of the caseids lived in the environment of deposition, in which the scavengers or predators were also present (Olson, 1962).

Whatever the precise environmental circumstances, it seems that the eotheriodonts did develop in a complex, in which terrestrial plants formed the trophic base, and that their adaptations were to feeding on large, reptilian herbivores that predominated in biomass. Increasing efficiency in this role was probably accompanied by locomotor changes relating to increased activity, applicable to both the brithopodan and gorgonopsian eotheriodonts. The differences between the two remain to be explained.

The herbivores pose different problems. The general patterns of masticatory modification in the skulls of *Dimacrodon* and *Otsheria* are rather similar to those of the eotheriodonts, but were probably induced by adaptations to more efficient feeding on terrestrial plants. As in the eotheriodonts, the changes laid the foundation for development of some of the advanced characters found in dicynodont eutherapsids (Table 3). Although these genera presumably were derived from sphenacodonts, the possibility of an edaphosaurian ancestry cannot be completely ruled out (Fig. 8A, B). The dynamic changes from the basal reptilian pattern are somewhat similar in *Edaphosaurus* and *Otsheria,* although they are gross rather than detailed.

Finally, the eodinocephalians, Group II, have no evident base among the pelycosaurs if the caseids are ruled out, as they must be at least in the cases of *Driveria* and *Estemmenosuchus.* The eodinocephalians probably evolved in the same chronofaunal system as the other eotherapsids did, and—if the interpretation shown in Figure 10 is an approximation of the course of events—the presence of early links to ancestors would not be expected in any of the samples we know today. Whatever the source and the underlying nature of the adaptations of the skulls, jaws, and dentitions, it is apparent that eodinocephalians did not establish a basis for development of the suite of more advanced therapsid characters found in the other lines. Only the tendency to broaden the epipterygoid suggests one of the trends found in other lines of therapsids.

Summary and Conclusions

The scant evidence concerning the morphology, evolution, phylogeny, and ecology of the eotherapsids has been summarized. The morphological data are interpreted in relation to life conditions of the eotherapsids and their possible predecessors. Development of characters different from those of the presumed pelycosaurian ancestors are found in modifications of structures related to food procurement, preparation, and ingestion. The extent of integrated changes in locomotor structures is known in only a few eotheriodonts. Postcranial modifications in eodinocephalians are primarily related to size increases. The postcrania of the eodicynodonts are not known.

Modifications of the eotheriodont masticatory system appears to be related to a continued development of efficiency in the predation on large terrestrial animals. Similar adaptations, less fully expressed, were also developed in sphenacodontines such as *Dimetrodon,* inhabitants of an aquatic-food-based trophic system. Two lines of eotheriodonts, gorgonopsianlike and brithopodan forms, are known. From within the former, perhaps from a *Watongia*like animal, the gorgonopsians arose. Other members of this group, *Eotitanops, Phthinosuchus,* and *Biarmosuchus,* may also lie close to gorgonopsian ancestry. The brithopodans are less closely related to any known pelycosaurs, but may have had a common base with other eotheriodonts. Much the same may apply to *Dimacrodon* and *Otsheria,* but this is less clear.

From the data available, it seems that the masticatory changes and accompanying modifications of the postcranium in eotheriodonts provided an adaptive base in the context of predation, which set the stage for development of the therian trends in the therapsids. The eodicynodonts established a comparable base but in context of herbivory. The changes in skulls and skeletons almost certainly were accompanied by the beginning of the physiological changes that culminated in development of the mammalian grade. The proximate causes in physiological changes lay in improved feeding mechanisms and increased activity. Where these did not develop, as in the eodinocephalians, the trends found in more advanced therapsids were not established in the descendants.

References

Barghusen, H.
1968. The lower jaw of cynodonts (Reptilia, Therapsida) and the evolutionary origin of mammal-like adductor jaw musculature. *Postilla.* 116:1–49.
1973. The adductor jaw musculature of *Dimetrodon* (Reptilia, Pelycosauria). *Jour. Paleon.* 47: 823–34.
1976. Notes on the adductor musculature of *Venjukovia,* a primitive anomodont therapsid from the Permian of the U.S.S.R. *Ann. S. Afr. Mus.* 69:239–60.

Cope, E. D.
1878. Description of extinct Batrachia and Reptilia from the Permian formation of Texas. *Proc. Amer. Philos. Soc.* 27:505–30.

Chudinov, P. K.
1959. Discovery of new reptiles in the Upper Permian of the U.S.S.R. *Paleon. Jour.* No. 1:143–146. [In Russian]
1960. Upper Permian therapsids of the Ezhovo locality. *Paleon. Jour.* No. 4:81—94. [In Russian]
1965. New facts about the fauna of the Upper Permian of the U.S.S.R. *Jour. Geol.* 73:117–30.

Efremov, I. A.
1954. The fauna of terrestrial vertebrates in the Permian Copper Sandstones of the western Cis-Urals. *Tr. Paleon. Inst., Acad. Sci. U.S.S.R.* 54. [In Russian]
1956. American elements in the fauna of Permian reptiles of the U.S.S.R. *Dokl. Acad. Sci. U.S.S.R.* 111:1091–94. [In Russian]

Efremov, I.A., and Vjushkov, B. P.
1955. Catalogue of localities of Permian and Triassic terrestrial vertebrates in the territories of the U.S.S.R. *Tr. Paleon. Inst. Acad. Sci., U.S.S.R.* 46. [In Russian]

Lewis, G. E., and Vaughn, P. P.
1965. Early Permian vertebrates from the Cutler formation of the Placerville area Colorado. *Geol. Surv. Prof. Paper* 503-C.

Olson, E. C.
1944. Origin of mammals based upon the cranial-morphology of therapsid suborders. *Geol. Soc. Amer., Spec. Paper* 55.
1952. The evolution of a Permian vertebrate chronofauna. *Evol.* 6:181–96.

1957. Catalogue of localities of Permian and Triassic terrestrial vertebrates of the U.S.S.R. *Jour. Geol.* 65:196–226.

1959. The evolution of mammalian characters. *Evol.* 13:344–53.

1962. Late Permian terrestrial vertebrates, U.S.A. and U.S.S.R. *Trans. Amer. Philos. Soc.* 52 (pt. 2):3–224.

1968. The family Caseidae. *Fieldiana Geol.* 17:225–349.

1971. *Vertebrate Paleozoology.* New York: Wiley Interscience.

1974. On the source of therapsids. *Ann. S. Afr. Mus.,* 64:27–46.

1975a. The exploitation of land by early tetrapods. In *Morphology and Evolution of Reptiles,* ed. A. d'A.Bellairs and C. B. Cox, *Linnean Society Symposium Series* 3:1–30.

1975b. Permo-Carboniferous paleoecology and morphotypic series. *Amer. Zool.* 15:371–89.

1979. Biological and physical factors in the dispersal of Permo-Carboniferous terrestrial vertebrates. In *Historical Biogeography, Plate Tectonics, and the Changing Environment,* ed. J. Gray and A. J. Boucot, pp. 227–38. Corvallis, Oreg.: Oregon State University Press.

Olson, E. C., and Beerbower, J. R.
1953. The San Angelo formation, Permian of Texas and its vertebrates. *Jour. Geol.* 61:389–423.

Olson, E. C., and Vaughn, P. P.
1970. The changes of terrestrial vertebrates and climates during the Permian of North America. *Forma and Functio* 3:113–38.

Orlov, Y. A.
1958. The carnivorous dinocephalians of the Isheevo fauna (Titanosuchia). *Tr. Paleont. Inst. Acad. Sci. U.S.S.R.* 72. [In Russian]

Romer, A. S.
1966. *Vertebrate Paleontology,* 3d ed. Chicago: University of Chicago Press.

Romer, A. S., and Price, L. I.
1940. Review of the Pelycosauria. *Geol. Soc. Amer. Spec. Paper* 28:.

Rozhdestvenskii, A. K., and Tatarinov, L. P. (eds.)
1964. *Amphibians, Reptiles, and Birds,* unnumbered volume [twelfth in series] of *Fundamentals of Paleontology,* ed. Y. A. Orlov, pp. 1–722. Moscow: Paleont. Inst. Acad. Sci. U.S.S.R. [In Russian].

Sigogneau, D.
1970. Revision systematique des Gorgonopsiens Sud-Africains. *Cahiers de Paléontologie* (unnumbered), ed. J. P. Lehman, pp. 1–416. Paris: CNRS.

Sigogneau, D., and Chudinov, P.
1972. Reflections on some Russian Eotheriodonts (Reptilia, Synapsida, Therapsida). *Palaeovertebrata, Montpellier* 5:79–109.

Sigogneau-Russell, D., and Russell, D. E.
1974. Etude du premier Caseide (Reptilia, Pelycosauria) d'Europe occidentale. *Bull. Mus. Nat. Hist. Natur. Sci. de Terre* 38:145–205.

Smith, G. E.
1975. Depositional systems, San Angelo formation (Permian), North Texas: Facies control of red-bed copper mineralization. *Bur Econ. Geol., Univ. Texas, Austin. Rpt. Recent Investigations* 80.

Vaughn, P. P.
1969a. Upper Pennsylvanian vertebrates from the Sangre de Cristo formation of central Colorado. *Los Angeles Co. Mus. Contrib. Sci.* No. 164.

1969b. Early Permian vertebrates from southern New Mexico and their paleozoogeographic significance. *Los Angeles Co. Mus. Contrib. Sci.* No. 166.

E. C. OLSON

HANS-DIETER SUES
Museum of Comparative Zoology
Harvard University
Cambridge, Massachusetts 02138

Locomotion and Body Form in Early Therapsids (Dinocephalia, Gorgonopsia, and Therocephalia)

Introduction

It is now well established that mammals originated from mammal-like reptiles, more specifically, from the Cynodontia (Barghusen, 1968). This evolutionary transformation involved complex changes in the masticatory apparatus and middle ear, in the structure and replacement of teeth, and in the limbs, girdles, and axial skeleton (Crompton and Jenkins, 1979).

The study of therapsids has largely focused on the skull and dentition, which are traditionally accepted as having the greatest potential for distinguishing closely related taxa from one another. In general, the postcranial skeleton has received less attention, much of the information on noncynodont therapsids being ancedotal and appended to descriptions of the skull. Descriptions of unusually complete skeletons of individual taxa, representing all major groups of dinocephalians and theriodonts, are available, as are general treatments of limbs and girdles of dinocephalians and gorgonopsians. However, except for the Cynodontia and earliest mammals (Jenkins, 1970, *et seq.*), no group has as yet been covered in depth.

This paper reviews available data on body form in the Dinocephalia, Gorgonopsia, and Therocephalia, and general features of the locomotor apparatus as reflected by the structure of the appendicular skeleton. The Dinocephalia are treated here as a distinct monophyletic taxon within the Therapsida (*con.* Romer, 1956), characterized especially by the possession of peculiar, interlocking incisor teeth. The Biarmosuchidae, Eotitanosuchidae, and Phthinosuchidae are very primitive therapsids of uncertain affinities and are not included in the Dinocephalia (see Hopson and Barghusen, this volume). The postcranial skeleton of the dicynodonts is discussed by Hotton (this volume).

Historical Background

The data utilized in preparing this review were derived from numerous individual references that document the major advances in research on the postcranial anatomy of the Dinocephalia, Gorgonopsia, and Therocephalia.

Gregory (1926) described in great detail the postcranial skeleton of the tapinocephalid dinocephalian *Moschops capensis*. Boonstra (1955, 1966) published synoptic accounts on the girdles and limb bones of the South African dinocephalians and Orlov (1958) has given an excellent description of the postcranial structure of the primitive Russian Brithopodidae, especially *Titanophoneus*. Earlier references describing dinocephalian and other therapsid postcranial material have been summarized by Broom (1932) in his classic book on the South African mammal-like reptiles. Olson (1962) has discussed aspects of the postcranium of early therapsids and late pelycosaurs from the Upper Permian of the United States and the USSR.

The postcranial skeleton of the Gorgonopsia is comparatively well known, and Sigogneau (1970, pp. 383–96) has recently summarized much of the available information. Colbert's (1948) monograph on the skeleton of *Lycaenops ornatus* and Pravoslavlev's (1927) description of *Inostrancevia* are important as documentation of unusually complete specimens. Boonstra (1934a) and Broili and Schröder (1935) have given accounts of rather complete skeletons from South Africa, and von Huene (1950) published a detailed description of a skeleton from the Upper Permian of East Africa.

Information on the postcranial skeleton of the Therocephalia (including Bauriamorpha) is sparse. Kemp (1978), in his paper on postcranial remains of *Regisaurus jacobi* from the *Lystrosaurus* zone of South Africa, has listed most of the relevant references, to which should be added Attridge's (1956) description of a fairly complete skeleton of *Mirothenthes* and von Huene's (1950) account of numerous postcranial elements of *Notosollasia*. Cluver (1968) briefly described much of the postcranium of the small scaloposaurid *Zo-*

rillodontops, and, most recently, Hou (1979) has published a description of the incomplete skeleton of a bauriamorph from the Lower Triassic of Inner Mongolia.

General Habits

Gorgonopsia

The Gorgonopsia (Fig. 1B) were top predators in terrestrial environments during the Late Permian (Bakker, 1975). Their carnivorous habit, indicated by dental pattern and jaw structure, is supported by the discovery of an anomodont jaw between the ribs of the type skeleton of *"Scymnognathus" parringtoni* (Huene, 1950, p. 48). In general body form, the Gorgonopsia were quite different from the lizardlike sphenacodontid pelycosaurs that had been top predators in the Early Permian. The limbs of gorgonopsians are longer and were more nearly vertically oriented, carrying the gracile trunk well above the ground (Colbert, 1948). Footfall was closer to the midline, and the feet apparently pointed more directly forward than in sphenacodonts. The hind limb is longer than the forelimb, and the femur is only slightly longer than the tibia (Broili and Schröder, 1935; Colbert, 1948), suggesting more rapid locomotion than the antecedent sphenacodonts or the contemporary dinocephalians were capable of. The tail was proportionately shorter than that of sphenocodonts but did not show the marked reduction found in some dinocephalians and most therocephalians.

Dinocephalia

The tapinocephalid dinocephalians (Fig. 1A), which were probably herbivorous, were massively built, with a wide, deep thorax and a short tail (Gregory, 1926; Huene, 1931). As in gorgonopsians, limb pose was more nearly vertical than in sphenacodonts. Unlike gorgonopsians, front and hind limbs were subequal in length, extremely robust, with proximal segments much longer than distal. Manus and pes were broad and had very short digits (Gregory, 1926). The inference, from body form, of a hippopotamus-like, semiaquatic mode of life for *Moschops* and related genera (e.g., see Huene, 1931), is supported by taphonomic information presented by Boonstra (1955).

Titanosuchids, anteosaurids, and brithopodids were predatory dinocephalians, as indicated by their jaw structure and dentition. They were more gracile than the tapinocephalids (Broom, 1932; Orlov, 1958), and—as in theriodonts—the

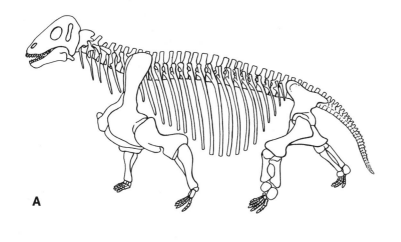

Figure 1. Skeletal reconstructions of: A, dinocephalian *Moschops;* and B, gorgonopsian *Lycaenops.* (A, slightly modified after Gregory, 1926; B, after Colbert, 1948.) Total length of A, about 2.4 m; of B, about 1.2 m.

front limbs were longer than the hind limbs. Predatory dinocephalians were larger than most theriodonts, however, and much more robustly built. The tail of the genus *Titanophoneus* was apparently very substantial.

Therocephalia

Most Therocephalia seem to have had relatively large heads, a deep thorax, and fairly slender limbs. The Scaloposauridae include a number of small, very lightly built forms, one of which, *Ericiolacerta,* is "remarkable for its large head . . . and for the length and delicacy of its limbs" (Watson, 1931, p. 1180). The Pristerognathidae, Whaitsiidae, and related groups, by contrast, include robust, short-legged forms such as the large *Pristerognathus* (Attridge, 1956) and *Whaitsia* (Broom, 1932), and the much smaller *Aneugomphius* (Brink, 1957). The tail is not known for certain, but is restored as being short in *Aneugomphius.*

Structure and Function

Shoulder girdle and forelimb

Shoulder girdles of the earliest therapsids such as *Brithopus,* (Watson, 1917 [as "*Rhopalodon*"];

Efremov, 1954) are comparable to the massive shoulder girdles of the Pelycosauria (Fig. 2A, B). The scapula is large and bladelike, with well-developed coracoid and procoracoid ossifications. The glenoid remains somewhat "screw-shaped" in *Brithopus,* though foreshortened.

Later therapsids (Fig. 2C) show a more or less semilunar glenoid that permitted much more freedom of movement, and the procoracoid becomes progressively excluded from the glenoid cavity. Jenkins (1971) has discussed the functional significance of the structural changes in the glenoid region of synapsids. In the forms with a screw-shaped glenoid (such as the pelycosaur *Dimetrodon*), the humerus was retracted in a nearly horizontal plane, driving the body forward, and rotated about its long axis to permit antebrachial elevation. The lateral and horizontal orientation of the humerus would have resulted in significant compressive forces acting on the thorax. The forces were accommodated by the large, platelike scapulocoracoids and the robust clavicles, acting as struts in transmitting forces to the opposite limb and linked by the expanded head of the interclavicle. With the reorientation of the limbs, the glenoid shortens anteroposteriorly and loses its complex structure. It

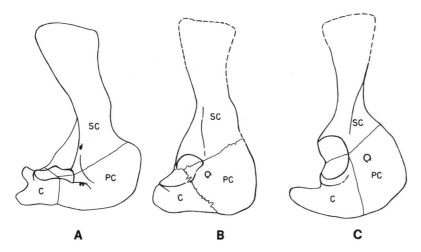

Figure 2. Scapulocoracoids of: A, pelycosaur *Dimetrodon;* B, dinocephalian *Brithopus;* and C, gorgonopsian *Aelurognathus,* in lateral view. (A, after Romer and Price, 1940; B, after Efremov, 1954; C, after Boonstra, 1934a.)

Key: **C,** coracoid; **PC,** procoracoid; **SC,** scapula.

comes to face more ventrally and posteriorly in, for instance, Dinocephalia (Watson, 1917; Gregory, 1926) and Gorgonopsia (Boonstra, 1965). By this structural change, the pectoral girdle is increasingly relieved of stresses that required massiveness of the bony elements.

The scapular blade in the Dinocephalia is relatively narrow (e.g., Orlov, 1958). In the Therocephalia (Watson, 1931; Boonstra, 1964) the scapula is slender, and the platelike coracoids are reduced.

In therapsids, the proximal articular surface of the humerus has lost the spiral shape seen in pelycosaurs (c.f., *Dimetrodon,* Jenkins, 1971). The convex articular surface still extends broadly across the proximal end but becomes increasingly concentrated in a medial caput (Gregory, 1926). There is less "twisting" of the distal articular end relative to the proximal end, compared to the condition in pelycosaurs (Romer, 1956). The radius is shorter than the humerus; in the tapinocephalid *Moschops,* the humerus is more than twice as long as the radius (Gregory, 1926), and, in the gorgonopsians (Colbert, 1948), the humerus is about 40 percent longer than the radius.

The pelycosaurian manus reflects the primitive reptilian phalangeal formula of 23453, but among therapsids where the manus is known, only the Biarmosuchidae (Sigogneau and Tchudinov, 1972) and some Gorgonopsia (Sigogneau, 1970) retain this formula. Different, presumably derived, counts are reported for certain Gorgonopsia, such as 23343 in *Lycaenops* (Colbert, 1948). In all other therapsid groups—including dinocephalians (Orlov, 1958; Boonstra, 1966)—the formula corresponds to that of mammals, 23333 (Fig. 3A). In the wrist of some gorgonopsians (Colbert, 1948) and therocephalians

(Boonstra, 1934b), the fourth and fifth distal carpals are fused (Fig. 3B).

Pelvic girdle and femur

Parrington (1961) and Jenkins (1971) have discussed in great detail the evolutionary development of the pelvis and femur in synapsid reptiles.

In the Pelycosauria (Fig. 4A) the iliac blade is not expanded, and the pubic plate is large, approaching the size of the ischium (Romer and Price, 1940). The femur (Fig. 5A) has a terminally positioned head and a roughly Y-shaped system of ridges on the ventral aspect of the shaft. The anterior branch of this Y has been interpreted as a trochanter internus for the insertion of *Musculus puboischiofemoralis externus* (Parrington, 1961).

A rugose area on the posterodorsal surface is interpreted as the insertion area of part of *M. puboischiofemoralis internus.* A distinct fourth trochanter is developed for the caudifemoralis muscle, which originated in the robust base of the long tail. In early dinocephalians, such as *Deuterosaurus* (Efremov, 1954), the femur is essentially similar to that of a sphenacodont pelycosaur, but a number of differences are manifest (Fig. 5B). A trochanter major is incipiently developed and, although the Y-shaped arrangement of ventral ridges is still visible, a distinct fourth trochanter, and the insertion area for *M. puboischiofemoralis internus,* on the posterodorsal aspect, appear to be absent.

In tapinocephalid dinocephalians (Fig. 5C), such as *Struthiocephalus* and *Avenantia* (Boonstra, 1955), the femur becomes very massive and has expanded ends; the primitive Y-shaped system of ridges is no longer apparent, but a trochanter major (for *M. iliofemoralis*) is differen-

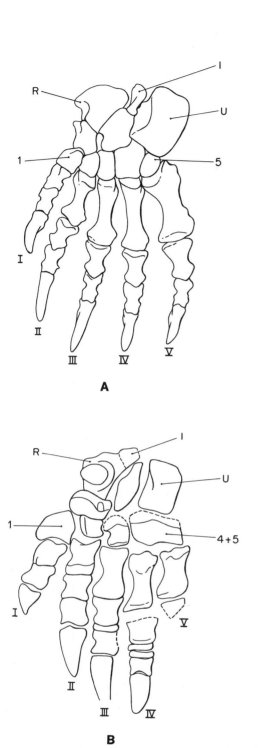

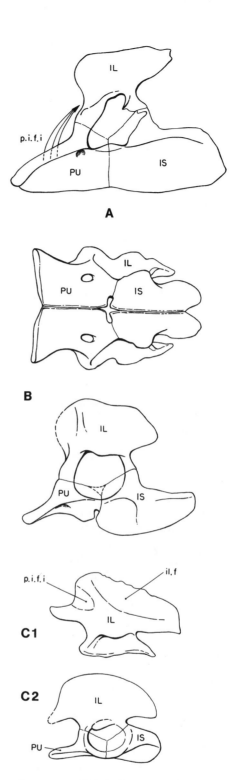

Figure 3. Manus of: A, dinocephalian *Titanophoneus;* and B, an indeterminate gorgonopsian, in dorsal view. (A, after Orlov, 1958; B, after Sigogneau, 1970.)

Key: **I,** intermedium; **R,** radiale; **U,** ulnare; Arabic numerals, distal carpals; Roman numerals, digits.

Figure 4. Pelvic girdles of: A, pelycosaur *Dimetrodon;* B, dinocephalian *Titanophoneus;* and two therocephalians—C1, *Regisaurus;* C2, *Alopecognathus*). (A) and (C) in lateral view; (B) in lateral and ventral view. (A, after Romer and Price, 1940; B, after Orlov, 1958; C1, after Kemp, 1978; C2, after Boonstra, 1964.)

Key: **IL,** illium; **IS,** ischium; **PU,** pubis, **il.f,** *M. iliofemoralis* (origin); **p.i.f.i,** *M. puboischiofemoralis internus* (muscle and origin).

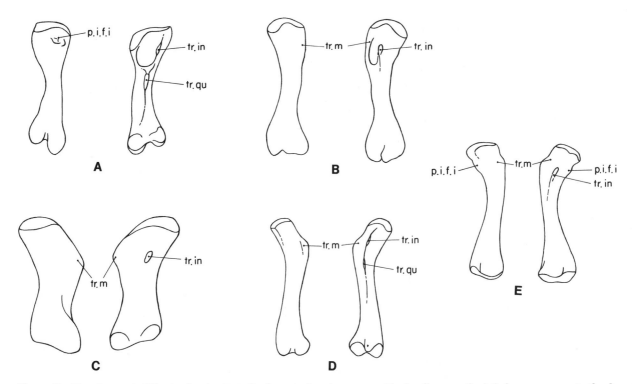

Figure 5.   Development of the trochanteres on the femora of various synapsids. In all cases, the left figure represents the dorsal view, and the right figure, the ventral view of the femur. A, *Dimetrodon* (Pelycosauria); B, *Deuterosaurus* (Dinocephalia); C, *Struthiocephalus* (Dinocephalia); D, gen. indet. (Gorgonopsia); and E, *Regisaurus* (Therocephalia). (A, after Romer and Price, 1940; B, after Efremov, 1954; C, after Boonstra, 1955; D, after Parrington, 1961; E, after Kemp, 1978.)

Key: **p.i.f.i,** insertion for *M. puboischiofemoralis internus;* **tr.in,** internal trochanter; **tr.m,** trochanter major; **tr.q,** fourth trochanter.

tiated. The pelvis in these forms shows a somewhat reduced pubis and a moderate expansion of the ilium (Boonstra, 1955). Some dinocephalians, such as *Titanophoneus* (Orlov, 1958), have a relatively more slender femur than pelycosaurs, with but a single ventral ridge and a sigmoidally curved shaft. The head is set at an angle to the shaft and there is some development of a trochanter major. The well-developed ventral ridge shows a proximal swelling and a more distal one, believed by Parrington (1961) to be homologous with the trochanter internus and fourth trochanter, respectively.

The femur of the Gorgonopsia (Parrington, 1961) and the Biarmosuchidae (Sigogneau and Tchudinov, 1972) is almost identical with that of *Titanophoneus*. It is slender, somewhat sigmoidally curved (Fig. 5D), and has a moderately developed trochanter major. The pelvic girdle (Fig. 4B) of *Titanophoneus* (Orlov, 1958) and gorgonopsians (Colbert, 1948) is little advanced beyond the primitive type found in pelycosaurs. It differs by a perceptible expansion of the iliac blade and a reduction of the pubis (c.f. Fig. 4A, B), matched in the femur by a moderately developed trochan-

ter major and the presence of an internal trochanter.

M. puboischiofemoralis externus of these early synapsids was probably an important adductor acting across the ventral aspect of the hip joint; adduction of the femur was probably the principal means for elevating the body off the ground in forms with femora oriented in a more-or-less horizontal plane (Jenkins, 1971). *M. puboischiofemoralis internus,* originating from the medial surface of the pubis, probably inserted onto the anterior aspect of the anteroventral trochanter and the dorsal surface of the proximal femoral shaft (Jenkins, 1971). If this reconstruction is correct, it seems likely that the muscle, extending almost horizontally, acted in femoral protraction by pulling the bone in a more-or-less horizontal arc (Jenkins, 1971).

The structure of the pelvic girdle and femur in the Therocephalia is still rather poorly documented, but the well-preserved ilium and femur in the holotype of *Regisaurus jacobi,* described by Kemp (1978), indicate a fairly advanced type of structural organization. This had been inferred by Parrington (1961) on the basis of less complete specimens. The ilium of *Regisaurus* (Fig. 4C1) and *Ericiolacerta* (Watson, 1931) has a posteriorly extended blade, probably for the origin of *M. iliofemoralis*. It also has a distinct anterior projection, which defines the ventral limit of a shallow depression interpreted as the origin of *M. puboischiofemoralis internus* (probably equivalent to *M. iliacus* in mammals) by Kemp (1978). The very slender femur of *Regisaurus* (Fig. 5E) closely resembles that of a crocodile in its distinct sigmoid curvature and the position of the inward-turned proximal head. The trochanter major is moderately developed. There is also a trochanter for *M. puboischiofemoralis* (possibly homologous to the mammalian trochanter minor?) and, posteromedial to it, a prominent internal trochanter *sensu* Parrington (Kemp 1978). The pubis and ischium were probably large, as in other therocephalians (Fig. 4C2) described by Watson (1931) and Boonstra (1964).

Kemp (1978) has presented a case for multigaited locomotion in *Regisaurus,* which he claimed was capable of both a sprawling, "lizard-like" gait and a more erect type of gait similar to the high walk of living crocodiles (see Brinkman, 1980). In Kemp's evolutionary scenario this would represent an intermediate stage during the evolution of the mammalian locomotory pattern. The apparent dorsal shift of the origin of *M. puboischiofemoralis internus* from the puboischial plate onto the iliac blade, together with the development of a trochanter on the anterodorsal edge of the femoral head, is of special interest. As hypothesized above for more primitive synapsids, the puboischiofemoralis internus muscle would have functioned as a protractor during sprawling locomotion, and also as a levator of the femur. If a more upright mode of locomotion, with femoral excursion in a parasagittal plane, was employed, this protracting ability could have been increased as the origin and insertion of the muscle would have been more widely separated (Kemp, 1978). The extensively developed *M. iliofemoralis* (homologous to the mammalian gluteal muscles) could also have shifted part of its function from long-axis rotation of the femur, during sprawling gait, to femoral retraction in the more erect, "mammal-like" gait (Kemp, 1978).

The distal (tibial) articular surface of the femur is more or less parallel to the long axis of the shaft in pelycosaurs (Romer and Price, 1940) but faces increasingly distally in therapsids (Kemp, 1978).

The significance of the erect gait is not at all clear. Bakker (1975) has produced some evidence demonstrating that neither top speed of locomotion nor efficiency differ significantly between Recent lizards and noncursorial, "primitive-limbed" mammals of comparable size. The most obvious distinction between the locomotor capability of the two groups is the endurance of mammals at high speeds, but this is due primarily to the higher rate of aerobic respiration in mammals. Kemp (1978) has suggested that a more erect gait would have reduced stresses on the ankle for any given amount of locomotory force. Placement of the hind feet closer to the body would also have enhanced maneuverability, one would presume. Using living crocodiles as analogues, Kemp postulates that the erect gait was used for more rapid locomotion and for longer journeys.

Pes

Schaeffer (1941b) and Jenkins (1971) have reviewed the structural changes in the pes from pelycosaurs to mammals. Kemp (1978) has discussed in particular the calcaneum and astragalus in *Regisaurus*.

Of particular importance is the development of a plantigrade pes. In the pelycosaurian pes, neither astragalus nor calcaneum had plantar contact; the cruro-pedal joint seems to be designed to transmit forces largely perpendicular to its articular facets (Jenkins, 1971). In mammals, the astragalus is removed from plantar contact by superposition on the calcaneum. The fibulotarsal articulation is displaced onto the dorsal aspect of the astragalus and calcaneum, and there is a lateral displacement of the articulation between the tibia and the astragalus onto the dorsum of the astragalus (Schaeffer, 1941b; Jenkins, 1971). Boonstra (1965) demonstrated that in the primitive therapsid *Hipposaurus,* from the *Tapinocephalus* zone of South Africa, the tibial and fibular facets were already situated on the dorsum of the astragalus and calcaneum (Fig. 6A). The Dinocephalia (Fig. 6B) reflect a pattern comparable to that of pelycosaurs (Boonstra, 1966).

Astragalar superposition was only partially achieved in *Hipposaurus* and in the Therocephalia; in *Bauria,* Schaeffer (1941a) noted that the calcaneo-astragalar superposition was "weak" and that the astragalus lies almost entirely medial to the calcaneum. *Hipposaurus* shows a distinct calcaneal process, apparently homologous to the mammalian sustentaculum tali—an unusual development in such an early therapsid (Boonstra 1965).

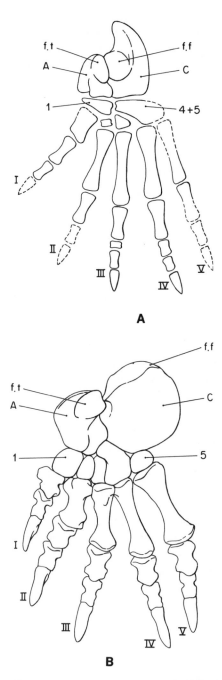

A

B

Figure 6.   Pes of: A, gorgonopsian *Hipposaurus;* and B, dinocephalian *Titanophoneus,* in dorsal view. (A, after Boonstra, 1965; B, after Orlov, 1958.)

Key: **A,** astragalus; **C,** calcaneum; **f.t,** facet for tibia; **f.f,** facet for fibula; Arabic numerals, distal tarsals; Roman numerals, digits.

Among therapsids, a trend towards the formation of a calcaneal tuber can be observed. This feature serves as the point of insertion for the tendon of *M. triceps surae,* resulting in an improved lever effect of this muscle on the foot. A tuber is present in *Hipposaurus* (Boonstra, 1965)

and in therocephalians (Kemp, 1978; Hou, 1979); the latter forms probably had a relatively consolidated metatarsus that could have acted as a propulsive lever.

Kemp (1978) has postulated mobility between the astragalus and calcaneum in *Regisaurus.* In his partial reconstruction, the two bones are linked by a prominent calcaneo-astragalar ligament. The astragalus is considered to be functionally part of the crus; the calcaneum—as a functional part of the pes—would have rotated against it. Further material is needed to test this interesting hypothesis.

An important aspect of the evolution of the mammalian pes is the consolidation of the tarsalia and the formation of intermetatarsal contacts. The pelycosaurian pes (Romer and Price, 1940) has five distal tarsals arranged in a broad arc and the digits are splayed, the first and fifth enclosing angles of 60° and more. The expanded proximal ends of the metatarsals overlap only slightly. The pes of dinocephalians (Orlov, 1958; Boonstra, 1966) closely resembles that of pelycosaurs in retaining five distal tarsals and in lacking intermetatarsal articulations (Fig. 6B). In the Gorgonopsia, *Hipposaurus* (Fig. 6A), and Biarmosuchidae, the number of distal tarsals is reduced to four, but the pedal digits still have a splayed arrangement and intermetatarsal contacts are poorly developed. The pes of the therocephalian *Bauria* appears to have acquired some degree of proximal contact between the metatarsals but not as much as in the later cynodonts (Jenkins, 1971).

Little is known about the phalangeal formula of the gorgonopsian pes; it is supposedly identical with that of the manus (Sigogneau, 1970), but available specimens are inadequate to resolve this issue. In the dinocephalians (Orlov, 1958; Boonstra, 1966) and therocephalians (Boonstra 1964), the phalangeal counts are reduced to the mammalian formula 23333. The Biarmosuchidae, like the pelycosaurs, reflect the reptilian formula 23453 (Sigogneau and Tchudinov, 1972).

Concluding Remarks

The postcranial skeleton of the Dinocephalia, Gorgonopsia, and Therocephalia reflect features "intermediate" between the more primitive pelycosaurs and the more advanced cynodonts and mammals. Some of these features approximate the mammalian condition in parallel among distantly related groups; for example, the reduction of phalanges to the mammalian formula of 23333. Although their postcranial structure is still inadequately documented, the Therocephalia seem to approach the primitive mammalian condition in more features than do other noncynodont therapsids. This is consistent with the hypothesis (cf. Kemp, 1978), based on cranial features, that therocephalians are the sistergroup of the Cynodontia plus Mammalia.

Acknowledgments

I thank Professor F. A. Jenkins, Jr., Harvard University, for reading the manuscript, and The Zoological Society of London for copyright clearance for figures from the *Journal of Zoology*.

References

Attridge, J.
1956. The morphology and relationships of a complete therocephalian skeleton from the Cistecephalus zone of South Africa. *Proc. Roy. Soc. Edinburgh, B* 66:59–93.

Bakker, R. T.
1975. Experimental and fossil evidence for the evolution of tetrapod bioenergetics. In *Perspectives in Biophysical Ecology,* ed. D. Gates and R. Schmerl. Berlin: Springer-Verlag.

Barghusen, H. R.
1968. The lower jaw of cynodonts (Reptilia, Therapsida) and the evolutionary origin of mammal-like adductor jaw musculature. Postilla 166:1–49.

Boonstra, L. D.
1934a. A contribution to the morphology of the Gorgonopsia. *Ann. S. Afr. Mus.* 31:137–74.
1934b. A contribution to the morphology of the mammal-like reptiles of the suborder Therocephalia. *Ann. S. Afr. Mus.* 31:215–67.
1955. The girdles and limbs of South African Dinocephalia. *Ann. S. Afr. Mus.* 42:185–326.
1964. The girdles and limbs of the pristerognathid Therocephalia. *Ann. S. Afr. Mus.* 48:121–65.
1965. The girdles and limbs of the Gorgonopsia of the *Tapinocephalus* zone. *Ann. S. Afr. Mus.* 48:237–49.
1966. The dinocephalian manus and pes. *Ann. S. Afri. Mus.* 50:13–26.

Brink, A. S.
1957. On the skeleton of *Aneugomphius ictidoceps* Broom and Robinson. *Palaeont. Afr.* 5:29–37.

Brinkman, D.
1980. The hind limb step cycle of *Caiman sclerops* and the mechanics of the crocodile tarsus and metatarsus. *Can. J. Zool.* 58:2187–200.

Broili, F., and Schröder, J.
1935. Beobachtungen an Wirbeltieren der Karrooformation. XIII. Über die Skelettreste eines Gorgonopsiers aus den unteren Beaufort-Schichten. *Sitz.-Ber. Bayer. Akad. Wiss. München, math.-naturw. Kl.* (1935):279–330.

Broom, R.
1932. *The Mammal-like Reptiles of South Africa and the Origin of Mammals.* London: H. F. and G. Witherby.

Cluver, M. A.
1969. *Zorillodontops,* a new scaloposaurid from the Karoo. *Ann. S. Afr. Mus.* 52:183–88.

Colbert, E. H.
1948. The mammal-like reptile *Lycaenops. Bull. Amer. Mus. Nat. Hist.* 89:353–404.

Crompton, A. W., and Jenkins, F. A., Jr.
1979. Origin of mammals. In *Mesozoic Mammals. The First Two-Thirds of Mammalian History,* ed. J. A. Lillegraven, Z. Kielan-Jaworowska, and W. A. Clemens. Berkeley: University of California Press.

Efremov, J. A.
1954. Fauna nasemnikh posvonochnikh v permskikh medistikh peschankakh zapadnogo priural'ia. *Trudy Paleont. Inst. Akad. Nauk SSSR* 54.

Gregory, W. K.
1926. The skeleton of *Moschops capensis,* Broom, a dinocephalian reptile of South Africa. *Bull. Amer. Mus. Nat. Hist.* 56:179–251.

Hou, Lianhai
1979. [On a new theriodont from Inner Mongolia.] *Vertebrata Palasiat.* 17:121–30.

Huene, F. von
1931. Beitrag zur Kenntnis der südafrikanischen Karrooformation. *Geol. Paläont. Abh.* 18(3):159–227.
1950. Die Theriodontier des ostafrikanischen Ruhuhu-Gebietes in der Tübinger Sammlung. *N. Jb. Geol. Paläont. Abh.* 92:47–136.

Jenkins, F. A., Jr.
1970. Cynodont postcranial anatomy and the "prototherian" level of mammalian organization. *Evolution* 24:230–52.
1971. The postcranial skeleton of African cynodonts. *Bull. Peabody Mus. Nat. Hist., Yale Univ.* 36:1–216.

Kemp, T. S.
1978. Stance and gait in the hindlimb of a theroce-

phalian mammal-like reptile. *J. Zool. Lond.* 186:143–61.

Olson, E. C.
1962. Late Permian terrestrial vertebrates, U.S.A. and U.S.S.R. *Trans. Amer. Phil. Soc.*, n. s., 52(2):1–224.

Orlov, J. A.
1958. Khishnie deinocephali fauni Isheeva (Titanosukhi). *Trudy Paleont. Inst. Akad. Nauk SSSR* 72.

Parrington, F. R.
1961. The evolution of the mammalian femur. *Proc. Zool. Soc. Lond.* 137:285–98.

Pravoslavlev, P. A.
1927. Gorgonopsidae is severo-dvinskikh raskopok V. P. Amalitskogo. *Severo-dvinskie raskopoki Prof. V. P. Amalitskogo* III. Leningrad: Akademia Nauk SSSR.

Romer, A. S.
1956. *Osteology of the Reptiles.* Chicago: University of Chicago Press.

Romer, A. S., and Price, L. I.
1940. Review of the Pelycosauria. *Geol. Soc. Amer. Spec. Pap.* 28:1–538.

Schaeffer, B.
1941a. The pes of *Bauria cynops* Broom. *Amer. Mus. Novit.* 1103:1–7.
1941b. The morphological and functional evolution of the tarsus in amphibians and reptiles. *Bull. Amer. Mus. Nat. Hist.* 78:395–472.

Sigogneau, D.
1970. Révision systématique des gorgonopsiens Sud-Africains. *Cahiers de Paléontologie.* Paris: Éditions du C. N. R. S.

Sigogneau, D., and Tchudinov, P. K.
1972. Reflections on some Russian eotheriodonts (Reptilia, Synapsida, Therapsida). *Palaeovertebrata* 5:79–109.

Watson, D. M. S.
1917. The evolution of the tetrapod shoulder girdle and forelimb. *J. Anat.* 52:1–63.
1931. On the skeleton of a bauriamorph reptile. *Proc. Zool. Soc. Lond.* (1931):1163–205.

NICHOLAS HOTTON III
Department of Paleobiology
Smithsonian Institution
Washington, D. C. 20560

Dicynodonts and Their Role as Primary Consumers

Introduction

Dicynodonts are therapsids with distinctive specializations for herbivory. They were not the first tetrapods to exploit plants as food, having been anticipated by diadectid cotylosaurs, caseid pelycosaurs, and dinocephalian therapsids. However, they surpassed their predecessors in numbers, making up about 90 percent of the individuals in the rich and diversified therapsid faunas of South Africa. As the principal primary consumers, dicynodonts must have been a critical part of the environment of the predatory forms among which the ancestors of mammals arose. They are therefore as important to the origin of mammals, ecologically, as advanced Permian theriodonts are phylogenetically.

In this context, the present paper has two aims: the first, to present the general structure of dicynodonts; the second, to deduce feeding habits from skull morphology, body habitus, and foot structure of five of the most common genera, and to relate these features to a reconstruction of the contemporary flora. It would be useful to know what just one dicynodont actually ingested, but that must wait; fossilized stomach contents are extremely scarce, and none are yet known for these animals.

Abbreviations of special terms used in this paper

AL—axis of proximal limb element
BA—limits of bearing surface of articular
BC—basis cranii
BQ—limits of bearing surface of quadrate
CB—caniniform blade, anterior margin of caniniform
    process
CPT—caniniform process, tip

FAE—generalized direction of force of adductor exter-
   nus muscle group, prime movers of jaw eleva-
   tion
IAE—lateral insertion, adductor externus group
N—notch of caniniform blade
PA—proximal articular surface of proximal limb ele-
   ment
PP—position of secondary palate
TAE—generalized transverse component of force ex-
   erted by adductor externus muscle group.

Cranial Structure

The dicynodont skull shares basic features with primitive therapsids: the basipterygoid joint is fused, and the large stapes is in direct contact with the reduced quadrate. It remains pelyco-saurlike with respect to the number of bones, prominent parietal fenestra, and large postden-tary component of the lower jaw. A preparietal bone is shared with gorgonopsians.

The skull is uniquely defined as dicynodont by adaptations for feeding (Watson, 1948) that cen-ter on modification of the jaw joint for longitudi-nal motion in the bite. The lower component of the joint (angular and surangular, BA, Figs. 1A, B; 2B) is about twice as long as the upper (quadrate, BQ, Figs. 1A, 2A), and is convex as it curves around the back of the jaw. The en-larged adductor externus musculature has sup-planted the pterygoideus musculature as the prime mover of jaw elevation, and slopes forward from its origins around the temporal fenestra (tf, Fig. 1A) to its insertion on the dentary (IAE, Fig. 1B). Its force is generally directed backwards as well as upwards (FAE, Fig. 1A), so that retrac-tion is associated with elevation and is much more powerful than the protraction mediated by the reduced pterygoideus group (Crompton and Hotton, 1967). The anterior shift of the insertion of the prime movers precludes the "snap" of the jaws utilized by reptilian predators, but compen-sates by conferring great mechanical advantage: the dicynodont bite, though slow, was very pow-erful. It is this feature that indicates that dicy-nodonts subsisted chiefly on vegetation.

The face is shortened, while the marginal den-tition is reduced in most forms to a pair of max-illary tusks or is lost altogether, and is sup-planted by a horny beak superficially like that of a turtle. The distribution of horn across the short mouth and occlusal parts of the jaws is indicated by punctate sculpture on the surfaces of the fused dentaries, fused premaxillae, and maxillae (Fig. 1). In general, horn provided tough surfaces and trenchant edges for anterior cropping and lateral shear. In many forms the horny blade supported by the maxilla was extended down-ward by the caniniform process, so that its edge (CB, Figs. 1A, C, D, 2A) was at a right angle to

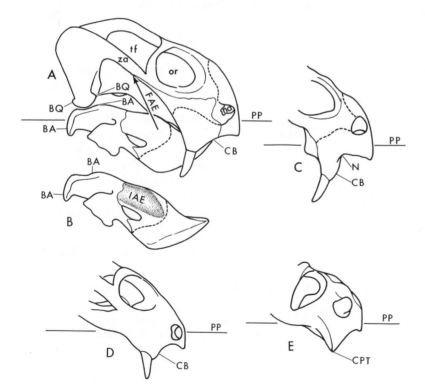

Figure 1. Skull, central dicynodonts, oriented by reference to bones surround-ing inner ear (Cox, 1962): A, *Dicynodon*, lateral aspect, lower jaw fully elevated and retracted; B, *Dicynodon*, lower jaw, lateral aspect; C–E, snout only: C, *Diic-todon;* D, *Kingoria;* E, *Oudenodon*. (A, B, and E redrawn from Culver and Hotton, 1981.)

Key for use in this and other figures: **ac,** acetabulum; **ch,** choana; **cl,** clavicle; **cor,** coracoid; **ds,** dentary symphysis; **dc₁,** 1st distal carpal; **gl,** glenoid; **icl,** interclavicle; **il,** ilium; **is,** ischium; **ls,** lateral shelf of dentary; **mc₁,** 1st metacarpal (other metacarpals arabic numerals 2–5); **na,** naris; **cf,** obturator foramen; **or,** orbit; **pb,** pubis; **r,** radius; **sc,** scapula; **t,** tusk; **tf,** temporal fenestra; **u,** ulna; **za,** zygo-matic arch.

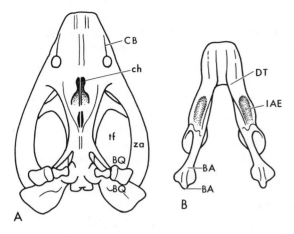

Figure 2. *Dicynodon* sp.: A, skull, palatal aspect; B, lower jaw, dorsal aspect. Choanae (ch) mark the posterior end of mouth and secondary palate, which consists mostly of premaxilla in central dicynodonts and *Lystrosaurus*. (Redrawn from Cluver and Hotton, 1981.)

the arc described by the dentary as it was being elevated and retracted. The dentary table (DT, Fig. 2B), a medial expansion of the dorsal rim of the dentary, probably provided for crushing action during late stages of retraction, when it occluded swellings on the secondary palate near the bases of the tusks (Cluver, 1971, 1975; King, 1981a).

Postcranial Structure

In dicynodonts, the atlas-axis complex conforms closely to a pelycosaurian pattern, and the deeply amphicoelous vertebral centra are probably notochordal. As in pelycosaurs, the zygapophyseal articular surfaces are close to the midline, sloping mediad; morphological change along the column is gradual.

The vertebral column of dicynodonts tends to be less flexible than that of pelycosaurs. Cervical vertebrae are reduced from seven (Romer and Price, 1940) to six, caudals from more than fifty to less than twenty, and a sternum, unossified in pelycosaurs, appears as a thin oval plate with dorsal facets or bosses for direct attachment of the first three pairs of dorsal ribs. These ribs are long and stout, and—being anchored ventrally to the sternum—provide a firm platform for the shoulder girdle.

The shoulder girdle and humerus are much more suggestive of the pelycosaurian than of the mammalian condition. The girdle (Fig. 3A) retains all elements except the cleithrum (Cox, 1959; Watson, 1960). Being firmly interconnected ventrally by a large interclavicle (see also

Cox, 1959; King, 1981a), the two halves probably had little independent motion. The humerus, like that of pelycosaurs, is short, with massive proximal and distal processes for muscle attachment; its proximal articulation is centered in line with the shaft (Fig. 3B). Scapular and procoracoid facets of the glenoid, however, are in line with one another, rather than being offset as in pelycosaurs, and the humeral component of the joint is cylindrical rather than strap-shaped. The glenoid fossa faces more to the rear, and was probably positioned more ventrally because of the curvature of the bottom of the girdle. Muscle attachments and the orientation of the proximal humeral articulation indicate that the arm motion of dicynodonts was still predominantly transverse, as in pelycosaurs, but the configuration of shoulder joint surfaces suggest that mobility was greater (King, 1981a). Orientation of the glenoid indicates a larger rearward and downward component in the habitual resting position of the humerus.

The dicynodont pelvis (Fig. 4) looks much more advanced than the column and shoulder girdle. The ilium, unlike that of pelycosaurs and primitive therapsids, is expanded to accommodate four or more large sacral ribs. The pubis

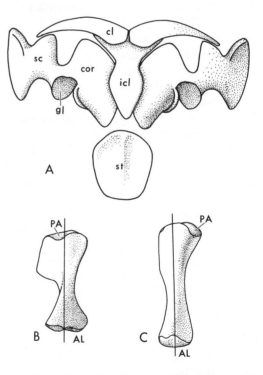

Figure 3. *Diictodon* cf. *grimbeeki*: A, pectoral girdle, ventral aspect; C, right femur, dorsal aspect. B and C from individuals of comparable size, smaller than individual represented by A.

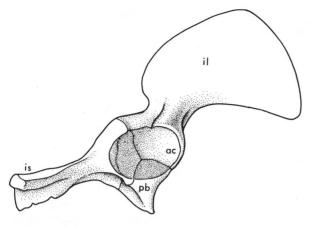

Figure 4. Right innominate, *Dicynodon leoniceps*. Oriented approximately as in life; note position of acetabulum (ac) *behind* expanded iliac blade (il).

and ischium are displaced so far backward relative to the ilium (Romer, 1956) that the acetabulum comes to lie nearly or quite behind the sacrum, in this respect surpassing even the Early Triassic theriodonts in mammal-like appearance. At the ventral midline, the pubes and ischia of dicynodonts meet not at all, or only at a thin edge, while those of pelycosaurs meet at a reinforced butt-joint. This difference has been related to the advent of viviparity (Watson, 1960; King, 1981a), but it is probably better accounted for by different postural and locomotor stresses at the ventral midline. In dicynodonts, the weight of the animal seems to have been transmitted laterally from sacrum to acetabulum, a condition that would subject midline structures to transverse tension. Such stresses would be readily resisted by ligaments, and differential movement between right and left innominates would be minimized by the anteroposteriorly expanded sacroiliac joint.

The femur (Fig. 3C) is a robust, slightly curved rod in small dicynodonts, whereas in large ones it is flattened in a plane through the axis of the tibial condyles. The proximal articular surface is spheroidally convex. It varies from a simple dome (King, 1981a) to a distinct spherical head (Cox, 1965; Cluver, 1978) and is offset dorsally from the tibial plane and anteriorly from the femoral axis at different angles in various taxa. Engaging the shallow acetabulum of the very mammal-like pelvis, it seems functionally analogous to the mobile and ubiquitous ball-joint hip of mammals, and the inference of parasagittal limb motion, comparable to that of mammals, is difficult to avoid. King (1981a), however, suggests that *Dicynodon* retained a transverse

power stroke with axial rotation of the femur, though with a greater vertical component than in the primitive condition. She emphasizes increased mobility rather than an approach to parasagittal motion. Resolution of this problem requires further study of the variability of femoral head shape and angulation.

The distal segments of front and hind limbs are robust, and shorter than the proximal segments. Weight would have been supported about equally by radius and ulna in front, and principally by the tibia in back. Manus and pes are remarkably short and stout, with metapodials but little longer than the short phalanges (Fig. 5). Metapodial I, in fact, is reduced to the length of the nearest phalanx, and seems to be replaced functionally by an elongate first distal podial (dc_1, Fig. 5A). Digits are subequal in length, the phalangeal formula being the primitive one for mammals, 23333. Kemp (1982) observes that this condition is not well understood in dicynodonts because the function of wrist and ankle joints remain obscure. He suggests that it is associated with parasagittal limb motion and plantigrade foot pose in some theriodonts. In dicynodonts, the axis of both manus and pes seems to run through digit III. Despite their shortness, manus and pes were apparently flexible, for when preserved in articulation they are often folded up like fists between proximal and distal rows of podial bones.

General Appearance and Locomotion

In their external appearance, dicynodonts were slab-sided animals with short, heavily muscled limbs and short tail. Their plantigrade feet no longer sprawled so far to the sides as those of

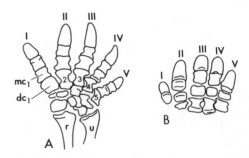

Figure 5. A, right forearm and hand, *Diictodon* cf. *grimbeeki*, dorsal aspect; B, left metacarpals and digits, natural articulation, *Oudenodon* sp., ventral aspect. Both individuals about the same size, skull length about 110 mm. The ungual phalanges of *Dicynodon* and *Lystrosaurus* resemble the short, spatulate unguals of *Oudenodon*.

their pelycosaurian forebears, but they had lost the lizardlike gracility of pelycosaurs without gaining the mammalian slenderness of living dogs and cats. The body form of dicynodonts is roughly comparable to that of such robust mammals as beavers *(Castor)* and New World badgers *(Taxidea),* but the limb bones of dicynodonts are more robust, and the feet are shorter and stouter than those of even the most stout-bodied mammals. There are no skeletal specializations to suggest the burrowing ability of beaver and badger, but the genera *Cistecephalus* and *Kawingasaurus* (see below) were specialized for a mole-like mode of life.

Increased robustness of dicynodont body form was accompanied by reduction of lateral undulation of the vertebral column that was only partly compensated by greater mobility of the limbs (Cox, 1959; King, 1981a). Although it reduced speed and agility, the robust build of dicynodonts made for a stable, plodding gait. King emphasizes stability as adaptive to feeding habits requiring a great deal of mechanical force, and endurance as essential to herbivory in a perhaps seasonally harsh climate.

King (1981a) also suggests that the dicynodonts' lack of speed and agility may have been compensated by cryptic or crepuscular habit that served as protection against predators, but this view is untenable for two reasons. First, it assumes that potential predators were significantly faster and more agile than their prey; they were not. The postcranial structure of primitive theriodonts is little more flexible and little less robust than that of dicynodonts. A dicynodont pursued by a therocephalian (Brink, 1958) would have fared no worse than a jackrabbit chased by a coyote. Second, reduction of flexibility of the dicynodont column is probably overemphasized. It is not unusual to find articulated columns in which the posterior part is gently curved as much as 30° or 40° with respect to the anterior. Reducing this value by half, to allow for postmortem exaggeration of maximum curvature, would still provide sufficient maximum abduction (or flexion) to lengthen the stride significantly. In addition to this degree of flexibility, the living column was probably springy because of its notochordal structure and the elasticity of the intercentral ligaments of the vertebrae. Such springiness would greatly enhance the efficiency of alternate lateral or dorsoventral bending as a means of increasing stride length, and therefore speed, when circumstances required it. Just as beavers and badgers engage in locomotion of this

kind when threatened, so it is probable that dicynodonts were briefly able to do likewise.

Diversity of Dicynodonts and Their Putative Food

The number of dicynodont taxa, reduced from a maximum (Haughton and Brink, 1954) by such revisions as those of Cox (1964), Cluver (1971), and Keyser (1975), currently includes about forty generic and more than one hundred specific names from Africa alone. Five genera, however, accomodate forty-nine of the specific names and represent a large majority of individuals. These genera are *Dicynodon, Diictodon, Oudenodon,* and *Kingoria* of the late Permian, redefined as the central dicynodonts by Cluver and Hotton (1981), and *Lystrosaurus* of the earliest Triassic, a very close derivative of *Dicynodon.* Since these animals were the predominant dicynodonts when the suborder was most diverse and abundant, their herbivory is treated as representative.

Among the majority of taxa omitted by concentrating on the central dicynodonts are contemporaries and antecedents (Keyser, 1973; King, 1981b), as well as later Triassic forms presumably derived from *Dicynodon* (Cox, 1965). It is therefore to be expected that some aspects of herbivory, not clearly documented by the material at hand, may have been missed.

Floral remains directly associated with dicynodont fossils consist of little except bamboo-size equisetalean stems (Plumstead, 1969; Keyser, 1970) and petrified logs of conifers and perhaps *Glossopteris.* Such poverty may be more apparent than real, however, for the association of diverse dicynodont genera, and evidence of tusk wear, suggest that fodder may have been quite varied, at least seasonally. In addition to the coarse material of the actual record, the flora probably included groups that preceded and survived the Late Permian in South Africa, but were too delicate to be preserved in the existing conditions. These groups include algae, fungi, lichens, and mosses and liverworts, as well as herbaceous and shrubby equisetaleans, lycopods, ferns, and a greater variety of seed ferns.

Morphological Indicators of Feeding Diversity

The morphological diversity of the central dicynodonts and *Lystrosaurus* reflect differences in feeding levels, in basic shear mechanisms of the jaws, and in the physical nature of the food. The

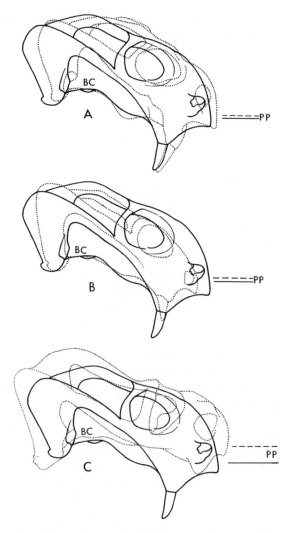

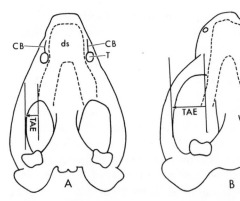

Figure 7. Palatal aspect of skull with lower jaw in place, protracted and elevated (broken lines): A, *Dicynodon;* B, *Oudenodon.* (*Dicynodon* redrawn from Cluver and Hotton, 1981.)

Figure 6. Habitual attitude of head and level of palate in central dicynodonts. *Dicynodon* (solid lines) overlies other genera (broken lines) by reference to basis cranii and quadrates. A, *Diicytodon;* B, *Kingoria;* C, *Oudenodon.* Not to scale; length of lateral exposure of basis cranii held constant. (*Dicynodon* and *Kingoria* redrawn from Cluver and Hotton, 1981.)

tusk-bearing genera *Dicynodon, Lystrosaurus, Diictodon,* and *Kingoria* differ among themselves in details related to the nature of the food, but collectively are separated from the tuskless *Oudenodon* by the entire feeding complex.

When the head is oriented in its habitual position by reference to the horizontal semicircular canal (Cox, 1962), the palate of *Dicynodon, Lystrosaurus, Diictodon,* and *Kingoria* lies below the quadrates and basis cranii (Fig. 6). The effect of this feature is to direct the mouth and tusks toward the substrate, which therefore was probably the primary target of foraging in these animals. Tusk wear indicates that the tusks were

utilized in foraging a good part of the time. In the shearing mechanism, transverse displacement of the dentary symphysis was prevented by the close fit of the prominent caniniform processes (Fig. 7A), and of the tusks (when present), against the flat, parallel sides of the symphysis. The transverse component of force exerted by jaw musculature was minimized (TAE: Fig. 7A), for the origins of the prime movers of elevation of the zygomatic arches lay almost directly above their insertions on the jaw rami. Shear took place at the lateral margins of the mouth as the angular dorsal edges of the symphysis were drawn longitudinally up and back, past the sharp, blade-like anterior margins of the caniniform processes (CB: Figs. 1A, C, D; 7A).

In *Dicynodon* and *Lystrosaurus,* the caniniform blade curves smoothly up to the tip of the premaxilla (CB, Fig. 1A), and is mechanically similar to a paper cutter. In *Diictodon* the blade is set off from the front edge of the maxilla by a distinctive notch (N, Fig. 1C); its closest mechanical analogue is a wire cutter. The difference suggests that *Dicynodon* and *Lystrosaurus* fed more frequently on foliage, while *Diictodon* foraged principally on stems, rhizomes, roots, and the like. In *Kingoria,* the caniniform blades are prominent, sharp, and smoothly curved (Fig. 1D), as in *Dicynodon.* The edges and tip of the symphysis, however, are rounded and blunt, and the mouth is short, which suggest that shear was less significant. The transverse component of force exerted by jaw musculature was sharply curtailed: prime movers were confined to a longitudinal pull not only by unflared zygomatic origins, but also by a shift of insertions laterally onto a dentary shelf. The configuration of the symphysis suggests a crushing function, but the palate seems to have lacked the horn covering of other dicynodonts, and so did not provide a tough surface against which the symphysis could work. Whatever the food of *Kingoria,* it must have been of small size, soft, and abundant.

All of the tusk-bearing genera were substrate feeders, but not all were grubbers. *Diictodon* was probably most closely tied to a grubbing mode, as indicated not only by its putative preference for roots and rhizomes, but also by its long, claw-like ungual phalanges (Fig. 5A). These were better suited for digging than the spatulate, hoof-like unguals of *Dicynodon* and *Lystrosaurus* (cf. *Oudenodon,* Fig. 5B), and would have compensated for the lack of tusks in some individuals of *Diictodon. Dicynodon* and *Lystrosaurus* reflect greater flexibility, for their grubbing was augmented by the foliage-cropping facility of the caniniform blade. *Kingoria,* though a substrate feeder, probably did not do much grubbing: tusks are absent in a majority of individuals and small in those that possess them (Cox, 1959); ungual phalanges are unknown.

Dicynodon and *Lystrosaurus* may have been more flexible than other dicynodonts with respect to foraging in or near standing water. *Lystrosaurus* is widely accepted as the more highly aquatic (e.g., Broom, 1932; Camp, 1956; Cox, 1965; Cluver, 1971). Since depression of its palatal plane has taken place below the nares, *Lystrosaurus* could forage in mud or shallow water without submerging the nostrils. At the same time, however, striae on the tusks suggest that *Lystrosaurus* also foraged under drier conditions. Conversely, the most terrestrial *Dicynodon* carries hints of aquatic habit. Ewer (1961) infers the presence of a valvular nostril in *"Daptocephalus"* (= *Dicynodon leoniceps*), and in *D. leoniceps* the naris is modestly higher than in most dicynodonts.

In the tuskless *Oudenodon,* the plane of the palate passes through the quadrates and lies only slightly below the basis cranii (Fig. 6C), so that the mouth was directed forward. *Oudenodon* therefore probably foraged habitually at levels from about 20 cm to something more than 100 cm above the substrate, depending on individual size. In its shearing mechanism, transverse displacement of the dentary symphysis was not restricted, for the caniniform processes are reduced and slope laterally, away from the sides of the symphysis (Fig. 7B). The transverse component of muscular force was enhanced by the lateral flare of the zygomatic arches, which carried the origins of the prime movers well lateral to their insertions (TAE, Fig. 7B). Transverse motion would have involved alternate movement of opposite rami, one side being protracted and elevated while the other was retracted and depressed. As a consequence, the symphysis rotated in the direction of displacement, so that its beak produced shear across the anterior margin of the mouth, in an arc from the tip of one caniniform process to the tip of the other.

Tusks

The tusks, which inspired the name *Dicynodon* (Owen, 1845) share major features of persistently growing tusks of mammals. They show little evidence of replacement; they lack enamel when mature (Poole, 1956; King, 1981a; but see also Watson, 1960); and their pulp cavities are wide open at the base. In mammals, persistent growth accomodates wear, and wear is clearly shown on the tusks of *Dicynodon, Lystrosaurus,* and *Diictodon* by facets, microscopic scratches, and polish.

Lateral wear facets testify to the noncyclic and strenuous nature of food grubbing in their irregularity and occasional origin as a consequence of trauma. Lateral facets in *Dicynodon* and *Lystrosaurus* are slightly concave, are commonly restricted to the distal third of the tusks, and may be developed anteriorly, posteriorly, or both. They are rare in *Diictodon;* but, in one individual, a slightly concave facet, in a exactly lateral position, occupies nearly the full length of one tusk. This specimen may record a traumatic spalling, the edges of the injury having become rounded by subsequent wear. A similar facet is present on a large tusk of *Dicynodon leoniceps.*

Medial facets, on the other hand, reflect the regularity of jaw action in their uniformity. Medial facets result from the close fit of the tusks against the sides of the moving dentary symphysis, and are uniformly single, flat, and of a size directly proportionate to the size of the tusks on which they are formed.

In *Dicynodon, Lystrosaurus,* and *Diictodon,* and perhaps in *Kingoria,* mature tusks are long enough that, when the jaw is fully retracted and elevated, one-third to one-half of their length projects below the dentary symphysis (Fig. 1A). Since the projecting length of tusks corresponds to the distribution of lateral wear facets of nontraumatic origin, it is likely that grubbing took place with the jaw retracted and elevated. The horn-covered anteroventral surface of the sym-

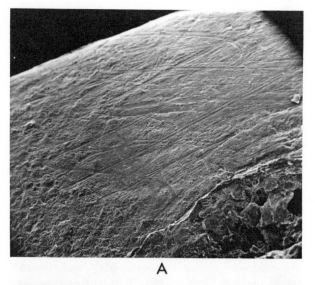

A

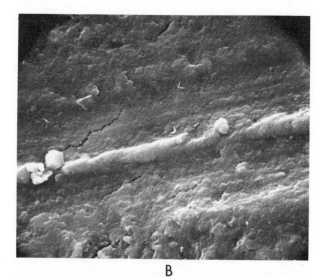

B

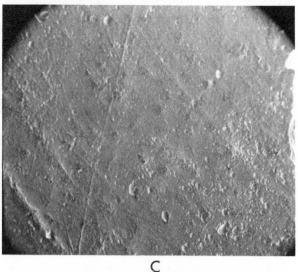

C

Figure 8. Striated surfaces of medial wear facet in *Lystrosaurus,* by scanning electron microscope. A and B, same specimen, different magnifications. In A (× 45), note regularity of abundant, coarse axial and oblique striae. In B (× 2000), note that coarse striae have sharp margins, and that dentinal tubules are not apparent. B and C, different specimens, same magnification. C (× 2000) contrasts with B in that coarse striae are rare and have rounded margins (lower right corner); most of the surface is smooth with very fine striae, and dentinal tubules are manifest as shallow, rounded pits. (A, field number 208/64, × 45; B, field number 208/64, × 2000; C, field number 207/64, × 2000.)

physis would have formed a sort of skid-plate, bracing the tusks against breakage as they were applied to the substrate in diverse directions and angles.

If the tusks were to be cleared for grubbing by opening the mouth, dicynodonts would have had to depress the jaw to at least 70° from full elevation (90° in some specimens). This is extremely unlikely, as it is close to twice the maximum gape determined by the detailed studies of Cluver (1971) of such disparate forms as *Lystrosaurus* and *Emydops.* Nor is it any more likely, by analogy of the dicynodont jaw joint to the "freefloating" hinge of herbivorous mammals, that dicynodonts normally depressed the jaw more than 20° or 30° in any circumstances. (It is only mammalian predators, with very different, anatomically circumscribed jaw hinges, that indulge in gapes on the order of 40° or 50°.) A small gape

would not preclude digging with the mouth open, using the upper beak, or the lower beak, in the scooping action ascribed to *Dicynodon* (King, 1981a), *Lystrosaurus* (Cluver, 1971), and *Endothiodon* (Cox, 1964).

Microscopic scratches on all tusk surfaces are reminiscent (except for scale) of the long, straight, parallel striae formed on bedrock by glaciers (Fig. 8A). Striae are distinct and commonly parallel over distances of several millimeters, and are more regular on the medial sides of the tusks, where, for the most part, they seem to reflect jaw action. In a few cases, however, the condition of striae seems related to food-gathering or to the nature of the food.

Striae vary in individual width from a fraction of a micron to about 40 μ, and the distribution of widths and distances apart is usually random. This implicates silt as the principle abrasive ma-

N. HOTTON III

terial, supporting other indications that tusked dicynodonts fed at or just below the surface of the substrate. On a single medial facet of *Lystrosaurus,* however, width and distance apart are nonrandom. Striae parallel to the axis of the tusk are consistently coarser and further apart than those that are oblique to the axis (Fig. 8A), indicating regularity in the distribution of abrasive material in the animal's jaws. Phytoliths in the tissue of the plant being ingested are the most obvious source of this regularity, and Equisetales are the most obvious choice of plants, but phytoliths have also been inferred in lycopods and seed ferns (Retallack, 1977; verbal comm., 1982). Nonrandom striae are therefore inconclusive with respect to the hypothesis that the chief fodder of dicynodonts was equisetaleans (Keyser, 1970). Distances between nonrandom striae suggest that the plant in question was small, a finding inconsistent with the suggestion of Watson and Romer (1956) that dicynodonts tore open the trunks of cycads to get at the nutritive pith.

Commonly, the edges of striae are angular (Fig. 8B), and the spaces between large striae are occupied by smaller ones. In some tusks, however, the edges of large striae are rounded, as if by polishing, and the spaces between them are smooth, even at high magnification (Fig. 8C). Polish is corroborated by a specimen of *Lystrosaurus* in which the entire surface is smooth, the edges of a medial wear facet barely discernible. Magnification of about × 2000 shows the remains of striae of normal size and orientation that have been nearly obliterated by a new surface marked by very fine, ungrouped striae.

The obliteration of striae by polishing indicates a change in the nature of the food, perhaps associated with changed circumstances of feeding. It may well reflect seasonal alternation of harsh and succulent foliage or of subsurface and aboveground parts of plants. It is presumed that the changes in available plants were controlled by a periodically varying supply of water, which might also change the abundance of incidental abrasives, such as clay or silt, in the feeding environment. At the very least, the presence of polish suggests that dicynodonts were by no means dependent on a single kind of plant as food. Such an interpretation would probably apply to tuskless as well as tusk-bearing dicynodonts, since all were subject to the same environmental periodicity.

Environmental Correlates of Morphological Indicators

As terrestrial grubbers, *Dicynodon, Lystrosaurus,* and *Diictodon* would have had access to subterranean food items such as fungi and underground storage structures of vascular plants. They would also have had access to algae, fungi, and other organisms growing in the litter, and ground cover such as the equisetalean creeper *Sphenophyllum,* mosses, and herbaceous lycopods and ferns. *Lystrosaurus* would have foraged on algae and vascular plants growing in shallow water, as would some *Dicynodon* and, perhaps, a few species of *Diictodon.* In *Diictodon,* however, the combination of jaw adaptations for shearing roots and rhizomes, with the use of the feet in grubbing, would seem to be more effective on dry ground than in water.

Kingoria, as a substrate feeder of uncertain grubbing ability, may have concentrated on thick litter in relatively dry circumstances. Here it would have foraged not only for plants, but also for slow-moving arthropods, molluscs, and annelids that should have been common. Such habits are consistent with its small stature (Table 1). *Kingoria* would of course have exploited fallen fruit and seeds in season, as would all of the ground-foraging dicynodonts.

The browsing *Oudenodon* would have concen-

Table 1.—Central dicynodonts

	Basal length of skull, mm	Body bulk comparable to:	Number of named Karroo species	Other species
Dicynodon	100–450	beaver to brown bear	20	E. Africa, USSR
Diictodon	70–120	marmot to beaver	21	China
Oudenodon	100–300	beaver to black bear	2	Zimbabwe, USSR, India
Kingoria	100–150	beaver	6	Tanzania

trated on shoots, leaves, seeds, and fruit of shrublike plants, such as *Glossopteris* and other seed ferns, lycopods, equisetaleans, and ferns. It could also have exploited foliage and shoots of saplings of larger *Glossopteris* and conifers; large individuals could have reached the seeds and fruit of low trees. *Oudenodon* probably overlapped the domain of substrate feeders only to the extent that small individuals might have sought to feed on tall ground cover. The largest *Dicynodon* and *Lystrosaurus* were big enough (Table 1) to encroach upon levels utilized by *Oudenodon,* but their combined ground-foraging and aquatic tendencies suggest that they did not do so very often.

A Putative Sequence of Plant Utilization

Diictodon preceded the other central dicynodonts by more than one-third of the Late Permian (Fig. 9), and during that interval was very abundant. Most dicynodonts of the time were morphologically similar to *Diictodon,* except that they had teeth on the dentary and on the maxilla behind the tusk position. A few, though not similar to *Diictodon,* were nevertheless also grubbers. One such is *Endothiodon,* a large animal in which the principal grubbing tool was a peculiarly conical symphysial beak (Cox, 1964). The mouth was directed toward the substrate (Broom, 1932), and although *Endothiodon* had neither tusks nor caniniform processes, jaw motion was restricted to a longitudinal path as in the tusk-bearing dicynodonts. Shear was anterolateral, at the sharp margins of a large trough in the premaxilla, where the conical beak was received.

The feeding mechanisms of *Diictodon* and its early contemporaries suggest that subterranean food sources were the first to be heavily exploited. Ground cover and litter were utilized less frequently by a few small animals that seem to foreshadow *Dicynodon* and *Kingoria,* and higher levels were virtually untouched.

When *Dicynodon, Kingoria,* and *Oudenodon* appeared (Fig. 9), *Diictodon* declined somewhat in numbers of individuals, and most of its early contemporaries became extinct. The advent of the new forms signaled increased exploitation of ground cover and litter, and initiated the use of higher levels of vegetation. The survival of *Diictodon* and the grubbing potential of *Dicynodon* indicate continued utilization of subterranean food sources.

So also does the appearance of small burrowers, such as *Cistecephalus* and *Kawingasaurus.*

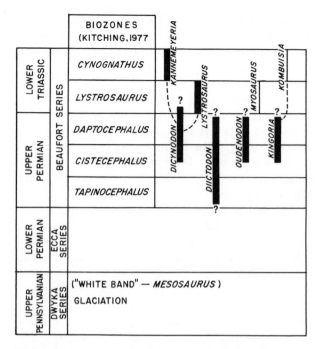

Figure 9. Stratigraphic distribution of central dicynodonts and some Early Triassic successors in South Africa.

In *Cistecephalus,* postcranial structure approaches that of moles or chrysochlorids in adaptation for fossorial life (Cluver, 1975), and the skull reflects this specialization in the modified occiput. The small caniniform processes, wide palate, and flared zygomae indicate that shear took place across the front of the mouth by transverse displacement of the stout dentary, much as in *Oudenodon. Cistecephalus* therefore probably fed on underground vegetation. *Kawingasaurus* was equally specialized for burrowing, but Cox (1972) suggests that it may have foraged for subterranean invertebrates.

The simultaneous extinction of *Diictodon* and *Oudenodon,* at the beginning of the Triassic, marks a narrowing of the utilization of the flora from both ends of the range. *Lystrosaurus,* the only dicynodont to survive in abundance, was probably more flexible than either extreme, but it was not such a grubber as *Diictodon,* nor such a browser as *Oudenodon. Lystrosaurus* was followed by *Kannemeyeria,* a large animal presumably derived from *Dicynodon,* which, superficially at least, seems to have continued the tradition of combined grubbing and ground-cover foraging. Each was accompanied by a small, rare contemporary with *Kingoria*like feeding structure—*Lystrosaurus* by *Myosaurus,* of uncertain affinity (Cluver, 1974), and *Kannemeyeria* by *Kombuisia,* plausibly derivable from *Kingoria*

(Hotton, 1974). The adaptations shared by these small relicts suggests continued litter foraging, but their record ends with the Early Triassic. *Kannemeyeria,* however, was followed by a succession of large dicynodonts—apparently derived from its stock—that persisted, world-wide, until the end of the Triassic. In this lineage, Cox (1965) identified both browsing and "grazing" forms, but most of these animals seem rather *Kannemeyeria*like by the criteria used here. They were probably flexible feeders, but lacked the morphological diversity of Late Permian dicynodonts.

Epilogue

The attenuation of dicynodont lineages to two genera at the beginning of the Triassic may not have been as abrupt as it seems. The lithology of the *Lystrosaurus* Zone is quite different from that of earlier deposits (Hotton, 1967), and as a limited facies may be only part of the record of an interval of gradual decline. In these circumstances, dicynodont decline may be largely accounted for by the emergence of new competitors and predators.

Competition probably arose among the therapsids themselves. By the time of *Kannemeyeria,* gomphodont cynodonts and bauriamorph therocephalians had become ground-foraging omnivores or herbivores; and, a little later, tritylodonts were doing likewise. The predecessors of these forms were low-slung animals of small-to-moderate size that had been evolving more advanced systems of locomotion and, perhaps, thermoregulation. These advantages would have allowed theriodonts to penetrate the niche occupied by substrate-foraging dicynodonts, which would be gradually replaced as theriodonts became better able to exploit vegetable food.

The Triassic was also a time when therapsid predators were being progressively replaced by archosaurs. In addition to being more agile, archosaurs probably became uricotelous very early, which would have predisposed them to move into drier environments. Here, browsers such as *Oudenodon* would have been easy prey while they lasted, even as the therapsid predators, with which they had grown up, were failing in competition.

With the increasing diversity and abundance of archosaurs and other reptiles of diapsid grade, the wonder is not that dicynodonts went into decline, but that Triassic forms held on so long. One factor in their survival may have been their large size, and another may have been their flexibility in the choice of foraging level or environment, presumably similar to that of their Permian ancestor *Dicynodon.*

Acknowledgments

The author wishes to thank Anna K. Behrensmeyer, Robert J. Emry, and Francis M. Hueber for taking the time to read and criticize the manuscript, and Dolores E. Larkie for the multiple typing jobs that were required. Illustrations were prepared by Lawrence B. Isham. The field work upon which this study was based, together with the collection and preparation of therapsid specimens in the National Museum of Natural History, was supported by National Science Foundation Grants G 14709 and GB 1647.

References

Brink, A. S.
1958. Notes on some whaitsiids and moschorinids. *Palaeont. Afr.* 6:23–49.

Broom, R.
1932. *The Mammal-like Reptiles of South Africa.* London: H. F. and G. Witherby.

Camp, C. L.
1956. Triassic dicynodont reptiles. Part 2. Triassic dicynodonts *compared. Memoirs of the University of California* 13(4):305–48.

Cluver, M. A.
1971. The cranial morphology of the dicynodont genus *Lystrosaurus. Ann. S. Afr. Mus.* 56(5): 155–274.
1974. The cranial morphology of the Lower Triassic dicynodont *Myosaurus gracilis. Ann. S. Afr. Mus.* 66(3):35–54.
1975. A new dicynodont reptile from the *Tapinocephalus* Zone (Karoo System, Beaufort Series) of South Africa, with evidence of the jaw adductor musculature. *Ann. S. Afr. Mus.* 67(2):7–23.
1978. The skeleton of the mammal-like reptile *Cistecephalus* with evidence for a fossorial mode of life. *Ann. S. Afr. Mus.* 76(5):213–46.

Cluver, M. A., and Hotton, Nicholas III
1981. The Genera *Dicynodon* and *Diictodon* and their bearing on the classification of the Dicynodontia (Reptilia, Therapsida). *Ann. S. Afr. Mus.* 83(6):99–146.

Cox, C. B.
1959. On the anatomy of a new dicynodont genus, with evidence of the position of the tympanum. *Proc. Zool. Soc. London* 132(3):321–67.

1962. A natural cast of the inner ear of a dicynodont. *Amer. Mus. Nov.* 2116:1–6.

1964. On the palate, dentition, and classification of the fossil reptile *Endothiodon* and related genera. *Amer. Mus. Nov.* 2171:1–25.

1965. New Triassic dicynodonts from South America, their origins and relationships. *Phil. Trans. Roy. Soc. London,* B, Biological Sciences 248(753):457–516.

1972. A new digging dicynodont from the Upper Permian of Tanzania. In *Studies in Vertebrate Evolution,* ed. K. A. Joysey and T. S. Kemp, pp. 173–89. Edinburgh: Oliver and Boyd.

Crompton, A. W., and Hotton, Nicholas III.
1967. Functional morphology of the masticatory apparatus of two dicynodonts (Reptilia, Therapsida). *Postilla* 109:1–51.

Ewer, R. F.
1961. The anatomy of the anomodont *Daptocephalus leoniceps* (Owen). *Proc. Zool. Soc. London* 136(3):375–402.

Haughton, S. H., and Brink, A. S.
1954. A bibliographic list of reptilia from the Karroo Beds of South Africa. *Palaeont. Afri.* 2:1–187.

Hotton, Nicholas III.
1967. Stratigraphy and sedimentation in the Beaufort Series (Permian-Triassic), South Africa. In *Essays in Paleonotology and Stratigraphy, Raymond C. Moore Commemorative Volume,* ed. C. Teichert and E. L. Yochelson, pp. 390–428. *University of Kansas Department of Geology Special Publications* 2.

1974. A new dicynodont (Reptilia, Therapsida) from *Cynognathus* Zone deposits of South Africa. *Ann. S. Afri. Mus.* 64:157–65.

Kemp, T. S.
1982. *Mammal-like Reptiles and the Origin of Mammals.* London: Academic Press.

Keyser, A. W.
1970. Some ecological aspects of the *Cistecephalus* Zone of the Beaufort Series of South Africa. *Proc. Papers, Second Gondwana Symp., S. Afr.* (1970):687–689.

1973. A re-evaluation of the genus *Tropiodostoma* Seeley. *Palaeont. Afr.* 16:25–35.

1975. A re-evaluation of the cranial morphology and systematics of some tuskless Anomodontia. *Memoir of the Geological Survey, South Africa* 67:1–110

King, G. M.
1981a. The functional anatomy of a Permian dicynodont. *Phil. Trans. Roy. Soc.,* B, Biological Sciences 291(1050):243–322.

1981b. The postcranial skeleton of *Robertia broomiana,* an early dicynodont (Reptilia, Therapsida) from the South African Karoo. *Ann. S. Afr. Mus.* 84(5):203–31.

Kitching, J. W.
1977. The distribution of the Karroo vertebrate fauna. *Bernard Price Institute for Palaeontological Research, Memoir* 1:1–131.

Owen, R.
1845. Report on the reptilian fossils of South Africa. Part I. Description of certain fossil crania discovered by A. G. Bain, Esq., in sandstone rocks in the southeastern extremity of Africa, referable to different species of an extinct genus of reptiles, *Dicynodon,* and indicative of a new tribe or suborder of Sauria. *Trans. Geol. Soc. London* Series 2, 7:59–84.

Plumstead, E. P.
1969. Three thousand million years of plant life in South Africa. Geological Society of South Africa Annexure to Volume 72. *Alex L. du Toit Memorial Lectures* 11:1–72.

Poole, D. F. G.
1956. The structure of the teeth of some mammal-like reptiles. *Quarterly Journal of Microscopical Science* 97:303–12.

Retallack, G. J.
1977. Triassic palaeosols in the Upper Narrabeen Group of New South Wales. Part I. Features of the palaeosols. *Journal of the Geological Society of Australia* 23:383–99.

Romer, A. S.
1956. *Osteology of the Reptiles.* Chicago and London; The University of Chicago Press.

Romer, A. S., and Price, L. I.
1940. Review of the Pelycosauria. *Geological Society of America Special Papers* 28:1–538.

Watson, D. M. S.
1948. *Dicynodon* and its allies. *Proc. Zool. Soc. London* 118(3)823–77.

1960. The anomodont skeleton. *Trans. Zool. Soc. London* 29(3):131–208.

Watson, D. M. S., and Romer, A. S.
1956. A classification of therapsid reptiles. *Bull. Mus. of Comp. Zool.* 114(2):37–69.

JAMES A. HOPSON
Department of Anatomy
University of Chicago
1025 East 57th Street
Chicago, Illinois 60637

and

HERBERT R. BARGHUSEN
Departments of Oral Anatomy
and Anatomy
University of Illinois Medical Center
801 South Paulina Street
Chicago, Illinois 60612

An Analysis of Therapsid Relationships

Addendum

Recent study of new therocephalian and cynodont material indicates that the cladograms in figures 10 and 12 may require modification. New specimens of hofmeyriid therocephalians indicate that the presence of a postfrontal bone is doubtful and that the lack of fusion of the anterior processes of the vomers, seen with certainty only in young *Hofmeyria* skulls, may be a juvenile feature rather than a primitive retention in adults. Therefore, the primitive nature of the Hofmeyriidae with respect to the three remaining eutherocephalian groups is questionable. Our knowledge of the interrelationships of these four eutherocephalian taxa is best represented at this time by a tetrachotomy in the cladogram of figure 10.

New preparation of the basicrania of *Probainognathus* and *Chiniquodon* reveals the presence of internal carotid foramina in these chiniquodontoid cynodonts. Therefore, loss of the internal carotid foramina characterizes only the Cynognathia. This weakens the basis for allying the Chiniquodontoidea with the Cynognathia rather than with the Ictidosauria + Mammalia. Under the alternative hypothesis of relationships (discussed on page 18), a squamosal-surangular accessory jaw joint would be a synapomorphy of *all* post-thrinaxodontid cynodonts (node 41 in Figure 12), including the ancestors of Ictidosauria + Mammalia. This leaves only characters 42.2 and 42.3 to link the Chiniquodontoidea with the Cynognathia, but these features are balanced by character 46.1 and loss of costal plates which link the Chiniquodontoidea with Ictidosauria + Mammalia. Because character 46.1 no longer represents a synapomorphy uniting only Probainognathidae and Chiniquodontidae, the monophyletic nature of the Chiniquodontoidea is thrown into question. At present, then, the relationships of these two families to each other and to the Cynognathia and Ictidosauria + Mammalia must be considered uncertain.

Introduction

The hypothesis of relationships of the Therapsida presented here is based on a cladistic analysis; for detailed discussions of cladistic theory and methodology see Platnick (1979), Eldredge and Cracraft (1980), and Wiley (1981). Briefly stated, "cladistic analysis is seen as a method of discerning phylogenetic pattern, namely the hierarchical arrangement of taxa as it is reflected by the hierarchical distribution of postulated shared derived characters" (Cracraft, 1981, p. 459). The pattern of phylogenetic relationship so determined is usually expressed by means of dichotomously branching diagrams called cladograms (for example, Fig. 1); the nodes in cladograms represent evolutionary novelties that arose in the common ancestor of the organisms linked at the node and are thus shared by these descendant organisms. Such novelties, or derived characters, are termed "apomorphies," and it is their sharing, as *synapomorphies,* that permits us to recognize groups and to arrange the groups in a hierarchical relationship to one another. The primitive states of these characters are termed "plesiomorphies." They cannot be used to delimit the groups under consideration because they are shared, as *symplesiomorphies,* with groups outside the scope of our analysis and so lack phylogenetically relevant information.

Assessment of the primitive state of each character is, nevertheless, essential to the determination of the derived state. With fossil taxa, primitive character states can be determined only by comparison with outgroups; i.e., related taxa lying outside the limits of the analysis (see Watrous and Wheeler, 1981). Use of related outgroups requires a provisional classification as a starting framework within which the detailed analysis is carried out. The analysis proceeds in stepwise fashion, later decision as to whether a character is primitive or derived depending on taxonomic grouping established by earlier decisions.

The classification used as a framework for the present analysis groups all living nonmammalian amniotes together as the Sauropsida. This conclusion is based primarily on the large numbers of shared derived features in the central nervous system of diapsids (including birds) and turtles (see Ulinski, this volume). The Synapsida (Mammalia plus mammal-like reptiles) is the sister group of the Sauropsida. A consequence of this classification is that the lateral temporal openings of the skull are convergent (i.e., they were independently evolved) in diapsids and synapsids. Therefore, the presence of a lateral temporal fenestra is synapomorphic within diapsids and synapsids, but it defines neither group uniquely.

The only groups considered to be "natural" in cladistic classification (and in this paper) are those that are strictly monophyletic in the sense that all descendants of a common ancestor (known or hypothesized) are included within the group. Groups from which some descendants of the ancestral species are excluded are termed "paraphyletic" and are not considered to be natural groups. For example, the Amniota is a monophyletic group because it contains all descendants of the ancestral species in which the characterizing synapomorphy (the amnion) arose; the Reptilia, on the other hand, is a paraphyletic group because it excludes certain descendants (birds and mammals) of the ancestral species. Inasmuch as the Reptilia, as currently delimited, is defined solely by the absence of synapomorphies—for instance, reptiles are amniotes lacking the derived features of both birds and mammals—it is not a natural group.

Our analysis and presentation are subject to the following constraints:

1. Only characteristics of the skull and lower jaws have been used. This is the only portion of the skeleton that is adequately known in most groups, and it is the portion with which we have greatest familiarity. Over the last twenty years, we have examined most of the relevant material in museums throughout the world.

2. The quality of preservation and preparation, as well as the number of specimens available, is much less adequate for primitive than for advanced therapsids. Therefore, some major relationships are insecure, as evidenced by low numbers of synapomorphies used to define certain taxa.

3. A full formal classification of the Synapsida has not been attempted because the relationships expressed in the cladograms are necessarily provisional. We have given new names to some groups in order to characterize them in the tables and in the discussion.

4. Because such traditional names as Synapsida, Therapsida, Theriodontia, and Cynodontia

denote paraphyletic taxa, they represent concepts that are not accepted here. In order to form monophyletic groups, yet minimize the number of new names created for what may prove to be provisional taxa, we have extended the definition of many traditional taxa to include all descendant groups. For example, Therapsida is used to denote the monophyletic taxon represented by all non-"pelycosaurian" synapsids, including mammals.

The results of our analysis are conveyed primarily by the cladograms (Figs. 1, 4, 10, 12), which are based on the derived characters listed in tables 1–4 and illustrated in the semidiagrammatic figures of skull morphology (Figs. 2, 3, 5–9, 11, 13, 14). Characters that evolved independently in two or more groups are indicated in the tables by "Conv." (= convergent on). The derived character states are indicated in the figures by numbers that refer to the tables. The groups listed in the tables are, in turn, keyed to the cladograms. The following section on the major groups deals primarily with controversial aspects of classification or of interpretation of characters, but does not represent a full discussion of these topics.

Analysis and Discussion of Taxa

Sphenacodontids as the sister group of the Therapsida

The sphenacodontids have long been recognized as the nearest relatives of the therapsids, primarily on the basis of the joint possession of a reflected lamina on the angular bone (Romer and Price, 1940) but also on the basis of the features listed in Table 1 (Fig. 2; see also Reisz, 1980). The detailed analysis of haptodontine sphenacodontids by Currie (1979) suggests that some of the features indicated here as synapomorphies of advanced sphenacodontids and therapsids may be convergences (Table 1, characters 1.3, 1.4).

Therapsida

The most primitive of post-sphenacodontid synapsids are the genera *Biarmosuchus* (Fig. 2C) of Russia and *Hipposaurus, Rubidgina, Ictidorhinus,* and related forms from South Africa. Relative to sphenacodontids, they and more derived therapsids share a large number of apomorphic states, many of which can be related to intensification of the predaceous adaptations first seen in sphenacodontids. *Biarmosuchus* and

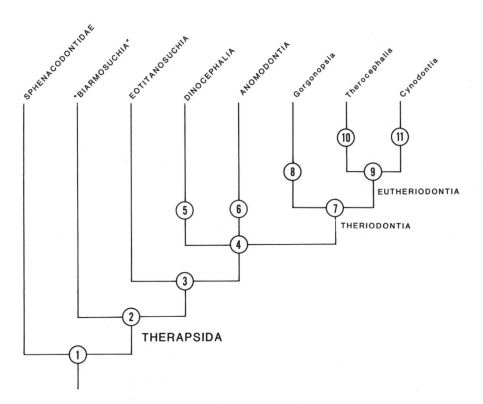

Figure 1. Cladogram of the principal groups of Therapsida, plus the Sphenacodontidae, the sister group of the Therapsida. Circled numbers indicate natural groups as defined by character states listed under these numbers in Table 1. The Mammalia are included within the Cynodontia as a derived subgroup.

Table 1.—Character states of the principal groups of Therapsida plus Sphenacodontidae

1. Sphenacodontid + Therapsid
    1. Angular bone with reflected lamina.
    2. Zygomatic process of quadratojugal lost, replaced by process of squamosal.
    3. Canine teeth enlarged, transversely compressed, with mesial (anterior) and distal (posterior) cutting edges.
    4. Maxilla increased in height, eliminating lacrimal contact with external naris.
    5. Retroarticular process of articular turned downward.
    6. Paroccipital process elongated and directed ventrolaterally.
2. Therapsid
    1. Lateral temporal fenestra enlarged. [Conv. *Edaphosaurus*]
    2. Septomaxilla with posterodorsal process extending onto face between nasal and maxillary bones
    3. Supratemporal bone lost.
    4. Squamosal with groove on posterior surface, the "external auditory meatus" of many authors.
    5. Reflected lamina of angular, deeply notched dorsally.
    6. Upper canine further increased in length.
    7. Dorsal process of premaxilla greatly elongated.
    8. Parietal foramen raised on a prominent boss.
    9. Maxilla increased further in height to eliminate contact of nasal and lacrimal bones.
    10. Interpterygoidal vacuity reduced in size.
    11. Vomer transversely widened between internal nares.
3. Eotitanosuchian + Advanced Therapsid
    1. Temporal fenestra and temporal fossa posterodorsally enlarged so that area of origin of *Musc. adductor mandibulae externus* (MAME) is visible in dorsal view.
4. Advanced Therapsid
    1. Temporal roof further reduced in width.
    2. Temporal fossa expanded laterally.
5. Dinocephalian
    1. The MAME takes extensive origin from dorsal surface of temporal roof, including dorsal surface of postorbital bar.
    2. Incisor teeth interlock.
    3. Incisor teeth with lingual heels.
6. Anomodont
    1. Zygomatic arch displaced dorsally.
    2. Dentaries fused at symphysis. [Unfused in some dromasaur specimens that appear to be juvenile individuals. Conv. 42.2]
    3. Articular surface of lower jaw slopes steeply posteroventrally.

Table 1 (continued)

    4. Fenestra between dentary and angular bones.
    5. Facial region shortened.
    6. Lower canine reduced in size. [Conv. 17.2]
    7. Posterodorsal part of dentary with fossa for insertion of MAME. [Conv. 11.1]
    8. Palatal portion of premaxilla greatly expanded posteriorly to closely approach palatine bone.
    9. Palatal teeth lost. [Conv. some therocephalians and all cynodonts]
    10. Coronoid bone lost.
7. Theriodont
    1. Postdentary bones reduced in height and posterodorsal part of dentary increased in height so that the latter is left as a free-standing coronoid process.
    2. Quadrate and quadratojugal reduced in height.
    3. Quadrate and quadratojugal lie in a depression in the anterior face of the squamosal, with no sutural union with the squamosal.
    4. Dorsal process of premaxilla reduced in length. [Reversal of primitive therapsid condition. Conv. some dicynodonts.]
    5. Skull reduced in height. [Conv. many dicynodonts.]
8. Gorgonopsian
    1. Palatine bones meet on ventral midline, separating vomer from contact with pterygoid on palatal surface.
    2. Anterior portion of vomer greatly expanded transversely. [Conv. 23.2, including less derived condition 10.4]
    3. Premaxilla with prominent vomerine process broadly overlapping ventral surface of vomer. [Conv. 23.3]
    4. Fossa for lower canine confluent with internal naris. [Conv. 10.5]
    5. Quadrate with broadly rounded dorsal surface.
    6. Articular bone with prominent posterolateral process ("dorsal process" of Parrington, 1955), which contacts the posterior surface of the quadrate above the lateral quadrate condyle.
    7. Preparietal bone present. [Conv. ictidorhinid "biarmosuchians," 21.6]
    8. Reflected lamina lies far anterior to jaw articulation.
    9. Reflected lamina lacks free dorsal margin. [Reversal to pretherapsid condition.]
    10. Lateral surface of reflected lamina with characteristic morphology, a robust near-vertical ridge anteriorly bordering a deep fossa.

Table 1 (continued)

11. Number of postcanine teeth greatly reduced. [Conv. several groups of therocephalians and dicynodonts]
12. Vomers fused [Conv. 11.18 and 11.19, 22.2, 26.2]
13. Precanine maxillary teeth lost. [Conv. *Eotitanosuchus,* Anteosauridae, 29.2, 35.2, 38.5]

9. Eutheriodont (Therocephalian + Cynodont)
    1. Temporal roof completely eliminated so that temporal fossa is completely open dorsally.
    2. Postorbital bone shortened so that it does not contact squamosal medial to temporal fossa.
    3. Parietal expanded posteriorly on midline behind parietal foramen, increasing length of sagittal crest.
    4. Epipterygoid expanded anteroposteriorly.
    5. Rudimentary osseous secondary palate ("crista choanalis") on maxilla and palatine. [Conv. some ictidorhinid "biarmosuchians"]
    6. Postfrontal reduced in size. [Conv. some dicynodonts]
    7. Loss of teeth on palatine bone. [Conv. 6.9]
    8. Squamosal emarginated from below lateral to quadratojugal so that much of quadratojugal is exposed in lateral view. [Conv. anomodonts]
    9. Posteroventral portion of dentary forms a thickened lower border that extends below the angular bone and supports the latter in a trough on its medial surface.
    10. Prootic with a laterally directed process lying anterior to the paroccipital process; in therocephalians, called the "central process," and in cynodonts, the "lateral flange." [The presence of this process in pristerognathid therocephalians is uncertain, although it appears to be present in *Ptomalestes.*]
    11. Ventral edge of squamosal with a V-shaped notch posterior to the quadrate. [A notch is present in pristerognathids, the whaitsiid *Theriognathus,* the euchambersiid *Annatherapsidus,* and cynodonts; in other therocephalians, this region is usually damaged, but the notch appears to be absent in baurioids; this is interpreted as a secondary loss, for the alternative interpretation requires at least three independent origins of the notch.]

10. Therocephalian
    1. Suborbital vacuities in palate.
    2. Stapes lacks stapedial foramen. [Conv. dicynodonts and, apparently, anteosaurids]

Table 1 (continued)

3. Well-developed anteroventral ("prootic") process of squamosal lying anterior to the posttemporal foramen. [It forms most of the anterior border of the pterygo-paroccipital foramen in all therocephalians with the possible exception of pristerognathids; see 24.4.]
4. Vomer moderately expanded and widest at anterior end. [Whaitsiid vomer widest behind its anterior end due to development of unique lateral process. Conv. 8.2 in part]
5. Fossa for lower canine confluent with internal naris. [Conv. 8.4].
6. Dorsal process of stapes reduced or absent.

11. Cynodont
    1. Fossa on dorsolateral surface of coronoid region of dentary for insertion of portion of MAME, which develops into masseter muscle of more derived cynodonts.
    2. Zygomatic arches flared laterally and pterygoid flanges reduced in transverse dimension so that posterior half of lower jaw lies near the center of the temporal fossa, rather than at its lateral margin.
    3. Posterior half of nasal bone expanded at expense of facial portion of prefrontal so that nasal contacts lacrimal and excludes prefrontal from contact with maxilla.
    4. Reflected lamina of angular greatly reduced in size.
    5. Lateral flange of prootic expanded anteroposteriorly and contacts quadrate ramus of epipterygoid.
    6. Postorbital and prefrontal bones meet on orbital margin and exclude frontal bone from orbital rim.
    7. Occipital condyles double.
    8. Supraoccipital bone narrow, excluded from posttemporal fossa by expanded tabular bone.
    9. Well-developed palatal processes formed by palatines as well as by maxillae. [Palatine forms minor part of palatal process in therocephalians.]
    10. Basioccipital tubera lost.
    11. Anterodorsal portion of prootic overlaps external surface of posterior border of epipterygoid.
    12. Quadrate with a posterior process that lies in the posterior notch of the squamosal.
    13. Stapes narrowest in dorsoventral rather than anteroposterior dimension, and stapedial foramen oriented dorsoventrally rather than anteroposteriorly.
    14. Jugular foramen faces ventrally rather than posteriorly.

Table 1 (continued)

15. Parietal extends well down lateral wall of braincase.
16. Frontal contacts epipterygoid.
17. Prootic with flanges that overlie grooves for (most likely) vascular structures.
18. Posterior processes of vomers fused on midline. [Conv. 8.12, 22.2]
19. Anterior (interchoanal) processes of vomers fused. [Conv. 8.12, 22.2, 26.2]
20. Posterior part of dentary elongated to broadly overlap the surangular. [Conv. 24.1]
21. Lower part of surangular and anterodorsal part of angular emarginated to produce a gap between them. [Conv. 24.2, but differing in that the gap is covered laterally by the dentary.]
22. Postfrontal bone lost. [Conv. 26.1]
23. Teeth on pterygoid bone lost. [Conv. 6.9, 27.6, some baurioids.]
24. Incisors spatulate. [Conv. 27.4]
25. Epipterygoid greatly expanded anteroposteriorly. [Conv. 28.2]
26. Sagittal crest extends far forward to incorporate the parietal foramen. [Conv. 28.4]
27. Palatal exposure of the maxilla behind the upper canine is greater than 20% of the distance from the canine to the posterolateral edge of the palatine bone. [Conv. 30.1]
28. Postcanine teeth possess mesial and distal accessory cusps and lingual cingulum cusps. [Conv. derived baurioids.]

related African forms are considered to be the most primitive therapsids on the basis, primarily, of the relatively small size of the temporal fenestra and only slight emargination of the temporal roof as compared with other therapsids.

"Biarmosuchia"

The primitive therapsid families Biarmosuchidae (Sigogneau and Tchudinov, 1972) and Ictidorhinidae, including Hipposauridae and Rubidginidae (Sigogneau 1970), are here tentatively united as the "Biarmosuchia." This group is characterized only by possession of primitive therapsid characters; therefore, we do not know whether it is monophyletic or paraphyletic. This uncertainty is expressed by placing the name in quotation marks. The genus *Phthinosuchus* may also fall within this group, but the only skull is so incomplete that we cannot eval-

uate its systematic position. Published figures of *Phthinosuchus* are extensively reconstructed.

Eotitanosuchia

This group contains only the genus *Eotitanosuchus* (Fig. 2D) of Russia. It is more derived in size and degree of expansion of the temporal opening than the "biarmosuchians," but, insofar as its cranial morphology is known, it is less derived than the most primitive members of the three groups discussed below as "advanced therapsids." Sigogneau and Tchudinov (1972) provide the most recent description of *Eotitanosuchus*.

Advanced Therapsids

Because the three traditional groups of therapsids—Dinocephalia, Anomodontia, and Theriodontia (Fig. 3)—are more derived in temporal morphology than *Eotitanosuchus*, they are united here as a monophyletic taxon. The resemblance of *Eotitanosuchus* to the theriodont group Gorgonopsia is considered to be due to the retention of a large number of primitive therapsid character states in the latter, rather than being an indication of special relationship. Likewise, Boonstra's (1972) grouping of the Eotitanosuchia (including forms included here in the "Biarmosuchia"), Gorgonopsia, and Dinocephalia into a higher taxon, the Alphatherapsida, is based entirely on the retention of primitive characters.

Watson (1948) and Watson and Romer (1956) considered the primitive dicynodont relatives, the venjukovioids, to have been derived from tapinocephaloid dinocephalians; therefore, they grouped the dinocephalians, venjukovioids, and dicynodonts together as the Anomodontia. In addition to the shared herbivorous specializations, all were considered to share a uniquely derived feature among non-mammalian synapsids, namely, the loss of the coronoid bone in the lower jaw (Romer, 1966). The coronoid is indeed lacking in venjukovioids and dicynodonts, but not in titanosuchid dinocephalians (Boonstra, 1962). Orlov's (1958) figures of the lower jaws of the primitive anteosaurids (= brithopodids) *Syodon* and *Titanophoneus* show differences that may be due to the coronoid being mistaken for part of the surangular in the former and for part of the dentary in the latter. We conclude that all dinocephalians, more likely than not, possessed a coronoid bone, and that the herbivorous specializations of tapinocephalians are highly derived within the Dinocephalia. Thus, dinocephalians show no special resemblances to venjukovioids and dicynodonts and should not be in-

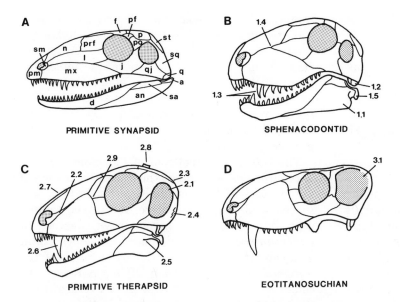

Figure 2. Diagrammatic representations of skulls of primitive members of the Synapsida. A, Primitive synapsid ("pelycosaur"), with bones labeled; B, sphenacodontid; C, primitive therapsid (based on *Biarmosuchus*); D, Eotitanosuchian (based on *Eotitanosuchus*). (A and B, after Romer and Price, 1940; C, original; D, after Sigogneau and Tchudinov, 1972.)

Key: **a,** articular; **an,** angular; **d,** dentary; **f,** frontal; **j,** jugal; l, lacrimal; **mx,** maxilla; **n,** nasal; **p,** parietal; **pf,** postfrontal; **pm,** premaxilla; **po,** postorbital; **prf,** prefrontal; **qu,** quadrate; **qj,** quadratojugal; **sa,** surangular; **sm,** septomaxilla; **sq,** squamosal; **st,** supratemporal.

Note: In this and following figures, the character states that define given groups are indicated with numbers separated by periods (i.e., 1.1, 1.2); the first number refers to the numbered groups in the cladograms and tables, and the second number refers to the character states listed under each group in the tables.

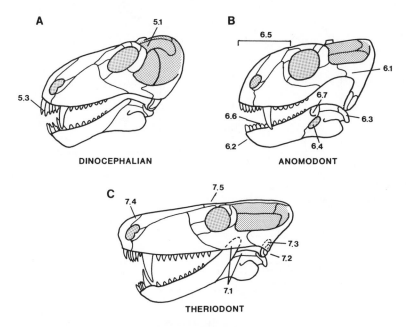

Figure 3. Diagrammatic representations of skulls of three principal groups of advanced therapsids: A, Dinocephalian (based primarily on *Titanophoneus*); B, Anomodont (based primarily on *Venjukovia*); C, Theriodont. (A, modified from Orlov, 1958; B, modified from Barghusen, 1976; C, original.)

cluded with them in the Anomodontia. The term "Anomodontia" should, therefore, refer only to the Venjukovioidea and Dicynodontia.

We have not found synapomorphies that link any two of the three groups of advanced therapsids with one another. For the present, then, we express the interrelationships of the Dinocephalia, Anomodontia, and Theriodontia as a trichotomy.

Dinocephalia

Most workers accept the close relationship of the Russian brithopodids and *Estemmenosuchus* with the anteosaurids, titanosuchids, and tapinocephalids of South Africa. All are characterized by the possession of heeled incisor teeth (Table 1, 5.3, Fig. 3A) which interlock when the jaws are closed (Table 1, 5.2), and in all but *Estemmenosuchus* and the most derived of tapinocephalids the area of origin of the external adductor jaw muscles extends onto the dorsal surface of the postorbital bar (Table 1, 5.1, Fig. 3A).

We recognize two monophyletic subgroups of Dinocephalia: the Anteosauria (= Brithopia of Boonstra, 1972), comprising a single family that we choose to designate the Anteosauridae, (including the Brithopodidae); and the Tapino-

cephalia (= Titanosuchia of Boonstra, 1972), comprising the families Estemmenosuchidae, Titanosuchidae, and Tapinocephalidae. Anteosaurians (Fig. 5A) are the more plesiomorphic group, retaining carnivorous adaptations, and, as such, are more difficult to characterize. The herbivorous tapinocephalians modify the dentition and temporal region to a much greater degree (Fig. 5B, C, D).

The broad temporal roof of *Estemmenosuchus* is regarded as secondary, the narrow condition of anteosaurians, titanosuchids, and primitive tapinocephalids being primitive. In derived tapinocephalids and, to a much lesser degree, in *Anteosaurus*, the development of supraorbital weaponry resulted in partial overgrowth of the temporal fossa (Barghusen, 1975); moreover, we consider that a similar secondary overgrowth of the temporal fossa also occurred in the bizarrely horned *Estemmenosuchus*.

Anomodontia

As has long been recognized, the venjukovioids *Otsheria* and *Venjukovia* are related to the Dicynodontia on the basis of a number of unique synapomorphies (Fig. 3B), notably the upward arching of the zygomatic arch (Table 1, 6.1) and the posterior expansion of the premaxilla on the

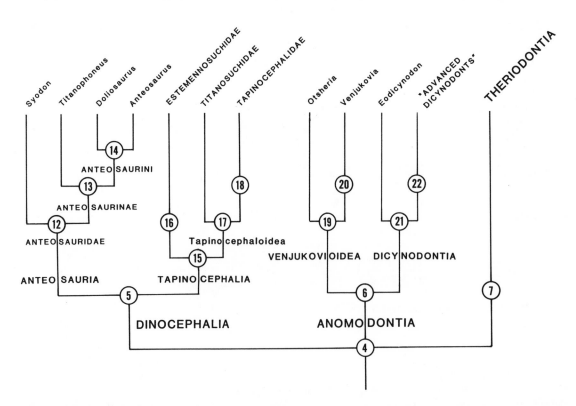

Figure 4. Cladogram of the subgroups of Dinocephalia and Anomodontia. See Table 2 for definition of character states.

HOPSON AND BARGHUSEN

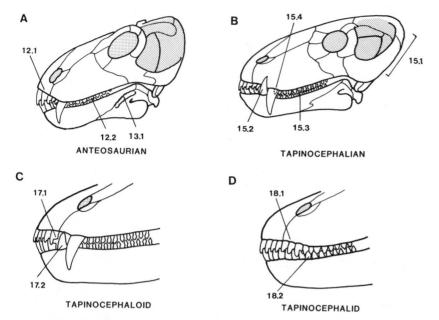

Figure 5. Diagrammatic representations of skulls and teeth of the major subgroups of Dinocephalia: A, Anteosaurian (based primarily on *Titanophoneus*); B, Tapinocephalian (based primarily on *Jonkeria*); C, Tapinocephaloid (based on *Jonkeria*); D, Tapinocephalid (based primarily on *Struthiocephalus*). (A, after Orlov, 1958; B, after Boonstra, 1969; C, after Boonstra, 1962; D, after Boonstra 1962, 1965.)

palate (Table 1, 6.8). Though generally plesiomorphic relative to dicynodonts, the venjukovioids are specialized in reducing the height of the upper canine (Table 2, 19.1) and increasing the size of the incisors (Table 2, 19.2); the dentition thus bears a superficial resemblance to that of tapinocephalids, although the teeth do not intermesh in true dinocephalian fashion.

Venjukovia shares, with certain advanced dicynodonts, a contact of palatine with premaxilla (Table 2, 20.1) and an anteroposterior reorientation and reduction in size of the transverse flange of the pterygoid (Table 2, 20.2; Fig. 6B). However, a number of advanced dicynodonts lack a palatine-premaxilla contact, and the most primitive dicynodont, *Eodicynodon* (Barry, 1974; Cluver and King, 1983) retains well-developed pterygoid flanges of primitive morphology (Fig. 6C). Therefore, these derived features of *Venjukovia* are convergences. Likewise, its possession of a shelf on the palatine, such as characterizes all dicynodonts (Table 2, 21.4, Fig. 6D), must also be regarded as a convergence.

Three genera of small primitive anomodonts, associated by Broom as the Dromasauria, are interpreted here as probable venjukovioids. They are perhaps based on juvenile individuals and may not constitute a monophyletic taxon distinct from the Venjukovioidea; for this reason, they are not dealt with further here. They have recently been restudied by Brinkman (1981).

Table 2.—Character states of the subgroups of Dinocephalia and Anomodontia

Dinocephalia (for characters see Table 1).

12. Anteosaurian (including Anteosauridae only)
    1. Exaggerated upturning of the alveolar margin of the premaxilla.
    2. Postcanine teeth with bulbous crowns.
13. Anteosaurinae (includes *Titanophoneus, Doliosaurus, Anteosaurus*)
    1. Lateral surface of angular bone with a thickened region ("boss") adjacent to dentary.
14. Anteosaurini (includes *Doliosaurus, Anteosaurus*)
    1. Boss on angular very prominent.
    2. Dorsal surface of nasal, frontal, and postfrontal bones thickened and rugose ("pachyostotic"). [Conv. tapinocephalids]
15. Tapinocephalian (includes Estemmenosuchidae, Titanosuchidae, Tapinocephalidae)
    1. Pronounced anteroventral rotation of occiput, suspensorium, and subtemporal region.
    2. Lower canine passes external to lateral border of maxilla.
    3. Postcanine teeth spatulate with cuspidate mesial and distal ridges.
    4. Anterior end of postcanine tooth row passes lingual to canine.
    5. Pterygoids with pronounced horizontal shelf extending posteriorly from the transverse processes.
16. Estemmenosuchid
    1. Postfrontal bones form horns. [Conv.

Table 2 (continued)

Burnetia, Proburnetia, and *Styracocephalus* of uncertain affinities]

    2. Jugal with massive, transversely oriented boss.

    3. Dorsal surface of temporal roof expanded, muscle attachment area eliminated from temporal roof. [Secondary reversal to predinocephalian condition. Conv. some tapinocephalids]

17. Tapinocephaloid (includes Titanosuchidae, Tapinocephalidae)

    1. Incisor heels greatly enlarged.

    2. Lower canine reduced in height. [Conv. 6.6]

18. Tapinocephalid

    1. Canines incisiform.

    2. Pattern of interlocking extends to canines and postcanines.

    3. Anterior end of postcanine row does not extend lingual to the canine. [Reversal to pre-tapinocephalian condition.]

Anomodontia (for characters see Table 1).

19. Venjukovioid (includes *Otsheria, Venjukovia*)

    1. Upper canine reduced in height.

    2. Incisor teeth enlarged and spatulate.

20. *Venjukovia*

    1. Premaxilla contacts palatine. [Conv. some dicynodonts]

    2. Transverse process of pterygoid oriented anteroposteriorly. [Conv. 22.3]

    3. Palatine forms shelf ventral to internal naris. [Conv. 21.4]

21. Dicynodont

    1. Edentulous beak formed by premaxilla and dentary.

    2. Facial region further shortened beyond primitive anomodont condition.

    3. Vomer excludes pterygoid from anterior border of interpterygoidal vacuity.

    4. Palatine forms shelf ventral to internal naris. [Conv. 20.3]

    5. Dorsal process of quadratojugal greatly expanded mediolaterally.

    6. Preparietal bone present. [Conv. ictidorhinid "biarmosuchians," 8.7]

    7. Dorsal process of squamosal expanded laterally, serves as extensive area of origin of MAME.

    8. Lateral articular facet of articular bone anteroposteriorly convex.

    9. Medial articular facet of articular bone on a distinct medial process.

22. Post-*Eodicyndon* Dicynodont

    1. Premaxillae fused completely.

    2. Vomers fused on midline. [Conv. 8.11, 11.18, 11.19., 26.2]

    3. Transverse flange of pterygoid reoriented anteroposteriorly and reduced in size. [Conv. 20.2]

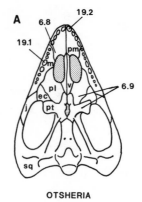
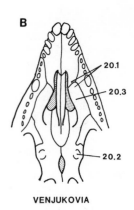

OTSHERIA   VENJUKOVIA

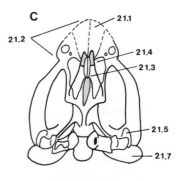
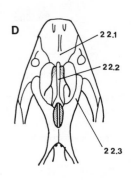

EODICYNODON   ADVANCED DICYNODONT

Figure 6. Diagrammatic representations of palates of major subgroups of Anomodontia: A, *Otsheria;* B, *Venjukovia;* C, *Eodicynodon;* D, advanced dicynodont. (A, after Chudinov, 1965; B, after Efremov, 1940; C, after Barry, 1974, and original; D, after Cluver and Hotton, 1981.)

Key: **ec,** ectopterygoid; **pl,** palatine; **pt,** pterygoid; **v,** vomer; other abbreviations as in Figure 2.

A cladistic analysis of dicynodont interrelationships was recently published by Cluver and King (1983).

Theriodontia

The Theriodontia is a persistently carnivorous therapsid group that contains the Mammalia as its most derived subgroup. Theriodonts are characterized primarily by two specializations retained by mammals (Fig. 3C): a free-standing coronoid process on the dentary (Table 1, 7.1) and a quadrate of reduced size, which has been freed from sutural union with the skull (Table 1, 7.2, 7.3). Also, the skull takes on a more mammalian form than is seen in other therapsids by becoming lower, with a flatter dorsal profile (Table 1, 7.5). More primitive therapsids, because of their general resemblance to carnivorous theriodonts, have often been classified as members of the Theriodontia (Boonstra, 1952; Olson, 1962; Hopson, 1969). The primitive carnivorous ther-

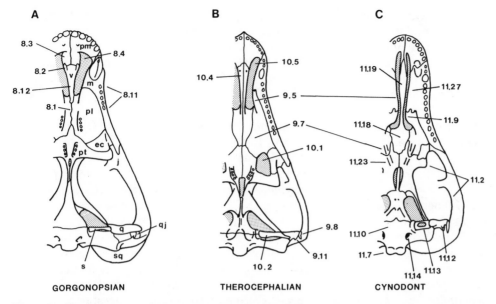

Figure 7. Ventral views of diagrammatic skulls of major subgroups of Theriodontia: A, Gorgonopsian (based on *Arctognathus*); B, Therocephalian (based primarily on *Ictidosuchoides*); C, Cynodont (based on *Procynosuchus*). (A, after Kemp, 1969; B, after Mendrez-Carroll, unpublished; C, after Kemp, 1979.)

Key: **s,** stapes; other abbreviations as in Figures 2 and 6.

apsids of Russia, grouped as Eotheriodontia by Olson (1962), are here distributed among the "Biarmosuchia," Eotitanosuchia, and Dinocephalia.

Gorgonopsia

Among the theriodonts, the Gorgonopsia (Fig. 7A) are the most plesiomorphic group. As such, they have not always been clearly separated taxonomically from the primitive non-theriodont

Ictidorhinidae (= Hipposauridae; see Boonstra, 1963; Romer, 1966), here placed in the "Biarmosuchia." Sigogneau (1970), Sigogneau and Tchudinov (1972), and Mendrez-Carroll (1975) have advocated an increasingly greater separation of the Ictidorhinidae from the Gorgonopsia.

The isolated position of the Gorgonopsia within the Theriodontia has been emphasized by Kemp (1969). Gorgonopsians share a number of derived features with therocephalians, notably

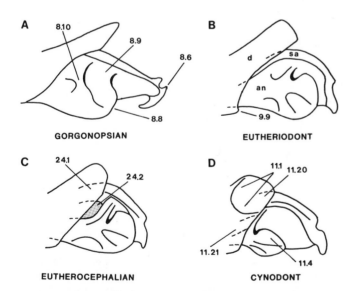

Figure 8. Posterior portions of diagrammatic lower jaws of Theriodontia: A, Gorgonopsian; B, primitive eutheriodont (based on the pristerognathid therocephalian *Ptomalestes*); C, Eutherocephalian (based on *Theriognathus*). D: Cynodont (based on *Procynosuchus*). (A, after Kemp, 1969; B, original; C, after Kemp, 1972; D, original.)

Abbreviations as in Figure 2.

with pristerognathids. These features include: anterior expansion of the vomer and of the vomerine process of the premaxilla; development of a fossa—for reception of the lower canine—which is confluent with the internal naris; reduction in postcanine tooth number; and, perhaps, development of serrations on the teeth. Our analysis indicates that these shared features are most parsimoniously regarded as convergences.

Eutheriodontia (= Therocephalia + Cynodontia)

The Therocephalia and Cynodontia (including the Mammalia as a derived subgroup) are herein united on the basis of a relatively large number of synapomorphies. Broom (1938) and, more recently, Brink (1960, 1965) have advocated a close relationship between therocephalians (notably, scaloposauroids) and cynodonts, a concept to which Romer (1969a) has taken exception. Romer argued that most of the resemblances between scaloposauroids (primitive baurioids in this paper) and cynodonts are primitive retentions and that the former possess a number of

derived, typically therocephalian, features that are not to be expected in a cynodont ancestor. We agree with Romer that cynodonts are not derived from therocephalians, but disagree that the two groups are related only at a basal therapsid level. The two have a sister-group relationship within a monophyletic Theriodontia—a relationship that we express by adopting Olson's (1962) term "Eutheriodontia," from which we exclude the Gorgonopsia.

Kemp (1972, p. 33) has recently proposed that "cynodonts arose from therocephalians and that among the latter the whaitsiids are the closest known forms to the actual cynodont ancestor." This proposal is adopted by Gaffney (1980), but the supposed synapomorphies linking whaitsiids with cynodonts are most parsimoniously interpreted either as primitive retentions from the pre-therocephalian common ancestor or as convergences.

Therocephalia

The Therocephalia (Fig. 7B, 9A, B) have long been recognized as theriodonts showing complete

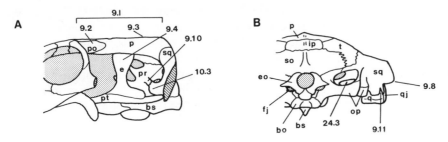

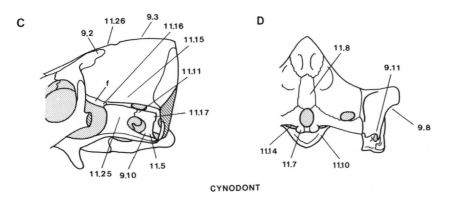

Figure 9. Diagrammatic lateral views of braincases (with zygomatic arches removed) and posterior views of occiputs of Eutheriodontia: A, therocephalian braincase (based on *Ictidosuchoides*); B, therocephalian occiput (based on *Ictidosuchoides*); C, cynodont braincase (based on *Dvinia* and *Procynosuchus*); D, Cynodont occiput (based on *Dvinia* and *Procynosuchus*). (A and B, after Mendrez-Carroll, unpublished; C and D, original.)

Key: **bo,** basioccipital; **bs,** basisphenoid; **e,** epipterygoid; **eo,** exoccipital; **fj,** jugular foramen; **ip,** interparietal; **op,** opisthotic; **pr,** prootic; **so,** supraoccipital; other abbreviations as in figures 2 and 6.

Hopson and Barghusen

elimination of the temporal roof but retaining a generally primitive palate and possessing unique paired openings in the palate—the suborbital vacuities (Table 1, 10.1). Recent studies of Mendrez (1972, 1975) have added other unique features of the palate (Table 1, 10.4) and of the braincase (Table 1, 10.3). *Bauria* (Fig. 11F) and related Triassic forms that possess a secondary palate and multicusped postcanine teeth are usually separated from the Therocephalia as the Bauriamorpha. Watson and Romer (1956) added to this group the related but more primitive forms generally called "scaloposaurs." Brink (1965) used the term "Scaloposauria" as a synonym for "Bauriamorpha."

In the current work, the Bauriamorpha and Scaloposauria of older classifications are recognized as a subgroup of the Therocephalia and are called "Baurioidea." The term "Scaloposauria" should not be used to designate a taxonomic group, because the characters that define it are

juvenile, and the species in which they are expressed are not all baurioids. Traditionally, these features include small size, broad intertemporal region, incomplete postorbital bar, and absence of well-defined canines. Because they change during ontogeny, such features do not define natural groups.

The current study demonstrates the isolated postions of the primitive family Pristerognathidae with respect to the remaining therocephalians, which are allied on the basis of synapomorphies 24.1–6 (Table 3, Figs. 8C, 9B, 11A) as the Eutherocephalia. Among the latter, the genera *Hofmeyria* and *Ictidostoma* (united here as Hofmeyriidae *fam. nov.*) are primitive in retaining a postfrontal bone and divided vomers. The three groups of advanced eutherocephalians—Euchambersiidae (= Moschorhinidae, Annatherapsidae, Akidnognathidae), Whaitsiidae, and Baurioidea—show three distinct modifications of the palate related to separation of the internal nares

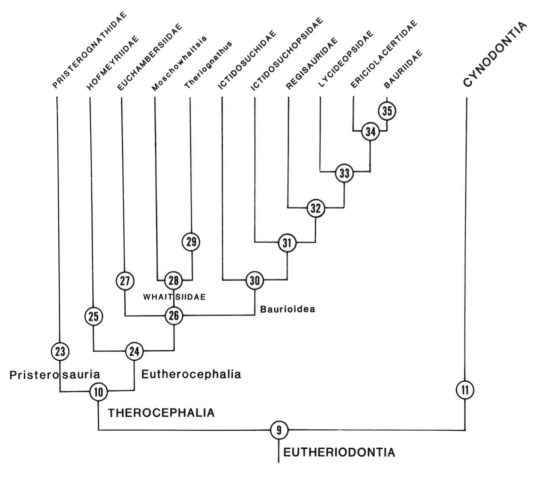

Figure 10.   Cladogram of the subgroups of Therocephalia. See Table 3 for definition of character states.

(For therocephalian characters see Table 1).

23. Pristerosaurian (includes Pristerognathidae only)
    1. Lower incisor number reduced from 4 to 3. [Conv. 35.4, 38.4]
    2. Vomers transversely expanded beyond the primitive therocephalian condition. [Conv. 8.2, 27.1 in part]
    3. Premaxilla with prominent vomerine process broadly overlapping ventral surface of the vomer. [Conv. 8.3]

24. Eutherocephalian
    1. Posterior part of dentary extended posteriorly to broadly overlap the surangular. [Conv. 11.20]
    2. Lower part of surangular and anterodorsal part of angular emarginated to produce a fenestra between them and dentary. [Conv. 11.21]
    3. Dorsal surface of paroccipital process deeply hollowed in floor of posttemporal fossa.
    4. Well-developed prootic process of the squamosal meets the "central process" of the prootic to enclose the pterygo-paroccipital foramen. [Condition uncertain in pristerognathids, see 10.3; this may be a primitive therocephalian condition.]
    5. Pterygoids with a prominent ventromedian crest on rear of palate anterior to the interpterygoidal vacuity.
    6. Incisors with longitudinal ridges and grooves. [Incisors are ridged in Hofmeyria, Theriognathus, and primitive, but not derived, euchambersiids and baurioids.]

25. Hofmeyriid (includes Hofmeyria and Ictidostoma)
    1. Postfrontal contacts prefrontal on orbital margin, with a greater amount of contact within the orbit.
    2. Dentary with characteristic boomerang, or banana, shape.

26. Advanced Eutherocephalian
    1. Postfrontal bone lost. [Conv. 11.22]
    2. Anterior processes of vomers fused on midline. [Conv. 8.11, 11.19, 22.2]

27. Euchambersiid (= Moschorhinidae, Annatherapsididae, Akidnognathidae)
    1. Anterior part of vomer greatly expanded transversely, more so than in any other therocephalian group, and broadly overlapping the ventral surface of the premaxilla.
    2. Fossa in palate for lower canine partially or completely roofed by premaxilla and maxilla.
    3. Coronoid process of dentary with a broadly convex lateral surface that extends anteroventrally above the angular region [The primitive condition for therocephalians appears to be a flat lateral surface of the coronoid process.]
    4. Incisors spatulate, with mesiolingual and distolingual crests and concave lingual surface. [Conv. 11.24]
    5. Canines and postcanines with unserrated crest on distal (posterior) border of crown.
    6. Teeth on pterygoid bone lost. [Conv. 6.9, 11.23]
    7. Reduction in number of precanine maxillary teeth from 2 to 1. [Loss of precanine maxillary teeth is too common in therapsids to warrant its use as sole evidence for a sister group relationship between euchambersiids and whaitsiids. Conv. Eotitanosuchus, Anteosauridae, 8.13, Dvinia, 38.5, some pristerognathids, some hofmeyriids, some bauriids]

28. Whaitsiid (includes Moschowhaitsia, Theriognathus)
    1. Vomer with lateral process that contacts a medially directed process of the maxilla to separate foramen for lower canine from internal naris.
    2. Epipterygoid greatly expanded anteroposteriorly. [Conv. 11.25]
    3. Separate foramen formed in epipterygoid for maxillary branch of trigeminal nerve (V^2). [Conv. some cynognathian cynodonts]
    4. Sagittal crest extends forward to incorporate parietal foramen. [Conv. 11.26]

29. Theriognathus
    1. Loss of postcanine teeth. [Conv. some dicynodonts]
    2. Loss of precanine maxillary teeth. [Conv. Eotitanosuchus, Anteosauridae, 8.13, 35.2, 38.5]
    3. Closure of suborbital vacuities [Conv. Euchambersia]
    4. Closure of interpterygoidal vacuity. [Conv. 38.8]

30. Baurioid
    1. Palatal exposure of the maxilla behind the upper canine is greater than 20% of the distance from the canine to the posterolateral edge of the palatine bone. [In all other therocephalians, excepting Theriognathus but including Moschowhaitsia, the maxilla is less than 20% of the distance from canine to rear of palatine; this is also the condition in all more primitive therapsids. Conv. 11.27]

31. Post-Ictidosuchid Baurioid
    1. Palatal process of maxilla nearly, or just, contacts vomer, but sutural connection is

Table 3 (continued)

Table 3 (continued)

lacking. [This condition superficially resembles that of primitive cynodonts, but is different in detail.]

32. Post-Ictidosuchopsid Baurioid
   1. Palatal process of maxilla contacts lateral margin of vomer to form a short osseous secondary palate; connection may be sutural.
33. Post-Regisaurid Baurioid
   1. Palatal process of maxilla contacts lateral margin of vomer to form long osseous secondary palate.
34. Post-Lycideopsid Baurioid (including *Ericiolacerta*)
   1. Palatal processes of maxillae meet on the midline ventral to anterior half of vomer.

35. Bauriid
   1. Palatal processes of maxillae completely cover vomer on osseous secondary palate, except, in some specimens, for a small exposure of vomer anteriorly between premaxilla and maxilla.
   2. Precanine maxillary teeth lost. [Conv. *Eotitanosuchus,* Anteosauridae, 8.13, 29.2, 38.5]
   3. Upper incisor number reduced from 6 to 4. [Conv. 38.3]
   4. Postcanine teeth greatly expanded transversely with crown-to-crown occlusion. [Conv. 45.1, in part]

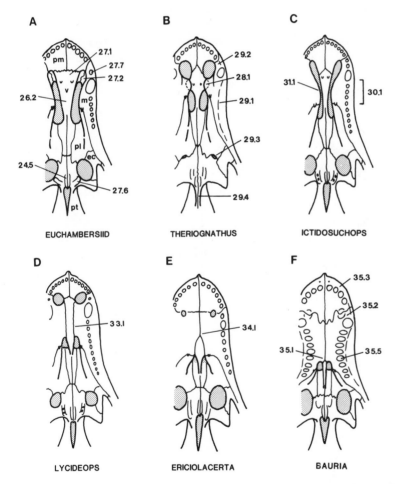

Figure 11. Diagrammatic representations of palates of Therocephalia: A, Euchambersiid (based on *Promoschorhynchus*); B, *Theriognathus;* C, *Ictidosuchops*; D, *Lycideops*; E, *Ericiolacerta*; F, *Bauria*. (A, B, D, E, and F, after Mendrez, 1975; C, after Mendrez-Carroll, unpublished.)
   Abbreviations as in figures 2 and 6.

from the oral cavity (Table 3, 27.1, Fig. 11A; Table 3, 28.1, Fig. 11B; Table 3, 31.1, Fig. 11C). The most primitive baurioids, however, are not advanced in secondary palate development much beyond that considered primitive for the Therocephalia.

The Euchambersiidae and Whaitsiidae share derived characters that are also shared with at least some members of every other group of therocephalians and are, therefore, not strong indicators of relationship. They also possess five upper incisors, but we are unable to decide if this feature is primitive or derived among therocephalians. Therefore, for the present, we consider a special relationship between these two families to be uncertain and, in the cladogram, represent the interrelationships of the advanced eutherocephalians as a trichotomy.

Cynodontia

The Cynodontia (Figs. 7C; 8D; 9C, D), including the Mammalia, are characterized by an extraordinarily large number of apomorphies (Table 1, 11.1–11.28), of which the first seventeen are unique to this group among theriodonts, and the remaining eleven are shared with one or another group of therocephalians. Of the latter, seven characters are shared with euchambersiids, seven with whaitsiids, and six with advanced baurioids.

Kemp (1972) has presented a detailed argument for the sister-group relationship of cynodonts and whaitsiids. The present analysis indicates that of the seven apomorphies shared by cynodonts and whaitsiids, only two are unique to these groups: (1) epipterygoid greatly expanded anteroposteriorly, and (2) sagittal crest extending far forward to incorporate the parietal foramen. (An additional resemblance—the accommodation of the dorsal process of the quadratojugal in a deep slit in the squamosal—was not observed in numerous specimens of *Theriognathus* (= *Whaitsia*) examined by Hopson in South Africa, and must be either unique to the specimen described by Kemp or an artifact of preservation). For cynodonts to be considered the sister group of whaitsiids, the seven presumed synapomorphies would have to be balanced against a total of ten to twelve convergences of whaitsiids with other therocephalian groups, or

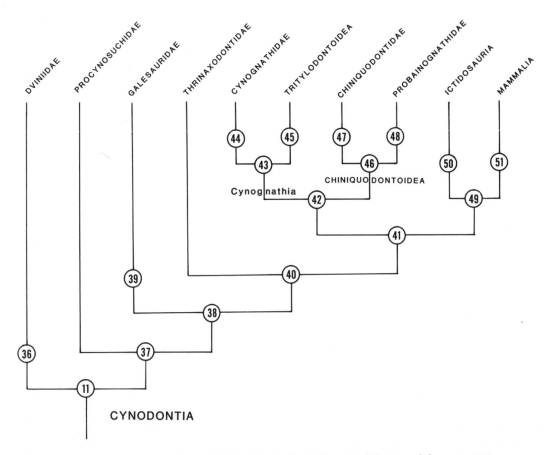

Figure 12.   Cladogram of the subgroups of Cynodontia. See Table 4 for definition of character states.

Table 4.—Character states of the subgroups of Cynodontia

(For cyndont characters see Table 1).

36. Dviniid
    1. Postcanine teeth greatly expanded transversely with numerous accessory cusps. [But lacking crown-to-crown occlusion as in 35.5, 45.1]
    2. Sagittal crest very high.
    3. Palatal processes of maxilla and palatine meet on midline. [This is uncertain due to inadequate preservation. Conv. 40.1]
    4. Lower incisor number increased from 4 to 6. [4 lower incisors considered primitive for cynodonts by outgroup comparison and presence of 4 in procynosuchids.]
37. Post-Dviniid Cyndont
    1. Anterodorsal process of prootic with extensive epipterygoid contact.
    2. Posttemporal foramen reduced in size.
    3. Squamosal flares posteriorly in rear wall of temporal fossa.
    4. Paroccipital process expanded anteroposteriorly.
38. Post-Procynosuchid Cynodont
    1. Masseteric fossa extends to lower border of dentary.
    2. Coronoid process much increased in height.
    3. Upper incisor number reduced from 6 to 4. [Conv. 35.3]
    4. Lower incisor number reduced from 4 to 3. [Conv. 23.1]
    5. Frecanine maxillary teeth lost. [Conv. 8.13, 29.2, 35.2]
    6. Descending flange of squamosal lateral to quadratojugal increased in size.
    7. Quadrate reduced in height with less exposure below squamosal in occipital view.
    8. Closure of interpterygoidal vacuity. [Vacuity may be present in juveniles. Conv. 29.4]
39. Galesaurid (includes *Cynosaurus*, *Galesaurus*)
    1. Cingulum cusps on postcanine teeth lost. [Reversal to a precynodont condition. Conv. 44.2, and the chiniquodontid *Probelesodon*]
    2. Anterior accessory cusp on postcanines reduced or lost.
40. Post-Galesaurid Cynodont
    1. Palatal processes of maxilla and palatine meet on the midline to form a complete osseous secondary palate. [Possibly conv. 36.3]
41. Post-Thrinaxodontid Cyndont
    1. Dentary greatly enlarged so that it closely approaches the jaw articulation and also forms a distinct posteroventral angular region.
    2. Vertical portion of surangular and angular reduced in height, and postdentary series becomes more rodlike and obliquely oriented.

Table 4 (continued)

    3. Reflected lamina of the angular further reduced in size from the primitive cynodont condition.
    4. Quadrate ramus of the pterygoid greatly reduced or absent.
42. Cynognathian + Chiniquodontoid
    1. Secondary jaw articulation formed between the surangular and a flat facet on the descending flange of the squamosal.
    2. Dentaries fused at the symphysis. [Conv. 6.2]
    3. Pterygoids and basisphenoid form an elongate ventral basicranial girder.
    4. Internal carotid foramina lost, it is presumed that internal carotid arteries entered pituitary fossa from cavum epiptericum lateral to basisphenoid.
43. Cynognathian (Cynognathid + Tritylodontoid)
    1. Jugal with descending flange on the anterior root of the zygomatic arch.
44. Cynognathid (includes *Cynognathus* only)
    1. Postorbital bone greatly expanded anteroposteriorly, broadly contacting squamosal on zygomatic arch.
    2. Cingulum cusps on postcanine teeth lost. [Conv. 39.1, and the chiniquodontid *Probelesodon*]
45. Tritylodontoid (includes Diademodontidae, Trirachodontidae, "Traversodontidae," and Tritylodontidae)
    1. Postcanine tooth crowns greatly expanded transversely, with crown-to-crown occlusion well developed. [Conv. 35.5, in part]
    2. Descending flange of jugal greatly enlarged. [Secondarily lost in some "traversodontids" and in tritylodontids]
46. Chiniquodontoid (includes Chiniquodontidae and Probainognathidae)
    1. Osseous secondary palate extends to posterior end of the tooth row. [Conv. 49.1]
47. Chiniquodontid
    1. Distinct angulation between ventral edge of zygomatic process of the maxilla and the anteroventral margin of the zygomatic arch.
48. Probainognathid
    1. Descending flange of squamosal lateral to quadratojugal with a glenoidlike depression for reception of a rounded articular facet on the posterodorsal tip of the surangular.
    2. Cingulum cusps reduced.
49. Ictidosaurian + Mammalian
    1. Osseous secondary palate extends to posterior end of the tooth row. [Conv. 46.1]
    2. Basicranium shortened anteroposteriorly beyond thrinaxodontid condition.
    3. Enamel prismatic.
    4. Upper postcanine teeth with an external cingulum.
    5. Postorbital bar lost. [Conv. Tritylodontidae]

Table 4 (continued)

      6. Postorbital bone lost. [Conv. Tritylodontidae]

      7. Prefrontal bone lost. [Conv. Tritylodontidae]

      8. Quadrate with a dorsomedial concavity. [Conv. Tritylodontidae]

      9. Zygomatic arch slender along entire length.

50. Ictidosaurian (includes Tritheledontidae only)

      1. Upper incisor number reduced from 4 to 3. [Conv. some "traversodontids" and tritylodontids]

      2. First lower incisor enlarged. [Conv. some "traversodontids" and tritylodontids]

      3. Upper postcanine teeth with lateral surface of the principal cusp bulging laterally.

      4. Palatal process of palatine bone extremely long.

51. Mammalian

      1. Dentary with distinct, ovoid articular condyle contacting a distinct, concave glenoid cavity on the squamosal.

      2. Postcanine teeth differentiated into premolars, which undergo a single replacement, and molars, which are not replaced.

      3. Postcanine teeth with divided roots. [Conv. Tritylodontidae]

      4. Molar teeth with well-developed shear surfaces that form a consistent pattern of wear facets. [Conv. with some or all Tritylodontoidea]

      5. Quadrate with elongate stapedial process, the crus longus of the mammalian incus.

reversals in the ancestral cynodont to a pretherocephalian condition (i.e., loss of six therocephalian and four eutherocephalian apomorphies, and, perhaps, two whaitsiid apomorphies). Consideration of *Theriognathus* as the sister group of cynodonts requires that an additional primitive whaitsiid character (Table 3, 28.1) be either secondarily lost in cynodonts or convergently acquired in *Theriognathus* and *Moschowhaitsia*.

Derivation of cynodonts from baurioids (as suggested by Brink, 1960), or from any other therocephalian group, would involve equally great numbers of convergences or reversals relative to synapomorphies. Parsimony dictates that cynodonts be regarded as having a sister-group relationship with the Therocephalia as a whole rather than with any subgroup of therocephalians.

Kermack, Mussett, and Rigney (1981) have recently argued that the early true mammal *Morganucodon* and the prototherian ("atherian" of their terminology) mammals could not have been derived from nonmammalian cynodonts because this would involve reversal of the condition of the primitive cynodont epipterygoid (= alisphenoid) to the even more primitive, precynodont, condition present in *Morganucodon*. Nineteen of the twenty-eight apomorphies of primitive cynodonts listed in Table 1 occur in *Morganucodon* (Table 1, 11.1–5, 11.7, 11.9, 11.10, 11.13–16, 11.20–23, 11.26–28) and an additional twenty or more are shared between *Morganucodon* and more derived nonmammalian cynodonts. This makes at least thirty-nine characters shared between nonmammalian cynodonts and *Morganucodon*. We can compare this with a maximum of thirteen characters (most of which also occur in nonmammalian cynodonts) shared between therocephalians (including bauriamorphs) and *Morganucodon*. Among more primitive therapsids, we find no unique synapomorphies with *Morganucodon*. Our conclusion from these data is that *Morganucodon* and the prototherian mammals are part of a monophyletic taxon—herein called the Cynodontia—containing only the nonmammalian cynodonts and the Mammalia.

Primitive Cynodonts (Dviniidae and Procynosuchidae)

The genera *Dvinia* and *Procynosuchus* (Fig. 9C, D) are both very primitive cynodonts, but, as pointed out by Kemp (1979), the skull of *Dvinia* is the more primitive of the two. Primitive features of *Dvinia* are: restricted sutural contact of the prootic with the epipterygoid above the trigeminal foramen; relatively large size of the posttemporal foramen; paroccipital process anteroposteriorly narrow and lying almost entirely behind the level of the fenestra ovalis; and absence of a posterior flare of the squamosal in the rear wall of the temporal fossa. Preservation of the two known specimens of *Dvinia* is generally poor, and some of the features described by Tatarinov (1968, and references cited therein) could not be verified by Hopson when he restudied them in 1973. Two of the presumed primitive features of *Dvinia* cited by Kemp (1979)—paired vomers and supraoccipital broader than the postparietal—cannot be verified. A third feature considered by Kemp to be primitive—the possession of six lower incisors—is interpreted here as an autapomorphy (Table 4, 36.4). *Dvinia* possesses additional autapomorphies (Table 4, 36.1—3), which set it well off from the expected primitive morphotype of cynodonts. *Procynosuchus*, to the contrary, shows no cranial features that appear to be autapomorphic, and it is probably close to the expected primitive morphotype for all later cynodonts (Kemp, 1979).

Galesauridae and Thrinaxodontidae

Members of the Galesauridae and Thrinaxodontidae represent the next clear advance beyond the *Procynosuchus* level of cynodont evolution. The genera *Cynosaurus* and *Galesaurus* are more primitive than *Thrinaxodon* in that the osseous secondary palate is incomplete, as in *Procynosuchus*. They are set off as a natural group, the Galesauridae, by several synapomorphies in the cheek dentition. *Thrinaxodon* (Fig. 13A) is more advanced only in its possessing a complete osseous secondary palate (Table 4, 40.1). Lacking definite autapomorphies, the cranial skeleton of *Thrinaxodon* has often been treated as an ancestral cranial morphotype from which later cynodonts, including mammals, could easily be derived.

Although we have not utilized postcranial characters in our analysis, it should be pointed out that galesaurids and *Thrinaxodon* possess expanded thoracic and lumbar ribs, the costal plates of Jenkins (1971). In *Cynognathus,* and all but the most derived tritylodontoids, the poste-rior thoracic and lumbar ribs possess costal plates (Jenkins, 1970, 1971). On the other hand, costal plates are lacking in Chiniquodontidae, Ictidosauria, and primitive Mammalia (the ribs are unknown in *Probainognathus*). The implication of this analysis of cranial characters is that the absence of costal plates in chiniquodontids, ictidosaurs, and mammals is due to secondary loss, the conclusion being supported by the documented gradual loss of costal plates within the "traversodontid" tritylodontoid clade (Jenkins, 1970). The cladogram of cynodonts (Fig. 12) indicates that costal plates were lost independently in chiniquodontoids and in the ictidosaur-mammal clade.

Post-thrinaxodontid cynodonts

All cynodonts beyond the level of the Thrinaxodontidae share characters 41.1—4 (Table 4, Figs. 13B, 14B) and are regarded here as a natural group. Beyond node 41 in Figure 12, however, there are two possible hypotheses of relationship that, within the limit of our analysis, appear to be of nearly equal likelihood, although the one illustrated in this paper (Fig. 12) is slightly more parsimonious than the other. Here, the Chiniquodontidae and Probainognathidae are united as the Chiniquodontoidea and are placed with the Cynognathia as a clade distinct from a sister clade comprised of the Ictidosauria and Mammalia. The Chiniquodontoidea and Cynognathia are set off from the ictidosaur-mammal clade on the basis of four characters (Table 4, 42.1–4) in which the latter clade shows a more primitive condition. The principal implication of this hypothesis is that the ancestors of mammals never possessed the accessory jaw articulation between surangular and squamosal (Table 4, 42.1; see below). Accordingly, the glenoid cavity in the squamosal of *Probainognathus* was derived independently of that of mammals. Likewise, the posterior elongation of the secondary palate (and the loss of costal plates) occurred independently in the chiniquodontoids and the ictidosaur-mammal clade.

The alternative hypothesis of interrelationships within the advanced cynodonts (not illustrated in this paper) is that the ictidosaur-mammal clade shared an ancestor with the Cynognathia and Chiniquodontoidea, which possessed characters 42.1—4, (Table 4), but that these were subsequently lost in the common ancestor of ictidosaurs and mammals. One can imagine the surangular-squamosal jaw articulation (Table 4, 42.1, Fig. 13B) being lost in mam-

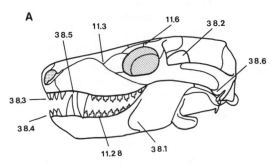

THRINAXODONTID CYNODONT

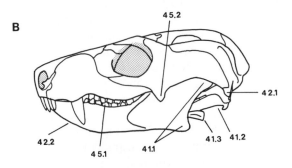

TRITYLODONTOID CYNODONT

Figure 13. Diagrammatic representations of skulls of Cynodontia: A, Thrinaxodontid cynodont (based on *Thrinaxodon*); B, Tritylodontoid cynodont (based on *Trirachodon*). (A, after Estes, 1961; B, original.)

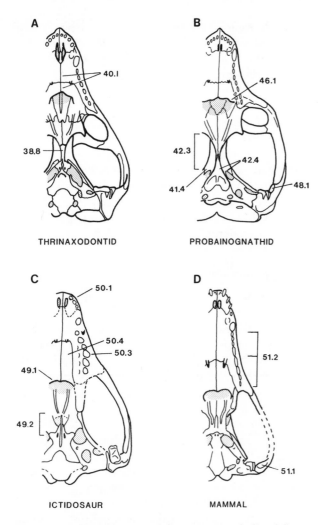

Figure 14. Ventral views of diagrammatic skulls of Cynodontia: A, Thrinaxodontid (based on *Thrinaxodon*); B, Probainognathid (based on *Probainognathus*); C, Ictidosaur (based primarily on *Pachygenelus*); D, primitive mammal (based on *Morganucodon*). (A, after Parrington, 1946; B, after Romer, 1970; C, original; D, after Kermack, Mussett, and Rigney, 1981.)

mals as a consequence of the establishment of the dentary-squamosal articulation, but ictidosaurs seem to have lacked both articulations. The remaining three characters (Table 4, 42.2–4; Figs. 13B, 14B) could have been reversed to a more primitive condition as a consequence of paedomorphosis accompanying the trend toward very small adult body size. Under this hypothesis of relationships, *Probainognathus* and the Chiniquodontidae would form a clade with the ictidosaurs and mammals (with elongation of the secondary palate and loss of costal plates as synapomorphies). The squamosal glenoid of *Probainognathus* is doubtfully homologous with that of mammals because of its absence in ictidosaurs.

Therefore, it is not clear under this hypothesis whether *Probainognathus* or the Chiniquodontidae would be the sister group of ictidosaurs plus mammals.

Cynognathia (= Cynognathidae + Tritylodontoidea)

The Cynognathidae and the Tritylodontoidea are united by a single apomorphy: the presence of a ventrally directed process on the jugal (Table 4, 43.1), which has been interpreted by Barghusen (1968) as the site of tendinous origin of the superficial masseter muscle. Both groups retain a number of primitive characters relative to the Chiniquodontoidea; notably, the secondary palate terminates anterior to the end of the tooth row, and the ribs bear costal plates.

The Cynognathidae are a monotypic family, containing only *Cynognathus*, a large carnivore possessing numerous autapomorphic cranial features.

The Tritylodontoidea are, by contrast, the largest group of nonmammalian cynodonts, comprising the so-called gomphodonts (Fig. 13B), a diverse radiation of predominantly herbivorous forms that are usually placed in four families: Diademodontidae, Trirachodontidae, Traversodontidae, and Tritylodontidae. Hopson's cladistic analysis of the tritylodontoids is in progress, but is insufficiently advanced to permit the delimitation of a complete series of monophyletic groups. Because the Tritylodontidae are considered to be derived from within the Traversodontidae, the latter are a paraphyletic group and require subdivision into additional family level clades.

The tritylodontids are extremely mammal-like in cranial and postcranial anatomy, much more so than any of the other gomphodonts. Watson (1942) was the first to regard them as derivatives of gomphodonts, a view supported by most subsequent workers. Crompton and Ellenberger (1957) noted the resemblance of the complex cheek teeth of tritylodontids to those of traversodontids, and Crompton (1972b) further documented the morphological transition between the traversodontid and tritylodontid cheek dentitions. As the most derived subgroup of the herbivorous radiation of gomphodont cynodonts, it follows that all of the features, in which tritylodontids most closely resemble ictidosaurs and mammals, are due to convergence.

Recently, Kemp (1982, 1983) has argued that the mammalian features of tritylodontids are evidence of close relationship with ictidosaurs and mammals. Under this interpretation, the gomphodont features are convergences. In the absence of a cladogram of the gomphodonts, it is not possible for us to rigorously defend our preferred hypothesis that tritylodontids have a sister-group relationship with some, at present unspecifiable, "traversodontids," and that the special resemblances of tritylodontids to mammals are convergently derived.

Chiniquodontoidea

The Chiniquodontoidea, according to our preferred hypothesis of cynodont relationships (Fig. 12), are the sister group of the Cynognathia and are defined by the possession of a secondary palate that extends to the posterior end of the tooth row (Table 4, 46.1).

The Chiniquodontidae are the more diverse and widespread family of chiniquodontoids, with at least three valid genera: *Probelesodon* and *Chiniquodon* (possibly including *Belesodon*) of South America and *Aleodon* of East Africa. In *Aleodon* and *Chiniquodon* the cheek teeth are lingually expanded and possibly possessed a primitive form of crown-to-crown occlusion.

The Probainognathidae (Fig. 14B) contain only the genus *Probainognathus*, described by Romer (1969b, 1970) as possessing a glenoid cavity on the squamosal, which received both a posterior process of the dentary and a portion of the surangular. This contrasts with the accessory jaw articulation of cynognathians and chiniquodontids, in which a flat facet on the squamosal contacts the surangular alone. Crompton (1972a) initially affirmed Romer's interpretation of the accessory jaw articulation in *Probainognathus*, but has since determined that the dentary did not actually reach the squamosal glenoid—the accessory articulation was with the surangular only (see Crompton and Hylander, this volume). Thus, *Probainognathus* is like cynognathians and chiniquodontids in possessing a surangular-squamosal accessory jaw articulation, and is unlike mammals that have a dentary-squamosal articulation, and ictidosaurs that seem to have neither.

Ictidosauria and Mammalia

As the skull and dentition of ictidosaurs—principally *Pachygenelus* and *Diarthrognathus* (Gow, 1980; Hopson and Crompton, in progress)—become better understood, their resemblance to those of true mammals becomes increasingly apparent. Hopson (in progress) has restudied the skull of *Diarthrognathus*, described by Crompton

(1958, 1963), and has concluded that its supposedly primitive characters, which Crompton believed precluded a close relationship with cynodonts, are either juvenile features or are doubtfully present. Thus, the numerous cynodont characters of *Diarthrognathus*, which Crompton interpreted as convergences, are best regarded as synapomorphies.

Ictidosaurs share numerous features with primitive mammals (Table 4, 49.1—9) of which four are also shared with tritylodontids (Table 4, 49.5—8). In the remaining five characters (Table 4, 49.1–4, 49.9), however, ictidosaurs and mammals are more derived than are tritylodontids. A unique feature (Table 4, 49.3) shared only by ictidosaurs and mammals among synapsids is prismatic enamel (Grine and Vrba, 1980).

Crompton (1958, 1963) described a dentary contact with the squamosal in *Diarthrognathus*, but the more primitive ictidosaur *Pachygenelus* seems to lack this contact (Gow, 1980), and the presence of such a contact in *Diarthrognathus* is uncertain (Gow, 1980; Hopson, personal observation). Therefore, a dentary-squamosal contact is not a primitive ictidosaurian character and cannot be regarded as a synapomorphy linking ictidosaurs and mammals.

Mammals possess a number of unique features that strongly indicate they are a strictly monophyletic group. A well-developed articulation between the dentary and squamosal (Table 4, 51.1) is known with certainty only in mammals. In contrast, the articulation described in *Diarthrognathus* is questionable, as is that inferred for the tritylodontid *Tritylodontoideus* by Fourie (1968). Diphyodonty (Table 4, 51.2) and a quadrate (incus) with a well-developed stapedial process (crus longus, Table 4, 51.5) also appear to be unique mammalian apomorphies. As noted earlier, the hypothesis proposed by Kermack, Mussett, and Rigney (1981) that prototherian and therian mammals had separate origins from noncynodont and cynodont ancestors respectively, is without support.

Acknowledgments

Thanks are due the following colleagues for facilitating access to material in their care and for providing generous hospitality: Drs. T. H. Barry, J. F. Bonaparte, A. J. Charig, P. K. Chudinov, M. A. Cluver, F. E. Grine, J. van Heerden, J. A. van den Heever, K. A. Joysey, T. S. Kemp, J. W. Kitching, A. C. Milner, M. A. Raath, L. P. Tatarinov, E. S. Vrba, P. Wellnhofer, and F. Westphal.

We also acknowledge the help of Dr. R. L. Carroll for making available unpublished results of the research of the late Dr. C. Mendrez-Carroll. Welcome comments on the manuscript were provided by Drs. E. F. Allin, M. A. Cluver, F. E. Grine, and J. A. van den Heever. Special thanks are due Dr. A. W. Crompton for providing access to material and for continued encouragement and stimulation.

The research on which this study is based has been supported by a series of grants from the National Science Foundation. The most recent grant to Hopson is DEB 80-22183, that to Barghusen is GB-40061.

References

Barghusen, H. R.
1968.   The lower jaw of cynodonts (Reptilia, Therapsida) and the evolutionary origin of mammal-like adductor jaw musculature. *Postilla* 116:1–49.
1975.   A review of fighting adaptations in dinocephalians (Reptilia, Therapsida). *Paleobiology* 1:295–311.
1976.   Notes on the adductor jaw musculature of *Venjukovia*, a primitive anomodont therapsid from the Permian of the U.S.S.R. *Ann. S. Afr. Mus.* 69:249–60.

Barry, T. H.
1974.   A new dicynodont ancestor from the Upper Ecca (Lower Middle Permian) of South Africa. *Ann. S. Afr. Mus.* 64:117–36.

Boonstra, L. D.
1952.   Die gorgonopsiër-geslag *Hipposaurus*, en die familie Ictidorhinidae. *Tydskr. Wet. Kuns.* 12:142–49.
1962.   The dentition of the titanosuchian dinocephalians. *Ann. S. Afr. Mus.* 46:57–112.
1963.   Early dichotomies in the therapsids. *S. Afr. J. Sci.* 59:176–95.
1965.   The skull of *Struthiocephalus kitchingi. Ann. S. Afr. Mus.* 48:251–65.
1969.   The fauna of the *Tapinocephalus* Zone (Beaufort Beds of the Karoo). *Ann. S. Afr. Mus.* 56:1–73.
1972.   Discard the names Theriodontia and Anomodontia: a new classification of the Therapsida. *Ann. S. Afr. Mus.* 59:315–38.

Brink, A. S.
1960.   A new type of primitive cynodont. *Palaeont. Afr.* 7:119–54.
1965.   A new ictidosuchid (Scaloposauria) from the *Lystrosaurus*-Zone. *Palaeont. Afr.* 9:129–38.

Brinkman, D.
1981.   The structure and relationships of the dromasaurs (Reptilia: Therapsida). *Breviora* 465: 1–34.

Broom, R.
1938.   The origin of cynodonts. *Ann. Transvaal Mus.* 19:279–88.

Chudinov, P. K.
1965.   New facts about the fauna of the Upper Permian of the U.S.S.R. *J. Geol.* 73:117–30.

Cluver, M. A., and Hotton, N., III.
1981.   The genera *Dicynodon* and *Diictodon* and their bearing on the classification of the Dicynodontia (Reptilia, Therapsida). *Ann. S. Afr. Mus.* 83:99–146.

Cluver, M. A., and King, G. M.
1983.   A reassessment of the relationships of Permian Dicynodontia (Reptilia, Therapsida) and a new clasification of dicynodonts. *Ann. S. Afr. Mus.* 91:195–273.

Cracraft, J.
1981.   Pattern and process in paleobiology: the role of cladistic analysis in systematic paleontology. *Paleobiology* 7:456–68.

Crompton, A. W.
1958.   The cranial morphology of a new genus and species of ictidosaurian. *Proc. Zool. Soc. London.* 130:183–216.
1963.   On the lower jaw of *Diarthrognathus broomi* and the origin of the mammalian jaw. *Proc. Zool. Soc. London.* 140:697–750.
1972a. The evolution of the jaw articulation of cynodonts. In *Studies in Vertebrate Evolution,* ed. K. A. Joysey and T. S. Kemp, pp. 231–51. Edinburgh: Oliver and Boyd.
1972b. Postcanine occlusion in cynodonts and tritylodontids. *Brit. Mus. (Nat. Hist.) Bull. (Geology).* 21:27–71.

Crompton, A. W., and Ellenberger, F.
1957.   On a new cynodont from the Molteno Beds and the origin of the tritylodontids. *Ann. S. Afr. Mus.* 44:1–14.

Currie, P. J.
1979.   The osteology of haptodontine sphenacodonts (Reptilia: Pelycosauria). *Palaeontographica* A 163:130–68.

Efremov, I. A.
1940.   Preliminary description of new Permian and Triassic terrestrial vertebrates from the U.S.S.R. *Trudy Paleon. Inst.* 10:1–140.

Eldredge, N., and Cracraft, J.
1980.   *Phylogenetic Patterns and the Evolutionary Process.* New York: Columbia University Press.

Estes, R.
1961. Cranial anatomy of the cynodont reptile *Thrinaxodon liorhinus*. *Mus. Comp. Zool. Bull.* 125:165–80.

Fourie, S.
1968. The jaw articulation of *Tritylodontoideus maximus*. *S. Afr. J. Sci.* 64:255–65.

Gaffney, E. S.
1980. Phylogenetic relationships of the major groups of amniotes. In *The Terrestrial Environment and the Origin of Land Vertebrates,* ed. A. L. Panchen, pp. 593–610. London: Academic Press.

Gow, C.
1980. The dentitions of the Tritheledontidae (Therapsida: Cynodontia). *Proc. R. Soc. London.* B 208:461–81.

Grine, F. E., and Vrba, E. S.
1980. Prismatic enamel: a pre-adaptation for mammalian diphyodonty? *S. Afr. J. Sci.* 76:139–41.

Hopson, J. A.
1969. The origin and adaptive radiation of mammal-like reptiles and non-therian mammals. *Ann. N. Y. Acad. Sci.* 167:199–216.

Jenkins, F. A., Jr.
1970. The Chañares (Argentina) Triassic reptile fauna. VII. The postcranial skeleton of the traversodontid *Massetognathus pascuali* (Therapsida, Cynodontia). *Breviora* 352:1–28.
1971. The postcranial skeleton of African cynodonts. *Bull. Peabody Mus. Nat. Hist.* 36:1–216.

Kemp, T. S.
1969. On the functional morphology of the gorgonopsid skull. *Phil. Trans. R. Soc.* B 256:1–83.
1972. Whaitsiid Therocephalia and the origin of cynodonts. *Phil. Trans. R. Soc.* B 264:1–54.
1979. The primitive cynodont *Procynosuchus:* functional morphology of the skull and relationships. *Phil. Trans. R. Soc.* B 285:73–122.
1982. *Mammal-like Reptiles and the Origin of Mammals.* London: Academic Press.
1983. The relationships of mammals. *Zool. J. Linn. Soc.* 77:353–84.

Kermack, K. A.; Mussett, F.; and Rigney, H. W.
1981. The skull of *Morganucodon. Zool. J. Linn. Soc.* 71:1–158.

Mendrez, C. H.
1972. On the skull of *Regisaurus jacobi,* a new genus and species of Bauriamorpha Watson and Romer 1956 (= Scaloposauria Boonstra 1953), from the *Lystrosaurus*-zone of South Africa. In *Studies in Vertebrate Evolution,* ed. K. A. Joysey and T. S. Kemp, pp. 191–212. Edinbrugh: Oliver and Boyd.

1975. Principales variations du palais chez les thérocéphales sud-africains (Pristerosauria et Scaloposauria) au cours du Permien supérieur et du Trias inférieur. In *Problèmes actuels de Paléontologie—Evolution des Vertébrés,* Colloque international C.N.R.S. 218: 379–408.

Mendrez-Carroll, C.
1975. Comparaison du palais chez les thérocéphales primitifs, les gorgonopsiens et les Ictidorhinidae. *C. R. Acad. Sci. Paris.* D 280:17–20.

Olson, E. C.
1962. Late Permian terrestrial vertebrates, U.S.A. and U.S.S.R. *Amer. Phil. Soc. Trans.* 52:1–224.

Orlov, Y. A.
1958. The carnivorous dinocephalians of the Isheevo fauna (titanosuchians). *Trudy Palaeont. Inst., Akad. Nauk* 72:1–114. (In Russian)

Parrington, F. R.
1946. On the cranial anatomy of cynodonts. *Proc. Zool. Soc. London.* 116:181–97.
1955. On the cranial anatomy of some gorgonopsids and the synapsid middle ear. *Proc. Zool. Soc. London,* 125:1–40.

Platnick, N. I.
1979. Philosophy and the transformation of cladistics. *Syst. Zool.* 28:537–46.

Reisz, R. R.
1980. The Pelycosauria: a review of phylogenetic relationships. In *The Terrestrial Environment and the Origin of Land Vertebrates.* ed. A. L. Panchen, pp. 553–91. London: Academic Press.

Romer, A. S.
1966. *Vertebrate Paleontology, 3d. ed.* Chicago: University of Chicago Press.
1969a. The Chañares (Argentina) Triassic reptile fauna. V. A new chiniquodontid cynodont, *Probelesodon lewisi* – cynodont ancestry. *Breviora* 333:1–24.
1969b. Cynodont reptile with incipient mammalian jaw articulation. *Science* 166:881–82.
1970. The Chañares (Argentina) reptile fauna. VI. A chiniquodontid cynodont with an incipient squamosal-dentary jaw articulation. *Breviora* 344:1–18.

Romer, A. S., and Price, L. I.
1940. Review of the Pelycosauria. *Spec. Paper Geol. Soc. America* 28:1–538.

Sigogneau, D.
1970. Revision systématique des gorgonopsiens sud-africains *Cahiers de Paléontologie* (unnumbered), ed. J. P. Lehman, pp. 1–416. Paris: CNRS.

Sigogneau, D., and Tchudinov, P. K.

1972. Reflections on some Russian eotheriodonts (Reptilia, Synapsida, Therapsida) *Palaeovertebrata* 5:79–109.

Tatarinov, L. P.

1968. Morphology and systematics of the northern Dvina cynodonts (Reptilia, Therapsida; Upper Permian) *Postilla* 126:1–51.

Watrous, L. E., and Wheeler, Q. D.

1981. The out-group comparison method of character analysis. *Syst. Zool.* 30:1–11.

Watson, D. M. S.

1942. On Permian and Triassic tetrapods. *Geol. Mag.* 79:81–116.

1948. *Dicynodon* and its allies. *Proc. Zool. Soc. London.* 118:823–77.

Watson, D. M. S., and Romer, A. S.

1956. A classification of therapsid reptiles. *Mus. Comp. Zool. Bull.* 114:37–89.

Wiley, E. O.

1981. *Phylogenetics, the Theory and Practice of Phylogenetic Systematics.* New York: John Wiley and Sons.

OF TIME
AND PLACE

J. MICHAEL PARRISH[1]
Department of Anatomy
University of Chicago
Chicago, Illinois 60637
and
JUDITH TOTMAN PARRISH
and
A. M. ZIEGLER
Department of Geophysical Sciences
University of Chicago
Chicago, Illinois 60637
and
U.S. Geological Survey
M.S. 940
Denver, Colorado 80225

Permian-Triassic Paleogeography and Paleoclimatology and Implications for Therapsid Distribution

Introduction

In the history of life, never have the continents been united in a single land mass as they were in the Permian-Triassic. At that time, the supercontinent, Pangaea, had marked effects on world climate and biogeography. This paper, a collaborative effort, considers the biogeographical implications of trends in world paleogeography and climate during the geologic range of the mammal-like reptiles.

A. M. Ziegler prepared the paleogeographic maps; J. T. Parrish was responsible primarily for interpreting the paleoclimatology; and J. M. Parrish contributed the vertebrate paleobiogeography and prepared the manuscript.

Paleogeography

Paleogeographic maps included in this paper were produced as part of the Paleogeographic Atlas Project of the Department of Geophysical Sciences at the University of Chicago. Publications of the project, dealing with Paleozoic paleogeography, include the following: Ziegler et al. (1979); Ziegler, Bambach, Parrish, Barrett, Gierlowski, Parker, Raymond, and Sepkoski (1981); Ziegler, Hansen, Johnson, Kelley, Scotese, and Van der Voo (1977); Bamach, Scotese and Ziegler (1980); and Scotese et al. (1979). Mesozoic and Cenozoic paleogeography have been dealt with in abstract (Scotese, Van der Voo, and Ross, 1981; Ziegler, Bambach, Barrett, McKerrow, Scotese, Kazmer, and Parrish, 1981; Ziegler, Scotese, and

---
[1]Current address:
University of Colorado Museum
Boulder, Colorado 80309

Barrett, 1983). A brief description follows of the techniques used in the preparation of the paleogeographic maps:

1. Worldwide lithologic data were collected for the geologic stage to be mapped, and localities were plotted on recent world maps. Lithologic data were compiled only for the stage being mapped, so that each map was representative of a fairly narrow, five- to ten-million-year span. Key lithologies were plotted on the finished maps.

2. Fits of continents and determination of continental paleolatitudes were accomplished using polar-wander curves, compiled from continental paleomagnetic data.

3. Major changes in continental plate configuration also were determined by dating rifts and collisional orogenies.

4. Finally, biogeography and the distribution of climatically sensitive lithologies, such as tillites and coals, were used as a check of the independently determined continental positions. When other data were lacking, biogeography and climatically sensitive sediments were used for the initial placement of particular blocks.

The Mollweide projection used for these maps offers the following features:

1. Projections are equal-area; therefore, area data can be taken by planimeter directly from the finished maps.

2. Projections are whole-earth; all land and sea areas are visible on a single map.

3. Lines of latitude are parallel, making paleolatitudinal distributions of plotted data easy to obtain.

Modern shorelines and five-degree grid points for modern longitudes and latitudes are plotted on the paleocontinents to aid in orientation. Lithologies, areas of mountains, and continental shelves are plotted on each map.

Maps presented here are those that have been completed to date within the general geologic range of the therapsids. On some maps, the stages shown are not those of highest therapsid diversity but they bracket the desired temporal range, demonstrating paleogeographic trends over all during the reign of the mammal-like reptiles.

The Westphalian Stage (Late Carboniferous, ca. 300 million years B.P.) map (Fig. 1) represents the world about fifty million years before the appearance of the first therapsids. Pangaea lay mostly in the Southern Hemisphere, with considerable land area over the south paleopole. Glaciation occurred in the Southern Hemisphere,

as evidence by the presence of abundant tillites. The equatorial region was humid, as indicated by the equatorial coal belt; evaporites, which generally indicate warm, at least seasonally dry conditions, are restricted north and south to a zone at 30° latitude (the "horse latitudes").

Figure 2 is the map for the Kazanian Stage (Late Permian, ca. 250 million years B.P.), a time of high diversity of therapsids. This map shows the northward movement of Pangaea (cf. Fig. 1). Glaciation was greatly reduced, being restricted to one area in Australia, and evaporites were prominent at low latitudes.

The first two maps (Scotese et al., 1979) show a less reliable portrayal of what is now China than do the second two (Ziegler, Bambach, Barrett, McKerrow, Scotese, Kazmer, and Parrish, 1981). China was affected by a series of continental collisions—the Hercynian Orogeny, along the northern border during the Paleozoic, and the Indosinian Orogeny, between north and south China during the Mesozoic—and few paleomagnetic data are available. All that can be said with certainty is that the faunas, floras, and the sedimentary facies associated with China indicate that the land mass was considerably farther south in the late Paleozoic and early Mesozoic than is indicated on most published reconstructions.

Figure 3 shows the paleogeography of the Induan Stage, (earliest Triassic, ca. 240 million years B.P.). Pangaea had moved farther northward since the Kazanian, and the land mass was more or less symmetrically disposed about the equator. Pangaea had rotated somewhat clockwise as well. During the Induan and throughout the Triassic, tillites were absent, indicating a period without glaciation. Coals were scarce in the Induan, with but a single locality in Antarctica. Evaporite distribution was as in the Kazanian. Although equatorial evaporites were not prominent in the Induan Stage, we know from the work of others, notaby Robinson (1973) and Briden and Irving (1964), that they were common and widespread during other stages of the Triassic.

The last paleogeographic map (Fig. 4) is for the Pliensbachian Stage (late Early Jurassic, ca. 185 million years B.P.). Continued northward movement and clockwise rotation of Pangaea had occurred since the Induan. Coals were abundant in the northern hemisphere in the Pliensbachian, especially in the USSR and China. However, according to Robinson (1973), in the Late Triassic, during the end of the therapsids'

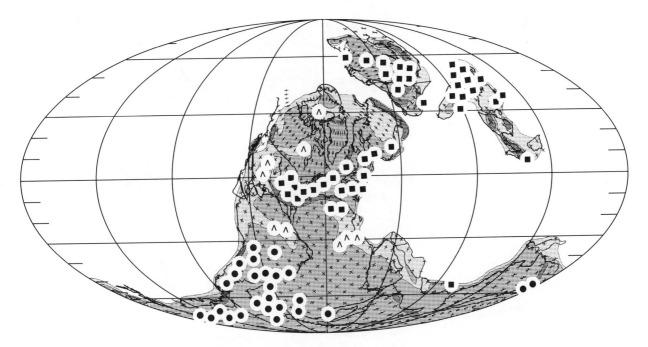

Figure 1. Westphalian (Late Carboniferous) paleogeography and distribution of climatically controlled sediments. (From Scotese et al., 1979; and Ziegler et al., 1979.)

Key: circles, tillites; squares, coals; inverted "v", evaporites; dark shading, highland; medium shading, lowland; light shading, continental shelf.

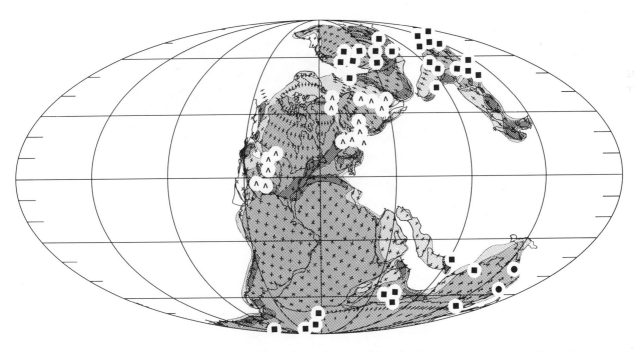

Figure 2. Kazanian (Late Permian) paleogeography and distribution of climatically controlled sediments. (From Scotese et al., 1979; and Ziegler et al., 1979.) Symbols and shading as in Figure 1.

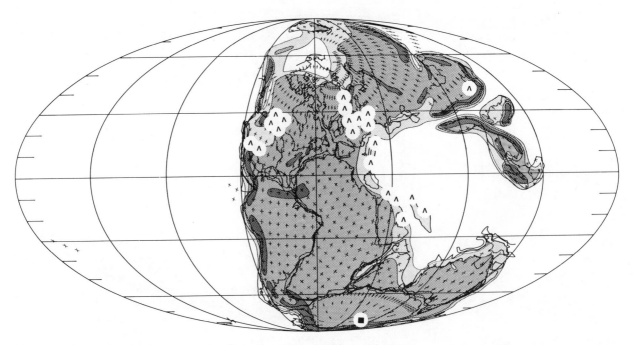

Figure 3. Induan (earliest Triassic) paleogeography and distribution of climatically controlled sediments. (From Ziegler et al., 1981a.) Symbols and shading as in Figure 1.

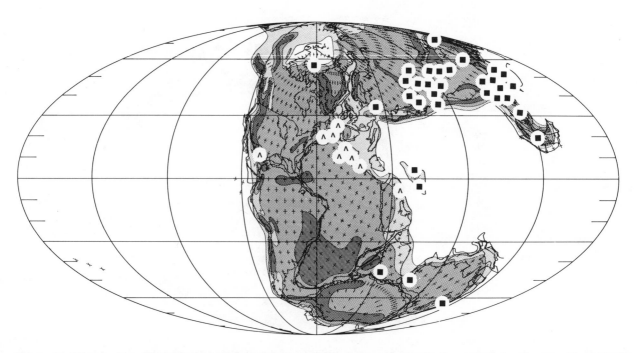

Figure 4. Pliensbachian (Early Jurassic) paleogeography and distribution of climatically controlled sediments. (From Ziegler et al., 1981a.) Symbols and shading as in Figure 1.

PARRISH, PARRISH, AND ZIEGLER

existence, these areas were apparently still quite warm and dry, with no coals, but with abundant evaporites. North and south China collided in the late Early Triassic, producing the Chinling Orogeny.

In summary, the following trends are observed in world paleogeography through the Permian and Triassic:

1. Pangaea moved progressively northward, with decreased glaciation, exclusion of coals from equatorial regions, and spread of equatorial and subequatorial evaporites.

2. Pangaea rotated progressively clockwise.

3. The land masses now constituting north and south China collided in the Late Triassic, forming the Chinling Mountains.

We emphasize that the maps presented are still tentative, as all paleogeographic maps must be to some extent. In particular, we lack extensive lithologic data from South America and Africa. Additional information about the Mesozoic of those regions will greatly improve map reliability.

Paleoclimatology

The Permian to Jurassic was a time of transition for global climate, from the extensive continental glaciations of the Late Carboniferous to the warm equable conditions characteristic of the later Mesozoic. We analyzed Permian to Jurassic climates using three independent approaches. The first was to study the distribution of paleoclimatically controlled sediments—especially evaporites, which indicate dry and usually warm climate, and coals, which indicate wet climate. The second approach was to model atmospheric circulation on theoretical grounds, based on the assumption that controls on general circulation patterns have not changed through time. Such models are independent of the sediment data, which can then be used to test the models. The third approach was to quantify some aspect of paleoclimate. We chose the global heat budget— the amount of heat absorbed by the earth's surface. We will explain each of these approaches.

Sediments

Generally, evaporites form in the subtropical belts between 10° and 30° latitude, and coals occur along the equator and at about 50°–60° latitude. These zones correspond to the high- and low-pressure belts characteristic of the most general features of atmospheric circulation (see, for example, the discussion in Ziegler Bambach,

Parrish, Barrett, Gierlowski, Parker, Raymond, and Sepkoski, 1981). Broadly speaking, as the world warmed during the late Paleozoic and early Mesozoic, the subtropical dry belts expanded in the Permian and Triassic and then contracted again by the Early Jurassic. Coal belts, which had heretofore been prominent along the equator as well as in the high-latitude wet belts, became confined to the high latitudes. Several workers have described these changes, notably Briden and Irving (1964), Robinson (1973), Drewry, Ramsey, and Smith (1974), and Frakes (1979). Their conclusions were based on data that represented the whole of each geologic period. The lithologic and paleogeographic maps compiled for much narrower time spans by Ziegler, Bambach, Barrett, McKerrow, Scotese, Kazmer, and Parrish (1981); Ziegler et al. (1979), and for this paper reveal the same climate changes. The distribution of coals, evaporites, and tillites are shown in figures 1–4.

Atmospheric circulation

In modeling the atmospheric circulation and climate on theoretical grounds, we use what we known about the factors that control the major features of present-day atmospheric circulation. This approach has produced consistent results in predicting ocean currents and explaining biogeographic patterns in the Paleozoic (Ziegler et al., 1979; Ziegler, Bambach, Barrett, McKerrow, Scotese, Kazmer, and Parrish, 1981; Parrish, 1982; Parrish and Curtis, 1982). The technique, described in detail by Parrish (1982), is summarized briefly here. The atmospheric circulation maps for the Kazanian, Induan, and Pliensbachian Stages are presented in Figures 5–10. On an earth with a homogeneous surface, the following pressure and precipitation systems would exist: low pressure (ascending air) and high precipitation at the equator and at about 50°–60° latitude, and high pressure (descending air) and low precipitation at about 30° latitude and at the poles. The winds would consist of the equatorial easterlies between about 20° north and south latitude, westerlies between about 35° and 50° latitude, and the polar easterlies at latitudes higher than 65°. These patterns are all zonal, that is, parallel to latitude, and they represent the effects of the rotation of the earth and of the heat exchange between the equator and the poles. The heterogeneities of the earth's surface create a thermal regime that complicates the one created by the equator-to-poles temperature gradient. Hence, the zonal patterns are disrupted over and

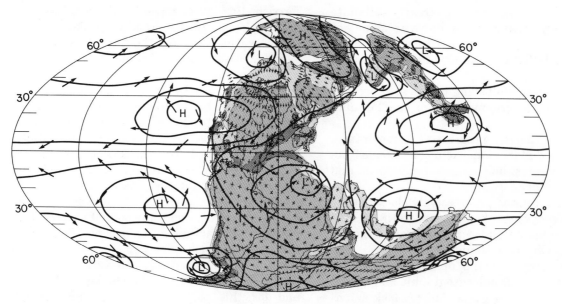

Figure 5. Atmospheric circulation in the Kazanian (Late Permian) for the northern winter. (From J. T. Parrish, 1982.)
Key: thick lines, isobars; arrows, surface winds; **H**, relative high pressure; **L**, relative low pressure.

around the continents by the effect of land-sea temperature contrasts. The dominance of the zonal system must be emphasized. The atmospheric circulation of the present-day world still retains a strong zonal component, most clearly seen over the Pacific and Southern oceans, despite the predominance of latitudinally extensive continents.

The distinctive paleogeography that existed from the Permian to the Early Jurassic was likely to have produced a climate pattern comparable to that of today in the vicinity of Asia. The separate continental masses were virtually all assembled into one huge continent stretching from pole to pole. In the Permian, 64 percent of the exposed land mass was south of the equator. By the Early Triassic, however, the land area was almost symmetrically disposed about the equator (45 percent north of the equator), and by the Early Jurassic still more of the exposed land (51 percent) was north of the equator—the result of the northward movement of Pangaea. The climatic result of this paleogeography was likely to have been the existence of a strong monsoonal (that is, seasonally alternating) circulation, strengthening through time from the Permian through the Triassic.

Because land absorbs and radiates heat much more readily than water does, land areas respond more strongly to seasonal changes in solar radiation. The continent becomes warm in the summer, possibly establishing a low-pressure cell, and cool in the winter, with the possible de-velopment of a high-pressure cell. Seasonal changes over a large continent will be greater than over a small continent, because the interior of a large continent is more isolated from the ameliorating influences of the surrounding oceans. The response is even stronger if mountains are situated in such a way as to further isolate the interior of the continent.

Asia is today an ideal continent for the fullest development of a monsoonal circulation. It is large, lies at mid-latitudes, and has mountains to the south and east. Asia's position at mid-latitudes maximizes the effects of seasonality—at higher latitudes the continent would be cool the year round and at lower latitudes it always would be warm. The mountains on the south and east maximize the isolation of the interior of the continent from the warmest ocean (the western Pacific and the Indian Ocean), which results in a cold interior and a strong winter monsoon. In summer, the warmest area of the continent, south of the Himalayas, is protected from the cooling influences of the air farther north, permitting the development of a low-pressure belt over Pakistan. Furthermore, the presence of mountains (the Himalayas and the mountains in Southeast Asia) enhances rainfall, which strengthens the summer monsoon over northern India through the release of latent heat. Finally, many workers believe that the summer monsoon also is strengthened by the Tibetan Plateau, which acts as a high-level heat source. The release of latent heat and the presence of a high-

PARRISH, PARRISH, AND ZIEGLER

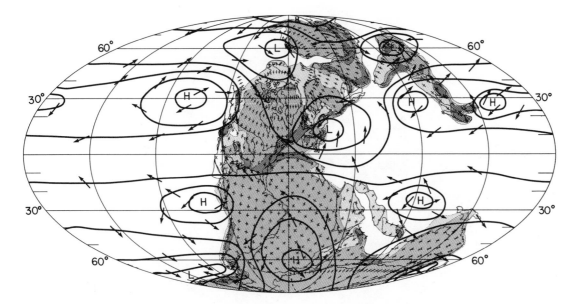

Figure 6. Atmospheric circulation in the Kazanian (Late Permian) for the northern summer. (From J. T. Parrish, 1982.) Symbols as in Figure 5.

level heat source are responsible for much of the system depicted as an area of low pressure on general global circulation maps.

The north and south halves of Pangaea had some of the features instrumental in the establishment of a monsoonal circulation. The land mass was large and most of its area was situated at mid-latitudes. Throughout the time considered here, more than half the exposed land area lay between 20° and 60° latitude. In the Permian, the part of Pangaea north of the equator, although not constituting as large a land area as in subsequent intervals, was shielded from the ameliorating effects of Tethys by what is now the Appalachian Mountains. Highlands in the vicinity of Tethys were not prominent in the Triassic, but in the Early Jurassic the northern part of Pangaea had several mountain chains, and the southern half contained a plateau (not as high as the Himalayas) centered at 40° south latitude.

The presence of large land masses on both sides of the equator permitted the possibility of a strong monsoonal circulation in both hemispheres, a circulation that does not exist today. In the northern winter, the northern part of Pangaea would have been dominated by a high-pressure cell; whereas a strong low-pressure cell would have been developed over the southern part of the continent, farther south of the equator than would be expected over a smaller land mass (e.g., present-day Africa, where the low-pressure cell that forms in the southern summer laps over the equator). The opposite would have

occurred in summer (cf. Figs. 5–10). If the low-pressure cells that developed during the summer in each hemisphere were of sufficient strength to disrupt the Intertropical Convergence Zone (ITCZ)—the normal area of ascending air near the equator—then a fully developed monsoonal circulation similar to that found over Asia today would have existed, but in both hemispheres. This means that cross-equatorial flow of wind and water currents would have been strong during both the winter and summer, a point we will return to later.

The monsoonal system would have been developed most fully after the Permian, when the land was more symmetrically disposed about the equator. This possibility accords well with Robinson's (1973) concept of Triassic monsoons. In the Permian to Jurassic world, the absence of an equivalent to the Tibetan Plateau may have been compensated by the unique distribution of large, contiguous land masses in both hemispheres. This distributional pattern would have tended to maximize the contrast between the summer and winter hemispheres, thereby reinforcing monsoonal circulation. Therefore, we believe that the proposal of a strong monsoonal circulation over Pangaea is reasonable.

Several lines of indirect evidence suggest that monsoonal circulation was a significant process in the Permian to Jurassic. First, an unusual association of evaporites and coals occurs at mid-latitudes in many stages of the Triassic. This association appears in the maps of Robinson

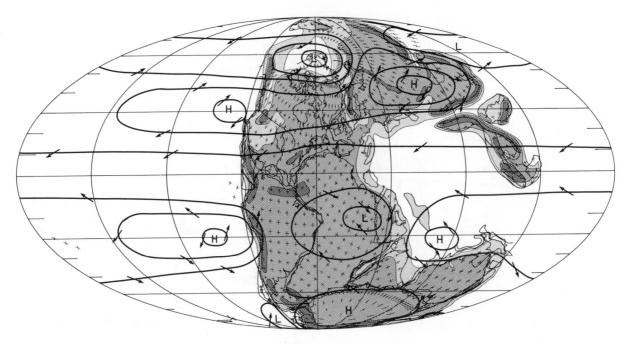

Figure 7. Atmospheric circulation in the Induan (earliest Triassic) for the northern winter. (From J. T. Parrish and Curtis, 1982.) Symbols as in Figure 5.

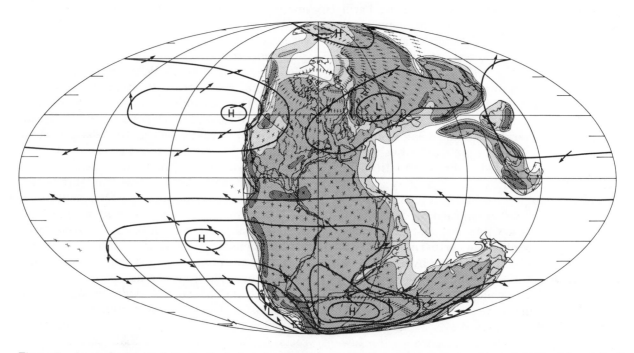

Figure 8. Atmospheric circulation in the Induan (earliest Triassic) for the northern summer. (From J. T. Parrish and Curtis, 1982.) Symbols as in Figure 5.

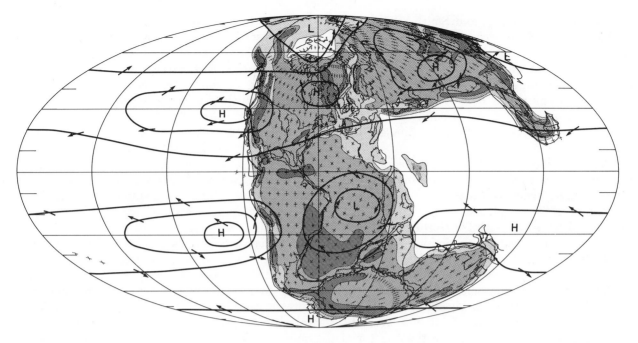

Figure 9.   Atmospheric circulation in the Pliensbachian (Early Jurassic) for the northern winter. (From J. T. Parrish and Curtis, 1982.) Symbols as in Figure 5.

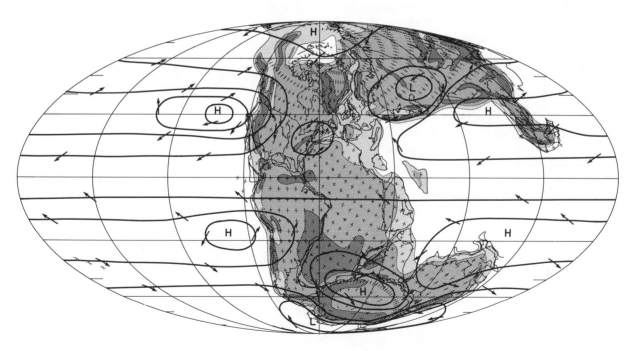

Figure 10.   Atmospheric circulation in the Pliensbachian (Early Jurassic) for the northern summer. (From J. T. Parrish and Curtis 1982.) Symbols as in Figure 5.

(1973), Drewry, Ramsey, and Smith (1974), and Frakes (1979), which encompass long time intervals, although it is not shown in Figure 3, which is limited to a much shorter time interval. Robinson's (1973) suggestion that alternating wet and dry seasons might have occurred describes precisely what a monsoonal circulation would be expected to bring about (Parrish, Ziegler, and Scotese, 1982).

Evaporites formed very close to the equator on the east side of Pangaea. This is difficult to explain without invoking a monsoonal circulation. A circulation that is almost a normal zonal pattern would have equatorial easterlies impinging on the coast and would release much rain (as in the East Indies and the Amazon Basin today), thus preventing the deposition of evaporites. However, a strong monsoonal circulation of the type proposed for Pangaea would create an almost year-round cross-equatorial flow over the adjacent ocean that would bypass the equatorial region on the continent. The rain would be released farther north or south, depending on the season, and the equatorial region would thus be dry, permitting evaporite deposition. Indeed, even in its present-day form, the monsoonal circulation keeps the equatorial region of East Africa dry (Petterssen, 1969).

Finally, cross-equatorial winds, which would have paralleled the east coast of Pangaea, would have created seasonal oceanic upwelling currents: north of the equator in the northern summer and south of the equator in the southern summer. Such an upwelling current occurs off Somalia during the northern summer today. Upwelling currents are regions of high biologic productivity and are believed to be a setting for the deposition of petroleum source beds (e.g., Dott and Reynolds, 1969; Dow 1978; Parrish, 1982; Parrish and Curtis, 1982). The area of the Persian Gulf, the richest oil-bearing region in the world, would have been under the upwelling current created by the southern summer monsoon during the Triassic and Jurassic; the Persian Gulf oil source beds are believed to be Jurassic in age (Murris, 1980; Ayres et al., 1982).

The climatic asymmetry of Pangaea, unrelated to the monsoon, must be considered for its potential influence on the distribution of terrestrial organisms. The eastern side of Pangaea would have been warm relative to the western side at any given latitude between 40° north and 40° south. Similar climatic asymmetry is present across north–south trending continents today because the ocean currents, carrying warm equa-

torial water into high latitudes, flow along the east coasts of continents and cold water flows towards the equator on the west coasts. The low temperature of this water is enhanced further by upwelling, driven by longshore winds that are stronger on the eastern sides of the ocean basins (e.g., off Peru and California today).

On land, the effects of asymmetry are to move the equator (hence equatorial evaporites on the west side of Pangaea in the Permian) and to make the west sides of the continents generally much cooler. Climatic asymmetry would have been particularly strong across Pangaea because—it is presumed—most of the cross-latitudinal oceanic heat exchange would have occurred along the two coasts, in contrast to the present-day world in which the heat exchange is effected along four coasts in two oceans. The equatorial current would have had almost 300° of longitude in which to warm up before reaching Tethys, making Tethys an extremely warm ocean. Tethys was almost enclosed, prohibiting the entry of cold currents and requiring the establishment of two extremely warm, Gulf Stream–type gyres (Ziegler, Bambach, Barrett, McKerrow, Scotese, Kazmer, and Parrish, 1981.

The Permian asymmetric climate pattern is reflected in marine invertebrate biogeographic patterns; warm water faunas were extremely widespread in Tethys and occurred only at the equator on the west side of Pangaea (Humphreville and Bambauch, 1979; R. K. Bambach and R. Humphreville, unpublished data). The relatively large cross-continental temperature gradient may have reinforced the monsoonal circulation, especially during summer, because of the contrast between the cool west-coast water and the adjacent warm land.

Global heat-budget

A third approach to viewing paleoclimates is to try to make a quantitative estimate of paleoclimatic parameters. One parameter that can be estimated, given only the paleogeography, is the global heat budget. Global heat-budget can be calculated from the fraction of incoming solar radiation absorbed over each 10° of latitude, totaled for the entire earth. The amount of solar radiation absorbed is dependent on surface characteristics (water, land, snow, ice) as well as on the level of radiation itself, which varies with latitude, decreasing towards the poles. The technique of determining global heat-budget and the assumptions involved are described in detail in Barron, Sloan, and Harrison (1980). The calcu-

Table 1.—Values of Q(1 = a_T) for the Permian (Kazanian Stage), Early Triassic (Induan Stage), and Early Jurassic (Pliensbachian Stage)

Time	Assumptions		
	Present Q Snow and ice above 70° Deserts 10°–30°	Ancient Q Snow and ice above 70° Deserts 10°–30°	Ancient Q Snow and ice and desert varied
Permian	11.715	11.545	11.652
Triassic	11.658	11.501	11.742
Jurassic	11.705	11.596	11.892

[1]See text for variations in Q and for the assumptions upon which the calculation of the last column is based.

lation is Q(1 − a_T), where Q is the incoming solar radiation for a ten-degree-wide latitudinal belt, a_T is the total albedo (reflectivity) of the surface within that belt, and the values for all the latitude bands are totaled. Various assumptions can be made about the amount of snow and ice cover, variations in land albedo (for example, whether they are extensive deserts that have high albedo), and the value of Q. Q is dependent largely on solar luminosity, which may have increased through time during the sun's stellar evolution cycle (Sagan and Mullen, 1972). Heat-budget calculations for the Permian, Triassic, and Jurassic are presented in Table 1.

Assuming a current solar luminosity value, and, by convention, snow and ice at latitudes above 70° and deserts between 10° and 30° latitude, we infer a decrease in absorbed solar radiation from the Late Permian to the Early Triassic and then a slight increase to the Early Jurassic. If we assume that solar luminosity has increased linearly 30 percent since the formation of the solar system (Sagan and Mullen, 1972), and if we project values for the late Paleozoic and early Mesozoic, we see that the pattern is the same for both eras, but the value is higher for the Early Jurassic than for the Permian, as would be expected. Since the conventional albedo assumptions probably are not adequate for the Permian to Jurassic paleogeography and climates, we also calculated the heat budget based on the following assumptions, which may be more realistic:

1. Values of Q appropriate for each interval, projected from 75 percent of present value at 4.5 billion years.

2. Permian: narrower desert belts (based on the distribution of evaporites), snow and ice cover above 70° latitude (toward the end of a glacial epoch).

3. Triassic and Jurassic: wider desert belts (10° to 30° latitude), no snow and ice.

There is strong evidence from plant (Retallack, 1975) and amphibian (Colbert and Cosgriff, 1974) data that the Triassic polar regions were too warm for any significant ice and snow cover. Widespread glaciation in Gondwana in the Carboniferous has been well-documented (Frakes, 1979). Frakes documented abundant glacial deposits, dated with marine invertebrates, of Early to Late Permian age in Australia. In addition, he described Early Permian continental tillites, glacial-marine and fluvial deposits containing dropstones, and striated floors in South America, South Africa, Antarctica, and India. The transition from widespread glaciation in the Carboniferous and Early Permian to warm polar climate in the Early Triassic probably would have included a time of widespread snow cover, which would not have left a record in the rocks, but would have affected the albedo. Given these assumptions, a rise in absorbed solar radiation occurred between the Permian and Triassic and a still greater rise to the Early Jurassic. The rise between the Triassic and Jurassic is due entirely to the northward movement of Pangaea, whereas the difference between the Late Permian and the Early Triassic seems to be due largely to assumed variations in snow and ice cover. The results from this latter set of global heat-budget calculations tend to confirm previous ideas about climatic trends from the Permian to the Jurassic, although caution must be used to avoid overinterpreting their significance.

In conclusion, the three approaches to determining Permian to Jurassic climates—distribution of climatically controlled sediments, atmospheric circulation models based on the paleogeography, and global heat-budget calculations—tend to give consistent results. The distribution of climatically controlled sediments derives from data used somewhat successfully by other workers to determine the general climatic patterns.The atmospheric circulation modeling confirms and supplements Robinson's (1973) proposal of past monsoonal circulation. Finally, the heat-budget calculations provide some quantitative support for the view that the Permo-Jurassic was a time of increasing warmth on the earth's surface.

Therapsid Distributions

Data on faunas of the Permian and Triassic are plotted on the paleogeographic map that is temporally closest to the time period of each fauna. Lower Permian data are plotted on the Westphalian map (Fig. 11), lower Upper and upper Upper Permian data are plotted on Kazanian maps (Figs. 12 and 13), the Lower and Middle Triassic data on Induan maps (Figs. 14 and 15), and the Upper Triassic-Liassic data on the Pliensbachian map (Fig. 16). Deposits of the indicated ages that lack therapsids, but include other tetrapods, are plotted on each map as well. Therapsid categories reflect the phylogeny pre-

sented by Hopson and Barghusen (this volume). A few categories do not reflect established taxonomic groups; these are detailed in Table 2. In addition, therapsid distributional data are listed in Table 3, along with supporting references. Distributions of cosmopolitan therapsid genera are listed in Table 4.

Table 2.—Constitution of nontraditional phylogenetic groupings used in this paper[1]

Group Name	Taxonomic Constitution
"Biarmosuchia"	*Biarmosuchus, Hipposaurus, Burnetia,* Ictidorhinidae
"nondicynodont anomodonts"	*Otsheria, Venyukovia,* Dromasauria
"mammal-like cynodonts"	Chiniquidintidae, Trithelodontidae

[1]Categories listed were chosen to represent phylogenetic relationships of taxa not commonly allied into unique taxa (Hopson and Barghusen, this volume). No attempt was made to organize formal taxonomic categories for these groupings.

Table 3.—Stratigraphic and geographical distribution of therapsids

Time, Place, Taxon	Reference
Lower upper Permian	
South Africa—Karroo Basin	
"Biarmosuchia"	Hopson and Barghusen (this volume), Sigoneau and Tchudinov (1972),
Dinocephalia	Boonstra (1969)
Gorgonopsia	Boonstra (1969)
nondicynodont anomodonts	Boonstra (1969)
Therocephalia	Boonstra (1969)
Dicynodontia	Anderson and Cruickshank (1978)
Rhodesia—Zambesi Valley	
Dicynodontia	Kitching (1977)
USSR	
Eotitanosuchia	Olson (1962), Sigoneau and Tchudinov (1972)
"Biarmosuchia"	Hopson and Barghusen (this volume), Sigoneau and Tchudinov (1972)
Therocephalia	Boonstra (1969)
nondicynodont anomodonts	Boonstra (1969)
Dinocephalia	Anderson and Cruickshank (1978)
USA	
Therapsida (?)	Olson (1962; see text)
Uppermost Permian	
South Africa—Karroo Basin	
"Biarmosuchia"	Hopson and Barghusen (this volume), Anderson and Cruickshank (1978)
Gorgonopsia	Anderson and Cruickshank (1978)
Therocephalia	Anderson and Cruickshank (1978)
nondicynodont anomodonts	Broom (1932)
Dicynodontia	Anderson and Cruickshank (1978)
procynosuchid cynodonts	Anderson and Cruickshank (1978)
galesaurid cynodonts	Anderson and Cruickshank (1978)
Tanzania—Ruhuhu Valley	
Dicynodontia	Anderson and Cruickshank (1978)

Table 3.—Continued

Time, Place, Taxon	Reference
Therocephalia	Anderson and Cruickshank (1978)
Gorgonopsia	Anderson and Cruickshank (1978)
Zambia—Luangwa Valley	
Therocephalia	Anderson and Cruickshank (1978)
Dicynodontia	Anderson and Cruickshank (1978)
Madagascar	
Therapsida	Carroll (1981)
Brazil—Parana Basin	
Dicynodontia	Keyser (1980)
India	
Dicynodontia	Keyser (1980)
Scotland	
Dicynodontia	Rowe (1980)
USSR	
Dicynodontia	Anderson and Cruickshank (1978)
Gorgonopsia	Anderson and Cruickshank (1978)
Therocephalia	Anderson and Cruickshank (1978)
procynosuchid cynodonts	Anderson and Cruickshank (1978)
China—Sinkiang	
Dicynodontia	Sigoneau-Russell and Sun (1981)
—North China	
Dinocephalia (?)	Young (1979), Sigoneau-Russell and Sun (1981)
Gorgonopsia	Young (1979), Sigoneau-Russell and Sun (1981)
cynodonts (?)	Young (1979), Sigoneau-Russell and Sun (1981)
Lower Triassic	
South Africa	
Therocephalia	Anderson and Cruickshank (1978)
Dicynodontia	Anderson and Cruickshank (1978)
galesaurid cynodonts	Anderson and Cruickshank (1978)
diademodontid cynodonts	Anderson and Cruickshank (1978)
cynognathid cynodonts	Anderson and Cruickshank (1978)
Antarctica	
Therocephalia	Colbert and Kitching (1981)
Dicynodontia	Colbert (1974)
galesaurid cynodonts	Colbert and Kitching (1981)
Argentina	
Dicynodontia	Anderson and Cruickshank (1978)
galesaurid cynodonts	Anderson and Cruickshank (1978)
diademodontid cynodonts	Anderson and Cruickshank (1978)
cynognathid cynodonts	Anderson and Cruickshank (1978)
India	
Dicynodontia	Anderson and Cruickshank (1978)
Laos	
Dicynodontia (?)	Repelin (1923)
USSR	
Therocephalia	Anderson and Cruickshank (1978)
Dicynodontia	Anderson and Cruickshank (1978)
galesaurid cynodonts	Anderson and Cruickshank (1978)
China—Sinkiang	
Dicynodontia	Sigoneau-Russell and Sun (1981)
Therocephalia	Sigoneau-Russell and Sun (1981)
—North China	Hou (1979)
Middle Triassic	
Tanzania and Zambia	
Dicynodontia	Anderson and Cruickshank (1978)

Table 3.—Continued

Time, Place, Taxon	Reference
diademodontid cynodonts	Hopson and Kitching (1972)
mammal-like cynodonts	Hopson and Kitching (1972)
India	
Dicynodontia	Anderson and Cruickshank (1978)
diademodontid cynodonts	Anderson and Cruickshank (1978)
South America	
Dicynodontia	Anderson and Cruickshank (1978)
diademodontid cynodonts	Anderson and Cruickshank (1978)
mammal-like cynodonts	Anderson and Cruickshank (1978)
USSR	
Therocephalia	Anderson and Cruickshank (1978)
Dicynodontia	Anderson and Cruickshank (1978)
diademodontid cynodonts	Tatarinov (1973)
China—Sinkiang	
Dicynodontia	Sigoneau-Russell and Sun (1981)
—North China	
Therocephalia	Sigoneau-Russell and Sun (1981)
Dicynodontia	Sigoneau-Russell and Sun (1981)
cynognathid cynodonts (?)	Sigoneau-Russell and Sun (1981)
diademodontid cynodonts	Sigoneau-Russell and Sun (1981)
Upper Triassic-Liassic	
South Africa	
diademodontid cynodonts	Anderson and Cruickshank (1978)
tritylodontid cynodonts	Anderson and Cruickshank (1978)
mammals	Anderson and Cruickshank (1978)
Morocco	
Dicynodontia	Dutuit (1965)
India	
diademodontid cynodonts	Chatterjee (1982)
Argentina	
Dicynodontia	Anderson and Cruickshank (1978)
diademodontid cynodonts	Anderson and Cruickshank (1978)
mammal-like cynodonts	Anderson and Cruickshank (1978)
tritylodontid cynodonts	Anderson and Cruickshank (1978)
Brazil	
Dicynodontia	Anderson and Cruickshank (1978)
mammal-like cynodonts	Anderson and Cruickshank (1978)
England and Central Europe	
tritylodontid cynodonts	Anderson and Cruickshank (1978)
mammals	Anderson and Cruickshank (1978)
U.S.A.—Arizona and Texas	
Dicynodontia	Camp and Welles (1956)
tritylodontid cynodonts	Lewis (this volume)
mammals	Jenkins (1981)
—North Carolina	
Cynodontia incert. sed.	Carroll et al. (1972); Baird and Patterson (1967)
Dicynodontia	Carroll et al. (1972); Baird and Patterson (1967)
Nova Scotia	
diademodontid cynodonts	Carroll et al. (1972)
China—Yunnan	
tritylodontid cynodonts	Young (1946)
mammals	Anderson and Cruickshank (1978)

Table 4.—Cosmopolitan therapsid taxa

Time	Taxa	Localities	Reference
Lower Upper Permian	No cosmopolitan therapsids reported, but Boonstra (1969) notes close similarity between southern dinocephalian genera and their northern counterparts, e.g. *Moschops* (South Africa) and *Ulemosaurus* (USSR); *Anteosaurus* (South Africa) and *Doliosauriscus* (USSR).		
Uppermost Permian	Dicynodontia		
	Endothiodon	South Africa, India, South America	Keyser (1980)
	Diictodon	South Africa, China	Cluver and Hotton (1977)
	Cistecephalus	South Africa, India (?)	Anderson and Cruickshank (1978)
Lower Triassic	Dicynodontia		
	Lystrosaurus	South Africa, India, USSR, China, Antarctica	Kalandadze (1975), Colbert (1974)
	Myosaurus	South Africa, Antarctica	Hammer and Cosgriff (1981)
	Cynodontia		Colbert and Kitching (1977)
	Thrinaxodon	South Africa, Antarctica	
	Cynognathus	South Africa, South America	Hopson and Kitching (1972)
	Therocephalia		
	Ericolacerta parva	South Africa, Antarctica	Colbert and Kitching (1981)
Middle Triassic	Dicynodontia		
	Kannemeyeria	South Africa, India, South America, very similar genera from USSR	Keyser and Cruickshank (1979)
	Cynodontia		
	Scalenodon	South Africa, USSR	Tatarinov (1973)
Upper Triassic/Liassic	Mammals		
	Eozostrodon	China, western Europe	Rigney (1963); Kermack et al. (1981)

Lower Permian

Although there are no Lower Permian therapsids, the distribution of sphenacodontid pelycosaurs during that epoch is of interest, as the prevailing opinion today is that all therapsids originated from a sphenacodontid stock (Hopson and Barghusen, this volume). Lower Permian sphenacodontids are known from numerous localities throughout the United States and from England, France, and Germany (Fig. 11). The observed distribution is equatorial to subequatorial. Lower Permian deposits that do not contain pelycosaurs are known from the Russian Platform, India, South America, and South Africa (Anderson and Cruickshank, 1978). Assuming that sphenocodontids were true ectotherms, then their restriction to the equatorial regions, and to the eastern side of Pangaea at other paleolatitudes, is not surprising for two reasons. First, cool conditions are suggested for the Late Carboniferous-Early Permian by distributions of coals, tillites, and evaporites. Second, the eastern coast of Pangaea was warmed by the circumequatorial currents impinging on that coast and being diverted north and south.

The absence of sphenacodontid pelycosaurs from South Africa and the USSR, the two regions where therapsids first occur, is notable. This may be facies-related phenomenon, as the taxa known from those areas are amphibians (USSR) and aquatic mesosaurs (South Africa; Anderson and Cruickshank, 1978).

Lower Upper Permian

In the lower Upper Permian, there are two undoubted regions of therapsid-bearing deposits—South Africa and the Russian Platform (Fig. 12, Table 3). A third area of synapsid-bearing deposits is in the southwest United States (Olson,

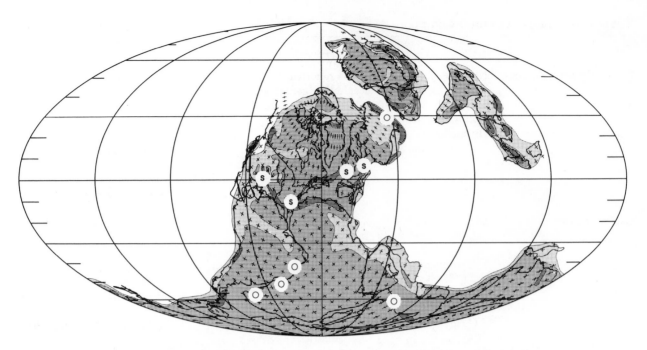

Figure 11.   Distribution of sphenacodontid pelycosaurs in the Lower Permian. Base map is for the Westphalian (Upper Carboniferous).

Key: **S,** sphenacodontid pelycosaurs; open circles, Lower Permian terrestrial deposits that do not contain sphenacodontids.

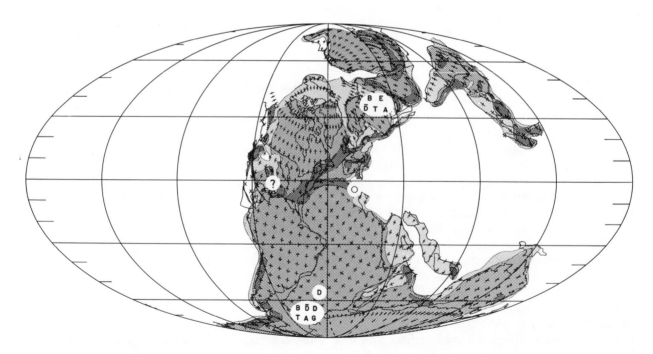

Figure 12.   Distribution of therapsids in the lower Upper Permian. Base map is for the Kazanian (Upper Permian).

Key; **A,** nondicynodont Anomodontia; **B,** "Biarmosuchia;" **Ð,** Dinocephalia, **D,** Dicynodontia; **E,** Eotitanosuchia; **G,** Gorgonopsia; **T,** Therocephalia; open circles, lower Upper Permian terrestrial deposits that do not contain therapsids.

PARRISH, PARRISH, AND ZIEGLER

1962), but the forms from that region are of uncertain taxonomic affinities because of poor preservation. Lower Upper Permian therapsid faunas from South Africa and the USSR are quite similar and contain "biarmosuchians," dinocephalians, therocephalians, and nondicynodont anomodonts. Dicynodonts and gorgonopsians are known only from South Africa, whereas eotitanosuchians are known only from the USSR. No genera are currently recognized as being found in both South Africa and the USSR. This may be because the taxa in the two regions were usually described by different workers. Boonstra (1969) noted marked similarities between the tapinocephalid genera *Moschops* (South Africa) and *Ulemosaurus* (USSR), and the anteosaurid genera *Anteosaurus* (South Africa) and *Doliosauriscus* (USSR).

Paleoclimatological evidence suggests that the Russian and South African deposits were in temperate and fairly moist climates that resulted from the joint effects of fairly high paleolatitudes and locations near the warmer eastern side of Pangaea (in the Russian deposits). As a whole, lower Upper Permian therapsid distributions seem controlled largely by the distribution of continental sedimentary deposits of that age that have yielded fossil vertebrates. To our knowledge, the only tetrapod-bearing deposit of that age that does not contain therapsids is the Moradi Formation of Algeria, from which a captorhinid is known (Taquet, 1969). The significance of the observed distributional pattern is that, within the level of resolution afforded us by fossil record, therapsids are cosmopolitan from their first appearance.

Uppermost Permian

In the uppermost Permian, therapsid-bearing deposits are widely distributed throughout Pangaea. In addition to deposits in South Africa and the USSR, therapsids are known from India, South America, Madagascar, Europe, and China (Fig. 13, Table 3). Dicynodonts are especially widespread and are known from all therapsid-bearing localities of latest Permian age except north China. The genus *Endothiodon* is known from Brazil, India, and several South African localities (Keyser, 1980). The best-known uppermost Permian localities are from South Africa and Russia, and similar assemblages are seen from each of the areas. Dicynodonts, gorgonopsians, therocephalians, and procynosuchid cynodonts are known from all regions. An uppermost Permian therapsid fauna from China is now in

the process of being described; but, so far, dicynodonts are known from Sinkiang, and indeterminate cynodonts, dinocephalians, and gorgonopsians are known from north China, indicating a fauna similar to those in South Africa and Russia (Young, 1979; Sigoneau-Russell and Sun, 1981).

No equatorial or subtropical therapsid localities are known from the uppermost Permian; localities are restricted to the paleolatitudes 25° to 70° north and south. If hot and seasonally arid conditions prevailed in the tropics and subtropics as predicted by the global circulation model for this period, the absence of equatorial and subequatorial therapsids is not surprising. However, the areas near the Late Permian equator lack vertebrate-bearing beds of that age, suggesting that the absence of therapsids in that place and time may be a preservational artifact. The high degree of faunal similarity observed in deposits north and south of the paleoequator indicates that free migration across that zone must have been possible, at least periodically.

The therapsid-bearing localities in China, India, and the USSR coincide geographically with coal deposits, which suggests that moist conditions prevailed in those regions, at least seasonally. The therapsids are concentrated at high mid-latitudes in moderately warm regions that have abundant annual rainfall, but without the extreme temperatures and marked seasonality expected on the eastern side of Pangaea at lower paleolatitudes.

Lower Triassic

Therapsids are widely distributed in the Lower Triassic, even occurring near the south paleopole (Antarctica; Fig. 14, Table 3). The lowermost Triassic genus *Lystrosaurus* has a Pangaean distribution, as its remains have been found in the U.S.S.R., India, South Africa, China, and Antarctica. A highly questionable dicynodont, referred to by Keyser and Cruickshank (1979) as *"Lystrosaurus,"* is known from the "Lower Triassic" of Laos (Repelin, 1923); but both the age and identity of the single specimen seem to be in question, and no further material of that age, from Southeast Asia, has been described. Similar dicynodont-cynodont faunas of latest Early Triassic age are preserved in South Africa, South America, and the USSR.

No Lower Triassic therapsids are reported from areas within the paleolatitudes 35° north to 35° south, although Lower Triassic amphibians within these paleolatitudes occur in the Lower

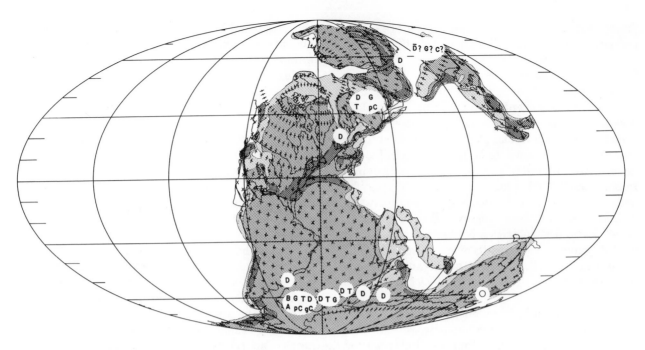

Figure 13. Distribution of therapsids in the uppermost Permian.
  Key: **A,** nondicynodont Anomodontia; **B,** "Biarmosuchia;" **D̄,** Dinocephalia; **D,** Dicynodontia; **G,** Gorgonopsia; **T,** Therocephalia; **pC,** procynosuchid cynodonts; **gC,** galesaurid cynodonts; **C?,** indet. cynodonts; open circles, uppermost Permian terrestrial deposit that does not contain therapsids.

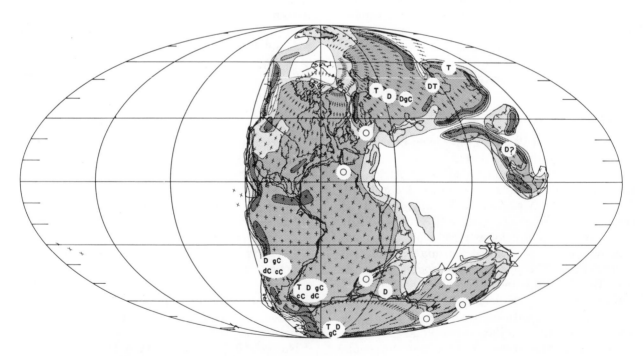

Figure 14. Distribution of therapsids in the Lower Triassic.
  Key: **T,** Thercephalia; **D,** Dicynodontia; **dC,** diademodontid cynodonts; **cC,** cynognathid cynodonts; **gC,** galesaurid cynodonts; open circles, Lower Triassic terrestrial deposits that do not contain therapsids.

126

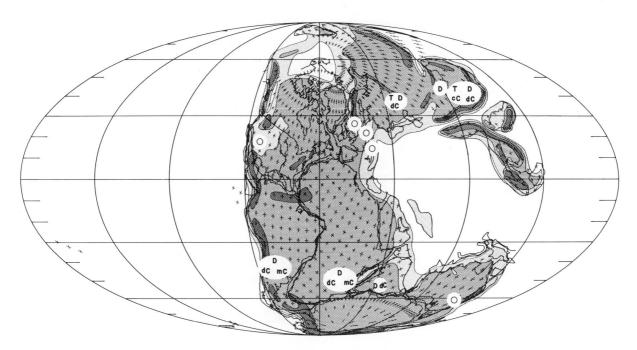

Figure 15.   Distribution of therapsids in the Middle Triassic. Base map is for the Induan (Lower Triassic).

Key: **T**, Therocephalia, **D**, Dicynodontia; **dC**, diademodontid cynodonts; **cC**, cynognathid cynodonts; **mC**, mammal-like cynodonts; open circles, Middle Triassic terrestrial deposits that do not contain therapsids.

Triassic of Algeria and Central Europe. Therapsid-bearing deposits cluster around the paleolatitudes 55° to 60° north and south, but range widely across the longitudinal extent of Pangaea. The presence of therapsids (as well as the possibly more climatically sensitive thecodontians and amphibians) near the south paleopole supports the predictions made on the basis of paleoclimatological criteria discussed earlier—that temperate-to-warm, worldwide climatic conditions prevailed in the Early Triassic.

Middle Triassic

Middle Triassic therapsid distributions (Fig. 15) are similar to those for the Lower Triassic, except for Antarctica and Laos. Dicynodonts, diademodont cynodonts, and mammal-like cynodonts are distributed worldwide. The large dicynodont *Kannemeyeria* is found in South Africa, South America, India, and the USSR, whereas the diademodontid cynodont genus *Scalenodon* is represented in South Africa and (by teeth only) in the USSR (Table 4).

As in the Lower Triassic, the absence of tropical therapsid faunas is notable, although amphibians and a poorly understood diapsid fauna occur in the upper, Middle Triassic part of the Moenkopi Formation of Arizona (Welles and Estes, 1969; Welles and Cosgriff, 1965; Welles, 1947; McKee, 1954) within 10° of the paleoequa-

tor, and there is a near-equatorial marine reptile fauna from Israel and Tunisia. The additional distribution of the marine reptile fauna around the eastern coast of Pangaea in Europe and central China supports the suggestion that the equatorial currents impinging on the eastern coast of Pangaea warmed most of that coast, allowing a wide peri-Tethyan distribution of these presumably thermophilic reptiles. Nonetheless, the absence of therapsids from equatorial and near-equatorial regions in the Lower and Middle Triassic could be a result of their temperature tolerances or the absence of terrestrial tetrapod-bearing beds of the appropriate ages, or both.

Upper Triassic

In the Upper Triassic, therapsid-bearing deposits are more numerous near the paleoequator, but there are none at paleolatitudes above 60° (Fig. 16). Subtropical faunas are reported from North Carolina and the southwestern United States, but not from the warmer, drier eastern half of Pangaea. In the lower Upper Triassic, dicynodonts are known from South and North America; and diademodontid cynodonts, from India, Nova Scotia, South America, and South Africa. The tritylodontid cynodont-mammal-protosuchid crocodilian faunas of Arizona, China, South Africa, and Europe have been interpreted variously as uppermost Triassic (Colbert, 1981; Simmons,

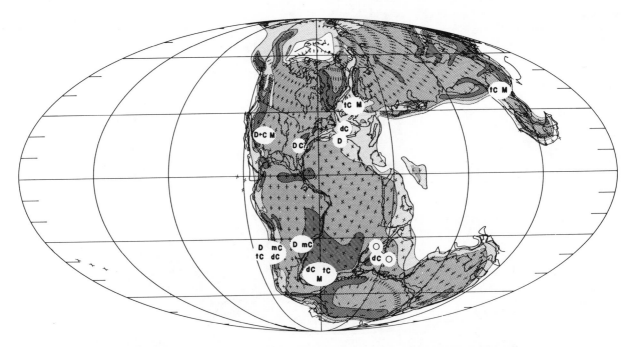

Figure 16.   Distribution of Upper Triassic therapsids. Base map is for the Pliensbachian (Lower Jurassic).

Key: **D,** Dicynodontia; **dC,** diademodontid cynodonts; **mC,** mammal-like cynodonts; **tC,** tritylodontid cynodonts; **C?,** indet. cynodonts; **M,** mammals.

1965) and as lowermost Jurassic (Olsen and Galton, 1977; Clemens, et al. 1979), but the high degree of faunal similarity among these faunas requires that Pangaea-wide migrations were still possible at the time they were deposited. The only cosmopolitan synapsid genus reported for the Upper Triassic-Liassic is *Eozostrodon,* from both China and Europe. The increase of therapsid faunas towards the equator in the Late Triassic suggests a cooling trend that is not predicted by any of the paleoclimatological criteria, although Frakes (1979, his Fig. 9-1) suggested a temperature drop in this period. Again, the observed distributional pattern may reflect preservational biases imposed on the actual distributions of taxa. As has been noted, the sub-equatorial therapsid-bearing deposits in the lower Upper Triassic are from the United States and, thus, from the relatively cool, wetter western half of Pangaea.

In summary, the observed distributions of therapsids suggest their exclusion from hot equatorial and dry regions throughout their existence, but that warm-to-temperate worldwide climatic conditions allowed the therapsids to exist at very high paleolatitudes, such as in Antarctica in the Lower Triassic. The similarities of distribution of taxa worldwide suggest that no marked barriers to migration existed throughout the Permian-Triassic. The observed distributions

probably represent the distribution of known tetrapod-bearing terrestrial sediments of various ages as strongly as they represent actual faunal ranges.

Acknowledgments

Drs. James A. Hopson and Herbert R. Barghusen offered much assistance in clarifying affinities of therapsid taxa, and provided preliminary versions of the therapsid phylogeny they prepared for this symposium. Dr. Yin Hongfu graciously translated a Chinese manuscript. S. Chatterjee, P. Olsen, E. McKee, and B. Wardlaw made many helpful comments on the manuscript. Ms. Rebecca Curtis drafted the figures, and Ms. P. Worl and Ms. G. Pilcher typed various versions of the manuscript.

References

Anderson, J. M., and Cruickshank, A. R. I.
1978.   The biostratigraphy of the Permian and Triassic. Part 5. A review of the classification and distribution of Permo-Triassic tetrapods. *Palaeontologica Africana* 21:15–44.

Ayres, M. G.; Bilal, M.; Jones, R. W.; Slentz, L. W.; Tartir, M.; and Wilson, A. O.
1982.   Hydrocarbon habitat in main producing areas,

PARRISH, PARRISH, AND ZIEGLER

Saudi Arabia. *Amer. Assoc. Petrol. Geol. Bull.* 66:1–9.

Baird, D., and Patterson, O. F., III
1967. Dicynodont-archosaur fauna in the Pekin Fm. (Upper Triassic) of North Carolina. *Geol. Soc. Amer. Abst. Prog.*, South Central Sec., p. 11.

Bambach, R. K.; Scotese, C. R.; and Ziegler, A. M.
1980. Before Pangaea: the geographies of the Paleozoic world. *Amer. Sci.* 68:26–38.

Barron, E. J.; Sloan, J. L.; and Harrison, C. G. A.
1980. Potential significance of land-sea distribution and surface albedo variations as a climatic forcing factor, 180 m.y. to the present. *Palaeogeog., Palaeoclim., Palaeoecol.* 30:17–40.

Boonstra, L. D.
1969. The fauna of the *Tapinocephalus* zone (Beaufort beds of the Karroo). *Ann. S. Afr. Mus.* 56:1073.

Briden, J. C. and Irving, E.
1964. Paleolatitude spectra of sedimentary paleoclimatic indicators. In *Problems in Paleoclimatology,* ed. A. E. M. Nairn, pp. 199–224. London: Interscience Publishers, John Wiley and Sons Ltd.

Broom, R.
1932. *The Mammal-like Reptiles of South Africa and the Origin of Mammals.* London: H. F. and G. Witherby.

Camp, C. L., and Welles, S. P.
1956. Triassic dicynodont reptiles. *Univ. Calif. Mem.* 13:255–348.

Carroll, R. L.
1981. Plesiosaur ancestors from the Late Permian of Madagascar. *Phil. Trans. Roy. Soc. Lond.* Ser. B. 293:315–383.

Carroll, R. L.; Belt, E. S.; Dineley, D. L.; Barid, D.; and McGregor, D. C.
1972. Vertebrate paleontology of eastern Canada. *Guidebook for Field Excursion A59*, 24th Int. Geol. Cong., Montreal.

Chatterjee, S.
1982. A new cynodont reptile from the Triassic of India. *J. Paleo.* 56:203–14.

Clemens, W. A.; Lillegraven, J. A.; Lindsay, E. H.; and Simpson, G. G.
1979. When, where, and what—a survey of known Mesozoic mammal distribution. In *Mesozoic Mammals: The First Two-thirds of Mammalian History*, ed., J. A. Lillegraven, Z. Kielen-Jaworowska, and W. A. Clemens, pp. 7–58. Berkeley: University of California Press.

Cluver, M. A., and Hotton, N., III.
1977. The dicynodont genus *Diictodon* (Reptilia, Therapsida) and its significance. *Fourth Gond-wana Symposium, Papers,* vol. 1:176–83. Delhi: Hindustan Publishing Corporation.

Colbert, E. H.
1974. *Lystrosaurus* from Antarctica. *Amer. Mus. Novit.* 2535:1–44.
1981. A primitive ornithischian dinosaur from the Kayenta Formation of Arizona. *Bull. Mus. No. Ariz.* 53:1–61.

Colbert, E. H., and Cosgriff, J. W.
1974. Labyrinthodont amphibians from Antarctica. *Amer. Mus. Novit.* 2522:1–20.

Colbert, E. H., and Kitching, J. W.
1977. Triassic cynodont reptiles from Antarctica. *Amer. Mus. Novit.* 2611:1–30.
1981. Scaloposaurian reptiles from the Triassic of Antarctica. *Amer. Mus. Novit.* 2709:1–22.

Dott, R. H., Sr., and Reynolds, M. J.
1969. *Sourcebook for Petroleum Geology.* Amer. Assoc. Petrol. Geol. Mem. 5.

Dow, W. G.
1978. Petroleum source beds on continental slopes and rises. *Amer. Assoc. Petrol. Geol. Bull.* 62:1584–606.

Drewry, G. E.; Ramsay, A. T. S.; and Smith, A. G.
1974. Climatically controlled sediments, the geomagnetic field, and trade wind belts in Phanerozoic time. *J. Geol.* 82:531–33.

Dutuit, J. M.
1965. Découverte de dicynodontes (reptiles therapsides) dans le Trias du couloir d'Argana (Atlas occidental marocain). *C. R. Acad. Sci. Paris* 260:3477–48.

Frakes, L. A.
1979. *Climates Throughout Geologic Time.* New York: Elsevier.

Hammer, W. R., and Cosgriff, J. W.
1981. *Myosaurus gracilis,* and anomodont reptile from the Lower Triassic of Antarctica and South Africa. *J. Paleo.* 55:410–24.

Hopson, J. A., and Kitching, J. W.
1972. A revised classification of cynodonts (Reptilia; Therapsida). *Paleontologica Africana* 14:71–85.

Hou, L.
1979. On a new theriodont from Inner Mongolia. *Vert. Palasiatica* 17:121–30. (Chinese, English summary).

Humphreville, R., and Bambach, R. K.
1979. Influence of geography, climate, and ocean circulation on the pattern of generic diversity of brachiopods in the Permian. *Geol. Soc. Amer. Abstr. Prog.* 11:447.

Jenkins, F. A., Jr.
1981. News note. *Soc. Vert. Paeo. News Bull.* 122:9–10.

Kalandadze, N. N.
1975. The first discovery of *Lystrosaurus* in the European regions of the U.S.S.R. *Paleont. J.* 4:557–60.

Kermack, K. A.; Mussett, F.; and Rigney, H. W.
1981. The skull of *Morganucodon. Zool. J. Linn. Soc.* 71:1–158.

Keyser, A. W.
1980. The stratigraphic distribution of the Dicynodontia of Africa reviewed in a Gondwana context. *Fifth Int. Gondwana Symp., Proceedings,* pp. 61–63. Rotterdam: A. A. Balkema.

Keyser, A. W., and Cruickshank, A. R. I.
1979. The origin and classification of Triassic dicynodonts. *Trans. Geol. Soc. S. Afr.* 82:81–108.

Kitching, J. W.
1977. The distribution of the Karroo vertebrate fauna. *Mem. Bernard Price Inst. for Paleont. Res.* 1:1–131.

McKee, E. D.
1954. Stratigraphy and history of the Meonkopi Formation of Triassic age. *Geol. Soc. Amer. Mem.* 61:1–133.

Murris, R. J.
1980. Middle East: stratigraphic evolution and oil habitat. *Amer. Assoc. Petrol. Geol. Bull.* 64:597–618.

Olsen, P. E., and Galton, P. M.
1977. Triassic-Jurassic tetrapod extinctions: are they real? *Science* 197:983–86.

Olson, E. C.
1962. Late Permian terrestrial vertebrates, U.S.A. and U.S.S.R. *Trans. Amer. Phil. Soc.* 52:1–224.

Parrish, J. T.
1982. Upwelling and petroleum source beds, with reference to the Paleozoic. *Amer. Assoc. Petrol. Geol. Bull.* 66:750–74.

Parrish, J. T., and Curtis, R. L.
1982. Atmospheric circulation, upwelling, and organic-rich rocks in the Mesozoic and Cenozoic. *Palaeogeog., Palaeoclim., Palaeoceol.* 40:31–66.

Parrish, J. T., Ziegler, A. M., and Scotese, C. R.
1982. Rainfall patterns and the distribution of coals and evaporites. *Paleogeogr., Paleoclimatol., Paleoecol.* 40:67–101.

Petterssen, S.
1969. *Introduction to Meteorology,* 3d ed. New York: McGraw-Hill.

Repelin, J.
1923. Sur un fragment de crane de *Dicynodon. Bull. Serv. Géol. L'Indochine* 12:5–9.

Retallack, G.
1975. The life and times of a Triassic lycopod. *Alcheringa* 1:3–29.

Rigney, H. W.
1963. A specimen of *Morganucodon* from Yunnan. *Nature* 197:1122–23.

Robinson, P. L.
1973. Palaeoclimatology and continental drift. In *Implications of Continental Drift to the Earth Sciences,* Vol. I, ed. D. H. Tarling and S. K. Runcorn, pp. 451–476. London: Academic Press.

Rowe, T.
1980. The morphology, affinities, and age of the dicynodont *Geikia elginensis.* In *Aspects of Vertebrate History,* ed. L. L. Jacobs, pp 269–294. Flagstaff: Museum of Northern Arizona Press.

Sagan, C. and G. Mullen.
1972. Earth and Mars: evolution of atmospheres and surface temperatures. *Science* 177:52–56.

Scotese, C. R.; Bambach, R. K.; Barton, C.; Van der Voo, R.; and Ziegler, A. M.
1981. Mesozoic and Cenozoic base maps [abstract]. *Amer. Assoc. Petrol. Geol. Bull.* 65:989.

Sigoneau-Russell, D., and Sun, A. L.
1981. A brief review of Chinese synapsids. *Geobios* 14:275–79.

Sigoneau, D., and Tchudinov, P. K.
1972. Reflections of some Russian Eotheriodonts (Reptilia, Synapsida, Therapsida). *Paleovert.* 5:79–109.

Simmons, D. J.
1965. The non-therapsid reptiles of the Lufeng Basin, Yunnan, China. *Fieldiana: Geol.* 15:5–93.

Taquet, M. P.
1969. Première découverte en Afrique d'un Reptile Captorhinomorphe (Cotylosaurine). *C. R. Acad. Sci. Paris* 268:779–81.

Tatarinov, L. P.
1973. Cynodonts of gondwanian habit in the Middle Triassic of the U.S.S.R. *Paleont. J.* 1973:200–204.

Welles, S. P.
1947. Vertebrates from the Upper Moenkopi Formation of northern Arizona. *Univ. Calif. Bull. Dept. Geol. Sci.* 27:241–94.

Welles, S. P., and Cosgriff, J.
1965. A review of the labyrinthodont family Capitosauridae and a description of *Parotosaurus peabodyi* from the Wupatki Member of the Moenkopi Formation of northern Arizona. *Univ. Calif. Publ. in Geol. Sci.* No. 54.

Welles, S. P., and Estes, R.

1969. *Hadrokkosaurus bradyi* from the Upper Moenkopi Formation of Arizona with a review of the brachyopid labyrinthodonts. *Univ. of Calif. Publ. in Geol. Sci.* No. 84.

Young, C. C.

1946. The Triassic vertebrate remains of China. *Amer. Mus. Novit.* 1324:1–14.

1979. A Late Permian fauna from Jiyuan, Henan. *Vert. Palasiatica* 17:99–114. (In Chinese)

Ziegler, A. M.; Bambach, R. K.; Barrett, S. F.; McKerrow, W. S.; Scotese, C. R.; Kazmer, C.; and Parrish, J. T.

1981. Mesozoic and Cenozoic paleogeography. [abstract] *Amer. Assoc. Petrol. Geol. Bull.* 65:1011.

Ziegler, A. M.; Bambach, R. K.; Parrish, J. T.; Barrett, S. F.; Gierlowski, E. H.; Parker, W. C.; Raymond, A.; and Sepkoski, J. J., Jr.

1981. Paleozoic biogeography and climatology. In *Paleobotany, Paleoecology, and Evolution,* Vol. 2, ed. K. J. Niklas, pp. 231–266. New York: Praeger Publishers.

Ziegler, A. M.; Hansen, K. S.; Johnson, M. E.; Kelley, M. A.; Scotese, C. R.; and Van der Voo, R.

1977. Silurian continental distributions, paleogeography, climatology, and biogeography. *Tectonophys.* 40:13–51.

Ziegler, A. M., Scotese, C. R., and Barrett, S. S.

1983. Mesozoic and Cenozoic paleogeograhic maps. In *Tidal Friction and the Earth's Rotation,* II, ed. P. Brosche and J. Sunderland pp. 240–52. New York: Springer Verlag.

Ziegler, A. M.; Scotese, C. R.; McKerrow, W. S.; Johnson, M. E.; and Bambach, R. K.

1977. Paleozoic biogeography of continents bordering the Iapetus (Pre-Caledonian) and Rheic (Pre-Hercynian) Oceans. In *Paleontology and Plate Tectonics,* ed. R. M. West pp. 1–22. *Milwaukee Museum Spec. Publ. Biol. Geol. 2.*

1979. Paleozoic paleogeography. *Ann Rev. Earth Planet. Sci.* 7:473–502.

EDWIN H. COLBERT
Museum of Northern Arizona
Flagstaff, Arizona 86001

Therapsids in Pangaea and Their Contemporaries and Competitors

Introduction

Geological and geophysical evidence indicates that at the end of the Paleozoic Era, present-day continents were conjoined into a vast supercontinent, Pangaea, which straddled the equator. Its northern and southern components are designated, respectively, Laurasia and Gondwanaland[1]. The rifting that led to more familiar continental configurations did not begin until the end of the Triassic Period. Terrestrial tetrapods were widely distributed in the ancient supercontinent, living under widely uniform climatic conditions, with few physical barriers to prevent their broad dispersal.

Among these tetrapods the therapsid reptiles were conspicuous during Late Permian time, and continued into the Triassic in declining numbers, diversity, and size. Some of the survivors became increasingly mammalian in structure, and gave rise to the first mammals during the Late Triassic.

Fossils that document this progressive evolution of morphology provide few clues regarding enlargement of the brain, except that it did not correspond to the advent of animals that were physiologically mammalian. However, the broad outlines of behavioral changes among the therapsids can be inferred from details of anatomy and distribution. In the present paper, some of the anatomical changes that took place are traced in the context of the adaptive radiation and distribution of therapsids generally, and of contemporaries with which therapsids had to compete, upon which they might have fed, and from which they had to hide. Interactions between therapsids and their physical and biological environments are especially relevant to major changes in locomotor and feeding systems, to the final decline and extinction of the therapsid line, and to the origin and survival of their daughters, the mammals.

Ancient Pangaea

Evidence from sea-floor spreading and paleomagnetism accumulated in the past two decades indicates, beyond much doubt, that at the end of the Paleozoic Era and at the beginning of the Mesozoic Era the land masses of the earth were conjoined into a single supercontinent, styled by Wegener (1966) "Pangaea" (see also Parrish, Parrish, and Ziegler, this volume). This great continental mass extended from northern to southern high latitudes, and from east to west across perhaps 180° longtitude (Fig. 1).

The cosmopolitan aspect of Permo-Triassic tetrapod faunas is consistent with this interpretation. The terrestrial vertebrates of those distant days roamed widely across their broad continental habitat, evidently with few barriers to obstruct their spread from one region to another (Colbert, 1980). Local and regional differences can be identified, but in broad terms the differences are less striking than the resemblances.

Upper Permian tetrapod faunas are found today in nothern Russia between latitudes of about 50° and 65° north, particularly along the Mesen and Dvina Rivers and in the region of the Province of Perm (the original type area for the Permian System), and in South Africa at a latitude of 30° south—a spread of some 90°. Triassic tetrapod faunas are equally widely dispersed from north to south, from northern Russia to the southern tip of Africa, and in the New World from Nova Scotia to a southern latitude even somewhat higher than the African occurrences (Fig. 2). In Permo-Triassic times, these north and south extremes, collectively, were probably somewhat farther south than in later times, most of the fragments of Pangaea having slid north since the Triassic. The north-south spread, however, was comparable to what it is today.

The widely uniform climate and the lack of natural barriers in Permo-Triassic Pangaea are indicated by closely related and frequently identical tetrapod genera found in the Permian of Russia, South Africa, and China; in the Lower Triassic of all continents except North America; and in the Upper Triassic of all continents except (so far) Antarctica. It has been argued (Bakker, 1975) that the wide distribution of therapsids in-

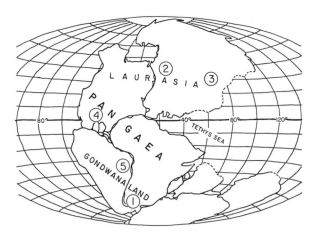

Figure 1. Therapsid localities in Permian Pangaea. 1. Lower Beaufort beds, South Africa. 2. Zones I–IV, USSR. 3. Lower Canfangou Formation, Sinkiang/Xinjiang. 4. Flower Pot and San Angelo Formations, Texas.

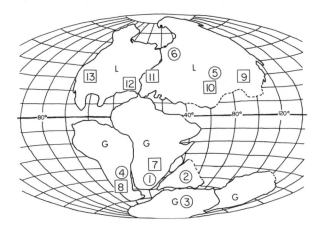

Figure 2. Therapsid localities in Triassic Pangaea. 1. Middle and Upper Beaufort beds, South Africa. 2. Panchet and Yerrapalli Formations, India. 3. Fremouw Formation, Antarctica. 4. Puesto Viejo and Chañares Formations, Argentina. 5. Jiucaiyan Formation, Sinkiang/Xinjiang. 6. Zones V–VI, USSR. 7. Stromberg Series and Manda beds, southern Africa. 8. Santa Maria Formation, Brazil; Ischigualasto and Los Colorados Formations, Argentina. 9. Ehrmaying Formation, Shansi/Shanxi. 10. Lufeng Series, Yunnan. 11. Keuper—Rhaetic sediments, Europe. 12. Newark Series, eastern North America. 13. Kayenta Formation, Arizona.

Key: **L**, Laurasia; **G**, Gondwana; circles, Lower Triassic; squares, Middle and Upper Triassic.

dicates the development of endothermy or homeothermy as an adaptation to varied climates in Pangaea. However, the presence in these faunas of tetrapods that had not departed from their primitive ectothermic inheritance (e.g., labyrinthodont amphibians, cotylosaurs, eosuchians, and thecodonts) negates such an argument. A large segment of the Permo-Triassic tetrapod

E. H. Colbert

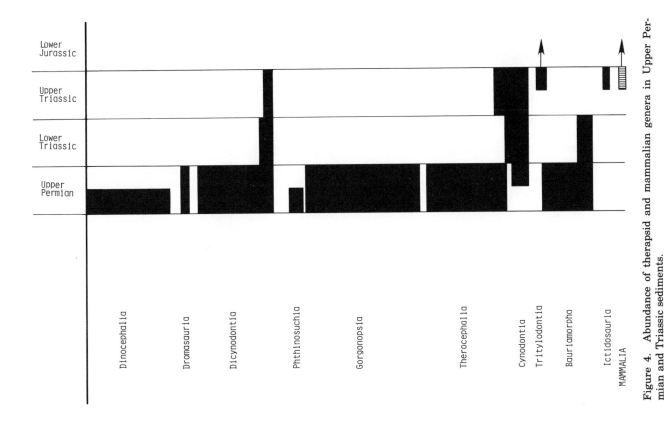

Figure 4. Abundance of therapsid and mammalian genera in Upper Permian and Triassic sediments.

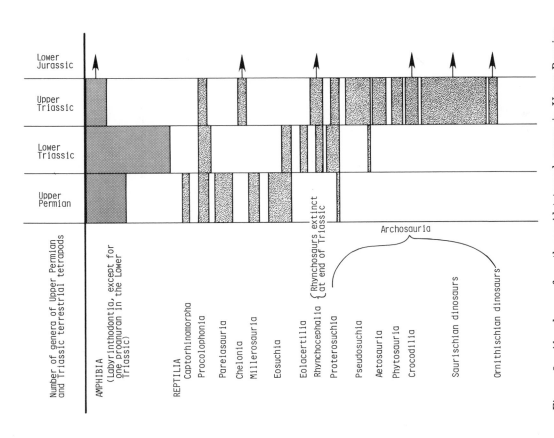

Figure 3. Abundance of nontherapsid tetrapod genera in Upper Permian and Triassic sediments.

faunas consisted of ectothermic animals that would of necessity have lived in tropical, subtropical, or warm temperate climates (Fig. 3). So Pangaea would seem to have been one world climatically as well as physiographically. In the great Southern Hemisphere, Permo-Carboniferous glaciation was a thing of the past.

Therapsids in Permo-Triassic Pangaea

The therapsids arose from pelycosaurian ancestors, a lineage of very ancient origin that was derived either from early cotylosaurs (Kemp, 1980) or independently from a common ancestor of amphibian grade (Carroll, this volume). Therapsids underwent the entire gamut of their evolutionary development during Permo-Triassic times (Fig. 4), passing into decline before that Late Triassic and leaving only a few lines, some of which gave rise to the first mammals, to persist to the end of the period.

This view is supported by simple analysis of the known tetrapod genera of Upper Paleozoic and Lower Mesozoic sediments. Therapsids constitute about four-fifths of all Upper Permian genera, less than a third of Lower Triassic genera, and less than a fourth of Upper Triassic genera (Appleby et al., 1967).

Correlatively, as therapsids decreased in number and variety during Triassic time, other tetrapods burgeoned. There was an almost exact reversal in the proportions of therapsids and other tetrapods between Late Permian and Late Triassic time (Tables 1 and 2). It should be said that the figures in Table 1 and 2 represent, so far as Permian deposits are concerned, essentially three general fossiliferous regions; southern Africa, northern Europe (mainly USSR) and inte-

Table 1.—Number of genera of Upper Permian and Triassic terrestrial tetrapods

Tetrapods	Upper Permian	Lower Triassic	Upper Triassic
Amphibia (Labyrinthodontia, except for one proanuran in the Lower Triassic)	25	52	12
Reptilia (other than therapsids)			
Captorhinomorpha	4		
Procolophonia	7	8	5
Pareiasauria	11		
Chelonia			6
Millerosauria	7		
Eosuchia	14	6	
Eolacertilia		4	
Rhynchocephalia		5	9
Proterosuchia	1	8	4
Pseudosuchia		1	16
Aetosauria			9
Phytosauria			6
Crocodilia			8
Saurischian dinosaurs			41
Ornithischian dinosaurs			6
Reptilia (Therapsida)			
Phthinosuchia	9		
Gorgonopsia	71		
Cynodontia	11	16	22
Tritylodontoidea			6
Therocephalia	52		
Bauriamorpha	31	10	
Ictidosauria			3
Dinocephalia	48		
Dromasauria	4		
Dicynodontia	46	8	6
Mammalia			4

E. H. COLBERT

Table 2.—Tetrapod genera

Time	Total number of genera	Genera of therapsids	Percentage of therapsids
Upper Permian	341	272	80
Lower Triassic	118	34	29
Upper Triassic	163	37	23

rior North America. The Triassic figures are worldwide, based upon fossils found in all of the continental regions. The numbers of genera are based upon Romer's (1966) classification of the vertebrates, and his synonymies are accepted.

The Succession of Faunas[2]

Therapsid reptiles are best known in greatest diversity from Permian sediments of South Africa, but the earliest examples are from Russia and the United States (Olson, this volume). The most primitive of these were the carnivorous phthinosuchians, showing characters annectent to sphenacodont pelycosaurs. From such beginnings, the therapsids of late Permian times evolved rapidly along several lines, notably the gorgonopsians, cynodonts, therocephalians and bauriamorphs, dinocephalians, and dicynodonts.

The initial Upper Permian fauna in South Africa was characterized by large, extremely robust dinocephalian therapsids. Within this taxonomic group, conveniently classified as an infraorder, there was an ecological dichotomy: on the one hand, clumsy herbivores, the tapinocephalids; and on the other, clumsy carnivores, the titanosuchids. It seems logical to suppose that within this broad zoological entity there was to some degree a "closed system" of herbivory and predation, in which tapinocephalids were primary consumers that provided the titanosuchids with a living. Sharing the scene with dinocephalians were the dicynodonts, smaller animals of markedly herbivorous adaptation, together with such predators as phthinosuchians, gorgonopsians, and therocephalians. The gorgonopsians and therocephalians were more gracile of body form and, therefore, presumably more agile than titanosuchids. They probably supplemented the titanosuchids as predators, preying perhaps on smaller tapinocephalids as well as on dicynodonts (Fig. 5) and a few nontherapsid reptiles. All predators may have preyed on one another to some extent. There is every reason to think that they also supplemented their diet by scavenging.

The most obvious interaction between the earliest African therapsids and contemporaneous nontherapsid reptiles involved parieasaurs—cotylosaurs that were large enough to compete with tapinocephalids and to be preyed upon by titanosuchians and others. Other nontherapsids—captorhinomorphs, procolophonids, millerosaurs, and younginids—were small animals of lizardlike body form, and so may have occupied somewhat different ecologic niches than most therapsids. In size, however, they were comparable to the smallest dicynodonts, and it is likely that the predators that hunted dicynodonts would also have caught nontherapsid reptiles when they found them.

During the final stages of Permian history in South Africa (Colbert, 1980) the phthinosuchians and dinocephalians had become extinct, but gorgonopsians, bauriamorphs, and dicynodonts expanded greatly, while the therocephalians continued with unabated vigor. At this time, the cynodonts made their appearance.

The disappearance of ungainly dinocephalian herbivores and carnivores suggests that selection pressures were favoring smaller and more active therapsids. However, a few giants survived for a time: the pareiasaurs persisted, to be stalked by certain large gorgonopsians, such as the huge *Rubidgea* of South Africa and *Inostrancevia* of Russia, both fearsome, saber-toothed predators.

Figure 5. Ecological relationships of late Permian therapsids in South Africa. A carnivorous gorgonopsian *(Lycaenops)* is shown stalking an herbivorous dicynodont (Dicynodon). (After Colbert, 1948.)

Still, as earlier, the therapsids lived largely within their own ecological system; the dicynodonts, now numerous and varied, formed the base of the food pyramid for the predatory theriodonts. The nontherapsid reptiles of this stage were the persistent procolophonids, millerosaurs and younginids, perhaps partly isolated from the therapsids by the ecological niches they inhabited. Labyrinthodont amphibians also survived, removed from many therapsids by their aquatic habits.

When viewed comprehensively, the tetrapod faunas of late Permian times are thus seen to have been essentially therapsid, with nontherapsid tetrapods occupying relatively minor roles. Competition was among the therapsids, except perhaps for such impact as the pareiasaurs might have had on tapinocephalids and dicynodonts for access to the vegetation on which they communally browsed. The therapsids lived in a therapsid world, and in that world they prospered.

The transition from Paleozoic to Mesozoic times was a period of biological stress throughout the world, as reflected in the record of therapsids. Gorgonopsians and therocephalians, numerous and varied during Late Permian time, became extinct. Bauriamorphs and dicynodonts were severely reduced in their generic diversity, although they maintain abundance of individuals into the earliest Triassic. Only the cynodonts showed an increase, and that, modest.

Pareisaurs became extinct toward the end of the Permian Period, thereby removing from the scene one group very characteristic of early tetrapod faunas. They were accompanied into extinction by two groups of nontherapsid reptiles, the captorhinomorphs and millerosaurs.

The decline in numbers of therapsid genera to somewhat less than a third of the Early Triassic census is due not only to therapsid extinctions, but also to an increase among amphibians brought about by the adaptive radiation of stereospondyls. This aspect of decline is merely an artifact of normalizing, a consequence of expressing numbers of genera as percentages of a whole. The fully aquatic stereospondyls, although numerous and often of large size, probably had little effect on therapsid evolution.

The truly significant development of Early Triassic time, so far as the therapsids were concerned, was the appearance of the thecodont reptiles. Although the Early Triassic thecodonts were not particularly large, numerous, or varied, they were, none the less, the harbingers of the

great archosaurian radiation that, during the course of the Mesozoic Era, was to dominate the continents in an unprecedented manner. The rise and deployment of the archosaurs, initiated in the Early Triassic and reaching very significant proportions by Late Triassic time, was accompanied by the decline and disappearance of the therapsids. There was probably a causal relationship in these processes, as we shall see.

Another reptilian order that made its appearance at the beginning of Triassic history was the Rhynchocephalia. Although never very diverse, the Rhynchocephalia were significant in Triassic faunas, especially those of Gondwanaland, because of the wide distribution of great numbers of rhynchosaurs. Rhynchosaurs were large, bulky herbivores with distinctive dentitions; to some extent they may have been competitors of the dicynodonts.

The extensive therapsid extinctions at the end of the Permian Period, and the appearance of such new reptiles as archosaurs and rhynchosaurs, gave Early Triassic faunas a composition quite different from that of late Paleozoic assemblages. Yet there were some holdovers from the Paleozoic, such as the labyrinthodont amphibians, in a marked expansion over their Permian predecessors, persistent cotylosaurs in the form of the little procolophonids, and small eosuchians. The procolophonids and eosuchians were both of lizardlike habitus. The therapsids that continued the history of the order into the Triassic were dicynodonts, cynodonts, and bauriamorphs.

Many of the holdovers continued into Late Triassic times in declining diversity. Yet despite the fact that these several groups lived on, often in great abundance so far as individuals were concerned, the later Triassic faunas were different, and perhaps as distinctive when compared with Early Triassic faunas, as the latter are when compared with Late Permian faunas. This new look was brought about by the remarkable expansion of the archosaurian reptiles. Whereas in Early Triassic time the archosaurs were moderately represented by proterosuchids and pseudosuchians, in the Late Triassic these groups were augmented by phytosaurs, crocodilians, and saurischian and ornithischian dinosaurs. The radiation of these saurischians was particularly varied and broad, so that numerous dinosaurs of this type wandered across the lands of Pangaea as forerunners of the great dinosaurian domination of Jurassic and Cretaceous continents. Ornithischian dinosaurs were present in the Late

E. H. COLBERT

Triassic in limited numbers, although they were destined for even greater success than saurischians in the later Mesozoic.

Other elements of Late Triassic faunas were newcomers. Although the remains of Upper Triassic frogs are as yet unknown, they must have been present in some of the faunal assemblages, since proanuran ancestors have been found in the Lower Triassic sediments of Madagascar. This was the time when the turtles appeared, to establish one of the longest lasting of tetrapod evolutionary lines. Among the therapsids, the highly specialized tritylodonts appeared as descendants from cynodont ancestors. They spread throughout the world, and continued in Europe into Jurassic time, the only therapsids to survive the end of the Triassic Period. The small, very mammal-like trithelodonts (Hopson and Kitching, 1972), formerly known as ictidosaurs (cf. Broom 1932), were another cynodont derivative that appeared late in the Triassic. Finally, the earliest mammals appeared in the Late Triassic, as very small descendants of cynodonts.

The Late Triassic tetrapod faunas were therefore more varied than the faunas that had gone before, and on top of this variety there was the dominating presence of the archosaurs. Late Permian time was the age of therapsids; Late Triassic time was the beginning of the long age of archosaurian rule.

The Success and Decline of the Therapsids

The foregoing review has attempted to show the succession of Upper Permian and Triassic terrestrial tetrapod faunas. As noted in the discussion of therapsid decline, this survey has been one of numbers, based upon the relative abundance or scarcity of genera during the geologic periods under consideration.

We now come to a consideration of the quality of therapsid life, to the factors that led to therapsid success, and subsequently to therapsid decline. In the primitive therapsid genus *Phthinosuchus,* from the USSR, the skull was narrow and deep, with a posteriorly placed orbit and a large lateral temporal fenestra (Fig. 6A). The dentition was somewhat differentiated, with small premaxillary and anterior dentary teeth, followed by large canines, which in turn were followed by sharp, compressed cutting teeth in the maxilla and middle section of the dentary. There were teeth on the palate. In these respects, the skull is reminiscent of the skull of the pelycosaur *Dimetrodon,* as though phthinosuchians

had inherited the basic skull pattern of sphenacodont pelycosaurs.

The postcranial form of the most primitive therapsids was apparently also inherited with little change from pelycosaurs. The trunk was elongate and the limbs comparatively slender. Five digits were retained, and the pose was quadrupedal.

Therapsid evolution was characterized by the following trends:

1. Retention of a quadrupedal pose in all evolutionary lines.
2. Adaptation of the limbs for an "upright" method of locomotion, with the body raised above the ground.
3. Expansion of the ilium and frequently of the scapula.
4. Retention of five digits in all evolutionary lines.
5. Loss of the intercentra and differentiation within the vertebral column into well-defined cervical, thoracic, and lumbar vertebrae.
6. Frequent differentiation of the dentition, with cheek teeth either drastically reduced (dicynodonts, gorgonopsians, therocephalians) or elaborated into complex forms (bauriamorphs, cynodonts, tritylodonts, and others).
7. Retention of an almost full complement of bones in the skull and mandible, but often with marked changes in proportions of the bones.
8. Expansion of the dentary bone in many evolutionary lines, at the expense of postdentary elements.
9. Development of a secondary palate.
10. Expansion of the lateral temporal fenestra in various evolutionary lines, often to incorporate the parietal bone into the margin of the fenestra.

Some evolutionary trends were conservative; for example, the retention of a quadrupedal stance and five digits in the feet. In contrast, the development of a pose with the body raised well off the ground was an advance over primitive reptiles. Such a pose introduced a mode of locomotion that was more effective for sustained activity, giving therapsids an advantage over the more primitive, "sprawling" types of tetrapods (Fig. 6B). Locomotor refinement was reflected elsewhere in the postcranial skeleton, by loss of the intercentra, by elongation of the sacrum and expansion of the ilium, by enlargement of the scapula, and by the limbs becoming more slender and reoriented so that the feet were brought beneath the body, close to the midline. The hind limbs were usually more advanced than the front

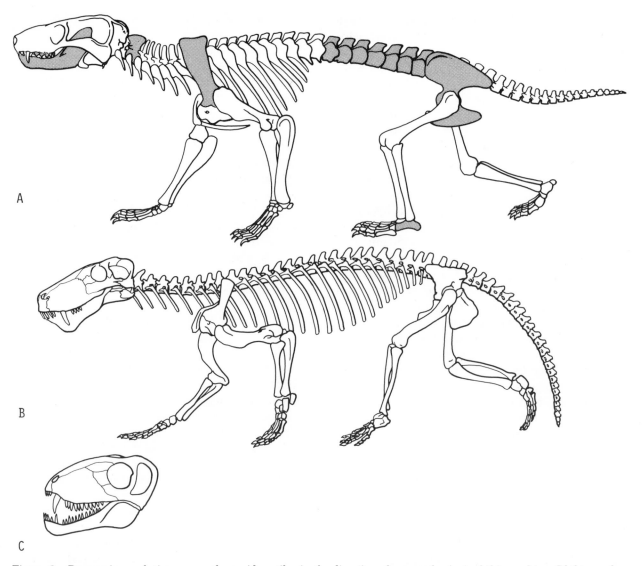

Figure 6. Progressive evolution among therapsid reptiles in the direction of mammals. A. A phthinosuchian, *Phthinosuchus,* forming a connecting link with the pelycosaurs. B. An Upper Permian gorgonopsian, *Lycaenops.* C. A Lower Triassic cynodont, *Thrinaxodon,* showing the development of strong mammal-like characters (shaded). These include: enlargement of the dentary; develoment of the spine on the axis vertebra; distinct lumbar vertebrae with reduction of the ribs; expansion of the scapula with the development of a scapular spine; enlargement of the ilium, and of the pelvis in general; and development of a tuber calcanei. (A, after Efremov, 1954; B, after Colbert, 1948; C, after Jenkins, 1971.)

in this respect: the head of the femur was offset to bring the shaft to a line parallel with that of the body axis, but the humerus was not greatly modified from its primitive shape, and the elbows generally remained everted. As a corollary to the raised locomotory pose, the digits, though remaining five in number, became subequal in length, a condition brought about by the reduction or elimination of phalanges.

In most therapsids, there was little differentiation of the trunk; the vertebrae and ribs formed a graded series from the back of the skull to the sacrum. In the cynodonts and tritylodonts, howver, differentiation was marked (Fig. 6C). In

these reptiles a well-defined boundary between thoracic and lumbar regions points to the possible existence of a diaphragm, which in turn implies a more mammal-like ventilatory mechanism, correlated with a high level of metabolism (but see Bennett and Ruben, this volume).

In the head, differentiation of teeth and the diversity of dentitions are vital clues to the ways in which therapsids exploited the various environmental opportunities open to them. Just as the postcranial skeleton reveals therapsids as active, highly mobile animals, so dentitions show that they were able to live on a great variety of foods acquired and processed in diverse ways.

E. H. COLBERT

Dentitions of the first cynodont therapsids foreshadow the primitive dental differentiation of mammals: small anterior incisors for nipping; large, daggerlike canines for piercing and slashing; and cheek teeth variously elaborated for crushing and shearing. Perhaps the ultimate is the rather rodent-like differentiation of tritylodonts, with a pair of pointed, peglike anterior teeth separated by a long diastema from the cheek teeth, which were broad and multicuspate, the cusps arranged in rows with grooves between them.

Little of the wide variety of dental differentiation manifest in earlier therapsids is especially mammal-like, and in few proper therapsids was the succession of teeth reduced to one or two generations as it is in mammals. Among primitive therocephalians, cheek teeth were commonly numerous and simple, and in many there were a pair of enlarged caniniform teeth, one behind the other, instead of a single one. One line of advanced therocephalians, the whaitsiids, enlarged the anterior incisiform teeth to match the caniniforms, and eliminated the cheek teeth altogether. The bauriamorphs, therocephalian derivatives, had a caniniform tooth little larger than the big incisiforms, but paralleled some cynodonts in their flat-crowned, crushing, cheek teeth. Gorgonopsians showed a strong emphasis on front teeth, but tended to enlarge the single caniniform tooth into a saber, anticipating the saber-toothed cats of the Pleistocene Epoch. Also, as in saber-toothed cats, the gorgonopsian caniniform tooth was commonly protected by a ventral flange on the dentary, the cheek teeth were reduced, and the joint was modified to accommodate an extraordinarily wide gape (Parrington, 1955). Dinocephalians tended to have large teeth, all of a size and shape, concentrated at the front of the jaws. In the herbivorous tapinocephalids, the teeth had peculiarly concave crowns and evidently provided a mechanism for cropping and crushing. In the predatory titanosuchians, the teeth were bladelike or conical and formed a tearing mechanism by which the animals dispatched prey of their own size. In dicynodonts, except for a pair of maxillary tusks in many forms, dentitions were effectively displaced by a horn-covered beak like that of a turtle. Although this pattern was most unmammal-like, tusk growth was very similar to a mode common among advanced mammals: it was continuous throughout the life of the individual, and the tusk was never replaced.

The evolution of the therapsid skull and jaw combined radical changes in proportion with a conservative tendency to retain the ancestral number of bones, which suffered neither loss nor fusion. Even that most mammal-like of trends, the rebuilding of the middle ear, was largely a matter of changing proportions. The dentary was enlarged at the expense of the postdentary bones; and stapes, quadrate, and quadratojugal were reduced concomitantly—but it was reduction, not loss, of postdentary bones that was characteristic of the process. Other changes of similar nature foreshadowing the mammalian condition were the development of special flanges on premaxilla, maxilla, and palatine to form a secondary palate, and the intrusion of the parietal, at the expense of the postorbital and squamosal, to form the medial border of the temporal fenestra.

Cephalic trends toward a mammalian morphology do not indicate any significant enlargement of the brain before a definitive mammalian condition was reached (Fig. 7). Jerison (1969) shows that there are two distinct correlations between brain and body size, one for "lower vertebrates"—fish, amphibians, and reptiles—the other for "higher vertebrates"—birds and mammals. Among the lower vertebrates, there is a single set of brain-to-body relationships, as though there were no selection for significant increase in the proportion of the brain through time. Jerison's work shows that all Mesozoic reptiles, therapsids as well as the giant dinosaurs, remained within the limits of brain-to-body-size characteristic of the lower vertebrates.

Evolutionary trends visible in the therapsids encourage speculation about certain developments that cannot be seen in the fossil remains, notably, endothermy. Highly evolved cheek teeth indicate that in Triassic times some of the advanced cynodonts and tritylodonts comminuted their food into small pieces before swallowing it, thereby making it available for quick transformation into energy. This interpretation is reinforced by the secondary palate, a device that allows for simultaneous breathing and eating, and by the differentiation of a lumbar region, pointing, albeit faintly, to the existence of a diaphragm. Collectively, these features suggest that advanced cynodonts and tritylodonts were active animals with a high rate of metabolism; therefore, it is quite possible that the later and more mammal-like of the therapsids were endothermic, or at least partially so.

Being small, would they not have needed an insulating coat of hair in order to maintain en-

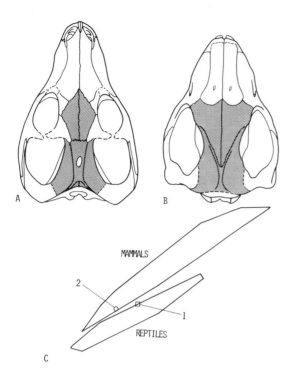

Figure 7. A. Dorsal view of the skull of the Lower Triassic theriodont, *Thrinaxodon*. B. Dorsal view of the skull of the Paleocene mammal, *Ptilodus*. The frontal and parietal bones forming the roof of the braincase are shaded. This indicates the much enlarged brain in an archaic mammal as compared with an advanced therapsid reptile. C. Brain-to-body-size relations shown as minimum convex polygons for living reptiles and mammals. The positions of an advanced Triassic therapsid reptile, *Thrinaxodon* (1), and a primitive Jurassic mammal, *Triconodon,* are superimposed on the reptile and mammal polygons, respectively. (A, after Estes, 1961; B, after Simpson; C, after Hopson, 1967.)

dothermy? It has been suggested that in certain therapsids, notably *Ericiolacerta,* the presence of minute foramina on the premaxilla and maxilla are possible indications "that the skin of the face was sensory" (Watson, 1931), and that perhaps vibrissae were present. If they were, then very probably there was a body covering of hair (but see Bennett and Ruben, this volume).

Thus, during the Triassic Period, certain therapsids were trending strongly toward a mammalian condition, just as the group as a whole was declining in diversity and abundance. To better understand this apparent anomaly, let us take a brief look at their rivals, the archosaurs, who were on the rise during this interval.

The Rise of the Archosaurs

A part of the concomitant rise of archosaurs and decline of therapsids can be explained in terms of energy. Pervasive evolutionary trends among theriodont therapsids toward higher rates of metabolism are not duplicated among archosaurs, which may have retained metabolic rates more nearly characteristic of the reptiles we know. In the worldwide tropical and subtropical climates of those days, the archosaurs were able to compete with theriodonts with the expenditure of much less energy.

The saurischian and ornithischian dinosaurs, which became totally dominant during later Mesozoic times, arose from Triassic bipeds (Fig. 8A). They walked and ran on long, birdlike hind limbs, which was a very effective means of getting around in open country, and may have given archosaurs a greater flexibility, including perhaps the freeing of the forelimbs for food gathering. The dinosaurs enjoyed a degree of mobility that was probably beyond the capabilities of most therapsids, which, being uncompromisingly quadrupedal, were probably not particularly agile. Dinosaurs, ranging far and wide, were able to preempt many of the available habitats, and thus were increasingly successful with time. Therapsids were progressively crowded from the lands.

Dicynodonts were among the last to go. Though reduced in numbers, these therapsids lived on into Late Triassic times as very large reptiles. They were herbivores, filling a role in Late Triassic faunas that was to be assumed by large herbivorous dinosaurs in later ages. Dicynodonts were extremely successful in this role, perhaps so much so that they were crowded out only after dinosaurs too had acquired the knack of subsisting on vegetation.

The First Mammals

Except for tritylodonts, which bridged the gap between the end of the Triassic and the beginning of the Jurassic, therapsids became extinct with the close of Triassic history. In a sense, however, their disappearance was not complete, because of the survival of their derivatives, the mammals (Fig. 8B, C) The first mammals, which appeared in late Triassic time, seem to have been derived from cynodont ancestors.

Several genera of late Triassic mammals, such as *Erythrotherium, Eozostrodon, Megazostrodon,* and *Morganucodon,* are known from Europe, South Africa, and Asia, and are styled "morganucodonts," collectively. All were very small, and they seem to have been able to isolate themselves from their larger cynodont relatives as

E. H. COLBERT

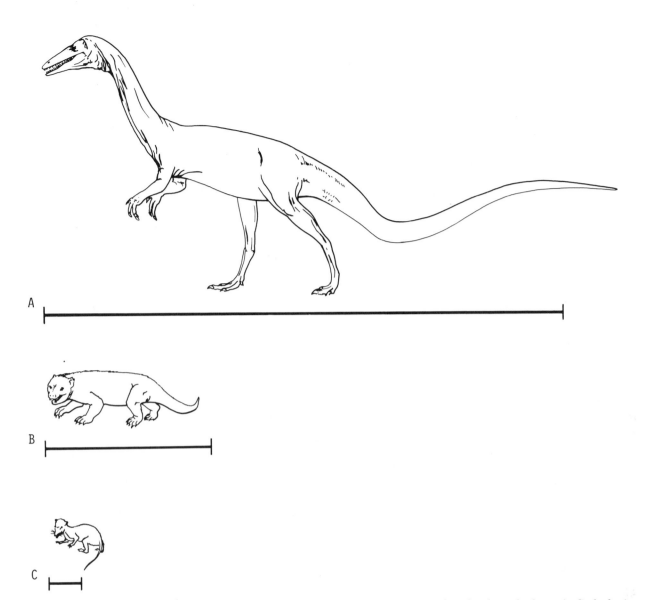

Figure 8. Late Triassic tetrapods, drawn approximately to scale, with comparative lengths shown by bars. A. *Coelophysis*, a carnivorous theropod dinosaur, one of the dominant members of its fauna. B. A herbivorous tritylodont, an advanced therapsid reptile, occupying a secondary ecological niche. C. *Megazostrodon*, a mammal, probably insectivorous and probably crepuscular, living in secluded microhabitats. (A, B, after Colbert, 1948; C, after Crompton, Taylor, and Jagger, 1978.)

well as from the ubiquitous early dinosaurs and other archosaurs.

Crompton, Taylor, and Jagger (1978) propose that the first Triassic mammals arose from their cynodont ancestors largely because of a change from a diurnal to a nocturnal style of life. The invasion of a nocturnal ecology niche, perhaps hitherto not widely exploited by tetrapods, may have been made possible by the development of endothermy, which released these first mammals from dependence upon the ambient temperatures of their environment. As suggested by Crompton, Taylor, and Jagger (1978) the relatively constant body temperature in the morganucodonts may

have been lower than in many modern mammals, by as much as 10° C. Nevertheless, the constancy of their temperatures would have enabled them to be active in chilly, nighttime environments. It is further suggested that being nocturnal, the visual sense was subordinated to hearing and smell, and consequently the brain was increased to cope with additional information received through the nostrils and the ears. This scenario is based on what is known of the morphology of the skeleton of Upper Triassic morganucodonts, on comparison of mammals with other living tetrapods with respect to the neuroanatomy of the special senses, and on details of thermoregulation in tenrecs and other "primitive" mammals.

Mammalian features of such Triassic genera as *Morganucodon* and *Megazostrodon* were probably coming into being in therapsids of which we have as yet no fossil remains. They clearly have roots in known advanced cynodonts. Such therapsids were evolving in a direction that was to assure the survival of their descendants through the long Mesozoic Period as contemporaries, but not as competitors, of the ascendant and dominant archosaurs.

Notes

1. The traditional usage of "Gondwanaland" is redundant, since Gondwana means "Land of the Gonds". "Gondwanaland" is, however, so firmly established in the literature that it probably will refuse to die.

2. Three general stratigraphic levels are recognized in this discussion: Upper Permian, Lower Triassic, and Upper Triassic. For the Permian, the major subdivisions are treated as Lower and Upper, following a stratigraphic convention in wide current use. The alternatives are to recognize three subdivisions, Lower, Middle, and Upper, a common practice among vertebrate paleontologists, or four subdivisions, Wolfcampian, Leonardian, Guadalupian, and Ochoan, an arrangement that is favored by American paleontologists, paleobontanists, and stratigraphers. In this paper, following Olson (1962), the division between the Lower and Upper Permian is drawn between the Leonardian and Guadalupian. This places the Lower Beaufort beds of South Africa and Zones I–IV of the USSR in the Upper Permian.

The type Triassic consists of the Buntsandstein, Muschelkalk, and Keuper, the first and third subdivisions being continental sediments containing terrestrial tetrapods, the middle subdivision being a marine facies with numerous invertebrates, fishes, and certain aquatic reptiles. It is difficult to equate terrestrial sediments containing tetrapods found in other parts of the world with the type Middle Triassic rocks and fossils. Such deposits as have been defined as of Middle Triassic age—for example, the Upper Ruhuhu and Manda beds of Africa and the Ischigualasto and Santa Maria beds of South America—can perfectly well be placed within the lower part of the Upper Triassic, as indeed has been done by various authorities.

Acknowledgments

The illustrations for this paper were made by Pamela Lungé, under the supervision of the author.

References

Appleby, R. M.; Charig, A. J.; Cox, C. B.; Kermack, K. A.; and Tarlo, L. B. H.
1967. Reptilia. In *The Fossil Record,* Geol. Soc. London, pp. 695–731. 1967.

Bakker, R. T.
1975. Dinosaur renaissance. *Scientific American* 232(4): 58–78.

Brink, A. S.
1956. Speculations on some advanced mammalian characteriatics in the higher mammal-like reptiles. *Palaeont. Africana* 4:77–96.

Broom, R.
1932. *The Mammal-like Reptiles of South Africa and the Origin of Mammals.* London: H. F. and G. Witherby.

Butler, P. M.; Clemens, W. A.; Graham, S. F.; Hooijer, D. A.; Kermack, K. A.; Patterson, B.; Ride, W. D. L.; Russell, D. E.; Savage, R. J. G.; Simons, E. L.; Tarlo, L. B. H.; Thaler, L.; and Whitworth, T.
1967. Mammalia. In *The Fossil Record,* Geol. Soc. London, pp. 763–87.

Colbert, E. H.
1948. The mammal-like reptile *Lycaenops. Bull. Amer. Mus. Nat. Hist.* 89:353–404.
1980. *Evolution of the Vertebrates.* Third Edition. New York: John Wiley and Sons.

Cox, C. B.
1967. Changes in terrestrial vertebrate faunas during the Mesozoic. In *The Fossil Record,* Geol. Soc. London, pp. 77–89.

Crompton, A. W.
1958. The cranial morphology of a new genus and species of ictidosaurian. *Proc. Zool. Soc. London* 130(2):183–216.
1968. The engima of the evolution of mammals. *Optima,* (Sept):137–51.

Crompton, A. W. and Jenkins, F. A., Jr.
1973. Mammals from reptiles: a review of mammalian origins. In *Ann. Rev. Of Earth and Planet. Sci.* 1:131–55.

Crompton, A. W.; Taylor, C. R.; and Jagger, J. A.
1978. Evolution of homeothermy in mammals. *Nature* 272:333–36.

Dietz, R. S., and Holden, J. C.
1970. The breakup of Pangaea. *Sci. Amer.* 223:30–41.

E. H. COLBERT

Efremov, I. A.
1954. Fauna of terrestrial vertebrates from the Permian copper sandstones of the U.S.S.R. *Trans. Paleont. Inst. Acad. Sciences U.S.S.R.* 54:1–416. (in Russian).

Estes, R.
1961. Cranial anatomy of the cynodont reptile *Thrinaxodon liorhinus. Bull. Mus. Comp. Zool.* 125:165–180.

Hallam, A.
1967. The bearing of certain palaeozoogeographic data on continental drift. *Palaeogeogr., Palaeoclimatol., Palaeoecol.* 3:201–41.

Haughton, S. H., and Brink, A. S.
1954. A bibliographical list of Reptilia from the Karroo beds of Africa. *Palaeont. Africana* 2.

Hopson, J. A.
1967. Mammal-like reptiles and the origin of mammals. *Discovery* 2:25–33.

Hopson, J. A., and Crompton, A. W.
1969. Origin of mammals. *Evolutionary Biology* 3:15–72.

Hopson, J. A., and Kitching, J. W.
1972. A revised classification of cynodonts (Reptilia; Therapsida). *Palaeontologica Africana* 14:71–85.

von Huene, F.
1940. Die Saurier der Karroo-Gondwana-und verwandten Ablagerungen in faunistischer, biologischer und phylogenetischer Hinsicht. *Neuen Jahrb. f. Min., Geol. und Pal.* 83(B):246–347.

Jenkins, F. A., Jr.,
1971. The postcranial skeleton of African cynodonts. *Bull. Peabody Museum of Natural History* 36:1–216.

Jerison, H. J.
1969. Brain evolution and dinosaur brains. *Amer. Nat.* 103:575–88.
1971. More on why birds and mammals have big brains. *Amer. Nat.* 105:185–89.

Kemp, T. S.
1980. Origin of the mammal-like reptiles. *Nature* 283:378–380.

Kitching, J. W.
1968. On the *Lystrosaurus* zone and its fauna with special reference to some immature Lystrosauridae. *Palaeont. Africana* 11:61–76.

Olson, E. C.
1957. Catalogue of localities of Permian and Triassic terrestrial vertebrates of the territories of the U.S.S.R. *Journal. Geol.* 65:196–226.
1962. Late Permian Terrestrial Vertebrates, U.S.A. and U.S.S.R. *Trans. Amer. Philos. Soc.,* N. S. 52(2):1–224.
1976. The exploitation of land by early tetrapods. In *Morphology and Biology of Reptiles,* ed. A. d'A Bellairs and C. Barry Cox, p. 1–30. *Linnean Soc. Symp. Series.* No. 3.

Parrington, F. R.
1955. On the cranial anatomy of some gorgonopsids and the synapsid middle ear. *Proc. Zool. Soc. London* 125(1):1–40.

Pivetau, J., ed.
1961. *Traité de Paléontologie,* Tome 6, vol. 1. Paris: Masson et Cie.

Romer, A. S.
1956. *Osteology of the Reptiles.* Chicago: University of Chicago Press.
1966. *Vertebrate Paleontology,* 3d ed. Chicago: University of Chicago Press.

Watson, D. M. S.
1931. On the skeleton of a bauriamorph reptile. *Proc. Zool. Soc. London* 1931(3):1163–1205.

Wegener, A.
1966. *The Origin of Continents and Oceans.* Transl. from 4th Ed. (1929) by John Biram. New York: Dover Publications, Inc.

BIOLOGICAL PROBLEMS
AND
THERAPSID SOLUTIONS

PHILIP S. ULINSKI

Department of Anatomy and Committee on
Neurobiology
The University of Chicago
Chicago, Illinois 60637

Neurobiology of the Therapsid–Mammal Transition

Introduction

There is good evidence that therapsids were experimenting with suites of structural changes in the late Permian and early Triassic and that one or more lineages of advanced therapsids underwent a transition from a reptilian grade of organization to a mammalian grade of organization by the late Triassic (e.g., Crompton and Jenkins, 1979; Kemp, 1982). This transition must have involved coordinated modifications in most of the organ systems. Modifications of the architecture of the limbs and vertebrae allowed increased flexibility of the shoulder and the adoption of a posture in which the limbs are held close to the body, in contrast to the sprawling posture seen in amphibians and reptiles (e.g., Jenkins and Parrington, 1976; Jenkins, 1973). Shifts in metabolic strategy reflected an increased ability for sustained activity (Regal, 1978; Bennett, 1980). A remodeling of inner and middle ears permitted an extension of the range of audible sounds (Stebbins, 1980). Development of morphologically heterogeneous teeth (e.g., Osborn, 1973) and changes in the musculoskeletal system of the jaws reflected changes in feeding mechanics (e.g., Crompton and Parker 1978). Changes took place in reproductive patterns and the endocrine system, with the development of viviparity and suckling (e.g., Lillegraven, 1979). The integument was modified by the appearance of hair. Each of these changes must have required significant, parallel changes in the central nervous system.

An understanding of these changes is important to an overall concept of the evolution of mammals and to an appreciation of the biology of mammals. However, it is clearly more difficult to study evolutionary changes in the nervous system than in skeletal systems. Can anything be said about the nature of neural changes in the therapsid-mammal transition?

Data from the Fossil Record

Fossil endocasts provide a sketch of the changes that took place in the shape of the brain from the stem reptiles, throughout the evolution of the diapsid and synapsid reptiles and in early mammals (see Hopson, 1979). Several relevant endocasts are shown in dorsal view in Figure 1. The endocast of *Diadectes,* a genus close to the stem reptiles, is shown at the bottom of the figure. It suggests a very narrow midbrain and forebrain (Hopson, 1979). If this condition held generally, members of the basal reptilian stock may have had tubular forebrains that anatomically resembled the forebrains of Recent lungfishes and amphibians. Unfortunately, it may be unwise to use amphibian forebrains as a model for the functional organization of the forebrains of stem reptiles because of the possibility that the central nervous system of Recent amphibians shows substantial secondary simplifications, comparable to those that occurred within their skeletal system. In any case, there is no sign in the stem reptiles of the forebrain shapes characteristic of either Recent reptiles or Recent mammals.

The stem reptiles gave rise to many lineages, three of which survive as Recent reptiles. In the archosaurian reptiles (now represented by crocodilians), it appears that some pseudosuchians of the Middle Triassic may have had a narrow midbrain and forebrain, while the aetosaurid *Desmatosuchus* (Fig. 1) of the Late Triassic and the crocodilian *Sebecus* of the Eocene show forebrain proportions comparable to those of Recent crocodilians (Hopson, 1979). There was a clear expansion of the forebrain in several lines of archosaurs by the Middle Jurassic (Hopson, 1979). The situation is not known in ancient lepidosaurs (which are survived by snakes, *Sphenodon,* and lizards). The turtles show an expansion of their forebrain by the Late Cretaceous (Hopson, 1979). It seems likely, then, that reptiles in at least several of the evolutionary lines leading to the Recent groups showed an expansion of the forebrain throughout the Mesozoic.

Within the synapsid reptiles (which include the therapsids), endocasts from pelycosaurs show a narrow midbrain and forebrain (Case, 1897; Hopson, 1979). Similarly, therapsid endocasts,

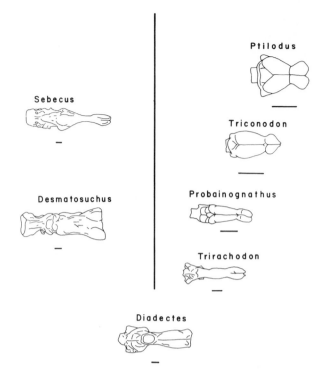

Figure 1. Endocasts of the brains of fossil reptiles and mammals. Drawings show the endocasts in dorsal view. *Diadectes* is a form close to the stem reptiles. Endocasts from diapsid reptiles are shown to the left of the vertical line. Endocasts from synapsid reptiles *(Trirachodon, Probainognathus)* and mammals *(Triconodon, Ptilodus)* are shown to the right of the line. The scale bars are all 1 cm. *(Diadectes, Desmatosuchus,* and *Sebecus,* based on figures in Hopson, 1979; *Trirachodon* and *Probainognathus,* based on Quiroga, 1979, 1980a; *Tricondon* and *Ptilodus,* on figures in Jerison, 1973.)

including those of the cynodonts *Probainognathus* (Fig. 1), *Trirachodon* (Fig. 1), *Massetognathus,* and *Probelesodon* (Quiroga, 1979, 1980a, b), show a telencephalon consisting of a pair of elongate tubes (Hopson, 1979).

By contrast, endocasts of Mesozoic mammals typically reveal an expansion or widening of the forebrain. The expansion is slight in the triconodont, *Triconodon* (Fig. 1), but more extensive in the multituberculate, *Ptilodus* (Fig. 1), and in later mammals (Simpson, 1927, 1937; Edinger, 1956, 1964; Jerison, 1973; Hopson, 1979; Quiroga, 1979, 1980a). Endocasts from placental mammals throughout the Cenozoic era show large cerebral hemispheres (Jerison, 1973). It is possible in some cases to trace the progressive development of the sulcal patterns that are characteristic of the various orders of marsupial (Haight and Murray, 1981) and placental mammals (e.g., Radinsky, 1975a, b; 1977).

It has been known for some time that there is an orderly relation between brain weights and body weights across the range of vertebrates. Jerison (1973) has shown in a recent formulation that brain weights and body weights for each class of vertebrates fall within a circumscribed area (called a minimum convex polygon) on double logarithmic plots of brain weight versus body weight. The polygon for reptiles lies significantly below the polygon for mammals (Platel, 1979). The ratios of brain weight to body weight for therapsids lie at the upper edge of, or perhaps slightly above, the polygon for reptiles (Hopson, 1980; Quiroga, 1979, 1980a, b) and may have overlapped those of mammals (Kemp, 1982).

To summarize, the data available from the fossil record suggest that the stem reptiles, pelycosaurs, and at least most of the therapsids had narrow forebrains, and that expansion of the forebrain coincided with the evolution of the Mesozoic mammals. There was likely a parallel but independent expansion of the forebrain in those evolutionary lines leading from the stem reptiles to the various groups of Recent reptiles.

Analyzing Changes in Neural Organization

Endocast data provide but a vague picture of the evolution of the brain through the therapsid-mammal transition. The greatest limitation is that the fossil record provides no information about the neuronal structure of the brains of extinct vertebrates. I have proposed (Ulinski, 1980a) that vertebrate nervous systems contain three levels of organization: The lowest level consists of individual neurons, the second level consists of groups of neurons that interact with each other to form functional units or modules, while the highest level is the network of interconnected nuclei and fiber pathways. Although evolutionary changes undoubtedly occur simultaneously at all three organization levels, it seems probable that changes at the network level are most characteristic of major evolutionary shifts, such as the therapsid-mammal transition. It is reasonable then to focus on changes in the network of neural connections related to the forebrain expansion that may have accompanied the therapsid-mammal transition.

Because of the ancestral relationship between reptiles and mammals, it may appear that the brains of living reptiles can be viewed as precursors of the brains of mammals, to be used to deduce the nature of neural changes involved in the therapsid-mammal transition. However, it is now accepted that synapsid reptiles diverged very early from the stem reptiles and therefore

from the evolutionary lines leading to the ancestors of the major groups of Recent reptiles. In particular, the fossil record suggests that the forebrain expanded independently in the synapsid reptiles, in the diapsid reptiles, and in turtles. There is no reason to assume a priori that the pattern of nervous system organization seen in Recent reptiles is anything like that found in therapsids, and every reason to think that patterns characteristic of Recent reptiles evolved in directions different from those of therapsids and mammals. It is sometimes argued (see Northcutt, 1971) that because turtles are closer than diapsid reptiles to the origins of the mammalian lineage, their pattern of brain organization is closer to that of remote mammalian ancestors. This argument is hard to challenge because of the obscurity of turtle ancestry (e.g. Carroll, 1969), but it does not indicate that turtles are close enough to the origin of pelycosaurs to warrant using their brain patterns as models for those of synapsids.

An alternative approach to the problem of understanding changes in the central nervous system during the therapsid-mammal transition is to examine the Recent mammals and ascertain which features of brain organization are unique to all of the three major groups. The first group are the prototherian mammals that at one time included diverse elements such as triconodonts and multituberculates, but are now represented only by the egg-laying monotremes (Giffiths, 1978), the duckbilled platypus and the echidnas of Australia. The second group consists of marsupial mammals that bear live, but very immature, young (e.g., Hunsaker, 1977). Third are the placental mammals that have relatively long intrauterine gestation periods.

The current view is that the prototherian and therian mammals (the marsupials and placentals) diverged from each other soon after the therapsid-mammal transition (Marshall, 1979), while the marsupial and placental lines diverged much later. It is likely that features found uniquely in all three groups of Recent mammals, but absent in other tetrapods, evolved within the lines leading to the prototherian and therian mammals. Similarly, features or characters common to both placental and marsupial mammals, but absent from monotremes, may have evolved after the differentiation of therian and prototherian mammals. The logic of this argument is borrowed from that of cladistics or phylogenetic systematics (see Eldredge and Cracraft, 1980). The basic idea of the cladistic approach is to use

Recent reptiles as an outgroup that can be compared to the two sister groups (prototherians and therians) of Recent mammals, rather than as representatives of the ancestors of mammals. The approach cannot recreate the history of the therapsid-mammal transition, but it can provide insights into the biology of mammals by helping to specify the cluster of neural characters that are distinctively mammalian, and to understand the functional implications of the mammalian pattern of neural organization.

The next section of the paper is, therefore, an analysis of some features of neural organization that are characteristic of Recent mammals. Although there are mammalian aspects to each of the brain's major systems, the most obvious differences between the brains of Recent mammals and Recent reptiles occur in the thalamus and the telencephalon. The thalamus is a major component of the diencephalon that links ascending pathways from the spinal cord, lower brainstem, and retina to the telecephalon. The traditional view has been that differentiation of sensory nuclei in the thalamus and telencephalon was the key step in the evolution of the mammalian pattern of brain organization (e.g., Herrick, 1948). However, I will argue that differentiated sensory regions of the thalamus and telencephalon are a basic tetrapod characteristic (see Northcut, 1981, and Ebbesson, 1972, for a review of this idea), and will instead emphasize differences between mammals and nonmammals in those forebrain structures that are directly involved in the control of movement. This leads to the speculation in the last section of the paper that functional changes in the organization of motor systems were a major correlate of the therapsid-mammal transition.

What is Different about the Brains of Mammals?

Thalamus

The thalamus in mammals is typically a large structure that contains a number of discrete nuclei (Fig. 2). Our conception of these nuclei has changed drastically during the past few years due to the application of the newer axonal tracing techniques (see Heimer and Robards, 1981). A formal classification of thalamic nuclei is consequently premature at this time. I will simply arrange thalamic nuclei into six groups on the basis of their afferent connections and relation to the telencephalon in a way that is convenient for this discussion (Fig. 3). We can then inquire

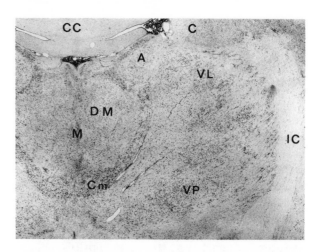

Figure 2. Thalamus in a monkey. A cross section through the thalamus in a rhesus macaque illustrates some of the major thalamic nuclei. The ventroposterior nucleus (VP) is a specific sensory nucleus. The ventrolateral nucleus (VL) is a specific motor nucleus. The centromedian nucleus (Cm) is an intralaminar nucleus. The anterior (A) and dorsomedial (DM) nuclei are limbic nuclei; the midline nuclei (M) are diffusely projecting nuclei. Other abbreviations: C, caudate nucleus; CC, corpus callosum; IC, internal capsule.

which of these groups of nuclei are unique to mammals.

1. Specific sensory nuclei are thalamic nuclei that receive afferents of a single sensory modality and project to a single, specific sensory area of the telencephalon. In placental mammals (see Jones, 1981, for a general review), they are situated caudally in the ventral half of the thalamus and include parts of the dorsal lateral geniculate nucleus (which receives direct retinal projections), the ventrobasal nucleus (which receives somatosensory information from both the head and postcranial body), and the ventral division of the medial geniculate nucleus (which receives auditory information from the inferior colliculus of the midbrain). In addition, certain parts of the pulvinar or lateral posterior nuclei are included in this category; they are "tectorecipient" nuclei that receive visual information from the pretectum (Graybiel and Berson, 1980). The same pattern of sensory nuclei is seen in the thalamus of marsupials (Johnson, 1977). The situation in monotremes is incompletely known, but dorsal lateral geniculate (Campbell and Hayhow, 1971, 1972) and ventrobasal (Welker and Lende, 1980) nuclei have been identified.

It is commonly assumed that these specific sensory nuclei are derived and typically mammalian characters. The dominant idea has been that the primitive condition was a thalamus that lacked segregated sensory nuclei and received,

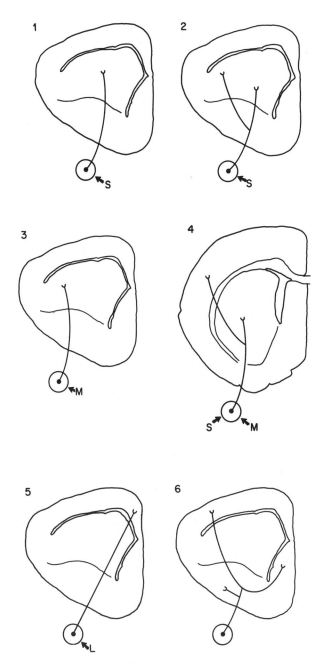

Figure 3.   Patterns of thalamotelencephalic projections. The projections of the six types of thalamotelencephalic projections are illustrated. Each figure shows projections from a thalamic nucleus (represented by a circle) to the telencephalon (represented by cross sections through the telencephalon of a lizard in numbers 1,2,3,5, and 6 and a rat in number 4).

Key: **S,** sensory inputs; **M,** cerebellar or striatal inputs; **L,** limbic system inputs.

instead, convergent inputs from the various sensory modalities (Herrick, 1922; Diamond and Hall, 1969). Evolution towards a mammalian grade involved the differentiation of specific sensory nuclei out of this multimodal matrix. A more recent variation of this idea considers that

the visual thalamus consisted at one stage of a pool of neurons that received convergent inputs from several visual pathways (Ebbesson, 1972, 1980). Specific nuclei, such as the dorsal lateral geniculate nucleus and the pulvinar, evolved by a process of parcellation or segregation from this common pool.

The idea of a multimodal thalamus was based on rather meagre evidence because it was impossible at the time of its formulation to trace out most of the pathways in the brains of nonmammals. However, the advent of Nauta degeneration and autoradiographic tracing techniques in the 1950s, 1960s, and 1970s made it possible to test the hypothesis of a multimodal thalamus by examining the afferents to the thalamus from each of the major sensory systems in a range of vetebrates. The hypothesis predicts that specific sensory nuclei would be present in derived forms and absent from primitive forms. The hypothesis has been essentially falsified in that specific sensory nuclei have been identified in each of the vertebrate groups that have been studied (Ebbesson, Jane, and Schroeder, 1972).

As an example, Figure 4 shows a section through the caudal thalamus of *Caiman,* a crocodilian reptile. A visual nucleus is situated medially in the thalamus and receives projections from the optic tectum. This is called nucleus rotundus in reptiles and birds (Fig. 4, Ro). An auditory nucleus, which has different names in different species, is generally identifiable near the midline of the caudal thalamus and receives projections from the auditory midbrain (e.g., Fig. 4, Re). Somatosensory nuclei have been less extensively studied, but a nucleus in the caudal (Fig. 4, MP) or the rostral ventral thalamus often receives ascending spinal projections. Again, the name of this nucleus varies among species. Finally, a second visual nucleus is situated immediately medial to the optic tract in the rostral thalamus. It receives direct retinal input and is usually called the *dorsolateral geniculate nucleus.* This nucleus is not shown in Fig. 4.

The pool parcellation hypothesis also now seems inapplicable to patterns of thalamic organization. It arose from the observation that certain vertebrates, such as sharks, snakes, and salamanders, lack distinct retinorecipient and tectorecipient thalamic nuclei (Ebbesson, 1972). Instead, a single thalamic nucleus seems to receive convergent projections from both the retina and optic tectum. However, reexamination of thalamic afferents in sharks and snakes, using more recent and sensitive tracing techniques,

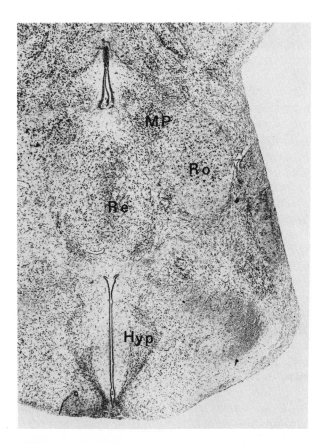

Figure 4. Thalamus in a reptile. A cross section through the thalamus in *Caiman* illustrates some of the major thalamic nuclei. Nucleus rotundus (Ro) receives visual input via the optic tectum. Nucleus reuniens (Re) receives auditory inputs via the torus semicircularis. Nucleus medialis posterior (MP) receives somatosensory inputs via the dorsal column nuclei and spinal cord. Other abbreviation: HYP, hypothalamus.

suggests that both retinorecipient and tectorecipient nuclei are present in both taxa. Smeets (1981a, b) and Luiten (1981a, b) have recently presented evidence that adjacent thalamic nuclei receive direct retinal and tectal projections, respectively, in sharks and rays. These two nuclei then project to distinct regions of the forebrain in nurse sharks. Dacey and Ulinski (1982) have shown that garter snakes have a distinct tectorecipient nucleus (nucleus rotundus) that is situated in the caudal thalamus and projects to the telencephalon. Nucleus rotundus is distinct from the dorsal lateral geniculate nucleus, which is present more rostrally and receives direct retinal input.

Thus, specific sensory nuclei can be defined on the basis of their afferent connections in all of the vertebrate groups that have been adequately studied. The efferent projections of the specific sensory nuclei cannot be treated until the organization of the telencephalon has been discussed,

but the basic point is that they have projections to specific sensory areas in the telencephalon. It would appear, then, that the existence of discrete channels, by which information from the visual, auditory, and somatosensory systems reach the telencephalon, is a basic, vertebrate characteristic and is not unique to mammals.

2. Multi-areal nuclei receive afferents from a particular sensory modality and project to two or more specific sensory areas of the telencephalon. They surround the specific sensory nuclei in the caudal thalamus and include the posterior nuclei and certain parts of the dorsal lateral geniculate complex. The medial component of the posterior nuclei, for example, receives projections from several somatosensory pathways and projects to two somatosensory areas in the cerebral cortex (e.g., Rockel, Heath, and Jones, 1972); Feldman and Kruger, 1980; Donoghue and Ebner, 1981a, b; Haight and Neylon, 1978; Spreafico, Hayes, and Rustioni, 1981). Lateral components of the posterior nuclear group receive projections from the inferior colliculus and project to several areas of auditory cortex (e.g., Anderson, Knight, and Merzenich, 1980; Andersen et al., 1980). The most ventral components of the dorsal lateral geniculate nuclei in cats (the C laminae) receive projections from specific groups of retinal ganglion cells and project to several of the visual areas in the cerebral cortex (e.g., Guillery et al., 1980; Geisert, 1980). Multi-areal nuclei have been identified in placental and marsupial mammals, but not—thus far—in monotremes (Ulinski, 1981). Experimental investigations of thalamotelencephalic projections in nonmammals have not yet been sufficiently detailed to determine if multi-areal nuclei are present.

3. Specific motor nuclei receive afferents from the cerebellum or basal ganglia and project to restricted regions of the telencephalon (e.g., Sakai, 1982; Grofova, 1979). They are situated rostrally in the ventral half of the thalamus and include the ventral lateral nucleus (which receives projections from the cerebellum) and the ventral anterior nucleus (which receive projections from the basal ganglia). They have been identified in placental, marsupial (e.g., Bodian, 1942), and monotreme (Welker and Lende, 1980) mammals. The efferent projections of the cerebellum and basal telencephalon have been studied only sporadically in nonmammals. Relatively small nuclei receive cerebellar or basal telencephalic projections in pigeons (Kitt and Brauth, 1981), but distinct thalamic nuclei that receive specific motor projections have not been generally identified

P. S. ULINSKI

in nonmammals. Well-developed specific motor nuclei may, then, be characteristic of mammals.

4. Intralaminar nuclei receive afferents from the various sensory modalities as well as from the cerebellum and basal ganglia. They lie embedded in a fibrous lamina, dorsal to the specific sensory and motor nuclei, and include the centromedian and centrolateral nuclei. Neurons in the intralaminar nuclei project to both the cerebral cortex and basal ganglia (Jones and Leavitt, 1975). Intralaminar nuclei are found in placental and marsupial (e.g., Donoghue and Ebner, 1981b) mammals, but have not been seen in monotremes (Ulinski, 1981). Although some authors have tentatively identified connectional or functional equivalents to the intralaminar nuclei of mammals in Recent reptiles (e.g., Belekhova, 1979), there is no consensus that these nuclei exist in nonmammals. The intralaminar nuclei may then be characteristic of at least placental and marsupial mammals.

5. Limbic nuclei receive afferents from specific pathways in the *limbic system*, a set of structures in the forebrain that play a general role in regulating the internal environment through the autonomic nervous and endocrine systems (e.g., Brodal, 1981). In mammals the limbic thalamic nuclei include the anterior nuclear group and the dorsomedial nucleus, and lie dorsal or medial to the intralaminar nuclei. Each nucleus projects to areas of the limbic cortex of the cingulate gyrus (e.g., Robertson and Kaitz, 1981). The limbic nuclei are present in all three groups of mammals. In reptiles, neither cortical areas corresponding to the limbic cortex of the mammalian cingulate gyrus, nor limbic nuclei have yet been identified with certainty. There are, however, indications of projections to the thalamus from possible limbic structures in recent reptiles (e.g., Halpern, 1980). Much more work is needed to confirm or deny the existence of limbic nuclei in reptiles, but it may be predicted tentatively that such nuclei will be found not unique to mammals.

6. Diffusely projecting nuclei have included intralaminar and reticular as well as midline nuclei at one time or another. Here the term is restricted to the nuclei that lie on the midline of the thalamus, including the ventromedial nucleus and nucleus reuniens, that have unusually widespread projections to the telencephalon (Herkenham, 1978, 1979). Diffusely projecting nuclei have been demonstrated in turtles (Balaban and Ulinski, 1981a) and tegu lizards (Lohman and van Woerden-Verkley, 1978) and, therefore, are not unique to mammals.

To tally the score, specific sensory nuclei, diffusely projecting nuclei, and perhaps limbic nuclei have been demonstrated in nonmammals and are probably general tetrapod, if not vertebrate, features. There is not enough information to decide the status of the multi-areal nuclei, but they may be characteristic of placental and marsupial mammals. There is no clear evidence for well-developed specific motor and intralaminar nuclei in nonmammals, and these may be typical of at least therian mammals. It is important to the central point here that the specific motor (e.g., Porter, 1975) and intralaminar (e.g., Schlag, Lehtinen, and Schlag-Rey, 1974) nuclei are involved in the neural circuits that control movement, but it is necessary to consider the organization of the telencephalon before discussing the functional implications of these differences in the thalamic nuclei of mammals and nonmammals.

Telencephalon

The telencephalon is a simple, closed tube in the early embryonic stages of all vertebrates that is modified into paired cerebral hemispheres during development (see Northcutt, 1981, for a general review). In sharks, lungfishes, and the tetrapods, the walls of the telencephalic vesicles evaginate or balloon out to form paired hemispheres, each of which contains a lateral ventricle. Each hemisphere is quadrangular in cross-section in early embryos (Fig. 5A, B). This configuration is retained into adulthood in lungfishes and amphibians. It is subsequently modified in reptiles, birds, and mammals, but the embryonic configuration serves to define three fundamental components of the telencephalon (Figs. 5C, 6, 7, 8). The pallium forms the upper half of the hemisphere. The septum forms the ventromedial wall of the hemisphere. The striatum forms the ventrolateral and rostrolateral walls of the vesicle (see MacLean, this volume).

Our ideas about the functional organization of the telencephalon were influenced by the substantial successes of the early comparative anatomists and embryologists in dealing with the rhombencephalon (Nieuwenhuys, 1974). They had argued that the dorsal walls of the rhombencephalon (derived from the alar plates) subserve sensory functions, while the ventral rhombencephalic walls (derived from the basal plates) subserve motor functions. The pallium was seen as a rostral continuation of the alar plates and as-

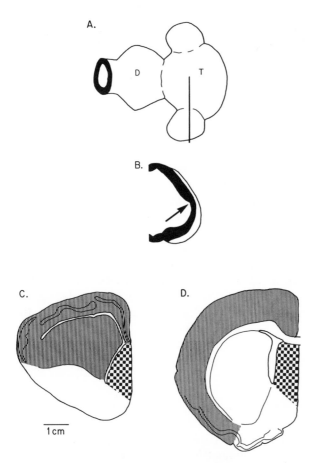

Figure 5. Organization of the telencephalon. The three major components of the telencephalon are illustrated in a reptile and a mammal. **A**, rostral end of the neural tube in an embryo illustrates the evaginated cereberal hemispheres (The diencephalon is marked by D; the telencephalon, by T. The line illustrates the plane of the sections shown in B. **B**, a cross section through the evaginated hemispheres shown in A. (The arrow marks the division between the pallium dorsally and the basal telencephalon ventrally.) **C**, cross section through the brain of an adult tegu lizard. (Vertical stripes indicate the region of the telencephalon derived from the pallium. Squares mark the septum. The clear area indicates the region of the telencephalon derived from the basal telencephalon.) **D**, cross section through the brain of an adult rat. (The regions of the telencephalon are indicated as in C.)

signed sensory functions that were mediated in mammals via the ascending projections from the specific sensory nuclei of the thalamus. The striatum was seen as a continuation of the basal plates and assigned motor functions. The data on hand indicated that the striatum was well developed in reptiles and birds, and this was consistent with the prevailing view that nonmammals were limited to stereotyped movement patterns (Ariëns Kappers, Huber, and Crosby, 1936). The pallium was thought to be well developed in mammals, serving as a substrate for increased sensory acuity and higher cognitive functions.

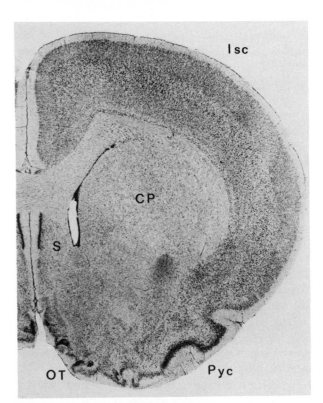

Figure 6. Rostral telencephalon of a rat.
Key: **CP**, caudatoputamen; **Isc**, isocortex; **OT**, olfactory tubercle; **Pyc**, piriform cortex; **S**, septum.

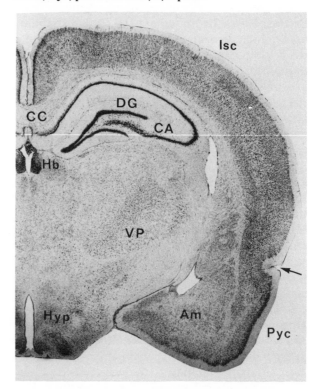

Figure 7. Caudal telencephalon and diencephalon of a rat.
Key: **Am**, amygdala; **CA**, hippocampus (cornu ammonis); **CC**, corpus callosum; **DG**, dentate gyrus; **Hb**, habenula; **Hyp**, hypothalamus; **Isc**, isocortex; **Pyc**, piriform cortex; **VP**, ventroposterior nucleus of thalamus. Arrow identifies rhinal sulcus.

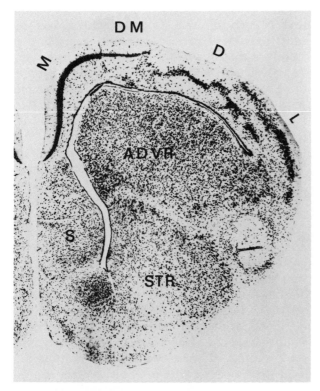

Figure 8. Telencephalon of tegu lizard.

Key: **ADVR,** anterior dorsal ventricular ridge; **D,** dorsal cortex; **DM,** dorsomedial cortex; **M,** medial cortex; **L,** lateral cortex; **S,** septum; **STR,** striatum.

The therapsid-mammal transition would then be characterized by a progressive elaboration of the specific sensory regions of the thalamus and pallium. Again, the results of more recent investigations have altered our views of both the pallium and the striatum.

PALLIUM

The nature of the pallium varies substantially between groups of vertebrates. In mammals, it is a cortex or laminated structure situated entirely above the lateral ventricle and containing three major constituents (Figs. 6 and 7). The traditional mission in comparative neurology has been to look for equivalents of these components of the mammalian pallium in nonmammals. This has been only marginally useful in that there does not now appear to be a one-to-one correspondence between pallial components in mammals and nonmammals. I will make this point here by discussing the organization of each of the components of mammalian pallium, and then inquiring if there are similar components in the pallium of Recent reptiles (Fig. 8).

Pallium of mammals.

The pallium in mammals has three major constituents: 1. isocortex; 2., piriform cortex, and

3. the hippocampal formation (see MacLean, this volume, for a differing view).

1. Isocortex. The first constituent of mammalian cortex is the isocortex that forms the dorsa-lateral and dorsal surfaces of the cerebral hemispheres (Figs. 6 and 7, Isc). It has a basic plan of six cellular layers, but there are regional variations in its laminar pattern (e.g., Ariëns Kappers, Huber, and Crosby, 1936). For the sake of simplicity, I am including cortical areas, such as some of the areas in the cingulate gyrus, within the isocortex. These are sometimes designated "mesocortex" or "juxtallocortex", and considered to be transitional between isocortex and the hippocampal formation.

An important organizational feature is that the isocortex can be divided by physiological techniques into a series of areas that correspond quite closely to those defined by variations in the laminar pattern. The first overall concept of these isocortical areas derives from the work of C. N. Woolsey (1958) and his colleagues. They showed—by recording from the cortex of anesthetized mammals subjected to somatosensory, auditory, or visual stimuli— that the isocortex contains a series of modality specific areas. They also delineated motor areas in which electrical stimulation evoked muscular movement. Study of common laboratory animals led to the generalization that each sensory modality was represented twice. Each sensory area contained a single, complete representation of a sensory-receptor surface or of the body. Similarly, two motor areas were identified. Regions of isocortex that were neither purely sensory nor motor in nature were classified as *association* cortex (see Diamond, 1979).

More recent studies, using smaller and more selective electrodes and sampling a wider range of mammals, have modified this picture (e.g., Merzenich and Kaas, 1980; Woolsey, 1981a, b, 1982). It is now clear that there is a rather wide range in the number of times a given sensory modility is represented. Echidnas (Lende, 1964) and platypuses (Bohringer and Rowe, 1977) seem to have a single representation of each sensory modality and a single motor area. Some placental and marsupial mammals have a double representation of each sensory modality (Lende, 1969), in accord with Woolsey's data. However, many placental mammals have multiple sensory or motor representations. Cats, for example, have as many as thirteen distinct visual areas (Van Essen, 1979). Each area contains a single representation of the sensory receptor surface that is topologically organized, even though the representation may be split or broken into pieces, or may greatly exaggerate a particular part of the receptor surface. In some cases, the use of microelectrodes shows that two or more representations lie within what larger electrodes indicated was a single representation (Kaas et al., 1981). Each representation corresponds to a single area as defined on histological grounds, so that each cytoarchitetonic area seems to have unique physiological properties.

We can now return to the issue (left unresolved in the last section) of how the various thalamic nuceli are related to the forebrain. The interrelation of thalamic nuclei and cortical areas was studied by workers such as Walker (1938), Bodian (1942), and Rose and Woolsey (1958). They assayed the extent of retrograde degeneration produced in thalamic nuclei by focal lesions of the cortex. The principal result was the ablation of a isocortical sensory or motor area produced intense degeneration in specific sensory or motor nuclei of the thalamus and less intense degeneration in multi-areal or intralaminar nuclei. However, larger lesions that involved several areas often produced retrograde degeneration in the latter two types of nuclei as well. Diamond and his colleagues extended retrograde degeneration studies to include marsupials and insectivores (e.g., Diamond and Hall, 1969). With the accumulation of data it was natural to extend the concept of a progressive evolution of a multimodal thalamus into specific sensory nuclei to include a model of cortical evolution and propose that the specific sensory areas of the isocortex evolved by a process of differentiation from a multisensory matrix (Diamond and Hall, 1969). Similarly, Lende (1969) proposed that the somatosensory and motor areas evolved by a differentiation out of a somatosensory-motor amalgam. His basic observation was that the primary somatosensory and motor cortices completely overlap in the American opossum, a wallaby, and a hedgehog. He suggested this was the primitive state.

This concept of cortical evolution by a progressive differentiation of areas has required modification in the face of results obtained during the last decade. Autoradiographic and horseradish peroxidase techniques have permitted a more detailed assessment of thalamocortical relationships and have revealed a complex network of interconnections between nuclei of the thalamus and cortical sensory and motor areas—making obsolete the concept of a simple relay of sensory information to a single, specific sensory nucleus and isocortical area. Diamond (1979) has recently reviewed various data and suggests that isocortex contains a "field" for each sensory modality. Each field comprises several cortical areas that have intricate and varied connections with the thalamus. Similarly, Graybiel and Berson (1981) define "families" of thalamic nuclei that are associated with the cortical representations of a single sensory modality through an intricate set of thalamocortical and corticothalamic projections. It may not be possible to show one-to-one correspondence of the areas within fields of different species.

Other difficulties with the theory that cortical areas evolved by a process of differentiation have been discussed by Kaas (1982). He points out that some of the overlap between adjacent areas discussed in the earlier literature could be due to the limited resolution of the techniques available at the time. He also notes that adjoining representations of the same modality are roughly mirror reversals of each other, and that it is not clear how a sensory representation with one intrinsic organization could gradually separate from a "parent" representation with a quite different organization. A revision may also be necessary for Lende's idea of the relation between somatosensory and motor cortices. It is difficult to argue that extensive somatosensory-motor overlap is a clearly primitive feature because variations in the relation of somatosensory and motor areas seem to occur in each major group of mammals. Echidnas and platypuses show different degrees of partial overlap (Lende, 1964; Bohringer and Rowe, 1977); some marsupials show a complete overlap (Lende, 1969) while others show little overlap (Haight and Neylon, 1978, 1981). The extent of overlap varies within the placental mammals so that rats, for example, show overlap between their somatosensory and motor areas only in the hind-limb representation.

It does seem, though, that there is an orderly relationship between thalamocortical projections and degree of overlap. Thus, the somatosensory-motor amalgam in opossums (Donoghue and Ebner, 1981a, b) receives convergent projections from the ventrobasal nucleus (a specific sensory nucleus), the ventrolateral nucleus (a specific motor nucleus), and the central lateral nucleus (an intralaminar nucleus). The hind-limb representation of rats receives a similar convergence of thalamic inputs, but the fore-limb and face representations have segregated projections from specific sensory and specific motor nuclei, respectively (Donoghue, Kerman, and Ebner, 1979). In echidnas, the somatosensory cortex defined electrophysiologically by Lende (1964) contains two histological areas (Ulinski, 1981). A large horseradish perioxidase injection that includes both areas retrogradely labels neurons in the ventrobasal nucleus, but fails to label neurons in other thalamic areas comparable to the labeling seen in multi-areal and intralaminar nuclei in marsupial and placental mammals. This suggests that modality-specific field containing several areas, all receiving projections from a multiareal nucleus, may be characteristic of therian mammals and are a derived, rather than a primitive feature.

In summary, it appears that models of the evolution of isocortex from a multimodal matrix are overly simplistic. Isocortical areas are now known to have varied and intricate relations with the thalamus, the pattern of variations does not bear a simple relation to phylogenetic lineages.

In addition to its affinities with the thalamus, an important feature of isocortex is that it gives rise to a large number of efferent projections that originate from pyramidal cells. Some cortical projections are back to thalamic nuclei while others project to the brainstem and spinal cord. These latter projections include the cortical projections to the spinal cord from the motor areas that are found in monotreme (Goldby, 1939), marsupial (see Johnson, 1977), and placental mammals (Phillips and Porter, 1977). Commissural projections to the contralateral cortex are present in all Recent mammals. In placental mammals, the connection is effected principally via the corpus callosum; in monotreme (Goldby, 1939) and marsupial (Johnson, 1977) mammals it is effected via a specific bundle of the anterior commissure.

2. Piriform cortex. The second constituent of mammalian cortex is the piriform cortex (Figs. 6 and 7, Pyc). It receives direct olfactory input and is characterized by pyramidal cells that send several dendrites towards the brain's surface (e.g., Skeen and Hall, 1977). The olfactory input terminates on the distal segments of these dendrites (Price, 1973) and is not topographically organized (Price and Sprich, 1975). The piriform cortex of both placental mammals (e.g., Skeen and Hall, 1977) and opossums (Haberly, 1973a, b; Haberly and Shepherd, 1973) has been studied in some detail and is basically the same. The piriform cortex of monotremes resembeles that of placental mammals histologically (Abbie, 1940),

but has not been completely studied. The piriform cortex in echidnas is extensively developed (Welker and Lende, 1979).

3. Hippocampal formation. The hippocampal formation makes up the medial edge of the cortex (Fig. 7, DG and CA). It contains a number of areas that have a basically trilaminar structure in which the central layer contains densely packed neurons whose dendrites extend radially into the first and third layers (Lorente de No', 1934). A major organizational feature of the hippocampal formation is that it receives information from several sensory systems. Olfactory projections originate directly from piriform cortex (e.g., Steward, 1976; Steward and Scoville, 1976), but the flow of information from the other sensory systems is more indirect. Each of the sensory areas of isocortex give rise to a stepwise sequence of projections that carry sensory information to the temporal cortex bordering the hippocampal formation, and ultimately to the hippocampus (e.g., Jones and Powell, 1970). It seems that the topographical representations of the receptor surfaces that are seen in isocortical sensory areas are absent in the hippocampal formation. Instead, many neurons in the hippocampal formation are multimodal (see Keefe and Nadel, 1978). The hippocampal formation is present in all three groups of mammals.

Pallium in nonmammals. Having gained some appreciation for the organization of the pallium in mammals, we can now try to determine if any of the mammalian pallial components can be identified in the Recent reptiles.

It was recognized by the late nineteenth century that a structural equivalent to the piriform cortex (e.g., the "paleocortex") is present in many vertebrates. In each case, this region of the brain receives direct projections from the olfactory bulbs. One viewpoint has been that the cerebral hemispheres were primarily olfactorecipient, and that there was a progressive invasion of the olfactory cortex by thalamic fibers with ascent of the "phylogenetic scale" (e.g., Herrick, 1948). This has turned out to be incorrect: olfactory projections are restricted to the rostral, basal telencephalon and the ventrolateral surface of the pallium in all of the vertebrates studied to date (see Northcutt, 1981). In particular Recent reptiles have a cortex that is divided into four longitudinal zones that are named *medial cortex, dorsomedial cortex, dorsal cortex,* and *lateral cortex,* according to their positions on the hemisphere (Ulinski, 1974). The lateral cortex (Fig. 8, L) receives direct projections from the olfactory bulbs (see Ulinski and Peterson, 1981). There is some variation in the internal organization of the lateral cortex, but the lateral cortex in snakes shares several structural features with the piriform cortex in mammals (Ulinski and Rainey, 1980). The efferent projections of the lateral cortex have not yet been studied and therefore cannot be compared to the projections of the piriform cortex of mammals.

It is also fairly obvious that the medial and dorsomedial cortices of reptiles (Fig. 8, M, DM) bear some resemblance to mammalian hippocampus (the "archicortex"). Classical descriptive studies indicated that both sets of structures are basically trilaminar cortices. Recent studies of these areas in snakes and lizards reveal some fairly close similarities in neuronal organization, including laminar and lamellar organization of afferents, and neuronal cytology. There are efferent projections to the septum and hypothalamus (Butler, 1978, 1980; Halpern, 1980; Ulinski, 1975, 1980c; Ulinski and Rainey, 1980), although the total set is less extensive than that seen in mammals (Swanson and Cowan, 1977). There is, then, an overall similarlity in the structure of the lateral and medial edges of the pallium in Recent reptiles and Recent mammals.

However, opinions have varied as to whether or not nonmammals have anything like isocortex. Some nineteenth-century authors suggested that isocortex is a neomorph characteristic of mammals (the "neocortex"). Other workers searched for an equivalent of isocortex in reptiles by looking for direct thalamic projections to the telencephalon (see Crosby, 1917). As of the early 1960s, the available experimental evidence failed to demonstrate direct projections from the thalamus to the pallium in lizards (Powell and Kruger, 1960), crocodilians (Kruger and Berkowitz, 1960), or pigeons (Powell and Cowan, 1961). However, the Nauta degeneration techniques being introduced at about that time led to the demonstration that specific thalamic nuclei project to two regions of the pallium of reptiles.

The first of these is a cortical structure, the dorsal cortex (Fig. 8, D). A thalamic projection to dorsal cortex has been best documented in turtles (Hall and Ebner, 1970; Ebner and Colonnier, 1975). The dorsal lateral geniculate complex receives a bilateral, retinotopically organized (Ulinski, 1980b) projection from the retina. The projection is organized so that the horizontal axis of the retina is represented along the rostrocaudal axis of dorsal cortex. The geniculate axons terminate on the distal dendrites of cortical cells

and on interneurons in its outer layer (Ebner and Colonnier, 1975; Smith, Ebner, and Colonnier, 1980). It is reasonable, then, to entertain the hypothesis that the dorsal cortex of Recent reptiles is equivalent to the isocortex of Recent mammals. A difficulty, however, is that dorsal cortex has some properties that are instead very much like those of limbic cortex. It is intricately involved in reciprocal projections with medial cortex (Ulinski, 1976). It projects to the septum in a way reminiscent of the projection of the hippocampal formation to the septum (Ulinski, 1975). Finally, the same distal dendrites that receive geniculate input are intersected by the axons of bowl cells carrying olfactory input medially from lateral cortex (Ulinski and Rainey, 1980; Orrego, 1961).

The second telencephalic target of thalamic nuclei in reptiles (and birds) is the dorsal ventricular ridge or DVR (Fig. 8, ADVR). This is a ridge of tissue that protrudes into the lateral ventricle medial to the lateral cortex (Ulinski, 1983). In contrast to isocortex, it is a nuclear structure that lacks obvious lamination and anything that resembles the pyramidal cells of isocortex. However, DVR does have several organizational features in common with isocortex.

First, DVR contains a series of modality-specific areas, each of which receives a direct input from a specific sensory nucleus of the thalamus. The basic pattern seems to be that a visual nucleus projects laterally within DVR (Karten and Hodos, 1970; Pritz, 1975; Balaban and Ulinski, 1981a, b), a somatosensory nucleus projects centrally within DVR (Pritz and Northcutt, 1980), and a auditory nucleus that recieves ascending projections from the auditory midbrain project medially within DVR (Karten, 1967; Pritz, 1974; Foster and Hall, 1978). The organization of these projections varies. The auditory area is tonotopically organized (Bonke, Scheich, and Langner, 1979). However, the visual area in lateral DVR receives a widely divergent projection from neurons in nucleus rotundus (Balaban and Ulinski, 1981b). Neurons in this area thus have very large receptive fields that respond well to small moving stimuli anywhere in visual space (Dünser et al., 1981).

On closer examination, it turns out that in most reptiles each area in DVR is divided into a series of zones that are oriented concentric with the ventricular surface (Ulinski, 1978; Balaban, 1978). The most obvious of these contains clusters of neurons with apposed somata. The lines of apposition are marked by specialized junctions that generally resemble gap junctions, suggesting that the clusters may consist of groups of electrotonically coupled neurons (Ulinski, 1976). Neurons situated outside of the zone of cell clusters have dendrites that extend long distances concentric with the ventricle. Those situated inside of the zone of cell clusters have stellate-shaped dendritic fields. The axons of these cells all tend to be vertically aligned so that information reaching a specific region of DVR would be relayed to adjacent zones in much the same way that the vertical connections in isocortex are a partial substrate for a columnar organization. Thus, afferents from the auditory thalamus of guinea fowl terminate in an intermediate zone within the auditory area of DVR (Bonke, Scheich, and Langner, 1979). Recordings made along electrode penetrations that proceed perpendicularly through the zones show that auditory information is relayed to zones both above and below the thalamic recipient zone, and that the characteristics of auditory neurons in each zone are different.

The DVR thus resembles isocortex in containing modality-specific sensory areas that may have a form of vertical organization similar to the columnar or bandlike organization seen in isocortex. However, it differs histologically from isocortex and occupies a topologically different position in the forebrain. Nauta and Karten (1970) and Karten (1979) have argued that DVR may be equivalent to at least parts of isocortex, regardless of its position, in that populations of neurons equivalent to DVR migrate into the isocortex during development in mammals. However, experiments that trace the migration of neuroblasts into isocortex during development have failed to confirm this hypothesis. Webster (1979) has provided a critical review of this idea.

In contrast to these demonstrations of modality-specific sensory areas in Recent reptiles, it has not been possible to find a region of the telencephalon that elicits movements upon stimulation and that projects directly to the vicinity of motoneurons in either the brainstem or spinal cord. Workers in several laboratories have searched for descending telencephalic projections in reptiles with no success.

There is, then, no structure in the brains of Recent reptiles that is clearly equivalent to mammalian isocortex. It appears, instead, that the central portion of the pallium has been elaborated differently in the diapsid reptiles and turtles, on the one hand, versus the mammals on the other hand. In fact, this part of the pallium

is elaborated differently in each major group of vertebrates (see Northcutt, 1981, for a general discussion). The history of pallial evolution in each line of reptiles is not known, but there are two relatively simple possibilities. The first is that DVR was elaborated in the stem reptiles, was retained throughout the history of the diapsids and turtles, but was lost somewhere along the pelycosaur-therapsid-mammal sequence and then was replaced by an isocortical pattern in the mammals. The second possibility is that pallial elaboration proceeded independently in the diapsid and synapsid reptiles. Thus, the diapsid reptiles plus turtles developed a DVR early in their evolution, while the pelycosaurs developed a cortical configuration in the central part of their pallium that was expanded and elaborated upon somewhere along the therapsid-mammal sequence. My guess is that the second alternative is correct. In that case, the therapsid-mammal transition would have involved a quantitative elaboration of a pattern that was already present at the therapsid (if not the pelycosaur) level. The scanty evidence available on cortico-thalamic organization in monotremes suggests that specific sensory nuclei and single modality specific areas in the cortex, as well as specific motor nuclei and a single motor area, were present prior to the divergence of the prototherian and therian mammals. The multi-areal and intralaminar nuclei are perhaps characteristic of therians and may have evolved later. An alternative hypothesis that cannot be excluded is that thalamocortical relations in monotremes are secondarily simplified.

STRIATUM

The striatum makes up the ventrolateral regions of the telencephalon in all tetrapods. There are some general similarlities in its anatomy and functional connections across the tetrapods, but it is best developed in the three groups of mammals. Simplified versions of the connections of the striatum are presented in Figure 9 for mammals and Figure 10 for reptiles.

Striatum in mammals. The striatum in mammals comprises a series of structures in the telencephalon that are called the basal ganglia because of their position in the base of the forebrain (Divac and Öberg, 1979). They protrude into the lateral ventricle and occupy much of the space that is occupied by DVR in Recent reptiles. (A complete account of the striatum is beyond the scope of this paper, and only those parts of the basal ganglia that are immediately relevant to the central point will be mentioned.) The most dorsal component of the basal ganglia consists of the caudate nucleus and the putamen (Fig. 6, CP), which are embryologically and functionally a single structure, and have high concentrations of dopamine and acetycholinesterase. This caudatoputamen contains, primarily, medium-sized neurons with dendrites that are heavily covered with dendritic spines and form spherical dendritic trees. It receives projections from three major sources (Fig. 9). First, the entire isocortex—and particularly the motor and premotor areas of the frontal lobes—projects to the caudatoputamen. There is a rough topography to the projection, but the cortical axons form fairly extensive, patchlike projection areas within the caudatoputamen (Goldman and Nauta, 1977). Second, the intralaminar nuclei of the thalamus project to the caudatoputamen, forming a link between the cerebellum, spinal cord, brainstem, and striatum (Kemp and Powell, 1971). Third, the substantia nigra of the midbrain projects to the caudatoputamen. It is known that some of its neurons use dopamine as a transmitter substance. The projection of the substantia nigra to the caudatoputamen accounts for the high concentration of dopamine in the caudatoputamen.

The medium-sized spiny neurons of the caudatoputamen project to two major targets. These targets are structurally similar and serve to link the striatum with two major structures. The first is the globus pallidus, which is a component of the basal ganglia. The axons of medium-sized spiny cells branch, entwining the dendrites of pallidal neurons in a plexus of collaterals (e.g., Grofova, 1978; Fox and Rafols, 1976). The principal targets for efferents from the globus pallidus are the intralaminar and specific motor nuclei of the ventral thalamus, especially the ventral anterior nucleus. Since these nuclei project to the motor areas of isocortex, the globus pallidus places the striatum in contact with the descending telencephalic pathways characteristic of mammals.

The second structure that receives projections from the caudatoputamen is the substantia nigra. The neurons of the pars reticulata of the substantia nigra resemble those of the globus pallidus and have the same relationship with the axons of medium-sized spiny neurons. Other than the caudatoputamen, the principal targets of the substantia nigra are thalamic nuclei (not shown in Fig. 9) and the intermediate layers of the superior colliculus (Graybiel, 1978). This lat-

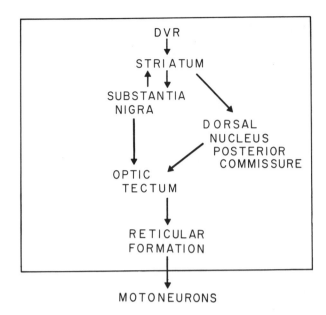

Figure 9. Summary of striatal connections in mammals. The major connections of the striatum (caudatoputamen and globus pallidus) and related structures are summarized. The interactions contained in the rectangle are generally equivalent to those contained in the rectangle in Figure 10 and represent interactions that are common to both reptiles and mammals. Those interactions that lie outside of the rectangle are characteristic of mammals.

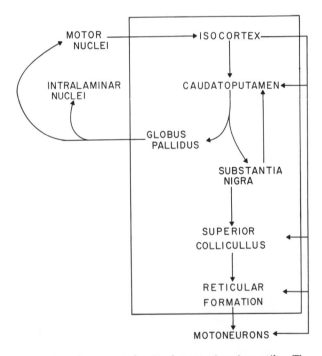

Figure 10. Summary of striatal connections in reptiles. The major connecitions of the striatum and related structures are outlined. The interactions contained in the rectangle are generally equivalent to those contained in the rectangle in Figure 9.

ter connection places the striatum in contact with the descending projections from the brainstem reticular formation.

These connections can be reduced, as a first approximation, to two components. First is the sequence of connection from the isocortex, through the basal ganglia and to the reticular formation that are enclosed in the rectangle in Figure 9. Second is the intralaminar and motor nuclei, which receive projections from the globus pallidus and project to the caudatoputamen in placental and marsupial mammals.

Striatum in nonmammals. A striatal region can be identified lying immediately ventral to the pallium in all tetrapods (e.g., Fig. 8). It typically contains a high concentration of dopamine and acetylcholinesterase (Parent, 1979). The best-understood connections of the striatum in Recent reptiles and birds (Ulinski, 1983) are summarized in Figure 10. The striatum receives projections from the modality-specific areas of DVR. In contrast to the striatum in mammals, however, there is no known projection from motor areas of the pallium.

It appears that the striatum typically projects to two targets. The first is a region in the mesencephalic tegmentum that resembles the substantia nigra in containing dopaminergic neurons (Parent, 1979). As in mammals, the substantia nigra projects back to the striatum and to the optic tectum (Reiner et al., 1980), establishing the same type of link with the reticulospinal systems (see Ulinski, 1977) that is seen in mammals. The second structure that receives striatal projections is the dorsal nucleus of the posterior commissure. It lies at the border of the thalamus with the mesencephalon and also projects to the optic tectum (Reiner et al., 1980). Although it is conceivable that the striatum additionally projects to thalamic nuclei that project to the telencephalon, it is unlikely that such pathways are very well developed.

Thus the striatum in reptiles, as in mammals, participates in a series of connections between the modality-specific areas of the pallium and the reticular formation. These connections are enclosed in the rectangle in Figure 10. Absent are feedback loops through the thalamus and direct pallial projections to motoneurons.

SUMMARY

It now appears that many aspects of telencephalic organization are general characteristics of tetrapods—and, in fact, probably, vertebrates. There is universally a strip of lateral pallium that receives direct olfactory projections. The medial edge of the pallium contains one or more cortical areas that receive both olfactory and nonolfactory sensory information and effect connections with the septum and hypothalamus. A central region of the pallium contains modality-specific sensory areas that receive afferents from the specific thalamic nuclei and project to the underlying striatum. The striatum has reciprocal connections with a mesencephalic structure that uses dopamine as a transmitter substance. This midbrain structure modulates the reticulospinal pathways via the optic tectum and the tectoreticular projections.

However, this basic pattern is elaborated differently in Recent reptiles and mammals. In reptiles, the central region of the pallium is dominated by the dorsal ventricular ridge and efferents from the the striatum are directed principally towards the optic tectum. In mammals, the central region of the pallium is the isocortex. The striatum is extensively developed and protudes into the lateral ventricle (which led to the misidentification of the dorsal ventricular ridge as a part of the striatum by early comparative anatomists). In addition to its influence on the superior colliculus, the striatum is linked with the specific motor areas of the isocortex via the specific motor nuclei of the thalamus. The isocortical motor areas give rise to direct projections to the vicinity of the spinal cord and brainstem motoneurons.

Most of the features of forebrain anatomy seen in placental mammals are also seen in marsupials and monotremes. Specifically, all three groups of Recent mammals have specific sensory nuclei, specific motor nuclei, and limbic nuclei in the thalamus. They have a cerebal cortex with an isocortex, piriform cortex, and hippocampal formation, and they have well-developed basal ganglia. A motor area of the isocortex projects to the spinal cord. One difference between placental and nonplacental mammals is the trajectory of commissural connections, but potentially more significant variations are that monotremes seem to lack intralaminar thalamic nuclei, multi-areal thalamic nuclei, and multiple sensory and motor areas in their isocortices.

Functional Correslates of the Therapsid—Mammal Transition

In the previous section I have dealt with the central nervous system of Recent mammals, pointing out structural differences between the various components of the brains of Recent mammals and Recent reptiles. The existence of such differences implies that there were changes in the organization of the central nervous system somewhere along the evolutionary sequences leading to the Recent reptiles, on the one hand, and to the Recent mammals, on the other. From a functional viewpoint, two changes seem particularly important.

First, we can speculate that there was a gradual elaboration of the sensory components of the telencephalon throughout the radiation of both the diapsids and synapsids. What we now know about the organization of the central nervous system in tetrapods makes it unlikely that the establishment of thalamotelencephalic projections occurred uniquely during the evolution of mammals. It is unlikely that there was a qualitative change in the organization of the sensory systems during the early evolution of mammals.

Rather, discrete modality-specific channels through the thalamus to the telencephalon were probably present throughout the evolution of the synapsid reptiles. The transition from therapsids to mammals quite likely involved some expansion of cortical sensory areas. It is possible that such expansions were related to modifications in the inner ear associated with an extension of the range of audible frequencies (e.g., Stebbins, 1980) and with the acquisition of hair. The apparent existence of only a single representation for each major modality in Recent prototherians suggests that the therian pattern of multiple sensory representations and multi-areal nuclei did not exist in the earliest mammals.

Second, the extensive differences between the brains of all Recent mammals on the one hand and all Recent reptiles on the other, with respect to neural systems that play direct roles in the control of movement, suggest that changes in motor control were an important concomitant of the therapsid-mammal transition. At the central level, these differences include the pattern of the precerebellar nuclei, such as the inferior olivary complex and the pontine nuclei (Holst, Ulinski, and Watson, in preparation), a well-developed caudatoputamen with relays through the specific motor nuclei, and the presence of descending pathways from the pallium to brainstem and spinal cord. All of these features are found in both prototherian and therian mammals, but may be absent from Recent reptiles. At more peripheral levels, the Golgi tendon organs (Proske, 1981) and muscle spindles are more elaborate in mammals than in nonmammals. Mammals have, for the most part, separate alpha and gamma motoneurons that innervate extrafusal and intrafusal muscle fibers, respectively. Nonmammals typically have beta motoneurons that innervate both extrafusal and intrafusal fibers via collaterals. It is generally thought that the existence of separate innervation of intrafusal and extrafusal fibers allows for a more flexible control of the state of muscular contraction (Prochazka, 1981).

All of these differences indicate that mammals have a series of neural systems that provides a relatively detailed regulation of on-going movement patterns. The current view is that the basic pattern of rhythmical movements is generated at the segmental level, either in the spinal cord or brainstem, by central pattern generators that can produce a correct sequence of motoneuronal activity independent of peripheral input (e.g., Stein, 1978; Goldberg and Chandler, 1981). The peripheral input can, however, serve to modulate the basic level of motoneural activity and to fine tune the control of movements (e.g., Prochazka, 1981). The activity of the various pattern generators is believed to be under the control of command systems orginating in the brainstem, probably in the reticular formation. Both pattern generators and command systems seem to be general tetrapod features. For example, electrical stimulation of descending brainstem projections can elicit coordinated swimming movements in turtles (Lennard and Stein, 1977) and walking in cats (Orlovsky and Shik, 1976).

However, the pathways from the cerebellum and basal ganglia to the specific motor nuclei of the thalamus seem to be characteristic of all three groups of mammals and probably play roles in the control of more flexible movement patterns. One formulation holds that these systems constitute a series of closed-loop and open-loop control systems (Evarts, 1981). Closed-loop control systems use peripheral feedback to evaluate the performance of movements, comparing the actual movements achieved to the intended movements. They are of primary use in regulating movements that are of sufficient duration to allow peripheral information to reach the control system and result in a correction during the execution of the movement. Open-loop systems operate with little peripheral input and are more useful in achieving the coordination of sets of central structures during movements that are too rapid to permit peripheral modulation.

There is evidence—from both clinical studies on human patients and from microelectrode recordings made from conscious monkeys during arm movements—that the cerebellum has some aspects of an open-loop control system that regulates rapid or ballistic movements, while the basal ganglia seem to function as a closed-loop control system during slower movements, such as precise movements of the hands or jaws (e.g., Kornhuber, 1971; Porter, 1975). The specific motor areas of the cortex also seem to be involved in closed-loop control in that recordings made from cortical neurons during hand movements in conscious monkeys indicate that these neurons can adjust their firing frequencies to compensate for sudden perturbations in a movement sequence (e.g., Evarts, 1981). Recordings from pairs or triplets of structures in awake monkeys indicate that both the cerebellum and basal ganglia become active in advance of a movement and prior to activity in the specific motor nuclei of the thalamus (Porter, 1975). The motor cortex becomes active immediately prior to the movement. Thus, the sequence of anatomical connections between the cerebellum and basal ganglia, the specific motor and intralaminar nuclei, and the motor cortex appear to underlie a functional sequence.

The fossil record shows changes in the skeletal systems of the vertebral column, the limbs, and the jaws during the evolution of the advanced therapsids and the transition to mammals (see Introduction, this paper, for references). All of these changes gradually led to a skeletomuscular system capable of more flexible movement sequences of the limbs and jaws than those usually seen in reptiles. These include the alteration of the shoulder in a way that permits extensive movements of the limbs in extrasomatic space and the alteration of the jaws in a way that involves the neural control of masticatory movements to achieve precise occlusion of the teeth. It is a reasonable conjecture that the somatic changes recorded by fossils conditioned parallel changes in the network of thalamotelencephalic connections, which resulted in the evolution of specific motor nuclei and elaboration of the basal ganglia. The growth of the basal ganglia may have resulted in some of the initial expansion of the forebrain seen in the endocasts of early mammals.

Acknowledgments

The author's work on reptiles has been supported by PHS Grant NS12518; his work on echidnas was supported by NSF Grant INT-8102645. Debra Randall and Dorothy Crowder typed the manuscript. Shirley Aumiller provided photographic assistance.

References

Abbie, A. A.
1940. Cortical lamination in the monotremata. *J. Comp. Neurol.* 72:429–67.

Andersen, R. A.; Knight, P. L.; and Merzenich, M. M.
1980. The thalamocortical and cortico-thalamic connections of Al, All, and the anterior auditory field (AAF) in the cat: evidence for two largely segregated systems of connections. *J. Comp. Neurol.* 194:663–701.

Andersen, R. A.; Roth, G. L.; Aitkin, L. M.; and Merzenich, M. M.
1980. The efferent projections of the central nucleus and the pericentral nucleus of the inferior colliculus in the cat. *J. Comp. Neurol.* 194:649–62.

Ariëns Kappers, C. U.; Huber, G. C.; and Crosby, E. C.
1936. *The Comparative Anatomy of the Nervous System of Vertebrates, Including Man.* Republished in 1967. New York: Hafner.

Balaban, C. D.
1978. Structure of anterior dorsal ventricular ridge in a turtle (*Pseudemys scripta elegans*). *J. Morphol.* 158(3): 291–322.

Balaban, C. D., and Ulinski, P. S.
1981a. Organization of thalamic afferents to anterior dorsal ventricular ridge in turtles. I. Projections of thalamic nuclei. *J. Comp. Neurol.* 200:95–130.
1981b. Organization of thalamic afferents to anterior dorsal ventricular ridge in turtles. II. Properties of the rotundo-dorsal map. *J. Comp. Neurol.* 200:131–50

Belekhova, M. G.
1979. Neurophysiology of the forebrain. In *Biology of the Reptila,* ed. C. Gans, R. G. Northcutt, and P. S. Ulinski, vol. 10, pp. 287–359. London: Academic Press.

Bennett, A. F.
1980. The metabolic foundations of vertebrate behavior. *Biosci.* 30: 452–56.

Bodian, D.
1942. Studies on the diencephalon of the Virginia opossum. III. The Thalamo-cortical projection. *J. Comp. Neurol.* 77:525–76.

Bohringer, R. C., and Rowe, M. J.
1977. The organization of the sensory and motor areas of cerebral cortex in platypus (*Ornithorhyncus anatinus*). *J. Comp. Neurol.* 174:1–14.

Bonke, D.; Scheich, H.; and Langner, G.
1979. Responsiveness of units in the auditory neostriatum of the Guinea fowl *(Numida meleagris)* to species-specific calls and synthetic stimuli. *J. Comp. Physiol.* 132A:243–55.

Brodal, A.
1981. *Neurological Anatomy in Relation to Clinical Medicine.* New York: Oxford University Press.

Butler, A. B.
1978. Forebrain connections in lizards and the evolution of sensory systems. In *Behavior and Neurology of Lizards,* ed. N. Greenberg and P. D. MacLean, pp. 65–78. Washington: National Institute of Mental Health.
1980. Cytoarchitectonic and connectional organization of the lacertilian telencephalon with comments on vertebrate forebrain evolution. In *Comparative Neurology of The Telencephalon,* ed. S. O. E. Ebbesson, pp. 297–329. New York: Plenum Press.

Campbell, C. B. G., and Hayhow, W. R.
1971. Primary optic pathways in the echidna *Tachyglossus aculeatus:* an experimental degeneration study. *J. Comp. Neurol.* 143:119–36.
1972. Primary optic pathways in the platypus *Ornithorhynchus anatinus:* an experimental degeneration study. *J. Comp. Neurol.* 145:195–208.

Carroll, R. L.
1969. Origin of Reptiles. In *Biology of the Reptilia,* ed. C. Gans, A. d; A. Bellairs, and T. S. Parsons, vol. 1, pp. 1–44. London: Academic Press.

Case, E. C.
1897. On the foramina perforating the cranial cavity of a Permian reptile and on a cast of its brain cavity. *Am. J. Sci.* 3:321–26.

Crompton, A. W., and Jenkins, F. A. Jr.
1979. Origin of Mammals. In *Mesozoic Mammals,* ed. J. A. Lillegraven, Z. Kielan-Jaworowska and W. A. Clemens, pp. 59–73. Berkeley: University of California Press.

Crompton, A. W., and Parker, P.
1978. Evolution of the mammalian masticatory apparatus. *Amer. Sci.* 66:192–201.

Crosby, E. C.
1917. The forebrain of *Alligator mississippiensis. J. Comp. Neurol.* 27:325–402.

Dacey, D. M., and Ulinski, P. S.
1982. Nucleus rotundus in a snake *(Thamnophis sirtalis).* J. Comp. Neurol. 216:175–191.

Diamond, I. T.
1979. The subdivision of neocortex: a proposal to revise the traditional view of sensory, motor, and association areas. Prog. Psychobiol. Physiol. Psychol. 8:1–43.

Diamond, I. T., and Hall, W. C.
1969. Evolution of neocortex. *Science* 164:251–62.

Divac, I., and Öberg, R. C. E.
1979. *The Neostriatum.* Oxford: Pergamon.

Donoghue, J. P., and Ebner, F. F.
1981a. The organization of thalamic projections to the parietal cortex of the Virginia opossum. *J. Comp. Neurol.* 198:365–88.
1981b. The laminar distribution and ultrastructure of fibers projecting from three thalamic nuclei to the somatic sensory-motor cortex of the opossum. *J. Comp. Neurol.* 198:389–420.

Donoghue, J. P.; Kerman, K. L.; and Ebner, F. F.
1979. Evidence for two organizational plans within the somatic sensory motor cortex of the rat. *J. Comp. Neurol.* 183:647–64.

du Lac, S., and Dacey, D. M.
1981. Relation of the retina and optic tectum to the lateral geniculate complex in garter snakes *(Thamnophis sirtalis). Neurosci. Abstr.* 7:460.

Dunser, K. R., Maxwell, J. H., and Granda, A. M.
1981. Visual properties of cells in anterior dorsal ventricular ridge of turtle. *Neuroscience Letters* 25:281–286.

Ebbesson, S. O. E.
1972. A proposal for a common nomenclature for some optic nuclei in vertebrates and the evidence for a common origin of two such cell groups. *Brain, Behav. Evol.* 6:75–91.
1980. The parcellation theory and its relation to interspecific variability in brain organization, evolutionary and ontogenetic development and neuronal plasticity. *Cell Tissue Res.* 213:179–212.

Ebbesson, S. O. E.; Jane, J. A.; and Schroeder, D. M.
1972. An overview of major interspecific variations in thalamic organization. *Brain, Behav. Evol,* 6:92–130.

Ebner, F. F., and Colonnier, M.
1975. Synaptic patterns in the visual cortex of turtle: an electron microscopic study. *J. Comp. Neurol.* 160:51–80.

Edinger, T.
1956. Objects et resultats de la paleoneurologie. *Ann. Paleontol.* 42:97–116.
1964. Midbrain exposure and overlap in mammals. *Am. Zool.* 4:5–19.

Eldredge, N., and Cracraft, J.
1980. *Phylogenetic Patterns and the Evolutionary Process.* New York: Columbia University Press.

Evarts, E. V.
1981. Functional studies of the motor cortex. In *The Organization of the Cerebral Cortex,* ed. F. O.

Schmitt, F. G. Worden, G. Adelman, and S. G. Dennis, pp. 263–284. Cambridge: MIT Press.

Feldman, S. G., and Kruger, L.
1980. An axonal transport study of the ascending projection of medial lemniscal neurons in the rat. *J. Comp. Neurol.* 192:427–54.

Foster, R. E., and Hall, W. C.
1978. The organization of central auditory pathways in a reptile, *Iguana iguana. J. Comp. Neurol.* 178:783–832.

Fox, C. A., and Rafols, J. A.
1976. The striatal efferents in the globus pallidus and in the substantia nigra. In *The Basal Ganglia,* ed. M. D. Yahr, pp. 37–55. New York: Raven Press.

Geisert, E. E., Jr.
1980. Cortical projections of the lateral geniculate nucleus in the cat. *J. Comp. Neurol.* 190:793–812.

Goldberg, L. J., and Chandler, S. H.
1981. Evidence for pattern generator control of the effects of spindle afferent input during rhythmical jaw movements. *Can. J. Physiol. Pharm.* 59:707–12.

Goldby, F.
1939. An experimental investigation of the motor cortex and pyramidal tract of *Echidna aculeatus. J. Anat.* (Lond.) 73:509–24.

Goldman, P. S., and Nauta, W. J. H.
1977. An intricately patterned prefronto-caudate projection in the rhesus moneky. *J. Comp. Neurol.* 171:369–86.

Graybiel, A. M.
1978. Organization of the nigrotectal connection: an experimental tracer study in the cat. *Brain Res.* 143:339–48.

Graybiel, A. M., and Berson, D. M.
1981. On the relation between transthalamic and transcortical pathways in the visual system. In *The Organization of the Cerebral Cortex,* ed. F. O. Schmitt, F. G. Worden, G. Adelman, and S. G. Dennis, pp. 286–319. Cambridge: MIT Press.

Griffiths, M.
1978. *The Biology of The Monotremes.* New York: Academic Press.

Grofova, I.
1979. Extrinsic connections of the neostriatum. In *The Neostriatum,* ed. I. Divac, and R. G. E. Öberg, pp. 37–51. Oxford: Pergamon.

Guillery, R. W.; Geisert, E. E., Jr.; Polley, E. H.; and Mason, C. A.
1980. An analysis of the retinal afferents to the cat's medial interlaminar nucleus and to its rostral thalamic extension, the "geniculate wing". *J. Comp. Neurol.* 194:117–42.

Haberly, L. B.
1973a. Unitary analysis of opossum prepiriform cortex. *J. Neurophysiol.* 36:762–74.
1973b. Summed potentials evoked in opossum prepiriform cortex. *J. Neurophysiol.* 36:775–78.,

Haberly, L. B., and Shepherd, G. M.
1973. Current-density analysis of summed evoked potentials in opossum prepiriform cortex. *J. Neurophysiol.* 36:789–802.

Haight, J. R., and Murray, P. F.
1981. The cranial endocast of the early miocene marsupial, *Wynardia basiana:* an assessment of taxonomic relationships based upon comparisons with recent forms. *Brain, Behav. Evol.* 19:17–36.

Haight, J. R., and L. Neylon.
1978. The organization of neocortical projections from the ventroposterior thalamic complex in the marsupial brush-tailed possum, *Trichosurus vulpecula:* a horseradish perioxidase study. *J. Anat.* (Lond.) 126:459–85.
1981. An analysis of some thalamic projections to parietofrontal neocortex in the marsupial native cat, *Dasyurus viverrinus* (Dasyuridae). *Brain, Behav. Evol.* 19:193–204.

Hall, W. C., and Ebner, F. F.
1970. Thalamotelencephalic projections in the turtle (*Pseudemys scripta*). *J. Comp. Neurol.* 140:101–22.

Halpern, M.
1980. The telencephalon of snakes In *Comparative Neurology of the Telencephalon,* ed. S. O. E. Ebbesson, pp. 257–95. New York: Plenum.

Heimer, L., and Robards, M. J.
1981. *Neuroanatomical Tract-Tracing methods.* New York: Plenum.

Herkenham, M.
1978. The connections of nucleus reuniens: evidence for a direct thalamo-hippocampal pathway in the rat. *J. Comp. Neurol.* 177:589–610.
1979. The afferent and efferent connections of the ventromedial thalamic nucleus in the rat. *J. Comp. Neurol.* 183:487–518.

Herrick, C. J.
1922. Some factors in the development of the amphibian nervous system. *Anat. Rec.* 23:291–305.
1948. *The brain of the Tiger Salamander.* Chicago: University of Chicago Press.
1969. *Brains of Rats and Men.* Chicago: University of Chicago Press.

Hopson, J. A.
1979. Paleoneurology. In *Biology of the Reptilia,* ed. C. G. Gans, R. G. Northcutt, and P. S. Ulinski, vol. 9, pp. 39–146. London: Academic Press.
1980. Relative brain size in dinosaurs: implications for dinosaurian endothermy. In *A Cold Look at the Warm-Blooded Dinosaurs,* ed. R. D. K. Thomas and E. C. Olson, pp. 287–310. Boulder: Westview Press.

Hunsaker, D.
1977. *The Biology of Marsupials.* New York: Academic Press.

Jenkins, F. A., Jr.
1973. The functional anatomy of the mammalian humero-ulnar articulation. *Am. J. Anat.* 137:281–97.

Jenkins, F. A., Jr., and Parrington, F. R.
1976. The postcranial skeletons of the Triassic mammals *Eozostrodon, Megazostrodon,* and *Erythrotherium. Roy. Soc. London Philos. Trans.,* B 273:341–87.

Jerison, H. J.
1973. *Evolution of The Brain and Intelligence.* New York: Academic Press.

Johnson, J. I., Jr.
1977. Central nervous system of marsupials. In *The Biology of Marsupials,* ed. D. Hunsaker II, pp. 157–278. New York: Academic Press.

Jones, E. G.
1981. Functional subdivision and synaptic organization of the mammalian thalamus. *Int. Rev. Physiol.* 25:173–245.

Jones, E. G., and Leavitt, R. Y.
1975. Retrograde axonal transport and the demonstration of non-specific projections to the cerebral cortex and striatum from thalamic intralaminar nuclei in the rat, cat and monkey. *J. Comp. Neurol.* 154:349–78.

Jones, E. G., and Powell, T. P. S.
1970. An anatomical study of converging sensory pathways within the cerebral cortex of the monkey. *Brain* 93:793–820.

Kaas, J. H.
1982. The segregation of function in the nervous system: why do sensory systems have so many subdivisions? *Contributions Sensory Physiol.* 7:201–40.

Kaas, J. H.; Nelson, R. J.; Sur, M.; and Merzenich, M. M.
1981. Organization of somatosensory cortex in primates. In *The Organization of The Cerebral Cortex,* ed F. O. Schmitt, F. G. Worden, G. Adelman, and S. G. Dennis, pp. 237–361. Cambridge: MIT Press.

Karten, H. J.
1967. The organization of the avian ascending auditory pathway in the pigeon *(Columba livia).* I. Diencephalic projections of the inferior colliculus (nucleus mesencephalicus lateralis, pars dorsalis). *Brain Res.* 6:409–27.
1969. The organization of the avian telencephalon and some speculations on the phylogeny of the amniote telencephalon. *Ann. N. Y. Acad. Sci.* 167:164–80.
1979. Visual lemniscal pathways in birds. In *Neural Mechanisms of Behavior in the Pigeon,* ed. A. M. Granda and J. H. Maxwell, pp. 409–30.

Karten, H. J., and Hodos, W.
1970. Telencephalic projections of the nucleus rotundus in the pigeon *(Columba livia). J. Comp. Neurol.* 140:35–52.

Keefe, J. O., and Nadel, L.
1978. *The Hippocampus as a Cognitive Map.* Oxford: Oxford University Press.

Kemp, J. M., and Powell, T. P. S.
1971. The connexions of the striatum and globus pallidus: synthesis and speculation. *Phil. Trans. Roy. Soc.* B 262:441–57.

Kemp, T. S.
1982. *Mammal-Like Reptiles and the Origin of Mammals.* London: Academic Press.

Kitt, C. A., and Brauth, S. E.
1981. A basal ganglia-thalamic-telencephalic pathway in pigeons. *Neurosci. Abstr.* 7:194.

Kornhuber, H. H.
1971. Motor functions of cerebellum and basal ganglia: the cerebellocortical saccadic (ballistic) clock, the cerebellonucleur hold regulator, and the basal ganglia ramp (voluntary speed smooth movement) generator. *Kybernetik* 8:157–162.

Kruger, L., and Berkowitz, E. C.
1960. The main afferent connections of the reptilian telencephalon as determined by degeneration and electrophysiological methods. *J. Comp. Neurol.* 115:125–41.

Lende, R. A.
1964. Representation in the cerebral cortex of a primitive mammal. *J. Neurophysiol.* 27:37–48.
1969. A comparative approach to neocortex: localization in monotremes, marsupials, and insectivores. Ann. N. Y. Acad. Sci. 167:262–75.

Lennard, P. R., and Stein, P. S. G.
1977. Swimming movements elicited by electrical stimulation of turtle spinal cord. I. Low spinal and intact preparations. *J. Neurophysiol.* 40:768–78.

Leonard, C. M.
1969. The prefrontal cortex of the rat. I. Cortical pro-

jection of the mediodorsal nucleus. II. Efferent Projections. *Brain Res.* 12:321–43.

Lillegraven, J. A.
1979. Reproduction in Mesozoic mammals. In *Mesozoic Mammals,* ed. J. A. Lillegraven, Z. Kielan-Jaworowska, and W. A. Clemens, pp. 259–76. Berkley: University of California Press.

Lohman, A. H. M., and van Woerden-Verkley, I.
1978. Ascending connections to the forebrain in the tegu lizard. *J. Cop. Neurol.* 182:555–94.

Lorente de Nó, R.
1934. Studies on the structure of cerebral cortex. II. Continuation of the study of the ammonic system. *J. Psychol. Neurol.* (Lpz.) 46:117–77.

Luiten, P. G. M.
1981a. Two visual pathways to the telencephalon in the nurse shark *(Ginglymostoma cirratum).* I. Retinal projections. *J. Comp. Neurol.* 196:531–38.
1981b. Two visual pathways to the telencephalon in the nurse shark *(Ginglymostoma cirratum).* II. Ascending thalamo-telencephalic connections. *J. Comp. Neurol.* 196:539–49.

Marshall, L. G.
1979. Evolution of metatherian and eutherian (mammalian) characters: a review based on cladistic methodology. *Zool. J. Linn. Soc.* 66:364–410.

Merzenich, M. M., and Kaas, J. H.
1980. Principles of organization of sensory-perceptual systems in mammals. *Proc. Psychobiol. Physiol. Psychol.* 9:1–42.

Nauta, W. J. H., and Karten, H. J.
1970. A general profile of the vertebrate brain, with sidelights on the ancestry of the cerebral cortex. In *The Neurosciences, Second Study Program,* ed F. O. Schmitt, pp. 7–26. New York: Rockefeller University Press.

Nieuwenhuys, R.
1974. Topological analysis of the brain stem: a general introduction. *J. Comp. Neurol.* 156:255–76.

Northcutt, R.G.
1971. The telencephalon of the western painted turtle *(Chrysemys picta belli). Illinois Biol. Monographs* 43:1–113.
1981. Evolution of the telencephalon in nonmammals. *Ann. Rev. Neurosci.* 4:301–50.

Orlovsky, G. N., and Shik, M. L.
1976. Control of locomotion: a neurophysiological analysis of cat locomotor system. *Int. Rev. Physiol.* 10:281–317.

Orrego, F.
1961. The reptilian forebrain. I. The olfactory path-

ways and cortical areas in the turtle. *Arch. Ital. Biol.* 99:425–45.

Osborn, J. W.
1973. The evolution of dentitions. *Amer. Sci.* 61:548–59.

Parent, A.
1979. Monoaminergic systems in reptile brains. In *Biology of the Reptilia,* ed. C. Gans, R. G. Northcutt, and P. S. Ulinski, vol. 10, pp. 247–85. London: Academic Press.

Phillips, C. G. and Porter, R.
1977. *Corticospinal Neurones.* London: Academic Press.

Platel, R.
1979. Brain weight-body weight relationships. In *Biology of the Reptilia,* ed C. G. Gans, R. G. Northcutt, and P. S. Ulinski, vol. 9, pp. 147–72. London: Academic Press.

Porter, R.
1975. The neurophysiology of movement performance. In *MTP International Review of Science,* Physiology Series One, ed. C. C. Hunt vol. 3, pp. 151–83. Baltimore: University Park Press.

Powell, T. P. S., and Cowan, W. M.
1961. The thalamic projection upon the telencephalon in the pigeon *(Columba livia). J. Anat.* (Lond.) 95:78–109.

Powell, T. P. S., and Kruger, L.
1960. The thalamic projection upon the telencephalon in *Lacerta viridis. J. Anat.* (Lond.) 94:528–42.

Price, J. L.
1973. An autoradiographic study of complementary laminar patterns of termination of afferent fibers to the olfactory cortex. *J. Comp. Neurol.* 150:87–108.

Price, J. L., and Sprich, W. W.
1975. Observations on the lateral olfactory tract of the rat. *J. Comp. Neurol.* 162:321–36.

Pritz, M. B.
1974. Ascending connections of a thalamic auditory area in a crocodile, *Caiman crocodilus. J. Comp. Neurol.* 153:199–214.
1975. Anatomical identification of a telencephalic visual area in crocodiles: ascending connections of nucleus rotundus in *Caiman crocodilus. J. Comp. Neurol.* 164:323–38.

Pritz, M. B., and Northcutt, R. G.,
1980. Anatomical evidence for an ascending somatosensory pathway to the telencephalon in crocodiles, *Caiman crocodilus. Exp. Brain Res.* 40:342–45.

Prochazka, A.

1981. Muscle spindle function during normal movement. *Int. Rev. Physiol.* 25:47–90.

Proske, U.

1981. The Golgi tendon organ. Properties of the receptor and reflex action of impulses arising from tendon organs. *Int. Rev. Physiol.* 25:127–71.

Quiroga, J. C.

1979. The brain of two mammal-like reptiles (Cynodontia-Therapsida). *J. Hirnforsch.* 20:341–50.

1980a. The brain of the mammal-like reptile *Probainognathus jenseni* (Therapsida, Cynodontia). A correlative paleo-neoneurological approach to the neocortex at the reptile-mammal transition. *J. Hirnforsch* 21:299–336.

1980b. Sobre un molde endocraneano del cinodonte *Probainognathus jeseni* Romer, 1970 (Reptilia, Therapsida) de la Formacion Ischichuca (Triasico medio), La Rioja, Argentina. *Ameghiniana* 17:181–90.

Radinsky, L.

1975a. Evolution of the felid brain. *Brain, Behav. Evol.* 11:214–54

1975b. Primate brain evolution. *Am.Sci.* 63:656–63.

1977. Brains of early carnivores. *Paleobiol.* 3:333–49.

Regal, P. J.

1978. Behavioral differences between reptiles and mammals: an analysis of activity and mental capabilities. In *Behavior and Neurology of Lizards,* ed. N. Greenberg and P. D. MacLean pp. 183–202. Bethesda; NIMH.

Reiner, A.; Brauth, S. E.; Kitt, C. A.; and Karten, H. J.

1980. Basal ganglionic pathways to the tectum: studies in reptiles. *J. Comp. Neurol.* 193:565–589.

Rockel, A. J.; Heath, C. J.; and Jones, E. G.

1972. Afferent connections to the diencephalon in the marsupial phalanger and the question of sensory convergence in the "posterior group" of the thalamus. *J. Comp. Neurol.* 145:105–30.

Robertson, R. T., and Kaitz, S. S.

1981. Thalamic connections with limbic cortex. I. Thalamocortical projections. *J. Comp. Neurol.* 195:501–26.

Rose, J. E., and Woolsey, C. N.

1958. Cortical connections and functional organization of the thalamic auditory system of the cat. In *Biological and Biochemical Bases of Behavior,* ed. H. F. Harlow and C. N. Woolsey pp. 127–50. Madison: University of Wisconsin Press.

Sakai, S. T.

1982. The thalamic connectivity of the primary motor cortex (MI) in the raccoon. *J. Comp. Neurol.* 204:238–52.

Schlag, J.; Lehtinen, J.; and Schlag-Rey, M.

1974. Neuronal activity before and during eye movements in thalamic internal medullary lamina of cat. *J. Neurophysiol.* 37:982–95.

Simpson, G. G.

1927. Mesozoic mammalia. IX. The brain of Jurassic mammals. *Am. J. Sci.* 14:259–68.

1937. Skull structure of the multituberculata. *Bull. Am. Mus. Nat. Hist.,* 73:727–63.

Skeen, L. C., and Hall, W. C.

1977. Efferent projections of the main and the accessory olfactory bulb in the tree shrew *(Tupai glis). J. Comp. Neurol.* 172:1–36.

Smeets, J. A. J.

1981a. Retinofugal pathways in two chondrichthyans, the shark *Scyliorhinus canicula* and the ray *Raja clavata. J. Comp. Neurol.* 195:1–12.

1981b. Efferent tectal pathways in two chondrichthyans, the shark *Scyliorhinus canicula* and the ray *Raja clavata. J. Comp. Neurol.* 195:13–24.

Smith, L. M.; Ebner, F. F.; and Colonnier, M.

1980. The thalamocortical projection in *Pseudemys* turtles: a quantitative electron microscopic study. *J. Comp. Neurol.* 190:445–62.

Spreafico, R.; Hayes, N. L.; and Rustioni, A.

1981. Thalamic projections to the primary and secondary somatosensory cortices in cat: single and double retrograde tracer studies. *J. Comp. Neurol.* 203:67–90.

Stebbins, W. C.

1980. The evolution of hearing in the mammals. In *Comparative Studies of Hearing in Vertebrates,* ed. A. N. Popper and R. R. Fay pp. 421–36. New York: Springer-Verlag.

Stein, P. S. G.

1978. Motor systems, with specific reference to the control of locomotion. *Ann. Rev. Neurosci.* 1:61–82.

Steward, O.

1976. Topographic organization of projections from the entorhinal area to the hippocampal formation of the rat. *J. Comp. Neurol.* 167:285–314.

Steward, O., and Scoville, S. A.

1976. Cells of origin of entorhinal cortical afferents to the hippocampus and fascia dentata of the rat. *J. Comp. Neurol.* 169:347–70.

Ulinski, P. S.

1974. Cytoarchitecture of cerebral cortex in snakes. *J. Comp. Neurol.* 158:243–66.

1975. Corticoseptal projections in the snakes *Natrix*

sipedon and *Thamnophis sirtalis. J. Comp. Neurol.* 164:375–388.

1976. Intracortical connections in the snakes *Natrix sipedon* and *Thamnophis sirtalis. J. Morph.* 150:463–84.

1977. Tectal efferents in the banded water snake, *Natrix sipedon. J. Comp. Neurol.* 173:251–74.

1978. Organization of anterior dorsal ventricular ridge in snakes. *J. Comp. Neurol.* 178(3): 411–50.

1980a. Functional morphology of the vertebrate visual system: an essay on the evolution of complex systems. *Am. Zool.* 20:229–46.

1980b. Organization of the retinogeniculate projection in pond turtles, *Pseudemys* and *Chrysemys. Neurosci. Absts.* 6:748.

1980c. Patterns of cortical organization. *Proc. Hines-Loyola Med. Conferences in Neurol.* 9:43–60.

1981. Thalamic projections to the somatosensory cortex of the echidna, *Tachyglossus aculeatus. Neurosci. Absts.* 7:757.

1983. *Dorsal Ventricular Ridge; a Treatise on Forebrain Organization* in Reptiles and Birds. New York: John Wiley and Son.

Ulinski, P. S., and Peterson, E. H.

1981. Patterns of olfactory projections in the desert iguana, *Dipsosaurus dorsalis. J. Morph.* 168:189–228.

Ulinski, P. S., and Rainey, W. T.

1980. Intrinsic organization of snake lateral cortex. *J. Morph.* 165:85–116.

Van Essen, D. C.

1979. Visual areas of the mammalian cerebral cortex. *Ann Rev. Neurosci.* 2:227–63.

Walker, A. E.

1938. *The Primate Thalamus.* Chicago: University of Chicago Press.

Webster, K. E.

1979. Some aspects of the comparative study of the corpus striatum. In *The Neostriatum,* ed. I. Divac and R. G. E. Öberg, pp. 107–26. New York: Pergamon Press.

Welker, W., and Lende, R. A.

1980. Thalamocortical relationships in echidna *(Tachyglossus aculeatus).* In *Comparative Neurology of the Telencephalon,* ed. S. O. E. Ebbesson, New York: Plenum.

Woolsey, C. N.

1958. Organization of somatic sensory and motor areas of the cerebral cortex. In *Biological and Biochemical Bases of Behavior,* ed. H. Harlow and C. N. Woolsey pp. 63–81. Madison: University of Wisconsin Press.

1981a. *Cortical Sensory Organization Vol. 1, Multiple Somatic Areas.* Clifton: Humana.

1981b. *Cortical Sensory Organization, Vol. 2, Multiple Visual Areas.* Clifton: Humana.

1982. *Cortical Auditory Organization, Vol. 3, Multiple Auditory Visual Areas.* Clifton, N. J.: Humana.

J. J. ROTH[1] AND E. C. ROTH[1]
former Staff Fellows
Laboratory of Brain Evolution and Behavior
National Institute of Mental Health
Bethesda, Maryland 20205
and
NICHOLAS HOTTON III
Department of Paleobiology
Smithsonian Institution
Washington, D. C. 20506

The Parietal Foramen and Eye: Their Function and Fate in Therapsids

Introduction

The parietal foramen, a midline opening in the parietal roof of the endocranial cavity, is present in nearly all Paleozoic vertebrates including synapsid reptiles, where it lies between the parietal bones. In many lizards, it lies at the confluence of the interparietal and frontoparietal sutures. The parietal foramen tends to disappear in advanced members of most lineages, and today is restricted to 11 of the 18 extant families of lizards (Gundy, Ralph, and Wurtz, 1975), the sole surviving rhynchocephalian *Sphenodon punctatus* (Dendy, 1911), and lampreys. In lizards, *Sphenodon,* and lampreys, the parietal foramen houses the parietal eye ("third eye"). In two genera of lizards, *Gerrhonotus* and *Aniella,* an eye is present despite the absence of a foramen. The parietal eye is characterized by a retina and a transparent lens and is spheroidal in shape; evidence of its photoreceptive function is summarized in detail by Quay (1979). In lizards, neural connection of the eye is to the left medial habenular nucleus (Engbretson, Reiner, and Brecha, 1981). In three families of frogs, the homologue of the parietal eye is the "stirnorgan", which, though photoreceptive, is not eyelike in structure; responses of the stirnorgan are different from those of the parietal eye (Ralph, Firth, and Turner, 1979). In frogs the parietal foramen is a microscopic canal through the frontoparietal bone that transmits a fine nerve from the stirnorgan to the habenula.

Because of its history and the obscurity of its function, the parietal eye was for many years regarded as a vestigial structure of no great functional significance in living species, and the

[1]Current address:
405 Hill Drive
Craig, Colorado 81625

question of its function in fossil species was largely dismissed. Edinger (1955) took exception to this attitude on the grounds that evolutionary retention of the eye by a variety of animals implies its continued functional significance in those animals. She emphasized the applicability of data from the living to the interpretation of fossil animals with the challenge: "If one doubts that this association [between the parietal foramen and a photoreceptive organ] existed also in extinct vertebrates, one may as well doubt that the orbits of fossil skulls contained eyes." Edinger's study marked a resurgence of interest in the function of the parietal eye, which began with Stebbins' classic work on lizards (e.g., Stebbins and Eakin, 1958) and continues to the present day. Recent advances are comprehensively reviewed by Quay (1979). The purpose of the present work is to utilize this information to interpret the parietal foramen of synapsid reptiles, in which the history of the foramen corresponds to that of tetrapods generally.

The parietal eye is associated with the glandular pineal body, which lies just behind it in the midline (Fig. 1). Together these structures make up the parietal-pineal complex, both elements being derived from the epiphyseal anlage. In all living animals in which it has been studied, the pineal body is predominantly secretory, but there is evidence of photoreceptive capacity as well in many lower vertebrates, including, but

not restricted to, species with a parietal eye (Ralph, Firth, and Turner, 1979).

Among extant vertebrates, so far as is known, the epiphyseal derivatives are expressed in three distinct adult conditions, which have been coded by Roth and Roth (1980) as follows:

Parietal eye	Pineal body	Code
present	present	E-2
absent	present	E-1
absent	absent	E-0

Eleven families of lizards and *Sphenodon* manifest condition E-2; lampreys appear to represent a very primitive condition in which both pineal body and parietal eye have an eyelike configuration. The status of frogs is equivocal. The great majority of living vertebrates manifest condition E-1, their ancestors having lost the parietal eye while retaining the pineal body. Crocodilian reptiles and edentate and sirenian mammals are a small minority that manifests condition E-0, having lost both elements of the parietal-pineal complex.

The function of the parietal eye is still incompletely understood, but includes an important role in thermoregulation; parietalectomized lizards consistently thermoregulate to a body temperature a degree or two higher than intact animals (Roth and Ralph, 1976, 1977). The parietal eye is also involved in coordination of cyclic aspects of reproduction with diurnal and seasonal periodicity (see Quay, 1979). The influence of the eye on reproduction may be a consequence of its thermoregulatory activity (Licht and Pearson, 1970; Engbretson and Hutchison, 1976). In any event, by means of its photoreceptive capacity and exposure to the environment, the parietal eye appears to monitor ambient radiation, which includes heat as well as light within the total spectrum of sunlight (Roth and Ralph, 1976, 1977).

The function of the pineal body appears to overlap that of the parietal eye in lower tetrapods, to the extent that both elements share secretory and photoreceptive capacities. The lateral eyes are also associated with the parietal-pineal complex in the coordination of cyclic physiology with periodic ambient radiation. The genus *Alligator* is an extreme example, in which production of the hormone melatonin, previously thought to be restricted to the pineal body, has been identified in the lateral retinae and in the harderian glands of the lateral orbits (Roth, Gern, Roth, Ralph, and Jacobson, 1980). Such

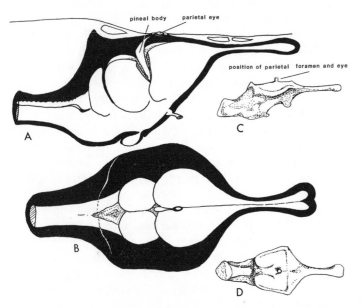

Figure 1. Brain, endocranial space, and endocranial cast of the iguanid lizard *Cyclura ornata*. A, lateral; B, dorsal; C, endocast, lateral; D, endocast, dorsal.

ROTH, ROTH, AND HOTTON

overlap of function may account for the wide range of expression of the parietal-pineal complex in lower tetrapods, to the extent that it enables compensation for evolutionary loss of various elements in different lineages, e.g. turtles (E-1) and crocodilians (E-0).

The parietal eye has a most reliable osteological correlate in the parietal foramen, a marker that is readily accessible for direct study in fossil vertebrates (Fig. 1C, D). The pineal body, on the other hand, has no such distinctive osteological correlate, regardless of whether the brain fills most of the endocranial cavity as in mammals and birds (Fig. 2A, B), or occupies but little more than half of it, as in adult reptiles (Fig. 2C-F). Exceptionally, in well preserved and carefully prepared therapsid skulls, the caudal endocranial border of the parietal foramen bears a slight indentation that suggests contact with a pineal body lying just behind the parietal eye, as in some lizards (Roth and Roth, personal observation). For the most part, however, the pineal body is separated from the bones roofing the endocranial cavity and so leaves no mark on them. In mammals it is deeply situated between the cerebral hemispheres, while in birds, and in reptiles lacking a parietal foramen, the pineal body is separated from the endocranial roof by tissue of the dorsal sagittal sinus. Reports of a large pineal body in certain dinosaurs (e.g. Swinton, 1958) are based on misidentification of the natural cast of a cartilagenous process of the supraoccipital bone, which, when preserved, is confluent with the endocranial cast.

Since the pineal body lacks any useful osteological marker, its presence in extinct animals must be inferred largely from the condition of extant animals, a condition that suggests that synapsid reptiles had a pineal body. If the parietal foramen is present, synapsids are identified as E-2 because of the universal association of the parietal eye with the pineal body in living species. If not, they are identified as E-1 because of the great preponderance of living species that lack a parietal eye but have a pineal body. The fact that the E-0 condition cannot be identified in fossil material by these criteria does not affect the interpretation of mammal-like reptiles, which are neither closely related to nor convergent toward the few living animals that are identified as E-0.

The Historical Problem

The loss of the parietal eye poses an evolutionary problem because the eye has a very long history as a basic vertebrate feature. Its first appearance is documented by the universal presence of a parietal foramen in the earliest jawless vertebrates, and its nature in these animals is indicated by the photoreceptive parietal eye of living lampreys. Whatever the modifications it may have undergone when vertebrates came out of water, the eye continued to be favored by selection in tetrapods until the end of the Permian. That these animals were ectothermic can be assumed on the grounds that ectothermy is the primitive condition of vertebrates. This assumption is supported, for all Paleozoic tetrapods except therapsids, by the histology of the long bones (de Ricqlès, 1976), by general body form, and by sprawled limb posture. The presence of a parietal eye in ectothermic tetrapods of the Paleozoic suggests that the eye functioned then as it does now. In Paleozoic tetrapods as in living lizards, the eye probably served to monitor ambient radiation in the control of body temperature, and in the coordination of cyclic reproductive physiology with environmental periodicity.

In synapsid reptiles, the history of the parietal eye, as indicated by the parietal foramen, can be divided into three stages: first, universal presence in pelycosaurs (Early Permian) and persistence in most therapsids of the Late Permian; second, absence in a few therapsids in the Late Permian and Early Triassic; third, absence in all advanced therapsids that survived beyond the Middle Triassic. These stages do not correspond to morphological changes that can be related to thermoregulation. Although the parietal eye remains an obvious feature of most therapsids un-

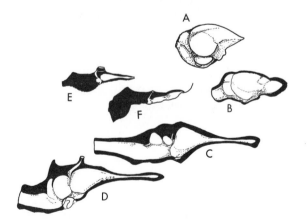

Figure 2. Diagrammatic representation, in lateral aspect, of volumetric relationships of brain (white) and endocranial space (black) in living and fossil tetrapods. A, eagle; B, opossum; C, alligator; D, lizard; E, dicynodont *(Diictodon);* F, theriodont. E and F, mid- and forebrain only.

til well into the Triassic, the basic morphological differences between pelycosaurs and therapsids (Olson, 1944) suggest that advent of 'incipient homoiothermy' with the origin of therapsids at the beginning of the Late Permian (Olson, 1959). This conclusion is supported by the work of de Ricqlès (e.g. 1976) on bone histology. The persistence of the foramen suggests that despite changes in synapsid thermoregulation, the ancient mechanism for monitoring ambient radiation continued to be an integral part of the system. On the other hand, although the parietal foramen had disappeared in advanced therapsids by the Middle Triassic, a definitive mammalian endothermy seems not to have been established until the appearance of true mammals near the end of the Triassic (e.g. Crompton, Taylor, and Jagger, 1978). This lack of coordination does little to clarify our earlier suggestion (Roth and Roth, 1980) that loss of the parietal eye may have coincided with or may have favored the origin of mammalian endothermy (see also Bennett and Ruben, this volume). Loss of the parietal eye in therapsids was probably not closely related to the attainment of mammalness, at least with respect to thermoregulation.

The parietal eye was also lost in a variety of tetrapods that were neither incipient endotherms nor mammal-like in any other respect, at the same time that it disappeared in therapsids. This temporal coincidence suggests that the search for causes of the loss of the parietal eye in therapsids should refer to the evolutionary fate of the eye in other lineages. Extant lizards are useful candidates for such a reference because some of them have a parietal eye while others do not, and because of their current diversity and geographic distribution. In addition, the tendency in some lizard species for developmental closure of the foramen suggests a possible model

of a proximate cause, as opposed to a history, of parietal eye loss. Edinger (1955) reports that in large individuals of *Iguana iguana,* the dorsal end of the parietal foramen becomes closed by bone, with a ventral remnant retained as a coincal hollow in the ceiling of the endocranial space. It was the observation of a similar condition in two large individuals out of 200 *Anolis carolinensis* (Roth and Roth), and in a very large individual of *Cyclura cornuta* (Hotton), that prompted us to examine this phenomenon in greater detail.

Developmental Closure of the Parietal Foramen in Lizards

In its external configuration, the parietal foramen of lizards mimics that of therapsids on a smaller scale. In many lizards, as in most therocephalians and cynodonts and in some dicynodonts and gorgonopsians, the foramen opens flush with the surface of the skull roof. In such large iguanid lizards as *Iguana iguana* and *Cyclura nubila,* but not *Cyclura cornuta,* the foramen opens into a shallow, bowl-shaped depression of slightly greater diameter. The depression is surrounded by a rim that rises slightly above the skull table; the rim is thick and boss-like in *I. iguana,* thin and ring-like in *C. nubila.* Comparable ornamentation is more elaborate in dinocephalians and many dicynodonts and gorgonopsians, in which it ranges from a low boss like that of *Iguana* to a volcano-shaped structure several millimeters high. The greater diversity of parietal ornament appears to reflect the greater diversity of therapsids in size and general osteology, rather than any significant difference between lizards and therapsids in content or function of the parietal foramen.

Details of foramen closure to be considered are

Table 1.—Parameters of regressions of greatest diameter of parietal foramen (PFD_g) on dorsal length of skull (SDL, back of parietal to premaxilla), $\log Y = \log b + a \log X$. Correlations are significant at a confidence level > 99.0%

Taxon	Sample size (N)	Correlation coefficient (r)	Slope (a)	Y-intercept (log b)
Anolis carolinensis	106	−.59	−2.3255553	2.3673303
Iguana iguana	20*	.61	0.8088282	−1.1637602
Captorhinus aguti	8	.93	0.8481464	−0.9913898
Diictodon sp., combined sample	32	.51	0.3158457	0.0890622

*Specimen with occluded foramen not used in computation; see Fig. 5.

ROTH, ROTH, AND HOTTON

based on four groups of parietal-eyed reptiles, two extant and two of Permian age, which were compared according to the following procedure.

Materials and methods

The extant iguanid lizard *Anolis carolinensis* (Table 1; Figs. 3 and 4) was chosen for the present study because of its availability in large samples of natural populations for which size parameters of growth and maturity are known. *A. carolinensis* arrives at sexual maturity (indicated by the initiation of ovarian follicular cycles) after about 3 years, when snout-vent length is about 46 mm and skull length equals or exceeds 12 mm. An initial sample, acquired in August, 1979, from a commerical supplier in Louisiana, ranged from young of the year (two or three months post-hatching) to fully mature adults.

Since *A. carolinensis* is much smaller than the smallest appropriate Permian reptiles, the extant *Iguana iguana* was incorporated into the quantitative study (Table 1; Fig. 5) to accommodate possible effects of size-scaling on foramen morphology. Data from *I. iguana* were supplemented by data from the similar-sized *I. delicatissima, Cyclura cornuta,* and *C. nubila* (Fig. 5). *Iguana* and *Cyclura* are represented by specimens in the osteological collections at the National Museum of Natural History, Smithsonian Institution; at the Museum of Comparative Zoology, Harvard; and at the University of Florida. With respect to determinable stages of life history, these animals range from small individuals (skull length < 40 mm) that are catalogued as juveniles on the basis of field data, to one of the larger adults of *I. iguana* (skull length 75.6 mm), which was more than 15 years old at death.

The Early Permian anapsid *Captorhinus aguti* and the Late Permian dicynodont genus *Diictodon* (Table 1; Fig. 5) were selected on a necessarily opportunistic basis. Few fossil taxa showing the appropriate details are abundant, and most are difficult to prepare. Specimens of *Captorhinus* from a system of fissure fills in limestone near Spur, Oklahoma, are unusually well preserved and easily prepared, and those of *Diictodon* are unusually abundant at certain stratigraphic levels in Cape Province, South Africa. The sample of *Captorhinus* was borrowed from the Field Museum of Natural History, and that of *Diictodon* was selected from the National Collection. There are no clear criteria other than size for judging maturity in Permian reptiles.

The lizard samples are monospecific, that of *A.*

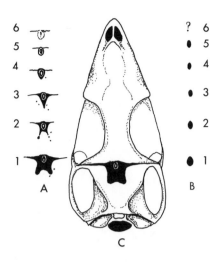

Figure 3. Changes in the parietal foramen with increase in size: A, living iguanid lizard, (♀) *Anolis carolinensis;* B, Early Permian anapsid reptile, *Captorhinus aguti.* A1 – A6 represent the parietal regions of growth stages of *A. carolinensis* with snout-vent lengths ranging from 35 mm to 54 mm, youngest to oldest. Stage A6 reflects complete closure of the foramen of an individual of 54 mm snout-vent length. B1 – B6 represent the foramina of skulls of *C. aguti* with lengths (back of parietal to premaxilla) ranging from 27.3 mm to 76.7 mm. These skull lengths correspond to snout-vent lengths of approximately 87 to 245 mm. Stage B6 is questionable, since closure was not observed in any specimen of *C. aguti.* C, relationships of skull, third eye, and parietal foramen in an immature female *A. carolinensis.*

carolinensis more clearly so than that of *I. iguana* because it was drawn from a more restricted geographic range. For the fossil populations, however, comparable taxonomic uniformity cannot be assured. *Captorhinus,* from a single locality of limited stratigraphic range, may approximate the lizard samples in uniformity, but *Diictodon,* being drawn from three localities of uncertain stratigraphic relationship, may represent one species or three. In the present case, however, taxonomic heterogeneity probably does not pose a problem, for all of the individuals in each fossil genus are of similar size and body form and would be expected to have similar thermoregulatory and reproductive requirements. The quantitative features that we have utilized reflect neither generic nor specific distinction in a variety of iguanid lizards (Hotton, unpublished data).

At the arrival of the initial sample of *A. carolinensis,* which consisted of 200 females, all animals were weighed (0.01 gm) on a Mettler balance, and snout-vent length measured with a

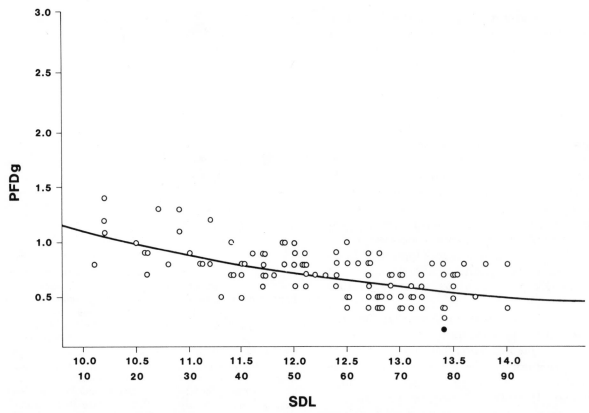

Figure. 4. Regression of PFD$_g$ on SDL (Y = bx^a) for *Anolis carolinensis*. Filled symbol indicates fully occluded foramen; value of PFD$_g$ is based on shallow pit in dorsum of parietals (see text). See Table 1 for parameters log Y = log b + alog X.

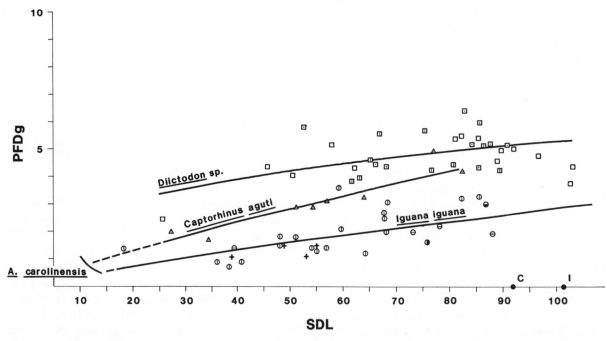

Figure 5. Regressions of PFD$_g$ on SDL (Y = bx^a) for the extant lizard *Iguana iguana* (◑, ◕, ●^{I}), the Early Permian anapsid reptile *Captorhinus aguti* (△), and the Late Permian dicynodont *Diictodon* sp. (□, ⊡, ⊞). For lizards, filled and partly filled symbols indicate occluded and partly occluded formina. For *Diictodon*, different symbols indicate different localities (see text). See Table 1 for parameters log Y = log b + a log X. *I. delicatissima* (+) and two species of *Cyclura* (⊖, ◐, ●^{C}) are plotted to show similarity to *I. iguana* in PFD$_g$ relative to SDL, but were not used in computation, nor was one specimen of *I. iguana* with occluded foramen (●^{I}). Vertical scale exaggerated X5 for clarity. The regression of *A. carolinensis* (Fig. 4) is also plotted to this scale to facilitate comparison.

ROTH, ROTH, AND HOTTON

metric rule. Weights and snout-vent lengths were normally distributed, with a central tendency grouped about a snout-vent length of 45 to 46 mm. This sample was culled by removing emaciated and obviously sick animals, male hatchlings, and animals with damaged third eyes, and was then subdivided. A large number of specimens were prepared histologically for study of the relationships among brain, endocranial cavity, and parietal-pineal complex, while skulls of 106 others were selected for osteological examination of the parietal foramen. Osteological specimen were prepared by removing the skin from the top and sides of the heads, which were then exposed to large populations of small (newly hatched) mealworms. By this means the skulls were cleared of muscle and brain tissue in about 15 minutes, after which they were immersed briefly in commercial bleaching fluid. To avoid damage to the bone, the material was monitored closely throughout these processes. The small size of *Anolis* required that skull dimensions, including those of the parietal foramen, be measured by a Zeiss binocular dissecting microscope fitted with an ocular micrometer, calibrated to 0.1 mm.

None of the specimens of the large iguanid lizards and Permian reptiles needed preparation for this study. Their size range is such that they can be easily measured by dial calipers accurate to 0.1 mm.

The samples were compared in terms of the greatest diameter of the parietal foramen (PFD_g) relative to an index of overall size, in this case the dorsal length of the skull (SDL: Table 1; Figs. 4 and 5). Anteroposterior and transverse diameters of the parietal foramen are subequal in about 33% of each sample, and where the disparity between them is 10% or more, it is the anteroposterior which is the greater. SDL was used as the independent variable because it is accessible in the greatest number of fossil specimens, and is least affected by the distortion to which fossils are subject.

It will be noted that in the specimen of *Anolis* in which the foramen is closed, the value of PFD_g is greater than zero (Fig. 4), whereas in comparable specimens of *Cyclura cornuta* and *Iguana iguana* the value is equal to zero (Fig. 5). The foramen is fully occluded in all three, but in *Anolis* the external position of the foramen is marked by a small pit, the superficial diameter of which can be measured. In *I. iguana*, the external position of the foramen is marked by a raised boss, but there is no depression left to me-

sure. In *C. cornuta* the external position of the foramen is undetectable; once occluded, the foramen leaves no more trace than if it had never existed.

Lizard specimens were examined for bone pathology, but no correspondence between general pathology and foramen closure was found. For example, in a specimen of *I. iguana* that is known to have lived in captivity for 15 years after its capture as a juvenile, fusion of the vertebral column is extensive and exostoses are common on ribs and neural spines. The partly-closed condition of the foramen, however, is the same as in a specimen of *C. nubila,* which, though larger, shows no pathology in the skeleton. Nor do individuals with a completely closed foramen show bone pathology other than healed injuries.

Results

Closure of the parietal foramen is complete in three specimens in our lizard samples, one each of *Anolis, I. iguana,* and *C. cornuta,* and earlier stages are indicated by two other specimens (Fig. 5). In one of the larger individuals of *I. iguana* and the larger of two specimens of *C. nubila,* the depression surrounding the foramen contains fine spicules, some of which partially occlude the foramen itself. Closure seems to occur about as frequently in *I. iguana,* in which the foramen opens into a depression with a prominent rim, as in *C. cornuta,* which lacks both depression and rim.

The lizard samples indicate that occlusion of the foramen accompanies large individual size (Figs. 4 and 5), and therefore, presumably, advanced age. In *Anolis,* closure does not appear to be an inevitable concomitant of growth (Fig. 4): the specimen in which the foramen is closed, though it falls within the largest 14% of the sample, is not the largest individual by a considerable margin. This relationship is probably a manifestation of the generally high variability of PFD_g in *Anolis.* In the large iguanids it is the largest representative of each genus that shows the greatest degree of occlusion (Fig. 5). In *Iguana,* however, the specimen that shows partial occlusion is smaller than some that do not, and the sample, though small, suggests a variability of PFD_g that is comparable to the variability of *Anolis.*

In the smallest representatives of both samples of lizards, a fontanelle at the junction between the parietal and frontal bones indicates delayed ossification in the midline of the skull. The fontanelle surrounds the parietal eye (Fig.

3) and thereby enlarges the measurable dimensions of the parietal foramen in very small individuals. In *Anolis* the fontanelle persists in diminishing size almost to sexual maturity, a circumstance that produces a negative slope in the regression of PFD_g on SDL (Fig. 4; Table 1). In large iguanids the fontanelle does not persist as long as in *Anolis* and the margins of the parietal foramen can be identified accurately in individuals of relatively smaller size. In consequence the slope of the regression for *I. iguana* is positive (Fig. 5; Table 1). PFD_g of *Anolis* is absolutely smaller than PFD_g of *I. iguana*, but is slightly larger relative to SDL.

In *Captorhinus* and *Diictodon* the parietal foramen is both absolutely and relatively larger than in lizards. The largest individuals show none of the signs of occlusion that are encountered in lizards, although the largest specimens of *Diictodon* from a single locality (□, Fig. 5) suggest a downward trend in PFD_g. The significance of this trend, however, is uncertain without much larger samples than are currently available, and without indication of incipient closure in large individuals, it is very doubtful that occlusion of the foramen occurred in these animals.

The smallest skulls of *Captorhinus* and *Diictodon* show no trace of a fontanelle, although the loosely sutured condition of the dermal bones confirms the presumptive immaturity of small specimens. The regression of PFD_g on SDL for these animals therefore has a slope that is positive, though of very low value, like that of *I. iguana* (Fig. 5; Table 1). In *Captorhinus*, variability (indicated by r = .93, Table 1) is much less than in *Diictodon* (r = .51), where it is comparable to the variability of lizards (*Anolis*, r = −.59); *Iguana*, r = .61). In view of the small size of the sample of *Captorhinus*, however, the significance of this difference is open to question.

Discussion

In its large size and lack of indication of closure, the parietal foramen of the Late Permian *Diictodon* illustrates the condition of therapsids during the first stage in the history of the synapsid parietal foramen. This condition is shared by Early Permian tetrapods that include *Captorhinus*, which is closer to the ancestry of lizards than to that of therapsids. It is probable that the larger size of the foramen in these animals involves a component of parietal eye function; a larger eye has a greater capacity to gather radiant energy (Edinger, 1955). Edinger, however, also warns against inferring parietal eye func-

tion from the size of the foramen, a warning that must be heeded in view of the limitations of current information. Accordingly, while size of the parietal foramen must be dealt with, it is presence or absence of the foramen that remains the most reliable datum.

The fontanelle, being present in extant lizards and absent in *Captorhinus* and *Diictodon*, probably reflects a difference between lizards and Permian reptiles in the timing or rate of bone formation. In small individuals of *Iguana* and *Cyclura* (SDL < 40 mm, fontanelle present), the skull bones are much thinner than those of small fossil individuals, but in the largest of these lizards (Fig. 5), skull bones are comparable in thickness to the largest *Captorhinus* and *Diictodon*. Assuming that size corresponds to age, ossification must either start later or proceed at a slower rate in young lizards than in the young of fossil species, but must accelerate at some point to a rate faster than that of fossil forms. Since the parietal foramen of lizards is small to begin with, occasional closure in large individuals may be expected as persistently high rates of ossification in mature animals overshoot the mark.

Such an effect cannot be expected in pelycosaurs and most therapsids, as much because of their large overall size and the relatively large size of the foramen as because of putatively lower adult rates of ossification. In smaller therapsids with smaller foramina, however, it is conceivable that the foramen could be occluded in the course of growth, as in lizards. None of the therapsids in which the foramen is certainly absent, the few of Late Permian and Early Triassic age (second stage) as well as the many of Middle Triassic and younger age (third stage), are larger than *Iguana* and *Cyclura* (length of adult skull 60 to 90 mm). In their closest kin, the foramen that is retained is small relative to head size.

The animals that represent the second stage in the history of the synapsid parietal foramen are largely restricted to scaloposaurs (Late Permian) and the dicynodont *Kombuisia* (Early Triassic). The Early Triassic genus *Bauria* also lacks a foramen, but may have inherited this condition from scaloposaurian ancestors. Scaloposaurs are small, predaceous (insectivorous?) therocephalians; in some the parietal foramen is present and in others absent (Broom, 1932). *Kombuisia*, perhaps a forager in ground litter (Hotton, this volume) lacks a foramen, in contrast to all other known dicynodonts (Hotton, 1974). In the Late Permian dicynodont *Dinanomodon*, the foramen is so small that Broom (1938, 1940) questions its existence, but *Dinanomodon* is a very large animal in which the temporal musculature encroached on the parietal region. This is a condition that commonly obscures the foramen without actually occluding it, and it is probable that *Dinanomodon* had a parietal foramen, albeit a small one (Haughton and Brink, 1954).

The question of developmental closure of the parietal foramen, on the lizard model, in scaloposaurs and other second-stage therapsids has not yet been addressed, but the evidence for it may lie in species-level taxonomy. Species-level taxonomy of most therapsids, as of many groups of Paleozoic tetrapods, is at best uncertain and at worst chaotic. It is entirely possible that non-fenestrate scaloposaur species include smaller individuals which, because they have a parietal foramen, have been misdiagnosed as members of a different species. Future inquiry should start with a review of the anatomical basis of the classification of these animals, without reference to the parietal foramen. The parietal region of fenestrate and nonfenestrate therapsids should eventually be compared with that of lizards of comparable size. Such comparison, however, must await details of the internal parietal sculpture of lizards, both those that lack a foramen and those in which the foramen is occluded in the course of growth.

Fate of the Parietal Eye of Therapsids

Since the most parsimonious explanation of parietal eye function in synapsids involves the periodicity of ambient radiation and of reproduction, the most obvious environmental factor favoring maintenance of the synapsid eye is seasonality. Seasonality is one feature the environments of pelycosaurs and therapsids had in common, although remains of pelycosaurs are distributed primarily at low paleolatitudes, while those of therapsids are found at high latitudes.

Pelycosaurs are best known from northcentral Texas, which during the Early Permian was equatorial; other localities where the remains of pelycosaurs are found also lie within a few degrees of the Permian paleoequator (Olson, 1976). The paleoclimate of Texas, though tropical, was highly seasonal, very wet seasons alternating with dry ones. Many pelycosaurs were riparian or aquatic in habit, and for such animals, being amniotes, the dry season would have been the best time for oviposition, when the eggs would be less likely to drown before hatching. For the inhabitants of interfluves or other high ground, the wet season would have been more favorable because of the greater productivity of food resources, and the smaller chance of having the eggs die from desiccation (Andrews and Rand, 1974). In either case, the ability to monitor seasonal changes of ambient light and temperature would permit physiological anticipation of favorable conditions, and may have been the critical advantage of the parietal eye. Since photic cues manifest less seasonal contrast in the tropics than in temperate regions, it may be that discriminative ability played a role in eye function in pelycosaurs.

Therapsids, on the other hand, are best known from South Africa, which today lies at about 30° south latitude and during the Late Permian lay much further south (Smith, Briden, and Drewry, 1973; Parrish et al., this volume). The potential of high latitude for seasonality is obvious, leading Bakker (1975) to illustrate the environment of early African therapsids with his "snows of Southern Gondwanaland." Such an inference is extreme, because the fauna also included large, non-therapsid reptiles that were clearly ectothermic. It seems probable that seasonal contrast involved water supply as much as temperature. In any event, rings in fossil wood indicate strong seasonal contrast, while high latitude implies periodic chill if not snow, together with variations in photoperiod comparable to those at high latitudes today.

Therapsids no doubt inherited their parietal eye from pelycosaurian ancestors. If they were the first tetrapods to penetrate high latitudes in numbers, which seems likely, the possession of a large, discriminative parietal eye would have been one of the features that enabled them to do so. Once they had established themselves at high latitudes, the harsh conditions of high seasonal contrast maintained the parietal eye through the Late Permian, despite changes in the therapsid internal milieu. Even if these changes included a trend toward homoiothermy, as suggested by Olson (1959) and de Ricqlès (1976), they did not make the eye less essential. A useful model of this phase is suggested by the present-day distribution of lizards (Gundy, Ralph, and Wurtz, 1975). Lizards living at the highest latitudes today are restricted to those that have a parietal eye, while a significant majority of lizards that lack a parietal eye is restricted to a few degrees north and south of the equator. Gundy et al. suggest that thermoregulation and reproductive synchrony are critical to lizards living in the seasonally harsh climate and varying photoperiods characteristic of high latitudes. They infer, therefore, that the parietal eye, which mediates control of these functions by detection of environmental radiation, is of decisive advantage to such animals, and those that lack an eye are able to survive only at much lower latitudes.

No Late Permian analogue can be identified that corresponds to the preponderance of parietal-eyeless lizards reported in the tropics, because low latitude terrestrial faunas of appropriate age are unknown. However, northward drift of Africa after the Permian brought about climatic improvement, which was probable enhanced by a worldwide trend toward milder climates that outlasted the therapsids. Such a trend may well have produced subtropical or tropical conditions of low seasonal contrast in southern Africa by the Middle Triassic. This was the time, it will be recalled, that not only therapsids, but also a broad range of non-therapsid tetrapods were losing the parietal foramen.

We therefore suggest that until the end of the Permian, the rigors of a high latitude environment gave the therapsid parietal eye a strong selective value. With worldwide climatic improvement, including reduction of seasonal contrast, during the Triassic, environmental selection to maintain the parietal eye became progressively weaker. As the eye approached a neutral selective value, its evolutionary loss was probably compensated by the functional overlap between elements of the parietal-pineal complex and the lateral eyes, on the model of living tetrapods. At no time did loss of the eye require that it be selectively disadvantageous. In synapsids, the easing of selective pressure maintaining the eye may have involved evolution of the internal milieu as well as changes in the environment, but analogous internal changes are unknown in nonsynapsid tetrapods that lost the eye during the same interval.

In an environment in which selection to maintain the parietal foramen is neutral, closure is most likely to take place in small animals with a small foramen. Occlusion requires less bone in such animals, and is therefore more probable for any given increase in the rate of ossification. This suggests a proximate cause for the disappearance of the therapsid foramen and eye, by analogy with the closure of the parietal foramen in lizards, here attributed to a developmentally late acceleration of the ossification rate. Like other developmental rates, rate of ossification can be expected to fluctuate on a small scale be-

cause of minor and random genetic changes within a population. Such fluctuation may in fact be documented by the high variability of PFD_g in *Anolis* (Fig. 4; Table 1), and in *Iguana* and *Diictodon* (Fig. 5; Table 1). In such a case, an opening as small as the parietal foramen of lizards is at continual risk of being closed up. All of the therapsids in which the parietal foramen was lost are small, as are their closest relatives that retained a foramen, and in the latter the foramen is small relative to head size. These animals conform closely to the lizard model in their potential for occlusion of the parietal foramen by changes in rates of ossification.

In conclusion, we must note the reptiles in which, contrary to the prevailing trend, the parietal foramen remained patent after the Early Triassic. These include the earliest lizards and the rhynchocephalian ancestors of *Sphenodon* on the one hand, and nothosaurs, plesiosaurs, and their euryapsid allies on the other. The early lizards and rhynchocephalians were terrestrial animals but little larger than *Anolis carolinensis*, while the euryapsids in question were mostly aquatic or marine and ranged from the size of small lizards to that of small whales.

Because terrestrial animals as small as early lizards and rhynchocephalians would gain and lose heat rapidly, the effect of periodicity in their microenvironments would be extreme, and selection would continue to favor the parietal eye. This inference is supported by the history of the lineage, in which the foramen was retained in species that remained small (lizards and *Sphenodon*), but was lost in those that approached the size of sheep or cows (Middle Triassic rhynchosaurs).

Retention of the foramen in euryapsids (except for a few of the largest plesiosaurs), and in their contemporaries the mosasaurs, which were sea-going lizards in the size range of porpoises, seems not to conform to the hypothesis being proposed here. The watery environment of these animals was buffered against fluctuation of temperature and so should have been conducive to early loss, rather than to retention of the parietal eye. Euryapsids and mosasaurs, however, were probably obligate egg-layers, and their locomotor anatomy of indicates that they were at least as competent on land as sea turtles, suggesting that the females came ashore to lay their eggs. Since oviposition is closely constrained by seasonality, the need to monitor seasonal changes in ambient radiation, from a fathom or two below the surface of the sea, may have been a decisive factor in preserving the parietal eye in euryapsids and mosasaurs.

Summary

The parietal foramen, and with it the parietal eye, is pervasive in therapsids and is shared by a wide variety of contemporary tetrapods. We suggest that its persistence reflects a functional significance common to the economy of all Late Permian forms. In therapsids, which lived at high latitudes in a probably harsh and seasonal climate, the parietal eye was strongly favored by selection as a photothermal monitor of environmental change, mediating thermoregulation and coordinating reproductive periodicity. A functional analogy is drawn between phylogenetic loss of the foramen in therapsids and developmental closure in present-day lizards. Noting that foramen loss is not restricted to therapsids in the Middle Triassic, we relate it to a broader and more explicit phenomenon than the mere accession of another "mammalian attribute" by advanced therapsids. That phenomenon was a worldwide reduction of climatic seasonality, which eased the selection that had maintained the parietal eye, and allowed its foramen eventually to be closed off by the dynamics of ossification.

Acknowledgments

The authors wish to thank Walter Auffenberg and E. E. Williams for the use of skulls of *Iguana* in collections under their custody, respectively at the University of Florida and the Museum of Comparative Zoology. Thanks are also due to John R. Bolt for the use of skulls of *Captorhinus* at the Field Museum of Natural History. The specimens of *Diictodon* utilized for this paper were acquired in the course of research supported by National Science Foundation Grants G 14705 and GB 1647 to the third author. We are indebted to Dolores E. Larkie for her patience in typing reworked manuscript, and to Lawrence B. Isham for the preparation of figures 4 and 5.

References

Andrews, R., and Rand, A. S.
1974. Reproductive effort in anoline lizards. *Ecology* 55:1317–27.

Bakker, R. T.
1975. Dinosaur renaissance. *Scientific American* 232:58–78.

Broom, R.
1932. *The Mammal-like Reptiles of South Africa and the Origin of Mammals.* London: H. F. and G. Witherby.
1938. On two new anomodont genera. *Ann. Transvaal Mus.* 19:247–50.
1940. On some new genera and species of fossil reptiles from the Karroo beds of Graaff-Reinet. *Ann. Transvaal Mus.* 20:157–92.

Crompton, A. W., Taylor, C. R., and Jagger, J. A.
1978. Evolution of homeothermy in mammals. *Nature* 272:333–36.

Dendy, A.
1911. On the structure, development, and morphological interpretation of pineal organs and adjacent parts of the brain in the tuatara (*Sphenodon punctatus*). *Phil. Trans. Roy. Soc. London,* ser. B 201:227–331.

Edinger, T.
1955. The size of parietal foramen and organ in reptiles. A rectification. *Mus. Comp. Zool. Bull.* 114:3–34.

Engbretson, G. A., and Hutchison, V. H.
1976. Parietalectomy and thermal selection in the lizard *Sceloporus magister. J. Exp. Zool.* 198:29–38.

Engbretson, G. A., Reiner, A., and Brecha, N.
1981. Habenular asymmetry and the central connections of the parietal eye of the lizard (*Uta stansburiana*). *J. Comp. Neurol.* 198:155–66.

Gundy, G. C., Ralph, C. L., and Wurst, G. Z.
1975. Parietal eyes in lizards: zoogeographical correlates. *Science* 190:671–73.

Haughton, S. H., and Brink, A. S.
1954. A bibliographical list of Reptilia from the Karroo beds of Africa. *Palaeontologia Africana* 2:1–187.

Hotton, N.
1974. A new dicynodont (Reptilia, Therapsida) from the Cynognathus Zone deposits of South Africa. *Ann. So. Afr. Mus.* 64:157–65.

Licht, P., and Pearson, A. K.
1970. Failure of parietalectomy to affect the testes in the lizard *Anolis carolinensis. Copeia* 1970:172–73.

Olson, E. C.
1944. The origin of mammals based on the cranial morphology of therapsid suborders. *Geol. Soc. Amer. Spec. Papers* 55:1–136.

1959.   The evolution of mammalian characters. *Evolution* 13:344–53.
1976.   The exploitation of land by early tetrapods. In *Morphology and Biology of Reptiles,* ed. A. d'A. Bellairs and C. B. Cox. *Linnaean Soc. Symposium* 3:1–30.

Quay, W. B.
1979.   The parietal eye-pineal complex. In *Biology of the Reptilia, Vol. 9, Neurology A,* ed. C. Gans, R. G. Northcutt, and P. S. Ulinski. New York: Academic Press.

Ralph, C. L., Firth, B. T., and Turner, J. S.
1979.   The role of the pineal body in ectotherm thermoregulation. *Amer. Zool.* 19:273–93.

de Ricqles, A. J.
1976.   On bone histology of fossil and living reptiles, with comments on its functional and evolutionary significance. In *Morphology and Biology of Reptiles,* ed. A. d'A. Bellairs and C. B. Cox. *Linnaean Soc. Symposium* 3:123–50.

Roth, J. J., Gern, W. A., Roth, E. C., Ralph, C. L., and Jacobson, E.
1980.   Nonpineal melatonin in the alligator *(Alligator mississippiensis). Science* 210:548–50.

Roth, J. J., and Ralph, C. L.
1976.   Body temperature of the lizard *(Anolis carolinensis):* effect of parietalectomy. *Exp. Zool.* 198:17–28.
1977.   Thermal and photic preferences in intact and parietalectomized *Anolis carolinensis. Behavioral Biol.* 19:341–48.

Roth, J. J., and Roth, E. C.
1980.   The parietal-pineal complex among paleovertebrates: evidence for temperature regulation. In *A Cold Look at the Warm Blooded Dinosaurs,* ed. R. D. K. Thomas and E. C. Olson. *AAAS Selected Symposium* 28:189–231. Boulder, Colorado: West View Press.

Smith, A. G., Briden, J. C., and Drewry, G. E.
1973.   Phanerozoic world maps. In *Organisms and Continents through Time,* ed. N. F. Hughes. *Palaeontological Assoc. Spec. Papers in Palaeontology* 19:1–42.

Stebbins, R. C., and Eakin, R. M.
1958.   The role of the "third eye" in reptilian behavior. *Amer. Mus. Novitates* 1870:1–40.

Swinton, W. E.
1958.   Dinosaur brains. *New Scientist* 4:707–9.

J. SCOTT TURNER[1]
and
C. RICHARD TRACY
Department of Zoology and Entomology
Colorado State University
Fort Collins, Colorado 80523

Body Size, Homeothermy and the Control of Heat Exchange in Mammal-like Reptiles

Body Size and Endothermy among Mammal-like Reptiles

Dramatic changes in body size are a striking feature in the phylogeny of several lineages of mammal-like reptiles. Early Pennsylvanian pelycosaurs weighed less than 1 kg. By the early Permian, pelycosaurs such as the conservative *Ophiacodon* and the advanced genera *Dimetrodon* and *Edaphosaurus,* were as big as 250 kg (Romer and Price, 1940; Romer, 1966). Later Permian therapsids, such as dinocephalians, some gorgonopsians, and some dicynodonts, were even larger (Romer, 1966). In the Triassic, however, body size declined as the dominant therapsids of the Late Permian became extinct. Cynodonts such as *Thrinaxodon* and the Tritylodontia, were much smaller, less than 50 kg in body mass (Romer, 1966). Cynodont body size eventually declined to that of the diminutive mammals that shared the earth with the Archosauria during the Jurassic and Cretaceous periods (Romer, 1966; McNab, 1978).

Various authors have proposed that endothermy in mammals had its origin among the mammal-like reptiles (Bakker, 1971; McNab, 1978). McNab has suggested that the large changes in body size that occurred during the evolution of this group were crucial to the development of endothermy. His thesis is that large body size conferred homeothermy on the large mammal-like reptiles of the Permian. Later reductions in body size of the group were accompanied by rates of total metabolism that remained constant or slightly increased, and by simultaneous development of a lower thermal

[1]Current address:
Department of Zoology
Duke University
Durham, North Carolina 27706

conductance through the origin of fur. This would have resulted in small animals that were essentially mammalian in their energetics, and presumably also in their thermoregulatory capabilities (McNab, 1978).

Crucial to this scenario is the contention that large body size necessarily renders an animal homeothermic. In general, this is true; when subjected to a change in evironmental temperature, large reptiles change body temperature more slowly than do small reptiles. Consequently, the body temperatures of large ectotherms would be expected to exhibit less variation through the day than would those of small ectotherms—large reptiles would be "inertial homeotherms" (McNab, 1978; Spotila et al., 1973; Spotila, 1980).

Homeothermy is too widespread among living taxa to dispute its value, and there is little reason to believe that it did not occur among large mammal-like reptiles. High body temperature is also important (Heinrich, 1977); both extant classes of endothermic vertebrates have high, as well as constant, body temperatures. Many extant lizards regulate body temperatures at the highest level that energetic and ecological constraints will allow (Huey and Slatkin, 1976).

Yet homeothermy and high body temperature need not go together. For example, Galapagos land iguanas *(Conolophus pallidus)* regulate body temperatures in a way that makes the period of constant temperature during the day as long as possible, even though the animals are capable of attaining higher body temperatures. The actual body temperature regulated in these animals seems to be a secondary consideration (Christian, Tracy, and Porter, 1983).

If the large mammal-like reptiles of the Permian were inertial homeotherms, they probably were constrained to homeothermy at a relatively low body temperature (25°–30°C; Spotila et al., 1973; Tracy, Turner, and Huey, this volume). For mammal-like reptiles to become "mammalian" with respect to body temperature and energetics, they would have had to become homeothermic at a higher body temperature (35°–40°C).

Many extant reptiles have considerable control over rates of heat exchange with the environment. This control occurs through behavioral thermoregulation, which involves selection of favorable microclimates. It also can occur through physiology, most importantly through varying patterns of blood flow within the body (Templeton, 1970; Smith, 1979; Bartholomew, 1982;

Turner, 1982; Turner and Tracy, 1983). Utilizing these avenues of control, an animal can attain a high body temperature more quickly than its body mass might suggest. If it then could lose heat at a very slow rate, its body temperature would stay high for a long time. During this time, such an animal could spend time moving about, hunting prey and defending territories, with all the benefits a high body temperature might bring with it.

We might expect that control over heat exchange would be particularly useful to an animal with large thermal mass. It might enhance the inertial homeothermy presumed to exist among the large mammal-like reptiles, so that they were homeothermic at a high body temperature.

Thus, there are two possible ways the large mammal-like reptiles of the Late Permian could have been homeothermic. If their large size was crucial to the evolution of endothermy, as McNab (1978) proposes, two possible scenarios for the origin of endothermy are suggested. If large therapsids were simply inertial homeotherms, their body temperatures would have been relatively low. In this case, it is likely that endothermy envolved first, with the attainment of a high body temperature appearing later in the evolution of mammals. If, on the other hand, large therapsids could exert control over heat exchange, they could have been homeothermic at high body temperatures. In this event, high body temperature would have appeared first, with endothermy being a later development to maintain high body temperature and whatever benefits accrue to it. To choose between these alternatives, we must know the extent to which large reptiles are able to control rates of heat exchange.

One of the important ways heat exchange can be controlled is through variations of blood flow within the body (Smith 1979; Bartholomew, 1982; Turner, 1982). In living reptiles, this is almost always manifest as higher rates of heating than of cooling. The appendages (limbs and tail) of small, "lizard-shaped" reptiles (those reptiles with limbs, a long tail, and a fusiform torso) are the most important sites for the control of heat exchange by blood flow (Turner and Tracy, 1983; Turner, 1982). The surface area of appendages can account for more than half of the total surface area available for heat exchange. The appendages are always better heat exchangers than the torso is, because of their larger surface-volume ratios and smaller convective boundary layers. Finally, conduction heat transfer between the torso and appendages is low. Thus, variation in blood flow to appendages can exert considerable control over the flow of heat between the torso and appendages and hence the environment.

In the following section, we assess possible relationships between body size and the effectiveness of control of heat exchange at appendages. Then we consider the implications of these relationships for the physiological control of heat exchange among mammal-like reptiles.

A Model of Heat Transfer at Appendages

The transfer of heat between the core of the body and the environment, via an appendage, is opposed by an internal resistance to heat transfer (r_i; K W^{-1}) and an external resistance to heat transfer (r_e; K W^{-1}). The total resistance to heat transfer (r_{tot}) is simply the sum of the internal and external resistances (Appendix 1; Fig. 1).

We define control of heat exchange as the capability to effect large changes in total resistance to heat transfer. In our simple model, changes in total resistance can come about through changes in either internal or external resistances, or both. To assess an animal's capabilities to control heat exchange by blood flow, we need to ask: "Under what conditions will a change in internal resistance bring about a substantial change in total resistance?" A useful tool to address this question is the dimensionless Biot number (Tracy, 1972; Thomas, 1980) defined as:

$$Bi = r_i/r_e$$

A Biot number of 0.1 or less signifies that external resistance is at least ten times greater than internal resistance. In this circumstance, the resistance controlling heat transfer is that between the animal and its environment; a change in internal resistance (such as a change in blood flow) has essentially no effect on total resistance. Significant changes in total resistance can occur only through changes in external resistance, such as a change in wind speed, or in radiant heat load.

When Biot numbers are between 0.1 and 10, internal and external resistances are within an order of magnitude of each other, and neither predominates; changes in either resistance can cause notable changes in total resistance.

When Biot numbers are greater than 10, internal resistance is the limiting factor in heat transfer, and so the control of heat exchange resides with control of internal resistance (such as

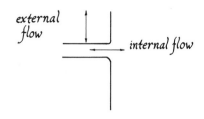

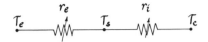

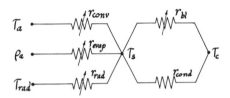

Figure 1. The interaction of internal and external resistance to heat transfer. Top drawing: schematic depiction of the flow of heat from the body core through an appendage (horizontal arrow), and to the environment (vertical arrow). Middle drawing: equivalent circuit diagram of the flow of heat in the upper diagram, with internal (ri) and external (re) resistances to heat transfer in series. Core temperature, T_c; surface temperature of torso, T_s; environmental temperature, T_e. Bottom drawing: a more detailed equivalent circuit, with external resistance resolved into parallel resistances arising from evaporation (revap), radiation (rrad), and convection (rconv), and internal resistance resolved into two parallel resistors arising from conduction (r cond) and blood flow (r_{bl}). T_e resolved into ambient air temperature, T_a; ambient vapor density, ρ_a; and radiant temperature of environment, T_{rad}.

control of blood flow). Total resistance is relatively insensitive to changes in external resistance.

Calculations of heat transfer resistance require information on such bodily dimensions as length of torso and diameter, length, volume, and surface area of the appendages. We constructed allometric equations for the relationships of these parameters (fore and hind limbs) to torso length up to 0.3 m in American alligators (see Appendix 1). There are no such data available for therapsids, but Romer and Price (1940) present data on both the body and limb lengths of pelycosaurs, which are similar to American alligators in these dimensions (Fig. 2). If this similarity in linear dimensions reflects similarities in body stature and size and location of muscles, then the alligator provides a satisfac-

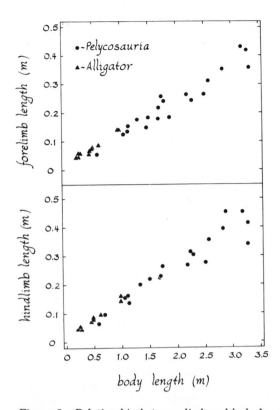

Figure 2. Relationship between limb and body lengths for pelycosaurs (circles) and the American alligator (triangles). Body length does not include the length of the head. Fore-limb lengths were defined as the sum of the humerus and radius lengths. Hind-limb lengths were defined as the sum of the femur and tibia lengths. Data for pelycosaurs were taken from Romer and Price (1940). Data for alligators were taken from living specimens.

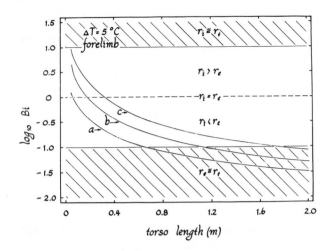

Figure 3. The relationship between the Biot number and the torso length for the fore-limb of pelycosaurs. Curve a, Biot numbers in still air; curve b, Biot numbers at a wind speed of 0.2 m/s; curve c, Biot numbers at a wind speed of 1.0 m/s. Wind speeds are normal to the long axis of the appendage. Temperature differential in all cases is 5° Celsius.

tory template for describing limb dimensions as they relate to body size in the Pelycosauria.

Details of the calculation of both external and internal resistances may be found in Appendix 1. Many possible permutations of both external and internal resistance could be explored, but we have limited ourselves to a few that we consider important. Temperature differentials between the animal and its environment was set at 5° C for all simulations. Wind speeds normal to the long axis of the appendages were varied from 0.0 to 1.0 m s^{-1} in our simulations. Finally, blood flow through the appendage was assumed to be the "normal" rate for reptilian white muscle ($9.67 \cdot 10^{-4}$ cm^3 s^{-1} g tissue $^{-1}$; Berger and Heisler 1977).

Scaling of Heat Exchange at the Fore Limb

In both still (Fig. 3; curve a) and moving air (Fig. 3; curves b and c), the Biot number for the fore limb declines as body size increases. The same general pattern is evident for the hind limb (not shown). Thus, as body size increases, external resistance to heat transfer comes more and more to dominate total resistance. From this, we may infer that any increase in size within a lineage of mammal-like reptiles would reduce capacity to control heat exchange by blood flow.

This point is quantified by claculating the change in blood flow to an appendage required to bring about a given change in total resistance. The percent change in blood flow required to produce either a ten-percent increase or decrease in total resistance to heat transfer is plotted against torso length (Fig. 4). As body size increases, the change in blood flow required to bring about a ten-percent change in total resistance increases (Fig. 4), reflective of the greater importance of external resistance at larger and larger body sizes. Consequently, large body size may have rendered the mammal-like reptiles of the Late Permian unable to control heat exchange by blood flow. If these animals were homeothermic, they probably did not maintain the high body temperatures of modern mammals.

Thermal Biology of Mammal-like Reptiles

Our model suggests that large body size among mammal-like reptiles favored homeothermy at low body temperatures. This prediction is very explicit, but it applies only to limited circumstances of body morphology and environmental conditions. By exploring the departures of mam-

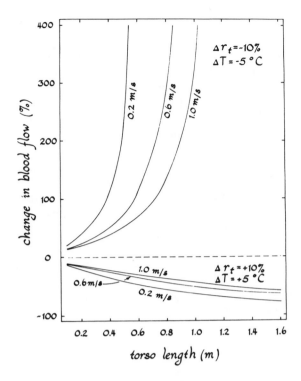

Figure 4. Percent change in mass = specific blood flow required for a +/− 10% change in total resistance to heat transfer. Three conditions of wind speed are shown: 0.2 m/s, 0.6 m/s, and 1.0 m/s.

mal-like reptiles from these conditions, we can infer other possible patterns of thermoregulation in the group. Mammal-like reptiles departed from the postulated conditions by reducing external resistance to heat transfer, thus making internal resistance more important (that is, Biot numbers for the appendages increased). They may have done so either by physiological or behavioral means, or by evolutionary modification of body form. We will consider each of these possibilities in turn, to see how they may explain observed features in the evolution of the mammal-like reptiles, particularly in the transition from Pelycosauria to Therapsida.

External Resistance to Heat Transfer

External resistance to heat transfer can be resolved into three major components (Fig. 1); convection, radiation and evaporation (conduction is considered relatively unimportant for an appendage). Anything that reduces resistance in any of these modes will make internal resistance a more important component of total resistance. This leaves us with the curious result that animals may actually sacrifice conservation of heat, reducing external resistance to achieve greater internal control over total resistance.

The effect of altering convection heat transfer is explicitly considered in Fig. 3. Increased wind speed will increase heat exchange through convection; as a result, Biot numbers for the appendage increase for all body sizes (Fig. 3). If air flow past the appendage is turbulent, heat exchange through convection is enhanced even more. Thus, large mammal-like reptiles may have sought turbulent or windy areas as a behavioral adjunct to the control of heat exchange.

Perhaps a more effective way to accomplish this would be to live in a different fluid—water as opposed to air. This is the behavior of many of the largest extant reptiles, such as crocodilians and marine turtles. Convection resistance in water is considerably less than in air, and a large animal in water can effect considerably more control over heat exchange by blood flow than it can in air.

Large, active predators, such as the sphenacodonts (Romer, 1966) were presumably faced with two opposed, but simultaneous, alternatives. Probability of success in finding and subduing prey was probably enhanced by high body temperature, as it is for modern reptiles (Werner 1972; Greenwald 1974; Huey 1982). At the same time, capture of prey can be a vigorous business, and in a large animal it can impose a substantial burden of metabolic heat production, with consequent increase in body temperature. If body temperature is already high to maximize success in predation, dangerous overheating can result unless there is a way to quickly dump large amounts of heat.

We argue that the amphibious lifestyles of modern crocodilians are a compromise solution to just this dilemma. Warming can occur quickly on land, in a setting of intense solar radiation. Activity in these situations is minimal, and precise and rapid variation in heat exchange may not be necessary. Control of heat exchange is important when the animals are active, however, and extended activity occurs almost solely in the water, where control of heat exchange will be most effective. This may explain why many of the fossils of the advanced pelycosaurs are found in deposits indicating a formerly copious water supply (see Olson, this volume), suggesting that these animals had a relatively amphibious lifestyle.

External resistance can also be modified by changes in the radiative properties of the animal's surface. The emissivity of reptile skin is probably not amenable to control, being constant at 0.9–1.0 (Campbell, 1977), and our simulations suggest that the small changes in temperature that an animal would exhibit likewise does not affect emission of radiation much. Thus, mammal-like reptiles may not have had much control over heat loss by radiation.

Finally, internal control of heat transfer could be enhanced by making evaporation heat exchange more important. Among extant reptiles, such as the alligator, all avenues of evaporation account for less than two percent of the animal's steady-state energy balance (Terpin, Spotila, and Foley, 1979; Tracy, 1982). Evaporative conductance of reptilian skin is very low, and modern reptiles do not sweat (Campbell, 1977; Spotila and Berman, 1976; Davis, Spotila, and Schaefer, 1980; Tracy, 1982). However, evaporative heat exchange varies in response to shedding cycles (Zucker and Maderson, 1980) and changes in the lipid content of the skin (Roberts and Lillywhite, 1980), and by control of respiration and oxygen consumption (Duvdevani and Borut, 1974), by control of evaporation from the surfaces of the eyes (Mautz, 1980), and by control of blood flow through the skin (Cohen, 1975). Evaporation can be important to the animal for local control of brain temperature while gaping (Spotila, Terpin, and Dodson, 1977) or panting (Templeton, 1971; Pough and McFarland, 1976; Crawford, Palomeque, and Barber, 1977) or for cooling the appendages during thermal crises, such as when the animal urinates or defecates on its hind limbs (Riedesel, Cloudsley-Thompson, and Cloudsley-Thompson, 1971; Cloudsley-Thompson, 1974; Sturbaum and Riedesel, 1974). By far the most significant control of evaporative heat exchange originates with behavioral selection of hydric microclimates (Davis, Spotila, and Schaefer, 1980; Thorpe and Kontoginnis, 1977; Spotila and Berman, 1976; Mautz, 1980; Cohen, 1975). Some mammal-like reptiles had skin with numerous and conspicuous glandlike structures (Chudinov, 1968), which suggests that some of these animals may have had the capacity to sweat.

Adjustments in Body Shape

The simulations reported here assume that the dimensions of the appendages, on which all the resistances to heat transfer depend, are in scale with body size in much the same way as those of an alligator. Among the Pelycosauria, for example (Fig. 2), this is probably a good assumption; the relationship between the dimensions of the locomotory appendages and body remained relatively constant throughout their evolutionary history.

However, there are two ways to subvert this limitation: develop ancillary appendages, separate from the locomotory appendages, designed mostly for the control of heat exchange; or modify the shape and structure of the locomotory appendages, to make control of heat exchange at them more effective.

The larger and more advanced pelycosaurs, such as *Dimetrodon* and *Edaphosaurus,* may have pursued the first strategy during their evolution, developing an ancillary heat exchanger in the form of a dorsal sail. The thermal consequences of possession of a sail are substantial, allowing the members of these genera to heat quickly and cool slowly and so remain homeothermic at a high body temperature, despite large body size (Tracy, Turner, and Huey, this volume).

The sphenacodonts that eventually gave rise to the therapsids did not include animals with sails. In the predecessors of the therapsids, we see little evidence of the morphological features that may have enabled *Dimetrodon* to be ectothermic and yet to have a high, relatively constant body temperature. These transitional animals, if ectothermic, would have been homeothermic at a relatively low body temperature (Tracy, Turner, and Huey, this volume).

Restructuring of the locomotory appendages for better control of heat exchange probably did not occur in the Pelycosauria (Fig. 2). However, the limbs underwent considerable change during the evolution of the Therapsids. They rotated ventrally so that therapsids stood more erect than their "sprawling" predecessors, in a more nearly "mammalian" posture (Bakker, 1971). This allowed a more mammalian locomotion, with the limbs moving in a parasagittal plane during walking and running. Accompanying these shifts was relocation of the appendicular muscles closer to the limb girdles. Simultaneously, the caudo-femoralis musclulature of the tail was greatly reduced, because of the reduction of lateral vertebral flexion (Sues, this volume). The result was that the limbs became more slender, and the tail became greatly reduced in mass.

These changes principally reflect the development of a new mode of locomotion. However, a change in the heat exchange properties of the appendages would have accompanied these locomotory alterations. Reducing the diameter of the appendages increases the Biot number, enhancing the importance of internal resistance in heat transfer (Fig. 3). Further, the relocation of the appendicular muscles into the body would have enabled these muscles to be nourished by blood flow without the blood having to flow out into the appendages, where it could exchange its heat readily with the environment. This also increases the Biot numbers of the appendages. In both cases, the capabilities for physiological control of heat exchange at the apendages are enhanced. The thermoregulatory significance of these changes is unknown but can be surmised: the more slender limbs of the Gorgonopsia, the Therocephalia, and perhaps the Dicynodontia could well have been exploited as controlled heat-loss fins if the animals were highly active and maintained high body temperatures.

Acknowledgments

We are grateful to Dr. John Mitchell, Department of Mechanical Engineering, University of Wisconsin, for the intellectual stimulus that started us thinking about appendages as heat exchange fins. We thank Colorado State University for partial financial support for this project. We thank the several reviewers of the early versions of this manuscipt, including Drs. J. Lillegraven, D. Duvall, and R. Huey, for their extremely valuable comments and criticisms.

Appendix 1. Model of thermal resistance of appendage

Circuits for Resistance to Heat Transfer

Circuits for the transfer of heat are analagous to circuits for the transfer of electrical energy (Fig. 1). For thermal circuits, we may use an analogy of Ohm's Law to express the relations between heat flow, temperature difference and resistance to heat transfer:

$$\dot{q} = dT/r \tag{1}$$

where $\ddot{q}$ = heat flow (W; J s^{-1}), dT = temperature difference (°C), and r = resistance to heat transfer (°C/W).

Calculating resistances in thermal circuits is done the same way that resistance is calculated in an electrical circuit. For the circuit in Figure 1, external and internal resistances to heat transfer are arranged in series. Therefore,

$$r_{tot} = r_i + r_e \tag{2}$$

where r_{tot}, i.e = total, internal and external resistances, respectively. Both internal and external resistances can be further resolved into different modes of heat exchange, each of which is arranged in parallel with the other resistances in its circuit. Thus, internal resistance can be resolved into parallel resistances arising from conduction heat transfer (r_{cond}) and arising from heat transfer by blood flow (r_{b1});

$$1/r_i = 1/r_{cond} + 1/r_{b1} \tag{3}$$

Resistance arising from blood flow is variable. Likewise, external resistance can be resolved into the parallel resistances associated with convection (r_{conv}), evaporation (r_{evap}) and radiation (r_{rad}):

$$1/r_e = 1/r_{conv} + 1/r_{evap} + 1/r_{rad} \tag{4}$$

Total resistance can be calculated from the component resistances associated with the simultaneous process of internal conduction, blood flow, evaporation, convection and radiation.

Calculation of Internal Resistances

Conduction

The appendage was considered to be a single homogeneous node. Conduction heat transfer within a cylindrical fin is:

$$\dot{q}_{cond} = l\,k_{app}\,dT \tag{5}$$

where l = characteristic length (m; V_{app}/A_{app}), and k_{app} = thermal conductivity of the composite material (W m^{-1} °C^{-1}, assumed to be 0.5). Conduction resistance is therefore;

$$r_{cond} = 1/l\,k_{app}. \tag{6}$$

Blood Flow

Heat transfer arising from blood flow is calculated by:

$$\dot{q}_{b1} = m\,c_{b1}\,dt \tag{7}$$

where $\dot{m}$ = mass flow rate of blood (g s^{-1}), and c_{b1} = specific heat of blood (J g^{-1} °C^{-1}). Resistance arising from blood flow is, therefore:

$$r_{b1} = 1/m\,c_{b1} \tag{8}$$

Calculation of External Resistance

Evaporation

Evaporation was considered to be a negligible source of heat exchange at appendages.

Radiation

Heat transfer arising from radiation is calculated as:

$$q_{\mathrm{rad}} = A_{\mathrm{app}} \, \epsilon \, \sigma \, (\mathrm{T}_s^4 - \mathrm{T}_j^4) \qquad (9)$$

where A_{app} = surface area of the appendage (m²), σ Stefan-Boltzmann constant ($5.67 \ 10^{-8}$ W m⁻² K⁻⁴), ϵ emissivity (assumed to be 0.95), and $\mathrm{T}_{s,j}$ = absolute temperature of surfaces s and j, respectively. Because radiation is proportional to the fourth power of the absolute temperature, resistance to heat transfer will depend partly upon temperature differences between the surfaces exchanging radiation. Resistance for radiation heat transfer is calculated as:

$$r_{\mathrm{rad}} = 1/[A_{\mathrm{app}} \, \epsilon \, \sigma \, (\mathrm{T}_s + \mathrm{T}_j)(\mathrm{T}_s^2 + \mathrm{T}_j^2)] \qquad (10)$$

Convection

Heat transfer arising from convection is described by;

$$\dot{q}_{\mathrm{conv}} = A_{\mathrm{app}} \, h_c \, dT \qquad (11)$$

where h_c = convection coefficient (W m⁻² °C⁻¹). Therefore, resistance to heat transfer by convection is:

$$r_{\mathrm{conv}} = 1/A_{\mathrm{app}} \, h_c \qquad (12)$$

The calculation of the convection coefficient partly depends upon the speed of air moving past the appendage, which will determine whether the air is still, or is moving past the appendage in laminar or turbulent flow. The choice of equations for still air is trivial. The choice between the equations for laminar or turbulent flow depends upon the Reynolds number, Re (dimensionless);

$$Re = u \, l/\nu \qquad (13)$$

where u = wind speed normal to the long axis of the appendage (m s⁻¹), l = diameter (m), and ν = kinematic viscosity of the air (m² s⁻¹). Generally is Re τ 10^5, air flow past the appendage will be turbulent. If $Re < 10^5$, air flow past the appendage will be laminar.

If $Re < 10^5$, the convection coefficient is calculated by;

$$h_c = [(0.04 \, Re^{1/2} + 0.06 \, Re^{2/3}) \, (\mu_\infty / \mu_0) \\ Pr^{0.4} \, \mathrm{k}_{\mathrm{air}} \, l \qquad (14)$$

where Pr = Pradtl number (dimensionless; $Pr = \nu/(c_p \, k_{\mathrm{air}})$, where c_p = specific heat of the air [J m⁻³ K]), and $\mu_{0,\infty}$ = dynamic viscosity of the air in the region of fully developed flow (∞) and at the surface of the limb (0).

If $Re > 10^5$, the convection coefficient can be estimated by;

$$h_c = (430 + 0.005 \, Re + 0.025 \ 10^{-9} \, Re \\ - 3.1 \ 10^{-17} \, Re) \, \mathrm{k}_{\mathrm{air}} \, l \qquad (15)$$

In still air, the convection coefficient is estimated by;

$$h_c = [0.54 \, (Gr \, Pr)^{1/4}] \, \mathrm{k}_{\mathrm{air}} \, l \qquad (16)$$

where Gr = Grashof number (dimensionless; $Gr = g \, \beta \, l^3 \, (\mathrm{T}_s - \mathrm{T}_f) / \mu_0$, where g = gravitational acceleration (9.8 m s⁻²), β = volume coefficient of expansion for air (°C⁻¹), l = diameter (m), and $\mathrm{T}_{s,f}$ = temperatures of the surface and fluid, respectively (°C).

A fairly complete discussion of the principles of heat transfer outlined here may be found in Thomas (1980). Many of the quantitative properties of air required for these calculations were calculated from subroutines provided in Tracy et al. (1978).

Calculation of Appendage Dimensions

Allometric equations for limb diameter, volume, and surface area, as functions of torso legnth, were formulated using the alligator as a model. For the forelimb:

$$\log d_f = -0.960 + 1.010 \log L_{\mathrm{torso}} \qquad (17)$$
$$\log V_f = -2.379 + 2.994 \log L_{\mathrm{torso}} \qquad (18)$$
$$\log A_f = -0.817 + 4.984 \log L_{\mathrm{torso}} \qquad (19)$$

where d = diameter (m), V = volume (m³), and A = surface area (m²) of the appendage, and L_{torso} = torso length (m).
For the hind limb:

$$\log d_h = -0.781 + 1.066 \log L_{\mathrm{torso}} \qquad (20)$$
$$\log V_h = -1.873 + 3.239 \log L_{\mathrm{torso}} \qquad (21)$$
$$\log A_h = -0.490 + 2.173 \log L_{\mathrm{torso}} \qquad (22)$$

Calculation of Appendage Blood Flow

Blood flow in the appendage was calucated as a function of the volume of the appendage and the mass specific perfusion rate for reptilian muscle (Berger and Heisler 1977):

$$Q_{\mathrm{app}} = V_{\mathrm{app}} \, \rho_{\mathrm{app}} \, Q_{\mathrm{muscle}} \qquad (23)$$

where V_{app} = volume of appendage (m³), ρ = density of the appendage (g m⁻³), and Q = mass specific volume flow rate for reptilian muscle ($9.67 \ 10^{-4}$ cm³ g⁻¹).

References

Bakker, R. T.
1971. Dinosaur physiology and the origin of mammals. *Evolution* 25:636–58.

Bartholomew, G. A.
1982. Physiological control of body temperature. In *Biology of the Reptilia,* vol. 12, ed. F. H. Pough and C. Gans. London: Academic Press.

Berger, P. J., and Heisler, N.
1977. Estimation of shunting, systemic and pulmonary output of the heart and regional blood flow distribution in unanaesthetized lizards *(Varanus exanthematicus)* by injection of radioactively labelled microspheres. *J. Exp. Biol.* 71:111–21.

Campbell, G. S.
1977. *An Introduction to Environmental Biophysics.* New York: Springer Verlag.

Christian, K. A., and Tracy, C. R.
1981. The effect of the thermal environment on the ability of hatchling Galapagos land iguanas to avoid predation during dispersal. *Oecologia* 49;218–23.

Christian, K. A., Tracy, C. R., and Porter, W. P.
1983. Seasonal shifts in body temperature and in the use of microhabitats by the Galapagos land iguana. *Ecology* 64:463–68.

Chudinov, P. K.
1968. Structure of the integuments of theriomorphs. *Doklady Akad. Nauk SSSR* 179:207–10. (Transl. by American Geological Institute).

Cloudsely-Thompson, J. L.
1974. Physiological thermoregulation in the spurred tortoise *(Testudo graeca). J. Natural Hist.* 8:577–87.

Cohen, A. C.
1975. Some factors affecting water economy in snakes. *Comp. Biochem. Physiol.* 51A:361–68.

Crawford, E. C.; Palomeque, J.; and Barber, B. J.
1977. A physiological basis for head body temperature differences in a panting lizard. *Comp. Biochem. Physiol.* 56A:161–63.

Davis, J. E.; Spotila, J. R.; and Schaefer, W. C.
1980. Evaporative water loss from the American alligator, *Alligator mississippiensis.* The relative importance of respiratory and cutaneous components and the regulatory role of the skin. *Comp. Biochem. Physiol.* 67:439–46.

Duvdevani, I., and Borut, A.
1974. Oxygen consumption and evaporative water loss in four species of *Acanthodactylus* (Lacertidae). *Copeia* (1974): 155–64.

Greenwald, O. E.
1974. Thermal dependence of striking and prey capture by gopher snakes. *Copeia* (1974):141–48.

Heinrich, B.
1977. Why have some animals evolved to regulate a high body temperature? *Amer. Naturalist* 111:623–40.

Huey, R. B.
1982. Temperature, physiology and the ecology of reptiles. In *Biology of the Reptilia,* vol. 12, ed. F. H. Pough and C. Gans. London: Academic Press.

Huey, R. B., and Slatkin, M.
1976. Costs and benefits of lizard thermoregulation. *Quart. Rev. Biol.* 51:363–84.

McNab, B. K.
1978. The evolution of endothermy in the phylogeny of mammals. *Amer. Naturalist* 112:1–21.

Mautz, W. J.
1980. Factors influencing evaporative water loss in lizards. *Comp. Biochem. Physiol.* 67A:429–38.

Pough, F. H., and MacFarland, W. N.
1976. A physical basis for head body temperature differences in reptiles. *Comp. Biochem. Physiol.* 53A:301–3.

Riedesel, M. L.; Cloudsley-Thompson, J. L.; and Cloudsley-Thompson, J. A.
1971. Evaporative thermoregulation in turtles. *Physiol. Zool.* 44:28–32.

Roberts, J. B., and Lillywhite, H. B.
1980. Lipid barrier to water exchange in reptile epidermis. *Science* 207:1077–79.

Romer, A. S.
1966. *Vertebrate Paleontology.* Chicago: University of Chicago Press.

Romer, A. S., and Price, L. L.
1940. Review of the Pelycosauria. *Special Papers of the Geological Society of America* 28:1–621.

Smith, E. N.
1979. Behavioral and physiological thermoregulation of crocodilians. *Amer. Zool.* 19:239–47.

Spotila, J. R.
1980. Constraints of body size and environment on the temperature regulation of dinosaurs. In *A Cold Look at the Warm-Blooded Diosaurs,* ed. R. D. K. Thomas and E. C. Olson. Boulder, Colorado: Westview Press.

Spotila, J. R., and Berman, E. R.
1976. Determination of skin resistance and the role of the skin in controlling water loss in amphibians and reptiles. *Comp. Biochem. Physiol.* 55A:407–11.

Spotila, J. R.; Lommen, P. W.; Bakken, G. S.; and Gates, D. M.
1973. A mathematical model for body temperatures of large reptiles. Implications for dinosaurian ecology. *Amer. Naturalist* 107:391–404.

Spotila, J. R.; Terpin, K. M.; and Dodson, P.
1977. Mouth gaping as an effective thermoregulatory device in alligators. *Nature* 265:235–36.

Sturbaum, P. A., and Riedesel, M. L.
1974. Temperature regulation responses of ornate box turtles, *Terrapene ornata,* to heat. *Comp. Biochem. Physiol.* 48A:527–38.

Templeton, J. R.
1970. Reptiles. In *Comparative Physiology of Thermoregulation,* vol. 3, ed. G. C. Whittow. London: Academic Press.
1971. Peripheral and central control of panting in the desert iguana, *Dipsosaurus dorsalis. J. Physiol.* (Paris) 63:439–42.

Terpin, K. M.; Spotila, J. R. and Foley, R. E.
1979. Thermoregulatory adaptation and heat energy budget analyses of the American alligator, *Alligator mississippiensis. Physiol. Zool.* 52:296–312.

Thomas, L. C.
1980. *Fundamentals of Heat Transfer.* Englewood Cliffs, N.J.: Prentice Hall.

Thorpe, G. S., and Kontogiannis, J. E.
1977. Evaporative water loss in isloated populations of the coastal side-blotched lizard *Uta stansburiana hesperis. Comp. Biochem. Physiol.* 57A:133–37.

Tracy, C. R.
1972. Newton's Law. Its applicability for expressing heat loss from homeotherms. *BioScience* 22:656–59.

1982. Biophysical modelling in reptilian physiology and ecology. In *Biology of the Reptilia,* vol. 12, ed. F. H. Pough and C. Gans. London: Academic Press.

Tracy, C. R., Welch, W. R., and Porter, W. P.
1978. Properties of air: a manual for use in biophysical ecology. *University of Wisconsin Laboratory in Biophysical Ecology Technical Report* 1. Madison, Wisconsin.

Turner, J. S.
1982. *The Relationship between Heat Exchange and Blood flow in Reptiles.* Ph.D. dissertation, Colorado State University, Ft. Collins.

Turner, J. S., and Tracy, C. R.
1983. Blood flow to appendages and the control of heat exchange in American alligators. *Physiol. Zool.* 56:195–200.

Werner, Y. L.
1972. Temperature effects on inner ear sensitivity in six species of iguanid lizards. *J. Herpetol.* 6:147–77.

Zucker, A. H., and Maderson, P. F. A.
1980. Cutaneous water loss and the epidermal shedding cycle in the tokay *(Gekko gekko). Comp. Biochem. Physiol.* 65A:381–92.

C. RICHARD TRACY
and
J. SCOTT TURNER[1]
Department of Zoology and Entomology
Colorado State University
Fort Collins, Colorado 80523
and
RAYMOND B. HUEY
Department of Zoology NJ-15
University of Washington 98195

A Biophysical Analysis of Possible Thermoregulatory Adaptations in Sailed Pelycosaurs

Introduction

The spectacular dorsal sails of some members of the synapsid order Pelycosauria have placed these animals among the most easily recognized of fossil tetrapods. Not surprisingly, these structures have generated much conjecture regarding their function. The large surface area of the sail is suspected to have been useful in temperature regulation—specifically in increasing rates of heat gain and loss (Romer, 1948), 1966; Bramwell and Fellgett, 1973; Spotila, 1980). However, it has also been suggested that the sail could have been used in intraspecific displays (Bakker, 1971).

Although a direct resolution of the function of a sail is impossible, we can apply biophysical models of heat transfer to analyze the conditions under which a sail might have functioned in thermoregulation. With the advanced sphenacodont pelycosaur *Dimetrodon* as an example, specific questions to be entertained are: Does the sail play a role in promoting homeothermy? How do body size, body form, and sail size interact to determine the body temperature at which *Dimetrodon* habitually may have regulated? What bearing does thermoregulation in *Dimetrodon* have on the ultimate attainment of endothermic homeothermy by early mammals?

Regulation of Heat Exchange in Reptiles

Modern reptiles are known for their ability to control heat exchange with the environment,

[1]Current Adress:
Department of Biology
Franklin and Marshall College
Lancaster, Pennsylvania 17604

and hence body temperature, by behavioral mechanisms such as regulating time of activity, microhabitat selection, basking, and postural orientation with respect to the sun or wind (Cowles and Bogert, 1944); Bogert, 1949; Brattstrom, 1965; Health, 1965; Huey and Pianka, 1977; Muth, 1977; James and Porter, 1979; Huey, 1982). Reptiles also supplement behavioral adjustments with sophisticated physiological adjustments that influence rates of heat exchange by altering distributions of blood flow within the body, evaporative heat loss through panting, and control of body color (Cowles, 1958; Bartholomew and Lasiewski, 1963; Bartholomew and Tucker, 1963; Norris, 1967; Baker and White, 1970; Weathers, 1970, 1971; Weathers and White, 1971; Smith, 1979; White, 1976; Voight and Johnson, 1977; Grigg, Drane, and Courtice, 1979). Indeed, except for a few very small species, reptiles use this physiological control so that the rates at which they cool are almost always lower than the rates at which they warm (Fig. 1; Table 1).

Difference in rates of warming and cooling have been explained as resulting from control of blood flow between the core and skin of the torso of an animal (Cowles, 1958). Subsequently, it has been argued on theoretical grounds that blood flow to the appendages is probably more important in controlling heat exchange than is blood flow between the core and skin of the torso (Turner, in press). Empirical evidence from *Alligator,* and from two genera of lizards, support this hypothesis (Turner, Hamond, and Tracy, 1980; Turner and Tracy, 1983; Turner, unpublished data). These recent findings, combined with morphological evidence that the sails of pelycosaurs were well supplied with blood (Romer and Price, 1940), feed the suspicion that pelycosaur sails—in essence, accessory heat exchangers—had an important role in thermoregulation.

The size of a reptile influences its heat exchange with the environment. For example, very large reptiles have capacities for storage of thermal energy, and, consequently, fluctuations in their body temperatures are invariably smaller than fluctuations in the thermal environment; this has been called "inertial homeothermy" (McNab, 1978; Spotila, 1980). Additionally, large reptiles can control thermal exchange with the environment by shunting heat around their bodies by varying the distribution of blood flow (Turner and Tracy, this volume). In contrast, very small reptiles have small capacities for storage of thermal energy and, therefore, a limited

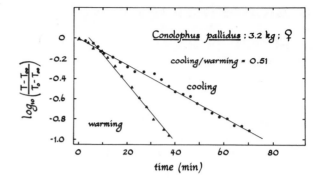

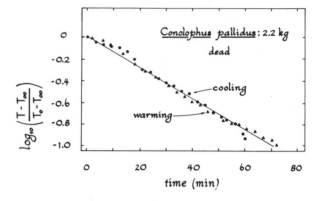

Figure 1. The body temperatures of Galapagos land iguanas *(Conolophus pallidus)* while cooling and warming in a water bath. *Top:* cooling and warming curves for a 3.2kg female; *bottom:* cooling and warming curves for a 2.2 kg dead lizard. (Tracy and Christian, unpublished data.)

Key: T = cloacal temperature, T_0 = body temperature at the beginning of the temperature transient, $T_{-\infty}$ = equilibrium body temperature at any time during the transient.

ability to regulate heat exchange within the body; they must rely primarily upon behavioral adjustments to restrict fluctuations in body temperature. Between extremes of size, reptiles can effectively use both behavioral and physiological mechanisms to regulate body temperature.

Homeothermy

Recent studies (Christian, Tracy, and Porter, 1983) have suggested that homeothermy, per se, plays an important role in the animal's life history. Indeed, actual body temperature may be less important than the ability to maintain a given body temperature for a long period of time (Christian, Tracy, and Porter, 1983). This suggets that selection favors homeothermy. While hypotheses have been advanced to explain the advantage of homeothermy (Alexandrov, 1967; Prosser, 1973; Hochachka and Somero, 1973; Heinrich, 1977; Else and Hulbert, 1981), the

TRACY, TURNER, AND HUEY

Table 1.—Ratios of cooling to warming in some lizards

Species	Mass(kg)	Cooling/warming	Source
Varanidae			
Varanus acanthurus	0.016	1.13	(a)
Varanus gouldii	0.094	0.94	(a)
Varanus gouldii	0.144	0.83	(a)
Varanus punctatus	0.186	0.94	(a)
Varanus varius	0.735	0.74	(a)
Varanus gouldii	0.736	0.85	(a)
Varanus varius	0.774	0.85	(a)
Varanus gouldii	1.060	0.72	(a)
Varanus varius	4.008	0.89	(a)
Agamidae			
Amphibolurus barbatus	0.294	0.74	(b)
Amphibolurus barbatus	0.520	0.76	(b)
Teiidae			
Cnemidophorus sexlineatus	0.005	0.80–1.01	(c)
Iguanidae			
Sceloporus undulatus	0.010	0.73–0.80	(c)
Dipsosaurus dorsalis	0.050	0.75	(d)
Amblyrhynchus cristatus	0.652	0.50	(e)
Amblyrhynchus cristatus	1.360	0.55	(e)
Conolophus pallidus	3.200	0.51	(f)
Conolophus pallidus	2.900	0.53	(f)

(a) Bartholomew and Tucker, 1964; (b) Bartholomew and Tucker, 1963; (c) McKenna and Packard, 1975; (d) Turner *et al.*, unpublished; (e) Bartholomew and Lasiewski, 1965; (f) Tracy and Christian, unpublished data.

principal advantage is probably biochemical conservatism. In the animal that maintains body temperature within narrow limits, biochemical function can specialize for greater efficiency within those limits than at other temperatures. Such an animal has an advantage, at its preferred temperature, over another with a more elaborate biochemical makeup, which, though effective over a broad spectrum of temperatures, may be especially efficient at none. Specialization for high efficiency in a narrow range of temperatures presumably requires but a single set of isozymes, and avoids the genetic and developmental expense of producing multiple sets to accomodate a broad range of body temperatures. In any case, constancy of body temperature is such a common pattern in nature that it would be difficult to dispute that it has adaptive value (Cowles and Bogert, 1944; Bartholomew and Tucker, 1963; MacKay, 1964; Hutchinson, Dowling, and Vinegar, 1966; DeWitt, 1967; Fry, 1967; Heath, 1968; Templeton, 1970; Edney, 1971; Bartholomew, 1972; Nagy, Odell, and Seymour, 1972; Whittow, 1970, 1973; Heinrich, 1974; Crompton, Taylor, and Jagger, 1978). Since homeothermy at some stage in life history is almost ubiquitous among extant mammals, but is not restricted to higher vertebrates, it is instructive to seek evidence for this characteristic among the reptilian progenitors of mammals.

Biophysical Models

Most biophysical models of energy exchange deal with animals in which rates of influx and efflux of energy are equivalent, and body temperature is constant with respect to time; these are "steady-state" or equilibrium models. More complex biophysical models (Spotila et al., 1973; Porter et al., 1973) deal with animals in which rates of influx and efflux are not equal, and body temperature changes with time (Fig. 2a). Such "transient-state" models are especially important for analyses of large animals, such as pelycosaurs, because large animals are often out of equilibrium with their environment due to their large thermal inertia. Control of blood flow to facilitate heat exchange is probably a crucial adaptation for the regulation of body temperature in large animals; and thus models of energy exchange in pelycosaurs must be transient-state models that include control of blood flow.

We base our analyses for pelycosaurs on a "three-lumped" model (Fig. 2b; Tracy et al., 1980), which tracks the temperatures of three regions (lumps) of the body (torso, shell or skin of

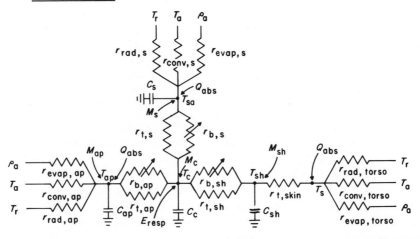

Figure 2. Three transient state energy balance models illustrated like "thermal circuits" (*i.e.,* diagrammed like an electrical circuit, but energy rather than electricity is the current transferred; see Campbell, 1977, for discussion of thermal circuit).

A. A two-layer model, described in Beckman, Mitchell, and Porter (1973), that has been used for describing small lizards as essentially consisting of a core (center of torso) with a temperature T_c and a shell (surrounding the core) with a temperature of T_{sh}.

B. A three-layer model, after Tracy et al. (1980), that has been used to describe large lizards as essentially consisting of a core and shell, as in the two-layer model, and appendages with a temperature T_{ap}.

C. A four-layer model used here to describe pelycosaurs as essentially consisting of a core, shell, and appendages, plus a sail with temperature T_{sa}.

In all models, energy can enter the animals as absorbed radiation, Q_{abs} at the torso, appendages, and sail. These regions can also exchange energy as thermal radiation, convection, and evaporation, depending upon the temperatures and vapor density of the environment (T_r, the radiant tempera-

ture of the environment; T_a, the ambient air temperature; and ρ_a = ambient vapor density) and the surface temperatures of the animal (T_s = surface temperature of the torso). Energy can be generated via metabolism in the four layers (M = metabolic heat production) and stored in the tissues of the layers, according to the capacitances of the layers (C = the capacitance for heat storage, which is the product of the mass of the layer and the specific heat of the tissues in the layer).

Finally, the rate of heat transfer from the environment to the animal, or between layers of the animal, is governed by the physical processes of heat transfer. This is represented as a thermal resistance to heat transfer. Thus, r_{rad} is the resistance of thermal radiative heat transfer; r_{evap} is the resistance to evaporative heat loss; r_t is the resistance to conductive heat transfer through tissues; and r_b is the resistance due to blood flow between layers. (Actually blood flow is more easily thought of as facilitating heat transfer than of resisting it, but the electrical analogy forces representation as in this figure. Thus, when blood flow is very high, resistance to heat transfer is very low).

torso, and appendages). This model is converted to a "four-lumped" model to deal with energy exchange in sailed pelycosaurs (Fig. 2c). In this model, all surfaces of the body (torso surface, **sh**; appendages, **ap**; and sail, **sa**) exchange heat with the environment by radiation, convection, and evaporation. Each surface also exchanges heat with the core of the torso via blood flow and conduction between the core and skin.

Metabolic heat is generated in the torso surface (M_{sh}) and core (M_c), and in the appendages (M_{ap}) and sail (M_{sa}), although this source of energy is usually small in reptiles (Bennett and Dawson, 1976). Solar radiation is absorbed, Q_{abs}, by the skin of the torso, appendages, and sail.

Although our model treats the sail as an accessory appendage, heat exchange involving the sail differs from that involving the true appendages. An important difference is that the sail ordinarily sits well above ground where the ambient air temperature is often relatively low, and where the wind speed is relatively high. Thus, the sail is exposed to a different thermal environment from that of the rest of the body.

Model Simulations of Large Extant Lizards

The prediction, by biophysical models, of body temperatures of pelycosaurs obviously cannot be verified directly. Nevertheless, our confidence in such models is fortified by demonstrating that slightly simpler models (Fig. 2b) do accurately predict body temperatures of large extant reptiles.

We initially test the ability of the three-lump, transient-state model (Fig. 2b) to predict body temperatures of adult green iguanas (*Iguana iguana*) during heating and cooling in the laboratory. Parameters of the model are from Christian, Tracy, and Porter, 1983, except for the rates of blood flow to the periphery (skin of the torso and appendages), which are taken from Baker and White (1970). The simulation (Fig. 3) predicted that the ratio of the rates of cooling and of heating should be 0.70, which compares favorably with ratios calculated from data on living green iguanas of 0.70, by Baker and White (1970), and 0.72, by Turner (unpublished). Furthermore, the model accurately simulates the observed phenomenon (Turner and Tracy, 1983; Turner and Tracy, this volume) that blood flow to appendages accounts for most of the differences in rates of warming and cooling in reptiles (Fig. 3).

The three-lump model (Fig. 2b) also accurately

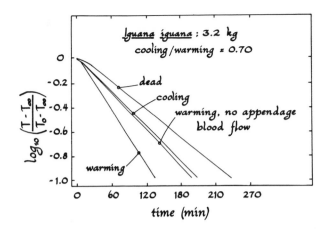

Figure 3. A computer simulation (using the model in Figure 2b) of temperature transients in a 3.2 kg green iguana (*Iguana iguana*). Simulations were for normal cooling and warming of a living lizard, cooling or warming of a dead lizard, and warming in a living lizard where blood flow between appendages and torso had been abrogate. Symbols are as in Figure 1.

predicts the body temperatures of large lizards during heating and cooling in nature. Christian and Tracy (unpublished) monitored the body temperatures of adult Galapagos land iguanas (*Conolophus pallidus*) that were tethered in full sun and later transferred to deep shade. Relevant meteorological data necessary for the model were recorded simultaneously (Christian, Tracy, and Porter, in press). Calculated and measured body temperatures were virtually identical during heating as well as cooling (Fig. 4).

Finally, Christian, Tracy, and Porter) (1982) used the three-lump model to predict the maximum and minimum attainable body temperatures of Galapagos land iguanas in nature. Additionally, they used radio-telemetry to measure temperatures of free-ranging lizards. Measured temperatures were always bracketed by the predictions (Fig. 5). Lizards maintained a constant body temperature (homeothermy) during midday even when their thermal environment was changing dramatically.

Both the thermal environment and the temperatures selected by the Galapagos land iguanas change seasonally (Christian, Tracy, and Porter, 1982). Interestingly, the particular temperature selected during each season maximized the length of time during a day that a constant, high body temperature could be maintained. For example, the land iguana in Figure 5 would necessarily have shortened its period of homeothermy if it had selected either a higher or lower body temperature (see Christian, Tracy, and Porter, 1982).

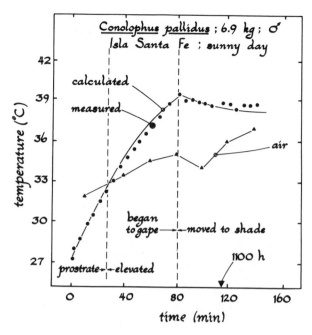

Figure 4. Measured and predicted body temperatures of a 6.9 kg Galapogos land iguana *(Conolophus pallidus)*, tethered with a rope so that it had to remain in the microclimatic conditions of the experiment. Initially, the lizard was cool from overnight climatic conditions. At around 9:00 A.M., the lizard was tethered in full sunlight. The tethered lizard was not prevented from posturing or moving about, but it was prevented from moving to the shade. When the lizard reached a body temperature of around 39.5° C, it was moved to deep shade created by two layers of canvas tarp held 2 m above the ground surface with tent poles. Dots represent cloacal temperatures measured with a thermocouple held in place (approximately 6 cm into the cloaca) with tape. Model predictions of body temperature are represented with the solid line. Also presented are air temperature and notes of a change in behavior.

These findings challenge our traditional view of thermoregulation. Most discussions of temperature regulation assume that ectotherms attempt to regulate to some "optimal" body temperature, the level of which is largely independent of the amount of time that the animal spends at that temperature. In contrast, land iguanas appear to select a body temperature that maximizes the amount of time (during the day) when body temperature can be held constant.

Hypotheses Concerning Thermoregulation in Pelycosaurs

With extant animals, one deduces patterns of temperature regulation by monitoring body temperatures in the field and laboratory and by analyzing the properties of the animal's natural environment (Fig. 5). Such patterns and properties serve as analogues with respect to extinct animals, and are then examined in terms of the pecularities—such as body size and dorsal sail—of the extinct forms themselves. In this way, circumstantial evidence for or against a particular hypothesis is gathered. In this paper, we propose *a priori* hypotheses concerning thermoregulation in pelycosaurs and then use biophysical simulation to determine whether evolutionary trends in body size and elaboration of dorsal sail are consistent with these hypotheses. We start with alternative propositions:

1. Pelycosaurs were large enough to be "inertial homeotherms" (see Spotila, 1980). In the extreme, this hypothesis assumes that the sail has no significant thermoregulatory function (see below).

2. The sail of pelycosaurs facilitated regulation of body temperature by serving as a heat exchanger that could be used to expedite heat exchange with the environment (Bramwell and Fellgett, 1973). In this hypothesis, both body size

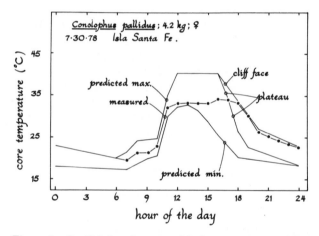

Figure 5. Predicted and measured body temperatures of the Galapagos land iguana *(Conolophus pallidus)* on Isla Santa Fe, Galapagos, in the cool season (July 30, 1978). Actual body temperatures were measured using radio telemetry. Predictions of body temperature were made using the model in Figure 2b (see Chrisitan, Tracy, and Porter, 1982). Predictions were made for the minimum attainable body temperature (that which would occur when the lizard was in deep shade, where the wind speed was greatest and air temperature lowest) and the maximum attainable body temperature (that which would occur when the lizard was in full sunlight and postured so that the maximum of its surface area would receive direct solar radiation). In addition, predictions of maximum attainable body temperature were made for the lizards found in two microhabitats: a plateau that received the full force of the revailing winds at all times; and a cliff face that was shielded from the prevailing wind. During the cool season, the lizards all retreated to the warmer cliff face in afternoon.

TRACY, TURNER, AND HUEY

and the sail jointly promote homeothermy (see below).

Both of these alternatives deal with the constraints that condition different ways of evolving homeothermy. thus, we are not directly asking "did homeothermy exist?" Instead, we are asking, "How will the use of a dorsal sail help an animal to maintain homeothermy?" and "Are the evolutionary trends in the evolution of body and sail size consistent with the best method of attaining homeothermy?"

This approach also requires consideration of the possibility that pelycosaurs could have regulated their body temperatures at two alternative levels: at relatively low body temperature (ca. 30° C, Bakker, 1971); and a temperature that is higher than ambient air temperature (ca. 35° C).

Allometry of the Sail in Pelycosaurs

The dorsal sail appeared early in the history of two lines of pelycosurs. The earliest members of the genus *Dimetrodon* were small (mass approximately 50 kg) and had proportionally smaller sails than did later and larger members of the genus (Fig. 6). Indeed, the allometric relationship between area of the sail, A_{sail} (m^2), and body mass, m (kg), for six species of *Dimetrodon* is:

$$A_{sail} = 0.005 \; m^{1.13}$$

(explained variance = 0.928). The pattern for *Edaphosaurus* was similar, but there are too few data to compute an allometric constant with confidence. These patterns imply that sail area did not evolve in direct relation to the area of the rest of the body, but rather it became proportionately much larger in large pelycosaurs (Fig. 6). A first guess, then, is that the sail was used as a heat exchanger to dissipate heat generated during exercise, but metabolic heat is generally proportional to $m^{0.75}$ (Schmidt-Nielsen, 1979; but see Heusner, 1982a, b), and the sail area is proportional to $m^{1.13}$.

Alternatively, the sail could have been important to large pelycosaurs while these animals were storing heat (during thermal transients), because the rate of storage of heat is proportional to $m^{1.0}$.

Modeling the Environment of Sailed Pelycosaurs

Dimetrodon and *Edaphosaurus* lived near the equator of the Lower Permian. *Dimetrodon*, which appears to have been primarily a predator

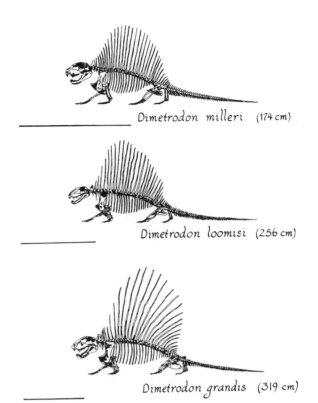

Dimetrodon milleri (174 cm)

Dimetrodon loomisi (256 cm)

Dimetrodon grandis (319 cm)

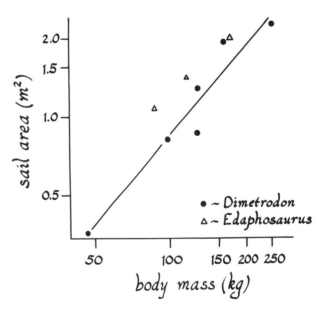

Figure 6. The relationship between the size of dorsal sails and the size of the body in some sailed pelycosaurs. *Top:* reconstructions of three members of *Dimetrodon* that differed greatly in size (the length of the bar in each case is 1m); and, *graph,* the relationship between the surface area of the dorsal sail and body mass in pelycosaurs of the genera *Dimetrodon* and *Edaphosaurs.*

of amphibians, would have spent much of its time near marshes and along streams. *Edaphosaures*, an herbivore, is most commonly found in deposits typically associated with standing water.

The environments of *Dimetrodon* and *Edaphosaurus* were, therefore, probably not heavily forested. The climate should have been warm, sunny, and without great daily or seasonal variation in temperature (Olson, this volume; Colbert, this volume; Parrish, this volume; Bakker, 1982). Additional support for the idea that sailed pelycosaurs lived in open habitats is suggested by the potential difficulties of maneuvering a large sail through a brushy or forested habitat.

We infer, therefore, that contemporary climates in open habitats in the tropics closely approximate conditions experienced by pelycosaurs during the Permian. Climate data from the Galapabos during the warm season (Christian, Tracy, and Porter, 1982) provide the basis of our simulations, but our conclusions are relatively insensitive to uncertainties in evaluating Permian climates.

Possible Thermoregulatory Significance of Size and Sails

Body size and sail area increase during the evolutionary history of sailed pelycosaurs. To evaluate the thermoregulatory significance of these trends, we examine a primitive and an advanced representative of this dynasty. The simulations for these forms suggest a scenario for the evolution of homeothermy at high body temperature in the Pelycosauria.

The earliest pelycosaurs were extremely small and had no sails (Reisz 1972). The earliest sailed forms, such as *Dimetrodon milleri*, were larger (ca. 50 kg). Nevertheless, they still could not have been inertial homeotherms because they were too small to dampen the effects of daily fluctuations in their thermal environments. Consequently, they could not have maintained a low body temperature (ca. 30° C) during the day (Fig. 7a). They could, however, have easily maintained homeothermy for much of the day by regulating at a high body temperature (ca 35° C). The sail of this reptile could have extended the period of daytime homeothermy at any temperature by perhaps as much as one hour (Fig. 7a), although its effectiveness would have been greater at high body temperatures.

The later sailed pelycosaurs *(D. grandis)* were

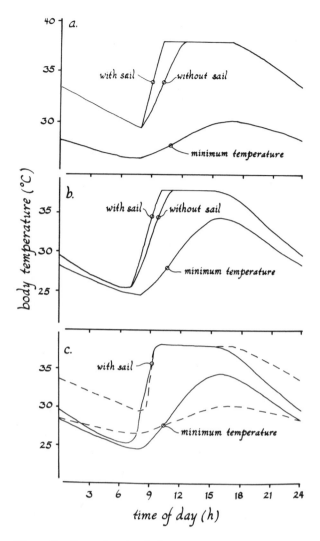

Figure 7. Computer simulations (using the model in Figure 2c) of the maximum and minimum attainable body temperatures of *Dimetrodon grandis* and *Dimetrodon milleri* in their presumed natural environments: A, body temperatures of *D. milleri* with and without benefit of a dorsal sail as an auxiliary heat exchanger; B, body temperatures of *D. grandis* with and without a dorsal sail; and C, body temperatures of *D. grandis* (solid line) and *D. milleri* (dashed line) superimposed for comparison. Both animals have benefit of their sails in this graph.

very large (250 kg), and as a result could have been inertial homeotherms at low body temperatures (ca. 30° C) for perhaps the entire day (Fig. 7b). In this case, the sail would have conferred no thermoregulatory advantage. This inference suggests a trend towards lower daytime body temperatures during the evolution of the sailed pelycosaurs, as *D. milleri* would have had a difficult time escaping high body temperatures at midday (Fig. 7a). Perhaps a more parsimonious interpretation is for the evolution of extended homeothermy at high body temperatures during

TRACY, TURNER, AND HUEY

daylight hours, which would encompass evolutionary trends in both body size and in sail size. The large sail of advanced pelycosaurs would have enabled large reptiles to retain the ability to warm up quickly, an attribute otherwise restricted to very small animals (Fig. 7c), thereby increasing the period of homeothermy by more than one hour (Fig. 7b). Moreover, the large body size of late pelycosaurs should have further extended the period of homeothermy at high body temperatures. For example, large size alone could have enabled *D. grandis* to remain homeothermic at 35° C for three hours longer than *D. milleri* (Fig. 7c) once its body temperature had attained that level by virtue of the sail.

The simulations suggest that evolutionary trends in body size, sail size, and energy exchange with the environment in sailed pelycosaurs were related to promoting homeothermy at high body temperature. If this hypothesis is correct, it means that homeothermy at high body temperature occurred early in the history of the mammal-like reptiles. It must be noted, however, that therapsids did not arise from *Dimetrodon,* but rather from a more primtive, unsailed sphenacodont such as *Haptodus* (see Carroll, this volume). Thus, while our analysis does not imply that the predecessors of therapsids were homeothermic, it does suggest that advanced sailed pelycosaurs, and perhaps synapsids as a whole, had extensive potential to evolve sophisticated thermoregulatory adaptations.

Acknowledgments

This work was supported by a Guggenheim Fellowship, the National Science Foundation (DEB 8109667), the University of Washington Graduate School Research Fund, and the Department of Zoology and Entomology of Colorado State University. We appreciate the loan of a digitizer, used to measure sail areas of pelycosaurs, from R. T. Paine and M. Denny. We especially thank J. Lillegraven for enormously helpful comments on the manuscript. We owe particular thanks to Dr. Keith Christian whose work in the Galapagos was so important to the maturation of ideas expressed here.

References

Alexandrov, V. Y.
1967. Protein thermostability of a species and habitat temperature. pp. 53–59. In *Molecular Mechanisms of Temperature Adaptation,* ed. C. L. Prosser, pp. 53–59. Pub. No. 84, American Association for the Advancement of Science, Washington, D.C.

Baker, L. A., and White, F. N.
1970. Redistribution of cardiac output in response to heating in *Iguana iguana. Comp. Biochem. Physiol.* 35:253–62.

Bakken, G. S., and Gates, D. M.
1975. Heat transfer analysis of animals: some implications for field ecology, physiology and evolution. In *Perspectives in Biophysical Ecology,* ed. D. M. Gates and R. B. Schmerl, pp. 255–90. New York: Springer-Verlag.

Bakker, R. T.
1971. Dinosaur phylogeny and the origin of mammals. *Evolution* 25:635–58.
1982. Juvenile-adult habitat shift in Permian fossil reptiles and amphibians. *Science* 217:53–55.

Bartholomew, G. A.
1972. Body temperature and energy metabolism. In *Animal Physiology: Principles and Adaptation,* ed. M. S. Gordon, pp. 298–368. New York: MacMillan.

Bartholomew, G. A., and Lasiewski, R. C.
1965. Heating and cooling rates, heart rate and simulated diving in the Galapagos marine iguana. *Comp. Biochem. Physiol.* 16:573–82.

Bartholomew, G. A., and Tucker, V. A.
1963. Control of changes in body temperature, metabolism and circulation by the agamid lizard, *Amphibolurus barbatus. Physiol. Zool.* 36:199–218.

Bartholomew, G. A., and Tucker, V. A.
1964. Size, body temperature, thermal conductance, oxygen consumption, and heart rate in Australian varanid lizards. *Physiol. Zool.* 37:341–54.

Bartlett, P. N., and Gates, D. M.
1967. The energy budget of a lizard on a tree trunk. *Ecology* 48:316–22.

Bechman, W. A.; Mitchell, J. W.; and Porter, W. P.
1973. Thermal model for prediction of a desert iguanas daily and seasonal behavior. *Journal of Heat Transfer Paper No. 71-WA/HT-35.*

Bennett, A. F., and Dawson, W. R.
1975. Metabolism. In Biology of the Reptilia, vol. 5, ed. C. Gans and W. R. Dawson, pp. 127–223. New York: Academic Press.

Birkebak, R. C.
1966. Heat transfer in biological systems. *Int. Rev. Gen. Exp. Zoology* 2:269–344.

Bogert, C. M.
1949. Thermoregulation in reptiles, a factor in evolution. *Evolution* 3:195–211.

Bramwell, C. D. and Fellgett, P. B.
1973. Thermal regulation in sail lizards. *Nature* 242:203–5.

Brattstrom, B. H.
1965. Body temperatures of reptiles. *Amer. Midl. Naturalist* 73:376–422.

Campbell, G. S.
1977. *An Introduction to Environmental Biophysics.* New York: Springer Verlag.

Christian, K. A.; Tracy, C. R.; and Porter, W. P.
1983. Seasonal shifts in body temperature and in the use of microhabitats by the Galapagos land iguana. *Ecology* 64:463–68.

Cowles, R. B.
1958. Possible origin of dermal temperature regulation. *Evolution* 12:347–57.

Cowles, R. B., and Bogert, C. M.
1944. A preliminary study of the thermal requirements of desert reptiles. *Bull. Amer. Museum Natural Hist.* 83:265–96.

Crawford, E. C., Jr.
1972. Brain and body temperatures in a panting lizard. *Science* 177:431–32.

Crompton, A. W.; Taylor, C. R.; and Jagger, J. A.
1978. Evolution of homeothermy in mammals. *Nature* 272:333–36.

DeWitt, C. B.
1967. Precision of thermoregulation and its relation to environmental factors in the desert iguana, *Dipsosaurus dorsalis. Physiol. Zool.* 40:49–66.

Edney, E. B.
1971. The body temperature of tenebrionid bettles in the Namib desert of southern Africa. *J. Exp. Biol.* 55:253–73.

Else, P. L., and Hulbert, A. J.
1981. Comparison of the "mammal machine" and the "reptile machine": energy production. *Amer. J. Physiol.* 240:R3–R9.

Fry, F. E. J.
1967. Responses of vertebrate poikilotherms to temperature. In *Thermobiology,* ed. A. H. Rose, pp. 374–409. New York: Academic Press.

Gans, C.
1970. Respiration in early tetrapods—the frog is a red herring. *Evolution* 24:723–34.

Grant, P. R.
1983. Lizard ecology, viewed at a short distance. In *Lizard Ecology: Studies of a Model Organism,* ed. R. B. Huey, E. R. Pianka, and T. W. Schoener. Cambridge: Harvard University Press.

Grigg, G. C.; Drane, C. R.; and Courtice, G. P.
1979. Time constants of heating and cooling in the eastern water dragon, *Physignathus lesuerii. J. Thermal Biol.* 4:354–60.

Heath, J. E.
1965. Temperature regulation and diurnal activity in horned lizards. *Univ. Calif. Publ. Zool.* 64:97–136.

1968. The origin of thermoregulation. In *Evolution and Environment,* ed. E. T. Drake, pp. 259–78. New Haven, Conn.: Yale University Press.

Heinrich, B.
1974. Thermoregulation in endothermic insects. *Science* 185:747–55.

1977. Why have some animals evolved to regulate a high body temperature? *Amer. Naturalist* 111:623–40.

Heusner, A. A.
1982a. Energy metabolism and body size. I. Is the 0.75 mass exponent of Kleiber's equation a statistical artifact? *Resp. Physiol.* 48:1–12.

1982b. Energy metabolism and body size. II. Dimensional analysis and energetic non-similarity. *Resp. Physiol.* 48:13–25.

Hochachka, P., and Somero, G. N.
1973. *Strategies of Biochemical Adaptation.* Philadelphia: Saunders.

Huey, R. B.
1982. Temperature, physiology and the ecology of reptiles. In: *Biology of the Reptilia,* vol. 12, ed. C. Gans and F. H. Pough, London: Academic Press.

Huey, R. B., and Pianka, E. R.
1977. Seasonal patterns of thermoregulatory behavior and body temperature of diurnal Kalahari lizards. *Ecology* 58:1066–75.

Hutchison, V. H.; Dowling, H. G.; and Vinegar, A.
1966. Thermoregulation in a brooding female Indian python, *Python molurus. Science* 151:694–96.

James, F. C., and Porter, W. P.
1979. Behavior-microclimate relationships in the African rainbow lizard. *Copeia* (1979):585–93.

Kreith, F., and Black, W. Z.
1980. *Basic Heat Transfer.* New York: Harper and Row.

MacKay, R. S.
1964. Galapagos tortoise and marine iguana deep body temperatures measured by radio telemetry. *Nature* 204:355–58.

McKenna, T. M., and Packard, G. C.
1975. Rates of heat exchange in the lizards *Cnemidophorus sexlineatus* and *Sceloporus occidentalis. Copeia* (1975):162–69.

McNab, B. K.
1978. The evolution of endothermy in the phylogeny of mammals. *Amer. Naturalist* 112:1–21.

TRACY, TURNER, AND HUEY

Mitchell, J. W.
1976. Heat transfer from spheres and other animal forms. *Biophys. J.* 16:561–69.

Muth, A.
1977. Thermoregulatory postures and orientation to the sun: A mechanistic evaluation for the zebra-tailed lizard, *Callisaurus draconoides*. *Copeia* (1977):710–20.

Nagy, K. A.; Odell, D. K.; and Seymour, R. S.
1972. Temperature regulation by the inflorescence of *Philodendron. Science* 178:1195–97.

Norris, K. S.
1967. Color adaptation in desert reptiles and its thermal relationships. In *Lizard Ecology: A Symposium,* ed. W. W. Milstead, pp. 162–229. Columbia: University of Missouri Press.

Porter, W. P.; Mitchell, J. W.; Beckman, J. M.; and DeWitt, C. B.
1973. Behavioral implications of mechanistic ecology. *Oecologia* 13:1–54.

Porter, W. P., and Tracy, C. R.
1983. Biophysical analyses of energetics, time-space utilization and distributional limits of lizards. In *Lizard Ecology: Studies of a Model Organism,* ed. R. B. Huey, E. R. Pianka, and T. Schoener. Cambridge, Mass.: Harvard University Press.

Prosser, C. L.
1973. Temperature. in *Comparative Animal Physiology,* ed. C. L. Prosser, pp. 362–488. Philadelphia: Saunders.

Reisz, R.
1972. Pelycosaurian reptiles from the Middle Pennsylvanian of North America. *Bull. Mus. Comp. Zool.,* Harvard 144:27–62.

Romer, A. S.
1966. *Vertebrate Paleontology,* 3d ed. Chicago: University of Chicago Press.

Romer, A. S., and Price, L. L.
1940. Review of the Pelycosauria. *Spec. Publ. Geol. Soc. Amer.* 28:1–621.

Schmidt-Nielsen, K.
1979. *Animal Physiology: ADaptation and Environment.* Cambridge: Cambridge University Press.

Scott, J. R.; Tracy, C. R.; and Pettus, D.
1982. A biophysical analysis of daily and seasonal utilization of climate space by a montane snake. *Ecology* 63:482–93.

Smith, E. N.
1979. Behavioral and physiological thermoregulation of crocodilians. *Amer. Zool.* 19:239–47.

Spotila, J. R.
1980. Constraints of body size and environment on the temperature regulation of dinosaurs. In *A Cold Look at the Warm-Blooded Dinosaurs,* ed. R. D. K. Thomas and E. C. Olson, pp. 233–252. AAAS Selected Sympposium 28. Boulder, Colorado: Westview Press.

Spotila, J. R.; Lommen, P. W.; Bakken, G. S.; and Gates, D. M.
1973. A mathematical model for body temperature of large reptiles: implications for dinosaur ecology. *Amer. Naturalist* 107:391–404.

Spotila, J. R.; Soule, O. H.; and Gates, D. M.
1972. The biophysical ecology of the alligator: heat energy budgets and climate spaces. *Ecology* 53:1094–102.

Templeton, J. R.
1970. Reptiles. In *The Comparative Physiology of Thermoregulation,* ed. G. C. Whittow, pp. 167–221. New York: Academic Press.

Tracy, C. R.
1978. The evolutiono-engineering approach. In *The Behavioral Significance of Color,* ed. E. H. Burtt. New York: Garland Publishers.
1982. Biophysical modelling in reptilian physiology and ecology. In *Biology of the Reptilia,* vol. 12, ed. F. H. Pough and C. Gans. London: Academic Press.

Tracy C. R.; Christian, K. A.; Turner, J. S.; and Porter, W. P.
1980. A new transient-state energy budget model of a reptile *(Conolophus pallidus)* which employs physiological control of energy exchange. *Bull. Ecol. Soc. Amer.* 61:93.

Turner, J. S.
In press. Cardiovascular control of heat exchange: interactions with body shape and size. *Amer. Zool.*

Turner, J. S.; Hammond, K. A.; and Tracy, C. R.
1980. Energy flux at the appendages and trunk of the American alligator during heating and cooling. *Anat. Rec.* 196:192A.

Turner, J. S., and Tracy, C. R.
1983. Blood flow to appendages and the control of heat exchange in American alligators *Physiol. Zool.* 56:195–200.

Waldschmidt, S., and Tracy, C. R.
1983. Interactions between a lizard and its thermal environment: implications for sprint performance and space utilization in the lizard *Uta stansburiana. Ecology* 64:476–84.

Weathers, W. W.
1970. Physiological thermoregulation in the lizard *Dipsosaurus dorsalis. Copeia* (1971):548–51.
1971. Some cardiovascular aspects of temperature regulation in the lizard, *Dipsosaurus dorsalis. Comp. Biochem. Physiol.* 40A:503–15.

Weathers, W. W., and White, F. N.
1971. Physiological thermoregulation in turtles. *Amer. J. Physiol.* 221:704–10.

White, F. N.
1976. Circulation, In *Biology of the Reptilia, Vol. 5,* ed. C. Gans and W. R. Dawson, pp. 257–344. New York: Academic Press.

Whittow, G. C.
1970. *Comparative Physiology of Thermoregulation, Vol. 1.* New York: Academic Press.

1973. Comparative Physiology of Thermoregulation, Vol. 3. New York: Academic Press.

Voight, W. G., and Johnson, C. R.
1977. Physiological control of heat exchange rates in the Texas tortoise, *Gopherus berlandieri. Comp. Biochem. Physiol.* 56A:495–98.

ALBERT F. BENNETT

School of Biological Sciences
University of California
Irvine, California 92717
and
JOHN A. RUBEN

Department of Zoology
Oregon State University
Corvallis, Oregon 97331

The Metabolic and Thermoregulatory Status of Therapsids

Introduction

Endothermy, the internal production of heat, entails essentially constant high rates of metabolism that are costly in energy: birds and mammals typically consume at least ten times as much food as do ectothermic vertebrates. Independently attained in the mammalian and avian lineages, endothermy required quantitative and qualitative changes in nearly all systems related to energy utilization. Its acquisition involved major alterations in anatomy, physiology, behavior, and ecology. In view of its costs, the advantages of endothermy are not fully understood. Various authors have dealt with such desirable attributes as high body temperature (Heinrich, 1978), homeothermy (Crompton, Taylor, and Jagger, 1978), and expanded behavioral capacity (Bennett and Ruben, 1979); while others have noted that ectothermy has compensatory advantages of its own (e.g., Pough, 1980a). What is clear is that an early commitment to endothermy was made in two vertebrate lineages and that the subsequent radiations of those lineages have been very successful.

The question arises as to whether or not the reptilian ancestors of mammals and birds were also endothermic. There has been much recent debate about the existence of endothermy in dinosaurs (see Thomas and Olson, 1980), but it is the therapsid-mammalian lineage with which are concerned. An inquiry into the thermoregulatory status of therapsids is desirable not only because of its bearing on mammalian evolution, but also because of the significance of therapsids as a major faunal component in the late Paleozoic and early Mesozoic. The Therapsida comprise one of the largest and most diverse of the reptilian radiations, dominating vertebrate terrestrial communities from the mid-Permian through the Early Triassic. The diversity of body sizes and feeding types reflects occupation of a wide variety of environments and ecological niches. The cause of their decline is not known, but their direct descendents, the Mammalia, survived and comprise a still more diverse and successful group.

It is obviously difficult to ascertain physiological characters from dead animals. It is even more difficult to infer those characters from fossilized bones. There is consequently little agreement about the acceptability of various characteristics that have been advanced as evidence of thermoregulatory status, but, in contrast to the often acrimonious dissension about endothermy in dinosaurs, there is rather remarkable agreement that the advanced therapsids were in some degree endothermic. This view was first advanced by Brink (1956) in a paper that, while highly speculative, was influential in reorienting thought about the anatomical and physiological capacities of these animals. Others have also advocated some endothermic status for therapsids (Olson, 1959), 1971; Van Valen, 1960; Reed, 1960; Simpson, 1959; Parrington, 1967; Heath, 1968; Hopson, 1969, 1973; de Ricqles, 1969b; Geist, 1972; McNab, 1978; Benton, 1979; Hotton, 1980; Baur and Friedel, 1980). In contrast, Crompton, Taylor, and Jagger (1978) maintain that endothermy was in fact a mammalilan invention and that therapsids were ectothermic. Bakker has suggested that therapsids were essentially ectothermic (Bakker, 1971), that they were essentially endothermic (Bakker, 1975), and that they had a metabolic status intermediate between ecotothermy and endothermy (Bakker, 1980). His work illustrates the elusiveness of the subject. As yet there has not been a concerted effort to reconcile different arguments. Here we review the assorted evidence and arrive at our own evaluation.

In order for an anatomical structure or other criterion to be diagnostic of a high metabolic rate or of endothermy, it must satisfy at least the following three conditions: it should have a clear and logical association with high rates of metabolism; it should not be explicable in terms unrelated to high levels of metabolism; and it should be absent in ectotherms. We have used these conditions to evaluate eight lines of reasoning that have been applied to the question of therapsid thermoregulation: the histological structure of therapsid bone; the pattern of posture and limb support; the presence of hair; brain size; other anatomical features, including the presence of a diaphragm, a turbinal complex within the nasal cavity, a bony secondary palate, and a parietal foramen; predatory/prey ratios of therapsid communities; biogeographic distribution of therapsids; and the comparative physiology of monotremes and therians.

Evidence for Endothermy in Therapsids

Histological structure of bone

A great diversity of organizational types of bone is found in extant and extinct vertebrates. Two types of compact bone have been recognized, differing quantitatively in their fibral organization and degree of vascularization (Foote, 1916; Gross, 1934; de Ricqles, 1969a). In one type, currently termed *lamellar-zonal,* compact bone is formed principally by periosteal deposition. Primary osteons are few. The bone has a layered appearance from which growth lines are sometimes adduced, and is poorly vascularized. In the other, termed *fibro-lamellar,* most of the matrix is deposited by numerous primary osteons, producing a woven fibrous appearance. Fibro-lamellar bone is well vascularized and is often reworked into extensive Haversian systems (secondary bones). However, there are numerous intermediate patterns that make clear distinctions difficult. Bone type varies with such factors as the aquatic, aerial, or terrestial habits of the animal, body size, age of the individual, and area of bone examined (de Ricqles, 1976b, 1977).

Differences in bone structure have been correlated with the taxonomic position of different vertebrate groups (de Ricqles, 1969a, 1972a, b). Lamellar-zonal bone is found in most ectothermic vertebrates such as amphibians and extant reptiles. Fibro-lamellar bone is present in mammals and birds. Bone from most therapsids resembles that of modern mammals more closely than the bone of extant ectothermic reptiles. Pelycosaurs possessed typical lamellar-zonal bone (Enlow and Brown, 1956, 1957, 1958; Peabody, 1961; Enlow, 1969; de Ricqles, 1974, 1978a). The diaphyses of their long bones show growth rings and are poorly vascularized. The only osseous tissue with a fibro-lamellar structure is found in the neural spines of some species. In contrast, the bony tissues of therapsids as a group show considerably more vascularity and different types of structural organization (Enlow and Brown, 1956, 1957, 1958; de Ricqles, 1969b,

1972c, 1978a, b). There is, however, considerable diversity among therapsids. Bone from the eotheriodont *Biarmosuchus* is only slightly more vascular than that of pelycosaurs (de Ricqles, 1974), and the gorgonopsian(?) *Watongia* had typically lamellar-zonal bone (de Ricqles, 1976a). The anomodonts possessed several types of fibro-lamellar bone, each given its own designation. A common type has a very dense, thickened, and well-vascularized cortex, reminiscent of that of modern artiodactyls. Within some titanosuchids and dicynodonts, distinct growth rings are apparent. In the more advanced therapsids, and therocephalians, bauriamorphs, cynodonts, and tritylodonts, the bone has a more typically fibro-lamellar organization. Bone in these groups may be composed of very numerous and densely packed osteons and may show considerable Haversian substitution. Considerable differentiation is found among advanced therapsid groups.

Fibro-lamellar bone has been associated with endothermy and lamellar-zonal bone with ectothermy (de Ricqles, 1969a, 1972a, b). The relationship of bone histological structure to thermoregulatory status are not direct and are consequently controversial. As bone is not itself a thermogenic tissue, the presence of highly vascularized and metabolically active bone is not *a priori* evidence of endothermy. Nor is absence of vascularity necessarily indicative of ectothermy, since small mammals and birds (under 1 kg in body mass) lack fibro-lamellar bone. De Ricqles (1976a, 1978a, 1980) has maintained that fibro-lamellar bone is associated with rapid growth that requires rapid deposition and extensive reworking of primary bone tissue. He believes that such rapid growth is possible only in systems with the high metabolic rates associated with endothermy. Thus the primary correlation is held to be between growth rate and bone structure. It has also been suggested that with a higher rate of metabolism there is accelerated modilization of calcium and phosphate salts from bone tissue. The high vascularization of fibro-lamellar bone, with its extensive Haversian network of vessels, might seem to permit more rapid release and deposition of these molecules (Bakker, 1975), but calcium can be released from bone very quickly even in ectotherms (Ruben and Bennett, 1981) and is probably rapid regardless of bone type. Diversity of bone types in therapsids may reflect a range of thermoregulatory strategies. De Ricqles (1978a) believes that the anomodonts were not stable endotherms, whereas the advanced therapsids were endothermic. These are reasonable

conclusions if indeed bone structure indicates a particular kind of thermoregulation. Some workers (Bouvier, 1977; Reid, 1981) dispute these correlations. There are indeed some disquieting discontinuities in these patterns, such as the absence of fibro-lamellar bone in small (and rapidly growing) endotherms and its presence in a labyrinthodont (Enlow, 1969). It is clear that the bone of therapsids is very different from that of their pelycosaurian ancestors and is more like that of their mammalian descendents. We believe that this line of evidence is suggestive of endothermy in advanced therapsids. However, because correlation between these characters and thermoregulatory status is not direct, and the bone of living endotherms and ectotherms does not separate into distinct and mutually exclusive types, we are inclined to regard this line of reasoning as inconclusive.

Posture and limb support

Limb suspension has been used as evidence both for and against endothermy in therapsids. Heath (1968) and Bakker (1971) agree that an erect posture, with limbs held vertically and directly under the body, is evidence for endothermy. Heath maintains that in contrast to the sprawling limb suspension characteristic of most modern reptiles, therapsids stood with a "fixed pillar stance." He argues that this fully erect stance is energetically more expensive because of increased muscle tonus, and is in fact a major source of heat production. Increased heat production from this source is seen as the cause of therapsid endothermy. Bakker, on the contrary, argues that therapsids had a sprawling, not an erect, limb suspension, and that in consequence they were ectothermic, being rather similar to modern monitor lizards in their thermoregulatory capacities. Bakker does not, however, maintain that there is a direct causal connection between posture and metabolic rate.

The purported associations between limb support and thermoregulatory pattern have been criticized elsewhere (Bennett and Dalzell, 1973; Feduccia, 1973). Contrary to Heath's opinion, mammalian endothermy does not depend primarily on heat production by skeletal muscle. Liver, kidney, brain, and heart metabolism account for the major portion of total resting rate of heat production. At rest, skeletal muscle tissue has a relatively low utilization of energy and a correspondingly small effect on total metabolic rate. It is doubtful that endothermy or a greatly increased metabolic rate could have been achieved by muscular rearrangements alone. Without a causal connection, the associations of posture and thermoregulation are only correlations that are not distinct among modern animals. For instance, chameleons and crocodilians, strict ectotherms, possess a semi-erect stance, intermediate in condition between sprawling and fully erect posture (Bakker, 1971). So do modern monotremes, which are competent endotherms. Jenkins (1970, 1971) presents evidence that advanced therapsids (cynodonts) also had a semi-erect stance (contrary to both Bakker and Heath). Were they ectothermic as crocodilians are or endothermic as monotremes? Given the controversy concerning the actual form of limb suspension in therapsids and the tenous associations between posture and thermoregulation, we believe that these arguments are also inconclusive.

Hair

The discovery of therapsid hair would probably be the most unequivocal and decisive evidence for therapsid endothermy. The presence of hair is one of the most dignostic mammalian traits and is clearly linked with thermoregulation. Such insulation would be primarily beneficial to an animal with an internal heat source in a cool environment. It might also serve as a shield against solar radiation and thus help prevent overheating. The most commonly cited evidence suggesting the presence of hair or hairlike structures are foramina on the facial portion of skulls of many therocephalians, gorgonopsians, and cynodonts (see Van Valen, 1960, for references). These foramina have been interpreted as passages for nerves and blood vessels supplying rostral sensory vibrissae (Watson, 1931; Broili, 1941; Brink, 1956), which Broili and Brink contended would indicate hair on the rest of the body. However, rostral foramina do not necessarily indicate the presence of vibrissae. Similar foramina are present in the skulls of living ectotherms whose scaly skins lack both vibrissae and hair (Estes, 1961, 1964); in the lizard *Tupinambis*, rostral foramina are almost identical in shape, number, and distribution to those of the cynodont *Thrinaxodon*. Nor is it clear that sensory hairs on the snout indicate a pelage. We do not understand the origin of hair, but if its initial function were sensory, it is quite possible that vibrissae reflect the primitive condition and so could have appeared long before an insulative pelage had evolved.

Thus there is no good evidence that therapsids possessed either vibriassae or pelage. On the contrary, a remarkable sample of fossilized skin from the dicynodont *Estemmenosuchus* shows neither hair impressions nor hair follicles (Chudinov, 1970). The epidermis of the skin was smooth and undifferentiated and lacked scales. The skin was well supplied with glands and was probably soft and pliable. No fossil traces of skin have been found in therapsid genera closer to the mammalian condition.

Brain Size

In relation to body size, the brains of mammals and birds are approximately ten times greater in volume than those of extant reptiles (Jerison, 1973; Hopson, 1980). It has been suggested that the greater levels of activity associated with high metabolic rates require larger brain capacities than are found in modern reptiles (Feduccia, 1973), and that high metabolic heat production may be a precondition for neocortical elaboration (Bakker, 1980).

Cranial volume has been calculated for only about six cynodonts and one dicynodont (Jerison, 1973; Quiroga, 1979, 1980; Hopson, 1980). The encephalization coefficients (= ratio of observed value to a typical value for an advanced mammal of equal size) in these skulls are about 0.1–0.2, that is, ten to twenty percent of modern mammalian volumes. These cranial capacities are similar to encephalization coefficients of monitor and teiid lizards, which are known to be intelligent and active animals but are strictly ectothermic. Jerison (1973) believes that therapsids were largely still reptilian in their degree of brain evolution. Hopson agrees that their brains are more reptile-like than mammal-like (Hopson, 1969), but interprets their degree of brain development as indicating an intermediate status (Hopson, 1980).

Encephalization coefficients reported for Mesozoic mammals exceed 0.2, but are not substantially greater than those of therapsids (Jerison, 1973; E. Allen, personal communication.) Thus the attainment of mammalian status was not accompanied by a quantum jump in brain size. Comparison of brain size of therapsids and early mammals provide no evidence of thermoregulatory modes.

Other Anatomical Features

Other anatomical features proposed as indicators of high metabolic rates and endothermy in therapsids include a muscular diaphragm, bony secondary palate, nasal turbinal complex, and loss of the parietal foramen. The first three features are associated with ventilation and the provision of air to the lungs. It was on the basis of these structures that Brink (1956) originally claimed endothermy in therapsids. The oxygen extraction efficiencies (ratio of volume of oxygen removed to volume of air ventilated) of modern reptiles and mammals are quite similar (Bennett, 1973: Wood and Lenfant, 1976). Mammals must, therefore, exchange considerably more air to meet their metabolic requirements. The following alterations in ventilatory mechanisms within the mammalian ancestry might well have been associated with the attainment of endothermic metabolic rates.

DIAPHRAGM

The muscular diaphragm is the primary means of ventilation of mammalian lungs, and its presence in therapsids might signify increments in ventilation rates necessary to support higher metabolic rates. Brink (1956) inferred its presence from the reduction of the lumbar ribs among advanced theriodonts; in both cynodonts and bauriamorphs, the lumbar ribs become greatly shortened, and the rib cage assumes a more typically mammalian form.

The reduction of lunbar ribs give the skeletons of advanced therapsids a more mammal-like appearance, but it need not be associated with diaphragmatic breathing and endothermy. Rather, the reduction of lumbar ribs might be better correlated with locomotory refinements. Late theriodonts were developing capacities for greater activity and agility, which involved skeletomuscular modifications related to rotation and flexion of the spinal column. Nor does the presence of a diaphragmlike mechanisms necessarily indicate endothermy. Several living reptiles, including crocodilians and some teiid lizards, possess diaphragmlike structures (for summary, see Goodrich, 1930, pp. 640–42). These structures are not homologous to the mammalian diaphragm, but they do function in ventilation although their possessors are clearly ectothermic.

BONY SECONDARY PALATE

In animals with confluent nasal and buccal cavities, ventilation may be blocked when the mouth is full, which may be expected to embarrass the respiration of animals with high metabolic rates. It is argued that the separation of air and food passages by the bony secondary palate has obviated this problem for mammals, and that the similar palate of advanced therapsids is therefore evidence of more continuous ventilation demanded by endothermic metabolic rates (Brink, 1956; McNab, 1978). However, living tetrapods other than mammals do not support this line of argument: a bony secondary palate is present in the ectothermic crocodilians and teiid lizards, but is lacking in the endothermic birds. Separation of the ventilatory stream is equally effective with a fleshy partition, which is present in many modern ectotherms. The primary function of the bony palate appears to be masticatory, as it serves as a platform for manipulation of the food by the tongue.

NASAL TURBINAL COMPLEX.

The nasal cavities of advanced therapsids approach a mammalian condition (Parsons, 1970). Casts of the nasal cavities of advanced theriodonts (*Diademodon, Watson, 1931; Nythosaurus,* Hopson, 1969; *Thrinaxodon,* Brink, 1955) show clear points of attachmnent of extensive ethmoturbinal bones or cartilages. Cynodont nasal cavities are more highly modified than those of other therapsids. The primary palate has been reduced, and the internal space is capacious enough to have permitted considerable elaboration of turbinal structures. Turbinals in modern mammals are covered with a moist epithelium and serve two primary functions, namely the conditioning of air incurrent to the lungs and the reclamation of water vapor from exhaled air. External air is warmed (or cooled) and humidified during its passage through the turbinal complex and is filtered by these structures so that dust and other debris does not enter the lung tissue. During exhalation, water is condensed on the turbinals as a result of cooling in the nasal cavity (Schmidt-Nielsen, Hainsworth, and Murrish, 1970), and is absorbed rather than being lost to the environment. Turbinals do not have any obvious function other than air conditioning. Their size is unrelated to the excellent olfaction of mammals, which is localized in rather small, nonturbinal areas of the nasal cavity. Turbinals are absent in living reptiles, which instead possess a series of conchae that are much less elaborate in form (Parsons, 1970).

Since the turbinals serve primarily to warm inspired air and to conserve water in living mammals, and since they are totally lacking in living ectotherms, we believe that the presence of complex turbinal structures constitutes the best anatomical evidence of endothermy in therapsids.

The parietal foramen lies on the midline of the skull between the parietal bones, and is the aperature through which the parietal eye gains access to the external environment. The parietal eye is part of the epiphyseal complex that includes the pineal body, which gives evidence of its presence in ancient fossils by distinctive sculpture on the ventral surfaces of the parietal bones near the foramen.

A parietal foramen, accompanied by a complete epiphyseal complex, is manifest in such conservative living reptiles as the rhynchocephalian *Sphenodon* and some lizards. The foramen and associated sculpture are present in all primitive tetraods including captorhinomorphs, pelycosaurs, and most therapsids, which are therefore presumed to have had a complete epiphyseal complex. In the course of evolution, the external connection has declined and disappeared in all major lineages, but most living tetrapods retain an epiphysis or pineal body. The entire complex is lost only in a very few mammals and in the crocodilians as a group.

Experimental ablation of parts or all of the epiphyseal complex of living ectotherms and endotherms seems to affect thermoregulation or circadian rhythms. Roth and Roth (1980) have suggested that the original function of the complex was control of body temperature, when the chief basis of thermoregulation was behavioral. From this it is argued that progressive loss of the external connection of the epiphyseal complex indicates the advent of endothermy, in forms in which the pineal part of the complex is retained.

The difficulty with this line of reasoning is twofold. First, the function of pineal and parietal bodies remains poorly understood in detail. Second, although all living groups with a parietal foramen and complete epiphyseal complex are ectothermic, loss of foramen and parietal eye has taken place many times in tetrapod history, and the majority of living ectothermic tetrapods, as well as living endotherms, lack both foramen and eye. We therefore feel that it is premature to adduce definitive metabolic or thermoregulatory function from any particular epiphyseal configuration.

Predator-prey ratios

Because they must expend so much energy on thermoregulation, endotherms (mammals and birds) typically direct only from one to three percent of their assimilated energy to secondary productivity (tissue formation in reproduction and growth; Golley, 1968). In ectothermic vertebrates, secondary productivity is often more than twenty percent of total assimilated energy, but there can be considerable overlap between the ranges of endotherms and ectotherms in this respect.

Bakker (1972, 1975, 1980) has proposed that these ratios are reflected in the standing crops of animal communities that are in steady state, and that they can be identified in fossil assemblages of predators and their prey. He argues that an assemblage in which the predators constituted only 2 to 3 percent of the animal biomass indicates endothermy in the predators, while a substantially greater ratio indicates ectothermic predators, the thermoregulatory status of the prey being irrelevant. Summaries of his analysis (Bakker, 1975, 1980) indicate that predaceous sphenacodont pelycosaurs constituted 35 to 60 percent of the biomass of their prey (mean ratio = 45% in 12 assemblages without predator concentrations). These ratios are interpreted as a typical ectothermic thermoregulatory pattern in sphenacodont predators. Ratios of 10 to 15 percent are reported for communities of therapsids, but the incision of a single "predator trapping" assemblage would increase the ratio to 24 percent (S.D. = 32.8, n = 6). Ratios of 0.8 and 3.4 percent, respectively, are reported as typical of communities of living and fossil mammals. Bakker (1980) therefore suggests that therapsids had metabolic levels intermediate between those of living endotherms and ectotherms, perhaps being endothermic but regulating body temperature at a lower level than that maintained by most extant birds and mammals.

Both the practicability of estimating community biomasses from fossil assemblages and the interpretation of such estimates have been criticized by Charig (1976), Tracy (1976), Béand and Russell (1980), Farlow (1980), and Hotton (1980), among others. Objections include the difficulty of determining what predators ate which prey; the dependence of biomass turnover on body size; and the questionable reliabiliy of fossilization in preserving true community structure. Predator-prey ratios thus constitute one of the least reliable lines of evidence adduced for endothermy in fossil organisms, and we do not feel that they can be used to draw conclusions about thermoregulatory capacities of therapsids.

Biogeographic Distribution

Large reptiles are currently restricted to tropical and warm temperate areas, and it is generally assumed that only endotherms can occupy areas with protracted cold seasons. Bakker (1975, 1980) argues that therapsids could never have dominated the Late Permian faunas of South Africa unless they had been endothermic, because Southern Gondwana lay at high southern latitudes during the Late Permian, and therefore had a very cold climate.

While it is true that South Africa was glaciated near the end of the Late Carboniferous, the ice sheets had disappeared by the beginning of the Early Permian. Many lines of evidence indicate a warm and generally equable climate by Late Permian time (Charig, 1976; Parrish, Parrish, and Ziegler, this volume; Hickey, personal communication, 1981). Marked seasonality is indicated by tree rings, but it was probably wet-dry rather than warm-cold. In addition to the dominant therapsids, the fauna included many large tetrapods that were doubtlessly ectothermic. Such large ectotherms among the Late Permian tetrapods in South Africa negate a cold climate of the time as evidence for therapsid endothermy.

Comparative Physiology of Prototherian and Therian Mammals

After attaining mammalian status, prototherians did not contribute to the evolutionary sequence leading to marsupials and placentals. Either they had arisen independently from therapsids (Olson, 1959; Simpson, 1959; Kermack, 1967; Mills, 1971), or they diverged from a common stock shortly after it arose from cynodonts in the Middle Triassic (Hopson and Crompton 1969; Crompton and Jenkins 1973, 1979). The traits common to prototherians and therians, therefore, must have either existed in common therapsid ancestors, evolved convergently, or evolved very quickly in concert during the short period before prototherian divergence (Carter, 1957; Hopson, 1969; Jenkins, 1970; Hulbert, 1981). If the number of features shared by prototherians and therians is large, the probability of convergence is small. Are the thermoregulatory mechanisms of extant monotremes similar to those of therians, or do they differ in numerous aspects?

THERMOREGULATORY ASPECTS

The body temperature of echidnas and the platypus is maintained at 30°–32° C in their thermal neutral zones (Schmidt-Nielsen, Dawson, and Crawford, 1966; Dawson, 1973; Dawson and Grant, 1980). Although these temperatures are considerably below those of most advanced placentals (38+° C) and marsupials (~ 35° C), they

are similar to those reported for several insectivores and edentates (Dawson, 1973; Eisenberg, 1980). Echidnas and the platypus are good thermoregulators during acute cold exposure, maintaining temperature and increasing heat production to match heat loss down to, or below, freezing. However, during long-term exposure to cold, echidnas experience nocturnal decrements of as much as 10° C in body temperature (Augee, 1978). They become torpid when deprived of food. Monotremes are not tolerant of heat stress and become hyperthermic when ambient temperatures rise above 30° C. Standard metabolic rates are low in comparison to those of placentals and marsupials; however, a lower metabolic rate is to be expected as a result of their lower body temperatures. If metabolic rates of all mammals are adjusted to a common temperature, the metabolic levels of echidnas are 46–90 percent of those of advanced eutherians (Schmidt-Nielsen, Dawson, and Crawford, 1966; Augee, 1976; Dawson and Grant, 1980) and those of the platypus are 114 percent (Dawson and Grant, 1980). In comparison, mean values of metabolic levels (after similar thermal correction) of marsupials, edentates, and insectivores are, respectively, 90 percent, 80 percent, and 109 percent (Hulbert, 1980). In contrast, corrected metabolic values of reptiles are only 10–20 percent (Bennett and Dawson, 1976). Since there is considerably variability in metabolic level among different mammalian groups, there is little to differentiate the thermoregulatory ability or metabolic level of monotremes from that of "primitive" mammals in the marsupial-eutherian lineage (Griffiths, 1978). The comparatively low metabolic rates of monotremes seem to be largely a function of body temperature regulated at a low level. A large increment above reptilian metabolic levels has occurred in all mammalian groups, suggesting that this metabolic adjustment was already present in their common ancestors.

OXYGEN CONSUMPTION AND TRANSPORT

The levels of oxygen consumption required to support thermoregulation and activity in mammals are beyond the capacities of reptilian systems (Bennett and Ruben, 1979). The evolution of endothermy required an increase in capacities for oxygen delivery and utilization. The increments attained in monotremes are of the same order as in eutherians (summarized in Jenkins, 1970, and Griffiths, 1978). Monotremes possess typical mammalian lungs with intrapulmonary bronchi and alveolar sacs. These lungs are ventilated with a muscular diaphragm. The respiratory physiology of echidnas seems to conform to that of typical eutherians (Bently, Herreid, and Schmidt-Nielsen, 1967; Parer and Hodson, 1974). The hematological characteristics of monotremes are typically mammalian. Erythrocytes are non-nucleated, and hematocrits and blood oxygen capacities are equal to, or greater than, those of most eutherians (Johansen, Lenfant, and Griggs, 1966; Parer and Metcalfe, 1967a, b) and are substantially greater than those of reptiles (Pough, 1980b). The monotreme heart is four-chambered, although it retains a distinct sinus venosus (Rowlatt, 1968). Stroke volume and tissue oxygen extraction are similar in echidnas and eutherians (Parer and Metcalfe, 1967c). Heart rate is low in echidnas, in keeping with lower body temperature. Thus, in nearly all features of their oxygen delivery systems, monotremes are essentially similar to eutherians.

OTHER FEATURES

In contrast to their similarities in thermoregulatory and aerobic ability, monotremes differ from therians in other features of physiology and anatomy, which supports the idea of a long interval of independent evolution. These features include the neuroanatomical organization of the central nervous system, details of the immune and endocrine systems (e.g., the structure and function of the adrenal cortex), structure of the eye, and myological organization, among others (Jenkins, 1970). A particular feature of differentiation is the oviparous reproductive mode, accompanied by numerous differences in anatomy and physiology. It is noteworthy that these characters, which mark the uniqueness of monotremes, are largely dissociated from thermoregulatory ability and rate of energy utilization, whereas the characters that are shared by extant monotremes and therians involve oxygen transport and metabolic performance.

If the latest common ancestory of monotremes and therians were ectothermic, it would be necessary to postulate independent evolution of a very great number of similar characters in the monotreme and therian lines. These include hair, sweat glands, a four-chambered heart, non-nucleated blood cells, high hematocrit and oxygen-carrying capacity of the blood, alveolar lungs, a diaphragm, and a greatly enhanced metabolic level. Moreover, these features would have had to evolve independently in a very short time, when little change was taking place except in jaw and brain morphology. Such an interpretation is less parsimonious than the view that

physiological and morphological systems associated with endothermy were inherited from advanced therapsids, at least at the level of cynodonts. The gross pattern of mammalian origin indicates that the common features present in the ancestral group were primarily thermoregulatory and energetic, and that modifications of the reproductive, endocrine, nervous, and skeletomuscular systems (Jenkins, 1970) arose after divergence of prototherians and therians.

Conclusions

Our conclusions regarding the various lines of evidence adduced for therapsid endothermy are summarized in Table 1. Two lines of reasoning strongly support the attainment of endothermy in this group: the very large number of traits shared by monotremes and therians that relate to metabolic rate and oxygen transport; and the presence of nasal turbinals in advanced therapsids. We also believe that bone histology is somewhat suggestive of the existence of endothermy. There is clearly a major change that occurred early in therapsid evolution that made the structure of cortical bone more mammal-like. Other lines of evidence are either inconclusive or untenable.

It seems probable that at least the advanced theriodonts had high rates of metabolism and were endothermic. It is not clear, however, whether or not these therapsids were also homeothermic. Monotremes are not homeothermic, at least in continuing cold (Augee, 1978), and the temperatures of many "primitive" therians ap-

Table 1.—Summary of features proposed to indicate high metabolic rates and endothermy in therapsids

Feature	Status as indicator
Histological structure of bone	Suggestive
Posture and limb attitude	Inconclusive
Hair	Untenable
Brain size	Untenable
Other anatomical features	
Reduction of lumbar ribs	Untenable
Secondary palate	Untenable
Nasal turbinals	Very suggestive
Epiphyseal complex	Inconclusive
Predator-prey ratios	Inconclusive
Biogeographical distribution	Untenable
Comparative physiology of monotremes and therians	Very suggestive

pear to be rather labile, particularly during activity (Dawson, 1973; Crompton, Taylor, and Jagger, 1978; Dawson and Grant, 1980; Eisenberg, 1980). If therapsid thermoregulation were endothermic, body temperatures may have been low as in living monotremes. However, therapsid body temperatures could also have been as high as those of therians, or higher if the general environment were warmer than it is today, for regulation below ambient temperatures would probably be prohibitively expensive in water loss.

What more general adaptations would have favored the origin of endothermy among therapsids? Skeletal alterations suggestive of increased agility and a more active existence have long been noted as trends typical of advanced therapsids (Colbert, 1958; Olson, 1959, 1971; Van Valen, 1960; Parrington, 1967; Hopson, 1969; Geist, 1972). Limbs were lengthened and rotated under the body, girdles were lightened and reoriented, and the spinal column became more regionally differentiated. These changes occurred in parallel in many independent phylogenetic lines (Olson, 1959). To the differentiation of skeletal features suggesting enhanced levels of activity, Olson (1959, 1971) related incipient endothermy or progressively more mammal-like thermoregulation.

Both enhanced activity and endothermy are linked to the expansion of aerobic ability (Bennett and Ruben, 1979). Modern reptiles have only very modest capacities for aerobically sustainable activity, and must utilize anaerobic metabolism for even limited levels of exertion beyond slow walking. Such anaerobically supported behavior cannot be sustained, and exhaustion ensues fairly rapidly. Expanded aerobic capacities, involving the enhancement of both resting and maximal rates of oxygen consumption, greatly enlarge the capacities of endotherms for routine activity, and give them a great range of endurance at near-maximum effort.

We believe that it was pressure for increased capacity for activity that selected for higher metabolic rates in this lineage. Increased activity may well have been more important than thermoregulatory considerations, if very warm and equable climates prevailed during the Early Triassic.

Acknowledgments

We thank R. C. Berkelhamer, T. J. Bradley, R. Huey, E. C. Olson, and D. Wake for providing helpful comments on the manuscript. Financial support for the authors was provided by NSF grants PCM 77-24208 and 81-02331, and NIH Grant K04 AM00351 to A.F.B., and NSF Grant DEB 78-10837 and PCM 8022980 to J.A.R.

References

Augee, M. L.
1976. Heat tolerance of monotremes. *J. Thermal Biol.* 1:181–84.
1978. Monotremes and the evolution of homeothermy. *Austral. Zool.* 20:111–19.

Bakker, R. T.
1971. Dinosaur phylogeny and the origin of mammals. *Evolution* 25:636–58.
1972. Anatomical and ecological evidence of endothermy in dinosaurs. *Nature* 238:81–85.
1975. Dinosaur renaissance. *Sci. Am.* 232:58–78.
1980. Dinosaur heresy-dinosaur renaissance. In *A Cold Look at the Warm-Blooded Dinosaurs*, ed. R. D. K. Thomas and E. C. Olson, pp. 351–462. Am. Assoc. Adv. Sci. Select Symp. Ser. Boulder, Colo.: Westview Press.

Baur, N. E., and Friedl, R. R.
1980. Application of size-metabolism allometry to therapsids and dinosaurs. In *A Cold Look at the Warm-Blooded Dinosaurs*, ed. R. D. K. Thomas and E. C. Olson, pp. 253–86. Am. Assoc. Adv. Sci. Select Symp. Ser. Boulder, Colo.: Westview Press.

Béland, P., and Russell, D. A.
1980. Dinosaur metabolism and predator/prey ratios in the fossil record. In *A Cold Look at the Warm-Blooded Dinosaurs*, ed. R. D. K. Thomas and E. C. Olson, pp. 85–102. Am. Assoc. Adv. Sci. Select Symp. Ser. Boulder, Colo.: Westview Press.

Bennett, A. F.
1973. Ventilation in two species of lizards during rest and activity. *Comp. Biochem Physiol.* 46A:653–71.

Bennett, A. F., and Dalzell, B.
1973. Dinosaur physiology: a critique. *Evolution* 27:170–74.

Bennett, A. F., and Dawson, W. R.
1976. Metabolism. In *Biology of the Reptilia, Vol. 5 (Physiology A)*, ed. C. Gans and W. R. Dawson, pp. 127–223. New York: Academic Press.

Bennett, A. F., and Ruben, J. A.
1979. Endothermy and activity in vertebrates. *Science* 206:649–54.

Bentley, P. J.; Herreid, C. F., II; and Schmidt-Nielsen, K.
1967. Respiration of a monotreme, the echidna,

Tachyglossus aculeatus. Am. J. Physiol. 212:957–61.

Benton, M. J.
1979. Ectothermy and the success of dinosaurs. *Evolution* 33:983–97.

Bouvier, M.
1977. Dinosaur Haversian bone and endothermy. *Evolution* 31:449–50.

Brink, A. S.
1955. A study on the skeleton of *Diademodon. Paleont. Afr.* 3:3–39.
1956. Speculations on some advanced mammalian characteristics in the higher mammal-like reptiles. *Paleont. Afr.* 4:77–95.

Broili, F.
1941. Haare bei Reptilien. *Anat. Anz.* 92:62–68.

Carter, G. S.
1957. The monotremes and the evolution of mammalian organization. *Proc. Zool. Soc. Calcutta (Mookerjie Mem. Vol.),* pp. 195–206.

Charig, A. J.
1976. Dinosaur monophyly and a new class of vertebrates: a critical review. In *Morphology and Biology of Reptiles,* ed. A. d'A. Bellairs and C. B. Cox, pp. 65–104. London: Academic Press.

Chudinov, P. K.
1970. The skin covering of therapsids. [In Russian]. In *Data on the Evolution of Terrestrial Vertebrates,* ed. K. K. Flerov, pp. 45–50. Moscow: Nauka.

Colbert, E. H.
1958. The beginning of the Age of Dinosaurs. In *Studies on Fossil Vertebrates,* ed. T. Stanley Westoll, pp. 39–58. London: The Athlone Press.

Crompton, A. W., and Jenkins, F. A., Jr.
1973. Mammals from reptiles: a review of mammalian origins. *Ann. Rev. Earth Planet. Sci.* 1:131–55.
1979. Origin of mammals. In *Mesozoic Mammals,* ed. J. A. Lilligraven, Z. Keilan-Jaworowska, and W. A. Clemens, pp. 59–73. Berkeley: University of California Press.

Crompton, A. W.; Taylor, C. R.; and Jagger, J. A.
1978. Evolution of homeothermy in mammals. *Nature* 272:333–36.

Dawson, T. J.
1973. "Primitive" mammals. In *Comparative Physiology of Thermoregulation, Vol. 3. Special Aspects of Thermoregulation,* ed. G. Causey Whittow, pp. 1–46. New York: Academic Press.

Dawson, T. J., and Grant, T. R.
1980. Metabolic capabilities of monotremes and the evolution of homeothery. In *Comparative Physiology: Primitive Mammals,* ed. K. Schmidt-Nielsen, L. Bolis, and C. R. Taylor, pp. 140–47. Cambridge: Cambridge University Press.

Eisenberg, J. F.
1980. Biological strategies of living conservative mammals. In *Comparative Physiology: Primitive Mammals,* ed. K. Schmidt-Nielsen, L. Bolis, and C. R. Taylor, pp. 13–30. Cambridge: Cambridge University Press.

Enlow, D. H.
1969. The bone of reptiles. In *Biology of the Reptilia, Vol. 1 (Morphology A),* ed. C. Gans, A. d'A. Bellairs, and T. S. Parsons, pp. 45–80. New York: Academic Press.

Enlow, D. H., and Brown, S. O.
1956. A comparative histological study of fossil and recent bone tissues, Part I. *Texas J. Sci.* 8:405–43.
1957. A comparative histological study of fossil and recent bone tissues, Part II. *Texas J. Sci.* 9:186–214.
1958. A comparative histological study of fossil and recent bone tissues, Part III. *Texas J. Sci.* 10:187–230.

Estes, R.
1961. Cranial anatomy of the cynodont reptile *Thrinaxodon liorhinus. Bull. Mus. Comp. Zool. Harvard* 125:163–80.
1964. Fossil vertebrates from the Late Cretaceous Lanee Formation, Eastern Wyoming. *Univ. Calif. Pub. Geol. Sci.* 49:1–180.

Farlow, J. O.
1980. Predator/prey biomass ratios, community food webs, and dinosaur physiology. In *A Cold Look at the Warm-Blooded Dinosaurs,* ed. R. D. K. Thomas and E. C. Olson, pp. 55–83. Am. Assoc. Adv. Sci. Select Symp. Ser. Boulder, Colo.: Westview Press.

Feduccia, A.
1973. Dinosaurs as reptiles. *Evolution* 27:166–69.

Foote, J. S.
1916. A contribution to the comparative histology of the femur. *Smithsonian Contributions to Knowledge* 35:1–242.

Geist, V.
1972. An ecological and behavioral explanation of mammalian characteristics, and their implication to therapsid evolution. *Z. Säugetier.* 37:1–15.

Golley, F. B.
1968. Secondary productivity in terrestrial communities. *Am. Zool.* 8:53–59.

Goodrich, E. S.
1930. *Studies on the Structure and Development of*

Vertebrates. London: Constable and Company Ltd.

Griffiths, M.
1978.   *The Biology of the Monotremes.* New York: Academic Press.

Gross, W.
1934.   Die Typen des mikroskopischen Knobenbaues bei fossilen Stegocephalen und Reptilien. *Z. Anat.* 103:731–64.

Heath, J. E.
1968.   The origins of the thermoregulation. In *Evolution and the Environment,* ed. E. T. Drake, pp. 259–78. New Haven, Conn.: Yale University Press.

Heinrich, B.
1977.   Why have some animals evolved to regulate a high body temperature? *Am. Nat.* 111:623–40.

Hopson, J. A.
1969.   The origin and adaptive radiation of mammal-like reptiles and non-therian mammals. *Ann. N. Y. Acad. Sci.* 167:199–216.
1973.   Endothermy, small size, and the origin of mammalian reproduction. *Am. Nat.* 107:446–52.
1980.   Relative brain size in dinosaurs. In *A Cold Look at the Warm-Blooded Dinosaurs,* ed. R. D. K. Thomas and E. C. Olson, pp. 287–310. Am. Assoc. Adv. Sci. Select. Symp. Ser. Boulder, Colo.: Westview Press.

Hopson, J. A., and Crompton, A. W.
1969.   Origin of mammals. In *Evolutionary Biology,* vol. 3, ed. T. Dobzbansky, M. K. Hecht, and W. C. Steere, pp. 15–72. New York: Appleton-Century-Crofts.

Hotton, N., III.
1980.   An alternative to dinosaur endothermy. In *A Cold Look at the Warm-Blooded Dinosaurs,* ed. R. D. K. Thomas and E. C. Olson, pp. 311–50. Am. Assoc. Adv. Sci. Select. Symp. Ser. Boulder, Colo.: Westview Press.

Hulbert, A. J.
1980.   The evolution of energy metabolism in mammals. In *Comparative Physiology: Primitive Mammals,* ed. K. Schmidt-Nielsen, L. Bolis, and C. R. Taylor, pp. 129–39. Cambridge: Cambridge University Press.
1981.   Evolution from ectothermia towards endothermia. In *Contributions to Thermal Physiology,* ed. Z. Szelnyi and M. Szekeley, pp. 237–47. Oxford: Pergamon Press.

Jenkins, F. A., Jr.
1970.   Cynodont postcranial anatomy and the "prototherian" level of mammalian organization. *Evolution* 24:230–32.
1971.   The postcranial skeleton of African cynodonts. *Peabody Mus. Nat. Hist.* 36:1–216.

Jerison, H. J.
1973.   *Evolution of the Brain and Intelligence.* New York: Academic Press.

Johansen, K.; Lenfant, C.; and Grigg, G. C.
1966.   Respiratory properties of blood and responses to diving of the platypus, *Ornithorhynchus anatinus* (Shaw). *Comp. Biochem. Physiol.* 18:597–608.

Kermack, K. A.
1967.   The interrelations of early mammals. *J. Linn. Soc. (Zool.)* 47:241–49.

McNab, B. K.
1978.   The evolution of endothermy in the phylogeny of mammals. *Am. Nat.* 112:1–21.

Mills, J. R. E.
1971.   The dentition of *Morganucodon. J. Linn. Soc. (Zool.)* 50 (Suppl. 1):29–63.

Olson, E. C.
1959.   The evolution of mammalian characters. *Evolution* 13:304–53.
1971.   *Vertebrate Paleozoology.* New York: Wiley-Interscience.

Parer, J. T., and Hodson, W. A.
1974.   Respiratory studies of monotremes. IV. Normal respiratory functions of echidnas and ventilatory response to inspired oxygen and carbon dioxide. *Respir. Physiol.* 21:307–16.

Parer, J. T., and Metcalfe, J.
1967a. Respiratory studies of monotremes. I. Blood of the platypus *(Ornithorhynchus anatinus). Respir. Physiol.* 3:136–42.
1967b. Respiratory studies of monotremes. II. Blood of the echidna *(Tachyglossus setosus). Respir. Physiol.* 3:143–50.
1967c. Respiratory studies of monotremes. III. Blood gas transport and hemodynamics in the unanesthetized echidna. *Respir. Physiol.* 3:151–59.

Parrington, F. R.
1967.   The origins of mammals. *Adv. Sci.* 24:1–9.

Parsons, T. S.
1970.   The nose and Jacobson's organ. In *Biology of the Reptilia, Vol. 2B (Morphology),* ed. C. Gans and T. S. Parsons, pp. 99–191. New York: Academic Press.

Peabody, F. E.
1961.   Annual growth zones in living and fossil vertebrates. *J. Morphol.* 108:11–62.

Pough, F. H.
1980a. The advantages of ectothermy for tetrapods. *Am. Nat.* 115:92–112.
1980b. Blood oxygen transport and delivery in reptiles. *Am. Zool.* 20:173–85.

Quiroga, J.
1979.   The brain of two mammal-like reptiles (Cyno-

dontia-Therapsida). *J. Hirnforschung* 20:341–50.

1980. Sobre un molde endocraniano del cinodonte *Probainognathus jenseni* Romer 1975 (Reptilia:Therapsida) de la formation Ischichuca (Triasico Medio), La Rioja, Argentina. *Ameghiniana* 17:181–90.

Reed, C. A.
1960. Polyphyletic or monophyletic ancestry of mammals, or: what is a class? *Evolution* 14:314–22.

Reid, R. E. H.
1981. Lamellar-zonal bone with zones and annuli in the pelvis of a sauropod dinosaur. *Nature* 292:49–51.

Ricqles, A. de.
1969a. L'Histologie osseuse envisagée comme indicateur de la physiologie thermique chez les tétrapodes fossiles. *C. r. hebd. Séanc. Acad. Sci. Paris (Ser. D)* 268:782–85.
1969b. Recherches paléohistologiques sur les os longs des tétrapodes. II. Quelques observations sur la structure des os longs des thériodontes. *Annls. Paléont. (Vétebrés)* 55:1–52.
1972a. Vers une histoire de la physiologie thermique. Les données histologiques et leur interprétation fonctionnelle. *C. r. hebd. Séanc. Acad. Sci. Paris (Ser. D)* 275:1745–49.
1972b. Vers une histoire de la physiologie thermique. L'apparition de l'endothermie et le concept de reptile. *C. r. hebd. Séanc. Acad. Sci. Paris (Ser. D.)* 75:1875–78.
1972c. Recherches paléohistologiques sur les os longs des tétrapodes. III. Titanosuchiens, dineocéphales, dicynodontes. *Annls. Paléont. (Vertébrés)* 58:17–60.
1974. Recherches paléohistologiques sur les os longs des tétrapodes. IV. Eothériodontes et pélycosaures. *Annls. Paléont. (Vertébrés)* 60:1–39.
1976a. On bone histology of fossil and living reptiles, with comments on its functional and evolutionary significance. In *Morphology and Biology of Reptiles,* ed. A. d'A. Bellairs and C. B. Cox, pp. 123–50. London: Academic Press.
1976b. Recherches paléohistologiques sur les os longs des tétrapodes. VII. Sur la classification, la signification fonctionnelle et l'histoire des tissus osseux des tétrapodes. *Annls. Paléont. (Vertébrés)* 62:71–126.
1977. Recherches paléohistologiques sur les os longs des tétrapodes. VII. Sur la classification, la signification fonctionelle et l'histoire des tissus osseux des tétrapodes. *Annls. Paléont. (Vertébrés)* 63:33–56.
1978a. Recherches paléohistologiques sur les os longs des tétrapodes. VII. Sur la classification, la signification fonctionelle et l'histoire des tissus osseux des tétrapodes. *Annls. Paléont. (Vertébrés)* 64:85–111.

1978b. Recherches paléohistologiques sur les os longs des tétrapodes. VII. Sur la classification, la signification fonctionelle et l'histoire des tissus osseux des tétrapodes. *Annls. Paléont. (Vertébrés)* 64:153–84.
1980. Tissue structures of dinosaur bone: functional significance and possible relation to dinosaur physiology. In *A Cold Look at the Warm-Blooded Dinosaurs,* ed. R. D. K. Thomas and E. C. Olson, pp. 103–39. Am. Assoc. Adv. Sci. Select. Symp. Ser. Boulder, Colo: Westview Press.

Roth, J. J., and Roth, E. C.
1980. The parietal-pineal complex among paleovertebrates: evidence for temperature regulation. In *A Cold Look at the Warm-Blooded Dinosaurs,* ed. R. D. K. Thomas and E. C. Olson, pp. 189–231. Am. Assoc. Adv. Sci. Select. Symp. Ser. Boulder, Colo.: Westview Press.

Rowlatt, U.
1968. Functional morphology of the heart in mammals. *Am. Zool.* 8:221–29.

Ruben, J. A., and Bennett, A. F.
1981. Intense exercise and blood calcium levels in vertebrates. *Nature* 291:411–13.

Schmidt-Nielsen, K.; Dawson, T. J.; and Crawford, E. G., Jr.
1966. Temperature regulation in the echidna (*Tachyglossus aculeatus*). *J. Cell. Physiol.* 67:63–72.

Schmidt-Nielsen, K.; Hainsworth, F. R.; and Murrish, D. E.
1970. Countercurrent heat exchange in the respiratory passages: effect on water and heat balance. *Respir. Physiol.* 9:263–76.

Simpson, G. G.
1959. Mesozoic mammals and the polyphyletic origin of mammals. *Evolution* 13:405–14.

Thomas, R. D. K., and Olson, E. C., eds.
1980. *A Cold Look at the Warm-Blooded Dinosaurs.* Am. Assoc. Adv. Sci. Select. Symp. Ser. Boulder, Colo.: Westview Press.

Tracy, C. R.
1976. Tyrannosaurs: evidence for endothermy? *Am. Nat.* 110:1105–6.

Van Valen, L.
1960. Therapsids as mammals. *Evolution* 14:304–13.

Watson, D. M. S.
1931. On the skeleton of a bauriamorph reptile. *Proc. Zool. Soc. London* 1931:1163–205.

Wood, S. C., and Lenfant, C. J. M.
1976. Respiration: mechanics, control, and gas exchange. In *Biology of the Reptilia, Vol. 5 (Physiology A),* ed. C. Gans and W. R. Dawson, pp. 225–74. New York: Academic Press.

DAVID DUVALL
Department of Zoology and Physiology
University of Wyoming
Laramie, Wyoming 82071

A New Question of Pheromones: Aspects of Possible Chemical Signaling and Reception in the Mammal-like Reptiles

Introduction

The question of social behavior and communication in mammal-like reptiles is an exciting one, for these animals were among the earliest completely terrestrial vertebrates, and included the earliest ancestors of mammals (Crompton and Jenkins, 1979). Although the last of the mammal-like reptiles became extinct well over 150 million years ago (Kemp, 1982; Romer, 1966), it is possible to develop provocative inferences concerning their ethological interactions, following models developed for other extinct animals (e.g., Bakker, 1980; Colbert, 1958; Galton, 1970; Greene and Burghardt, 1978; Hopson, 1975, 1977; MacLean, 1978; Molnar, 1977; Simpson, 1958). The criteria for such models are commonalities of morphology, physiology, and behavior of a broad range of living tetrapods. By the identification of key morphological traits in fossil animals, associated physiological and behavioral characters are inferred.

Inferences about the ethology of extinct animals must be based on questions that are definitive and specific. The following questions about social communication and behavior, as mediated by conspecific chemical signals, or pheromones (Karlson and Lüscher, 1959), apply to living tetrapods:

1. What is the nature of substances that function as pheromones?

2. What are the behavioral correlates of pheromone production and detection?

3. Is there a structural complex that functions specifically in the detection of pheromones?

4. What is the anatomy, embryology, and distribution of that structure?

Synapsids are then referred to this living background by the answers to two further questions:

1. With reference to question 3, above, what is the evidence for such a structural complex in pelycosaurs and therapsids?

2. What specific potential can be inferred regarding the production of sociochemical signals in synapsids?

With constraints on inference thus established, more speculative questions can be entertained, concerning the spectrum of interactions that characterized chemical communication among the mammal-like reptiles.

Sociochemical Production and Release

Almost any exudate can serve as a signal

It is an axiom among investigators of chemical communication that almost any exudate can serve a signal function. Such function is identified by a change in behavior or physiological state of the recipient as the exudate is detected (e.g., see Duvall, 1979, 1981; Shorey, 1976; Weldon, 1983). Exudates can be products of metabolism, such as endocrine function, nitrogenous waste excretion, or bulk waste excretion, and they can be chemicals derived from wounds or osmoregulation. Feces and urine long have been known to function as pheromones and allelochemicals (the latter interspecific chemical signals; see Duvall, Chiszar, Trupiano, and Radcliffe, 1978; Duvall, Schmitt, Erpino, and Rabedeau, 1978; Duvall, Herskowitz, and Trupiano-Duvall, 1980; Duvall, Scudder, and Chiszar, 1980; Weldon, 1980; Wilson, 1970) among mammals (Grau, 1976; Hediger, 1949; MacKay-Sim and Laing, 1981), certain lizards (Duvall, 1979, 1981), and rattlesnakes (Chiszar, Wellborn, Wand, Scudder, and Smith, 1980; King, McCarron, Duvall, Baxter, and Gern, 1983). The maternal pheromone present in the cecotroph that covers a mother rat's fecal boli, and which facilitates aggregation and nest location in newborn rat pups (Leon, 1974), may be a transformation product of cholic acid (Moltz and Lee, 1981). Saliva is also known to function as a pheromone, with an important role in mammalian behavior (e.g., see Blass and Teicher, 1980; Blass, Hall, and Teicher, 1979, Block, Volpe, and Hayes, 1981; Duvall, Scudder, Southwick, and Schultz, 1982; Schultz, 1979). Saliva may function as a pheromone in spacing (Simon et al.,

1981) and in more physically proximate interactions, such as mating and fighting, of some iguanid lizards (Duvall, 1982).

The efficiency of basic chemical exudates predisposes them to evolve signal function. Such materials are inexpensive, in the sense that they are continually available for use as chemical signals. If routinely produced metabolic and regulatory byproducts are exuded, and are deposited consistently in the environment, the necessary chemical preadaptation for the derivation of signal function exists. Because many chemical signaling systems are so inexpensive energetically, and common in virtually every kingdom of life (see Sondheimer and Simeone, 1970), it has been argued that chemical signaling may be the most primitive form of social communication (e.g., Shorey, 1976; Weldon, 1983).

In the case of vertebrates, especially tetrapods, the phylogenetic importance of olfaction is widely accepted (e.g., Jerrison, 1971, 1973; Romer and Parsons, 1977). Presumably the first tetrapod to walk on land already had the sensory and brain structures necessary to respond to energetically inexpensive pheromones or allelochemicals. The evolution by many animals of complex and specialized exocrine sources of pheromones (e.g., see Eisenberg and Kleiman, 1972; Garstka and Crews, 1981; Grau, 1976; Mykytowycz, 1970; Quay, 1977; Thiessen, 1977; Thiessen and Yahr, 1977) confirms the importance of the chemical channel in animal communication.

Pheromonal signaling is especially useful in a terrestrial environment because conditions often favor signal persistence long after the signaler is no longer physically present. This feature appears to contribute to spacing and territory maintenance among several terrestrial tetrapods (e.g., see Auffenberg, 1978; Bekoff, 1979a,b; Berry, 1974; Duvall, 1979, 1981; Kleiman, 1966; Madison, 1977; Simon, in press; Wells and Bekoff, 1981). Some fecal pheromone(s) of western fence lizards probably persist for up to two to three weeks even at relatively high ambient temperatures (Duvall, 1979, 1981; Auffenberg, 1978). One effect of these cues on recipient western fence lizards, is a significant increase in the frequency of assertion push-up displays (Duvall, 1979, 1981), which are known to affect spacing (see Stamps, 1977, for a discussion).

Active and passive marking

Many tetrapods "passively mark" or deposit secretions, such as those described above, as they move through their habitat (e.g., Duvall, 1980,

1981; Eisenberg and Kleiman, 1972; Mykytow-ycz, 1970; Shorey, 1976). For example, as a breeding western fence lizard runs across a large rock to capture an insect, pheromonal exudates from the cloaca are rubbed onto the stone simultaneously (Duvall, 1979; see also Bissinger and Simon, 1981). Passive marking is qualitatively different from "active marking," which is the "focused" deposition of a pheromonal cue on particular objects in the environment—including conspecifics, often while simultaneously exhibiting visually conspicuous postures or displays (e.g., see Bekoff, 1979a, b; Berry, 1974; Eisenberg and Kleiman, 1972; Grau, 1976; Kleiman, 1966; Simon et al., 1981). Active marking (Mykytowycz, 1970; Shorey, 1976; but see also Eisenberg and Kleiman, 1972) comes quite close to what some have referred to as *multimodal, composite signaling* (Bekoff, 1979a,b; Duvall, 1979, 1981; Wickler, 1978), in which both chemical and visual signals are emitted, roughly simultaneously. Finally, many tetrapods also have evolved specialized exocrine gland sources of pheromones that are used in active marking or composite visual and chemical signaling (e.g., Grau, 1976; Graves and Duvall, 1983 Mykytowycz, 1970; Quay, 1977; Thiessen, 1977; Thiessen and Yahr, 1977).

Aggregation

One of the simplest classes of group behavior known to be mediated by pheromones, at several levels of animal organization, is aggregation. For example, several species of lizards in the North American genus *Eumeces* aggregate in or near hibernacula as winter approaches (see Duvall, Herskowitz, and Trupiano-Duvall, 1980; Fitch, 1954). It has long been suspected that these lizards use pheromones to locate conspecifics and hibernacula (Fitch, 1954; see also Breckenridge, 1943; Scott and Sheldahl, 1937). In experimental olfactometer tests on the five-linked skink, *Eumeces fasciatus,* we confirmed this hypothesis in nonbreeding males and females tested in the late summer/early fall, the time at which the search for hibernacula presumably begins in nature (Duvall, Herskowitz, and Trupiano-Duvall, 1980a). Pheromonal mediation of aggregation also is common in other reptiles (Burghardt, 1970; Heller and Halpern, 1982; Madison, 1977; Scudder et al., 1980), amphibians (Madison, 1975, 1977), and mammals (see Shorey, 1976, for a discussion).

Several extant amphibians, reptiles, and mammals exude sex attractants, a more specific ag-gregation factor. Typically, at a time of sexual receptivity, females produce chemical cues that facilitate their location by males (e.g., see Crews, 1976; Dunbar, 1977; Estes, 1972; Garstka and Crews, 1981; Garstka, Camazine, and Crews, 1982; Kubie, Cohen, and Halpern, 1978; Madison, 1977; Shorey, 1976). Recently Duvall, Guillette, and Jones (1982) predicted that some reptiles will be found to employ reproductive "priming" pheromones (Bronson and Coquelin, 1980; Vandenbergh, 1975, 1980), commonly observed among mammals, in which chemical signals affect complex physiological processes directly and behavior secondarily. Releasing pheromones (Wilson and Bossert, 1963), or sociochemicals that affect behavior directly, seems to be involved in close social encounters, such as fighting and mating in mammals and various reptiles (Auffenberg, 1978; Burghardt, 1970; Duvall, 1979, 1981; Garstka and Crews, 1981; Madison, 1977; Ross and Crews, 1977; Simon, in press). In some sceloporine lizards, exudates that may be Harderian gland secretions or saliva (Duvall, 1982) may be involved in fighting and coitus.

Avoidance, the converse of aggregation, also occurs commonly as a function of chemical signaling. For example, both nonbreeding ground skinks, *Scincella lateralis* (Duvall, Herskowitz, and Trupiano-Duvall, 1980), and prairie rattlesnakes, *Crotalus viridis viridis* (the latter tested in midsummer; King, McLarron, Duvall, Baxter, and Gern, 1983), employed pheromones to avoid physical proximity of conspecifics (see also Porter and Czaplicki, 1974). Territoriality, or spacing maintenance, is a more complex manifestation of avoidance frequently affected by pheromones in mammals (e.g., Bekoff, 1979a, b; Eisenberg and Kleiman, 1972; Epple, 1976; Grau, 1976; Jolly, 1972; Kleinman, 1966; Mykytowycz, 1974; Wells and Bekoff, 1981). Among reptiles, several species of *Sceloporus* lizards use cloacal exudates in spacing (e.g., see Duvall 1979, 1981; Bissinger and Simon, 1981; Simon et al., 1981; see also Berry, 1974; Simon, in press). Such pheromones also may affect the frequency of occurrence of visual displays known to mediate spacing in these lizards (Duvall, 1979, 1981). Duvall and Guillette (unpublished results; see Table 1) also have found that naive, neonatal *Sceloporus jarrovi* respond to exudates collected from conspecific adults with tongue-vomeronasal organ investigation and visual signaling, suggesting that some degree of behavioral responsiveness to such "spacing pheromones" may be innate (see also

Table 1.—Responses of naive neonatal *Sceloporus jarrovi* to conspecific adult and control chemical Cues ($\bar{X} \pm SE$)[1]

Chemical-cue type	Tongue flicks[2]	Substrate licks[2]	Push-ups[2]
Conspecific adult	14.7 ± 4.0^a	2.3 ± 0.8^a	1.3 ± 0.4^a
Distilled water	1.5 ± 0.4^b	0.7 ± 0.4^a	0.2 ± 0.2^b
1:1 Cologne-water	2.0 ± 0.8^b	1.2 ± 0.2^a	0.0^b

[1]Neonatal lizards, isolated from conspecific adults from birth, were exposed to the conditions listed in column one, at 5 days of age and for 25 minutes, in a randomized, repeated measures design. Methods basically were similar to Duvall, 1981. (From Duvall and Guillette, unpublished.)

[2]Within a column of data, values with different superscripts are significantly different at $P < 0.05$, based upon t-tests.

Bissinger and Simon, 1981; Duvall, Guillette, Pierce, Swain, and Scudder, 1979).

Sociochemical Signal Reception: The Vomeronasal Organ in Tetrapods

Anatomy and occurrence of the vomeronasal organ

In tetrapods, it is the vomeronasal organ (of Jacobson) which has been implicated in the detection of pheromonal signals. This paired structure opens either into the mouth, the nasal cavity itself, or the paired nasopalatine canals (Allison, 1953; Bertmar, 1981; Estes, 1972; Negus, 1958; Parsons, 1959a, 1967, 1970, 1971; this paper, Figs. 1 and 2).

In testudines and urodele amphibians, well-developed, paired vomeronasal organs form distinctive regions of chemosensory mucosa in the ventral or ventrolateral portions of the main nasal cavities (Graziadei, 1971, 1977; Parsons, 1959a, 1967; Scott, 1979). Apodans, anurans, and the tuatara possess vomeronasal organs that occur as outpocketings or pouchlike folds emanating from the main nasal cavities (Negus, 1958; Parsons, 1959a). As in living amphibians and testudines, the vomeronasal organ probably opened into the nasal cavity during the amphibian-reptile transition hundreds of millions of years ago (Bertmar, 1981).

Among squamate reptiles, paired vomeronasal organs are blind and mushroom-shaped; they open into the mouth through the vomeronasal ducts, which pass through a cartilaginous portion of the primary palate (Bellairs and Boyd, 1950; Parsons, 1970; Pratt, 1948; Stebbins, 1948; see Fig. 2C, this paper).

The presence of vomeronasal organs is the rule among the majority of adult mammals; exceptions are certain higher primates, (Epple, 1976), some bats (Bhatnagar, 1980), cetaceans (Allison, 1953; Bertmar, 1981; Estes, 1972; Negus, 1958; Parsons, 1971; Tucker and Smith, 1976), and manatees. Most extant mammals possess a pair of tubular vomeronasal organs housed primarily in cartilaginous capsules that lie along either side of the nasal septum in the palatal region. These structures open at the anterior end only. The opening may connect exclusively with the nasal cavity, with a false "nasopalatine" canal that connects with the nasal cavity directly, or with a true nasopalatine canal between the mouth and nasal cavity. In their course from oral to nasal chambers, the nasopalatine canals pass through the incisive foramina in the premaxillary/maxillary region of the secondary palate (Fig. 3). In mammals with patent nasopalatine canals, the vomeronasal organs open directly into the nasal cavity at some locus apart from the openings of the nasopalatine canals. Nevertheless, materials picked up orally (e.g., by licking) are readily transmitted to the vomeronasal organs via the nasopalatine canals (Beauchamp et al., 1980; Meredith, 1980; Wysocki, Wellington, and Beauchamp, 1980). Incisive foramina and associated nasopalatine canals have apparently maintained the "mouth-smelling function" of the reptilian vomeronasal organ during the evolution of the mammalian secondary palate, as suggested by Estes (1972) and Negus (1958).

Embryology

Embryologically, the vomeronasal organ is represented as an anlage in all tetrapods thus far studied. In some, such as the mammalian orders cited above, and birds, the anlage atrophies before the animal becomes adult. The embryology of the testudine vomeronasal organ differs slightly from that of other extant amniotes (Parsons, 1967), but the adult organ conforms to other amniotes in most respects. This commonality throughout the amniotes supports the idea of phylogenetic continuity of the vomeronasal organ.

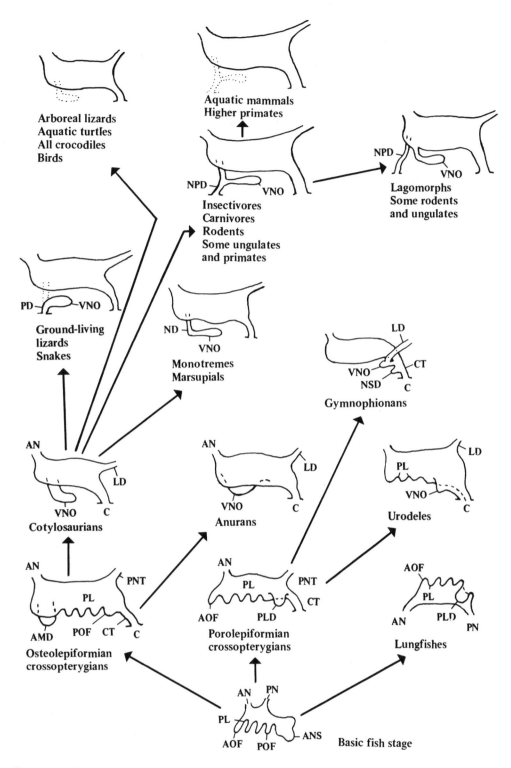

Figure 1. Schematic gross morphology and evolution of the vomeronasal organ (VNO), from Bertmar (1981). Other abbreviations: AMD, anteromedial diverticule; AN, anterior nostril; ANS, anterior nasal sac; AOF, anterior olfactory fold; C, choana; CT, choanal tubes; LD, lacrimal duct; ND, nasal duct; NPD, nasopalatine ducts; NSD, nonsensory diverticule; PD, palatine duct; PL, primary lamella; PLD, posterolateral diverticule; PN, posterior nostril; PNT posterior nasal tube; POF, posterior olfactory fold. Phylogenetic continuity of the vomeronasal organ in vertebrates is probable; for an alternative interpretation of the morphology of monotremes, marsupials, and testudines, see text and cited references. The iguanid lizard *Anolis carolinensis* is an exception to the rule for arboreal lizards (upper left), in having a well developed sensory vomeronasal organ mucosa which connects with the mouth through the vomeronasal duct (Roth, Roth, and Duvall, unpublished findings.)

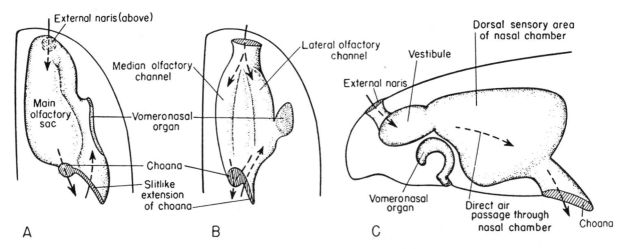

Figure 2. Gross morphology of the vomeronasal organ or pouch in: **A**, urodele; **B**, anuran; and **C**, squamate reptile. Generally, testudines are similar to A and B. (From A. S. Romer and T. S. Parsons, 1977.)

Histological and cytological conservatism

The sensory mucosa of the vomeronasal organ is never ciliated in tetrapods, whereas the bipolar sensory cells in the olfactory epithelium virtually always have cilia projecting into the mucous-covered lumen. This difference has been observed in amphibians (Allison, 1953; Tucker and Smith, 1976), reptiles (Allison, 1953; Altner and Müller, 1968; Bannister, 1968; Graziadei, 1971, 1977; Guillette and Duvall, unpublished observations; Scott, 1979; Tucker and Smith, 1976; Wang and Halpern, 1980), and mammals (Allison, 1953; Graziadei, 1977; Negus, 1958; Steinbrecht, 1969; Tucker and Smith, 1976), Similarly, Bowman's glands are never found in

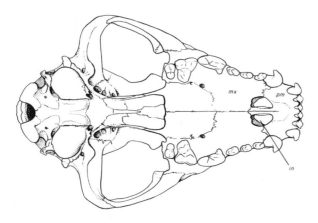

Figure 3. Incisive foramina (**in**) in the secondary palate of the skull of the African hunting dog, *Lycaon pictus*. Note position between maxilla (**mx**) and premaxilla (**pm**). In most extant mammals, **in** houses true nasopalatine ducts, which connect oral and nasal cavities, allowing oral access to the vomeronasal organs. See T. A.Vaughan, 1978, for other abbreviations. (From T. A. Vaughn, 1978.)

vomeronasal sensory epithelium, but are a distinctive feature of nasal sensory mucosa in all tetrapods (Allison, 1953; Parsons, 1967, 1971; Scott, 1979; Tucker and Smith, 1976; Wang and Halpern, 1980). The consistency, throughout the tetrapods, of the difference between vomeronasal sensory epithelium and nasal sensory mucosa with respect to both ciliation and Bowman's glands renders independent origin unlikely.

Olfactory and accessory olfactory projections

The pattern of sensory mucosal and central nervous projections of the main and accessory olfactory systems is also in agreement with the hypothesis of phylogenetic continuity. In virtually all tetrapods that possess these two chemosensory systems as adults, the projections from the vomeronasal organ synapse in the accessory olfactory bulb, and those from the nasal sensory mucosa, terminate in the main olfactory bulb (Allison, 1953; Cooper and Bhatnagar, 1976; Frahm and Bhatnagar, 1980; Halpern, 1976; Meredith, 1980; Parsons, 1959a, 1976; Scalia and Winans, 1976; Scott, 1979; Tucker and Smith, 1976; Wang and Halpern, 1980; see Fig. 4, this paper). The separation of the two systems is maintained in the secondary projections to the olfactory areas of the brain.

In squamate reptiles, the accessory olfactory bulbs establish ipsilateral connections with the nucleus sphericus (Halpern, 1976; Northcutt, 1978), while the main olfactory bulb projects to the olfactory tubercle and piriform cortex of both hemispheres (Northcutt, 1978; cf. Burghardt, 1980). The nucleus sphericus of squamates is

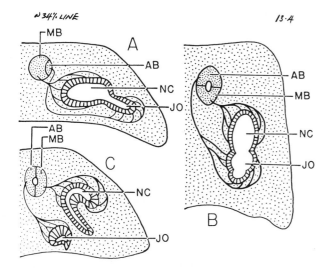

Figure 4. Innervation of the nasal cavity (NC) and vomeronasal or Jacobson's organ (JO) in: **A,** urodele; B, turtle; and C, snake. Vomeronasal organ sensory bipolar nerves project to the accessory olfactory bulb (AB) and nasal cavity sensory bipolar nerves project to the main olfactory bulb (MB). In mammals and reptiles, ascending brain projections from the two bulbs retain significant autonomy. (From T. S. Parsons, 1959.)

considered by some to be homologous to the mammalian amygdala (see Burghardt, 1980).

In mammals, the strict separation of the two systems is manifest by their amygdalar connections; the accessory olfactory bulb projects to the medial nucleus and to the posteromedial cortical nucleus, while the main olfactory bulb connects with the anterior and posterolateral cortical nuclei (Allison, 1953; Scalia and Winans, 1976; Winans and Powers, 1977; Winans and Scalia, 1970; see also Griffiths, 1978; Johnson, 1977). Through tertiary projections, however, the two systems may exert an overlapping influence on parts of the preoptic and hypothalamic regions involved in reproductive physiology and behavior. The resulting interplay of the two systems has important implications with respect to conspecific chemical signaling.

The vomeronasal organ and pheromone reception

Recent experimental work focuses on the different behavioral functions of the main olfactory and vomeronasal systems. Kubie, Vagvolgyi, and Halpern (1978) found that transection of the accessory olfactory nerves (from the vomeronasal organs) blocked precoital and coital activity in male garter snakes *(Thamnophis radix),* but that transection of the main olfactory nerves (from the nasal sensory mucosa) did not. These findings indicate that the vomeronasal system is critical in the male garter snake's response to

sex pheromones exuded by receptive females (Crews, 1976; Garstka and Crews, 1981; Kubie, Cohen, and Halpern, 1978). The vomeronsal organ of snakes also may be relatively more sensitive to less volatile chemical cues than the main olfactory system is (Burghardt, 1980; Halpern and Kubie, 1980; Kubie and Halpern, 1979; Wilde, 1938).

Powers and Winans (1973, 1975) found significant decrements in male hamster copulatory behavior and response to sex pheromones of receptive females after cutting the accessory olfactory nerves, but not to the same extent after section of the main olfactory nerves (see also Epple, 1976; Johns, 1980; Meredith, 1980; Meredith et al., 1980; Murphy, 1976; Mykytowycz, 1977; Poduschka, 1977; Poduschka and Firbas, 1968; Winans and Powers, 1977).

Cowles and Phelan (1958) hypothesized that in rattlesnakes, nasal olfaction serves more of a distance-sensing function than does vomeronasal olfaction, which is more discriminating. They also postulated that the distance-sensing, nasal olfactory system initiated further chemosensory investigation via the more discriminating vomeronasal organ complex. These novel and interest-

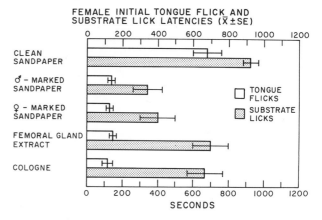

Figure 5. Female *Sceloporus occidentalis* initial tongue flick and substrate lick latencies. In successive discrimination procedures, in which lizards were exposed to conspecific and control chemical cues one at a time, any odor other than suspension vehicle (distilled water) resulted in significantly shorter latencies to initial lingual extrusions. The latter is indicative of chemosensory investigation via the tongue-vomeronasal organ system, since these lizards normally respire through the external nares with lips tightly shut when first placed in the test arena. Appropriately, Guillette and Duvall (unpublished) have found that the sensory nasal mucosa of sceloporine lizards is well developed. These data indicate that chemical stimulation of the sensory nasal mucosa elicits further investigation with the tongue-vomeronasal system. A plot of data for males is similar. (From Duvall, unpublished; but see Duvall, 1980, 1981, 1982, for further details and discussion.)

ing ideas were tested only indirectly by Cowles and Phelan (1958), but are currently being examined in a series of studies of the conspecific chemical signaling habits of the western fence lizard, *Sceloporus occidentalis* (Duvall, 1979, 1980, 1981, 1982). Nasal and vomeronasal olfactory responses to conspecific chemical cues and control odors were teased apart by successive discrimination procedures that avoided the use of invasive techniques that often disrupt normal behavior (see Chiszar, Duvall, Scudder, and Radcliffe, 1980; Duvall, 1981; Duvall, Scudder, and Chiszar, 1980).

Strong support for the Cowles and Phelan (1958) hypothesis was obtained. Any pungent chemical cue elicited tongue flicks or substrate licks of shorter latency than did a nonodorous suspension vehicle alone (Fig. 5). Further, once lingual-vomeronasal investigation was initiated, only "biologically appropriate" orders, such as pheromones, were investigated significantly (Fig. 6). Lizards were observed in a visually equivalent test arena from test to test, and were exposed to only one odor-type per test. Since western fence lizards respire typically through narial openings with lips tightly closed when first placed in the test area, the only cross-test stimulus that could have resulted in latency differences was the type of chemical cue present in any particular trial. In these circumstances, the nasal olfactory mucosa would have been the first chemosensory epithelium to be stimulated in both a spatial and temporal sense.

Johns (1980; see also Estes, 1972) has argued similarly that among mammals nasal olfaction may be critical in orienting the animals to the odoriferous pheromone source, so that it can utilize the vomeronasal organ, presumably with direct contact by tongue and mouth, or snout and nostril. Johns et al. (1978) found that direct contact with chemical cues in male rat urine may induce reflex ovulation in females, via stimulation of the vomeronasal system. Rather than nasal olfaction, therefore, vomeronasal olfaction may mediate some of the well-known reproductive and regulatory effects of some mammalian pheromones (cf. Poduschka, 1977; Poduschka and Firbas, 1968).

Aggregation in some lizards (Duvall, Herskowitz, and Trupiano-Duvall, 1980) and snakes (King McCarron, Duvall, Baxter, and Gern, 1983; Noble and Clausen, 1936) is known to be mediated by pheromones, and Heller and Halpern (1982) have obtained strong evidence for a critical role of the vomeronasal system in aggre-

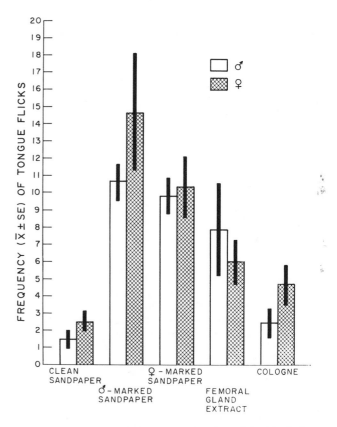

Figure 6. Tongue flick frequency of male and female *Sceloporus occidentalis* exposed to conspecific and control chemical cues in successive discrimination procedure. Although any odorous compound elicited initial tongue flicks of short latency (Fig. 5), once tongue flicking was initiated, only chemical cues derived from conspecifics elicited significantly elevated frequencies. Extracts made from femoral pore or gland exudate elicited marginally significantly greater (depending on the degree of stringency of the *post hoc* multiple comparison test employed), tongue flicking frequencies, when compared to levels exhibited in response to vehicle. (From Duvall, unpublished; but see Duvall, 1981, 1982, for further details and discussion.)

gation in garter snakes (cf. Burghardt, 1980, for a discussion). Duvall, Graves, and King (unpublished) have found that neonatal prairie rattlesnakes must contact skin-derived, lipoidal aggregation pheromones with the tongue directly, for these signals to be detected. The tongue-vomeronasal organ system is important in feeding among reptiles (e.g., see Burghardt, 1967, 1970; Halpern and Kubie, 1980; Kubie and Halpern, 1978, 1979), and in other sorts of interspecific chemical-cue or allelochemical interactions (Chiszar, Duvall, Scudder, and Radcliffe, 1980; Duvall, Chiszar, Trupiano, and Radcliffe, 1978; Duvall, Herskowitz, and Trupiano-Duvall, 1980; Duvall, Scudder, and Chiszar, 1980; Halpern, 1980; Weldon, 1980; Weldon and Burghardt, 1979).

In summary, the difference between vomeronasal and nasal olfaction with respect to pheromone detection seems to be consistent throughout a wide variety of tetrapods. These include a diversity of extant amphibians and reptiles, as well as representatives of seven orders of mammals.

Sociochemical Signaling in Mammal-like Reptiles: Bases for Speculation

Pheromonelike substances today are so ubiquitous, so energetically cheap, and so effective as terrestrial signals that we may take their presence in Permo-Triassic environments as a given. Similarly, vomeronasal structure and function are so widely comparable among living tetrapods as to suggest their existence at least as early as the Paleozoic. It remains to be seen, however, what evidence there is for the presence in synapsid reptiles of structures for the detection and production of pheromones.

Synapsid vomeronasal structure and its distribution

In fossil tetrapods, evidence for a vomeronasal organ, as distinct from the nasal apparatus, is limited by the fact that the nasal capsule is not ossified in lower amniotes and amphibians (Parsons, 1959a, 1967, 1970), and only partially in most mammals (Negus, 1958). However, there is general consensus that a membrane bone, the septomaxilla, ossifies in a consistent relationship to the vomeronasal organ and, therefore, indicates the likely existence of the latter as a distinct entity. An elaborate septomaxilla is characteristic of both pelycosaurian (Watson, 1921; Romer and Price, 1940) and therapsid mammal-like reptiles (Watson, 1921; Kemp, 1979; cf. Fig. 7, this paper), and of captorhinomorph stem reptiles as well (Romer, 1956). Based on this evidence, the vomeronasal organ was as widely distributed in Paleozoic as in present-day tetrapods.

In cynodonts and advanced therocephalians, in which a very mammal-like secondary palate had evolved, the existence of a vomeronasal organ is confirmed by the presence of incisive foramina near the junction of maxilla and premaxilla. Incisive foramina are well defined in the cynodonts *Probelesodon lewisi minor* (Fig. 8), *Thrinaxodon liorhinus* (Fig. 9), *Massetognathus teruggi, M. pascuali,* and *Probainognathus jenseni* (Fig. 10), and have been reported in the cynodont *Diademodon mastacus* (Brink, 1957), the tritylodonts *Oligokyphus* sp. and *Bienotherium* sp. (Romer,

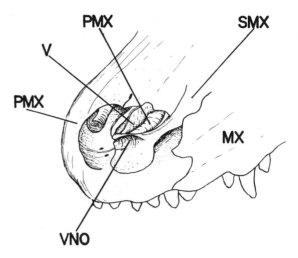

Figure 7. An anterior, and dorso-lateral cut-away view of the snout of the primitive cynodont *Prosynosuchus delaharpeae*. Note the anterior-most, scroll-shaped portion of the septomaxilla (SMX), which likely housed a vomeronasal (VNO) or Jacobson's organ. V, vomer; PMX, premaxilla; MX, maxilla. (Modified from Kemp, 1979.)

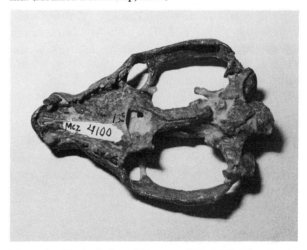

Figure 8. Ventral view of the secondary palate, showing incisive foramina, of the advanced cynodont *Probelesodon lewisi minor,* MCZ 4100. The incisive foramina of these animals probably housed nasopalatine canals, which allowed access to the vomeronasal organs from the mouth.

1956, 1966; Lewis, this volume), and the advanced therocephalian *Bauria cynops* (Broom, 1937). Broom suggests that the incisive foramina of *Bauria* were "probably for the ducts of Jacobson's organ." In other bauriamorphs, however, no incisive foramina have been reported (Romer, 1966).

In dicynodonts, evidence for a vomeronasal organ consists not only of an elaborate septomaxilla, but also of nasoseptal grooves (Fig. 11) in the nasal cavities of *Dicynodon* (King, 1981) and *Lystrosaurus* (Cluver, 1971). The organ may

Figure 9. Anteriodorsal view of the snout region, showing incisive foramina, of the cynodont *Thrinaxodon liorhinus,* USNM 22812.

Figure 10. Ventral view of the secondary palate and a large anterior pit in the advanced cynodont *Probainognathus jenseni,* MCZ 4021, that probably once housed incisive foramina. A septum comprised of maxillary and premaxillary components appears to have been broken away in this specimen.

have opened into the nasal cavity only, or, as in *Sphenodon* (Romer, 1956), into the mouth via the choanae, which lay rather far forward at the back of the short secondary palate. Dicynodonts lack incisive foramina (Cluver, 1971; King, 1981), perhaps because of their unique jaw and snout specializations for feeding on tough or fibrous plants (Hotton, this volume). However, if they also possessed a strong and flexible tongue (Hotton, personal communication), they may have utilized it to convey chemical signals from the mouth to the vomeronasal organ via the external naris, much as cattle do.

Thus a distinct vomeronasal organ appears to have been a characteristic of synapsid reptiles generally, and the indication of glandular integument in a primitive therapsid (Chudinov, 1968) suggests a potential among synapsids for production of pheromonal substances. These probabilities support the view that the vomeronasal organ functioned in the behavior of synapsids much as it does in that of living reptiles and mammals. The persistence of pheromonal signals in a terrestrial environment would have been useful to synapsids for such social interactions as spacing, aggregation, and maintenance of territory. This behavior would have been manifest as both active and passive marking, the latter in connection with everyday activities of excretion, locomotion, and feeding (Fig. 12).

Several mammals actively mark with specialized exocrine sources of pheromones in the snout (e.g., see Grau, 1976; Stoddart, 1980a,b), frequently associated with distinct patches or tufts

of modified hair. One probable function of hair-exocrine structural amalgams in pheromone systems is purely thermodynamic; the greater the surface area, the greater the rate of pheromone evaporation (Guthrie, 1976). Another function is that of a simple brush; hair tuft-exocrine gland combinations can facilitate efficient marking of objects in the environment in a single pass or wipe, since the chemical signal is present in great quantities as a function of greater surface area. Brink (1957) and Van Valen (1960) have emphasized pits and elongate grooves on the snouts of the advanced cynodonts *Diademodon* and *Cynognathus,* which may have housed specialized exocrine glands. The facial pits in the snout of several advanced cynodonts are also treated as evidence for the presence of vibrissae,

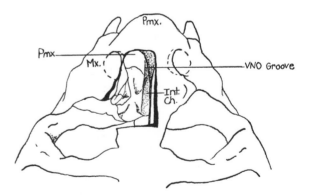

Figure 11. A dorsal, cut-away view of the left nasal cavity of the dicynodont *Dicynodon.* King (1981) and Cluver (1971) believe that the VNO groove housed the vomeronasal organ in life. Pmx, premaxilla; Mx, maxilla; Int. Ch., internal choana. (Redrawn and modified from King, 1981).

Figure 12. Ethological speculation. *Passive marking* and tongue-vomeronasal organ investigation in *Thrinaxodon*. In passive marking, animals deposit chemical cues in the course of routine daily activities. Here, as an individual rubs passively against a rock (upper and middle panels), pheromones are deposited that are investigated by conspecifics (lower panel). Passive marking is common among living tetrapods, and doubtless occurred among synapsids as well. Such chemical signaling could have affected aggregation, avoidance, spacing, and perhaps even reproductive activities.

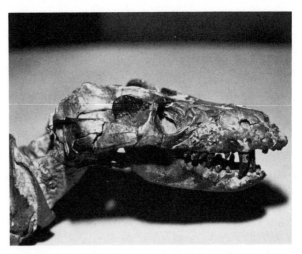

Figure 13. A lateral view of the skull of the *Thrinaxodon liorhinus*, USNM 22812. Although the large, round pit directly dorsal to the upper canine is probably due to injury, the several small pits in this region are not. The latter housed vessels and nerves that may have supplied glands, snout hairs, and vibrissae.

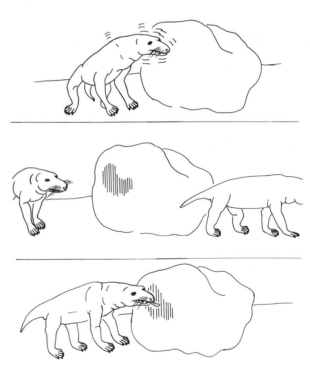

Figure 14. Ethological speculation. Among animals with more specialized chemical signaling systems, *active marking* often takes place. Here, a *Thrinaxodon liorhinus* individual actively snout-rubs on rock, depositing pheromanal exudates (upper panel). Another conspecific approaches the labeled rock (middle panel), and investigates the deposit with tongue and vomeronasal organ (lower panel). Reconstruction is based on the fact that several advanced cynodonts such as *Thrinaxodon* possessed facial pits and grooves that may have housed exocrine glands, which suggest active marking by pheromone deposition.

facial hairs of some sort, or both (Brink, 1957; Olson, 1959; Van Valen, 1960; Watson, 1931). The facial pits of *Thrinaxodon* are distinct (Fig. 13), and may have housed neural and vascular connections to glands, and, perhaps, to hair follicles as well. Such cynodonts as *Thrinaxodon, Diademodon,* and *Cynognathus* may have rubbed or marked objects or conspecifics with actions similar to snout-marking by domestic cats (Fig. 14).

Alternatively, Bennett and Ruben (this volume) refer to extant reptiles with facial sculpture which is described as comparable to cynodonts, but without glandular integument or vibrissae. The lack of agreement in this matter merely reminds us that the time of acquisition of a mammal-like integument remains uncertain. Regardless of the time of origin of hair and mammal-like skin glands, and of the original function of those glands, exuded chemicals would have possessed potential signal function from their first appearance. It is likely that prior to the origin of a glandular skin and hair, cynodonts and other therapsids utilized nonspecific substances such as saliva and nasal secretions in active marking, as certain extant lizards seem to do (Berry, 1974; Simon, in press; Simon et al., 1981). The first animals with hair and skin glands would have utilized more specific chemicals with but little change in behavior.

Aggregation pheromones and the derivation of nutrient-producing glands

Basic similarities of development and structure suggest that sweat and sebaceous glands gave origin to mammary glands (Darwin, 1859; Espe, 1938; Long, 1969; Smith, 1959). Features present in certain advanced therepsids have been adduced as evidence that the young of these animals fed by suckling (cf. Lillegraven, 1979). Such features are the reduction of tooth replacement (Brink, 1957; Hopson, 1973; Lillegraven, 1979; Pond, 1977) and a well-developed infraorbital foramen like that of mammals, the latter suggesting muscular lips and a sensory rhinarium (Lillegraven, 1979; Pond, 1977; Simpson, 1933; Van Valen, 1960).

To this morphological argument must be added the ethological events associated with mother-offspring chemical signaling that probably were related to the origin of mammary glands, the most definitive feature of extant mammals. For example, it is established that olfactory cues or pheromones are critical to mammalian maternal care, for the reciprocal recognition of offspring and mother (e.g., Blass and Teicher, 1980; Blass, Hall, and Teicher, 1979; Grau, 1976; Leon, 1974, 1979). The production of pheromones from skin glands of the mother's ventrum that facilitate aggregation in this region of the mother's body, and consequent location of the nipples, is under the control of the hormone oxytocin (Hofer, Shair, and Singh, 1976; Singh and Hofer, 1978)—the same hormone that controls milk ejection (see Norris, 1980). Might not some aggregation pheromone exuded from glands of the maternal ventrum, perhaps under the control of oxytocin or other neurohypophysial octapeptides, have facilitated aggregation of the young (Fig. 15) and have given rise to a ventral gland with nutritive function? If the secretion of this gland were nuzzled or licked by the young (presumably stimulated by vomeronasal olfaction), its potential advantage as a nutrient would be established. Once it became significantly nutritious, refinement of lingual and labial function on the part of the young, and of glandular function on the part of

Figure 15. Ethological speculation. Maternal care of young in the advanced cynodont *Probelesodon lewisi*. Rudiments of maternal care of eggs and young is widespread in living reptiles, and since such parental investment in young is highly developed in mammals, the cynodont reptiles—which gave rise directly to mammals—may have exhibited maternal care more definitive than that seen in extant lizards and crocodilians. Skin glands—regardless of type or derivation—on the ventrum of the mother could have exuded chemical materials that functioned as aggregation pheromones for young, cementing a bond between offspring and the mother's ventrum. The acquisition of nutritive function by these secretions likely led to the production of milk, the most distinctive feature of mammals.

the mother, would follow in a "coevolutionary" fashion. Glands performing a strictly pheromonal, nonnutritive function apparently continued to exist along with mammary glands, for potent "nonteat" pheromones are exuded from the ventrum of some living mammalian mothers.

Parental care of eggs and offspring is another form of vertebrate social behavior often affected by signaling or releasing pheromones. Many examples exist of the important role of chemical cues in the mammalian parent-offspring nexus (e.g., see Blass, Hall, and Teicher, 1979; Blaxter, 1971; Duvall, Scudder, and Chiszar, 1982; Grau, 1976; Leon, 1974, 1979; Moltz and Lee, 1981). Pheromones would likewise have been important to mammal-like reptiles in maternal care of eggs or young.

In summary, it is likely that pheromones played a role among mammal-like reptiles generally, in mediating such common group phenomena as aggregation and avoidance (e.g., Shorey, 1976). If, as seems probable, advanced cynodonts possessed specialized exocrine sources of sociochemical exudation, then they probably exhibited active marking and some degree of pheromonal control of spacing. Since living mammals and some living reptiles utilize pheromones in parental care of eggs or young, it is probable that the reptilian predecessors of mammals would have done likewise. Finally, the function of pheromones in maternal-offspring ag-

D. DUVALL

gregation, and in care of young, may well have been a necessary prior condition for the appearance of milk production.

Acknowledgments

Several individuals helped considerably by providing critical comments on other and earlier versions of this manuscript, including Thomas Parsons, Mimi Halpern, Bud Lindstedt, Jim Stewart, Gordon Burghardt, Lou Guillette, Paul Weldon, Alan MacKay-Sim, Dick Jones, Hank Harlow, Hobart Smith, Dave Chiszar, Jay Lillegraven, and especially Bill Gern. I thank Nick Hotton (The Smithsonian Institution), A. W. Crompton (The Museum of Comparative Zoology, Harvard University), Jan and Carol Roth and Paul MacLean (Laboratory of Brain Evolution and Behavior, National Institute of Mental Health), and Gillian King and Tom Kemp (Oxford University Museum of Natural History) for allowing me to examine specimens in their care. My wife, Jeanne Trupiano-Duvall, as well as my students, Geoff Carpenter, Brant Graves, and Mike King, also helped immeasurably. Mary David kindly typed the manuscript. This work was supported in part by funds from the Department of Zoology, University of Wyoming.

References

Allison, A. C.
1953. The morphology of the olfactory system in the vertebrates. *Biol. Rev.* 28:195–244.

Altner, H. and W. Müller.
1968. Electrophysiologische and Elektronemikroskopische Untersuchungen an der Riechschleimhaut des Jacobsonschen Organs von Eidechsen *(Lacerta). Z. Vergl. Physiol.* 60:151–55.

Auffenberg, W.
1978. Social and feeding behavior of *Varanus komodoensis.* In *Behavior and Neurology of Lizards,* ed. N. Greenberg and P. D. MacLean, pp. 301–331. Washington: National Institute of Mental Health, U.S. Department of Health, Education, and Welfare.

Bakker, R. T.
1980. Dinosaur heresy—dinosaur renaissance: why we need endothermic archosaurs for a comprehensive theory of bioenergetic evolution. In *A Cold Look at the Warm-Blooded Dinosaurs,* ed. D. K. Thomas and E. C. Olson. Boulder, Colo.: Westview Press.

Bannister, L. H.
1968. Fine structure of the sensory endings in the vomeronasal organ of the slow-worm *Anguis fragilis. Nature* (London) 217:275–76.

Barnes, R. D.
1977. The special anatomy of *Marmosa robinsoni.* In *The Biology of Marsupials,* ed. D. Hunsaker II. New York: Academic Press.

Beauchamp, G. K.; Wellington, J. L.; Wysocki, C. L.; Brand, J. C.; Kubie, J. L.; and Smith, A. B., III.
1980. Chemical communication in the guinea pig: urinary components of low volatility and their access to the vomeronasal organ. In *Chemical Signals,* ed. D. Müller-Schwarze and R. M. Silverstein. New York: Plenum.

Bekoff, M.
1979a. Scent-marking by free-ranging dogs: olfactory and visual components. *Biol. of Behav.* 4: 123–39.
1979b. Ground scratching by male domestic dogs: a composite signal. *J. Mammal.* 60:847–48.

Bellairs, A. D'As. and Boyd, J. D.
1950. The lachrymal apparatus in lizards and snakes. II. The anterior part of the lachyrmal duct and its relationship with the palate and with the nasal and vomeronasal organs. *Proc. Zool. Soc. Lond.* 120:269–310.

Berry, K. H.
1974. The ecology and social behavior of the chuckwalla, *Sauromalus obesus obesus* Baird. *Univ. California Publ. Zool.* 101:1–60.

Bertmar, G.
1981. Evolution of vomeronasal organs in vertebrates. *Evolution* 35:359–66.

Bhatnagar, K. P.
1980. The chiropteran vomeronasal organ: its relevance to the phylogeny of bats. In *Proceedings of the Fifth International Bat Research Conference,* ed. D. E. Wilson and A. L. Gardner. Lubbock: Texas Tech Press.

Bissinger, B. E., and Simon, C. A.
1981. The chemical detection of conspecifics by juvenile Yarrow's spiny lizard, *Sceloporus jarrovi. J. Herpetol.* 15:77–81.

Blass, E. M.; Hall, W. G.; and Teicher, M. H.
1979. The ontogeny of suckling and ingestive behaviors. In *Progress in Psychobiology and Physiological Psychology,* vol. 8, ed. J. M. Sprague and A. N. Epstein. New York: Academic Press.

Blass, E. M., and Teicher, M. H.
1980. Suckling. *Science* 210:15–22.

Blaxter, K. L.
1971. The comparative biology of lactation. In *Lactation,* ed. I. R. Falconer. University Park, Penn.: The Pennsylvania State University Press.

Block, M. L.; Volpe, L. C.; and Hayes, M. J.
1981. Saliva as a chemical cue in the development of social behavior. *Science* 211:1062–64.

Breckenridge, W. W.
1943. The life history of the black-banded skink *Eumeces sepentrionalis* (Baird). *Amer. Midl. Nat.* 29:591–606.

Brink, A. S.
1957. Speculations on some advanced mammalian characteristics in the higher mammal-like reptiles. *Paleontol. Afric.* 4:77–96.

Broman, I.
1920. Das Organon vomero-nasale Jacobsoni ein Wassergeruchsorgan! *Anat. Hefte.* 58:137–91.

Bronson, F. H.
1974. Pheromonal influences on reproductive activities in rodents. In *Pheromones,* ed. M. C. Birch. New York: American Elsevier.

Bronson, F. H., and Coquelin, A.
1980. The modulation of reproduction by priming pheromones in house mice: speculations on adaptive function. In *Chemical Signals,* ed. D. Müller-Schwarze and R. M. Silverstein. New York: Plenum.

Broom, R.
1937. On the palate, occiput and hind foot of *Bauria cynops* Broom. *Amer. Mus. Nov.* No. 946:106.

Burghardt, G. M.
1967. Chemical-cue preferences of inexperienced snakes: comparative aspects. *Science* 157:718–21.
1970. Chemical perception in reptiles. In *Advances of Chemoreception,* ed. J. W. Johnston, Jr., D. G. Moulton, and A. Turk. New York: Appleton-Century-Crofts.
1980. Behavioral and stimulus correlates of vomeronasal functioning in reptiles: feeding, grouping, sex, and tongue use. In *Chemical Signals,* ed. D. Müller-Schwarze and R. M. Silverstein. New York: Plenum.

Cagle, F. R.
1940. Eggs and natural nests of *Eumeces fasciatus.* *Univ. Florida Publ. Biol., Sci. Ser.* 3:1–118.

Chiszar, D.; Duvall, D.; Scudder, K.; and Radcliffe, C. W.
1980. Simultaneous and successive discriminations between envenomated and nonenvenomated mice by rattlesnakes (*Crotalus durisus* and *C. viridis*). *Behav. Neur. Biol.* 29:518–21.

Chiszar, D.; Wellborn, S.; Wand, M. A.; Scudder, K. M.; and Smith, H. M.
1980. Investigatory behavior in snakes, II: Cage cleaning and the induction of defecation in snakes. *Anim. Learn. Behav.* 8:505–10.

Chudinov, P. K.
1968. Structure of the integuments of theriomorphs. *Doklady Akad. Nauk SSSR* 179:207–10. (Translation by Amer. Geol. Inst.).

Cluver, M. A.
1971. The cranial morphology of the dicynodont genus *Lystrosaurus. Ann. S. Afr. Mus.* 56:155–274.

Colbert, E. H.
1958. Morphology and behavior. In *Behavior and Evolution,* ed. A. Roe and G. G. Simpson. New Haven, Conn.: Yale University Press.

Cooper, J. G., and Bhatnagar, K. P.
1976. Comparative anatomy of the vomeronasal organ complex in bats. *J. Anat.* 122:571–601.

Cowles, R. B.
1944. Parturition in the yucca night lizard. *Copeia* (1944):98–100.

Cowles, R. B., and Phelan, R. L.
1958. Olfaction in rattlesnakes. *Copeia* (1968):77–83.

Crews, D.
1976. Hormonal control of male courtship behavior and female attractivity in the garter snake (*Thamnophis sirtalis sirtalis*). *Horm. Behav.* 7:451–60.

Crompton, A. W., and Jenkins, F. A., Jr.
1979. Origin of Mammals. In *Mesozoic Mammals,* ed. J. A. Lillegraven, Z. Kielan-Jaworowska, and W. A. Clemens. Berkeley: University of California Press, 1979.

Darwin, C.
1859. *The Origin of Species by Means of Natural Selection, or The Preservation of Favoured Races in the Struggle for Life.* (Reprinted by Doubleday, Garden City, N.Y., 1960.)

De Boer, J. N.
1977. The age of olfactory cues functioning in chemocommunication among male domestic cats. *Behav. Proc.* 2:209–25.

Distel, H.
1978. Behavioral responses to the electrical stimulation of the brain in the green iguana. In *Behavior and Neurology of Lizards,* ed. N. Greenberg and P. D. MacLean. Poolesville, Md.: NIMH, 1978.

Doty, R. L., ed.
1976. *Mammalian Olfaction, Reproduction Processes, and Behavior.* New York: Academic Press.

Dunbar, I. F.
1977. Olfactory preference in dogs: the response of male and female beagles to conspecific odors. *Behav. Biol.* 20:471–81.

Duvall, D.

1979. Western fence lizard (Sceloporus occidentalis) chemical signals. I. Conspecific discriminations and release of species-typical visual display. *J. Exp. Zool.* 210:321–26.

1980. *Pheromonal Mechanisms in the Social Behavior and Communication of the Western Fence Lizard, Sceloporus occidentalis biseriatus.* Ph.D. dissertation, University of Colorado.

1981. Western fence lizard (Sceloporus occidentalis) chemical signals. II. A replication with naturally breeding adults and a test of the Cowles and Phelan hypothesis of rattlesnake olfaction. *J. Exp. Zool.* 218:351–61.

1982. Western fence lizard (Sceloporus occidentalis) chemical signals. III. An experimental ethogram of conspecific body licking. *J. Exp. Zool.* 221:23–26.

Duvall, D., Chiszar, D., Trupiano, J., and Radcliffe, C. W.

1978. Preference for envenomated rodent prey by rattlesnakes. *Bull. Pschon. Soc.* 11:7–8.

Duvall, D., Guillette, L. J., Jr., and Jones, R. E.

1982. Environmental control of reptilian reproductive cycles. In *Biology of the Reptilia*, vol. 13, ed. C. Gans and F. H. Pough, pp. 301–31. London: Academic Press.

Duvall, D., Guillette, L. J., Jr., Pierce, B., Swain, T., and Skudder, K. M.

1979. Neonatal behavior of Yarrow's spiny lizard, Sceloporus jarrovi. *J. Colo. Wyo. Acad. Sci.* 11:81.

Duvall, D., Herskowitz, R. L., and Trupiano-Duvall, J.

1980. Responses of five-lined skinks (Eumeces fasciatus) and ground skinks (Scincella lateralis) to conspecific and interspecific chemical cues. *J. Herpetol.* 14:121–27.

Duvall, D., Scudder, K. M., and Chiszar, D.

1980. Rattlesnake predatory behavior: mediation of prey discrimination and release of swallowing by cues arising from envenomated mice. *Anim. Behav.* 28:674–83.

Duvall, D., Scudder, K. M., Southwick, C. H., and Schultz, N. J.

1982. Paternal urine elicits increased maternal care in grasshopper mice. *Behav. Neur. Biol.* 34:221–25.

Duvall, D., Schmitt, C. V., Erpine, M. J., and Rabedeau, R. C.

1978. Androgen and concurrent androgen-progesterone maintenance of attack-eliciting characteristics in male mouse urine. *Behav. Biol.* 22:343–53.

Duvall, D., Trupiano, J., and Smith, H. M.

1979. An observation of maternal behavior in the Mexican desert spiny lizard, Sceloporus rufidorsum. Trans. Kansas Acad. Sci. 82:60–62.

Eisenberg, J. F., and Kleiman, D. G.

1972. Olfactory communication in mammals. In *Annual Review of Ecology and Systematics*, vol. 3, ed. R. G. Johnston, P. W. Frank, and C. D. Michener. Palo Alto, Calif.: Annual Reviews, Inc.

Epple, G.

1976. Chemical communication and reproductive processes in non-human primates. In *Mammalian Olfaction, Reproductive Processes, and Behavior*, ed. R. L. Doty. New York: Academic Press.

Espe, D. L.

1938. *Secretion of Milk*. Ames, Iowa: Collegiate Press.

Estes, R. D.

1972. The role of the vomeronasal organ in mammalian reproduction. *Mammalia* 36:315–41.

Evans, L. T.

1959. A motion picture study of maternal behavior of the lizard, Eumeces obsoletus Baird and Girard. *Copeia* (1959):103–10.

Fitch, H. S.

1954. Life history and ecology of the five-lined skink, Eumeces fasciatus. *Univ. Kan. Publ. Mus. Nat. Hist.* 8:1–156.

1970. Reproductive Cycles in Lizards and Snakes. *Univ. Kans. Mus. Nat. Hist. Misc. Publ.* 52:1–156.

Frahm, H. D., and Bhatnagar, K. P.

1980. Comparative morphology of the accessory olfactory bulb in bats. *J. Anat.* 130:349–65.

Galton, P. M.

1970. Pachycephalosaurids—dinosaurian battering rams. *Discovery* 6:23–32.

Garstka, W. R., and Crews, D.

1981. Female sex pheromone in the skin and circulation of a garter snake. *Science* 214:681–83.

Garstka, W. R.; Camazine, B.; and Crews, D.

1982. Interactions of behavior and physiology during the annual reproductive cycle of the red-sided garter snake (Thamnophis sirtalis parietalis). *Herpetologica* 38:104–23.

Grau, G. A.

1976. Olfaction and reproduction in ungulates. In *Mammalian Olfaction, Reproductive Processes, and Behavior*, ed. R. L. Doty. New York: Academic Press.

Graves, B. M., and Duvall, D.

1983. Pheromonal mediation of defensive behavior in prairie rattlesnakes (abstr.). *J. Colo. Wyo. Acad. Sci.* 15:48.

Graziadei, P. P. C.

1971. The olfactory mucosa of vertebrates. In *Handbook of Sensory Physiology,* vol. IV., Chemical Senses, part 1, Olfaction, ed. L. M. Beidler. New York: Springer-Verlag.

1977. Functional anatomy of the mammalian chemoreceptor system. In *Chemical Signals,* ed. D. Müller-Schwarze and M. M. Mozell. (eds). New York: Plenum.

Greene, H. W., and Burghardt, G. M.

1978. Behavior and phylogeny: constriction in ancient and modern snakes. *Science* 200:74–77.

Griffiths, M.

1978. *The Biology of the Monotremes.* New York: Academic press.

Guthrie, R. D.

1976. *Body Hot Spots.* New York: Van Nostrand.

Halpern, M.

1976. The efferent connections of the olfactory bulb and accessory olfactory bulb in the snakes, *Thamnophis sirtalis* and *Thamnophis radix. J. Morphol.* 150:553–78.

1980. Chemical ecology of terrestrial vertebrates. In *Animals and Environmental Fitness,* ed. R. Gilles. New York: Pergamon Press.

Halpern, M., and Kubie, J. L.

1980. Chemical access to the vomeronasal organs of garter snakes. *Physiol. Behav.* 24:367–71.

Hediger, H.

1949. Saugetier Territorien und ihre Markierung. *Bijdr. Dierk.* 28:172–84.

Heller, S. B., and Halpern, M.

1982. Laboratory observations of aggregative behavior of garter snakes, *Thamnophis sirtalis:* roles of the visual, olfactory and vomeronasal senses. *J. Comp. Physiol. Psychol.* 96:874–999.

Hofer, M. A.; Shair, H.; and Singh, P. J.

1976. Evidence that maternal ventral skin substances promote suckling in infant rats. *Physiol. Behav.* 17:131–36.

Hopson, J. A.

1973. Endothermy, small size, and the origin of mammalian reproduction. *Amer. Nat.* 107:446–52.

1975. The evolution of cranial display structure in hadrosaurian dinosaurs. *Paleobiology* 1:21–43.

1977. Relative brain size and behavior in archosaurian reptiles. *Ann. Rev. Ecol. Syst.* 8:429–48.

Jerison, H. J.

1971. More on why birds and mammals have big brains. *Amer. Nat.* 105:185–89.

1973. *Evolution of the Brain and Intelligence.* New York: Academic Press.

Johns, M. A.

1980. The role of the vomeronasal system in mammalian reproductive physiology. In *Chemical Signals,* ed. D. Müller-Schwarze and R. M. Silverstein. New York: Plenum.

Johns, M. A.; Feder, H. H., Komisaruk, B. R.; and Mayer, A. D.

1978. Urine-induced reflex ovulation in anovulatory rats may be a vomeronasal effect. *Nature* (London) 272:446.

Johnson, J. L., Jr.

1977. Central nervous sytem of marsupials. In *The Biology of Marsupials,* ed. D. Hunsaker II. New York: Academic Press.

Jolly, A.

1972. *The Evolution of Primate Behavior.* New York: Macmillan.

Karlson, P., and Lüscher, M.

1959. "Pheromones:" a new term for a class of biologically active substances. *Nature* (London) 183:55–56.

Kemp, T. S.

1979. The primitive cynodont *Procynosuchus:* functional anatomy of the skull and relationships. *Phil. Trans., Royal Soc. London, B. Biol. Sci.* 285:73–122.

1982. *Mammal-like Reptiles and the Origin of Mammals.* New York: Academic Press.

King, G. M.

1981. The functional anatomy of a Permian dicynodont. *Phil. Trans., Royal Soc. London, B. Biol. Sci.* 291:243–322.

King, M.; McCarron, D.; Duvall, D.; Baxter, G.; and Gern, W.

1983. Group avoidance of conspecific but not interspecific chemical cues by prairie rattlesnakes *(Crotalus viridis viridis). J. Herpetol.* 17:196–98.

Kleiman, D.

1966. Scent marking in the Canidae. In *Play, Exploration and Territory in Mammals, Symp., Zool. Soc. London, No. 18,* ed. P. A. Jewell and C. Loizos. London: Academic Press.

Kubie, J. L., and Halpern, M.

1978. Garter snake trailing behavior: effects of varying prey-extract concentration and mode of prey-extract presentation. *J. Comp. Physiol. Psychol.* 92:362–73.

1979. Chemical sense involved in garter snake prey trailing. *J. Comp. Physiol. Psychol.* 93:648–67.

Kubie, J. L.; Cohen, J.; and Halpern, H.

1978. Shedding enhances the sexual attractiveness of oestradiol treated garter snakes and their untreated penmates. *Anim. Behav.* 26:562–70.

D. DUVALL

Kubie, J. L.; Vagvolgyi, A.; and Halpern, M.
1978. Roles of the vomeronasal and olfactory systems in courtship behavior of male garter snakes. *J. Comp. Physiol. Psychol.* 92:627–41.

Leon, M.
1974. Maternal pheromone. *Physiol. Behav.* 13:441–53.
1979. Mother-young reunions. In *Progress in psychobiology and Physiological Psychology,* vol. 8, ed. J. M. Sprague and A. N. Silverstein. New York: Academic Press.

Lillegraven, J. A.
1979. Reproduction in Mesozoic mammals. In *Mesozoic Mammals,* ed. J. A. Lillegraven, Z. Kielan-Jaworowska, and W. A. Clemens. Berkeley: The University of California Press.

Long, C. A.
1969. The origin and evolution of mammary glands. *Bioscience* 19:519–23.

MacKay-Sim, A., and Laing, D. G.
1981. The sources of odors from stressed rats. *Physiol. Behav.* 27:511–13.

MacLean, P. D.
1978. Why brain research on lizards? In *Behavior and Neurology of Lizards,* ed. N. Greenberg and P. D. MacLean. Poolesville, Md. NIMH.

Madison, D. M.
1975. Intrapsecific odor preferences between salamanders of the same sex: dependence on season and proximity of residence. *Can. J. Zool.* 53:1356–61.
1977. Chemical communication in amphibians and reptiles. In *Chemical Signals,* ed. D. Müller-Schwarze and M. M. Mozell. New York: Plenum.

Meredith, M.
1980. The vomeronasal organ and accessory olfactory system in the hamster. In *Chemical Signals,* ed. D. Müller-Schwarze and R. M. Silverstein. New York: Plenum.

Meredith, M.; Marques, D. M.; O'Connell, R. J.; and Stern, F. L.
1980. Vomeronasal pump: significance for male hamster sexual behavior. *Science* 207:1224–26.

Molnar, R. E.
1977. Analogies in the evolution of combat and display structures in ornithopods and ungulates. *Evol. Theory* 3:165–90.

Moltz, H., and Lee, T. M.
1981. The maternal pheromone of the rat: identity and functional significance. *Physiol. Behav.* 26:301–6.

Müller-Schwarze, D.; and Mozell, M. M., eds.
1977. *Chemical Signals.* New York: Plenum.

Müller-Schwarze, D., and Silverstein, R. M., eds.
1980. *Chemical Signals.* New York: Plenum.

Murphy, M. R.
1976. Olfactory impairment, olfactory bulb removal, and mammalian reproduction. In *Mammalian Olfaction, Reproductive Processes, and Behavior,* ed. R. L. Doty. New York: Academic Press.

Mykytowycz, R.
1970. The role of skin glands in mammalian communication. In *Advances in Chemoreception,* ed. J. W. Johnston, Jr., D. G. Moulton, and A. Turk. New York: Appleton-Century-Crofts.
1974. Odor in the spacing behavior of mammals. In *Pheromones,* ed. M. C. Birch. New York: American Elsevier.
1977. Olfaction in relation to reproduction in domestic animals. In *Chemical Signals,* ed. D. Müller-Schwarze and M. M. Mozell. New York: Plenum.

Negus, V.
1958. *The Comparative Anatomy and Physiology of the Nose and the Paranasal Sinuses.* Edinburgh and London: E. & S. Livingstone Ltd.

Noble, G. K., and Clausen, H. J.
1936. The aggregation behavior of *Storeria dekayi* and other snakes with especial reference to the sense organs involved. *Ecol. Monogr.* 6:269–316.

Noble, G. K., and Kumpf, K. F.
1936. The function of the Jacobson's organ in lizards. *J. Genet. Psychol.* 48:371–82.

Noble, G. K., and Mason, E. R.
1933. Experiments on the brooding habits of the lizards *Eumeces* and *Ophisaurus. Amer. Mus. Novitates* 619:1–29.

Norris, D. O.
1980. *Vertebrate Endocrinology.* Philadelphia: Lea & Febiger.

Northcutt, R. G.
1978. Forebrain and midbrain organization in lizards and its phylogenetic significance. In *Behavior and Neurology of Lizards,* ed. N. Greenberg and P. D. MacLean. Poolesville, Md.: NIMH.

Olson, E. C.
1959. The evolution of mammalian characteristics. *Evolution* 13:344–53.

Parsons, T. S.
1959a. Nasal anatomy and the phylogeny of reptiles. *Evolution* 13:175–87.
1959b. Studies on the comparative embryology of the reptilian nose. *Bull. Mus. Comp. Zool. Harvard Univ.* 120:101–377.
1967. Evolution of the nasal structure in the lower tetrapods. *Amer. Zool.* 7:397–413.

1970. The nose and Jacobson's organ. In *Biology of the Reptilia,* vol. 2, Morphology B, ed. C. Gans and T. S. Parsons. London: Academic Press.

1971. Anatomy of nasal structures from a comparative viewpoint. In *Handbook of Sensory Physiology,* vol. IV, Chemical Senses, part 2, Olfaction, ed. L. M. Beidler. New York: Springer-Verlag.

Poduschka, W.
1977. Insectivore communication. In *How Animals Communicate,* ed. T. A. Sebeok. Bloomington: Indiana University Press.

Poduschka, W., and Firbas, W.
1968. Das Selbstebespeicheln des Igels, *Erinaceus europaeus* Linnè, 1758, steht in Verbindung zur Funktion des Jacobsonschen Organes. *A. Säugetierk.* 33:160–72.

Pond, C. M.
1977. The significance of lactation in the evolution of mammals. *Evolution* 31:177–99.

Porter, R. H., and Czaplicki, J. A.
1974. Response of water snakes *(Natrix r. rhombifera)* and garter snakes *(Thamnophis sirtalis)* to chemical cues. *Anim. Learn. Behav.* 2:129–32.

Powers, J. B., and Winans, S. S.
1973. Sexual behavior in peripherally anosmic male hamsters. *Physiol. Behav.* 10:361–68.

1975. Vomeronasal organ: critical role in mediating sexual behavior in the male hamster. *Science* 187:961–63.

Pratt, C. W. McE.
1948. The morphology of the ethmoidal region of *Sphenodon* and lizards. *Proc. Zool. Soc. London* 48:171–201.

Quay, W. B.
1977. Structure and function of skin glands. In *Chemical Signals,* ed. D. Müller-Schwarze and M. M. Mozell. New York: Plenum.

Rasmussen, L. E.; Schmidt, M. J.; Henneous, R.; Groves, D.; and Daves, G. D., Jr.
1982. Asian bull elephants: Flehmen-like responses to extractable components in female elephant estrous urine. *Science* 217:159–62.

Romer, A. S.
1956. *Osteology of the Reptiles.* Chicago: The University of Chicago Press.

1966. *Vertebrate Paleontology,* 3d ed. Chicago: The University of Chicago Press.

Romer, A. S., and Parsons, T. S.
1977. *The Vertebrate Body,* 5th ed. Philadelphia: Saunders College Publishing.

Romer, A. S., and Price, L. I.
1940. Review of the pelycosauria. *Geol. Soc. Amer. Sp. Papers* 28:1–538.

Ross, P., Jr., and Crews, D.
1977. Influence of the seminal plug on mating behavior in the garter snake. *Nature* (London) 367:34–45.

Scalia, F., and Winans, S. S.
1976. New perspectives on the morphology of the olfactory system: olfactory and vomeronasal pathways in mammals. In *Mammalian Olfaction, Reproductive Processes, and Behavior,* ed. R. L. Doty. New York: Academic Press.

Schultz, N. J.
1979. *Parental Role and Behavior of the Southern Grasshopper Mouse, Onychomys torridus.* Ph.D. dissertation, The Johns Hopkins University.

Schultz-Westrum, T. G.
1969. Social communication by chemical signals in flying phalangers *(Petaurus breviceps papuamus).* In *Olfaction and Taste III,* ed. C. Pfaffmann. New York: The Rockefeller University Press.

Scott, T. R., Jr.,
1979. The chemical senses. In *Turtles,* ed. M. Harless and H. Morlock. New York: John Wiley and Sons.

Scott, T. G., and Sheldahl, R. B.
1937. Black-banded skink in Iowa. *Copeia* (1937):192.

Scudder, K. M.; Stewart, N. J.; and Smith, H. M.
1980. Response of neonate water snakes *(Nerodia sipedon sipedon)* to conspecific chemical cues. *J. Herpetol.* 14:196–98.

Shorey, H. H.
1976. *Animal Communication by Pheromones.* New York: Academic Press.

Simon, C. A.
1983. Lizard Chemoreception: a review. In *Lizard Ecology: Studies of a Model Organism,* ed. R. B. Huey, E. R. Pianka, and T. W. Schoener. Cambridge, Mass.: Harvard University Press.

Simon, C. A.; Gravelle, K.; Bissinger, B. E.; Eiss, I.; and Ruibal, R.
1981. The role of chemoreception in the inguanid lizard *Sceloporus jarrovi. Anim. Behav.* 29:46–51.

Simpson, G. G.
1933. The ear region and the foramina of the cynodont skull. *Amer. J. Sci.,* ser. 5, 26:285–94.

1958. The study of evolution: methods and present status of theory. In *Behavior and Evolution,* ed. A. Roe and G. G. Simpson. New Haven, Conn.: Yale University Press.

Singh, P. J., and Hofer, M. A.
1978. Oxytocin reinstates maternal olfactory cues for nipple orientation and attachment in rat pups. *Physiol. Behav.* 20:385–89.

D. Duvall

Smith, V. R.
1959. *Physiology of Lactation,* 5th ed. Ames, Iowa: Iowa State University Press.

Sondheimer, E., and Simeone, J. B., eds.
1970. *Chemical Ecology.* New York: Academic Press.

Stamps, J. A.
1977. Social behavior and spacing patterns in lizards. In *Biology of the Reptilia,* vol. 7, ed. C. Gans and D. W. Tinkle. London: Academic Press.

Stebbins, R. C.
1948. Nasal structure in lizards with reference to olfaction and conditioning of the inspired air. *Amer. J. Anat.* 83:183–221. Steinbrecht, R. A.

Steinbrecht, R. A.
1969. Comparative morphology of olfactory receptors. In *Olfaction and Taste III,* ed. C. Pfaffmann. New York: The Rockefeller University Press.

Stoddart, D. M.
1980a. *The Ecology of Vertebrate Olfaction.* New York: Chapman and Hall.

Stoddart, D. M., ed.
1980b. *Olfaction in Mammals. Symp., Zool. Soc. London,* No. 45. New York: Academic Press.

Thiessen, D. D.
1977. Thermoenergetics and the evolution of pheromone communication. In *Progress in Psychobiology and Physiological Psychology,* vol. 7, ed. J. M. Sprague and A. N. Epstein. New York: Academic Press.

Thiessen, D., and Yahr, P.
1977. *The Gerbil in Behavioral Investigations.* Austin, Tex.: The University of Texas Press.

Tokarz, R. R., and Jones, R. E.
1979. A study of egg-related maternal behavior in *Anolis carolinensis* (Reptilia, Lacertilia, Iguanide). *J. Herpetol.* 13:283–88.

Tucker, D.
1963. Olfactory, vomeronasal and trigeminal receptor responses to odorants. In *Olfaction and Taste I,* ed. Zottermen. New York: Macmillan.

Tucker, D., and Smith, J. C.
1976. Vertebrate olfaction. In *Evolution of Brain and Behavior in Vertebrates,* ed. R. B. Masterson, M. E. Bitterman, C. B. G. Campbell, and N. Hotton. Hillsdale, N. J.: Lawrence Erlbaum Assoc.

Van Valen, L.
1960. Therapsids as mammals. *Evolution* 14:304–13.

Vandenbergh, J. G.
1975. Hormones, pheromones and behavior. In *Hormonal Correlates of Behavior,* vol. 2, ed. B. E. Eleftheriou and R. L. Sprott. New York: Plenum.

1980. The influence of pheromones on puberty in rodents. In *Chemical Signals,* ed. D. Müller-Schwarze and R. M. Silverstein. New York: Plenum.

Wang, R. T., and Halpern, M.
1980. Light and electron microscopic observations on the normal structure of the vomeronasal organ of garter snakes. *J. Morphol.* 164:47–67.

Watson, D. M. S.
1921. The bases of classification of the Theriodontia. *Proc. Zool. Soc. London* 1921:35–98.

1931. On the skeleton of a bauriamorph reptile. *Proc. Zool. Soc. London,* part 3:1163.

Weldon, P. J.
1980. In defense of "kairomone" as a class of chemical releasing stimuli. *J. Chem. Ecol.* 6:719–25.

1983. The evolution of alarm pheromones. In *Chemical Signals in Vertebrates,* III, ed. D. Müller-Schwartze and R. M. Silverstein pp. 309–12. New York: Plenum Press.

Weldon, P. J., and Burghardt, G. M.
1979. The ophiophage defensive response in crotaline snakes: extension to new taxa. *J. Chem. Ecol.* 5:141–51.

Wells, M. C., and Bekoff, M.
1981. An observational study of scent-marking in coyotes, *Canis latrans. Anim. Behav.* 29:332–50.

Whitten, W. K.
1963. Is the vomeronasal organ a sex chemoreceptor in mice? Second Asia and Oceanic Congress on Endocrinology, Sydney, Australia (as cited in Johns, 1980).

Wickler, W.
1978. A special constraint on the evolution of composite signals. *Z. Tierpsychol.* 48:345–48.

Wilde, W. S.
1938. The role of Jacobson's organ in the feeding reaction of the common garter snake, *Thamnophis sirtalis sirtalis* (Linn.). *J. Exp. Zool.* 77:445–65.

Wilson, E. O.
1970. Chemical communication within animal species. In *Chemical Ecology,* ed. E. Sondheimer and J. B. Simeone New York: Academic Press.

Wilson, E. O., and Bossert, W. H.
1963. Chemical communication among animals. *Rec. Prog. Horm. Res.* 19:673–716.

Winans, S. S., and Powers, J. B.
1977. Olfactory and vomeronasal deafferentation of male hamsters: histological and behavioral analyses. *Brain Res.* 126:325–44.

Winans, S. S., and Scalia, F.
1970. Anygdaloid nucleus: new afferent input from the vomeronasal organ. *Science* 170:330–32.

Wysocki, C. L.; Wellington, J. L.; and Beauchamp, G. K.
1980. Access of urinary non-volatiles to the mammalian vomeronasal organ. *Science* 207:781–83.

LOUIS J. GUILLETTE, JR.
Department of Biological Sciences
Wichita State University
Wichita, Kansas 67203
and
NICHOLAS HOTTON, III
Department of Paleobiology
The Smithsonian Institution
Washington, D.C. 20560

The Evolution of Mammalian Reproductive Characteristics in Therapsid Reptiles

Introduction

The origin of mammalian reproduction has been a topic of perennial interest ever since Darwin (1859) demonstrated that structures and processes are not created *in toto,* but arise from phylogenetically prior conditions. Emphasis has been largely on factors that produced the mammalian condition (for recent reviews, see Marshal, 1979; Lillegraven, 1979), such as homeothermy, endothermy, and decreasing body size (Hopson, 1973; Case, 1978; McNab, 1978). In this paper, we examine such characteristics of mammalian reproduction as egg retention, viviparity and placentation, reduced size of the egg, altricial young, mammary glands, and maternal care. Our purpose is to determine which traits may have arisen within the mammal-like reptiles and which at a later stage in phylogeny.

Characteristics of Reptilian and Mammalian Reproduction

The ancestral mode of reproduction in reptiles is oviparity, the deposition of a fertilized amniote egg (Smith, 1960; Romer and Parsons, 1977). Reptilian reproduction (Fig. 1) is commonly characterized by ovulation of relatively large megalecithal (large-yolked) eggs, lack of postpartum maternal care in most species, and precocial young—that is, young that require little maternal support after birth or hatching (Goin, Goin, Zug, 1978). In contrast, the most "primitive" reproductive pattern of extant mammals, that of the egg-laying monotremes (Prototheria), is characterized by: relatively small megalecithal

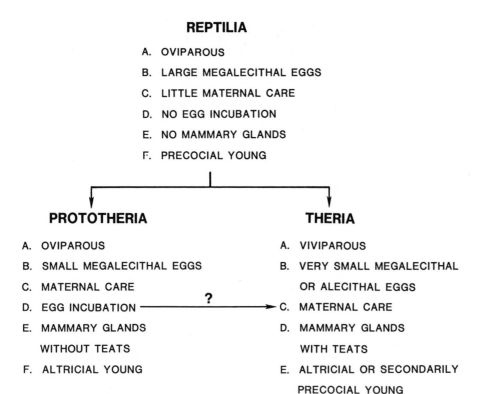

REPTILIA

   A. OVIPAROUS

   B. LARGE MEGALECITHAL EGGS

   C. LITTLE MATERNAL CARE

   D. NO EGG INCUBATION

   E. NO MAMMARY GLANDS

   F. PRECOCIAL YOUNG

PROTOTHERIA

A. OVIPAROUS

B. SMALL MEGALECITHAL EGGS

C. MATERNAL CARE

D. EGG INCUBATION ——————— **?** ——————→

E. MAMMARY GLANDS
   WITHOUT TEATS

F. ALTRICIAL YOUNG

THERIA

A. VIVIPAROUS

B. VERY SMALL MEGALECITHAL
   OR ALECITHAL EGGS

C. MATERNAL CARE

D. MAMMARY GLANDS
   WITH TEATS

E. ALTRICIAL OR SECONDARILY
   PRECOCIAL YOUNG

Figure 1. Schematized reproductive characteristics of the Reptilia, Prototheria, and Theria.

eggs at ovulation (small yolk mass); extensive maternal care before and after hatching; altricial young, requiring an extensive period of further development and maternal support after hatching; and the ability to produce milk as a postpartum food source (Griffiths, 1968). Marsupials and placentals (Theria) bear altricial young alive, having developed a placenta that mediates exchange of substances between the mother and fetus. Placental mammals (Eutheria) produce alecithal (yolkless) eggs.

Fossils tell us neither the order in which mammalian reproductive traits appeared among therapsid ancestors, nor the selective factors that produced the traits; these events and conditions must be inferred from the study of the reproductive anatomy, physiology, and behavior of extant organisms. The traditional therapsid-monotreme-marsupial-eutherian functional sequence (Morriss, 1975) implies the development of mammary glands, and presumably endothermy, prior to that of viviparity in all mammalian ancestors. Monotremes, however, apparently separated from the lineage that led to therians about the time it had attained definitive mammalian status (Crompton and Jenkins, 1979; Simpson, 1945). They are consequently the product of a very long interval of evolution independent of

therians, a consideration that undermines the utility of the monotreme model as a stage in the reproductive evolution of therians. Alternatively, the great variety of gestatory strategies of extant lizards and snakes (for review see Morriss, 1975; Tinkle and Gibbons, 1977) indicates clearly that elaborate maternal-"fetal" relationships arise in tetrapods without benefit of endothermy. It is therefore possible that poikilothermic synapsids first retained eggs in the oviduct, and evolved viviparity in a number of lines, much as have living squamate reptiles. Details of viviparity and placentation now coming to light in living reptiles lend support to this hypothesis.

Reptilian Viviparity and Placentation

Viviparity is a common reproductive mode in lizards and snakes, being exhibited by approximately fifteen percent of all extant species (Tinkle and Gibbons, 1977). Recently, several reviews have dealt with the subject in depth (Packard, Tracy, and Roth, 1977; Tinkle and Gibbons, 1977; Shine and Bull, 1979; Guillette et al., 1980; Guillette, 1982a). Reptilian viviparity ranges from simple egg retention to the development of placental structures and reduction of the yolk content of the egg, and its diversity indicates that viviparity evolved independently in a number of taxonomic groups (Weekes, 1933, 1935; Sergeev, 1940). This suggests a large number of pathways leading to viviparity and placentation, in which the most common sequence of events is reconstructed as follows.

From an oviparous ancestral mode of reproduction, reptilian viviparity begins with the holding of the eggs in the oviducts for a portion of the incubation period. Egg retention is advantageous in decreasing the time the egg is exposed to predation, soil organisms, and extremes of temperature and humidity (Tinkle and Gibbons, 1977). Furthermore, because its rate is temperature dependent, development of the embryo in the retained egg is accelerated by the female's customary behavioral thermoregulation. Egg retention taken to its extreme becomes ovoviviparity: the eggs are retained in the oviducts until they hatch. Once ovoviviparity is established, true viviparity may follow with the development of a placenta capable of functioning in the exchange of waste products, gases, and nutrients.

In all viviparous reptiles studied, two placentae of differing origins are present: a choriovitelline placenta (yolk-sac or omhaloplacenta) and a chorioallantoic placenta (Weekes, 1935; Bauchot, 1965). The choriovitelline placenta is believed to function in the transport of water (Weekes, 1935; Bauchot, 1965; Hoffman, 1970). In contrast, the chorioallantoic placenta may afford an exchange of gases and macromolecules (Bauchot, 1965; Yaron, 1977), and also may be steroidogenic (Guillette, Spielvogel, and Moore, 1981). Most marsupials possess only a choriovitelline placenta (Sharman, 1961). Several eutherians (Rodentia, Insectivora, and Chiroptera) have a transitory, but functional, yolk-sac placenta (Morriss, 1975; Hogarth, 1976, 1978). In fact, the yolk-sac placenta is the main nutritive organ during early embryonic development in the rat; it is replaced by the chorioallantoic placenta during the later stages of pregnancy (New, 1973). Thus, reptiles share some characteristics of placentation with metatherian and eutherian mammals.

Sceloporus aeneus, an iguanid lizard found at high elevations, confirms and extends this outline. *S. aeneus* consists of populations characterized exclusively by oviparous or viviparous females (Guillette, 1981a). Females that differ in reproductive mode also differ in reproductive strategy, oviductal and ovarian morphology, and oviductal vascularity (Guillette, 1981b). Oviparous females exhibit prolonged egg retention and

are characterized by spring reproductive activity, small ovulated eggs, and two clutches per year. Viviparous females exhibit the onset of vitellogenesis (yolking of eggs) in the autumn, ovulation during the winter—with fertilization by sperm stored in the oviducts—and parturition the next spring. They have larger eggs than oviparous females and produce only one clutch per breeding season. Oviparous females produce more eggs per clutch than viviparous females of the same size, indicating a decrease in clutch size with the evolution of viviparity. The oviducts of oviparous females include relatively thick layers of smooth muscle and a glandular endometrium absent in viviparous females, while the oviducts of viviparous females are reduced to thin, highly vascular membranes specialized for maternal-embryonic gas exchange. The embryos of viviparous females produce simple, but well-developed, choriovitelline and chorioallantoic placentae (Guillette, 1982a, b). The initial function of a chorioallantoic placenta seems to have subserved gas exchange rather than nutrition. The choriovitelline placenta is not more primitive evolutionarily than the chorioallantoic placenta; rather, the two evolve concomittantly. *Sceloporus aeneus* thus demonstrates that placental viviparity can evolve among poikilothermic tetrapods without ancillary physiological or anatomical specializations, such as the endothermy or nutritive glands found in mammals.

The Evolution of Mammalian Reproductive Traits: An Hypothesis

Egg retention

Because egg retention requires neither profound modification of the reproductive anatomy of lower tetrapods, nor endothermy, it is a logical first step in the evolution of mammalian reproductive traits. Moreover, it entails obvious advantages over the deposition of eggs on or in the ground, where they are subject to the hazards of predation, drying, flooding, and infection. Retained eggs are actively protected as the female makes good her escape from predators, and the eggs' environment is close to ideal as regards moisture and freedom from molds and bacteria.

Retained eggs are maintained more consistently at a thermal optimum, because the female behaviorally regulates her body temperature at higher than ambient temperatures. Embryonic development is temperature dependent (Bellairs, 1971), maximum rates being attained near the preferred body temperature of the appropriate amniote female (Licht and Moberly, 1965; Bustard, 1969; Rand, 1972). Thus egg retention accelerates development, reducing the time spent by the young in the most vulnerable stage of the life cycle, and the time in which the female herself is most vulnerable. If large-bodied early therapsids were inertial homeotherms, as McNab (1978) has suggested, their thermal constancy would further enhance the advantages of retention. However, as squamates demonstrate, physiologically constant body temperature, whether inertial or endothermic, is not prerequisite to the evolution of elaborate maternal-embryonic relationships.

Placentation

With egg retention, embryos must get their water and oxygen from maternal tissues. Water is readily transferred from the maternal oviduct, but the delivery of oxygen is complicated by the rising needs of the embryo as it develops (Ackerman, 1981). Metabolic demand for oxygen continues to increase from an initially high level because retained embryos grow at a relatively higher temperature. Diffusion distance increases with growth, and shell development and difficulties in gaseous diffusion are exacerbated by aqueous conditions within the oviduct (Guillette et al., 1980; Guillette, 1982a). If oviposition is to be delayed for any significant interval, the vascularity of the oviduct and embryonic membranes must increase with the growth of the embryo, and the thickness of the diffusion barrier must be reduced.

Hypervascularity of the oviduct and embryonic membranes is documented in a variety of egg-retaining oviparous reptiles (Clark, 1953; Guillette, 1981b), presumably in response to hypoxia induced by the initial conditions of egg retention and the prevailing hormonal conditions (Guillette, 1982a, b). Later, the diffusion distance between maternal and fetal tissue is diminished by reduction of oviductal glandular tissues and thinning of extraembryonic and shell membranes. This is most marked during the last third to the last half of embryonic development, an interval of exponential growth. In oviparous females of the reproductively bimodal lizard *Sceloporus aeneus,* oviductal vascularity increases during egg retention, but eggs are deposited just after the onset of exponential growth, and reduction of maternal and fetal membranes is not observed. Viviparous females of *S. aeneus,* on the other hand, exhibit not only hypervascularity of the

oviduct and embryonic membranes, but also massive reduction in tissue bulk.

The hypothetical origin of the chorioallantoic placenta, sketched above, may have been supplemented by the choriovitelline or yolk-sac placenta present in reptiles and many mammals (Pearson, 1949; Bauchot, 1965; Morriss, 1975). The mammalian yolk-sac placenta is capable of absorbing macromolecules, such as proteins and vitamins (Padykula, Deren, and Wilson, 1966), but the function of the reptilian choriovitelline membrane is not so certain. There is general agreement that the latter serves for the transport of water, perhaps as an active pump (Weekes, 1935; Hoffman, 1970), and it may normally serve as a water pump in deposited, as well as retained, eggs. Weekes (1935) suggests that it also may transport albumen, and Cate-Hoedemaker (1933), Boyd (1943), Kasturirangan (1952), and Hoffman (1970) propose a nutrient as well as water transport function for the reptilian choriovitelline placenta. The reptilian choriovitelline membrane undergoes little significant morphological change in the transition from an oviparous to a viviparous reproductive mode, as though it performs the same function in the new mode as in the old.

The source of nutrients for embryonic development and growth in extant metatherian and eutherian mammals is, of course, the maternal bloodstream, but an intermediate source may be uterine milk, a secretion of the oviduct or uterus or both. Uterine milk nourishes the retained young of many amphibians, sharks, and bony fish (Hogarth, 1976, 1978). It also occurs in monotremes and marsupials (Griffiths, 1968; Tyndale-Biscoe, 1973; Stivens, 1974); and, in reptiles, is believed to be absorbed by the choriovitelline membrane (Bauchot, 1965; Hoffman, 1970). Uterine secretion in reptiles is stimulated by the steroid hormones, estradiol-17β and progesterone (Fawcett, 1975; Mead, Eroschenko, and Highfall, 1981). These hormones are produced during pregnancy by the steroidogenic activity of the corpus luteum (Arslan et al., 1978). The corpus luteum is an evanescent, endocrine gland formed from the remains of the ruptured ovarian follicle (Rothchild, 1981). Extended activity of the corpus luteum is correlated with egg retention in reptiles (Jones and Guillette, 1982). It may also be hypothesized that activity is stimulated by the hypervascularity of the oviduct that follows egg retention, which, in turn, facilitates hormone delivery to the uterus.

Thus, all of these processes are interrelated,

and together suggest a multistaged model for the evolution of mammalian placentation. A system of brief and facultative egg retention led to hypervascularization of maternal and fetal membranes in response to hypoxia, which, in turn, permitted a longer period of retention. Thinning of the diffusion barrier introduced the potential for prolonged and obligatory egg retention, which was realized as the embryo found nutrition in uterine or oviductal secretions. A final stage, which is manifest in some reptiles and approaches that of metatherian mammals, is the reduction of yolk volume (Weekes, 1935; Blackburn, Vitt, and Beuchat, 1981).

All stages, starting with obligatory oviparity, were under the control of hormonal elements still at work in similar ways in living mammals. The diversity of reproductive modes in living lizards suggests that all stages were functionally competitive at any one time, given sufficient diversity of environments. By analogy with squamates, the sequence probably began independently many times among the therapsids and perhaps among pelycosaurs as well, since it did not require endothermy. Endothermy, however, would have enhanced the advantages of any stage in the development of placentation at which it appeared. On the other hand, the sequence did not necessarily go to completion in all the lines in which it appeared, even when, as in monotremes, its stages were associated with endothermy.

Care of nest and eggs

Care of the eggs entails the same advantages as egg retention and placentation: enhancement of survivorship of eggs and young. Like placentation, mammalian degrees of maternal care probably arose from the coalescence of various elements—in this case, behavioral—present in synapsid reptiles.

More primitive synapsids, which were presumably obligate egg layers, probably exhibited nesting and egg-guarding behavior in a range comparable to living reptiles. Though few of the latter guard their nests (Fitch, 1970), those that do tend to come into direct contact with the eggs (Fitch, 1954, 1970; Tinkle and Gibbons, 1977). The female of the lizard *Eumeces fasciatus,* for example, completely encircles the egg clutch with her body, a behavior that is common among oviparous species of *Eumeces* (Fitch, 1970). Heat exchange between female and eggs has not been demonstrated in this genus (Noble and Mason, 1933; Fitch, 1954), but the female's body may be large enough to provide a thermal buffer for the eggs. In addition, the female may control humidity in the immediate vicinity of the eggs (Fitch, 1954), as well as protect them against predators (Fitch, 1970). *Eumeces* also assists in hatching (Fitch, 1954). Several species *(Gerrhonotus coeruleus,* J. Stewart, personal communication; *Barisia moreleti,* H. Greene, personal communication; *Barisia imbricata,* Guillette, unpublished) of viviparous lizards exhibit postpartum behaviors reminiscent of those of mammals, such as assisting the young in breaking from the amnionic sac after birth, and eating the remnants of the sac.

Large reptiles, such as the snake *Python molurus,* and certain crocodilians exhibit behavior that goes well beyond simple nest guarding (Tinkle and Gibbons, 1977). *Python* provides a rudimentary incubation by converting itself into a low-grade endotherm during brooding, generating heat by muscular contraction (Hutchinson, Dowling, and Vinegar, 1966). Crocodilians pile up fermenting vegetation in which to lay their eggs, providing thereby an environment of constant high temperature that expedites development. They guard this nest until just before the eggs hatch, when they dig up the eggs, assist in hatching, and transport eggs or young to safe locations (Pooley and Gans, 1976). Moreover, adults provide a measure of protection after hatching by responding to alarm calls of the young. Strictly speaking, crocodilian solicitude for eggs and young is parental rather than exclusively maternal, for it is exhibited by males as well as females.

Endothermy and its effect on reproduction

The reproductive advantages of endothermy, noted in the discussion of egg retention, would have been realized most quickly in those animals in which physical contact between mother and young was prolonged. Oviparous therapsids which had already engaged in significant nest guarding or egg manipulation at the onset of endothermy could have shifted readily to true incubation, which in turn might be expected to set the stage for maternal care after hatching. For viviparous therapsids, the advantage of endothermy would have been manifest only until birth, unless they had evolved some form of postpartum maternal care prior to becoming endothermic. Living animals provide no good models for this stage of evolution, in particular for the very distinctive altricial condition of the young of primitive mammals.

It is likely, however, that the altricial state, unlike placentation, was a consequence of endothermy. The young of the earliest endotherms in the therapsid-mammal lineage, like the young of living endotherms, did not thermoregulate effectively. The altricial condition may, therefore, have originated as a mechanism that kept the young close to the mother for a time, utilizing her body heat to accelerate the development of the young after hatching or birth.

Once such a relationship was initiated, whether as a consequence of oviparity, as monotremes suggest, or as a new development in viviparous forms, modifications to facilitate the transfer of heat from mother to young would follow. A mammalian incubation patch on the ventral surface, marked by loss of hair and increased cutaneous vascularity (Long, 1972; Lehrman, 1961), is such a mechanism, as is the featherless brood patch of birds. The mammary glands of mammals and the brood patch of birds are under the control of similar hormones, such as estradiol, progesterone, and prolactin (Jones, 1971), further supporting the hypothesis of a parallel evolutionary scheme.

Since it is likely that, in therapsids, the integument was primitively glandular (Chidinov, 1968), undifferentiated cutaneous glands in the incubation-patch area might ultimately have given rise to mammary glands (for review, see Raynaud, 1961; Long, 1969, 1972). It has been suggested that, initially, the secretions of these glands served as an adhesive to hold eggs to the incubation patch, and as a source of moisture for the eggs (Long, 1969). If the secretion had a sebaceous component, it may also have afforded protection for the brood patch and adherent eggs (or young?) gainst drying. To the extent that these secretions included proteins, lipids, and sugars, they were potentially nutritive. Their ingestion, at first probably coincidental to the close contact between mother and young, would have extended the time that the young could remain altricial. The evolution of brood-patch secretions as an accessory food source for hatchlings has been suggested as a prerequisite for the development of the definitive mammalian jaw (Pond, 1977). Utilization of this material as food by active young would favor the evolution of secretions the primary function of which was nutritive; i.e., milk. Once the secretion of milk was well established, the extreme altricial condition of the young of living monotremes, marsupials, and primitive placentals became possible.

On the other hand, prolonged association between therapsid mother and young could have been eventuated regardless of the altricial state. Such association would have provided active young with a measure of protection and, after the advent of endothermy, would have insured access to warmth and food. It may have begun with maternal tolerance of the young after the seizure of prey, for the phylogeny leading to mammals seems to have been strongly predatory (Kurten, 1971; Colbert, 1980). Duvall (this volume) suggests that continuing association between therapsid mother and young could have been mediated by pheromones produced by a brood patch, and that it was this process that led to the origin of milk. Noting the evidence of vomeronasal organs in a variety of therapsids, Duvall proposes that the licking of brood-patch secretions for insertion into the vomeronasal organ would have encouraged their use as an accessory food source. The identification of the mother by this means would be reinforced by the satisfaction of obtaining food.

Summary

Ultimately, with the advent of endothermy, a stage was reached in which the female was characterized reproductively by egg retention, momentary or prolonged, and by maternal care, which included nourishment of the young by brood-patch secretions. In our opinion, this stage was reached by therapsids. Some of these animals were oviparous, as indicated by the condition of living monotremes, but by analogy with the pervasiveness of viviparity among squamate reptiles, many may have been viviparous. Viviparous therapsids would have possessed a placenta that functioned in fluid exchange and possibly in the supply of nutrients. Since the origin of a secretory brood patch requires endothermy, but does not require oviparity (Fig. 2), this state of affairs does not help resolve the relationship of prototherians to therians. However, it does allow for animals conforming to the hypothetical ancestors of Theria proposed by Lillegraven (1969, 1975, 1979).

Appearance of Mammal-like Reproductive Traits in Synapsid Reptiles

Of the mammal-like reproductive traits identified in this paper, egg retention, viviparity and placentation, and egg size at ovulation seem to be functionally interrelated but independent of endothermy. The others, namely the altricial state of the young, maternal care, and mammary

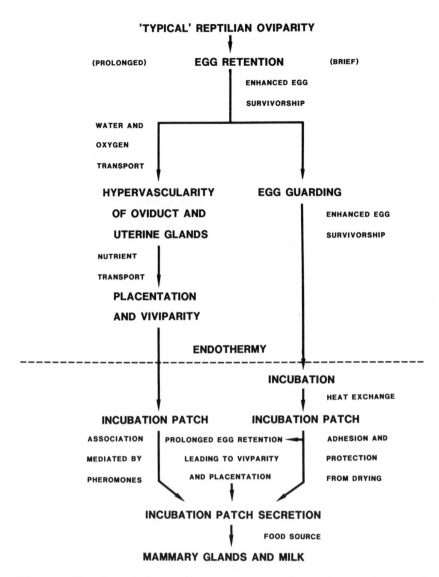

'TYPICAL' REPTILIAN OVIPARITY

↓

(PROLONGED)   **EGG RETENTION**   (BRIEF)

ENHANCED EGG

SURVIVORSHIP

WATER AND

OXYGEN

TRANSPORT

HYPERVASCULARITY   **EGG GUARDING**

OF OVIDUCT AND

UTERINE GLANDS   ENHANCED EGG

SURVIVORSHIP

NUTRIENT

TRANSPORT

PLACENTATION

AND VIVIPARITY

ENDOTHERMY

INCUBATION

HEAT EXCHANGE

INCUBATION PATCH   **INCUBATION PATCH**

ASSOCIATION   PROLONGED EGG RETENTION →   ADHESION AND

MEDIATED BY   LEADING TO VIVPARITY   PROTECTION

PHEROMONES   AND PLACENTATION   FROM DRYING

INCUBATION PATCH SECRETION

FOOD SOURCE

MAMMARY GLANDS AND MILK

Figure 2. Hypothetical schema of pathways in the evolution of mammalian reproductive traits. All three pathways were open to therapsids at large but were probably not followed to completion by many. At least two pathways were open to the direct ancestors of mammals.

glands, are interrelated by a common dependence on the origin of endothermy. This seems a likely reason why the putative distribution of these features resembles the actual distribution of mammal-like osteological features, which arose independently in different synapsid lines to form a variety of combinations (Olson, 1944, 1959). Reproduction, however, is even less directly reflected by osteology than is body temperature, and so is less clearly indicated by fossils. In consequence, reproductive characters are localized as to time of origin chiefly by reference to their varying relationships to the advent of endothermy.

Some widely accepted osteological indicators of endothermy are the elaboration of Haversian systems in cortical bone, the development of a secondary palate, modification of dentitions, and small body size. Elaboration of Haversian systems indicates extensive development of secondary bone, hence rapid growth rates and high metabolic rates (de Ricqles, 1974). A secondary palate separates food and air passage in the mouth so that feeding does not interfere with respiration, which implies increased ventilation required by endothermy (e.g., Stahl, 1967; Bennett, 1973). Differentiation of relatively homodont dentitions into incisiform, caniniform, and molariform teeth suggests more elaborate buccal processing of food for greater energy yield, as required by endothermy. The modification of tooth replacement (Hopson, 1973) from many sets (polyphydonty) to two (diphyodonty) may be related to suckling and the onset of rapid growth rates occasioned by endothermy (Brink, 1956). The supplanting of the reptilian mode of alternate tooth replacement by a mode in which molars were replaced from front to back—reflecting the more accurate occlusion of mammalian chewing (Crompton and Jenkins, 1973)—also indicates more nearly endothermic metabolic rates. Small body size, as manifest in late cynodonts, is construed as an indicator of endothermy of mammalian grade as it relates to the onset of a crepuscular or nocturnal habit (McNab, 1978; Crompton, Taylor, and Jagger, 1978).

No one of these above features, by itself, indicates endothermy. To the extent that all of them do so collectively, the manifestation of endothermy must have been highly variable in therapsids, and advent of the definitive mammalian condition protracted. The following is an approximate timing of relevant events in the evolution of synapsid endothermy:

Early Late Permian. Haversian patterns indicate a difference between pelycosaurs and therapsids (de Ricqles, 1974). The pattern of pelycosaurs is a reliable indicator of ectothermy because it conforms to the pattern of living ectotherms, as does much else of pelycosaur structure. There is less consensus in regard to the thermoregulatory systems of therapsids, that of primitive forms being regarded as transitional to endothermy (de Ricqles, 1980). A bony secondary palate appears in dicynodonts, which, however, are highly specialized for herbivory and show few mammal-like trends in their cranial osteology. A secondary palate is lacking in contemporary dinocephalians, pristerognathid therocephalians, and gorgonopsians. Much modification of ancestral dentitions is evident in dicynodonts, dinocephalians, gorgonopsians, and whaitsiid therocephalians, but none of it is especially mammal-like.

Late Late Permian. A body secondary palate, accompanied by other mammal-like trends in skull structure, appears in advanced therocephalians and primitive cynodonts. Differentiation of dentition into mammal-like incisiform, caniniform, and molariform patterns takes place in bauriid therocephalians and cynodonts, but these animals remain polyphodont. The earliest bauriids and cynodonts are small animals, as are many of their contemporaries, but they give rise to forms of moderate to large size in the Early and Middle Triassic.

Late Triassic. Diphyodonty, accompanied by distinctively small size and a squamoso-dentary joint, appears in late derivatives of the cynodont lineage.

Egg retention could have appeared among synapsids at any time during their history, from the first pelycosaurs in the Early Pennsylvanian to the last therapsids at the end of the Triassic, irrespective of degree of endothermy. At the outset, it would have been a facultative response to local extremes of rainfall or temperature, as it is in extant reptiles (Guillette, 1981a). In those lines in which egg retention became obligate, true viviparity, accompanied by chorioallantoic and choriovitelline placentation, could be expected. Which synapsids, pelycosaurian or therapsid, became viviparous are not known, but both groups may have been as diverse with respect to egg disposal as are living squamates. Nor do monotremes necessarily indicate that the cynodont lineage was exempt from this propensity to experiment, for they may be merely a surviving trace of cynodont diversity.

Egg guarding and nest care were presumably no less common among pelycosaurs before the end of the Early Permian than they are now among ectothermic tetrapods. Such behavior would have become more widespread during the Late Permian to the extent that rising metabolic rates, in the transition to therapsids, enhanced the survival value of contact between mother and eggs or nestlings. True incubation seems unlikely among the earlier therapsids, not because they may have been ectothermic, but because of their large size. However, even the largest could have manipulated eggs and young in the manner of living crocodilians. Egg guarding and nest care probably gave rise to true incubation of eggs or brooding of nestlings around the end of the Permian, when small bauriid therocephalians and primitive cynodonts were showing signs of heightened metabolic rates and, therefore, more constant body temperatures.

Maternal care of hatchlings or live-born young would have followed, incidental to incubation, especially if pheromones from the brood patch prolonged the association between mother and young (Duvall, this volume). Brink (1955) suggests that the fossil association of two individuals of the galesaurid cynodont *Thrinaxodon,* one mature and the other immature and about one-third the size, reflects a life association of mother and partly grown young. These specimens date from the earliest Triassic.

In conclusion, it seems likely that by the end of the Late Permian, some therapsids had evolved viviparity with simple, noninvasive placentation, while others remained oviparous. They would have tended to utilize the rudiments of homeothermy or endothermy for prolonged care of offspring, whether in or out of the egg. In time, the maternal secretions in some cynodont lineages may have become nutritive, but it is doubtful that at first such material could be called milk. The first appearance of suckling, and therefore of mammalian lactation, can be dated no earlier than early in the Late Triassic by the first appearance of diphyodonty and a squamoso-dentary joint. At present, refinements, such as invasive placentation, alecithal eggs, and teats, can be dated no closer than the first appearance of Theria, in the Late Cretaceous.

Acknowledgments

The primary author would like to thank Richard E. Jones, Hobart M. Smith, David Duvall, and Jason A. Lillegraven for their comments concerning portions of this manuscript, as well as for the many discussions concerning therapsid reproduction. The research on *Sceloporus aeneus* was supported by grants from the University of Colorado Museum and a doctoral dissertation improvement grant for NSF (DEB 80:01968). Thanks are due also to Dolores E. Larkie and Mary E. Parrish for their cheerful cooperation, respectively, in the retyping of manuscript and the preparation of illustration.

References

Ackerman, R. A.
1981. Oxygen consumption by sea turtle *(Chelonia caretta)* eggs during development. *Physiol. Zool.* 54:316–24.

Arslan, M.; Zaidi, P.; Lobo, J.; Zaidi, A. A.; and Quizi, M. H.
1978. Steriod levels in preovulatory and gravid lizards *(Uromastrix hardwicki)*. *Gen. Comp. Endocrinol.* 34:300–303.

Bauchot, R.
1965. La Placentation chez les Reptiles. *Ann. Biol.* 4:547–75.

Bellairs, R.
1971. *Developmental Process in Higher Vertebrates.* Coral Gables, Fla.: University of Miami Press.

Bennett, A. F.
1973. Blood physiology and oxygen transport during activity in two lizards, *Varanus gouldi* and *Sauromalus hispidus*. *Comp. Biochem. and Physiol.* 46A:653–71.

Blackburn, D. G.; Vitt, L. J.; and Beuchat, C. A.
1981. Nutritive viviparity and placentation in the skink *Mabuya heathi.* Unpub. Abst. Joint Annual meeting Society for the Study of Amphibians and Reptiles and the Herptotlogist's League, Memphis State University, August 4–14.

Boyd, M. M. M.
1943. The oviduct, foetal membranes and placentation in *Hoplodactylus maculatus* Gray. *Proc. Zool. Soc. London* 112A:65–104.

Brink, A. S.
1955. Note on a very tiny specimen of *Trinaxodon liorhinus*. *Palaeo. Africana* 3:73–76.
1956. Speculations on some advanced mammalian characteristics in the higher mammal-like reptiles. *Palaeo. Africana* 4:77–96.

Bustard, H. R.
1969. The micro-environment of a natural lizard nest. *Copeia* (1969):536–39.

Case, T. J.
1978. Endothermy and parental care in the terrestrial vertebrates. *Amer. Natur.* 112:861–74.

Cate-Hoedemaker, N. J.
1933. Beitrage zur Kenntnis der Plazentation bein Haien und Reptillien. *Zschr. Zellforsch. mikr-Anat.* 18:299–345.

Chudinov, P. K.
1968. Structure of the integuments of thermorphs. *Doklady Akad. Nauk SSSR* 179:207–10. (Translation by Amer. Geol. Inst.).

Clark, H.
1953. Eggs, egg-laying and incubation of the snake *Elaphe emoryi* (Baird and Girard). *Copeia* (1953):90–92.

Colbert, E. H.
1980. *Evolution of the Vetebrates,* 3d ed. New York: J. Wiley and Sons.

Crompton, A. W.; and Jenkins, F. A. Jr.
1973. Mammals from reptiles: a review of mammalian origins. *Ann. Rev. Earth and Planetary Sci.* 1:131–55.

Crompton, A. W., and Jenkins, F. A., Jr.,
1979. Origin of mammals. In *Mesozoic Mammals: the First Two-Thirds of Mammalian History,* ed. J. A. Lillegraven, Z. Kielan-Jaworowska, and W. A. Clemens, pp. 59–73. Berkeley: University of California Press.

Crompton, A. W.; Taylor, C. R.; and Jagger, J. A.
1978.   Evolution of homeothermy in mammals. *Nature* 272(5651):333–36.

Darwin, C.
1859.   *The Origin of Species by Means of Natural Selection*. London: John Murray.

Fawcett, J. D.
1975.   Effects of season, ovariectomy and hormone replacement therapy on the oviduct of *Anolis carolinensis* (Reptilia; Iguanidae). Ph.D. dissertation, University of Colorado, 1975.

Fitch, A. V.
1964.   Temperature tolerances of embryonic *Eumeces*. *Herpetologica* 20:184–87.

Fitch, H. S.
1954.   Life history and ecology of the five-lined skink, *Eumeces fasciatus*. *Univ. Kans. Publ. Mus. Nat. Hist.* 8:1–156.

Fitch, H. S.
1970.   Reproductive cycles in lizards and snakes. *Univ. Kans. Mus. Nat. Hist. Misc. Publ.* 52:1–156.

Goin, C. J.; Goin, O. B.; and Zug, G. R.
1978.   *Introduction to Herpetology*, 3d ed. San Francisco: W. H. Freeman and Company.

Griffiths, M.
1968.   *Echidnas*. Oxford: Pergamon Press.

Guillette, L. J., Jr.
1981a.   Reproductive strategies and the evolution of viviparity in two allopatric populations of the Mexican lizard, *Sceloporus aeneus*. Ph.D. dissertation, University of Colorado, Dissertation Abst. 8122285.
1981b.   On the occurrence of oviparous and viviparous forms of the Mexican lizard, *Sceloporus aeneus*. *Herpetologica* 37:11–15.
1982a.   The evolution of viviparity and placentation in the high elevation, Mexican lizard, *Sceloporus aeneus*. *Herpetologica* 38:94–103.
1982b.   Effects of gravity on the metabolism of the reproductively bimodal lizard, *Sceloporus aeneus*. *J. Exptl. Zool.* 223:33–36.

Guillette, L. J., Jr.; Jones, R. E.; Fitzgerald, K. T.; and Smith, H. M.
1980.   Evolution of viviparity in the lizard genus *Sceloporus*. *Herpetologica* 36:201–15.

Guillette, L. J., Jr.; Spielvogel, S.; and Moore, F. L.
1981.   Luteal development, placentation and plasma progesterone concentration in the viviparous lizard *Sceloporus jarrovi*. *Gen. Comp. Endocrinol.* 43:20–29.

Hoffman, L. H.
1970.   Placentation in the garter snake *Thamnophis sirtalis*. *J. Morphol.* 131:57–88.

Hogarth, P. J.
1976.   *Viviparity*. Baltimore, Md.: University Park Press.
1978.   *Biology of Reproduction*. New York: Harcourt Press, Inc.

Hopson, J. A.
1973.   Endothermy, small size and the origin of mammalian reproduction. *Amer. Natur.* 107:446–52.

Hutchinson, V. H.; Dowling, H. G.; and Vinegar, A.
1966.   Thermoregulation in a brooding female Indian python, *Python molurus birittatus*. *Science* 151:694–96.

Jones, R. E.
1971.   The incubation patch of birds. *Biol. Rev.* 46:315–39.

Jones, R. E., and Guillette, L. J.
1982.   Hormonal control of oviposition and parturition in lizards. *Herpetologica* 38:80–93.

Kasturirangan, L. R.
1952.   The allantoplacenta of the sea-snake *Hydrophis cyanocinctus* Daudin. *J. Zool. Soc. India* 3:277–90.

Kurten, B.
1971.   *The Age of Mammals*. New York: Columbia University Press.

Lehrman, D. S.
1961.   Gonadal hormones and parental behavior in birds and infrahuman mammals. In *Sex and Internal Secretions,* vol. 2, ed. W. C. Young. Baltimore: Williams and Wilkins Co.

Licht, P. and Moberly, W. R.
1965.   Thermal requirements of embryonic development in the tropical lizard *Iguana iguana*. *Copeia* (1965):515–17.

Lillegraven, J. A.
1969.   Latest Cretaceous mammals of the upper part of the Edmonton Formation of Alberta, Canada, and review of marsupial-placental dichotomy in mammalian evolution. *Univ. Kans. Paleont. Contrbs. Art.* 50 (Vertebrata 12):1–122.
1975.   Biological considerations of the marsupial-placental dichotomy. *Evolution* 29:707–22.
1979.   Reproduction in Mesozoic mammals. In *Mesozoic Mammals: The First Two-Thirds of Mammalian History,* ed. J. A. Lillegraven, Z. Kielan-Jaworowska and W. A. Clemens. Berkeley: University of California Press.

Long, C. A.
1969.   The origin and evolution of mammary glands. *BioScience* 19:519–23.
1972.   Two hypotheses on the origin of lactation. *Amer. Natur.* 106:141–44.

McNab, B. K.
1978. The evolution of endothermy in the phylogeny of mammals. *Amer. Natur.* 112:1–21.

Marshall, L. G.
1979. Evolution of metatherian and eutherian (mammalian) characters: a review based on cladistic methodology. *Zool. J. Linn. Soc.* 66:369–410.

Mead, R. A.; Eroschenko, V. P.; and Highfill, D. R.
1981. Effects of progesterone and estrogen on the histology of the oviduct of the garter snake, *Thamnophis elegans*. *Gen. Comp. Endocrinol.* 45:345–54.

Morriss, G.
1975. Placental evolution and embryonic nutrition. In *Comparative Placentation: Essays in Structure and Function*, ed. D. H. Steven. New York: Academic Press.

New, D. A. T.
1973. Studies on mammalian fetuses *in vitro* during the period of organogenesis. In *The Mammalian Fetus in Vitro*, ed. C. R. Austin. London: Chapman and Hall.

Noble, G. K. and Mason, E. R.
1933. Experiments on the brooding habits of the lizards *Eumeces* and *Ophisaurus*. *Amer. Mus. Nov.* 619:1–29.

Olson, E. C.
1944. Origin of mammals based upon the cranial morphology of the therapsid suborders. *Geol. Soc. Amer., Spec. Pap.* 55:1–136.
1959. The evolution of mammalian characters. *Evolution* 13:344–53.

Packard, G. C.; Tracy, C. R.; and Roth, J. J.
1977. The physiological ecology of reptilian eggs and embryos, and the evolution of viviparity within the class Reptilia. *Biol. Rev.* 52:71–105.

Padykula, H. A.; Deren, J. J.; and Wilson, T. H.
1966. Development of structure and function in the mammalian yolk sac. I. Developmental morphology and vitamin B12 uptake of rat yolk sac. *Dev. Biol.* 13:311–48.

Pearson, J.
1949. Placentation of Marsupialia. *Proc. Linn. Soc. London* 161:1–9.

Pond, C. M.
1977. The significance of lactation in the evolution of mammals. *Evol.* 31:177–99.

Pooley, A., and Gans, C.
1976. The Nile crocodile. *Sci. Amer.* 234:114–24.

Rand, A. S.
1972. The temperatures of *Iguana* nests ad their relation to incubation optima and to nesting sites and season. *Herpetologica* 28:252–53.

Raynaud, A.
1961. Morphogenesis of the mammary gland. In *Milk: The Mammary Gland and its Secretion*, vol. 1, ed. S. K. Kon and A. T. Cowie. New York: Academic Press.

Ricqles, A. J. de.
1974. Evolution of endothermy: histological evidence. *Evol. Theory* 1:51–80.
1980. Tissue structures of dinosaur bone: functional significance and possible relation to dinosaur physiology. In *A Cold Look at the Warm-Blooded Dinosaurs*, ed. R. D. K. Thomas and E. C. Olson. *AAAS Selected Symposium* 28:103–139. Boulder, Colo.: Westview Press.

Romer, A. S., and Parsons, T. S.,
1977. *The Vertebrate Body*, 5th ed. Philadelphia: W. B. Saunders Co.

Rothchild, I.
1981. The regulation of the mammalian corpus luteum. *Rec. Prog. Horm. Res.* 37:183–298.

Sergeev, A. M.
1940. Researches in the viviparity of reptiles. *Moscow Soc. Nat.* 1–34.

Sharman, G. B.
1961. The embryonic membranes and placentation in five genera of diprotodont marsupials. *Proc. Zool. Soc. London* 137:197–220.

Shine, R., and Bull, J. J.
1979. The evolution of live-bearing in lizards and snakes. *Am. Nat.* 113:905–23.

Simpson, G. G.
1945. The principles of classification and a classification of mammals. *Bull. Amer. Mus. Nat. Hist.* 85:1–350.

Smith, H. M.
1960. *Evolution of Chordate Structure: An Introduction to Comparative Anatomy*. New York: Holt, Rinehart and Winston, Inc.

Stahl, W. R.
1967. Scaling of respiratory variables in mammals. *J. Appl. Physiol.* 22:453–60.

Stivens, D.
1974. *The Incredible Egg: A Billion Year Journey*. New York: Weybright and Talley.

Tinkle, D., and Gibbons, J. W.
1977. The distribution and evolution of viviparity in reptiles. *Misc. Publ.; Mus. Zool., Univ. Mich.* No. 154.

Tyndale-Biscoe, H.
1973. *Life of Marsupials*. London: Edward Arnold Limited.

Weekes, H. C.
1933. On the distribution, habitat and reproductive

habits of certain European and Australian snakes and lizards with particular regard to their adoption of viviparity. *Proc. Linn. Soc. N.S.W.* 58:270–74.

1935. A review of placentation among reptiles with particular regard to the function and evolution of the placenta. *Proc. Zool. Soc. London* (1935):625–45.

Yaron, Z.

1977. Embryo-maternal interrelations in the lizard *Xantusia vigilis*. In *Reproduction and Evolution*. ed. J. H. Calaby and C. H. Tyndale-Brscoe. Canberra: Australian Academy of Science.

TRANSITION,
ADVANCED CYNODONTS
TO MAMMALS

HERBERT R. BARGHUSEN

Departments of Oral Anatomy and Anatomy
Colleges of Dentistry and Medicine
University of Illinois Medical Center
Chicago, Illinois 60612

On the Evolutionary Origin of the Therian Tensor Veli Palatini and Tensor Tympani Muscles

Introduction

Cynodonts show osteological changes in the lower jaw that indicate the partial acquisition of a mammalian arrangement of trigeminal jaw musculature (Barghusen, 1968). The characteristic morphology of the mammalian masseter and temporal muscles is largely established within this group, but other parts of the trigeminal jaw-elevating musculature were differentiated as in extant reptiles. Whatever the fate of these reptilian muscles during the evolution of mammalian trigeminal patterns, it is evident that many of the changes must have taken place after the appearance of definitive mammals.

This paper is concerned with the fate of the cynodont posterior pterygoid musculature (*sensu* Barghusen, 1973), reconstructed with characteristic reptilian origins and insertions in the cynodont, *Thrinaxodon* (Barghusen, 1968). Reptilian pterygoideus musculature has been suggested (e.g., Brock, 1938; Parrington and Westoll, 1940) as the source of the mammalian tensor veli palatini and tensor tympani muscles. This view is supported here, and an attempt is made to specify more completely the evidence for this transformation and the details of the process. Interpretations are also advanced concerning the evolutionary origin of the mammalian soft palate and auditory tube, to which the derivation of the mammalian tensors, from the reptilian posterior pterygoid muscle, is intimately related.

Ventral Aspect of the Cynodont Skull

General osteology

The ventral aspect of the skull of the moderately advanced cynodont *Thrinaxodon* (Fig. 1B) shows

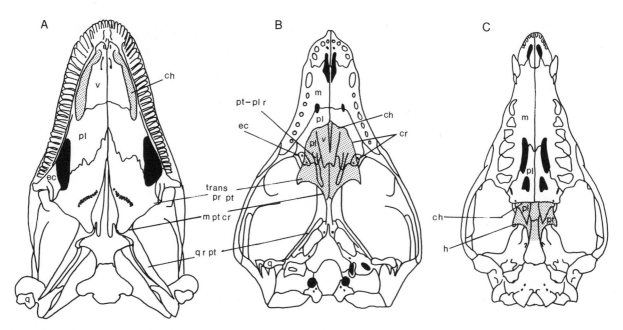

Figure 1. Ventral views of the skull to show the osseous morphology of the palate, nasopharynx, and pterygoid bones. **A,** the lizard *Ctenosaura;* **B,** the cynodont *Thrinaxodon;* and **C,** the therian *Didelphis.* In B and C, the extent of the nasopharynx is indicated by stippling. (Skull outlines in A, after Oelrich 1956; B, after Parrington, 1946.)

Key: **ch,** osseous choanal opening; **cr,** crest for the attachment of the soft palate; **ec,** ectopterygoid; **h,** hamulus of the therian pterygoid bone; **m,** maxilla; **m pt cr,** medial pterygoid crest for the attachment of the posterior pterygoid muscle; **pl,** palatine; **pt,** therian pterygoid; **pt-pl r,** pterygopalatine ridge; **q,** quadrate; **q r pt,** quadrate ramus of the reptilian pterygoid; **trans pr pt,** transverse process of pterygoid; **v,** vomer.

a combination of mammalian and reptilian features. Anteriorly, the oral cavity is separated from the nasal passages by an osseous secondary palate formed by the premaxilla, maxilla, and palatine bones, as in mammals (Fig. 1B, C). Posteriorly, however, the reptilian pterygoid bones approximate the configuration of extant lizards (Fig. 1A, B). The transverse processes (Fig. 1B) are prominent in all cynodonts, and in primitive and moderately advanced members of this group, quadrate rami (Fig. 1B) extend posterolaterally toward the quadrates, as in reptiles generally.

The vaulted region immediately behind the internal nares (Fig. 1B, C) and in front of the posterior edge of the transverse processes, occupies a position similar to the nasopharynx in therian mammals (stippled regions, Fig. 1B, C). The roof and walls of this vault are formed by parts of the vomer, palatine, and ectopterygoid and by the palatine rami of the pterygoid bones.

Reconstruction of posterior pterygoid muscle

Cynodonts show evidence strongly indicating the presence of a posterior pterygoid muscle as in extant reptiles (Barghusen, 1968, 1973, 1976). In *Thrinaxodon* (Fig. 2) the origin of this muscle mass is reconstructed as a tendinous attachment to the posterior edge of the transverse process,

including a heavy tendinous tie to the ventrolateral tip of the process. The origin extends onto the medial pterygoid crest (Fig. 2) and then onto the quadrate ramus. The insertion is reconstructed as attaching to the posteroventral sur-

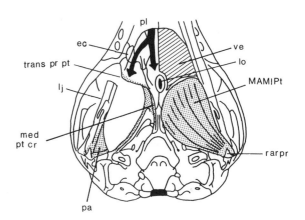

Figure 2. Ventral view of the skull and lower jaws of *Thrinaxodon* to show the reconstructed velum and posterior pterygoid muscle. The arrows indicate air passages. The stippled area on the right side of the skull indicates the areas of bony attachment of the reconstructed posterior ptyerygoid muscle.

Key: **lj,** lower jaw; **lo,** laryngeal opening; **MAMlPt,** posterior pterygoid muscle; **med pt cr,** medial ptyergoid crest **pa,** prearticular; **r ar pr,** retroarticular process of the articular; **ve,** velum. Other abbreviations as in Figure 1.

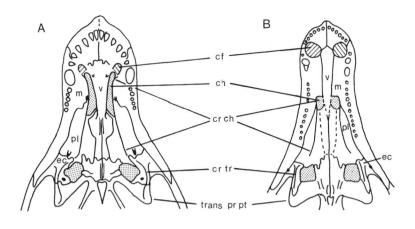

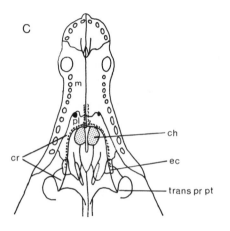

Figure 3. Ventral views of the palatal area to show structures pertinent to the reconstruction of the velum in therocephalians and cynodonts. **A,** the therocephalian *Promoschorhynchus;* **B,** the therocephalian *Lycideops,* showing an osseous secondary palate anteriorly (skull outlines in A and B after Mendrez, 1975); **C,** the cynodont *Cynognathus.*

Key: **cf,** fossa for the reception of the lower canine; **cr ch,** choanal crest; **cr tr,** ectopterygoidal crest. Other abbreviations as in Figure 1.

face of the lower jaw (Fig. 2) immediately adjacent to the jaw articulation. The bones involved are the articular, including at least part of its retroarticular process (Fig. 2), and the prearticular (Fig. 2). Allin (1975) has laid to rest the contention that the insertion also included the lateral surface of the body of the angular in therapsids (e.g., Barghusen, 1973).

Reconstruction of soft palate

Two osteological features associated with the vaulted region in cynodonts suggest the concentrated attachment of soft tissue. The first of these are the longitudinally oriented pterygopalatine ridges (Fig. 1B), which are found, one on either side, within the vaulted region stippled in Figure 1B. Parrington and Westoll (1940) and Fourie (1974) have interpreted these ridges as the site of attachments of a velum. In addition, there are two crests (Fig. 1B), one on either side, which form the lateral margins of the vaulted region shown in Figure 1B. Each crest is directly continuous with the posterior edge of the hard secondary palate and is formed on the palatine, ectopterygoid, and pterygoid bones of either side. The crests are very prominent in *Cynognathus*

(Fig. 3C) and *Diademodon;* they are present, but less developed, in all other appropriately preserved and prepared cynodonts that I have examined. Such crests have not, to my knowledge, been interpreted in cynodonts.

Morphological counterparts of these crests, styled *choanal crests* (Fig. 3A, B), have been extensively described by Mendrez (1975) in therocephalians (the sister group to "Cynodontia plus Mammalia"). They are interpreted as evidence of the presence of a soft palate by a number of workers (Broom, 1936; Crompton, 1955; Tatarinov, 1963). Tatarinov's paper is the most complete in giving reasons for the reconstruction, some of which are worth reiterating. First, the crests suggest the attachment of soft tissue; second, the deep groove for the air passage is positioned dorsal to the crests; and third, the choanal crests are continuous with the posterior border of the therocephalian hard secondary palate when this is present (Fig 3B). The third point indicates that the soft palate would be a direct posterior continuation of the hard palate.

The extant lizard *Tupinambis* serves as a model for the reconstruction of a soft secondary palate in therocephalians. A choanal crest (Fig.

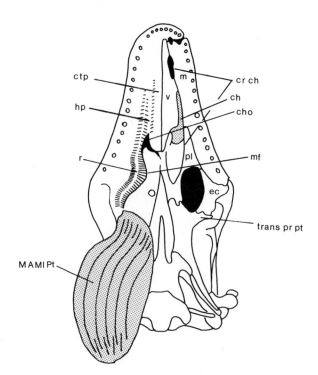

Figure 4. Ventral view of the head of *Tupinambis* to indicate soft structures of the palate. The underlying skeletal framework is shown on the left side of the head.

Key: **cho,** choanal opening posterior to the secondary palate; **ctp,** fibrous tissue pad; **hp,** horizontal fibrous tissue partition; **mf,** medially directed flange of fibrous tissue; **r,** vertically oriented ridge of fibrous tissue. Other abbreviations as in previous figures.

4) extends along most of the medial edge of the palatal surface of the maxilla. This crest forms part of the site of attachment of a horizontal fibrous tissue partition (Fig. 4) projecting medially to meet a median fibrous tissue pad (Fig. 4) supported dorsally by the expanded vomer. These soft partitions, one on either side, plus the vomer and its pad, form a functionally complete secondary palate anteriorly. Moreover, a flange of soft fibrous tissue (Fig. 4) projects medially from the lateral portion of the palatal surface of the palatine and forms an incomplete medially directed partition posterior to the choanal opening (Fig. 4).

Tupinambis also provides an explanation for the vertically oriented ridge (cr tr, Fig. 3A, B; crête transverse, Mendrez, 1975) which in therocephalians runs along the ventral surface of the ectopterygoid back to the base of the lateral terminus of the transverse process of the pterygoid. In *Tupinambis* a vertically oriented ridge (r, Fig. 4) of fibrous tissue, continuous with the medially directed flange, occupies this position. The ridge conforms to the mediodorsal surface of the lower jaw and guides the jaw when it is elevated. The ridge on the palatal surface of the ectopterygoid in therocephalians probably supported a similar fibrous tissue ridge with the same function.

The crests (Figs. 1B, 3C) in cynodonts appear to be a combined version of the choanal and ectopterygoidal crests of therocephalians (Figs. 3A, B, C). Tatarinov's reasons for reconstructing a soft palate in therocephalians apply as well to cynodonts, and *Tupinambis* also serves as a model because the critical anatomical relationships are similar in all three groups.

The structure of therian mammals is consistent with this reconstruction of the cynodont soft palate.[1] In typical therians, the soft palate arises from the continuous edge formed by the posterior border of the osseous secondary palate and the ventral borders of the osseous walls of the nasopharynx. The bones that support this edge are the palatines and the hamular portions of the pterygoids. If the reptilian ectopterygoid is homologous to the hamular moiety of the pterygoid bone in therians (Parrington and Westoll, 1940; Presley and Steel, 1978), the attachment of soft tissue indicated by the crest in cynodonts is exactly the same as the attachment of the soft palate in therians, excepting only that portion of the attachment extending into the cynodont pterygoid bone. The continuity of the crests with the posterior edge of the osseous secondary palate also conforms to the use of a therian model for the reconstruction.[2]

The reconstruction of a soft palate in cynodonts (Fig. 2), with a continuous attachment to the crests and posterior edge of the osseous secondary palate, defines the extent of the cynodont nasopharynx (stippled area, Fig. 1B). Its roof and walls are formed by the vomer, palatal rami of the cynodont pterygoids, and parts of the palatines and ectopterygoids.

A major difference between the cynodont and extant mammalian nasopharynx is the presence of the pterygopalatine ridges in cynodonts. These ridges subdivide the cynodont nasopharynx into median and lateral passages. The roof of the median passage (one half of which is represented by the medial arrow, Fig. 2) is deeply incised anteriorly to the level of the dorsal edge of the internal nares. The median passage and internal nares are directly confluent. Each shallower lateral passage (lateral arrow, Fig. 2) is also continuous with the internal nares via a route passing anterior to the anterior terminus of the pterygopalatine ridge. It appears certain that the median passage led directly to the entrance to the larynx (Fig. 2), which may have been positioned between the posterior termini of the pterygopalatine ridges. If so, the ventral edges of the posterior parts of these ridges may have served for the attachment of that part of the velum found on either side of the superior aspect of the larynx (i.e., a midline opening in the velum housed the superior part of the larynx). In front of the larynx, however, the velum would have extended from one side of the nasopharynx to the other without attaching to the pterygopalatine ridges. The ventral edges of the anterior parts of these ridges are smooth and do not project as far ventrally as the posterior parts. A possible major function of the posterior part of each pterygopalatine ridge was to support the velum and thereby maintain the patency of the lateral passage by resisting the tendency of the velum to collapse under the pressure of food being transmitted through the oropharynx. The significance of the lateral passage will be considered later.

The Derivation of the Mammalian Tensor Veli Palatini and Tensor Tympani Muscles

The tensor veli palatini and tensor tympani are both small muscles in extant therians. Their origins lie close together in the immediate vicinity of the osseous auditory tube (Fig. 5B). The two muscle masses may be connected by an intermediate tendon or, in some cases, directly by muscle fibers (see Kostanecki, 1891, for a review of earlier literature and an extensive description of these muscles in therian mammals). The proximity of the two muscles, and their innervation by the same branch of the mandibular division of the trigeminal nerve, suggest the derivation of the mammalian tensors from a single muscle mass.

The insertions of the therian tensors suggest

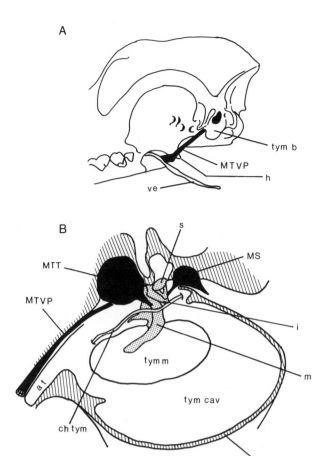

Figure 5. The tensor veli palatini and tensor tympani muscles in *Canis:* **A,** lateral aspect of the skull with the tensor veli palatini shown changing direction at the hamulus to enter the soft palate (displaced ventrally); and **B,** medial aspect of the right middle ear region showing the tensor muscles. (Outline in A, after Miller et al, 1964; in B, after Getty, 1975.)

Key: **at,** auditory tube; **ch tym,** chorda tympani nerve; **i,** incus; **m,** malleus; **MS,** stapedius muscle; **MTT,** tensor tympani muscle; **MTVP,** tensor veli palatini muscle; **s,** stapes; **tym b,** tympanic bulla; **tym cav,** tympanic cavity; **tym m,** tympanic membrane. Other abbreviations as in previous figures.

that the muscle in question was the cynodont posterior pterygoid muscle. The insertion of the tensor tympani, on the malleus at the base of the manubrium (Fig. 5B), is directly comparable to that of the posterior pterygoid reconstructed on the articular (= malleus), including the base of the retroarticular process (= manubrium). The insertion of the therian tensor veli palatini approximates the lateral most part of the origin of the posterior pterygoid. In therians, the tensor of the soft palate inserts by way of a tendon on the tip of the hamulus (= reptilian ectopterygoid) and/or on the soft palate proper, where it forms the palatal aponeurosis (Fig. 5A). In all cases, the tendon of insertion of part or all of the muscle uses the hamulus as a trochlea to change direction to enter the soft palate from its lateral side. Presumably, when the origin of the posterior pterygoid was eliminated by reduction of the reptilian pterygoid bone (see below), a small part of the muscle attachment was transferred to the nearby ectopterygoid and the lateral part of the soft palate (Fig. 2).

The fundamental assumption in the following discussion is that the tensor veli palatini muscle is not a therian neomorph but represents musculature present in cynodonts. This issue is raised because a tensor veli palatini muscle has not been described in monotremes. Conceivably, monotremes represent the primitive mammalian condition, in which the proximal portion of the posterior pterygoid muscle (i.e., that portion closest to the cynodont soft palate and ectopterygoid) was lost. At this stage of our knowledge, however, an equally likely and more parsimonious explanation is that the absence of a tensor veli palatini muscle in monotremes is a derived condition. Monotremes must be investigated more thoroughly to evaluate the possibility that the pterygospinosus muscle (Schulman, 1906), and the pharyngeal belly of the tensor tympani muscle (Eschweiler, 1899), are both remnants of a muscle mass that corresponds to the tensor of the soft palate in therians and the proximal portion of the posterior pterygoid in cynodonts.

If the reptilian posterior pterygoid gave rise to both therian tensors, it is reasonable that its proximal portion gave rise to the tensor veli palatini and its distal portion to the tensor tympani. If so, the following three changes must have taken place during the transition from cynodonts to extant therian mammals:

1. The pterygoideus musculature must have become much smaller. In their comprehensive study of the evolutionary origin of the mammalian palate, Parrington and Westoll (1940, Fig. 14) begin with a reconstructed pterygoid muscle in a cynodont. Their reconstruction differs in detail from that presented here for the posterior pterygoid muscle, but the two reconstructions are close enough so that their conclusions, explicit or implicit, apply to the present study. They relate the reduction in size of the reptilian pterygoid muscle to the reduction in size of the cynodont pterygoid and articular bones, which took place in the transition from cynodonts to mammals. Most of the areas of origin of the muscle from the reptilian pterygoid bones were eliminated during the transition (c.f. Fig. 1B, C, and

Fig. 2). The quadrate ramus was eliminated in advanced cynodonts. Most of the muscle-bearing portions of the transverse process must have disappeared because the ventrolateral part of the transverse process was replaced by the ectopterygoid in therians. Finally, the medial pterygoid crest and other immediately adjacent areas of muscle attachment were eliminated; Parrington and Westoll (1940) note a shortening of the skull in this region during the transition from the cynodont to the mammalian condition. It appears that the only portion of the cynodont pterygoid bone remaining in therian mammals is the palatal process, which in cynodonts and therians participates in the formation of the roof and wall of the nasopharynx.

2. The proximal portion of the posterior pterygoid muscle must have shifted its attachment from the transverse process to the ectopterygoid and lateral portion of the soft palate. Given the reconstruction of a soft palate, transfer of part of the muscle to the nearby velum could easily have occurred in cynodonts or any subsequent group of mammals. An implication of this putative shift in attachment is that during the formation of the tensor veli palatini only the lateral portion of the proximal part of the cynodont posterior pterygoid muscle survived (cf. Fig. 6A, C), because the ectopterygoid (= hamulus) is lateral in position in both cynodonts and mammals and serves for the attachment of, or as a trochlea for, the entire tensor muscle mass.

3. New bony attachments to the alisphenoid and petrosal must have been established somewhere along the midlength of the posterior pterygoid muscle. The development of these attachments would have established the areas of origin of both therian tensors. When this happened is unknown, but it may have been in association with the development of the narrow tubular middle and distal portions of the mammalian auditory tube.

Evolutionary Origin of the Entrance and Proximal Part of the Mammalian Auditory Tube

The foregoing inferences are consistent with the following interpretation of the lateral channel of the cynodont nasopharynx, as originally suggested to me by Edgar Allin. The function of the mammalian nasopharynx as an air passageway is twofold: first, it is a passage to the entrance of the larynx; second, it leads to the auditory tube connecting the nasopharynx with the tympanic

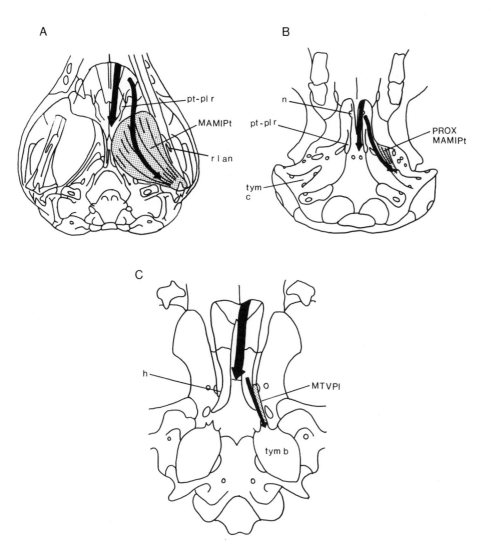

Figure 6. Ventral views of the skull with reconstructed musculature to illustrate the relationship between the lateral naso-pharyngeal passage, developing proximal part of the auditory tube (lateral arrow), and posterior pterygoid muscle. **A,** *Thrinax-odon;* **B,** *Kamptobaatar;* and C, *Canis* (representing a therian mammal with the position of the proximal portion of the auditory tube indicated by the lateral arrow). (Skull outline in B, after Kielan-Jaworowska, 1971.)

Key: **n,** incisure connecting lateral nasopharyngeal passage with internal naris; **PROX MAMIPt,** proximal part of posterior pterygoid muscle; **r l an,** reflected lamina of the angular; **tym c,** tympanic cavity. Other abbreviations as in previous figures.

cavity. Since the larynx is a single midline struc-ture in tetrapods, the median channel of the cy-nodont nasopharynx clearly led to it. There is reason to believe that each lateral channel serves the function of the mammalian nasophar-ynx, and reflects the development of an intercon-nection between the nasopharynx and the audi-tory structures.

In cynodonts, the lateral channel leads directly into a space, the sulcus pharyngis submandibu-laris (Shute, 1956), ventral to the ventromedial surface of the posterior pterygoid muscle (lateral arrow, Fig. 6A). As reconstructed by Shute

(1956) the sulcus pharyngis submandibularis ex-tended laterally from the pharynx, subjacent to the posterior pterygoid muscle, into a space, the angular cleft (see Allin, 1975), occupying the area lateral to the body of the angular bone. Shute (1956) suggested that the sulcus pharyn-gis submandibularis is implicated in the forma-tion of the mammalian auditory tube. Allin (1975) has concluded that the angular cleft and the adjacent postdentary bones of the lower jaw functioned in the reception of airborne sound. The implication of this is that the angular cleft developed into at least part of the mammalian middle ear cavity (Westoll, 1943; Shute, 1956). Therefore, given the conclusions of Shute and Allin, the evidence of the lateral nasopharyngeal passage suggests that a specialized interconnection between nasopharynx and auditory structures was already established in cynodonts.

Possible evidence of a similar interconnection is found in the illustrations and photographs of the multituberculate *Kamptobaatar* published by Kielan-Jaworowska (1971, fig. 4 and pl. 1). The morphology of the osseous nasopharynx illustrated in that paper is reinterpreted here (fig. 6B) as an elaboration of the condition in cynodonts.

In *Kamptobaatar,* the nasopharyngeal region consists of four passages—two medial and two lateral. The medial passages (one of which is indicated by the medial arrow, fig. 6B) are separated from each other along the anterior two thirds of their lengths by a midline partition formed by the vomer. Anteriorly each is confluent with the internal naris. Posteriorly these two passages are confluent with each other. The lateral passages (one of which is indicated by the lateral arrow, fig. 6B) are separated from the medial by strongly developed ridges (pt.-pl.r., fig. 6B) formed by the pterygoid and perhaps the palatine bones, and so styled "pterygopalatine". Each lateral passage communicates with the medial passage and internal naris via a specialized rounded incisure (n. fig. 6B), as well as by a gap anterior to the pterygopalatine ridge. The medial passages of *Kamptobaatar* clearly led to the midline glottis, which perhaps lay directly ventral to the region where the two passages join posteriorly. The medial channels are then a paired version of the cynodont median passage, and the pterygopalatine ridges occupy a position equivalent to the cynodont pterygopalatine ridges. Therefore the lateral passages of *Kamptobaatar* appear to be equivalent to the cynodont lateral passages albeit more specialized in their connection with the internal nares. Moreover, since the ventral edge of the lateral wall of each lateral passage is directly continuous with the posterior margin of the osseous secondary palate, this edge would mark the attachment of a velum. This inference plus the fact that the pterygopalatine ridge does not continue to the posterior margin of the osseous secondary palate strengthens the conclusion that each lateral passage was included in the nasopharynx of *Kamptobaatar* as were the lateral passages in cynodonts.

The lateral passage in *Kamptobaatar* exists in combination with what was, apparently, a fully formed mammalian middle ear cavity. Except for the coronoid bone in one genus, postdentary bones are unknown as such in multituberculates (Clemens and Kielan-Jaworowska, 1979). Presumably they had been converted into the tympanic annulus and ear ossicles as in monotremes and therian mammals. If so, the sulcus pharyngis submandibularis was no longer involved with part of the adult lower jaw as it had been in cynodonts, but had presumably followed the postdentary bones into the definitive mammalian tympanic cavity and formed part of the auditory tube (cf. Shute, 1956). In *Kamptobaatar,* the lateral nasopharyngeal channel leaves the osseous confines of the nasopharynx in the position where the entrance to the auditory tube is found in mammals. Posterior to the pterygopalatine ridge, the space into which the lateral passage leads can easily be interpreted as having flared laterally, thus leading directly to the tympanic cavity (lateral arrow, Fig. 6B). Alternative explanations of the lateral nasopharyngeal passage and the space into which it opens are not evident.

The conclusions concerning the lateral nasopharyngeal passage[3] and the proximal portion of the developing auditory tube integrate well with the inferred evolutionary development of the mammalian tensors. In cynodonts, the lateral nasopharyngeal passage leads directly to the space ventral to the ventromedial surface of the proximal portion of the posterior pterygoid muscle (Fig. 6A). This space is part of the sulcus pharyngis submandibularis, which would turn laterally toward the angular cleft at the level of the reflected lamina of the angular (Fig. 6A), and then pass under the distal end of the muscle. The space immediately behind the lateral nasopharyngeal passage is in the right position for the proximal portion of the mammalian auditory tube. It would come to lie progressively more medial to the posterior pterygoid muscle (Fig. 6B), as more medial portions of the latter were eliminated by reduction of the cynodont pterygoid bone. The space would then bear exactly the same relationship to the proximal remainder of the posterior pterygoid as the therian auditory tube (lateral arrow, Fig. 6C) does to the tensor veli palatini muscle. In addition, the inference that the sulcus pharyngis submandibularis would pass beneath the distal portion of the cynodont posterior pterygoid muscle is also consistent with the spatial relationships between the auditory tube and the tensor tympani in mammals (Shute, 1956). The distal part of the auditory tube lies ventral to the tensor tympani muscle.

Concluding Remark

Finally, the broader aim of this analysis is to call attention to the fact that the derivation of the mammalian tensors has considerable significance for understanding the evolutionary origin and development of the mammalian auditory apparatus as a functional unit. For example, the conclusion drawn by Allin (1975) that the postdentary bones in cynodonts and other therapsids functioned in sound reception indicates that any musculature that attached to these bones may have been important in auditory as well as other functions (e.g., feeding). If the mammalian tensors were derived from the posterior pterygoid muscle, their derivation in mammals may represent the direct continuation of a functional trend established much earlier in synapsids.

Notes

1. At this stage in the analysis, it is uncertain whether the cynodont velum was infiltrated by musculature as in mammals. It may have been composed solely of fibrous tissue. The determination of the composition of the soft palate in cynodonts seems to hinge upon whether or not a superior pharyngeal constrictor was developed. With the exception of the tensor veli palatini muscle, the superior pharyngeal constrictor seems to represent the original source of the extrinsic and intrinsic musculature of the velum (Kostanecki, 1891). An attempt to reconstruct pharyngeal musculature in cynodonts is currently being made by Edgar Allin.

2. Monotremes are not good analogues for the reconstruction of a soft palate in cynodonts because of a specialized condition in which much of the velum has been replaced by bone that results from a posterior extension of the hard palate. The hard palate extends back between the "echidna pterygoids," which Parrington and Westoll (1940) homologize with the reptilian ectopterygoids on the one hand and the therian hamular moieties on the other.

3. No attempt is being made here to homologize the lateral nasopharyngeal passage with any part of the mammalian auditory tube. Its value to the present study is that it provides evidence of a separate airway highly suggestive of a connection of the nasopharynx with the auditory structures.

Acknowledgments

Thanks are due Drs. Edgar Allin, Susan Herring, and Robert Scapino for critical reading of the manuscript. Drs. Edgar Allin and James Hopson discussed issues involved in this study and made many helpful suggestions.

This research was supported by NSF Grant GB-40061

References

Allin, E. F.
1975. Evolution of the mammalian middle ear. *J. Morph.* 147:403–38.

Barghusen, H. R.
1968. The lower jaw of cynodonts (Reptilia, Therapsida) and the evolutionary origin of mammal-like adductor jaw musculature. *Postilla* 116: 1–49.
1973. The adductor jaw musculature of *Dimetrodon* (Reptilia, Pelycosauria). *J. Paleonotol.* 47: 823–34.
1976. Notes on the adductor jaw musculature of *Venjukovia*, a primitive anomodont therapsid from the Permian of the U.S.S.R. Ann. S. Afr. Mus. 69:249–60.

Brock, G. T.
1938. The cranial muscles of the gecko. A general account with a comparison of the muscles in other gnathostomes. *Proc. Zool. Soc. Lond.* Ser. B. 108:735–61.

Broom, R.
1936. On some new genera and species of Karroo fossil reptiles, with notes on some others. *Ann. Transv. Mus. Pretoria* 18:349–86.

Clemens, W. A., and Kielan-Jaworowska, Z.
1979. Multituberculata. In *Mesozoic Mammals: The First Two-Thirds of Mammalian History*, ed. J. A. Lillegraven, Z. Kielan-Jaworowska, and W. A. Clemens. Berkeley: University of California Press.

Crompton, A. W.
1955. A revision of the Scaloposauridae with special reference to kinetism in this family. *Researches Nasionale Mus. Bloemfontein.* 1:150–83.

Eschweiler, R.
1899. Zur vergleichenden Anatomie der Muskeln und der Topographie des Mittelohres verschie-

dener Säugethiere. *Arch. milkroskop. Anat. und Entwicklungsgeschichte* 53:558–622.

Fourie, S.
1974. The cranial morphology of *Thrinaxodon liorhinus* (Seeley). *Ann. S. Afr. Mus.* 65:337–400.

Getty, R.
1975. *Sisson and Grossman's Anatomy of the Domestic Animal.* 5th Edition, 2 volumes. Philadelphia: W. B. Saunders Company.

Kielan-Jaworowska, Z.
1971. Skull structures and affinities of the Multituberculata. *Palaeo. Polonica* 25:5–41.

Kostanecki, K. V.
1891. Zur Morphologie der Tubengaumenmusculatur. *Arch. f. Anat. u. Phys.* 145–81.

Mendrez, C.
1975. Principales variations du palais chez les thérocéphales Sud-Africains (Pristerosauria et Scaloposauria) au cours du Permien Supérieur et du Trias Inférieur. In: *Problèmes actuels de Paleontologie-Évolution des Vertébrés.* Colloque international C. N. R. S., no. 218, Paris.

Miller, M. E., Christensen, G. C., and Evans, H. E.
1964. *Anatomy of the Dog.* Philadelphia: W. B. Saunders Company.

Oelrich, T. M.
1956. The anatomy of the head of *Ctenosaura pectinata* (Iguanidae). *Mus. Zool. Univ. of Michigan Misc. Publ.* 94:1–122.

Parrington, F. R.
1946. On the cranial anatomy of cynodonts. *Proc. Zool. Soc. London* 116:181–97.

Parrington, F. R., and Westoll, T. S.
1940. On the evolution of the mammalian palate. *Phil. Trans. Roy. Soc. London* Ser. B. 230:305–55.

Presley, R., and Steel, F. L. D.
1978. The pterygoid and ectopterygoid in mammals. *Anat. Embryol.* 154:95–110.

Romer, A. S.
1956. *Osteology of the Reptiles.* Chicago: University of Chicago Press.

Schulman, H.
1906. Vergleichende Untersuchungen über die Trigeminus-Musculatur der Monotremen. *Semon's Zoologische Forschungsreisen.* 3:300–400.

Shute, C. C. D.
1956. The evolution of the mammalian eardrum and tympanic cavity. *J. Anat.* 90:261–81.

Tatarinov, L. P.
1963. New Late Permian therocephalian. *Paleont. Zh.* 4:46–94.

Westoll, T. S.
1943. The hyomandibular of *Eusthenopteron* and the tetrapod middle ear. *Proc. Roy. Soc. Lond.* Ser. B. 131:393–414.

H. R. BARGHUSEN

A. W. CROMPTON
Museum of Comparative Zoology
Harvard University
Cambridge, Massachusetts 02138
and

W. L. HYLANDER
Department of Anatomy
Duke University
Durham, North Carolina 27710

Changes in Mandibular Function Following the Acquisition of a Dentary-squamosal Jaw Articulation

Introduction

The purpose of this paper is to discuss the changes in structure of the jaw joint, lower jaw, and dentition in the transition from advanced mammal-like reptiles to early mammals, and to reconstruct the loading of the jaw joint in advanced cynodonts and early mammals. Several conflicting views of the structure and loading of the jaw joint in these forms have been published and are reviewed in this section.

The morphological steps involved in the transition from a reptilian (articular-quadrate) to a mammalian (dentary-squamosal) jaw articulation are documented in a variety of specimens of mammal-like reptiles and early mammals. During the transition, the dentary increased in size at the expense of the accessory jaw bones (i.e., all lower jaw bones with the exception of the dentary) and the quadrate (Crompton, 1963a, b; Barghusen and Hopson, 1970; Crompton, 1972b; Allin, 1975; Crompton and Jenkins, 1979). In advanced cynodonts, an articular process of the dentary lies above the reduced accessory jaw bones; and, in a few specialized therapsids (Crompton, 1963a) and early mammals (Kermack, Mussett, and Rigney, 1973), this process contacts the squamosal to establish a new mammalian dentary-squamosal joint. Subsequent to the establishment of this new jaw articulation, the accessory jaw bones and quadrate become separated from the lower jaw and are included in the middle ear, which lies postero-medially to the dentary-squamosal joint. The structure of the angular, articular, and quadrate bones in an advanced therapsid and a Liassic mammal is remarkably similar to the structure of the tympanic ring, malleus, and incus of a typical mammal lacking a bulla (Allin, 1975; Crompton and Jenkins, 1979). The fossil record has thus confirmed the homologies of the mammalian ear ossicles established by Reichert (1837) and other comparative anatomists (see Goodrich, 1930, for review). An alternative view, recently summarized by Jarvik (1980), holds that the mammalian malleus and incus are derived from the hyoid rather than the mandibular arch. Jarvik claims that mammalian predecessors are of little help in establishing the origin of ear ossicles, but does not discuss the evidence of the fossil record.

In explaining why the dentary became larger while accessory jaw bones and quadrate became smaller, Crompton (1963a, b) postulated a selective advantage in having the adductor muscles insert on the bone bearing the teeth (the dentary) rather than on both dentary and accessories, as in typical reptiles. He suggested that the decrease in the size of the accessory jaw bones implies a progressive decrease in the load-bearing capacity of the articular-quadrate articulation. Reduction of accessories and quadrate was accompanied by dramatic increase in the bulk of adductor musculature in various therapsid lineages, being especially marked in cynodonts. Crompton (1963a, b) held that increase in muscle bulk was accompanied by changes in the organization of the adductor (levator) mass, which, while it increased bite force progressively in various lines, resulted in reduction of the forces to which the jaw articulation was subject.

Barghusen and Hopson (1970) suggested that mammalian organization of adductor muscles produced a temporalis and deep masseter, with a pronounced component of force directed to the rear. When subjected to this force, the articular process of the dentary was forced backwards, deflecting the accessory bones forward and downward, relative to the dentary. To restrict these motions, the contact between the articular process and the accessory jaw bones was strengthened. At the same time, the posterior process of the dentary was extended backward to gain contact with the squamosal, providing a buttress for the dentary, which minimized its tendency to force the postdentary bones forward. Crompton (1972b) showed that in all advanced cynodonts a secondary articulation was established between the surangular and the squamosal before any contact between the dentary and the squamosal

was established. The buttressing between the articular process of the dentary and the accessory jaw bones would, as Barghusen and Hopson (1970) suggested, prevent the accessory jaw bones from being forced forwards and the dentary backwards; the secondary articulation between an accessory jaw bone, the surangular, and the squamosal would help to reduce the backwardly directed force of the adductors being transferred from the lower jaw to the reduced and loosely suspended quadrate.

Kermack, Mussett, and Rigney (1973) compared the jaw joint of *Cynognathus* with that of an early mammal, *Eozostrodon (Morganucodon)*. They claimed that the jaw joint of *Cynognathus* was extremely powerful and did not reflect the reduction apparent in the postdentary bones. They held that reduction of the accessory bones was compensated by development of the articular process of the dentary, which buttressed the still large joint. Applying this line of reasoning to *Eozostrodon* as well as to *Cynognathus*, they viewed the expansion of the dentary and reduction of postdentary bones as a process that strengthened the articulation while it enlarged the insertions of the adductor muscles. Noting the tendency of the carnassial bite of terrestrial fissipedes to invert the mandible, Kermack, Mussett, and Rigney (1973) argued that the primary role of the dentary-squamosal articulation was to resist twisting during unilateral shear. They concluded that teeth and jaw joint are not independent, but that they evolved as parts of an integrated system.

Allin (1975) made an important contribution to the question of the jaw-joint transition. He suggested that in therocephalians, cynodonts, and dicynodonts, a mandibular tympanum was supported by, and included, the reflected lamina of the angular, and was situated anterior to the articular-quadrate jaw joint. He concluded that the middle ear of cynodonts was functionally similar to that of living mammals (especially monotremes). In Liassic mammals such as *Eozostrodon,* the angular, surangular, articular, and prearticular functioned essentially as parts of the middle ear, though they were still flexibly attached to the dentary. In more advanced mammals, these bones became separated from the mandible because the new mammalian dentary-squamosal articulation had taken over the jaw hinge function, which previously had been the role of the articular-quadrate joint. From Allin's thesis that the accessory jaw bones in therapsids were involved in hearing, it follows that progressive reduction in the size of these bones was correlated with improved auditory acuity. The smaller and looser the accessory jaw bones and the quadrate, the better they would transmit vibrations picked up by a mandibular tympanum (Crompton and Parker, 1978), and the better they would respond to higher sound frequencies (Allin, 1975). This implies progressive increase in the control of the forces acting through the reduced joint, suggesting that the reorganization of the jaw muscles in the course of therapsid evolution was related not only to the processing of food, but also to the control of forces acting through a jaw joint that became progressively smaller, relative to skull length.

In *Eozostrodon* and other triconodont mammals, the cochlear housing is a prominent feature of the skull base (Kermack, Mussett, and Rigney, 1981). In small cynodonts, tritylodonts (Sues, personal communication) and tritheledonts, on the other hand, the cochlear housing is not visible on the ventral surface of the skull. Some of the specimens of the latter groups approach the size of Mesozoic mammals, suggesting that the prominent cochlear housing of mammals is not simply the result of their small size. The prominence of the cochlear housing suggests increase in hearing acuity at this stage, which is consistent with the freeing of articular and quadrate from jaw joint function when a dentary-squamosal joint was established (Crompton, 1980). In a detailed description of the skull of *Eozostrodon (Morganucodon)*, Kermack, Mussett, and Rigney (1981) accept Allin's view that therapsid accessory jaw bones could move relative to the dentary, and that they and the homologous bones of *Eozostrodon* were involved in hearing. They reason that it was selection for improvement of high frequency response that freed the articular, quadrate, and stapes from the lower jaw hinge and sharply reduced their size. They cite intensity of selection to explain why this happened several times, but insist that it took place only after the morganucodontid-kuehneotherian level of organization had been attained. Kermack, Mussett, and Rigney argue that prior to and including *Morganucodon* the reptilian hinge is little smaller than in advanced cynodonts, and that the quadrate-articular component did not become smaller while remaining a functional jaw joint.

Bramble (1978), however, followed the traditional view that reduction of the accessory jaw bones and quadrate diminished the ability of the advanced theriodont jaw joint to withstand vertical forces. His suggestion that tensile loading of the jaw would have played a part in therapsid masticatory function supplemented the reasoning of earlier workers (Crompton, 1963a, b; Barghusen and Hopson, 1970), who tended to concentrate on compressive loading. By resolving hypothetical muscle forces acting about the point of bite, Bramble (1978) demonstrated that in all advanced cynodonts the main line of action of the temporalis placed the jaw joint under tension, which helped to balance the compressive forces delivered to the joint by the masseter and pterygoideus musculature. He suggested that compressive and tensile forces acting through the jaw joint could be balanced at all possible bite positions, provided only that differential activity within the temporalis muscle was possible. When the temporalis muscle contracted as a unit, its natural or resolved line of action maximized the moment arm of the coronoid process, but as Bramble pointed out, this line of action could be changed simply by relaxing parts of the temporalis.

This state of affairs would seem as likely in advanced cynodonts as in mammals, whose adductor musculature, except possibly for the medial pterygoid, was probably very similarly oriented (Barghusen, this volume). It is often assumed that during mastication there is little reaction force across the mammalian temporomandibular joint (see reviews by Hylander, 1975, 1978). On the basis of the direction of the bite forces during incisal biting in humans, Hylander (1978) concluded that the lower jaw essentially acts as a lever. In order to maintain static equilibrium, the downwards and backwards directed bite force on the mandible must be associated with a compressive reaction force on the mandibular condyles. These data, coupled with morphological considerations (Hylander, 1975), refute the hypothesis that the mammalian jaw joint is incapable of bearing stress.

Hylander (1979b) placed strain gauges on the lateral surfaces of the subcondylar region of the macaque mandible, and demonstrated four functional aspects of the temporomandibular joint (TMJ) in these animals:

1. The joint is loaded by a compressive reaction force during the power stroke of mastication and incision, and during isometric molar and incisor biting.

2. Average reaction forces at the joint are larger on the contralateral side during both mastication and isometric molar biting.

3. The ipsilateral joint is subject to compres-

sive reaction forces during biting along the premolars and first two molars.

4. The ipsilateral joint is subject to very little compression, no stress, or is loaded in tension during biting along M3.

Hylander's (1979a, b) data on feeding in macaques suggests a great deal of variation in the level of activities of the adductor muscles on the active and balancing sides. During isometric unilateral molar biting in these monkeys, the masseter and medial pterygoid muscle-forces on the active and balancing sides do not differ significantly; whereas during the mastication of soft food, such as apples, the forces on the active side are much greater than those on the balancing side. These data (Hylander, 1979b) suggest that relatively more contralateral (balancing) jaw-muscle activity is required for the comminution of hard objects or tough food than for that of soft food. In another study, mandibular bone-strain and bite-force values indicate that during isometric molar biting, the jaw adductors on the active side are twenty to forty percent more active than on the balancing side.

In addition to characterizing masticatory forces in macaques, which have a fused mandibular symphysis, Hylander (1979b, c) has attempted to infer the relative magnitude of masticatory forces in galagos. This was done indirectly by measuring bite-force and bone-strain values, from which it was concluded that in galagos the ipsilateral TMJ is loaded with the larger net reaction force during isometric molar biting. It may be that, in galagos, during unilateral biting of hard food (contrary to the case of macaques), there was less muscular activity on the balancing side. Preliminary data for isometric biting suggest that the active side generates two to three times more force than the balancing side does.

Weijs and DeJongh (1977) reported that, during chewing, the active side of the mandible is subject to three or four times as much strain as the balancing side. Strains produced by incisal biting are comparable to those produced on the balancing side during chewing, which suggests that it is primarily reaction forces exerted on the lower molars, rather than muscular forces, that caused the strain pattern on the active side. Weijs and DeJongh observe that the difference in transverse distance between the rows of upper and lower molars prevent molar contact on the balancing side through most of the chewing stroke. The forces of the active contralateral

muscles are balanced partially by reaction forces on the active side, which are transmitted through the symphysis because the balancing half of the mandible is supported only by the joint. From these relationships, they conclude that both halves of the jaw are subject to bending and torsional couples.

Weijs and Dantuma (1981), in a detailed analysis of activity in different muscles and in different parts of the same muscle, have shown that, in the rabbit, subtle changes in the timing and level of activity of the adductor and jaw opening muscles on the working and balancing sides can account for the complex movement of the lower jaw relative to the upper. During the power stroke, vertical forces on the balancing side amount to sixty-seven to sixty-nine percent of those on the working side. During incisal biting, the bilateral muscle resultant is about forty percent smaller than in pellet mastication, but reaction forces along both condyles are comparable to those exerted on the balancing condyle during chewing. Weijs and Dantuma conclude that, during chewing, the mandible seems to be supported entirely by the cheek teeth on the working side and the condyle on the balancing side. The condyle on the working side receives a negligible load, and the mandible operates purely as a lever.

Gorniak and Gans (1980) quantified electromyogram (EMG) activity of the adductors and digastric muscles in the cat, and the data show certain similarities to the rabbit data. Mean amplitudes and number of spikes of an entire reduction sequence were significantly greater for working than for balancing adductors. However, when the start, middle, and end of a reduction sequence were compared separately in terms of muscle activity, differences between working and balancing adductors were not always significant, nor were durations of activity per bite. In the cat, as in the rabbit, transverse movement of the mandible, especially during unilateral power stroke, is governed by differential activity of working- and balancing-side muscles. This implies loading of both the working and balancing temporomandibular joints, especially the joint on the balancing side.

It is difficult to avoid the conclusion that during incisal or canine biting, unilateral mastication, or unilateral molar biting, that the condyles are frequently subjected to loads that can approach about half that at the point of bite.

In view of the conflicting reports on the load-bearing capacity of the articular-quadrate articulation of advanced cynodonts, it is necessary to reexamine this articulation in selected cynodonts. Data on jaw-muscle activity and temporomandibular joint function in modern mammals help to assess mandibular function in advanced therapsids and early mammals.

Structure of the Jaw Articulation in Advanced Therapsids and Early Mammals

Thrinaxodon and *Probainognathus,* from the Early and Middle Triassic, respectively, seem in most aspects to represent morphological stages between a Late Permian cynodont, such as *Procynosuchus,* and an early mammal, such as *Eozostrodon (Morganucodon).* In *Thrinaxodon,* the postcanine teeth are remarkably like those of *Eozostrodon* (Crompton and Jenkins, 1968), and there are no obvious skeletal specializations to rule out a position close to the mammalian line (Jenkins, 1971; Jenkins and Parrington, 1976). In *Probainognathus,* an articular facet on the squamosal represents a significant advance in a mammalian direction. The facet appears to be very similar in structure and position to the glenoid of early mammals, although it is in contact with the surangular boss rather than the dentary. This joint was probably invaded by the dentary as the surangular became smaller. The cingular cusps of the postcanine teeth are reduced, suggesting that *Probainognathus* was probably a little removed from the phylogenetic line leading from primitive cynodonts to mammals.

In Figures 1 and 2, the drawings are scaled to lower jaws of the same length to show differences in the relative size of the articular region of different individuals. The specimens of *Thrinaxodon* and *Probainognathus* are about the same size, demonstrating that in the *Thrinaxodon-Probainognathus* sequence both the vertical (Fig. 1) and transverse (Fig. 2) dimensions of the accessory jaw bones and quadrate are reduced. Therefore, the area of the articular surfaces of the articular and surangular, on the one hand, and the quadrate and "glenoid," on the other (Fig 3A), is, in *Probainognathus,* about one-third of what it is in *Thrinaxodon.* This difference obtains even though the volume of adductor muscle, both in absolute and relative terms, was considerably greater in *Probainognathus* than in *Thrinaxodon.*

The accessory jaw complex is deep in *Thrinax-odon* and has a broad contact with the inner surface of the dentary. In *Probainognathus,* on the other hand, the articular, angular, surangular, and prearticular accessory jaw bones form a rod-like structure, most of the dorsal surface of which is overlain by the articular process of the dentary. Both this complex and the quadrate complex seem to have been less tightly bound to the dentary and squamosal, respectively, than in *Thrinaxodon.* This permitted the postdentary rod to rotate about its longitudinal axis. A small surangular boss is present in *Thrinaxodon;* it is directed towards, but does not meet, the articular flange of the squamosal. In *Probainognathus,* the articular flange of the squamosal is greatly enlarged and supports a slightly concave, longitudinally ovate "glenoid," which faces medio-ventrally (Figs. 2, 3A). The position, shape and orientation of the glenoid in *Probainognathus* is almost identical to the glenoid of *Eozostrodon* (Fig. 2, this paper; Kermack, Mussett, and Rigney, 1981) and distinct from the same area of other cynodonts such as *Diademodon, Trirachodon, Cynognathus, Massetognathus* and *Exaeretodon* (Crompton, 1972b). In *Probainognathus,* the basicranial region is wide, measured across the paroccipital processes, but the distance from the fenestra ovalis to the midline is about the same as in *Thrinaxodon.* Consequently, in *Probainognathus* the stapes, which in both genera firmly abuts the quadrate, is relatively long and slender.

In *Probainognathus,* relationships between the dentary, the accessory bones, and the quadrato-articular joint seem organized to compensate for the reduced load-bearing surfaces of the latter. First, the articular process of the dentary maintains a broad contact with the surangular, which resists horizontal displacement between dentary and accessories by forces acting on the mandible. Second, the surangular-glenoid contact absorbs some of the force transmitted to the quadrate via the accessory bones. Third, the horizontal orientation of the quadrate and quadratojugal enables the quadrato-articular joint to resist posteriorly directed forces.

The reconstruction of *Eozostrodon (Morganucodon)* by Kermack, Mussett, and Rigney (1981) is consistent with a trend toward reduction of the vertical dimension of the accessory jaw bones, and of the transverse dimensions of the quadrato-articular joint surface. The latter dimension is only about half that of *Probainognathus* (Figs. 2, 3A). the surangular boss seems to have van-

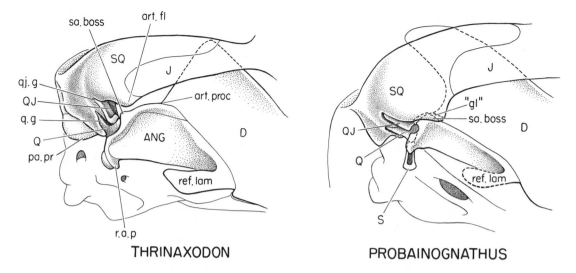

THRINAXODON

PROBAINOGNATHUS

Figure 1. Slightly oblique (from ventro-lateral aspect) views of the jaw articulation of *Thrinaxodon* and *Probainognathus*. Both drawings scaled to a lower jaw of standard length.

Abbreviations used in this and other Figures: **a.f,** articular facet of quadrate; **ANG,** angular; **ART,** articular; **art.fl,** articular flange; **art.proc,** articular process; **D,** dentary; **d.c,** dentary condyle; **ex.au.m?,** possible course of the external auditory meatus; **f.r,** foramen rotundum; **gl,** glenoid; **"gl",** articular surface for the surangular boss; **J,** jugal; **l.f,** lateral flange; **p.ant,** philaantotica; **pa.pr,** paroccipital process; **p.p.f,** pterygo paroccipital foramen; **Q,** quadrate; **q.g,** quadrate groove; **qj.g,** quadratojugal groove; **g r ep,** quadrate ramus of the epipterygoid; **QJ,** quadratojugal; **r.a.p,** retroarticular process; **ref.lam,** reflected lamina; **S,** stapes; **SA,** surangular; **sa.boss,** surangular boss; **SQ,** squamosal; **T,** tabular; **V,** foramen for the trigeminal nerve; **VII,** foramen for the facial nerve; **X,** jugular foramen.

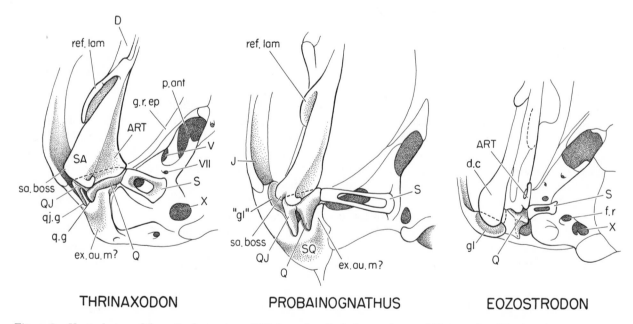

THRINAXODON

PROBAINOGNATHUS

EOZOSTRODON

Figure 2. Ventral view of the articular regions of *Thrinaxodon, Probainognathus,* and *Eozostrodon (Morganucodon)*. All figures scaled to a jaw of standard length (*Eozostrodon* [*Morganucodon*] after Kermack, Mussett, and Rigney, 1981.)

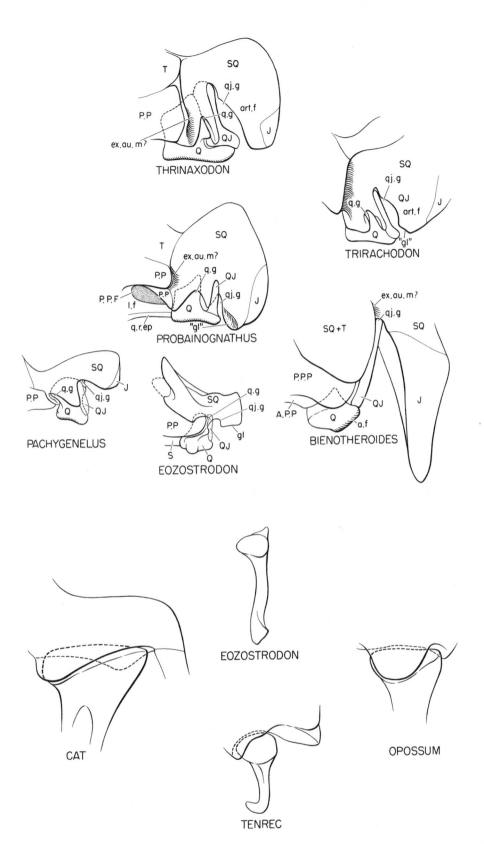

Figure 3. A. Posterior views of the quadrate-quadratojugal complexes of selected cynodonts *(Thrinaxodon, Trirachodon, Probainognathus),* a tritylodontid *(Bienotheroides),* a trithelodontid *(Pachygenelus)* and the early mammal *Eozostrodon (Morganucodon).* B. Posterior view of the dentary condyles in selected mammals. The size of these complexes and the dentary condyles are all scaled to a lower jaw of standard length. *Bienotheroides* after Sun Ai-Lin; personal communication.

ished, being replaced by a small but well-developed dentary condyle, which meets the glenoid. The postdentary bones and quadrate were probably very loosely held by the dentary and squamosal, respectively.

The sequence from *Thrinaxodon* to *Eozostrodon* demonstrates reduction of the accessory bones of the lower jaw together with the quadrate, while the quadrato-articular complex was still the functional jaw joint; i.e., prior to the development of a dentary-squamosal articulation. This evidence contradicts the view expressed by Kermack, Mussett, and Rigney (1981) that it was only after the acquisition of a dentary-squamosal articulation that the mass of the quadrate and accessory jaw bones was drastically reduced.

The accessory jaw bones were reduced independently in the gomphodonts and their presumptive derivatives, the tritylodonts, on the one hand, and in the line leading to the trithelodonts on the other (Fig. 3A). A surangular-squamosal contact was present in such gomphodont cynodonts as *Trirachodon* (Fig. 3A), but was lost in tritylodonts such as *Bienotheroides* (Fig. 3A), nor did the dentary invade the jaw joint in this lineage. In tritylodonts, moreover, the quadrate is supported loosely by the paroccipital process, having lost its contact with the squamosal (Crompton, 1964). Without the features that seem to protect the reduced articulation, tritylodonts must have had a jaw joint even more fragile than that of *Probainognathus*.

In the trithelodontids there is no evidence of a surangular boss, and in *Pachygenelus*, in which the articular facet of the quadrate is slightly smaller than that of *Probainognathus*, a "glenoid" facet on the squamosal is lacking (Fig. 3A). The well-preserved specimen of *Diarthrognathus* (Crompton, 1963a, 1970, 1972b) also lacks this facet, but the posterolateral region of the lateral ridge of the dentary is thickened, and may have made contact with the medial concave surface of the squamosal. This contact, however, is different from that of early mammals. Thus a mammalian dentary-squamosal joint cannot be derived from the conditions of tritylodonts or trithelodonts, though it could have stemmed from *Probainognathus*.

The lineages that paralleled one another in reduction in the size of the jaw joint are clearly differentiated by the features of dentition, jaw shape, and braincase structure. If the accessory jaw bones and quadrate were involved in hearing in the common ancestor of the tritylodontids, trithelodontids, and mammals (Allin, 1975, this

volume), and if a chain of lighter bones (postdentary rod, quadrate, and stapes) were more effective than a chain of heavy bones in transmitting vibrations picked up by a mandibular tympanic membrane, then the parallel reduction of the bones forming the joint in different therapsid lines would be expected. A reorganization of the orientation and changes in the activity pattern of the relatively larger adductor muscles in advanced therapsids could, as has been suggested (Crompton and Parker, 1978) and is elaborated upon in the next section of this paper, compensate for the reduced load-bearing capacity of the articular-quadrate joint.

Mandibular Adductor Activity in *Didelphis virginiana* and *Tenrec ecaudatus*

Condylar loading during feeding has so far been inferred from relatively highly specialized mammals, by measurement of mandibular strain in rabbits (Weijs and DeJongh, 1977) and macaques (Hylander, 1979a), and of muscle activity in cats (Gorniak and Gans, 1980). The American opossum, *Didelphis virginiana*, and the large Madagascan tenrec, *Tenrec ecaudatus*, are currently being examined as more nearly representative of the early mammalian condition. Data from the EMG activity of the adductor muscles on both sides of the head are as yet only partially analyzed, but initial results warrant tentative reconstruction of mandibular movement and adductor activity in early mammals and all advanced therapsids.

In the opossum, electrodes were placed in different regions of the adductor and hyoid muscles, symmetrically on both sides of the head. Synchronous recordings of 16 mm cineradiographs and electromyograms of twelve muscles were obtained. The recordings included chewing sequences in which the working side shifted from right to left or left to right. Amplification of the signals from individual EMG electrodes was kept constant during both recording and playback sessions, so that it is possible to compare the levels of activity of the same muscle when it is on the working side and when it is on the balancing side.

At the top of Figure 4, the gape/time plot, and below this the activity of several adductor muscles, are shown during four-and-a-half masticatory cycles. In the first three cycles, the animal was chewing on the right, and in the last two, on the left. The masticatory cycles—from maximum gape to maximum gape—are divided into the

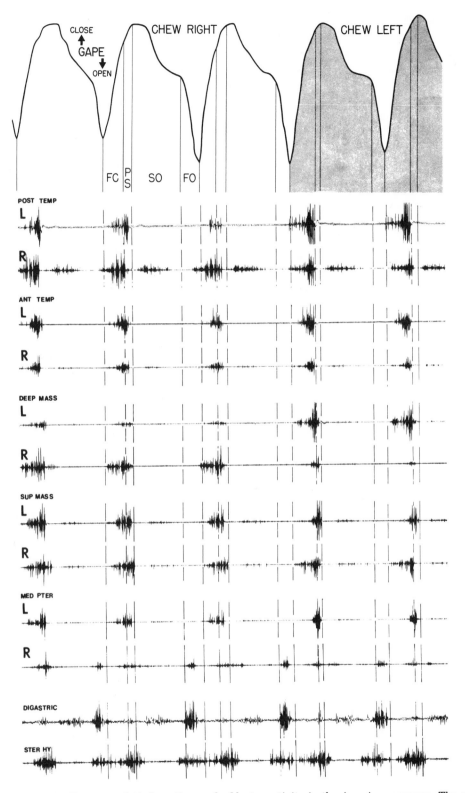

Figure 4. Jaw gape plotted vs. time and adductor activity in the American opossum. The gape for four-and-one-half cycles is shown in the top trace. The animal is chewing on the left for the first three and on the right for the remaining two. Each cycle is divided into 4 phases, FC (fast close), PS (power stroke), SO (slow open), and FO (fast open). The electromyograms for the main adductors on both sides are shown below to illustrate activity of muscles when they are on the balancing and working side.

four standard phases (Hiiemae, 1978); namely, fast close (FC), power stroke (PS), slow open (SO), and fast open (FO). At the time the recordings shown in Figure 4 were obtained, the animal was chewing on bone. Apparently there was a slight asymmetry in the placement of the electrodes in the temporalis and medial pterygoid. This is indicated by the fact that the right posterior temporalis shows activity during the slow opening phase whereas this activity is not present on the left. Activity in the left medial pterygoid is limited to the fast close and power stroke, whereas in the right medial pterygoid the major activity is during fast open, with a long burst of low activity during the power stroke and the first part of slow open. The levels of activity of the right medial pterygoid do not change during a side shift. In the left medial pterygoid, activity during the power stroke is more intense when the animal is chewing on the left than when chewing on the right. Although not all of the electrodes were completely symmetrical in placement, the following conclusions can be drawn from this preliminary experiment:

1. The level of activity of the anterior temporalis and superficial masseter, during fast close and the power stroke, is roughly the same for working and balancing sides. This suggests that when these muscles are on the balancing side they contract about as powerfully as they do when they are on the working side. Together, the anterior temporalis and the superficial masseter constitute about fifty percent of the adductor mass. There are, however, differences in the cut-off points of activity in these muscles. For example, electrical activity in the superficial masseter on the working side continues for 10 or 15 msecs after activity ceases in the muscle on the balancing side.

2. There is a marked difference in the level of activity of the deep masseter on the working side and balancing side. The same is also probably true for posterior temporalis, but the differences are not as pronounced. This suggests that these two muscles exert much more force on the working side. Furthermore, these two muscles make up about forty percent of the total adductor mass.

These data roughly approximate muscle force estimates made by Hylander (1979a) for the macaque, and by Weijs and Dantuma (1981) for the rabbit, showing that a large part of the adductor muscle force is contributed by the muscles of the balancing side. However, these data do not correspond as well to Hylander's estimates of mus-

cle force in galagos, which suggest that working-side muscle force exceeds balancing-side forces by a factor of two to three. On the other hand, Hylander's galago data are for isometric biting rather than mastication.

The opossum possesses a typical tribosphenic molar (Crompton and Kielan-Jaworowska, 1978) with the protocone fitting into a talonid basin. The earliest mammals, the Morganucodontidae and Kuehneotheriidae—together with the pantotheres, from which therian mammals are probably descended—lack both protocone and talonid basin. The molars of *Tenrec ecaudatus* are almost identical to those of pantotheres, probably being so because of the loss of protocone and talonid basin, not by retention of a primitive condition. However, similar molar structure implies similar masticatory function, and tenrec molars serve as a good model for the pattern of occlusion in the earliest mammals. In *T. ecaudatus*, occlusion consists of rather simple shearing of the anterior and posterior surfaces of the trigon of the uppers against the matching surfaces of the trigonid of the lowers. There is no mechanical "stop"—protocone in a talonid basin—which would have terminated jaw closure in tenrecs, pantotheres, or the earliest mammals.

Tenrecs have an extremely mobile symphysis (Crompton and Oron, in press), which is relatively smaller than that of the opossum, and during a masticatory cycle each hemimandible rotates independently around its longitudinal axis. Axial rotation, though slight, is perceptibly different on the working and balancing sides. During opening, the working hemimandible everts (dorsal edge moves laterally and ventral edge, medially). During the power stroke, the working hemimandible inverts, which enhances the upward and inward movement of the lower molar teeth across the uppers during occlusion. The posterior aspect of the articular surface of the mandibular condyle in the tenrec is gently convex (Fig. 3B) and, so, does not resist rotation of the mandible around its longitudinal axis during occlusion. The condyles of the earliest mammals, *Eozostrodon* and *Kuehneotherium*, were similar in shape to those of the tenrec and likewise did not resist hemimandibular rotation. The hemimandibles of early mammals are usually preserved separated, indicating that they possessed a loosely connected, probably mobile, symphysis. The shearing planes on the upper molars of eozostrodontids (and in the presumed descendants of this group, the triconodontids) are more horizontally orientated than those of the matching shearing surfaces on the lower molars, so that rotation of a hemimandible was necessary before the teeth could come into occlusion. This orientation contradicts the view of Kermack, Mussett, and Rigney (1981), that the original function of the dentary condyle was to prevent mandibular rotation. The condition of modern terrestrial carnivores (Fig. 3B), in which great transverse expansion of the condyle apparently prevents mandibular rotation, is a specialized feature not present in the earliest mammals (Fig. 3B). Hemimandibular rotation is more limited in the opossum than in the tenrec by the relatively greater transverse dimension of the condyle of the opossum.

In the tenrec, the temporalis musculature comprises about sixty-five percent of the adductor mass. When the tenrec is eating hard food, all parts of the temporalis musculature on both working and balancing sides are active during the power stroke. Moreover, there is no indication of one part of the muscle on one side showing a high level of activity during wide gape and another part of the muscle, intense activity during minimum gape. Neither is there any indication of a change in the level of activity of this muscle after a shift from the working to the balancing side and vice versa, provided that the animal is breaking down hard food with the molars. However, when the tenrec eats soft food, and the level of temporalis activity is considerably less than when eating hard food, a marked difference appears between the active and balancing sides.

The superficial masseter conforms to a somewhat similar pattern of activity: when the tenrec eats hard food, such as bone, there is little or no differential between active and balancing sides, but when it eats soft to medium-hard food, the working side dominates the balancing side. Bone, while it is being chewed, keeps the teeth apart throughout the power stroke until it is completely broken down. Occasionally bilateral biting is observed during feeding on bone, but usually biting with the molars is unilateral. During the power stroke, there is hardly any lateral shift of the mandible.

These data allow a comparison of extant mammals with advanced therapsids in the potential loading of the jaw joint during maximum adductor activity. Values of force are assigned to individual muscles or different regions of a single muscle, according to the cross-sectional area of the muscles or muscle regions in question. A first approximation of the reaction forces at the jaw

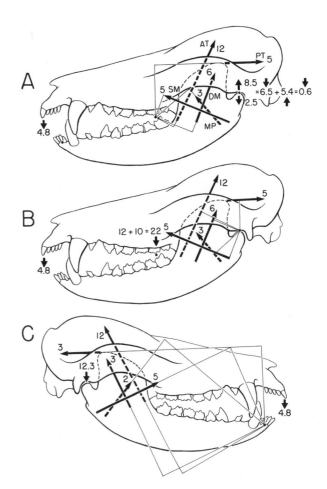

Figure 5. Arbitrary values for the resultant forces of the main adductor muscles in the American opossum. The resultants are shown in bold lines and the moment arms in faint lines. The force values are proportional to the relative mass of each of the muscles or parts of a muscle complex. The reaction forces generated by these values at the working side jaw joint (A), point of bite (B) and balancing side jaw joint (C) are also shown (see text for explanation). In order to compare these values with those shown in Figures 6–9, the calculations are based on the lower jaws being scaled to a standard of 10 units of length.

joint and point of bite that would be associated with these hypothetical muscle forces can be calculated from the lengths of the moment arms involved. To compare muscle forces and moment arms in different animals, skull shape and muscle origins and insertions must be standardized, in the present case by being drawn with lower jaws of the same length (Figs. 5–8). Moment arm lengths are based on a jaw length of ten units, in accordance with which moments are taken around various centers, and directions of average muscle pull are determined.

In the opossum, the moments acting around a bite point between the third molars (Fig. 5A) are developed from the following assumptions. The adductors of the active side are maximally active during the power stroke, arbitrary unit values of force being assigned to the muscles in proportion to their relative size (Turnbull, 1970): posterior temporalis, 5; anterior temporalis, 12: superficial masseter, 5; deep masseter, 6; medial pterygoid, 3. "Anterior temporalis" refers to the part of the muscle with a predominantly vertical vector, and "posterior temporalis," to the point with a more horizontal vector. This subdivision is functionally more significant for present purposes than the traditional separation of the temporalis into superficial and deep portions. Deep masseter includes the zygomatico-mandibularis.

Together the anterior temporalis, superficial masseter, deep masseter, and medial pterygoid on the active side generate 8.5 units of reactive compressive force at the working side condyle. The posterior temporalis, acting around the third molar (M3), tends to separate condyle from the glenoid and generates about 2.5 units of tensile force. The resultant load at the joint on the working side, imposed by the muscles on the same side, is about 6 units of compressive force.

In the muscles of the balancing side (Fig. 5C), the values for the anterior temporalis and superficial masseter are the same as those on the active side, while the values for posterior temporalis, deep masseter, and medial pterygoid are less: 3, 3, and 2 units, respectively (cf. Fig. 4). As there is no food between the teeth on the balancing side, the forces generated by its muscles would be transferred via the symphysis to the active side. If moments are taken around the jaw joint, about 4.6 units of vertically directed forced would be generated at the symphysis. In a static situation, with the bite point between the third molars on the active side, the force transferred from the balancing side muscles would, as Hylander (1979b) has suggested, rotate the active jaw around the point of bite and generate about 5.4 units of tensile force. This would nearly balance the 6 units of compressive force generated by the muscles on the active side, so that the active joint would probably be subjected to neither tensile nor compressive forces under these ideal conditions.

If the resultant bite were actually anterior to M3, as it probably is during mastication, both joints would be subjected to a compressive reaction force. Moreover, if the amount of muscle force on the balancing side has been overestimated in the above analysis, balancing condylar loads should be reduced and working condylar loads increased.

Such a condition would not apply to the balancing-side condyle. Moments taken around the symphyseal region on the balancing side (Fig. 5C) indicate that the compressive condylar reaction force associated with the anterior temporalis, deep masseter, superficial masseter, and medial pterygoid would be far greater than the tensile reaction force associated with the posterior temporalis. The resultant compressive force on the balancing condyle is about 12.3 units. The muscles on the working side generate about 12 units of force at the point of bite (Fig. 5B). The force from the balancing side would also add to the force generated at the point of bite. The length of input moment arm would be the hemimandible on the active side; the output moment arm would be the distance between the condyle and the point of bite. This arrangement generates an additional bite force of 10 units, a total bite force of about 22 units. Loading of the balancing condyle in this example would be a little over one-half of the force generated between the third molars. Consequently, when an opossum bites solely along the posterior molars, the balancing side jaw joint bears a compressive load equivalent to about one-half that generated at the point of bite. If the adductors on both sides are equally active when the animal bites food with the incisors and canines, compressive forces would then be generated at both condyles. These conclusions on joint loading in the opossum are in general agreement with the experimental evidence of joint loading in the macaque (Hylander, 1979b). The condyle and glenoid of the opossum, as is the case of virtually all mammals, are substantial structures, apparently designed to withstand large compressive forces.

The tenrec is analyzed in similar fashion, the bite point being between the third molars (Fig. 6). Arbitrary units of muscular force are: anterior temporalis, 12; posterior temporalis, 8; superficial masseter, 7; and medial pterygoid, 2. The tenrec lacks a deep masseter. When the animal bites unilaterally on hard food (bone), the adductors on both sides contract with nearly the same force. In a static situation, the adductors on the active side generate 2.9 units of compressive force at the condyle on the active side. Muscles on the balancing side will generate 5 units of force at the symphysis, and thereby tend to pivot the mandible about the point of bite and generate 5.8 units of tensile force at the condyle on the active side. The resultant compressive force at the active condyle is 3.8 units of tensile force. At the balancing condyle (Fig. 6C), on the other

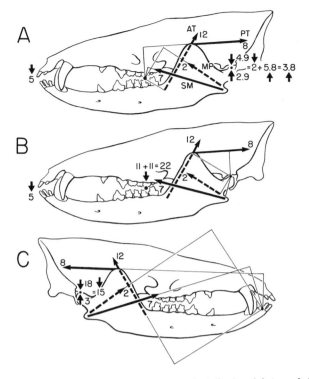

Figure 6. Reaction forces generated at the jaw joints, point and bite and symphysis by the adductor muscles in *Tenrec ecaudatus;* A and B working side; C balancing side. (See Figure 5 and text for explanation.)

hand, 15 units of compressive force are generated. The force at the point of bite (Fig. 6B) is 11 units generated by these muscles on the working side and 11 units generated by the muscles on the balancing side—a total of 22 units of force. The compressive force at the balancing condyle is about 3/4 of that at the point of bite between the molars. With the same muscle forces acting bilaterally during incisal and canine biting, the total bite force is about 10 units, with a compressive force of slightly larger magnitude (15 units) at each condyle. The tenrec, therefore, confirms the general mammalian pattern of substantial compressive loading of the balancing side condyle.

Mandibular Mechanics of *Probainognathus*

In *Probainognathus* (Fig. 7), the adductor fossa is not only long but also wide, since the zygoma is bowed away from the lower jaw. The temporalis and masseter complexes must have been very large. All parts of the adductor complex were large relative to skull size than in *Thrinaxodon.* In *Probainognathus,* the distance from the first incisor to the last molar is less than forty percent of the total mandible length, as opossed

to *Tenrec* and *Didelphis* in which this distance is about sixty percent. *Probainognathus* also differs from *Tenrec* and *Didelphis* in the orientations of the adductor muscles. The postero-ventral region of the adductor fossa (i.e., the region immediately above the jaw joint) lies well below the level of the dorsal tip of the coronoid process of the dentary, indicating a postero-ventral direction to the large posterior temporalis. The anterior temporalis and deep masseter are directed obliquely upwards and backwards. This, together with the more forward position of the dentition, means that the insertion of these muscles was relatively further forward on the dentary than in mammals such as the opossum and tenrec.

The postcanine teeth of *Probainognathus* are small, relative to skull size. As in "primitive"

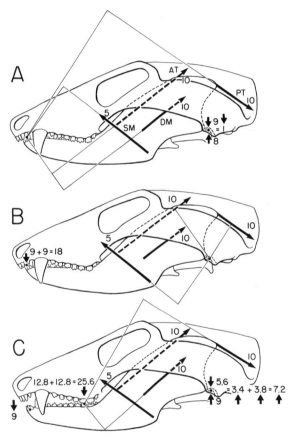

Figure 7. Forces generated by the adductor muscles in *Probainognathus.* A. Reaction forces at the jaw articulation during incisor-canine biting. If it is assumed that the adductors contact symmetrically, the forces generated at the opposite jaw articulation would be identical. B. Bite force with adductor muscles of both sides contributing to the total. C. In the unlikely event that the mandible was loaded unilaterally and the muscle on both sides contracted maximally, large tensile forces would be generated at the working side joint, whereas the balancing side would continue to show a small compressive load.

mammals, the upper postcanine tooth rows are further apart than are the lower. The buccal surface of the lower and the lingual surface of the upper postcanines lack wear surfaces. This suggests that in *Probainognathus* the mandible did not move extensively in a transverse plane, and unilateral occlusion of a mammalian type did not take place. Hence the postcanines probably did not play as important a role in the mechanical reduction of food in *Probainognathus* as they do in mammals. An animal such as *Probainognathus* has large canines and fairly substantial incisors. The front teeth were probably used for tearing flesh, which was then swallowed with little additional processing by the postcanines.

To compare *Probainognathus* with mammals and with other therapsids, on the basis of the form of the adductor region, the following values are assigned to the maximum forces that were probably generated by the adductor muscles in *Probainognathus* (Fig. 7): anterior temporalis, 10; posterior temporalis, 10; deep masseter, 10; superficial masseter, 5. The reptilian pterygoideus muscle was probably greatly reduced in *Probainognathus,* and it is doubtful that a mammalian medial pterygoid was present (Barghusen, this volume). Therefore, this muscle has been ignored in the following analysis.

In mammals such as the tenrec, the jaw adductors on both sides tend to show equal activity during incisal biting. If this was also true of *Probainognathus,* the relative muscle force values given above indicate that the bite force in the incisor-canine region (Fig. 7B) would be about 18 units (9 units contributed by each side), while the reactive force at the jaw joints would amount to only about 1 unit of compressive force (Fig. 7A). This is in marked contrast to mammals, in which incisor-canine bite force is less than the condylar reaction force.

In *Probainognathus,* a reduction in compressive forces at the condyles during incisal biting seems to have been achieved by moving the insertion of the anterior temporalis and deep masseter forward and by changing the orientation of the posterior temporalis. This apparent reduction of reaction force at the jaw joint coincides with the recorded decrease in the size of the articular-quadrate complex.

If *Probainognathus* had chewed hard food unilaterally between the posterior postcanines, powerfully, and if the muscles on both sides were equally active, the muscle forces given above indicate that the working-side condyle would be subjected to 7.2 units of tension—3.4 from active

and 3.8 from balancing sides (Fig. 7C). The balancing condyle would be subjected to 1 unit of compressive force. The total bite force at the postcanines would be 25.6—12.8 contributed by the working-side muscles, plus 12.8 by the balancing side muscles. Relative forces of similar magnitudes would probably also have been encountered in *Thrinaxodon.*

The structure of the joint in *Probainognathus* seems to be relatively resistant to compression, less so to tension; the articular-surangular complex does not clasp the quadrate as it does, for example, in some gorgonopsians. Tension could have been resisted by massive ligaments, but if the articular and quadrate were functioning as part of the middle ear, it is unlikely that these would have been present, nor is there any evidence suggesting that they were.

The absence of wear on the postcanine teeth suggests that occlusion was minimal, and the greater distance between the mandibular, than between the maxillary, postcanines effectively rules out bilateral occlusion. It is very probable that in *Probainognathus* the most powerful biting took place in the incisor-canine region and that the orientation of the jaw muscles and jaw shape excludes the possibility of major compressive or tensile force at the jont. The postcanine teeth were probably used to punture or crush food, without the teeth themselves ever coming into contact. If puncturing and crushing took place bilaterally, smaller tensile forces (3.4 units in the present example) would have been generated at the jaw joints. Unilateral loading would have produced larger forces, but these could have been minimized by reducing the level of adductor activity.

Mandibular Mechanics of *Tritylodontids*

The traversodont cynodonts and tritylodontids developed complex occlusion between the postcanine teeth. In the parallel postcanine rows of tritylodontids, two rows of crescent-shaped cusps on the lower postcanines occluded between three rows of crescentic cusps on the upper postcanines (Kühne, 1956; Crompton, 1972a). The cutting edge of the upper crescents faced forward and that of the lowers, backwards. The food was trapped between the cutting edges of the crescents and sheared by a backwardly directed power stroke. The extreme, oblique orientation of the articular-quadrate articulation, in dorsal aspect, would have permitted posterior movement of the mandible relative to the quadrate

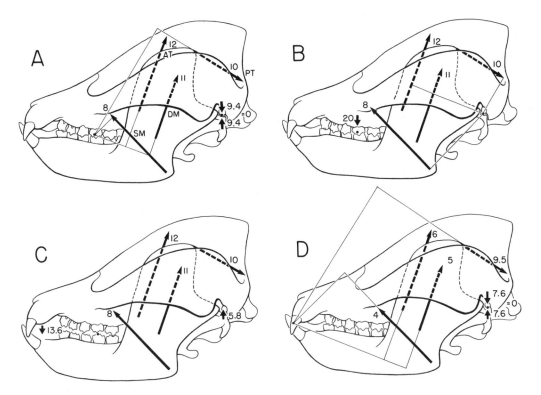

Figure 8. Forces generated by the adductor muscles in a tritylodontid. In Figures A and B, it is assumed that the level of activity of the muscle is the same on both sides. A. Reaction forces at the jaw joint during bilateral biting at the 4th postcanines on both sides. B. Bite force on one side during bilateral biting. C. In the unlikely event of unilateral biting the force of the balancing side muscles would be transmitted via the symphysis to the working side; as a result, the working side joint would be subject to tension and the balancing to compression. D. During incisal biting, compression at the jaw joint could be minimized by reducing the level of activity of the anterior temporalis and deep masseter.

during power stroke, and substantial rocking of the quadrate would not have been necessary to accommodate this movement. In tritylodontids it is virtually impossible to occlude the postcanine teeth of one side without also occluding the teeth on the opposite side, suggesting that bilateral chewing may have been the usual mode. These forms seem to have had a mobile symphysis, which probably accommodated minor differences in food size on either side and so maintained bilateral occlusal contact. Tritylodonts have either lost or reduced all but a single pair of enlarged incisors in both the upper and lower jaw. The lower incisors fit between the uppers, and wear facets are present on the lateral surface of the lowers and the medial surfaces of the uppers. The tips of the lower incisors do not seem to have worked against those of the uppers as they do, for example, in rodents. It is doubtful that major bite forces were developed between either the large lateral or small reduced incisors when they are present.

The jaw articulation of tritylodontids is extremely fragile, poorly designed to resist sub-stantial forces in any direction. It was even less capable of withstanding compressive forces than that of a cynodont such as *Probainognathus,* because the articular surfaces are further reduced, all contact between the surangular and the squamosal has been lost, and a dentary-squamosal joint was never developed. The joint is also poorly suited to resist tensile forces between the postdentary rod and articular are greatly reduced and the quadrate has lost its contact with the squamosal, being supported almost entirely by the paroccipital process.

The coronoid process (Fig. 8) of the dentary is extremely high and vertical. Its degree of verticality suggests a large vertically oriented anterior temporalis and deep masseter. The postero-dorsal tip of the coronoid process towers above the articular region, and the spatial arrangement of this area suggests a large, postero-ventrally directed, posterior temporalis. Units of force assigned to the muscles (Fig. 8A) are: anterior temporalis, 12; deep masseter, 11; superficial masseter, 8; and posterior temporalis, 10. Application of these values gives a force at the point of bite (situated at the fourth postcanine) of 20 units (Fig. 8B), and a reactive force at the jaw joint (Fig. 8A) of zero. The compressive reaction force at the jaw joint, associated with the masseter and anterior temporalis, would be balanced by a tensile reaction force at the joint by the posterior temporalis. Bilateral occlusion most probably involved identical muscular activity on both sides during the power stroke. Therefore, both sides can be considered as functioning in nearly identical fashion, much as in incisal biting in mammals.

Unilateral loading of the jaws and biting between the incisors were probably rare, but may have taken place momentarily from time to time. If unilateral loading took place with adductors on both sides maximally active (Fig. 8C), the balancing jaw joint would have been subjected to 7 units of compressive force, and 13.6 units would have been transferred via the symphysis to the active side. The active joint would be subjected to 5.8 units of tensile force. If the same values are applied to biting between the incisors, both joints would be subject to about 8 units of compressive force. These loads seem excessive for the structure of the joint, and could have been lightened by modifying the pull of the muscles. Enhanced activity of the posterior temporalis, relative to the remaining adductors (Fig. 8D), during unilateral loading would reduce the reaction force at the joints to zero, as would reducing the activity of all adductors during incisal bite. Bilateral occlusion most probably involved identical muscular activity on both sides during the power stroke. Therefore, both sides can be considered as functioning in a nearly identical fashion, much as in incisal biting in mammals.

Mandibular Mechanics of Early Mammals

If the skull of an early mammal, such as *Eozostrodon,* is compared with that of *Probainognathus,* several differences pertinent to the present discussion can be observed:

1. Unilateral mammalian-type occlusion between the molars was present in *Eozostrodon* but absent in *Probainognathus.*

2. A substantial, rounded dentary condyle and flat, squamosal glenoid was present in *Eozostrodon,* whereas no dentary-squamosal contact was present in *Probainognathus.*

3. The teeth occupy about fifty-one percent of the total lower jaw length in *Eozostrodon,* as compared with about forty percent in *Probainognathus.*

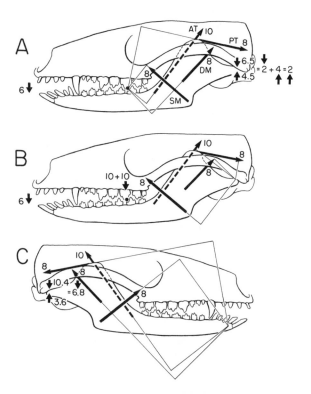

Figure 9. Reaction forces generated at the jaw joints and point of bite by adductor muscles during unilateral biting on hard food in the early mammal *Eozostrodon (Morganucodon).* (Reconstruction of skull after Kermack, Mussett, and Rigney, 1981.)

4. In *Eozostrodon,* the dentary insertion of the adductor muscles is relatively closer to the jaw joint than in *Probainognathus.*

Unit values of muscle force assigned to *Eozostrodon* (Fig. 9) are: anterior temporalis, 10; posterior temporalis, 8; superficial masseter, 8; and deep masseter, 8. A medial pterygoid was probably present but small, and has therefore been ignored in the present discussion. In a unilateral bite at the second molars, with adductors on both sides active to the same extent, about 7 units of compressive force would be generated at the balancing-side condyle (Fig. 9C) and about 2 units of tensile force at the active side.

The latter is based upon the adductor muscles on the active side contributing about 2 units of compressive force to the condyle, and the adductor muscles of the balancing side generating about 6 units of compressive force at the symphysis, which would pivot the active jaw about the point of bite to generate a total 4 units of tensile force at the joint (Fig. 9A). The force at the point of bite would be about 10 units each from the active and balancing sides, a total of 20 units. The ratio of force generated at the balancing condyle to that generated at a point between the molars in an early mammal such as *Eozostrodon* is 1:3. This is lower than in mammals such as the opossum and tenrec, where it is 1:1.8 and 1:1.5, respectively, indicating a relatively low level of joint loading in early mammals.

Thus in early mammals, at any position of bite, the balancing condyle during unilateral biting, and both condyles during incisor biting, are placed under greater compression relative to bite force than in advanced therapsids. This suggests that it was only with the acquisition of a joint between a dentary condyle and squamosal glenoid that compressive loading of the jaw joint became possible. By increasing the relative length of the tooth row, early mammals moved the insertion of the adductors closer to the joint. This, and the introduction of unilateral occlusion, resulted in an increase in the compressive loading of the balancing condyle during unilateral biting.

An interesting feature of the morganucodontids and kuehneotherids, each of which retained accessory jaw bones articulating with a quadrate alongside the dentary-squamosal articulation, in that they did not have matching shearing planes on newly erupted upper and lower molars (Crompton and Jenkins, 1968). Matching wear facets did form on upper and lower molars during occlusion, always at positions consistent within specific taxonomic groups, but a considerable part of the crown had to be worn away to produce them. In the Jurassic pantotheres and symmetrodonts, the morphology of the upper and lower molar crowns is such that they nearly "fitted" one another when they erupted, and only minimal wear was needed to acquire precisely fitting shearing surfaces. In the Morganucodontidae, there is considerable variation between taxa as to the relative positions of upper and lower molars. Therefore, in different taxa of this family, shearing facets are found in slightly different positions. The angle of the wear facets in both *Kuehneotherium* and *Eozostrodon* show that during occlusion the lower molars are drawn upwards and slightly inwards across the uppers, indicating that unilateral occlusion characterized these forms. The fact that the molars had to be worn to fit one another and the variation as to the location of the facets in different morganucodontid genera suggests that molar occlusion was a relatively recent acquisition of these early mammals.

Conclusions

In modern mammals, unilateral molar occlusion seems to generate compressive reaction forces, the temporomandibular joint balancing side, which are about one-half to one-third of those generated at the point of bite. When the ratio between muscle forces on the balancing and working side approaches unity, the balancing-side condylar reaction force exceeds that on the working side. During powerful incisal biting, the compressive force at each condyle exceeds that force at the point of bite. In advanced therapsids, the shape of the jaw and skull and the orientation and placement of the adductor muscles were such that compressive forces generated at the jaw joint seem to have been considerably less than those generated at the point of bite.

Several therapsid lineages are characterized by a progressive reduction in the size of the postdentary (articular, prearticular, angular, and surangular) and quadrate-quadratojugal complex. It seems likely that this reduction was related to the fact that these bones were involved in the transmission to the inner ear of vibrations picked by a mandibular tympanum (Allin, 1975). It is difficult to avoid the conclusion that the decrease in the size of the bones forming the reptilian jaw joint reduced the load-bearing capacity of this joint, and that the parallel changes—in different therapsid lineages—in the organization of the adductor muscles served in all cases to decrease compressive and tensile forces generated at the joint during all phases of mastication. The relative size of the load-bearing surface of the jaw joint of early cynodonts exceeds that of some mammals (cf. Fig. 3A and B). However, because the accessory jaw bones and the quadrate were not suturally connected, respectively, to the dentary and skull in therapsids, the relative load-bearing capacity of mammalian and therapsid jaw joints cannot be compared. Intuitively, the loose connections between the postdentary rod and dentary on the one hand, and the skull and quadrate on the other, seems to indicate a structure less well designed to resist compressive and tensile forces. Even if therapsid jaw joints of a size comparable to mammalian joints were capable of resisting mammalian-level forces, a reduction in loading of the joint may have been essential to maintain auditory function during mastication and other aspects of oral function.

There is no evidence in any mammal-like reptile of significant unilateral molar occlusion of the mammalian type. Such occlusion does not appear in the phylogenetic line leading from a primitive cynodont, such as *Thrinaxodon,* to mammals before the advent of the dentary-squamosal joint. It is concluded that in the therapsid part of this line, the postcanine teeth were not used extensively to comminute food, as they are in most mammals. They were probably used primarily to puncture and crush food bilaterally, and could also have been involved in shearing.

In the Tritylodontoidea (gomphodont cynodonts and tritylodontids), bilateral occlusion took place between the postcanine teeth, in conjunction with a posteriorly directed power stroke. If these forms had exerted great unilateral force in chewing, the jaw joint on the active side would have been subjected to tensile forces approaching one-quarter of the compressive force at the point of bite. Although this is not a large reaction force in modern mammals, it must be emphasized that the jaw joint in advanced therapsids does not appear adapted to withstand major tensile forces. Moreover, we suspect that massive restraining ligaments would not be compatible with the function of the reptilian jaw joint bones in the middle ear.

It is reasonable to assume that early mammals were similar to "primitive" living mammals, such as the tenrec and opossum, in adductor function. The adductor muscles on the balancing side were nearly as active as those on the working side during unilateral molar biting on hard food, and forces from the balancing side were transferred to the active side via the mobile symphysis. It is concluded that during unilateral biting in early mammals the balancing-side condyle was placed under compressive forces of about one-third of that at the point of bite. During incisal biting the compressive load on both condyles probably approached or exceeded that at the point of bite.

Recently Hylander (1979a) has found that during isometric molar biting on a transducer, *Galago crassicaudatus* seems to generate two to three times more muscle force on the working side. Unfortunately the approach utilized does not allow muscle force magnitudes to be estimated during actual mastication.

The masticatory apparatus of early mammals and "primitive" living mammals was almost certainly unlike that of advanced therapsids. The change in the orientation and the placement of the adductor muscles that accompanied the transition from mammal-like reptile *(Probainognathus)* to mammal *(Eozostrodon)* resulted in increased reaction forces at the jaw joint during all aspects of feeding. In particular, the acquisition of unilateral molar occlusion almost certainly increased compressive forces at the balancing-side condyle. The shift in muscular and dental elements probably also resulted in increased compressive loading at the active-side joint as well.

It is concluded that these changes in the loading pattern of the jaw joint were related to the acquisition of a dentary-squamosal jaw joint that was capable of withstanding compressive forces approaching one-third or more of those at the point of bite. There is a close functional correlation between unilateral occlusion and a dentary-squamosal joint. In the earliest mammals, the old articular-quadrate jaw joint was present together with the new dentary-squamosal articulation, but as the major support function of the jaw was taken over by the new joint, the articular-quadrate joint probably did not carry any part of the load to which the new joint was subjected. The marked relative increase in the cochlear housing in early mammals, over the condition seen in advanced large and small therapsids, suggests that an increase in auditory acuity accompanied the acquisition of the mammalian dentary-squamosal articulation. A further decrease in the size of the accessory jaw bones and their eventual separation from the lower jaw followed establishment of the new joint, as documented by the fossil record of most lines of Jurassic mammals.

Acknowledgments

This paper was in part made possible with the aid of grants from the National Institutes of Health (5RO1 DEO5738) and the National Science Foundation (DEB 8101094).

We wish to thank Mrs. Ai-lin Sun of The Peoples Republic of China for her kind permission to study the undescribed material of early Jurassic mammals and middle Jurassic tritylodontids, Mr. William Amaral for preparing much of the material cited in this paper, Mr. Laszlo Meszoly for preparing the drawings, Ms. Debra Sponder for her assistance with the experimental work, Mr. Al Coleman for the photography required, Dr. Uri Oron for permission to use the unpublished data on tenrec mastication, and Dr. Edgar Allin for his critical comment on the manuscript. We also wish to gratefully acknowledge our debt to Ms. Mary Reynolds for her help in preparing the manuscript.

References

Allin, E. F.
1975. Evolution of the mammalian middle ear. *J. Morph.* 147:403–37.

Barghusen, H. R., and Hopson, J. A.
1970. Dentary-squamosal joint and the origin of mammals. *Science* 168:573–75.

Bramble, D. M.
1978. Origin of the mammalian feeding complex: models and mechanisms. *Paleobiology* 4:271–301.

Crompton, A. W.
1963a. On the lower jaw of *Diathrognathus* and the origin of the mammalian lower jaw. *Proc. zool. Soc. Lond.* 140:697–753.
1936b. The evolution of the mammalian jaw. *Evolution* 17:431–39.
1964. On the skull of *Oligokyphus. Bull. Brit. Mus. (Nat. Hist.) Geol.* 9:69–82.
1972a. Postcanine occlusion in cynodonts and the origin of the tritylodontids. *Bull. Brit. Mus. (Nat. Hist.) Geol.* 21:27–71.
1972b. The evolution of the jaw articulation in cynodonts. In *Studies in Vertebrate Evolution,* ed. K. A. Joysey, and T. S. Kemp, pp. 231–51. Edinburgh: Oliver and Boyd.
1974. The dentitions and relationships of the southern African Triassic Mammals *Erythrotherium parringtoni* and *Megazostrodon rudnerae. Bull. Brit. Mus. (Nat. Hist.) Geol.* 24:397–437.
1980. Biology of the earliest mammals. In *Comparative Physiology: Primitive mammals,* ed. K. Schmidt-Nielsen, L. Bolis, and C. R. Taylor, pp. 1–12. Cambridge: Cambridge University Press.

Crompton, A. W., and Jenkins, F. A., Jr.
1968. Molar occlusioin in Late Triassic mammals. *Biol. Rev.* 43:427–58.
1979. Origin of mammals. In *Mesozoic Mammals: The First Two Thirds of Mammalian History,* ed. J. A. Lillegraven, Z. Kielan-Jaworowska, and W. A. Clemens, pp. 59–73. Berkeley: University of California Press.

Crompton, A. W., and Kielan-Jaworowska, Z.
1978. Molar structure and occlusion in Cretaceous mammals. In *Development, Function and Evolution of Teeth,* ed. P. M. Butler, and K. A. Joysey pp. 249–87. London: Academic Press.

Crompton, A. W., and Parker, P.
1978. Evolution of the mammalian masticatory apparatus. *Amer. Sci.* 66:192–201.

Goodrich, E. S.
1930. *Studies on the Structure and Development of Vertebrates.* London: Macmillan and Co.

Gorniak, G. C., and Gans, C.
1980. Quantitative essay of electromyograms during mastication in domestic cats *(Felis catus). J. Morph.* 163:253–81.

Hiiemae, K. M.
1978. Mammalian mastication: a revew of the activity of the jaw muscles and the movements they produce in chewing. In *Development, Function and Evolution of Teeth,* ed. P. M. Butler and K. A. Joysey, pp. 359–98. London: Academic Press.

Hylander, W. L.
1975. The human mandible: lever or link? *Am. J. Phys. Anthrop.* 43:227–42.
1978. Incisal bite force direction in humans and the functional significance of mammalian mandibular translation. *Am. J. Phys. Anthrop.* 48:1–8.
1979a. Mandibular function in *Galago crassicaudatus* and *Macaca fascicularis:* an in vivo approach to stress analysis of the mandible. *J. Morph.* 159:253–96.
1979b. An experimental analysis of temporomandibular joint reaction force in macaques. *Am. J. Phys. Anthrop.* 51:433–56.
1979c. The functional significance of primate mandibular form. *J. Morph.* 160:223–40.

Jarvik, E.
1980. *Basic structure and evolution of vertebrates,* vol. 2. New York: Academic Press.

Jenkins, F. A., Jr.
1971. The postcranial skeleton of African cynodonts. *Bull. Peabody Mus.* 36:1–216.

Jenkins, F. A., Jr., and Parrington, F. R.
1976. The postcranial skeleton of the Triassic mammals *Eozostrodon, Megazostrodon* and *Erythrotherium. Roy. Soc. Lond. Philos. Trans.* B (Biol. Sci.) 273:387–431.

Kermack, K. A.; Mussett, F.; and Rigney, H. W.
1973. The lower jaw of *Morganucodon. J. Linn. Soc. (Zool.)* 53:87–175.
1981. The skull of *Morganucodon. J. Linn. Soc. (Zool.)* 71:1–158.

Kühne, W. G.
1956. *The Liassic therapsid OLIGOKYPHUS.* London: British Museum (Natural History).

Mills, J. R. E.
1966. The functional occlusion of the teeth of Insectivora. *J. Linn. Soc. (Zool.)* 47:1–25.

Reichert, C.
1837. Über die Visceralbogen der Wirbeltiere im Allgemeinen und deren Metamorphosen bei den Vögeln und Säugetieren. *Archiv. fur Anatomie,*

Physiologie und Wissenschaftl. Medecin pp. 120–220.

Turnbull, W. D.
1970. Mammalian masticatory apparatus. *Fieldiana Geol.* 18:153–356.

Weijs, W. A., and Dantuma, R.
1981. Functional anatomy of the masticatory appa-ratus in the rabbit (*Oryctolagus cuniculus* L.) *Neth. J. Zool.* 31:99–147.

Weijs, W. A., and DeJongh, H. J.
1977. Strain in mandibular alveolar bone during mastication in the rabbit. *Arch. Oral Biol.* 22:667–75.

EDGAR F. ALLIN
Department of Anatomy
Chicago College of Osteopathic Medicine
Chicago, Illinois 60615

The Auditory Apparatus of Advanced Mammal-like Reptiles and Early Mammals

Introduction

Existing mammals are unique in ear structure and generally perceive sound frequencies far above the range of all other vertebrates (Bench, Pye, and Pye, 1975, Henson, 1974). In an attempt to elucidate the origin of these features, this paper deals with auditory morphology and inferred function in synapsids and early mammals. An analysis of jaw structure, also unique in extant mammals, in an essential part of this inquiry.

The external ear of living mammals has a mobile pinna and a tubular meatus. The middle ear has an externally concave eardrum supported by the intramembranous tympanic bone (Fig. 1). Vibrations are transmitted by three small bones: malleus, incus, and stapes. A muscle innervated by the trigeminal nerve inserts on the malleus. The inner ear has a very elongate cochlea, curved in monotremes and coiled in therians. Each hemimandible is a single bone that articulates with a fossa in the squamosal bone of the cranium.

In sauropsids, which have a distinct eardrum and middle ear cavity (Baird, 1970; Wever, 1978), there is no pinna and generally only a shallow meatus. The eardrum is externally convex and is supported by the endochondral quadrate bone (Fig. 2). Vibrations are transmitted by a single skeletal element, the stapes or columella, which is cartilaginous laterally and ossified medially. No muscle innervated by the trigeminal nerve attaches to it. The cochlea is short and uncurved. Each hemimandible consists of

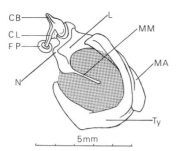

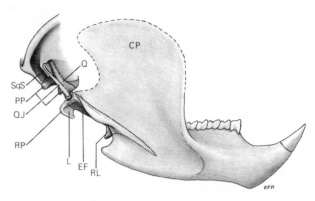

Figure 1. Right middle ear ossicles of an opossum, lateral aspect. Pars tensa of the tympanic membrane is stippled.

Key: **CB,** crus brevis of incus; **CL,** crus longus of incus; **FP,** footplate of stapes; **L,** lamina of malleus; **MA,** anterior process of malleus; **MM,** manubrium of malleus; **N,** neck of malleus; **Ty,** tympanic anulus (loosely suspended).

Figure 3. Mandible and posterior portion of the cranium of the tritylodont *Bienotherium,* right side. The hidden outline of the postdentary portion of the mandible is dotted. (Modifed after Hopson, 1965, 1966.)

Key: (and mammalian homologies): **CP,** coronoid process of dentary; **EF,** external fossa of body of angular (= tympanic) bone; **L,** thin plate (= lamina of malleus); **PP,** paroccipital process of petrosal; **Q,** quadrate (= incus); **QJ,** quadratojugal; **RL,** reflected lamina of angular bone—possibly incomplete; **RP,** retroarticular process of articular (= neck and manubrium of malleus); **SqS,** squamosal sulcus.

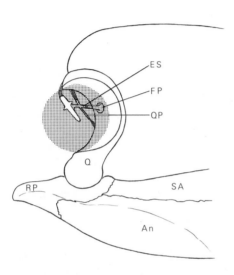

Figure 2. Right middle ear of a generalized lizard, lateral aspect. The tympanic membrane is stippled.

Key: **An,** angular bone of mandible; **ES,** shaft of extrastapes (cartilaginous portion of stapes); **FP,** footplate of stapes proper (ossified portion of stapes) seen through quadrate as if this bone were transparent; **Q,** quadrate bone of cranium; **QP,** quadrate (internal) process of extrastapes; **RP,** retroarticular process of articular bone; **SA,** surangular bone.

several elements, including the articular bone, which articulates with a condyle of the quadrate.

On the evidence of embryology Gaupp (1913) and Goodrich (1930) long ago demonstrated remarkable homologies (Fig. 3) which have since been confirmed by paleontologic evidence (see Allin 1975). The entire mammalian hemimandible corresponds to the dentary element of the compound mandible of other vertebrates, the tympanic bone to its angular element, and the malleus (except for its anterior process) to the articular bone; the incus is homologous with the

quadrate. The tensor tympani corresponds to a portion of the jaw-closing musculature (see also Barghusen, this volume). Thus, in the course of mammalian phylogeny, the angular bone and those skeletal structures that formed the original jaw articulation became incorporated into the middle ear as a new jaw articulation came into being.

When, how, and why the posterior portion of the mandible became associated with an air chamber, a tympanic membrane, and the reception of airborne sound remains questions open to debate. Previously, I (Allin, 1975) argued that these events long antedated the emergence of mammals; I also questioned (as did Tumarkin, 1955) the existence in any synapsids of a long external acoustic meatus, a tympanic membrane posterior to the quadrate, and a tympanic process of the stapes. This interpretation (criticized by Parrington, 1979), made the origin of the definitive mammalian middle ear understandable in terms of continued refinement of a preexisting structure-function complex, without the problem of accounting for the loss of a postquadrate tympanum. The considerations outlined below lead to a modification of my original view regarding the presence of a synapsid meatus, postquadrate drum, and tympanic process, but does not change the basic argument. The story thus becomes more complicated but, I hope, closer to what actually happened.

Survey of Information from Fossils

Evolutionary trends

My concern is with the functional correlates of structural change, which may provide intimations of causation. Especially attractive in this regard are instances of parallelism, convergence, and progressive change in successive lineages. An event that happens only once may depend on unique, undecipherable factors, but events that occur repeatedly are more interpretable. Perhaps the best means of recognizing trends is by constructing rigorous cladograms and sequences of nodal morphotypes. The first extensive cladistic analysis of the Synapsida is that of Hopson and Barghusen (this volume). The trends described below are consistent with their cladogram. Good general references for the rest of this section are Romer (1956) and Kemp (1982).

The mandible

GENERAL FEATURES

In all synapsids and in Early Mesozoic mammals, the mandible is compound, consisting, on each side, of the tooth-bearing dentary bone and several accessory jaw bones: the articular, prearticular, angular, and surangular, which I will call the postdentary bones, plus the coronoid and splenial, which assist in fastening the postdentary elements against the dentary.

THE ANGULAR COMPLEX

Sphenacodontids, all therapsids, and Rhaetic mammals display a characteristic configuration of the postdentary region (Figs. 3, 4, 5, 6). On the lateral aspect of the body of the angular bone is the external fossa, which extends back onto the outer side of the articular bone, including its ventrally projecting retroarticular process. Protruding lateral and ventral to this fossa is the reflected lamina of the angular bone, a flange observed in no other vertebrates. A rim bounding the external fossa, posteriorly and dorsally, continues as the margin of the reflected lamina; the incisure outlined by this rim and margin is the angular gap (Fig. 4). The pocketlike space deliminated by the external fossa medially and the reflected lamina laterally is the angular cleft.

DENTARY-POSTDENTARY INTERFACE

Whereas in sphenacodontids, like most present-day reptiles, the dentary has complex sutural connections with the angular and surangular, in

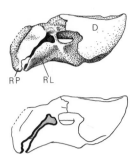

Figure 4. Mandible of the dicynodont *Stahlekeria*, right side. The lower drawing shows the angular gap in dark outline and the visible portion of the external fossa in stipple. (After a drawing of the Tubingen Museum display specimen by T. Rowe.)

Key: **D**, dentary; **RL**, reflected lamina; **RP**, retroarticular process.

theriodonts and early mammals these connections are simplified. In cynodonts, one lineage of which probably gave rise to the mammals, the dentary-postdentary interface is smooth except for an area of rugosity at its posterodorsal end in such Triassic genera as *Trirachodon, Diademodon,* and *Cynognathus.*

DENTARY DOMINANCE

All theriodonts show some enlargement of the dentary relative to the rest of the jaw. Only in cynodonts (including tritylodonts and tritheledonts) and mammals is this trend continued conspicuously (Barghusen and Hopson, 1970). In these forms the dentary develops a mammal-like shape (Figs. 3, 5), with a prominent angular process, high coronoid process, posterior process, and masseteric fossa (Barghusen, 1968, 1972). As the dentary expands, the postdentary bones are reduced and nestle into a medial trough in the dentary overhung by an eavelike ridge (Crompton, 1963).

MODIFICATIONS OF THE POSTDENTARY BONES

In therapsids the external fossa and angular cleft enlarge and the angular gap extends by encroachment on the dorsal portion of the reflected lamina. The gap becomes long and narrow in therocephalians (Fig. 6) and some dicynodonts (Fig. 4), but is long and broad in other dicynodonts and in cynodonts. The reflected lamina also expands and thins in most therapsids, including primitive cynodonts, but it is greatly reduced in area in later cynodonts. Rarely preserved in advanced cynodonts, its exact form is uncertain for most; however, complete or nearly complete examples are known for *Cynognathus,*

Diademodon, Trirachodon, Pachygenelus and Morganucodon, in all of which it is a splintlike projection. The rest of the postdentary unit is greatly diminished in height and mass in all later cynodonts and in early mammals. The retroarticular process is rarely intact in fossils. When preserved, it is often prominent. Its exact form is unknown for early mammals, but in the tritylodont *Bienotherium* (Hopson, 1965, 1966; Fig. 3, this paper) it is very similar to homologous parts of the malleus (neck and manubrium) of those living mammals in which the ossicles are thought to be most primitive (Fig. 1, this paper; Fleischer; 1978).

The suspensorium

In sphenacodontids, the quadrate is massive, with a high, broad dorsal portion in extensive rugose contact with the pterygoid and squamosal. Probably it had little mobility. Appended to it laterally is the smaller quadratojugal. In theriodonts and dicynodonts the quadrate is considerably reduced and is socketed in the squamosal; it was probably moveable in the former group. Re-

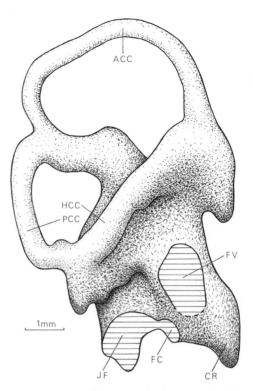

Figure 6. Right osseous labyrinth of the cynodont *Probainognathus* reconstructed from serial sections, lateral aspect. Apertures are cross-hatched.

Key: **ACC,** anterior semicircular canal; **CR,** cochleolagenar recess (the full length is not evident because it projects medially); **FC,** fenestra cochleae (round window) confluent with jugular foramen; **FV,** fenestra vestibuli (oval window); **HCC,** horizontal semicircular canal; **JF,** jugular foramen; **PCC,** posterior semicircular canal.

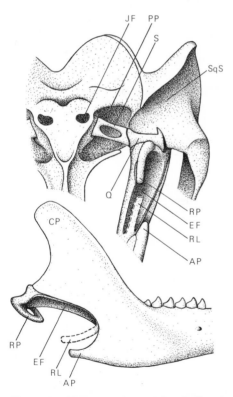

Figure 5. Reconstructions of the skull and mandible of the cynodont *Exaeretodon.* Top: Posterior portion of the skull in ventral view. Bottom: Mandible in lateral view. The reflected lamina (RL) is restored after a specimen of *Trirachodon.*

Key: **AP,** angular process of dentary; **JF,** jugular foramen; **S,** stapes; other abbreviations as in Figure 3.

duction continues in all cynodont clades. The Rhaetic mammal *Morganucodon (Eozostrodon)* has a quadrate similar to that of tritylodonts but with an incuslike stapedial process (Kermack, Mussett, and Rigney, 1981). The articular-quadrate joint is supplemented in advanced cynodonts by a surangular-squamosal abutment (Crompton, 1972), in more advanced cynodonts by a probable syndesmotic articulation between dentary and squamosal (tritheledonts) or jugal (tritylodonts, in my opinion), and in early mammals by a synovial dentary-squamosal joint.

The stapes

Throughout the Synapsida the stapes makes an end-on contact with the ventral portion of the quadrate (Fig. 5A). The sphenacodontid stapes was large and retained a suspensorial function, as in the earliest reptiles (Lombard and Bolt, 1979; Carroll, this volume). Reduction in stapedial mass occurs in all therapsids, but never to the extent observed in most sauropsids. Primitively there is a proximal dorsal process articulating with the skull, but in later forms this process shifts distally and may disappear. The anterior hyoid cornu appears to have attached to the ventral aspect of the stapes distally in sphenacodontids and in at least some therapsids, but possibly not in advanced theriodonts. No synapsid has a definite tympanic process, although one plausible candidate has been described (see below). Dorsal or quadrate processes have sometimes been regarded as tympanic processes.

The squamosal sulcus

A groove on the posterolateral aspect of the squamosal, ending at the paroccipital process of the opisthotic, is evident in most therapsids. This has generally been referred to as the meatal groove, but the noncommittal term *squamosal sulcus* seems preferable. Its form varies from group to group. Poorly defined in primitive cynodonts, it is conspicuous in more advanced cynodonts (Figs. 3, 5A, 7), curving downward from the dorsal portion of the zygomatic arch. It is less pronounced in morganucodontids.

Delimintation of the cavum tympani

Unlike most present-day mammals, no synapsid or early mammals has an auditory bulla so it is impossible to be certain of the size and form of the middle ear cavity.

The cochlea

The bony cochlea has been described for a few dicynodonts, gorgonopsians, and therocephalians (Olson 1944), in all of which it is essentially globular. The same is true of the early cynodont *Thrinaxodon*, in which it projects about 3 mm beyond the fenestra vestibuli (demonstrated in a sectioned skull). It is narrower and a bit longer in later cynodonts (Simpson, 1933), reaching 3.7 mm in *Bienotherium* (Hopson, 1965) and 3.8 mm in *Probainognathus,* as reconstructed from a sectioned skull (Fig. 8). In *Morganucodon* it is decidedly longer than wide but only a bit more than 2 mm long (based on figures in Kermack, Mussett, and Rigney, 1981) although the cochlear housing is more prominent than in any cynodont, partly as an allometric effect.

In none of these animals is the cochlea curved or as prolonged as in crocodilians. No estimate of the width of the basilar membrane and organ of Corti can be made for the therapsids mentioned, because there are no defined bony lamellae for their support as in modern mammals.

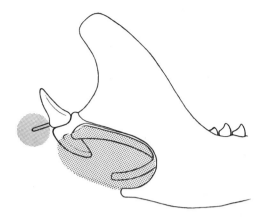

Figure 7.   A. Postulated mandibular (coarse stiple) and post-quadrate (fine stipple) tympana of the cynodont *Exaeretodon.* The stapes is hidden from view by the quadrate except for its hypothetical cartilaginous tympanic process. B. If the primitive hyo-stapedial connection persisted, the anterior hyoid cornu may have transmitted vibrations of an extension of the mandibular tympanum.

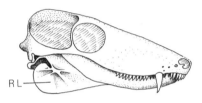

Figure 8.   Skull of the therocephalian *Ictidodraco* The large reflected lamina (**RL**) is very thin but stiffened by ridges. (After Broom and Robinson, 1948.)

Reconstruction and Functional Interpretation

Contents of the angular cleft

Neither a salivary gland nor muscle can account for the angular cleft and reflected lamina. A gland would not require so elaborate an accommodation. The prominent dorsal margin (Fig. 4) and sharp ventral border of the external fossa of many therapsids make it unlikely that a muscle entered from above (Kemp, 1972, 1979) or, less certainly, from below (Barghusen, 1968, 1972). A broad lamina would constrain the muscle from thickening as it shortened, while a thin one would give way under powerful traction. Also, there are no such rugosities on the walls of the cleft as are common at sites of muscle attachment.

However, an air-filled diverticulum of the pharynx, homologous to at least part of the mammalian cavum tympani and held open by the reflected lamina, is more likely. A ventrolateral recess of the pharynx subjacent to the pterygoideus muscle mass is present in reptiles (the sulcus pharyngis submandibularis; Shute, 1956). Extension of such a recess would bring it onto the outer aspect of the angular bone. The lateral nasopharyngeal passage of cynodonts and *Morganucodon* (Barghusen, this volume) is evidence for a pharyngeal diverticulum of this sort, probably continuous with the space around the stapes corresponding to the sauropsid cavum tympani. Westoll (1943, 1945) suggested an alternative in the form of a diverticulum (recessus mandibularis tympanicus) extending forward from the air space around the stapes. I will use the term *recessus mandibularis* for a pharyngeal extension of either kind.

Evidence for a mandibular tympanum in cynodonts

RESEMBLANCES OF HOMOLOGOUS STRUCTURES

The similarity in form of the postdentary elements and quadrate of advanced cynodonts and Rhaetic mammals to their homologs in the middle ear of conservative living mammals (Fleischer, 1978; Henson, 1974) is incompatible with a total change of function.

QUADRATO-STAPEDIAL ABUTMENT

The presence of a quadrato-stapedial abutment suggests that transmission of sound vibrations from quadrate to stapes was an important aspect of hearing in cynodonts (Fig. 5A). The only plausible area from which such vibrations could have come is the postdentary region of the jaw (airborne or otherwise).

SEGREGATION OF THE POSTDENTARY REGION

In therocephalians and cynodonts the mandible is partitioned into two structurally (and, presumably, functionally) distinct complexes, one composed of the dentary, coronoid, and splenial elements and the other of the four postdentary elements (articular, prearticular, angular, and surangular). The simplified interface between dentary and postdentary units implies significant flexibility and acoustic isolation of the postdentary complex from the tooth-bearing portion of the jaw.

TRANSFERENCE OF JAW MUSCULATURE TO THE DENTARY

Primitively, the jaw-elevating muscles largely inserted on the postdentary bones, but in therapsids, especially cynodonts, there was increased attachment to the dentary (Barghusen, 1968, 1972; Barghusen and Hopson, 1970). Such a shift would enhance acoustic damping of the dentary, which would reduce the transmission of feeding noises to the ear. At the same time it would diminish acoustic damping of the postdentary complex.

REDUCTION OF THE POSTDENTARY BONES AND QUADRATE

A reduction of the postdentary bones and quadrate would diminish acoustic impedance, facilitating reception of higher frequencies of sound.

PRESENCE OF A MANDIBULAR AIR CHAMBER

The tissues overlying a recessus mandibularis, including the reflected lamina and soft tissues bridging the angular gap, would be set into vibration by air-borne sound of appropriate wavelengths. Such a system could function as an acoustic receiver.

Trends toward extension of the angular gap and thinning of the reflected lamina would reduce the mass of the mandibular tympanum while rendering the reflected lamina better able to vibrate.

SEEMINGLY PERMISSIVE ASSOCIATED CHANGES

As the postdentary complex and quadrate and their moorings were reduced in size and strength (concurrent with a marked enhancement of jaw musculature and biting forces), several apparently complementary modifications took place. Rearward extension of the dentary and formation of its medial ridge braced the dwindling postdentary unit. Shifting of muscles reduced stresses on the postdentary bones. A high coronoid process and low posterior extension of the temporal fossa allowed reorientation of muscular forces to minimize reaction forces at the jaw articulation (Crompton, 1963, and this volume). A downward displacement of the quadrate rami of the epipterygoid in tritylodonts allowed an anteroventrad muscular pull on the posterior process of the dentary. Improved bracing of the quadrate by the squamosal, and formation of a surangular-squamosal articulation, permitted reduction of the quadrate. Finally, establishment of a joint between dentary and cranium paved the way for complete separation of the postdentary bones and quadrate from the feeding mechanism as parts of the definitive mammalian middle ear.

E. F. Allin

EXPLANATORY POWER OF THIS INTERPRETATION

While the features and trends described above surely did not occur solely for reasons of audition, the existence of a mandibular tympanum in cynodonts would help to make sense of a host of puzzling observations, including convergent or parallel evolution of many of these features. A mandibular tympanum also provides a simpler expalantion of the evolutionary origin of the mammalian middle ear (Crompton and Jenkins, 1980; Crompton and Parker, 1978) than does an exclusively postquadrate or sauropsidlike tympanum.

Hopson (1966) tried to accommodate the latter to the origin of the mammalian middle ear by postulating the following three steps. First, an attachment of the postquadrate eardrum to the vestigial articular bone provided a lever mechanism that improved hearing. Second, the stapedial and tympanic process disappeared because it "short-circuited" the lever. Third, continued posterior expansion of the dentary brought the vestigial reflected lamina close to the drum, which it could then support. This train of events is unlikely because surely a lever device would have already existed, and attachment of the drum to structures that moved with the jaw would exacerbate auditory interference during feeding.

The observed weakening of the dentary-postdentary articulation is contrary to Davis' (1961) assertion that dentary dominance could be explained as a means of strengthening the mandible by eliminating sutures, in effect, and transferring muscular forces to the tooth-bearing bone. In any case, synostosis of elements would accomplish Davis' postulate more simply.

The commonest objections to a postdentary tympanum are that feeding would generate an intolerable racket, and that the ear would be "too big." Because of the articulation of quadrate and stapes, feeding noises undoubtedly did interfere with hearing but that would be the case regardless of the presence of a mandibular tympanum; indeed, persistence of the stapedo-quadrate articulation suggests that the stapes could not be shifted onto a postquadrate eardrum without an auditory penalty. As for the second objection, the eardrum of an African elephant is about 31 mm in diameter (Fleischer, 1978). It is larger than the postulated mandibular tympanum of small cynodonts, and the ossicles are almost as massive as their homologs in *Probainognathus* (Romer, 1970). Furthermore, as argued

below, there is no reason to think that cynodonts perceived frequencies above the range of existing reptiles (about 10,000 Hz; Manley, 1972; Wever, 1978); the size of their tympanic apparatus would affect the reception of higher frequencies only. Indeed, snakes, which have no tympanum, are more sensitive to frequencies of air-borne sound below 400 Hz than many reptiles with tympanic ears (Wever, 1978). Given its compromise between auditory and suspensory roles, the cynodont mandibular tympanic apparatus would not have been optimal, but would have been effective nonetheless (Kermack and Mussett, 1983).

Presence of a postquadrate tympanum in therapsids

CONTRARY EVIDENCE

In several respects cynodonts do not have osteologic features expected in tympanic ear of the sauropsid type (Fig. 2). The quadrate shows no indication of an eardrum attachment, while the stapes is large and meets the ventral portion of the quadrate end-on (Fig. 5A). In no synapsid or captorhinomorph is there definite evidence for a tympanic process of the stapes. Lombard and Bolt (1979) and Carroll (this volume) argue that the common ancestor of synapsids and sauropsids probably did not possess a true tympanic membrane. I agree. Probably aerial sound was inefficiently received by unspecialized throat tissues and transmitted to the stapes mainly via the anterior hyoid cornu, as appears to be true in the most conservative living reptiles, *Sphenodon* (Gans and Wever, 1976). However, there are indications in most therapsid groups of an eardrum located posterior and medial to the quadrate. The stapes would have to be connected to such a drum by some sort of tympanic process or by a persisting hyo-stapedial connection.

SUPPORTING EVIDENCE

The best indication that a postquadrate tympanic membrane was present in therapsids is that the squamosal sulcus always extends to the lateral limit of the paroccipital process, posteromedial to the quadrate (Figs. 3, 5A). Some genera have characteristics suggestive of an eardrum attachment site in this location (e.g., certain dicynodonts; Cox, 1959). I have previously argued that the squamosal sulcus may have harbored a depressor mandibulae muscle (Allin 1975), but I no longer adhere to this view because: 1. It is not obvious why this muscle would be so large in dinocephalians and gomphodont cynodonts. 2. The course of the sulcus in cynodonts is less direct than usual for a muscle attachment but conforms well to the general course of the meatus of many mammals, especially monotremes. 3. The retroarticular process of cynodonts is sometimes too small to have been an isertion for a muscle of any size. 4. Most important, the shape of the sulcus in certain cynodonts seems too confining. The anterodorsal portion of the sulcus is almost tubular in two specimens of the tritylodont *Oligokyphus* figured by Kühne (1956), and in a large specimen of *Cynognathus* now being studied by Hopson. The posteroventral portion of the sulcus forms a narrow cleft in the tritylodont *Bienotherium* (Fig. 3, this volume; Hopson, 1965, 1966).

NATURE OF THE POSTQUADRATE TYMPANIC APPARATUS

Although a tympanic membrane in a position corresponding to that of sauropsids was probably present, there is no direct evidence that a stapedial tympanic process existed. A cartilaginous process would not ordinarily be preserved in fossils, but a facet or bump on the posterolateral angle of the stapes, as has been described in a few therapsids, may indicate that site of emergence of a tympanic process. However, there is no sign of a facet here or even a region lacking perichondral bone on the stapes of the gomphodont *Exaeretodon* (Fig. 5A). If the facet had been present, it probably projected across the postquadrate eardrum to its center, stiffening the drum while providing a lever mechanism to enhance auditory sensitivity (Fig. 7A).

For clarity, the following discussion assumes the postquadrate drum to be independent of the mandibular (postdentary) tympanum, but an equally plausible alternative is presented in Fig. 7B. Based on the ratio of drum area to stapedial footplate area in existing vertebrates (almost 20:1 in humans and rarely much less in others; Fleischer, 1978; Henson, 1974; Manley, 1972), most reconstructions of postquadrate tympana seem too small (e.g., Parrington, 1949). These ratios identify the primary transformer mechanism of the middle ear, which functions by concentrating sound energy from the large drum onto the small footplate (see also Bergeijk, Pierce, and David, 1960). Given the large footplate of the synapsid stapes, a postquadrate drum of no more than ten times this size would be much larger than in most extant tetrapods of comparable

body size. In view of the weight of the stapes, a drum less than ten times the area of the footplate seems unlikely (but see Hotton, 1959), and it is not apparent where an eardrum of this size could have been accommodated (Kermack, 1982). It is probable that the postquadrate tympanic apparatus of synapsids was not as effective as that of living reptiles.

Relationship to the recessus mandibularis. Living forms often show expansion of the cavum tympani, probably reflecting enhanced sensitivity to low sound frequencies (Fleischer, 1978). Improvement of low frequency sensitivity of a postquadrate tympanum does not explain the formation of the recessus mandibularis, however, because it fails to account for trends discussed in the preceding section, such as extension of the angular gap.

BIMODAL HEARING

Coexistence of mandibular and postquadrate tympana makes sense only if they received different spectra of sound frequencies. One may have received a broad range of frequencies while the other was more sensitive to a narrow band within that range, but it is more likely that one received lower frequencies, and the other, higher. Anuran amphibians provide an analog, responding optimally to higher frequencies—including mating calls—when the opercularis muscle is relaxed, and to lower frequencies when it is contracted (Lombard and Straughan 1974). Quantitative simulation of the acoustics of cynodont tympana is difficult, and so the bandwidths of the two receivers are uncertain.

FATE OF THE POSTQUADRATE TYMPANUM IN MAMMALS

If the cynodont postquadrate tympanum received higher frequencies, it may have become redundant as the range of the mandibular drum came to include higher frequencies *pari passu* with its reduction in size in the line that led to mammals. If the cynodont postquadrate tympanum was originally responsive to lower frequencies, then diminution during the origin of mammals may have decreased its effectiveness. Whether or not the postquadrate eardrum persisted as the pars flaccida of the mammalian tympanum (Westoll, 1945) is unclear; the postition of the chorda tympani suggests that it did not. The question is also obscure as to whether or not the cartilages of Paaw (commonly misspelled *Paauw*) and Spence are remnants of the stapedial tympanic process (Westoll, 1944). When the postquadrate

E. F. ALLIN

tympanic apparatus ceased to function cannot be determined; perhaps it was already vestigial in some advanced cynodonts and in the first mammals.

Vocal function of the recessus mandibularis

WESTOLL'S VOCAL RESONATOR HYPOTHESIS

In 1943 and 1945, Westoll suggested that the recessus mandibularis of therapsids functioned as a resonant vocal amplifier like the inflatable buccal chamber of anurans or the laryngeal pouches of gibbons. Initially, I did not find this idea attractive because it seemed unreasonable that a mandibular resonator existed in animals with a quadrato-stapedial abutment. I have since realized that during calls, acoustic uncoupling of the articular-quadrate linkage by contraction of the pterygoideus musculature (partly homologous with the mammalian tensor tympani; Barghusen, this volume) would, along with contraction of the stapedius muscle, eliminate this problem.

Any air chamber suitably situated would act as a resonator, selectively amplifying certain frequencies as do the human pharyngeal, oral, and nasal cavities, and as is obligatory for the oral and pharyngeal cavities of reptiles, such as crocodilians and gekkonid lizards, which vocalize. The size and shape of the air spaces largely determine the dominant frequencies of sounds produced, and thus account for individual-and species-specific voice characteristics. The reflected lamina would have imparted its own vibrational effects, amplifying certain frequencies in the manner of the sounding board of a violin (Hutchins, 1962) and, along with the rest of the tissues overlying the recessus, acting as an acoustic radiator, like the buccal floor of frogs (Gans, 1974).

SOUND PRODUCTION AND RECEPTION BY THE SAME SYSTEM

Westoll (1945) tentatively suggested that sound reception by the postdentary region may have begun in later therapsids but he did not suggest any specific relationship between vocal amplification and sound reception by this system. Such a relationship may well have been important. A thin-walled resonator will be most readily set into vibration by the same wavelengths it amplifies and radiates. Many bony fishes produce sounds by vibrating their air bladder, and receive sounds using the same air bladder (Henson, 1974). The recessus mandibularis in synapsids may have initially served as a focal

resonator, with subsequent elaboration of the overlying tissues, including the reflected lamina, serving as both vocal radiator and receiver in dicynodonts (Fig. 4), therocephalians (Fig. 6), and in at least the earlier cynodonts. The frequencies amplified and sensed would have depended on volume, pressure, and shape of the air chamber, as well as the area, mass, stiffness, and elasticity of the overlying tissues. A complex set of resonances would characterize such a system (Bergeijk, Pierce, and David, 1960; Hutchins, 1962). At some stage in mammalian phylogeny, the vocal radiator function would have been lost while the receiver function persisted. Perhaps this had already occurred in advanced cynodonts.

The external auditory meatus

The meatus that served the postquadrate tympanum of noncynodont therapsids certainly did not also cover the large postdentary region, as the mammalian external acoustic meatus does. The meatus of advanced cynodonts may have extended over the mandibular tympanum, as suggested by the large size of the squamosal sulcus in most gomphodonts and by the mediolateral width of the terminal portion of the sulcus of *Bienotherium* (Fig. 3). Advanced cynodonts often show a well-delimited posterior surface of the squamosal, which abruptly terminates laterally (Fig. 5A). If the meatus was as wide as shown, either it was open laterally or it continued onto the postdentary region.

A tubular meatus ending at the postquadrate drum and not covering the mandibular drum could not have expanded across the latter without interfering with its function. Therefore, it is likely that primitive cynodonts, in which the squamosal sulcus is ill defined, had a laterally open depression behind the squamosal, rather than a tubular meatus. In galesaurid cynodonts, the mandibular tympanum would have been in a depression posteroventral to the masseter muscle, and probably continuous with that in the squamosal sulcus. Merging of the margins of the combined C-shaped depression, beginning ventrally, would have resulted in a tubular meatus that covered both tympana and opened over the lateral aspect of the zygomatic arch.

The postulated intermediate stage, a long curving meatal depression with a raised posterior margin (primitive pinna), is much like the meatus of owls (Norberg, 1978) and would have served to protect the tympana and to gather sound. A deep meatus also acts as a broadly tuned resonator amplifying the frequency range of greatest acuity, in humans at least (Shaw, 1974). The large meatus of gomphodonts might indicate optimal sensitivity to frequencies decidedly lower than the human optimum (3,500–4,000 Hz).

A deep meatus is rarely present in living vertebrates other than mammals; perhaps ceruminous glands to repel parasites are not readily evolved. The shallow meatus of sauropsids is typically oriented posterolaterally. Cynodonts, like mammalian predators, may have made more use of hearing to locate prey than do most sauropsid predators.

Scale effects

So long as the postdentary unit and quadrate remained part of the feeding apparatus, they could not be optimized for hearing. They were necessarily larger in larger animals, although some degree of allometric compensation may have been possible. Large animals would have been less sensitive to high-frequency sound and more sensitive to low, and would have produced lower-pitched vocal sounds. Small advanced cynodonts would have had a greater capacity than large ones to perceive high frequencies. The diminutive Triassic mammals may have been sensitive to frequencies into the ultrasonic range (above the human and avian limit of 20,000 Hz), since their postdentary elements and quadrate are smaller than homologous structures in many living mammals that hear such sounds (e.g., cats).

The size and shape of the cochlea of *Probainognathus* and *Morganucodon* suggest capacity for discrimination of higher frequencies than have most reptiles, excepting gekkoes and crocodilians (above 10,000 Hz). Perhaps higher frequencies could be heard but not well discriminated. In modern mammals, perception of frequencies above 10,000 Hz, and usually well above 20,000 Hz, provides the ability to detect many sounds produced by insects, as well as high-pitched calls, such as the ultrasonic cries of baby mice, which are inaudible to nonmammalian predators. Whether upward extension of the hearing range was a causal factor in the miniaturization of the earliest mammals or merely a byproduct is impossible to determine.

Parallel origins of the mammalian middle ear

In the earliest known mammals, both therian *(Kuehneotherium)* and nontherian (morganucodontids), the postdentary elements were still part of the mandible and the quadrate part of the suspensorium (Kermack, Mussett, and Rigney,

1973). It is likely that these elements were separated from the feeding machinery to become strictly auditory structures by parallel evolution in therians and in at least one line of nontherian mammals.

Aside from the living monotremes, two extinct groups of nontherian mammals, the Triconodontidae and Multituberculata, seem to have had a middle ear of the definitive mammalian sort. Neither has a compound mandible. Presence of a fossa incudis on the crista parotica of the unnamed Cloverly triconodotid (A. W. Crompton, personal communication), a fossa for the origin of a tensor tympani muscle in triconodontids (Allin, unpublished), and a tympanic ring in the multituberculate *Ectypodus* (R. E. Sloan, personal communication) show that although no ossicles are preserved a full mammalian set was probably present in life.

Tricondontids are thought to be morganucodontid derivatives (Crompton and Jenkins, 1980; Hopson and Crompton, 1969). A still earlier separation of the line leading to the monotremes is indicated by their retention of certain postcranial characters more primitive (cynodontlike) than those of morganucodontids (form of the proximal end of the humerus in particular; see Jenkins and Parrington, 1976). Multituberculates are of uncertain affinity, but they share some derived features with monotremes and may be their sister group.

Thus the definitive mammalian middle ear may have arisen separately in the lines leading to therians, triconodontids, monotremes, and perhaps multituberculates. Kühne (1973) disagrees, and states that for such a complex outfit to have arisen more than once would be a tragedy for the concept of evolution. To my thinking, on the contrary, the commonality of antecedent morphology and function is so pervasive among cynodonts that a middle ear like that of mammals could have been expected to emerge in any cynodont derivative that survived long enough.

Final Comments

The major points of the present paper are that cynodonts and the earliest mammals were alike in the design of their auditory apparatus. They received sounds predominantly by a tympanum associated with the postdentary portion of the mandible. Westoll (1943, 1944) may well have been correct in his surmise that a major factor in the emergence of this unique system was vocal amplification.

Acknowledgements

I wish to thank Dr. H. R. Barghusen for critical reading of the manuscript and Dr. D. A. Allin for technical assistance.

This research was supported by an NIH GRS grant to the University of Illinois Medical Center and by a grant from the Chicago College of Osteopathic Medicine.

References

Allin, E. F.
1975. Evolution of the mammlian middle ear. *J. Morph. 147*:403–38.

Baird, I. L.
1970. The anatomy of the reptilian ear. In *Biology of the Reptilia,* vol. 2, ed. C. Gans. New York: Academic Press.

Barghusen, H. R.
1968. The lower jaw of cynodonts (Reptilia, Therapsida) and the evolutionary origin of mammal-like adductor jaw musculature. *Postilla* 116:1–49.
1972. The origin of the mammalian jaw appparatus. In *Morphology of the Maxillo-mandibular Apparatus,* ed. G. H. Schumacher. Leipzig: Thieme.

Barghusen, H. R., and Hopson, J. A.
1970. Dentary-squamosal joint and the origin of mammals. *Science* 168:573–75.

Bench, R.; Pye, A.; and Pye, J. D.
1975. *Sound Reception in Mammals.* New York: Academic Press.

Bergeijk, W. A. van; Pierce, J. R.; and David, E. E., Jr.
1960. *Waves and the Ear.* New York: Doubleday.

Broom, R., and Robinson, J. T.
1948. On some new types of small carnivorous mammal-like reptiles. In *Special Publication of the Royal Society of South Africa: Robert Broom Commemorative Volume,* ed. A. L. DuToit, pp. 29–44. Cape Town: Royal Society of South Africa.

Cox, C. B.
1959. On the anatomy of a new dicynodont genus with evidence on the position of the tympanum. *Proc. Zool. Soc. Lond.* 132:321–67.

Crompton, A. W.
1963. On the lower jaw of *Diarthrognathus* and the origin of the mammalian lower jaw. *Proc. Zool. Soc. Lond.,* 140:697–750.
1972. The evolution of the jaw articulation of cynodonts. In *Studies in Vertebrate Evolution,* ed. K. A. Joysey and T. S. Kemp. Edinburgh: Oliver and Boyd.

Crompton, A. W., and Jenkins, F. A., Jr.
1980. Origin of mammals. In *Mesozoic Mammals,* ed. J. A. Lillegraven, Z. Zielan-Jaworowska, and W. A. Clemens. Berkeley: University of California Press.

Crompton, A. W., and Parker, P.
1978. Evolution of the mammalian masticatory apparatus. *Amer. Scientist* 66:192–201.

Davis, D. D.
1961. Origin of the mammalian feeding mechanism. *Amer. Zool.* 1:229–34.

Fleischer, G.
1978. Evolutionary principles of the mammalian middle ear. *Adv. Anat., Embr. Cell Biol.* 55:1–70

Gans, C.
1974. *Biomechanics.* Toronto: Lippincott.

Gans, C., and Wever, E. G.
1976. Ear and hearing in *Sphenodon punctatus. Proc. Natl. Acad. Sci. USA* 73:4244–46.

Gaupp, E.
1913. Die Reichertsche Theorie. *Arch Anat u. Physiol., Abt. Anat.,* Supplement 4:1–417.

Goodrich, E. S.
1930. *Studies on the Structure and Development of Vertebrates.* London: Macmillan.

Henson, O. W., Jr.
1974. Comparative anatomy of the middle ear. In *Handbook of Sensory Physiology,* vol. 1., *Auditory System,* ed. W. D. Keidel and W. D. Neff. Berlin: Springer-Verlag.

Hopson, J. A.
1965. Tritylodontid therapsids and the cranial morphology of *Bienotherium.* PhD. dissertation, University of Chicago.
1966. The origin of the mammalian middle ear. *Amer. Zool.* 6:437–50.

Hopson, J. A., and Crompton, A. W.
1969. The origin of mammals. *Evol. Biol.* 3:15–72.

Hotton, N., III.
1959. The pelycosaur tympanum and the early evolution of the middle ear. *Evolution* 13:99–121.

Hutchins, C. M.
1962. The physics of violins. *Scient. American* (Nov.):79–93.

Jenkins, F. A., Jr., and Parrington, F. R.
1976. The postcranial skeletons of the Triassic mammals *Eozostrodon, Megazostrodon,* and *Erythrotherium. Phil. Trans. Roy. Soc. Lond.* B 273:387–431.

Kemp, T. S.
1972. Whaitsiid Therocehalia and the origin of cynodonts. *Phil Trans. Roy. Soc. Lond.* B 264:857–911.

Kemp, T. S.
1979. The primitive cynodont *Procynosuchus:* functional anatomy of the skull and relationships. *Phil Trans. Roy. Soc. Lond.* B 285:73–122.

Kemp, T. S.
1982. *Mammal-like Reptiles and the Origin of Mammals.* New York: Academic Press.

Kermack, K. A.; Mussett, F.; and Rigney, H. W.
1973. The lower jaw of *Morguanucodon. Zool. J. Linn. Soc.* 53:87–175.
1981. The skull of *Morguanucodon. J. Linn. Soc. (Zool.)* 71:1–158.

Kermack, K. A.
1982. The ear in the Theropsida *Geobios, mem. spec.* 6:151–56.
1983. The ear in mammal-like reptiles and early mammals. Acta Palaeont. Polon. 28:147–58.

Kühne, W. G.
1956. *The Liassic Therapsid Oligokyphus.* London: Adlard & Son Ltd.
1973. The systematic position of monotremes reconsidered (Mammalia) *Z. Morph. Tiere* 75:59–64.

Lombard, R. E., and Bolt, J. R.
1979. Evolution of the tetrapod ear: an analysis and reinterpretation. *Biol. J. Linn. Soc.* 11:19–76.

Lombard, R. E., and Straughan, I. R.
1974. Functional aspects of anuran middle ear structures. *J. Exp. Biol.* 61:71–93.

Manley, G. A.
1972. A review of some current concepts of the functional evolution of the ear in terrestrial vertebrates. *Evolution* 26:608–21.

Norberg, R. A.
1978. Skull asymmetry, ear structure and function, and auditory localization in Tengmalm's owl, *Aegolius funereus* (Linne). *Phil. Trans. Roy. Soc. Lond.* B 282:325–410.

Olson, E. C.
1944. Origin of the mammals based upon the cranial morphology of therapsid suborders. *Special paper, Geol. Soc. Amer.* 55:1–136.

Parrington, F. R.
1949. Remarks on a theory of the evolution of the tetrapod middle ear. *J. Laryngol. Otol.* 63: 580–95.
1974. The problem of the origin of monotremes *J. Nat. Hist.* 8:421–26.
1979. The evolution of the mammalian middle and outer ears: a personal review. *Biol. Rev.* 54:369–87.

Romer, A. S.
1956. *Osteology of the Reptiles.* Chicago: University of Chicago Press.
1970. The Chanares (Argentina) Triassic reptile fauna, VI. A chiniquodontid cynodont with an incipient squamosal-dentary jaw articulation. *Breviora, Mus. Comp. Zool.* 344:18.

Shute, C. C. D.
1956. The evolution of the mammalian eardrum and tympanic cavity. *J. Anat.* 90:261–81.

Shaw, E. A. G.
1974. The external ear. In *Handbook of Sensory Physiology,* vol. 1, *Auditory System,* ed. W. D. Keidel and W. D. Neff. Berlin: Springer-Verlag.

Simpson, G. G.
1933. The ear region and the foramina of the cynodont skull. *Amer. J. Sci.* 26:285–94.

Tumarkin, A.
1955. On the evolution of the auditory conducting apparatus: a new theory based on functional considerations. *Evolution* 9:221–42.

Watson, D. M. S.
1953. Evolution of the mammalian ear. *Evolution* 7:159–77.

Westoll, T. S.
1943. The hyomandibular of *Eusthenopteron* and the tetrapod middle ear. *Proc. Roy. Soc. Lond.* B 131:393–414.
1944. New light on the mammalian ear ossicles. *Nature, Lond.* 154:770–71.
1945. The mammalian middle ear. *Nature, Lond.* 155:114–15.

Wever, E. G.
1978. *The Reptile Ear.* Princeton: Princeton University Press.

E. F. ALLIN

G. EDWARD LEWIS[1]
U. S. Geological Survey, Retired

Nearctylodon broomi, the First Nearctic Tritylodont

Introduction

The Trilylodontidae is a family of mammal-like reptiles so advanced that they were long identified as mammals (e.g., Romer, 1933). They first appeared during the Late Triassic, and representatives survived into the Middle Jurassic. Tritylodonts have been known for more than a century from western Europe and England, and for a century from South Africa. About fifty years ago they were discovered in southwestern China, and undescribed fragments ascribed to the Tritylodontidae have been reported from northwestern Argentina. With the developing history of continental drift, it became reasonable to suppose that they should occur in rocks of the same age in North America, but despite assiduous search, it was not until 1953 that the first specimens were found.

North American Tritylodont Fossils

Discovery and collection

In the summer of 1953, Mr. Ben Hoy, of the Bureau of Indian Affairs, reported flecks of white material exposed in an outcrop atop Comb Ridge on the Navajo Indian Reservation. Mr. C. A. Repenning, of the U. S. Geological Survey, took me to the locality, which is 11.4 km airline, bearing 069° true, from Kayenta, Arizona. The outcrop is in the upper part of the Kayenta Formation, 2.5 to 3 m below the base of the overlying Navajo Sanstone. Here the Kayenta Formation is about 44.5 m thick.

Examination by hand lens showed that the flecks had bony structure; therefore, Mr. Glenn R. Scott and I quarried out a block of the rock matrix and took it to the Survey's Laboratory of Paleontology and Stratigraphy at the Federal

[1]Current address:
155 Brentwood Street
Lakewood, Colorado 80226

Center in Lakewood, Colorado. The bones exposed at the weathered rock surface proved to be small dermal scutes, and removal of the very refractory sandstone revealed the anterior portion of a skeleton of *Protosuchus,* a primitive crocodilian.

This success encouraged me to return to the quarry early in 1954, where, next to the spot from which the remains of *Protosuchus* had been collected, I removed a number of additional blocks. On the broken surface of these blocks were exposed a few sections on bone, unidentifiable in the field. Preparation of this unpromising material was begun at the Survey Laboratory in 1954 by Mr. William Aaron, whose work gradually revealed a long, relatively thin, curved, tapering tooth that projected from the symphyseal area of a lower jaw. Although this tooth looks more like the canine of a modern carnivore than the incisors of *Tritylodon* and *Bienotherium,* which are short, blunt, and subcircular in cross section, it aroused the expectation that we had at last found a tritylodont in North America.

This expectation was confirmed by Mr. Aaron's careful preparation that first exposed an upper cheek tooth, and by June, 1954, an outline of the skull of the first known members of the family Tritylodontidae from the Western Hemisphere. This discovery was announced in a press release, and informally at the 1954 meetings of the Society of Vertebrate Paleontology and the Geological Society of America; it was reported subsequently in the bulletin of the latter society (Lewis, 1958). Mr. Aaron was succeeded by Mr. Robert W. O'Donnell, who has done most of the preparation, devoting many years to the tedious, painstaking freeing of these fossils from the very refractory rock matrix, a task not yet finished.

My party returned to the field in 1955, prepared to make a more extensive collection by enlarging the quarry with blasting powder, and took out about 500 kg of fossiliferous blocks. An even larger collection was made the next year. In due course the U. S. Geological Survey collections will be deposited in the National Museum of Natural History, formerly the U. S. National Museum, and accordingly have been assigned National Museum catalogue numbers, prefix USNM.

One year later I invited Dr. E. H. Colbert and Mr. George Whittaker of the American Museum of Natural History to join the survey party at the quarry. Together with Dr. John Ostrom, then a student of Dr. Colbert, they packed and shipped that year's large collection to the American Museum for preparation. Some of these specimens, identified by American Museum catalogue numbers, prefix AMNH, provide data for the present study. Subsequently, Dr. David H. Dunkle, of the National Museum of Natural History, joined our survey party, and a large collection was deposited at the National Museum. Dr. William D. Turnbull, of the Field Museum of Natural History, accompanied me to the quarry during still another year, to make plans to collect for his institution.

Status of material in custody of the U. S. Geological Survey

The Survey's collection now includes ten skulls with associated mandibles. One of these specimens is part of a nearly complete articulated skeleton, USNM 317201, the genoholotype of the species established in this paper. Four other associated skulls and mandibles belong to incomplete articulated skeletons, two skulls are articulated with cervical vertebrae, and three have no other bones directly associated with them. Five specimens of upper jaw fragments, some of which are associated with lower jaw fragments, have been prepared. A specimen catalogued as USNM 317204, which consists of a maxillary and a dentary fragment with upper and lower incisors and cheek teeth, constitutes the remains of the smallest individual in the collection. The cheek teeth of this specimen are only 20 to 25 percent of the length of the cheek teeth of the largest specimen, and about 30 percent of that of AMNH 7650, the largest specimen treated in detail in this paper (Table 1). All told, the Survey collection represents the remains of more than twenty-four individual animals.

Tritylodont remains of comparable abundance and diversity from other localities have traditionally led to the establishment, chiefly on the basis of size, of multiple closely related species. Such an interpretation is not tenable in this case, because all of the Comb Ridge material comes from a single stratigraphic level, and there is no evidence that it was drawn from more than one life assemblage. By Matthew's (1930) analogy with assemblages of living tetrapods, species are not normally associated with closely related species of the same genus. I therefore think that all of the specimens at hand are members of a single species, preserved much as they had lived, at one stratigraphic position in the Kayenta Formation.

Table 1.—Upper cheek dentition of *Nearctylodon broomi* in serial succession. Length of the diastema and labial lengths of the first five teeth are tabulated to scale (left to right = front to back), and arranged in sequence of increasingly greater lengths of skull. The posterior end of the diastema, indicated by double vertical lines, is marked in actual specimens by the first tooth in the cheek series, but the teeth are plotted according to corresponding labial lengths. The nine specimens in this series include the type of *N. broomi*, USNM 317201. Catalogue numbers: 4 digits, AMNH; 6 digits, USNM

Stage no.	Skull length lambda to prosthion	Diastema	1	2	3	4	5	6	7	8	9	10	11	12	13	14	15
11	149	23									7.4	7.5	7.6	?	?		
10	142	22								7.0	7.4	7.5	8.0	8.5			
9	137	20							6.3	7.0	7.4	7.5	7.7				
8	119	16						5.8	6.5	7.0	7.4	7.5					
7	117	13					5.7	5.9	6.5	6.7	7.3						
6																	
5	105	12				4.6	5.2	5.7	6.0	6.5							
4	?	6			4.1	4.6	5.2	5.2	?								
3	90	9			3.0	4.0	4.5	5.0	5.7								
2																	
1	?	4.7	1.7	2.0	2.8	?	?										

UPPER CHEEK TEETH, SERIAL SUCCESSION (labial lengths in millimeters) — DEVELOPMENTAL TOOTH POSITION

Taxonomy

Class REPTILIA
Order **THERAPSIDA**
Infraorder Cynodontia
Superfamily Tritylodontoidea
Family **Tritylodontidae**
Genus *Nearctylodon,* new genus

Etymology: The name is formed by elision of "Nearctic," the present-day zoogeographic region where the genus was discovered, with *"Tritylodon",* a genus to which it is closely related.

Genotype: Nearctylodon broomi.

Included species: Only the genotype is known to date.

Diagnosis: Tritylodontidae in which the septomaxilla separates the premaxilla from the nasal, as in *Tritylodon,* but differing from *Oligokyphus* and *Bienotherium* in this respect; a lambdoid crest extends backward over the occipital region; the only incisors present are I^2 and I_1 (Fig. 1), which are long, thin, curved, and tapered rather than short, blunt, and subcircular in crosssection as in other tritylodonts; up to 7 cheek teeth have

cusp formula outside— $\dfrac{2\text{-}3\text{-}3}{3\text{-}3}$ —inside as in *Tritylodon;* the mandibular articulation is between the quadrate and the long, slim articular as in *Oligokyphus;* coronoid process not as restored in

Oligokyphus by Kühne (1956), and in *Bienotherium,* but with the top recurved and projecting backward beyond that part of the ascending ramus below it as in *Diarthrognathus* and in *Oligokyphyus* as restored by Crompton (1963); 7 cervical vertebrae, 19 dorsal vertebrae (the last 2 could be called *lumbar*), spinous processes of dorsal neural arches distinctively expanded transversely rather than long and laterally compressed, transverse expansion greatest in posterior dorsals, expecially in lumbars (Fig. 2), 4 sacral vertebrae, at least 19 caudal vertebrae; morphology of girdles and limbs therapsidlike,

Figure 1. Left lateral view of the skull of the type specimen of *Nearctylodon broomi* n. sp., USNM 317201.

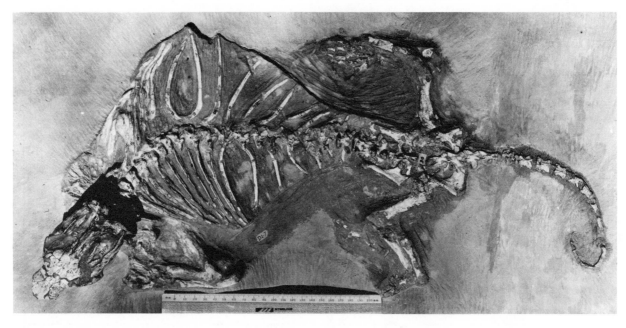

Figure 2.   Dorsal view of the type specimen of *Nearctylodon broomi* n. sp., USNM 317201.

with some ornithorhynchoid features but no epi-pubic bones, manus larger than pes, both clawed with phalangeal formula 2-3-3-3-3.

Nearctylodon broomi, new species

Etymology: Named in honor of the late Robert Broom, whose keen insight contributed so greatly to his studies of tritylodonts, ictidosaurs, and other therapsids.

Holotype: A nearly complete articulated skeleton with skull and mandible, USNM 317201 (Fig. 3).

Hypodigm: With the type, includes four incomplete articulated skeletons with skulls and mandibles, USNM 317201, 317202, 317207, 317208; two skulls with associated mandibles, articulated with cervical vertebrae, USNM 317209, 317210; three skulls with associated mandibles, USNM 317203, 317205, 317206; five palates or upper jaw fragments with associated lower jaw fragments, USNM 317204, 317211, 317212, 317213, 317214; and a number of more fragmentary specimens. In addition, there are numerous specimens from the same stratigraphic position in the same quarry, largely unprepared and un-catalogued, in the National Museum of Natural History, the Field Museum of Natural History, and the American Museum of Natural History.

Locality: U. S. Geological Survey Fossil Vertebrate Locality D1 on Comb Ridge, 11.4 km airline, bearing 069° true, from Kayenta, Arizona,

1,701 m above sea level, in the upper part of the Kayenta Formation, 2.5 to 3.0 m below the top of the formation and about 41.75 m above the base at the top of the Wingate Sandstone.

Diagnosis: The same as for the type genus.

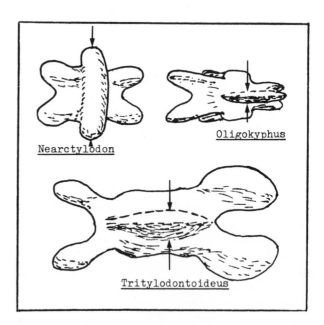

Figure 3.   Transversely expanded distal end of dorsal neural spine, presacral 25, *Nearctylodon broomi* n. sp., USNM 317201. Transverse distance 12.4 mm. Presacral vertebrae of *Oligokyphus* (After Kühne, 1956) and *Tritylodontoideus* (from cast) are shown to scale. All in dorsal aspect, anterior to right.

G. E. LEWIS

Growth and Tooth Replacement

The uniform preservation of the remains of *Nearctylodon*, together with the proximity, both lateral and vertical, of specimens in the field, indicate not that the individuals belong to a single species, but also that they probably died at about the same time. The individuals therefore serve collectively as a model of ontogenetic growth in the species *N. broomi,* their size range reflecting, from smallest to largest, a range of ages from youngest to oldest at time of death.

Ossification and adult size

None of the specimens from Comb Ridge seems to be fully ossified. In the holotype, USNM 317201, which falls about eighty-seven percent of the way from the smallest to the largest extremes at hand, carpals and tarsals are not preserved, though the fore and hind feet are preserved in articulation (Fig. 3). Likewise, the ends of the long bones and of many vertebral centra, and the basis cranii, are poorly preserved, as if they had consisted of cartilage rather than bone. Larger specimens show somewhat better preservation, but the condition of even the largest suggests persistently cartilagenous ends on the long bones. A single large femur, unassociated with other skeletal elements, has ends that are more completely finished in bone than any part of the holotype.

This condition probably indicates that the entire Comb Ridge collection consists of juveniles, the more complete, but still limited, ossification of the larger specimens foreshadowing the approach of maturity. If this is the case, the South African genus *Tritylodontoideus* Fourie (1962) provides an analogue of the adult size of *Nearctylodon*. With a skull length of 250 mm, *Tritylodontoideus* is nearly twice the size of its South African coeval *Tritylodon,* which has about the same size range as the Comb Ridge specimens. J. W. Kitching (personal communication, 1982) suggests that *Tritylodontoideus* represents a large adult individual of *Tritylodon,* and a comparable adult size for *Nearctylodon* is consistent with the evident immaturity of the American specimens.

An alternative possibility is that the poor ossification of the Comb Ridge material reflects adaptation to aquatic life. This explanation, however, is not supported by an morphological speciliazation of limbs, girdles, presacral vertebral column, or tail. On the evidence of these structures, *Nearctylodon* seems to be a rather generalized terrestrial tetrapod near the transition from therapsid to mammalian levels of organization.

Size and replacement of teeth

If the fossils from Comb Ridge are indeed the remains of immature animals, they represent a period of development during which replacement of teeth was most rapid. In order to exploit this condition to illustrate certain details of dental succession, specimens have been selected for measurement of representative growth stages (Tables 1 and 2). These specimens are chosen for the completeness of their dentition to assure maximum recovery of information, and, because this criterion overrides other considerations, the intervals between growth stages are not entirely uniform.

Measurements include length of skull from lambda to prosthion as an index of size over all, lengths of the first five cheek teeth along the labial margins of the crowns, and the length of the diastema from the base of the incisor to the actual position of the first tooth. The length of the row of cheek teeth is satisfactorily indicated by the sum of the labial lengths of the first five teeth, although it is short of being complete by the lengths of the last one or two teeth. Labial length of the last teeth was not measured, nor was the maximum anteroposterior diameter of any teeth, since these data are inaccessible in the majority of specimens because the jaws are tightly clenched and cannot be separated without excessive damage.

Each new cheek tooth of *Nearctylodon* erupts at the back of the tooth row while an old tooth is being shed at the front. The labial length of individual teeth increases from the front to the rear of each row, presumably because a given animal was larger when the last tooth erupted than it had been when more anterior teeth came in. In the sample at hand, the lengths of the row of cheek teeth and of the diastema increase with over-all size at comparable rates. The slope of linear regressions on skull length ($Y = a + bX$) is 0.29 for the tooth row (r = .97) and 0.25 for the diastema (r = .98). The length of the tooth-bearing ramus of the dentary does not increase fast enough to keep pace with the eruption of ever larger teeth at the back of the functional row, which in consequence is forced bodily forward. When they first erupt and come into occlusion, the crowns are at the gum line. As the teeth move forward, they rise higher and higher *pari passu* until they reach the front of the cheek

Table 2.—Lower cheek dentition of *Nearctylodon broomi* in serial succession. Format as in Table 1

Stage no.	Skull length lambda to prosthion	Diastema	1	2	3	4	5	6	7	8	9	10	11	12	13	14	15
11	149												8.3	8.4	?	?	?
10	142	26										7.5	7.7	8.6	?	?	
9	137	17									7.5	7.8	8.0	8.5	?		
8	119	13								6.0	7.1	7.8	7.9	?			
7	117	15							6.2	6.5	7.2	7.6	?				
6																	
5	105	10						5.8	6.6	7.2	7.3	?					
4	?	5				4.2	4.9	5.3	5.8	?							
3	90	5.3			3.6	4.6	5.2	5.9	6.7								
2																	
1	?	4.0	2.0	2.5	2.9	?	?										

LOWER CHEEK TEETH, SERIAL SUCCESSION (labial lengths in millimeters)

DEVELOPMENTAL TOOTH POSITION

series, where they appear to be standing on the tips of their roots just before being shed. This mode of replacement is common to tritylodonts generally (see Kühne, 1956, pp. 67–68) and their close relatives the gomphodont cynodonts, and resembles that of manatees and elephants. It contrasts sharply with tooth succession in other vertebrates, in which the new tooth erupts from the same position as the tooth being replaced.

Position of teeth

Teeth in a single row vary so consistently in labial length that some of them are more nearly similar to some of the teeth of larger or smaller specimens than they are to the rest of the teeth in their own row. For example (Table 1), the fifth upper cheek tooth of stage 7 corresponds in length to the fourth of stage 8, to the third of stage 9, to the second of stage 10, and to the first of stage 11, more closely than it does to the other teeth of stage 7. Similarly, the third upper cheek tooth of stage 3 corresponds to the second of stage 4 and to the first of stage 5.

In a sequence of increasingly larger specimens, the arrangement of teeth of corresponding labial length into vertical columns results in a distinctively staggered pattern of tooth rows (Tables 1 and 2). This pattern suggests that the diastema increases in length primarily by the shedding of anterior teeth, most of the dental ramus being occupied by teeth at all stages of growth. Extrapolation of the data to smaller sizes allows the possibility that the diastema of stage 1 attained its recorded length through the shedding of still smaller anterior teeth. In the lack of evidence to

the contrary, however, the diastema of stage 1 must be treated as though it had not previously been occupied by teeth, a condition which probably existed at some very small but currently indeterminate size.

Variation of the labial length of teeth in the same vertical column (Table 1) is smaller than it is in any individual tooth row (Table 3). The vertical columns therefore appear to mark "developmental" positions in the jaw, where teeth erupt at about the same developmental stage in all individuals. Developmental positions, determined solely by the labial length of the tooth that occupies them at some ontogenetic stage, contrast with the positions in specific individuals that are actually occupied by teeth, the most anterior marking the back of the diastema. No more than seven positions are actually occupied by teeth in any jaw, but from 13 to 15 developmental positions are identified by the progressive overlap of tooth rows in the sample at hand. The exact number of positions is uncertain because the difference between the labial lengths of adjacent teeth declines as the teeth get larger. One can be fairly confident of a difference of 1 mm between teeth in the range of 2 to 4 mm labial length (Table 1, columns 1–4), but a difference of 0.1 mm between teeth of 7.5 mm labial length (Table 1, columns 11 and 12) is more equivocal. It is possible that columns 11 and 12, and perhaps columns 7 and 8, represent single developmental positions from which, for currently unknown reasons, two teeth normally erupt. In any case, assuming the maximum of 15 developmental positions shown in Table 1, an in-

Table 3.—Variation $V = \dfrac{100X}{S_x}$ of labial length of teeth, from Tables 1 and 2

	Individual tooth rows, tabulated as horizontal rows		Developmental position, tabulated as vertical columns	
	Stage number (N = 5) except as noted	V	Column number (N variable)	V
Upper (Table 1)	10	7.6	13 (N = 3)	2.7
	9	7.7	12 (N = 4)	0
	8	10.3	11 (N = 5)	0.6
	7	10.0	10 (N = 4)	2.2
	5	13.1	9 (N = 4)	1.6
	4 (N = 4)	11.1	8 (N = 3)	1.7
	3	23.0	7 (N = 4)	4.5
Lower (Table 2) (N = 4 except as noted)	9	5.3	12 (N = 3)	1.2
	8	12.2	11 (N = 4)	3.1
	7	9.3	10 (N = 5)	2.8
	5	10.3	9 (N = 4)	2.4
	4	11.6	8 (N = 4)	4.8
	3 (N = 5)	22.9	7 (N = 4)	3.2

dividual of *Nearctylodon broomi* that lived to grow as large as stage 11 would have erupted 15 teeth, having shed eight and retained seven by the time it died.

Change in the actual position of the tooth row is evaluated by the increase in the length of the diastema, which, being mediated by the shedding of teeth at the front of the row, is stepwise, in contrast to over-all growth, which is essentially continuous. In two skulls of comparable lambda-to-prosthion length, the diastema can vary by the full labial length of a cheek tooth, depending on whether the tooth at the end of the row is still retained or has just been shed. In the sequence of stages 7, 8, and 9, for example, diastema length increases by twenty-five percent over each interval, whereas skull length increases by only two percent from stage 7 to 8, but by fifteen percent from stage 8 to 9. Thus the increments of change of diastema length and,

Table 4.—Summary to show measurements, growth stages, and serial succession of upper and lower cheek teeth at a glance

*NEARCTYLODON BROOMI — LENGTHS OF CHEEK TEETH IN MILLIMETERS, MEASURED ALONG LABIAL SIDES OF CROWNS. Upper cheek teeth (serial succession** arranged by increasing size) in columns U1–U15; lower cheek teeth in columns L1–L15.*

Specimen No.	Stage	U1	U2	U3	U4	U5	U6	U7	U8	U9	U10	U11	U12	U13	U14	U15	L1	L2	L3	L4	L5	L6	L7	L8	L9	L10	L11	L12	L13	L14	L15	CT^{1-3}	CT^{1-4}	DIASTEMA/	CT_{1-3}	CT_{1-4}	/DIASTEMA	LAMBDA-PROSTHION
7650	11											7.4	7.5	7.6	?	?											8.3	8.4	?	?	?	22	?	23	28	?	?	149
317202	10										7.0	7.4	7.5	8.0	8.5											7.5	7.7	8.6	?	?		20	29	22	23	32	26	142
317206	9									6.3	7.0	7.4	7.5	7.7											7.5	7.8	8.0	8.5	?			20	29	20	25	34	17	137
317201 (this specimen is the Type)	8								5.8	6.5	7.0	7.4	7.5											6.0	7.1	7.8	7.9	?				20	28	16	20	27	13	119
317205	7							5.7	5.9	6.5	6.7	7.3											6.2	6.5	7.2	7.6	?					18	24	13	19	27	15	117
	6											(this is a hypothetical stage, not represented in collections)																										
7651	5					4.6	5.2	5.7	6.0	6.5											5.8	6.6	7.2	7.3	?							17	24	12	20	28	10	105
7654	4				4.1	4.6	5.2	5.2	?											4.2	4.9	5.3	5.8	?								14	20	6	15	21	5	?
317203	3			3.0	4.0	4.5	5.0	5.7											3.6	4.6	5.2	5.9	6.7									12	17	9	14	20	5.3	90
	2											(this is a hypothetical stage, not represented in collections)																										
317204	1	1.7	2.0	2.8	?	?											2.0	2.5	2.9	?	?											6.8	?	4.7	6.5	?	4.0	?

*National Museum of the United States catalog, six 6-digit numbers; American Museum of Natural History catalog, three 4-digit numbers.

**Arranged according to increasing size.

therefore, of tooth position do not correspond precisely to the intervals between growth stages in the sample at hand.

This discrepancy is accommodated by inferring stages 2 and 6, which are unrepresented by specimens. Stages 2 and 6 are of limited value, however, for although they smooth out the pattern of overlap of the upper cheek teeth (Table 1), they do not improve that of the lowers (Table 2), which are generally less regular than the uppers. The lower teeth are consistently slightly longer than the uppers, as though their developmental succession lay one position to the rear with respect to the upper teeth.

Forward movement of the tooth row

The relationship between the actual and developmental positions of the first cheek tooth corroborates the forward movement of the tooth row during growth, and affords an estimate of its rate with respect to increase in size over all. This relationship is derived by reference to the smallest specimen, stage 1 (Table 4).

At stage 1, the beginning of the developmental sequence is identified by the labial length of the first tooth, the actual position of which defines the posterior end of the diastema as it does in all specimens. At stage 3, the developmental position of the first tooth, defined by labial length, coincides with the actual position defining the back of the diastema, perhaps because the diastemal increment corresponds closely to the sum of the labial lengths of teeth putatively shed since stage 1. By stage 5 this coincidence no longer exists, despite continued addition to diastemal length by the shedding of anterior teeth. The labial length of the first tooth is now greater than the length expected by comparison with

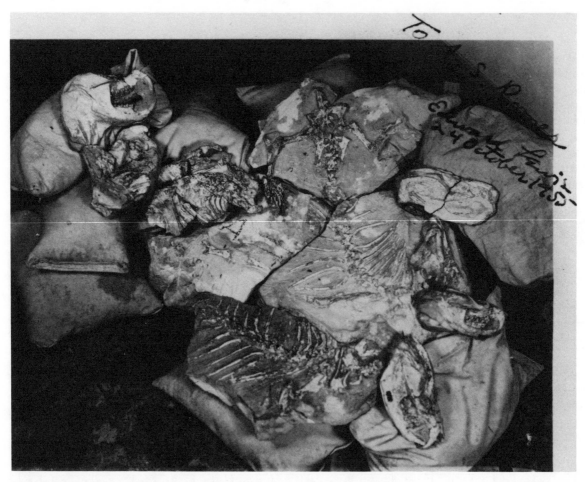

Figure 4. Thanks to Charles Schaff, Museum of Comparative Zoology, Harvard University, the editors obtained a photo of several blocks from the original find of tritylodonts at Comb Ridge that G. Edward Lewis inscribed for A. S. Romer. Dr. Lewis kindly gave permission to reproduce it at the end of his article. The photo shows the remains of five nearly complete specimen found in close proximity.

G. E. Lewis

smaller stages, and in still larger animals becomes progressively greater than expected values (Table 1, shaded zone tabulated to scale in terms of labial length of expected teeth). Thus the increase in length of the diastema fails to keep pace with the sum of expected labial lengths of shed cheek teeth. The most parsimonious explanation of the difference is that it represents the distance along which the tooth row moves to bring the most anterior cheek tooth to its actual position at the back of the diastema. Accordingly, as *Nearctylodon broomi* grew from an individual with a skull 90 mm long to one with a skull 149 mm long, the row of cheek teeth moved forward across more than four developmental tooth positions, a distance of about 27 mm. Distance of movement ranges from zero in the smallest specimens at hand to about forty percent of the length of the tooth-bearing ramus of the dentary in the largest.

References

Crompton, A. W.
1963. On the lower jaw of *Diarthrognathus* and the origin of the mammalian lower jaw. *Zool. Soc. London Proc.* 140:697–750.

Fourie, S.
1962. Notes on a new tritylodontid from the Cave Sandstone of South Africa. *Navorsinge Nasionale Mus. Bloemfontein,* 2(1):7–19.

Kühne, W. G.
1956. *The Liassic Therapsid* Oligokyphus. London: Trustees of the British Museum (Natural History).

Lewis, G. E.
1958. American Triassic mammal-like vertebrates. *Geol. Soc. America Bull.* 69:1735. [Abstract]

Matthew, W. D.
1930. Range and limitations of species as seen in fossil mammals faunas. *Bull. Geol. Soc. America* 41:271–74.

Romer, A. S.
1933. *Vertebrate paleontology,* 1st ed. Chicago: The University of Chicago Press.

SUMMARY

JOHN A. RUBEN
Department of Zoology
Oregon State University
Corvallis, Oregon 97331

Therapsids and Their Environment, A Summary

Introduction

A major incentive for producing this volume is the paradox that so many trained biologists know that dinosaurs may have been warm-blooded, yet are unaware of the very existence of the mammal-like reptiles, the Therapsida and their predecessors. Although this state of affairs may cause dismay in some quarters, it is hardly surprising: the mammal-like reptiles are less spectacular in appearance than dinosaurs, and good therapsid fossil localities are restricted primarily to the Southern Hemisphere. As a result, therapsids seldom become the subjects of museum displays or classroom student presentations, at least in North America. Moreover, biology textbooks, whether at the high school or college level, almost invariably devote more space for recounting the "dinosaur story" than to discussing the therapsid reptiles (see, e.g., Boolootian and Stiles, 1981). Consequently, although application of biological systems data to the fossil record has become increasingly popular and useful in the last decade, many neontologists who might potentially make substantial contributions to our knowledge of therapsid biology remain oblivious to the significance of these animals. This is doubly unfortunate, for therapsids encompass not only the phylogenetic predecessors of mammals, but also a very significant part of the biological environment in which the ancestors of mammals evolved. The better we understand the mammal-like reptiles, the more likely we are to understand the origins and functions of our own anatomical, physiological, and behavioral systems.

General interpretations of therapsid origins and phylogeny (Fig. 1) have, with a few excep-

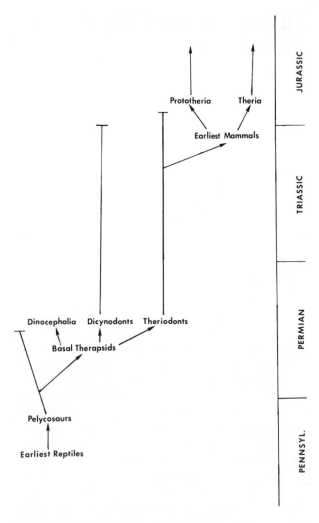

Figure 1. The evolution and relationships of the synapsid reptiles and early mammals. (From Hopson and Barghusen, personal communication; Romer, 1961; and Crompton and Jenkins, 1979.)

tions, remained essentially those of Romer (1961) and Boonstra (1963). Major groups of therapsid reptiles included the theriodonts, dicynodonts, and dinocephalians. Theriodonts were primarily carnivorous animals although a number of Triassic forms became specialized herbivores (see Lewis, this volume). Late Triassic therapsids were the most mammal-like of all, and a number of them were, in many respects, indistinguishable from early mammals.

Dicynodonts were exclusively herbivorous forms that were extremely abundant from the Late Permian to the Early Triassic. Distinctive dicynodont features included their edentulous trophic apparatus (except for the presence of a pair of enlarged maxillary tusks) and a beaklike rostrum. Dinocephalians were the earliest of the therapsids for which we can identify a significant

adaptive radiation, and for a time must have been the dominant land vertebrates. Most were enormous, ponderous creatures and included both herbivorous and carnivorous species.

My purpose is to review briefly our knowledge of the physical world of the therapsid reptiles, in the context of data presented in preceeding chapters concerning the evolution of therapsids, their ancestors, and the Permo-Triassic fauna and flora.

Review

The world of therapsid reptiles, from Middle Permian to Late Triassic times (about 240–190 M.Y.B.P.) was one of profound changes in the earth's crust and great diversification of the terrestrial vertebrate biota. Throughout this time period, although the continents remained coalesced as the "supercontinent" Pangaea, extensive epeirogenetic movements and orogenic disturbances transformed numerous geosynclines into mountain ranges. Thus, mountain ranges formed during the life of Pangaea included, among others, the Ouachita and Appalachian ranges of North America, the Urals of western Asia and the Varisca chain of England, northern France, and Germany.

These orogenic episodes and other crustal activities associated with them resulted in a rather continuous reduction in the extent of inland seas, especially in North America and Europe. For example, fairly extensive Middle Permian embayments in southwest North America connected broadly with extensive marine transgressions to the northwest via waterways in what is now California, Nevada, and Utah. By Late Triassic times these embayments had shrunk to roughly one-half their original size (Dunbar, 1964).

Permian and Triassic climates seem to have been increasingly equable, especially from Middle Permian times onward. Early Permian glaciation in South Africa apparently gave way to high-latitude temperate climates by Middle to Late Permian times, and faunal and floral evidence indicates that cosmopolitan subtropical to tropical climates persisted throughout the Triassic Period. Upper Permian-Triassic evaporites indicate that broad bands of seasonally dry regions existed to the east of more mesic areas of southwest and northwest Pangaea. These climatic conditions are hypothesized to have resulted, in part, from warm oceanic and wind currents approaching the equatorial region of eastern Pangaea, which were deflected into northern and southern gyres (Robinson, 1972; Parrish *et al.,* this volume). Additionally, the northward drift of Pangaea away from the southern polar influence probably also contributed to the overall warming trend.

Hickey (verbal communication, 1981) points out that in spite of contiguous land masses and broad bands of thermal equability, there seems to have been great variation between northern and southern floras of the Permian and Triassic Periods. Middle to Upper Permian Southern Hemispheric *Glossopteris* floras included conifers, sphenopsids, and abundant seed ferns. In contrast, northern floras from this time period contained varieties of seed ferns not found to the south, along with a far higher proportion of upland conifers. The contrast between northern and southern floras intensified into the Triassic Period. Early Triassic southern floras consisted primarily of different varieties of seed ferns and conifers, while the north became dominated by other conifers, bennettitaleans, and cycads. Seed ferns persisted as relatively minor constituents of northern floras throughout the Triassic and, in fact, survived, albeit at decreasing levels, into the Early Cretaceous in the Northern Hemisphere.

There seems to have been little general correlation between therapsid geographic distribution and particular types of seed or forage plants. For example, well-developed Early Triassic dicynodont faunas existed in regions dominated by conifers and cycads in the north and seed ferns in the south.

Therapsid predecessors, the pelycosaurs, originated in the Pennsylvanian Period and relatively quickly thereafter enjoyed spectacular early and continued dominance over the Pennsylvanian to Middle Permian terrestrial vertebrate biota. Carroll (this volume), enlarging on earlier work of Barghusen (1973), presents evidence that might account for this situation. Specifically, the adductor muscle mass, even in the earliest pelycosaurs, is thought to have inserted on the mandible in a manner that severely restricted the ability of struggling prey to cause anterior dislocation of the lower jaw. Such an arrangement of the jaw musculature can be analogized with the function of the temporalis muscle in modern Carnivora, and is hypothesized to have enabled early synapsids to become the first group of truly carnivorous (as opposed to insectivorous) reptiles. Carroll also emphasizes the architectural role of the massive stapes of early

reptiles and the probable absence of a refined tympanic ear.

Attainment of the dentary-squamosal jaw joint in the cynodont-mammal lineage has long been recognized as one of the hallmarks of the mammalian grade of evolution. What has not always been so clear is why such a major reorganization of the cynodont jaw and middle ear took place at all. Recent evidence, however, strongly indicates the mammalian ear is capable of audition over a far greater range of sound frequencies than any other group of vertebrates (Fleischer, 1978). Allin (1975; this volume) presents evidence that the ever-decreasing robustness of the jaw joint and postdentary bones in theriodonts and the eventual inclusion of quadrate and articular homologues into the mammalian middle ear may have been associated with continued selection for this capacity. According to his interpretation, the reflected lamina of the cynodont angular bone supported a tympanic membrane which transmitted sound vibrations to the inner ear via the reduced quadrate and articular bones. Allin now accepts the probable presence in cynodonts of an external acoustic meatus, postquadrate eardrum, and stapedial tympanic process. He also now considers Westoll's postdentary vocal resonator hypothesis attractive and consonant with reception of vocalizations by the mandibular tympanum.

In galesaurid cynodonts such as *Thrinaxodon,* reduction of the jaw articulation was compensated by suspension of the mandible in a mammal-like muscular sling. This configuration generated biting force at the teeth while simultaneously blocking significant stress at the articulation (Crompton and Parker, 1978). Crompton and Hylander (this volume) demonstrate that in advanced cynodonts, jaw joint reaction forces were also minimized by a bilaterally symmetrical bite, and that the asymmetrical chewing of mammals became feasible only with the advent of the squamosodentary joint. Eventual contact of the dentary with the squamosal, and incorporation of the quadrate and articular into the middle ear, strengthened the joint sufficiently to accomodate a broader repertoire of jaw motions. This, presumably, was the refinement that enabled mammals to evolve a wide variety of cheek teeth.

In association with the development of the mammalian middle ear, Barghusen (this volume) demonstrates the probable evolution of the anterior portion of the mammalian eustachian tube from evidence afforded by a lateral air channel found in the cynodont nasopharynx. Additionally, he details the probable homologous relationship of the tensor veli palatini and tensor tympani muscles with portions of the proximal and distal regions, respectively, of the reptilian posterior pterygoideus muscle. Consequently, the ancient but highly modified association of the pterygoid musculature with the articular bone has persisted in mammals.

Olson (1972; this volume) contrasts general patterns of pelycosaur and therapsid adaptive radiations. Pelycosaurs exhibit a relatively conservative morphology throughout their history. Major changes, such as they were, usually involved fluctuations in size. This was hypothesized to have been the result of carnivorous pelycosaurs having fed primarily on aquatic prey (e.g., fish, nectrideans), which resulted in little selection for postcranial morphological specialization in that group, although cranial morphology suggests that sphenacodontids were capable of feeding on terrestrial as well as aquatic prey.

In contrast, virtually all therapsids (including all dinocephalians, theriodonts, dicynodonts) exhibited changes in general morphology (cranial and postcranial) associated with either terrestrial herbivory or a terrestrial mode of predation. For example, the highly predaceous theriodonts assumed numerous specialized features foreshadowing many mammalian characteristics. Hotton (this volume) points out that Middle and Upper Permian dicynodonts possessed a variety of trophic and postcranial adaptations and had become specialized into at least three distinct modes of herbivory: grubbing or rooting (*Dicynodon, Diictodon*), fossorial (*Cistecephalus*), and "browsing" (*Oudenodon*). Even the earlier, cumbersome dinocehalians exhibited postcranial features indicative of a greater variety of feeding modes and more progressive modes of locomotion than any pelycosaurs (Sues, this volume). Thus, constant selection for more efficient terrestrial locomotion and herbivorous or predaceous trophic apparatus seems to have resulted in greater diversity of terrestrial forms of Permian synapsids.

Although therapsids underwent a great adaptive radiation, and were in fact, probably the dominant terrestrial vertebrate of their day, virtually all the vertebrate biota, especially the reptiles, experienced significant adaptive radiation during this time period. Reptiles expanded from six Middle Permian orders (Araeoscelidia, Captorhinomorpha, Mesosauria, Pelycosauria, Procolophonia, Therapsida) and attained their peak

ordinal diversity—thirteen orders (Araeoscelidia, Chelonia, Crocodilia, Eosuchia, Icthyosauria, Ornithischia, Procolophonia, Rhynchocephalia, Saurischia, Sauropterygia, Squamata, Thecodontia, Therapsida)—by the end of the Triassic. Major groups of reptiles that probably coexisted with late Permian therapsids included the Captorhinomorpha, Procolophonia, Eosuchia, and Araeoscelidia.

Most captorhinomorphs, Permian eosuchians and araeoscelidians were primariy lizardlike invertebrate feeders, although later captorhinomorphs have been among the earliest terrestrial herbivores.

Procolophonians, which were probably derived from the captorhinomorphs, were mostly small, slim-limbed creatures about 1–2 feet in length. Although early procolophonians were much like captorhinomorphs, many Triassic species possessed transversely expanded teeth probably adapted to a herbivorous mode of feeding. A specialized group of Middle to Late Permian procolophonians, the pareiasaurs, were among the largest of Permian reptiles. These thick-bodied, slow-moving herbivores attained lengths of three meters. Their fossilized remains are fairly comon in late Permian deposits in South Africa and Europe, and it seems likely that they were among the most abundant of Late Permian plant-eaters.

Representatives of all previously listed orders, except the captorhinomorphs, survived into the Triassic. These were joined by significant radiations of many of the more familiar reptiles, including the rhynchocephalians, lizards, thecodonts, crocodiles, dinosaurs, chelonians, sauropterygians, and icthyosaurs.

Most Triassic rhynchocephalians and lizards were, superficially at least, much like today's lizards. However, one group of rhynchocephalians, the rhynchosaurs, attained large size (many hundreds of pounds) and may have been very specialized frugivores. Additionally, even at this relatively early phase of lizard evolution, there were already specialized forms apparently capable of gliding, somewhat similar to extant *Draco*.

Thecodonts underwent a significant Triassic radiation. Major groups of thecodonts included: pseudosuchians—small, apparently bipedal ancestors of more specialized thecodonts, dinosaurs, pterosaurs, and crocodiles; phytosaurs—large crocodilelike animals; aetosaurs—heavily armored, medium-sized quadrupeds; and early, small crocodiles.

Dinosaurs, including herbivorous and carnivorous forms, were well differentiated by the Late

Triassic, although at that relatively early stage in their history they were far less specialized than they were to become in the Jurassic and Cretaceous Periods.

Triassic turtles, such as *Proganochelys,* though they retained teeth and could not retract their extremities, were nevertheless very turtlelike in their external appearance and probably in their habits as well.

Far less terrestrial in habitat were the sauropterygians. Triassic forms included the marine placodonts and the amphibious nothosaurs. Placodonts, most of which seem to have been mollusc-eaters, can best be likened to extant seals, although some very specialized forms were amazingly similar to marine turtles. Nothosaurs, the probable ancestors of the plesiosaurs, were large, long-bodied, semiaquatic fish feeders that perhaps resembled living sea-lions, at least in their habits.

A number of amphibians, including a wide variety of labyrinthodonts were contemporary with Permian therapsids, but by the end of the Triassic Period, only a few lepospondyls and the highly aquatic stereospondylous labyrinthodonts remained.

The great increase in the number of orders of Triassic reptiles, compared to those of the Permian, is somewhat decetive. Permo-Triassic ordinal expansion was not a steady, orderly process of adaptive radiation; and unexplained large-scale extinctions at the end of the Permian led to the disappearance of some seventy-five percent of Late Permian reptilian genera. Thus, subsequent Early to Middle Triassic radiation was primarily responsible for the great diversity of early Mesozoic reptiles (for a more complete account of Permo-Triassic vertebrates, see Romer, 1966, and Colbert, this volume).

Considering their longtime dominance and increasingly sophisticated anatomical and physiological systems, the extinction of the therapsids is something of an enigma. Many factors were undoubtedly involved, among which Colbert (this volume) cites competition from Late Triassic dinosaurs as having perhaps hastened the exit of therapsids.

Although a broad variety of topics are reviewed and updated in this volume, there remain numerous important areas yet to be fully investigated. Prime among them is the biological significance of the marked reduction in size of late cynodonts and early mammals. Early theriodonts the size of large dogs were not uncommon, but the last chiniquodontid cynodonts had skulls only about 70 mm in length, and the earliest mammals were no longer than that in total length! Clearly, there was chronic selection for decreasing size in early mammals and their predecessors. The specifics of such continued selection remain obscure, though small size doubtless entails advantages as well as liabilities.

Acknowledgment

This work was sponsored, in part, by NSF Grants No. DEB 78-10837 and PCM-8022980 (to JAR).

References

Allin, E. F.
1975. Evolution of the mammalian middle ear. *J. Morph.* 147:403–38.

Barghusen, H. R.
1973. The adductor jaw musculature of *Dimetrodon* (Reptilia, Pelycosauria). *J. Paleont.* 47:823–34.

Boolootian, R., and Stiles, K.
1981. *College Zoology.* New York: Macmillan Publishing Co.

Boonstra, L. D.
1963. Early dichotomies in the therapsids. *S. Afr. J. Sci.* 59:176–95.

Colbert, E. H.
1965. *The Age of Reptiles.* New York: Norton & Co.

Crompton, A. W., and Jenkins, F. A., Jr.
1979. Origin of mammals. In *Mesozoic Mammals,* ed J. A. Lillegraven, Z. Kielan-Jaworowska, and W. A. Clemens. Berkeley: University of California Press.

Crompton, A. W., and Parker, P.
1978. Evolution of the mammalian masticatory apparatus. *Amer. Sci.* 66:192–201.

Dunbar, C.
1964. *Historical Geology.* New York: Wiley and Sons, Inc.

Fleischer, G.
1978. Evolutionary principles of the mammalian middle ear. *Adv. in Anat., Embr. and Cell Biol.* 55(5):1–70.

Olson, E. C.
1971. *Vertebrate Paleozoology.* New York: John Wiley & Sons.

Robinson, P. L.
1972. Paleoclimatology and continental drift. In *Implications of Continental Drift to the Early Sciences,* Vol. I, ed. D. H. Tarline and S. Runcorn. London and New York: Academic Press.

Romer, A. S.

1961. Synapsid evolution and dentition. In *International Colloquium on the Evolution of Mammals,* part 1. Kon. Vlaamse Acad. Wetensch. Lett. Sch. Kunsten Belgie, Brussels.

1966. *Vertebrate Paleontology.* Chicago: University of Chicago Press.

J. A. RUBEN

DAVID CHALLINOR
Assistant Secretary for Science
Smithsonian Institution

Commentary on Continental Drift and Therapsid Evolution

For the past two days many of those present have been engrossed in giving and listening to papers dealing primarily with a group of long extinct reptiles, the therapsids. These mammal-like reptiles are of particular interest because evidence indicates that they included the forerunners—more than 200 million years ago—of mammals. It is particularly appropriate that the closing day of this conference is being held in this auditorium, for the Smithsonian Institution takes very seriously its charge from the will of James Smithson for the increase and diffusion of knowledge. Exchange of information among peers is certainly an appropriate example of such diffusion. Our principal task, then, is to share our findings with colleagues and to publish the results to record how we, in 1981, understand therapsid evolution. We must, however, keep in mind that such discussion may be a cause of unease to those who are unacquainted with, or who do not accept, most of the hypotheses that we take for granted.

Let us review briefly what scientists have discovered about the earth in the last thirty years. In the early 1950's, the structure of the earth's interior was not clear. Scientists are still not completely certain, but detailed topographic mapping of the ocean bottom, supplemented by cores, indicates that the relatively simple geology of the ocean floor is very different from that of the continents. The former seems to be underlain predominantly by basalt lava flows and a thin veneer of sediments, while the continents have granites and many other kinds of rocks that are much older, geologically speaking, than the ocean floor. For example, the exposed granite in central Canada is estimated to be over 3 billion years old, while the oldest known rock from the ocean floor is about 300 million years in age.

It is now generally agreed that convective currents occur within the mantle of the earth. Molten lava rises under the midocean ridges, causing the ocean floor to move away from either side of these ridges toward the continents. Where the ocean floor meets certain continental edges it is thought to descend under the continent. Such subduction often triggers volcanic activity, as, for example, along the west coast of the Americas.

I stress that data are still being accumulated to support the concept of moving continents. The long known variations in the earth's magnetic field has been used by geophysicists as a tool to track continental movement. When basalt lava is erupted to the sea floor, tiny grains of iron oxide are crystallized, and these grains become oriented by the earth's magnetic field, recording its configuration at the time that the lava solidifies.

In the 1960's Runcorn and his team, using the earth's past polarity as determined from rock cores, plotted on a map showing today's location of the continents, the position of the North Magnetic Pole as it appeared at intervals over a span of 600 million years. Cores from North American rocks described a path of successive magnetic poles that lay to the west of the path shown from rock cores collected in Europe. Results were puzzling, because they showed that either there were two north magnetic poles, or the continents had moved. The evidence seemed to support the latter because when Europe and North America were shifted from their present positions to lie adjacent to each other, the two paths were joined into one.

The evidence from rock cores, going back hundreds of millions of years, has shown that not only did polarity change, but also that it completely reversed itself. Polarity reversal did not occur regularly as it does every eleven years in the sun, but rather at intermittent intervals, often a million years apart. Use of potassium-argon dating techniques has allowed geophysicists to correlate polarity reversals with age. Furthermore, polarity patterns were found to be consistent with age regardless of where the rocks were formed. By plotting the irregular polarity reversal patterns in rocks over time, an efficient dating mechanism was developed for geological events, much as the irregularity of tree ring patterns permits dendrochronologists to date ancient wooden artifacts. Rock cores have fallen

into 16 periods of normal and reversed polarity in periods from fifty thousand years to more than one million years.

These cores suggest a tantalizing correlation between polarity reversal and animal extinction levels. James Hayes, at the Lamont Observatory, noted from a series of cores covering a span of 2.5 million years, that 8 species of radiolaria disappeared, and that 6 of these species vanished close to times of reversal of polarity. On further study he found that at the end of the Permian (225 million years ago) there were frequent polarity reversals, and that about this time half of the known families of animals became extinct. A similar interval of increased polarity reversal occurred at the end of the Cretaceous (65 million years ago), also a time of widespread extinction. Whether there is a causal connection between episodes of polarity reversal and episodes of extinction, or whether this hypothesis must give way to others, such as those which postulate extraterrestrial events, only a lot more investigation will tell.

It is incumbent on scientists to try to explain these matters to people who lack experience of the technology involved, a task that requires perceptiveness and sensitivity as well as persistence. This is an important challenge and one that I do not think we have yet met successfully. Happily, however, it seems as though scientific curiosity will exist as long as humans. The proliferation of magazines of popular science, the quality of imaginative television programs concerning science, and the non-technical reporting of science in daily newspapers all indicate a clear demand for scientific information. This demand for sound answers seems to me to be where the challenge lies. It clearly takes more energy to untangle a skein of competing ideas than to accept established imperatives. It also requires a healthy skepticism in the face of pronouncements on virtually all subjects, and finally, patience and willingness to await the accumulation of evidence. I suspect that it will be a long time before we can fathom what triggered the Permian and Cretaceous extinctions, just as we have had to wait more than half a century until Wegener's theory of the present configuration of continents and oceans became generally accepted by earth scientists. Furthermore, we must accept in principle the fact that we will never find the final answers to all the scientific questions raised.

But the joy is in the hunt, and the rewards are waiting to be claimed, with the potential for serendipity always an enticement. Peter Barrett's discovery of a labyrinthodont jaw fragment on Antarctica's Graphite Peak in late 1967 set the stage for further paleontological efforts there. The subsequent finds by E. H. Colbert and his colleagues linked Antarctica even closer with the Triassic deposits of the Karroo Basin in South Africa and added immensely to the supporting evidence for continental drift. There are undoubtedly other fossils waiting to be found in this now-inhospitable continent that should furnish a better understanding of how it fitted into Gondwanaland.

The search goes on and each new find adds a further piece to help complete the puzzle. When we think how hard fossils are to find, and how fragile they are when they are finally exposed at the present surface, it is truly amazing that so many thousands of them have been discovered. And fossils are all that remain of the therapsids, animals that literally ruled the land over 200 million years ago, before the beginning of the Age of Dinosaurs. How scanty are the clues to plot the pathways of mammalian origins! That mammals evolved from more primitive animals there is no doubt, but patience as well as insight will be needed to unravel the "how".

Where do we go from here? Most likely new Permian and Triassic outcrops will be discovered and the fossil record will expand. Dating techniques will improve and the technology to plot continental drift more accurately will rapidly increase. In fact, the Smithsonian has been involved for the last twenty years in a satellite tracking program to measure the earth. Through the use of laser beams, bouncing off a very stable satellite and back to an accuracy of a few tenths of a nanosecond (10^{-10} sec),* we can now plot the location of two points on earth 10,000 kilometers apart to within less than 10 cm. We expect to reduce this to about 5 cm in a year or two, at which point we should finally be able to measure accurately the actual movement of the continents. Just as it has become difficult today to defend a flat earth, and increasingly hard to believe in a young earth, I am optimistic that in the next generation or two, evolution will become in like manner generally accepted. The evolution I speak of refers to the idea that all life evolved from a common ancestor, even though precise evolutionary pathways may remain forever unclear. Nevertheless, the work of the past three days at Poolesville, and here, has opened our minds to some of the possible routes through which the therapsids led to mammals.

---

*The time of day has to be known to an accuracy of 1 microsecond (10^{-6} sec).

Index of Key Words

Preparation of this list was done with a computer assist. Key words are entered in the form used by individual authors. This provides direct access to subject matter, as each author's usage is strongly influenced by the individual subjects and disciplines. Names of bones are entered in the nominative form (postcranial bones) or adjectival form (most cranial bones), and are not collected under the term "bone." The names of glands, muscles, and neural elements such as nuclei are entered directly. Similar information may be entered under more than one key word, as in the case of Anomodontia and anomodont reptile, or Russia, Soviet Union, and USSR.

acetabulum, 39,74
acetylcholinesterase, 162, 163. *See also* cholinesterase
acoustic impedance, 288
acoustic meatus, 283, 284, 290, 291, 309
acoustic radiator, 291
activity, 196, 215
adaptive radiation, 133
adductor fossa, 275
adult size, 299
Adkinognathidae, 95
aerobic ability, 215
Aetosauria, 136
aetosaurid reptile, 150
aetosaurs, 310
Africa, 144
age of rocks, relative, 313
aggregation, 220, 221, 226, 228, 230
aggression, 11
agility, 75, 142, 215
air bladder, 291
air flow, climatic, 118, 189, 192
air passage, 255
alar plate, 155
albedo, 119
alecithal egg, 240, 247
Aleodon, 103
Algeria, 125, 127
alisphenoid, 100, 258
allantois, 42
allelochemical, 220, 226
Alligator, 174, 196

alligator, 43, 187, 190, 192
Alphatherapsida, 88
altricial young, 239, 240, 243, 244
Amazon Basin, 118
ambient radiation, 174–176
Amblyrhynchus, 197
amnion, 84
Amniota, 84
amniote vertebrate, 25, 27, 28, 32, 40, 41, 43, 222, 227
amniote egg, 239
Amphibia, 136
amphibian, 12, 25, 27, 28, 58, 119, 123, 125, 127, 134, 136, 138, 150, 155, 202, 208, 221, 224, 227, 242, 290, 311
Amphibolurus, 197
amphisbaenid reptile, 43
amygdala, 15, 225
anaerobic metabolism, 215
anapsid reptile, 6, 43
Aneugomphius, 63
Angelosaurus, 58
angular, 72, 86–88, 92, 95, 99, 255, 259, 264, 279, 285, 288, 309
  reflected lamina, 260, 264
angular cleft, 259, 260, 285, 287, 288, 290
angular flange, 54, 55
angular process of dentary, 285
Aniella, 173
ankle, 67
Annatherapsidae, 87, 95, 96
Anolis, 5, 176, 177, 179, 180, 182
anomodont reptile, 62, 86, 92, 120, 125, 209
Anomodontia, 6, 7, 88, 90, 92
Antarctica, 1, 2, 110, 119, 121, 123, 125, 128, 134, 315
anteosaur, 62, 87, 90, 91, 125
Anteosauria, 90
Anteosauridae, 87, 90, 92, 96
Anteosaurus, 52, 91, 92, 123, 125
anterior commissure, 159
anthracosaur, 27, 28
anuran amphibian, 222, 290, 291
apodan amphibian, 222
apomorphy, 83, 98, 100
Appalachian Mountains, 115
appendages, 186, 187, 188, 190–192, 199
  ancillary, 190
  locomotory, 190

aquatic habit, 77, 299
aquatic reptile, 144
Araeoscelidia, 310
Archaeosyodon, 49
Archaeothyris, 30–34
archicortex, 14, 160
archipallium, 14
archosaur, 27, 32, 42, 81, 138, 139, 142–144, 150
Archosauria, 185
area:
  cingulate, 14
  entorhinal, 14
  hippocampal, 14
  limbic, 14
  piriform, 14
Argentina, 121, 122, 295
aridity, seasonal, 125
Arizona, 122, 127
artery:
  internal carotid, 99
  lateral striate, 15
articular, 10, 12, 16, 86, 87, 92, 255, 257, 258, 264, 265, 267, 276, 277, 279, 284, 285, 288, 289, 309
articular condyle, dentary, 100
artiodactyl, 209
ascending pathways, 152
ascending spinal projection, 153
Asia, 142, 308
association cortex, 157
astragalus, 28, 39, 67, 68
atlas, 28, 34
atlas-axis complex, 27, 28, 34, 73
atmospheric circulation, 113, 119
attractants, sex, 221
auditory function, 279, 280, 289, 309
auditory structure:
  central, 154, 160
  peripheral, 253, 257–61, 287
Australia, 110, 119
autapomorphy, 100
autonomic nervous system, 155
Avenantia, 64, 66
avoidance, 221, 230
axis, 28, 34

badger, 9, 75
barriers to migration, 128, 134
basalt, 313
Bashkir, 48
basicranial girder, 99

basicranial region, 267
basicranium, 84, 99
basioccipital tubera, 87
basis cranii, 76, 299
basisphenoid, 99
basking, 196
bat, 222
Bauria, 67, 68, 180, 227
bauriamorph, 9, 10, 62, 81, 87, 94–98,
    100, 137–138, 141, 209, 211, 227,
    246
Bauriamorpha, 62, 95, 136
Baurioidea, 95
beak, 72, 80, 92, 141
bear, 9
Beaufort Series, 9, 144
beaver, 75
Belebei-Cotylosaur Complex, 49
Belesodon, 103
belt, low-pressure, 114
bennettitalean plant, 309
Biarmosuchia, 88, 92, 120
biarmosuchian reptile, 87, 88, 92, 125
Biarmosuchidae, 62, 64, 66, 68, 88
Biarmosuchus, 49, 57, 59, 85, 88, 120,
    209
Bienotherium, 227, 286, 287, 290, 291,
    296, 297
Bienotheroides, 270
biogeography, 109, 110
    marine invertebrate, 118
biogram, 5
biology textbooks, 307
Biot number, 187, 188, 191
biped, 142
bird, 3, 26, 84, 153, 155, 163, 175, 207–
    212, 222
bite, 72
    bilateral, 273, 274, 309
    canine, 266, 274, 275
    carnassial, 264
    incisor, 266, 274–276, 278–280
    incisor-canine, 276
    isometric, 266, 272, 280
    posterior molar, 274
    unilateral, 266, 273, 274, 278–280
bite point, 273, 274, 280
    fourth postcanine, 278
    third molars, 274
blood flow, 186–188, 190–192, 196, 199
body form, 137
body size, 185, 188, 196, 202, 203, 245,
    246, 299, 310, 311
body temperature, 186, 188, 190, 191,
    197, 199, 202, 203, 215
body weight, 151
bone histology, 40, 208, 209, 214
bones:
    girdle, 62
    postdentary, 259–261, 264, 279, 285,
    288, 292, 309
Bowman's glands, 224
brain, 2, 3, 5, 13, 41, 43, 133, 141, 143,
    150–152, 159, 161, 179, 210, 220
    triune, 3
brain size, 141, 150, 208, 210
brain temperature, 190
braincase, 28, 41, 87, 96, 270
brainstem, 14, 152, 159, 161–164
Brazil, 121, 122, 125
brithopodan reptile, 49, 51, 52, 54, 57–
    59, 63, 88, 90
Brithopodidae, 62, 90

Brithopus, 63
brood patch, 244, 246
brooding, 11, 243, 246
Brouffia, 33
browsing 81, 310
buccal cavity, 211
bulla, 264
Buntsandstein, 144
Burnetia, 92, 120
burrowing, 75, 80

Caiman, 153
calcaneal tuber, 68
calcaneum, 37, 67, 68
California, 308
calls:
    distress, 11
    isolation, 11
    separation, 11
Canada, 313
canals, haversian, 10
caniniform process, 72, 76, 77, 80
captorhinomorph, 25, 27, 28, 32, 34, 36,
    37, 40, 41, 43, 125, 137, 138, 212,
    227, 289, 310
Captorhinomorpha, 6, 136, 310
Captorhinus, 58, 177, 180
Carboniferous Period, 33, 37, 110, 113,
    119, 123, 213
care:
    maternal, 11, 12
    parental, 15
Carnivora, 309
carnivore, 7, 308
carnivorous tetrapod, 309
carpal bones, 64, 299
caseid, 28, 58, 71
Caseidae, 55
cat, 75, 154, 157, 164, 229, 266, 270,
    292
    saber-tooth, 141
caudate nucleus, 162
caudatoputamen, 162, 164
cavum epiptericum, 99
cavum tympani, 287, 290
cecotroph, 220
cells, atmospheric, 114, 115
Cenozoic Era, 109, 150
central nervous system, 149, 151
centrum, 34, 73
cerebellum, 154, 155, 162, 164, 165
cerebral cortex, 154, 155
cerebral hemisphere, 14, 150, 157, 159,
    175
cerebral region, 41
cervical vertebrae, 139
chameleon, 210
character states, 28
characters:
    mammalian, 152
    mosaic of, 47
cheek, of skull, 32
Chelonia, 136, 310
chemical signalling, mother-young,
    230
chewing, 266, 270, 276, 277, 280, 309
Chickasha, 39, 48, 49, 59
China, 110, 113, 121–123, 125, 127,
    134, 295
Chiniquodon, 83, 103
chiniquodont, 83, 99, 101, 103, 311

Chiniquodontidae, 83, 99, 102, 103, 120
Chiniquodontoidea, 83, 101, 103
Chinling Orogeny, 113
Chiroptera, 241
choanae, 228
cholinesterase, 3, 4, 15
chorda tympani, 290
choriovitelline membrane, 242
Choza Formation, 39
Chronofauna:
    Caseid, 57, 58
    Permo-Carboniferous, 57
chrysochlorid mammal, 80
Chthomaloporus, 49
cilia, 224
cingulate gyrus, 14, 155, 157
Cistecephalus, 75, 80, 123, 310
cladistic analysis, 84
cladistics, 151
cladogram, 83, 85, 98, 101, 103, 285
claustrum, 16
clavicle, 36, 63
cleithrum, 73
climate, 75, 109, 113, 118, 125, 128,
    136, 181, 202, 213, 215, 308
Cloverly Formation, 292
cnemial crest, 36
Cnemidophorus, 197
coal, 110, 113, 123, 125
coal belt, equatorial, 110
Coal Measures, 6
cochlea, 283, 287, 292
cochlear housing, 265, 280
cognitive function, 156
coital activity, 225
coitus, 221
Colorado, 57
columella, 283
Comb Ridge, 295, 296, 298, 299
commissural projection, 159
common ancestor, 213, 315
communication, 2, 3, 5, 11, 219, 220
community biomass, 212
compact bone, 208
competition, 81, 133, 138, 144, 311
conchae, 211
conduction, 189
    internal, 191
condyle:
    dentary, 270, 276, 278–280
    mandibular, 266
    quadrate, 284
coniferous tree, 309
Conolophus, 186, 197, 199
conservatism, evolutionary, 139
continent, 114
continental drift, 110, 182, 295, 314,
    315
continental sediments, 144
continental shelf, 110
convection, 189, 191, 192, 199
convection coefficient, 192
convective boundary layer, 186
convergence, evolutionary, 84–88, 91,
    92, 94, 103, 285, 289
coracoid, 64
coronoid, 86, 88
coronoid process of dentary, 86, 92, 95,
    99, 260, 265, 275, 277, 285, 288
coronoid region, 87
corpus callosum, 159
corpus luteum, 242
corpus striatum, 3, 16

cortex, 13, 15, 161
  cingulate, 14
  dorsal, 159, 160
  dorsomedial, 159
  entorhinal, 15
  insular, 15
  lateral, 159, 160
  medial, 159
  motor, 165
  piriform, 15
cosmopolitan distribution, 120, 123,
    125, 128, 134
costal plate, 83, 101, 102
Cotylorhynchus, 50, 54, 55, 58
cotylosaur, 71, 134, 136–138
Cotylosauria, 6
couples:
  bending, 266
  torsional, 266
cow, 182
coyote, 75
cranial volume, 210
crest, 255, 256, 258
Cretaceous Period, 13, 138, 150, 185,
    247, 309, 311, 314
crista parotica, 292
crocodile, 37, 67
Crocodilia, 136, 310
crocodilian reptile, 6, 26, 39, 41, 127,
    138, 150, 153, 160, 174, 175, 189,
    210–212, 243, 246, 287, 291, 310
Crotalus viridis viridis, 221
crus, 68
crus longus, incus, 100
cues, chemical, 221
currents, oceanic and wind, 308, 309
cusp formula, 297
cyclicity, reproductive, 175
Cyclura, 176, 177, 179, 180
cynodont reptile, 6, 7, 9–13, 39, 47, 68,
    81, 83, 86, 87, 94, 96, 98–103, 120–
    122, 125, 127, 137–142, 144, 150,
    176, 185, 209–211, 213, 227–230,
    246, 253, 254, 256–260, 263–265,
    267, 276, 277, 279, 280, 285–292,
    309, 311
Cynodontia, 2, 61, 68, 85, 94, 98, 100,
    122, 123, 136
Cynognathia, 83, 101–103
cynognathian reptile, 99, 103
cynognathid reptile, 99, 121, 122
Cynognathus, 101–103, 228, 255, 264,
    267, 285, 290
Cynosaurus, 99, 101
cytoarchitectonic area, 158

dating, potassium-argon, 314
decline:
  evolutionary, 139, 142
  of dicynodonts, 81
dental differentiation, 141
dental ramus, of dentary, 300, 303
dental succession, 299
dentary, 10, 56, 72, 73, 86–88, 92, 95,
    99, 100, 103, 139, 141, 263–265,
    267, 270, 278, 279, 285, 286, 288,
    289, 299, 309
  articular process, 264, 267
dentary shelf, 76
dentary symphysis, 76, 77, 86, 99
dentary table, 73
dentary-squamosal joint, 10, 16, 102

dentition, 51, 61, 73, 101, 102, 138–141,
    245, 246, 263, 270, 275, 296, 299
derived character, 84, 85
dermal scutes, 296
desert, 119
Desmatodon, 28
Desmatosuchus, 150
Deuterosaurus, 64
Diadectes, 28, 41, 57, 150
diadectomorph reptile, 28, 32
Diadectomorpha, 27, 28
Diademodon, 211, 227, 228, 255, 267,
    285, 286
diademodont reptile, 127
diademodontid reptile, 121, 122, 127
Diademodontidae, 99, 102
diaphragm, 140, 141, 210, 213, 214
diapsid reptile, 6, 27, 28, 32, 43, 81, 84,
    150, 151, 161, 164
diapsid fauna, 127
Diarthrognathus, 10, 103, 270, 297
diastema, 141, 296, 299–303
diazomethane, 14
dichotomy, 137
Dicynodon, 74–81, 227, 310
dicynodont reptile, 47, 55, 58, 61, 71,
    72, 74, 75, 77, 79–81, 86–88, 92,
    96, 125, 127, 137–139, 141, 142,
    176, 180, 185, 209, 210, 227, 228,
    246, 264, 285–287, 289, 291, 308–
    310
Dicynodontia, 90, 120–123, 136, 191
Didelphis, 13, 270, 275
diencephalon, 152
diffusion barrier, 242, 243
digits, 62, 139
Diictodon, 75–77, 79, 80, 123, 177, 180,
    182, 310
Dimacrodon, 49, 50, 54, 55, 58, 59
dimensions:
  limb, 187, 188
  torso, 187
Dimetrodon, 6, 41, 54, 57, 59, 64, 139,
    185, 190, 195, 201–203
Dinanomodon, 180, 181
Dinocephalia, 61, 62, 64, 67, 68, 88, 90,
    92, 120, 136
dinocephalian reptile, 47, 52, 56, 61–64,
    68, 71, 86, 88, 90, 123, 137, 141,
    185, 246, 290, 308, 310
dinosaur, 1, 6, 11, 25, 136, 138, 141–
    143, 175, 207, 208, 307, 310, 311,
    315
diphyodonty, 9, 16, 103, 246, 247
Dipsosaurus, 197
display behavior, 5, 220, 221
distribution of faunas, 123, 133, 212
dog, 75, 311
Doliosauriscus, 123, 125
Doliosaurus, 92
dominance, behavioral, 5
dopamine, 4, 16, 162, 163
dorsal crest, 5
dorsal sagittal sinus, 175
dorsal ventricular ridge, 3, 15, 160, 163
Draco, 310
Driveria, 49, 50, 52, 55, 58
dromasaur, 86
Dromasauria, 92, 120, 136
dropstones, 119
Dvina River, 134
Dvinia, 96, 100
dviniid, 99

Dviniidae, 100
DVR, 3, 15, 160–162

ear, 288
eardrum, 283, 289, 290
  mammalian, pars flaccida, 290
  mandibular, 290, 291
  postquadrate, 290, 309
Earth, measurement of, 315
East Africa, 62, 103, 118
East Indies, 118
echidna, 151, 157–159, 213, 214
ecological system, therapsid, 138
ectepicondyle, 36
ectopterygoid, 254–258, 261
ectotherm, 123, 136, 200, 212, 213, 246
ectothermy, 11, 40, 134, 175, 190, 207–
    212, 246
Ectypodus, 292
edaphosaur, 28, 36, 48, 55, 86
Edaphosaurus, 58, 185, 190, 201, 202
edentate, 174, 213
egg, amniote, 11, 27, 28, 43, 181, 239,
    240, 244
egg-guarding behavior, 230, 243, 246
egg retention, 239–244, 246
electromyogram, 270
elephant, 289, 300
embryonic membrane, 242
EMG, 270
Emydops, 78, 79
enamel, prismatic, 99
encephalization, 17
encephalization coefficient, 210
endocranial cast, 2, 12–14, 17, 41, 150,
    151, 165, 175
endocranial cavity, 173, 175, 179
endocrine system, 155
endotherm, 212, 213, 243
endothermy, 10, 11, 16, 47, 134, 141,
    143, 176, 185, 186, 207–215, 240,
    241, 243–247
Endothiodon, 78–80, 123, 125
endurance, 75
England, 122, 123, 295, 308
enkephalins, 4
Eocene, 150
Eodelphis, 13
Eodicynodon, 91
eodicynodont reptile, 49, 50, 54, 58, 59
eodinocephalian reptile, 49, 57–59
Eolacertilia, 136
Eosuchia, 136, 310
eosuchian reptile, 134, 138
Eosyodon, 30, 49, 50
eotherapsid reptile, 48, 49, 51, 52, 54,
    56–58
eotheriodont reptile, 49, 51, 52, 54, 57–
    59, 209
Eothyris, 33
Eotitanops, 49, 59
Eotitanosuchia, 61, 88, 92, 120
eotitanosuchian reptile, 86, 125
Eotitanosuchus, 87, 88, 96
Eozostrodon, 123, 128, 142, 264, 265,
    267, 272, 278–280, 286
epidermis, 210
epiphyseal complex, 212
epiphysis cerebri, 10, 174, 212
epipterygoid, 59, 87, 88, 96, 98, 100,
    288
epipubis, 298

epithelium, 211
equatorial region, 110, 113, 115, 118, 123, 125
Ericiolacerta, 63, 67, 96, 123, 142
Eryops, 57
Erythrotherium, 142
estemmenosuchid reptile, 92
Estemmenosuchidae, 88, 92
Estemmenosuchus, 48, 52, 56, 58, 88, 90, 210
estradiol, 242, 244
ethogram, 5
ethology, 219
Euchambersia, 96
euchambersiid reptile, 87, 95, 96, 98
Euchambersiidae, 95, 98
eudinocephalian reptile, 57
Eumeces, 11, 221, 243
Europe, 122, 125, 127, 142, 295, 308, 310, 314
euryapsid reptile, 6, 182
eustachian tube, mammalian, 309
eutherapsid reptile, 48, 49, 51, 52, 56, 58
Eutheria, 13, 240
eutherian mammal, 213, 241, 242
eutheriodont reptile, 49, 87
Eutheriodontia, 94
Eutherocephalia, 95
eutherocephalian reptile, 83, 95, 96, 98
evaporation, 189–191, 199
evaporites, 110, 113, 115, 118, 119, 123, 308
evolution, cortical, 158
Exaeretodon, 267, 290
excretion, 228
exoccipital, 32
exocrine glands, 228, 230
expense, energetic, 220, 227
external auditory meatus, 86
external naris, 86
extinction, 81, 137, 138, 314
extraembryonic membranes, 27
extraterrestrial events, 314
exudates, sociochemical, 220, 221, 230
Ezhovo, 39, 48

facial foramina, on skull, 210
facial region, skull, 33, 86
facial sculpture, 228, 229
facies, sedimentary, 110, 123
family, 2, 14
fauna, 110, 134
fauna and flora, Permo-Triassic, 308
faunal succession, 137
faunas:
    dicynodont-cynodont, 125
    warm water, 118
feeding, 134, 208, 228, 261, 288, 310
feeding apparatus, 292
feeding complex, 75
feeding preference, 77–80
femur, 36, 39, 49, 54, 55, 62, 64, 66, 67, 74, 140, 299
fenestra ovalis, 43, 100, 267
fenestra vestibuli, 287
fibula, 36
fighting, 220, 221
fish, 27, 32, 58, 144, 242, 291, 310
fish-eaters, 311
fissipede mammal, 264
flange, ventral, on dentary, 141

flocculus, 41
flora, 71, 75, 110
floras, Permian and Triassic, 309
fluvial deposits, 119
fold, gular, 5, 11
fontanelle, 179, 180
food, 75, 138, 140–142
    vegetable, 77, 79–81, 309
foraging, 76, 77, 79, 81
foramina, maxillary, 142
forebrain, 3, 5, 150–152, 155, 161, 165
forelimb, 36
fossa incudis, 292
fossorial habit, 310
France, 58, 123, 308
frog, 139
frontal, 87, 92
frontal lobe, 162
frugivory, 310

gait, 67, 75
galago, 266, 272
Galago crassicaudatus, 280
Galapagos, 186, 199
galesaurid, 99, 101, 120, 121, 246, 291, 309
Galesauridae, 101
Galesaurus, 99, 101
ganglia:
    basal, 154, 155, 161–165
    of DVR, 3
    retinal, 154
    telencephalic, 3
gape, 141, 190, 270, 273
Gekko gekko, 43
Gephyrostegus, 28
Germany, 123, 308
Gerrhonotus, 173
gibbon, 291
glacial deposits, 119
glacial-marine deposits, 119
glaciation, 110, 113, 119, 136, 308
gland, pineal, 10
glands:
    Harderian, 221
    skin, 10, 11, 16, 210, 221, 292
glenoid:
    shoulder, 36, 39, 73
    squamosal, 100–103, 267, 274, 278, 279
gliding, 310
globus pallidus, 4, 162, 163
Glossopteris, 75, 80, 309
glottis, 260
gomphodont reptile, 81, 102, 103, 270, 280, 290–292, 300
Gondwana, 119, 144, 213
Gondwanaland, 2, 133, 138, 144, 181, 315
Gorgodon, 54
Gorgonopsia, 61, 62, 64, 68, 88, 93, 120, 136, 191
gorgonopsian reptile, 9, 10, 39, 47, 49–52, 54, 56–59, 61–64, 66, 68, 72, 86, 125, 137–139, 141, 176, 185, 209, 210, 246, 276, 287
granite, 313
Graphite Peak, 315
Grashof number, 192
ground cover, 80
grubbing habit, 80, 310
Guadalupian Stage, 48, 57, 144

Gulf Stream, 118
gyrus:
    cingulate, 6
    hippocampal, 14

habit, 75, 80, 181, 189, 246
habits, feeding, 75
habitus, 71, 138
hair, 11, 16, 141, 149, 164, 208, 210, 214, 228
hamulus, 257, 258
haptodont reptile, 33, 54, 57, 85
Haptodus, 39, 203
hard palate, 261
harderian glands, 174
Harrismith, South Africa, 11
hatching, 181, 239, 243
hatchling, 11, 244, 246
Haversian system, 10, 208, 245, 246
hearing, 12, 143, 264, 265, 270, 288, 289, 292
heart, 214
heat budget, global, 113, 118, 119
heat exhange, 186–191, 195, 196, 199, 200, 243
heat exchanger, 201
heat loss, 189–191, 196, 213
heat transfer, 186–192, 195
hedgehog, 13, 158
hemimandible, 272, 283
Hemispheres, Northern, Southern, 110
herbivore, 7, 8, 28, 79, 138, 141, 202, 308
herbivory, 71, 75, 81, 102, 137, 246, 310
Hercynian Orogeny, 110
heterodonty, 56
hibernacula, 221
Himalayas, 114, 115
hind limb, 36
hippocampal formation, 15, 159, 163
hippocampus, 14, 160
Hipposauridae, 88, 93
Hipposaurus, 67, 68, 85, 88, 120
Hofmeyria, 83, 95
hofmeyriid reptile, 83, 95, 96
Hofmeyriidae, 83, 95
homeothermic physiology, 214
homeothermy, 41, 134, 181, 185, 186, 188, 190, 195, 197, 199, 201, 202, 247
horn, 72, 76, 77, 141
horse latitudes, 110
humerus, 33, 36, 37, 39, 64, 73, 140, 292
Hunter's eminence, 3
Hylonomus, 6, 33, 34, 36
hyoid arch, 264
hyoid, anterior cornu, 289
hypothalamic region, 225
hypothalamus, 160, 163

ice, 118, 119
ichthyosaur, 310
Ichthyosauria, 310
ictidorhinid reptile, 49, 87, 92
Ictidorhinidae, 88, 93, 120
Ictidorhinus, 85, 88
ictidosaur, 9, 10, 99, 101, 103, 298
Ictidosauria, 84, 101, 103, 136
Ictidostoma, 95

Iguana, 176, 177, 179, 180, 182, 199
iguana, land, 199, 200
ilium, 36, 64, 66, 67, 73, 139
incipient homoiothermy, 176
incisive foramen, 222, 227, 228
incubation, 241, 243, 246
incubation patch, 244
incus, 12, 103, 264, 283
India, 2, 114, 119, 121–123, 125, 127
Indosinian Orogeny, 110
Induan Stage, 110, 113
inertial homeothermy, 186, 196, 200, 202, 242
inferior colliculus, 152, 154
infraorbital foramen, 230
inner ear, 164, 309
Inner Mongolia, 62
innominate, 74
Inostrancevia, 62, 137
Insectivora, 241
insectivore, 13, 158, 213
insectivorous habit, 309
integument, glandular, 228, 229, 244
intercentrum, 28, 34, 139
interclavicle, 36, 64, 74
intermedium, 28
internal carotid foramen, 83, 99
interpterygoid vacuity, 49, 86, 92, 95, 96, 99
intertemporal, 28
intertemporal region, skull, 95
Intertropical Convergence Zone, 115
intraspecific display, 195
invertebrate animal, 80, 144
Ischigualasto, 144
ischium, 67, 74
isocortex, 14, 157–163
Israel, 127
ITCZ, 115

jackrabbit, 75
Jacobson's organ, 222, 227
jaw, 141, 149, 244, 266
jaw articulation, 12, 72, 83, 87, 99, 101, 103, 141, 255, 263, 264, 273, 275, 276, 280, 288
jaw bones, accessory, 264, 265, 267, 270, 279, 280, 285
jawless vertebrates, 175
jaws, edentulous, 308
Joggins, Nova Scotia, 25, 36
joint:
    ankle, 37
    articular-quadrate, 10, 16, 263, 264, 267, 276, 280, 286
    basipterygoid, 72
    cruro-pedal, 67
    dentary-postdentary, 289
    dentary-squamosal, 16, 103, 246, 247, 263–265, 270, 277–280, 309
    fibulotarsal, 67
    hip, 66
    jaw, *See* jaw articulation
    sacroiliac, 74
    squamoso-dentary, *See* joint, dentary-squamosal
    surangular-glenoid, *See* joint, surangular-squamosal
    surangular-squamosal, 83, 101, 267, 270, 286, 288
    temporomandibular, 265–267, 279
Jonkeria, 52

jugal, 91, 99, 102, 286
jugular foramen, 87
Jurassic climate, 119
Jurassic Period, 13, 110, 113–115, 118, 119, 128, 138, 142, 150, 185, 279, 280, 295, 311
juvenile individual, 33, 299
juxtallocortex, 157

Kamptobaatar, 260
Kannemeyeria, 80, 81, 123, 127
Karroo, 1, 6, 7, 16
Karroo Basin, 120, 315
Kawingasaurus, 75, 80
Kayenta Formation, 295, 296, 298
Kayenta, Arizona, 295, 298
Kazanian Stage, 48, 110, 113
Keuper, 144
Kingoria, 75–77, 79, 80
Knoxosaurus, 52
Kombuisia, 80, 180
Komodo dragon, 5
kuehneotherid reptile, 279
Kuehneotheriidae, 16, 272
Kuehneotherium, 16, 272, 279, 292

labyrinthodont amphibian, 134, 138, 209, 311, 315
lacrimal, 86, 87
lambda, 299
lambdoid crest, 297
lamina, dorsal medullary, 15
lamprey, 173–175
land, 115, 118
Laos, 121, 125
larynx, 257–259
lateral amygdala, 15
latitude, 110, 118, 125, 134, 182
Laurasia, 133
lens, 173
Leonardian Stage, 57, 144
lepidosaur, 27, 150
ligament, calcaneo-astragalar, 68
limb, 62, 75, 139, 299
    girdles, 297, 299
    motion, parasagittal, 190
    posture, 175, 208, 209
limbic cortex, 155, 160
limbic system, 6, 155
limnoscelid reptile, 30, 32
Limnoscelidae, 27
Limnoscelis, 28, 32
lineage, cynodont-mammal, 309
linkage, articular-quadrate, 291
lips, muscular, 11, 230
lithology, climatically sensitive, 110
litter, 80
lizard, 5, 6, 11, 25, 32, 33, 36, 37, 40, 42, 43, 67, 150, 155, 160, 173, 174, 176, 177, 179–182, 186, 196, 199, 209–212, 220, 221, 226, 230, 240, 241, 254, 255, 291, 310
locality, 110
locomotion, 9, 34, 37, 43, 58, 62, 66, 67, 73, 75, 81, 134, 139, 190, 211, 228, 310
locomotor system, 61
longitude, 110
lower jaw, 84, 88, 253, 255, 256, 258, 260, 263, 267, 270, 275, 277, 309
Luangua Valley, 121

lumbar region, 139–141
lumbar ribs, 211
lungfish, 150, 155
lungs, 211, 213, 214
Lycaenops, 62, 64
Lystrosaurus, 75–80, 123, 125, 227
Lystrosaurus Zone, 9, 62

macaque, 266, 270, 272, 274
Madagascar, 121, 125, 139
magnetic polarity reversal, 314
malleus, 12, 264, 283, 286
    manubrium of, 257, 286
MAME, 86, 87, 92
mammal, 3, 5, 6, 10, 37, 39, 67, 84, 85, 92, 99, 101, 103, 122, 123, 127, 133, 134, 136, 139, 142, 150–152, 155, 157, 159–161, 163–165, 175, 176, 185, 186, 195, 197, 207–213, 220–222, 225, 227, 228, 230, 241–243, 253, 254, 256, 258, 263, 265, 267, 270, 272, 273, 276, 279, 280, 283–288, 290, 292, 295, 309, 311, 315
Mammalia, 84, 92, 94, 98, 101, 103, 106, 208
mammals, origin of, 28, 71, 290
mammary glands, 230, 239, 240, 244
manatee, 222, 300
Manda Formation, 144
mandible, 139, 264–266, 267, 270, 273, 276, 284, 285, 288, 289, 292, 296, 309
mandibular arch, 264
mandibular condyle, 272, 274, 275
mandibular symphysis, 266, 274
mantle currents, convective, 314
manus, 64, 298
    and pes, 74, 75
mapping, ocean bottom, 313
maps, paleogeographic, 110, 113, 120
marine facies, 144
marine invertebrates, 119
marine reptile fauna, 127
marking behavior, 220, 221, 228, 229
marsupial mammal, 13, 16, 150–152, 154, 155, 157–159, 163, 213, 240–242
masseteric fossa, 99, 285
Massetognathus, 150, 227, 267
mastication, 265, 270, 272, 279, 280
masticatory system, 59, 61
maternal care, 2, 230, 239, 243, 244
maternal secretions, 247
mating, 220, 221
maxilla, 72, 86–88, 91, 95, 96, 99, 141, 227, 254, 256, 258
meatal groove, 287
meatus, tubular, 291
medial centrale, 37
megalecithal egg, 239
Megazostrodon, 142, 144
melatonin, 174
Mesen River, 134
mesencephalic tegmentum, 163
mesocortex, 14, 157
    limbic cingulate, 15
mesosaur, 123
Mesosauria, 310
Mesozoic Era, 13, 109, 110, 113, 119, 134, 136, 138, 139, 141, 144, 150, 151, 207, 210, 285

metabolism, 43, 140, 141, 149, 189, 199, 210–214, 245, 246
metapodials, 74
metatarsus, 37, 68
Metatheria, 13
metatherian mammal, 241, 242
methylazoxymethanol (MAM), 14
micrencephaly, 13, 14, 17
microenvironment, 182, 190, 196
microsaur, 28
midbrain, 4, 41, 150, 152, 153, 160, 162
middle ear, 16, 28, 43, 61, 141, 149, 258, 260, 263, 264, 276, 280, 283, 284, 286–290, 292, 309
midocean ridges, 314
migration, 125, 128
milk, 11, 230, 231, 240, 244, 247
    uterine, 242
millerosaur, 137, 138
Millerosauria, 136
minimum convex polygon, 151
Mirotenthes, 62
Moenkopi Formation, 127
mole, 75, 80
mollusc-eaters, 311
Mollweide projection, 110
moment arms, 273, 274
Mongolia, 13
monophyly, 61, 84, 85, 88, 100, 102, 103
monotreme, 11, 16, 151, 152, 154, 155, 159, 161, 163, 208, 210, 214, 239, 242, 244, 246, 258, 260, 261, 264, 283, 290, 292
monsoonal circulation, 114, 115, 118, 120
Moradi Formation, 125
Morganucodon, 16, 100, 142, 144, 264, 265, 267, 286–288, 292
morganucodont mammal, 142, 279, 287, 292
Morganucodontidae, 272, 279
Morocco, 122
mosasaur, 182
Moschops, 62, 64, 123, 125
Moschorhinidae, 95
Moschowhaitsia, 96, 100
motion:
    parasagittal, of limb, 74
    vertebral column, 75
motor area, 157, 158
motor cortex, neocortical, 4
mountains, 110, 114
Mountains:
    Appalachian, 308
    Ouachita, 308
    Ural, 57, 308
    Varisca, 308
mouse, 292
movement:
    lower jaw, 165, 266
    body, 165
mucosa, chemosensory, 222
Multituberculata, 292
multituberculate, 16, 150, 151, 260, 292
Muschelkalk, 144
muscle:
    adductor mandibulae externus, 86, 87, 92
    anterior temporalis, 272, 274–278
    caudifemoralis, 64
    deep masseter, 272, 274–278
    depressor mandibulae, 289

iliacus, 66
iliofemoralis, 64, 67
masseter, 87, 253, 264–266, 291
medial pterygoid, 265, 266, 272, 274, 276, 278
posterior pterygoid, 253, 254, 257–260, 310
posterior temporalis, 272, 274–278
pterygoid, reptilian, 258, 276
pterygoideus, 28
pterygospinous, 258
puboischiofemoralis externus, 64, 66
reptilian, 192
stapedius, 291
superficial masseter, 102, 272–274, 276–278
superior pharyngeal constrictor, 261
temporalis, 264, 265, 309
tensor tympani, 253, 257, 258, 261, 284, 291, 310
tensor veli palatini, 253, 257, 258, 260, 261, 310
triceps surae, 68
white, reptilian, 188
zygomatico-mandibularis, 274
muscle activity, 266
muscle force, 273
muscle mass, pterygoideus, 288
muscles:
    appendicular, 27
    axial, 27, 36, 37
    external adductor, 88
    hyoid, 270
    jaw, 56, 264, 278, 288
    transversospinalis, 44
musculature:
    adductor, 265, 267, 270, 279, 280, 309
    adductor externus, 72
    caudo-femoralis, 190
    masseteric, 275
    pterygoideus, 72, 253, 258, 265, 291
    temporalis, 181, 253, 272, 273, 275
    trigeminal, 253
Myosaurus, 80, 123

nares, internal, 87, 93, 94–96, 254, 257, 260
naris, 77
nasal, 86, 87, 92, 297
nasal capsule, 227
nasal cavity, 211, 222, 254
nasopalatine canal, 222
nasopharyngeal passage, 288
    lateral, 260
nasopharynx, 254, 256–261, 310
nasoseptal grooves, 227
natural selection, 182
Navajo Sandstone, 295
Nearctylodon broomi, 295, 297–299, 301, 303
nectrideans, 310
neocortex, 3, 13, 14, 160
neopallium, 14
nervous system, 151
nesting behavior, 243, 246
nestlings, 246
neural arch, 28, 34
neural organization, mammalian, 152
neuroblast, 14
neurohypophysial octapeptides, 230
neuron, 151
neuronal module, 151

Nevada, 308
nipples, 230
nocturnal habit, 11, 143
North America, 308, 314
North Carolina, 122, 127
North Magnetic Pole, position of, 314
nothosaur, 6, 182, 311
notochordal structure of column, 75
Notosollasia, 62
Nova Scotia, 6, 122, 127, 134
nuchal crest, 5
nuclear group, anterior, 155
nuclei:
    centrolateral, 155
    diffusely projecting, 155
    inferior olivary, 164
    intralaminar, 155, 158, 159, 161, 162, 163, 165
    lateral posterior, 152
    limbic, 155, 163
    pontine, 164
    posterior, 154
    sensory, 152
    specific motor, 154, 155, 158, 163, 165
    specific sensory, 152, 155, 158, 161, 163
    thalamic, 160, 163
nucleus:
    accumbens, 3
    anterior cortical, 225
    auditory, 153
    caudate, 3
    central lateral, 158
    centromedian, 155
    dorsal lateral geniculate, 152–154, 160
    dorsal, of posterior commissure, 163
    dorsomedial, 155
    habenular, 173
    medial, 225
    medial geniculate, 152
    posterolateral cortical, 225
    posteromedial cortical, 225
    reuniens, 155
    rotundus, 153, 154, 160
    somatosensory, 160
    sphericus, 224
    ventral anterior, 154, 162
    ventral lateral, 154
    ventrobasal, 152, 158
    ventrolateral, 158
    ventromedial, 155
    visual, 153
nursing habit, 2, 5, 11, 16
Nythosaurus, 211

occipital condyle, 16, 87
occipital region, 297
occiput, 28, 29, 32, 91
occlusion:
    dental, 103, 165, 272, 276, 278–280
    parietal foramen, 179, 180
ocean currents, 113, 118
oceans, 114
Ocher, 48, 57, 58
Ochoan Stage, 144
Oedaleops, 33
Oklahoma, 39, 48, 57
olfaction, 12, 211, 220
    nasal, 225, 227
    vomeronasal, 225–227

olfactory bulb, 12, 159
  accessory, 224
  main, 224
olfactory epithelium, 224
olfactory input, 159
olfactory mucosa, nasal, 226
olfactory nerve:
  accessory, 225
  main, 225
olfactory projection, 159
olfactory system, 2
  main, 225
olfactory tubercle, 224
olfactostriatum, 3
Oligokyphus, 227, 290, 297
omnivory, 81
ontogenetic growth, 299
Ophiacodon, 31, 34, 57, 58, 185
ophiacodont reptile, 28, 34, 57
Ophiacodontia, 28
opisthotic, 28, 32, 33, 287
opossum, 13, 158, 272–275, 279, 280
optic tectum, 153, 163
oral cavity, 254
organ of Corti, 287
Ornithischia, 136, 310
ornithischian, 138, 142
orogeny, 110, 308
oropharynx, 257
ossification, 180, 182, 183, 299
otic capsule, 32, 41
Otsheria, 49, 50, 54, 55, 58, 59, 90, 93, 120
Oudenodon, 75–77, 80, 310
oviduct, 11, 240–242
oviparity, *See* ovipary
ovipary, 11, 214, 239, 241, 242, 244, 247
oviposition, 181, 182, 242
ovoviviparity, 241
ovulation, 226, 239, 241
owl, 291
oxygen consumption, 213
oxygen demand, metabolic, 242
oxygen extraction efficiency, 211
oxygen transport, 213, 214
oxytocin, 230

Paaw's cartilage, 290
Pachygenelus, 103, 270, 286
Pakistan, 114
palate, 41, 76, 80, 88, 96
palatine, 86–88, 92, 96, 99, 100, 141, 254–256, 260
paleoclimate, 113, 125, 128, 181
paleocortex, 159
paleoequator, 125, 127, 181
paleogeography, 109, 110, 114, 118, 119
paleolatitude, 110, 125, 127, 181
paleomagnetism, 110, 134
paleopallium, 14
paleopole, 110, 125
paleostriatum, 15
Paleothyris, 31, 33
Paleozoic Era, 27, 41, 109, 110, 113, 119, 133, 134, 136, 138, 175, 181, 207, 227
pallidum, 4, 5
pallium, 14, 155, 157, 159, 161, 163, 164
Pangaea, 1, 109, 110, 114, 115, 118, 119, 125, 127, 128, 133, 134, 136,

138, 308
panting, 190, 196
pantothere, 13, 16, 272, 279
Pantylus, 28
parallelism, evolutionary, 47, 285, 289, 292
Parana Basin, 121
paraphyly, 84, 85, 88, 102
parcellation, 153
pareiasaur, 137, 138, 310
Pareiasauria, 136
parental care, 230, 243
parietal, 10, 28, 32, 33, 87, 139, 141, 212
parietal eye (third eye), 9–11, 173–177, 179–183, 212
parietal foramen, 9, 16, 41, 56, 72, 86–88, 96, 98, 173, 175, 176, 179–183, 208, 211, 212
parietal-pineal complex, 175, 179, 182
parietalectomy, 174
paroccipital process, 33, 86, 87, 95, 100, 267, 270, 277, 287, 289
pars reticulata, 162. *See also* substantia nigra
parsimony, 94, 100, 101
parturition, 241
pathology, bone, 179
pelage, 186, 210
pelvis, 36, 49, 64, 66, 73, 74
pelycosaur, 12, 27, 28, 32–34, 36, 37, 39–41, 43, 44, 47–49, 52, 54, 56–59, 62–64, 67, 68, 71–73, 75, 85, 123, 137, 139, 150, 151, 161, 175, 180, 181, 185, 187, 189, 190, 195, 199, 200–203, 209, 212, 227, 243, 246, 309, 310
Pelycosauria, 5, 6, 64, 188–190, 195, 202, 310
Pennsylvanian Period, 25, 28, 32–34, 36, 37, 39, 185, 246, 309
periodicity:
  environmental, 175, 181, 182
  reproductive, 181, 183
Perm, 134
Permian Period, 1, 6, 7, 28, 32, 33, 39, 42, 47, 57, 58, 62, 71, 75, 80, 81, 110, 113–115, 118, 120, 123, 125, 133, 134, 136–138, 144, 149, 175, 177, 179–183, 185, 186, 188, 201, 208, 213, 246, 247, 267, 308–311, 314, 315
Permian climate, 119
Permian faunas, 120
Permian-Triassic Periods, 109
Permo-Carboniferous interval, 136
Permo-Triassic interval, 134, 136, 227
Persian Gulf, 118
pes, 37, 39, 67, 68, 298
Petrolacosaurus, 31, 32
petroleum source beds, 118
petrosal, 258
phalanges, 9, 16, 56, 69, 74, 77, 140, 298
pharynx, 259, 287, 288
pheromones, 219–222, 225, 226, 228, 230, 245, 246
photoperiod, 181
photoreceptive function, 173, 174
Phreatosuchus, 48, 54–56
Phthinosaurus, 49
Phthinosuchia, 136
phthinosuchian reptile, 6, 52, 137

Phthinosuchidae, 62
Phthinosuchus, 48, 49, 59, 88, 139
phylogeny, 84, 151, 185, 284
physiology, 213
phytolith, 79
phytosaur, 138, 310
Phytosauria, 136
pigeon, 154, 160
piloerection, 11
pineal body, 174, 175, 212
pineal foramen, *See* parietal foramen
pinna, 283, 291
piriform cortex, 14, 15, 159, 163, 224
pituitary fossa, 99
placenta, 240–242, 244, 246
placental mammal, 16, 150, 152, 154, 155, 157–159, 163, 213, 240
placentation, 11, 16, 239–241, 243, 244, 247
Placerias, 54
placodont reptile, 6, 311
plantigrade, 75
plant life, 75, 79, 80, 119
platypus, 151, 157, 158, 213
play, 2, 5
Pleinsbachian Stage, 110, 113
Pleistocene Epoch, 141
plesiomorphy, 83
plesiosaur, 6, 182, 311
pleurocentrum, 28, 34
poikilothermy, 10
polar wander, 110
poles, 113, 118, 119, 139
polyphyodonty, 9, 246
pose, sprawling, 190
position of head, habitual, 76
postcranial structure, 33, 37, 39, 75, 101, 139, 296
postdentary bones, 86, 99, 139, 141, 267, 270, 277
posterior process of dentary, 285
postfrontal, 83, 87, 88, 92, 95
postorbital, 7, 28, 32, 33, 99, 100, 141
postorbital bar, 9, 16, 86, 90, 95, 99
postorbital region, skull, 33
postparietal, 28, 32, 100
posttemporal fossa, 28, 29, 32, 87, 95, 100
posture, 11, 13, 39, 43, 73, 139, 149, 196, 208, 209
Pradtl number, 192
preadaptation, chemical, 220
prearticular, 255, 264, 267, 279, 285, 288
precipitation system, 113
precocial young, 239
predation, 137, 310
predator, 81, 137, 189, 292
predator/prey ratio, 208, 212
predatory habit, 141
preferred temperature, 197
prefrontal, 87, 100
premaxilla, 72, 80, 86–88, 92, 94, 95, 141, 227, 254, 295, 297
preoptic region, 225
preparietal, 52, 72, 87, 92
pretectum, 152
prey, 81, 141, 189, 292, 309, 310
primary consumer, 71
primary palate, 222
primate, 5, 222
prismatic enamel, 103
pristerognathid reptile, 87, 94–96, 246

Pristerognathidae, 63, 95
Pristerognathus, 63, 95
pristerosaurian reptile, 95
proatlas, 28
Probainognathidae, 83, 99, 101, 103
Probainognathus, 14, 15, 83, 101–103, 150, 227, 267, 270, 275–278, 280, 287, 289, 292
Probelesodon, 99, 103, 150, 227
Proburnetia, 92
Procolophonia, 136, 310
procolophonian reptile, 137, 138, 310
procoracoid, 64
procynosuchid reptile, 99, 120, 125
Procynosuchidae, 100
Procynosuchus, 100, 267
productivity, biologic, 118
profile, behavioral, 5
Proganochelys, 311
progesterone, 242, 244
projections:
    accessory olfactory, 224
    olfactory, 224
prolactin, 244
prootic, 87, 95, 100
propulsion, 36
prosthion, 299
protanuran amphibian, 136, 139
Proterosuchia, 136
proterosuchid reptile, 138
Protorogyrinus, 28
protorothyrid reptile, 25, 27, 30, 32–34, 36, 37
Protosuchus, 296
Prototheria, 239
prototherian mammal, 100, 103, 151, 164, 213, 244
Pseudosuchia, 136
pseudosuchian reptile, 138, 150, 310
pterosaur, 310
pterygoid, 27, 28, 49, 87, 91, 92, 96, 99, 254–258, 260, 261, 286
pterygopalatine ridge, 255, 257, 260
pterygoparoccipital foramen, 87
pterygoparoccipital process, 95
Ptilodus, 150
Ptomalestes, 87
pubic tubercle, 36
pubis, 64, 66, 74
pulvinar, 152, 153
putamen, 3, 162
pyramidal cell, 159
Python molurus, 243

quadrate, 10, 12, 16, 28, 32, 72, 76, 77, 86, 87, 92, 98–100, 103, 141, 254, 263–265, 267, 270, 276, 277, 279, 283, 284, 286, 288, 289, 292, 309
quadrate rami of epipterygoid, 288
quadrato-stapedial abutment, 288
quadratojugal, 86, 87, 92, 98, 99, 141, 267, 279, 286
quadrupedal gait, 139, 142

rabbit, 266, 270, 272
radiation, 189, 191, 199
radiolaria, 314
radius, 63, 74
rainfall, 114, 118, 125
rat, 158, 220, 241

rattlesnake, 220, 221, 225, 226
ray, 154
R-complex, 4, 5
receptor:
    opiate, 4
    stretch, 27
recessus mandibularis, 12, 288, 290, 291
reflected lamina, angular, 85–88, 99, 285, 287, 288
reflectivity, 119
Regisaurus, 62, 66–68
reproduction, 43, 181, 225, 239, 244
reptile, 3, 4, 150, 151, 153, 155, 159–161, 163, 164, 181, 196, 197, 208, 210, 211, 213, 221, 224, 227–230, 242–244, 253, 254, 286, 288
Reptilia, 84, 136
reptilian complex, 3–5
resistance to thermal transfer, 191
resonator, 291
respiration, 67, 211, 245
reticular formation, 163, 164
reticulospinal system, 163
retina, 152, 160, 173, 174
retinal projection, 152
retroarticular process, articular, 86, 255, 257, 285, 286, 290
Reynolds number, 192
Rhaetic Stage, 285, 286, 288
rhinarium, 230
rhipidistian fish, 32
Rhodesia, 120
rhombencephalon, 155
Rhopalodon, 63
Rhynchocephalia, 6, 136, 138, 310
rhynchocephalian reptile, 6, 173, 182, 212, 310
rhynchosaur, 138, 310
ribs, 73, 101, 140
rift, 110
rings, fossil wood, 181
rodent, 13, 277
Rodentia, 241
rooting, 310
rostrum, 308
Rubidgea, 137
Rubidgina, 85, 88
Rubidginidae, 88
ruffing of feathers, 11
Ruhuhu, 120, 144
Russia, 6, 39, 62, 88, 125, 134, 137
Russian Platform, 123

saber-tooth, 137
sacral ribs, 36, 73
sacrum, 73, 139
sagittal crest, 87, 88, 96, 98, 99
sail, pelycosaurian, 190, 195, 196, 199, 200, 202, 203, 301
salamander, 28, 153
salivary gland, 287
San Angelo Formation, 48, 52, 58
Santa Maria Formation, 144
Santagulov mine, 48
Saurischia, 136, 310
saurischian reptile, 138, 139, 142
sauropsid reptile, 283, 286, 289, 290, 292
Sauropsida, 84
Sauropterygia, 310
sauropterygian reptile, 310, 311

Scalenodon, 123, 127
scales, 210
scaloposaur, 62, 95, 180, 181
Scaloposauria, 95
Scaloposauridae, 63
scapula, 36, 63, 139
scapulocoracoid, 34, 63
scavenging habit, 137
Sceloporus, 197, 221, 226, 241, 242
Scincella lateralis, 221
Scotland, 121
Scymnognathus parringtoni, 62
sea-floor spreading, 134
sea-lion, 311
seal, 311
seasonality, 114, 125, 181–183, 199, 202, 213, 301
sebaceous glands, 11, 230
Sebecus, 150
secondary palate, 9, 10, 16, 72, 95, 96, 99, 101–103, 139, 141, 208, 210, 222, 227, 228, 245, 246, 254–256, 260
secretory function, 174
sediments:
    climatically sensitive, 113, 119
    continental, 125
seed ferns, 309
semicircular canals, horizontal, 76
sensory area, 157
sensory modality, 153
sensory structures, peripheral, 142, 220, 224
septomaxilla, 86, 227, 297
septum, 155, 160
sequence, pelycosaur-therapsid-mammal, 161
serotonin, 4
sexual maturity, *Anolis,* 180
shark, 153–155, 242
shearing mechanism, 76
sheep, 182
shoreline, 110
shoulder girdle, 36, 63, 73
signalling, chemical, 220–222, 227
Sinkiang, 121, 122, 125
sinus venosus, 214
sirenian mammal, 174
size, body, 39, 43
skeleton, 61, 62
    appendicular, 61
    postcranial, 27
skid-plate, 78
skin glands, 190, 229
skull, 33, 56, 61, 71, 72, 85, 92, 139, 141, 175, 210, 246, 253, 258, 265, 296, 299, 310
smell, 143
snake, 6, 25, 43, 150, 153, 154, 160, 225, 226, 240, 289
snow, 118, 119, 181
social behavior, 219
soft palate, 253, 255, 256, 258, 261
solar radiation, 114, 118, 119, 189
Somalia, 118
somatosensory area, 152, 154, 158
somatosensory cortex, 159
sound reception, 291
sound, air borne, 43, 288–290, 292, 309
South Africa, 1, 2, 6, 7, 39, 52, 62, 67, 71, 75, 88, 90, 119–123, 125, 127, 134, 137, 142, 144, 181, 213, 295, 310, 315

South America, 2, 119, 122, 123, 125, 127, 144
Soviet Union, 48, 49, 52, 57, 58
spacing, 220, 221, 228, 230
Spence's cartilage, 290
Sphenacodon, 58
sphenacodont pelycosaur, 6, 32–34, 36, 39–41, 47, 54–58, 62, 64, 85, 86, 88, 123, 137, 189, 190, 195, 203, 212, 285, 286, 310
Sphenacodontia, 28
Sphenodon, 37, 40, 42, 43, 150, 173, 174, 182, 212, 228, 289
sphenodontid reptile, 25
Sphenophyllum, 79
sphenopsid plant, 309
spinal cord, 152, 159, 161, 162–164
splenial, 285, 288
Spur, Oklahoma, 177
Squamata, 6, 310
squamate reptile, 42, 222, 224, 240, 243, 246
squamosal, 7, 10, 28, 32, 86, 87, 92, 95, 98–101, 103, 141, 264, 267, 270, 277, 283, 286–288, 291, 309
squamosal sulcus, 287, 289, 291
stapedial process, quadrate, 100, 289
stapes, 28, 32, 43, 72, 87, 141, 265, 267, 270, 283, 284, 286, 288–290, 309
Stefan-Boltzmann constant, 192
stellar evolution, 119
stem reptile, 6, 150, 151, 227
Steppesaurus, 52
stereospondylous amphibian, 138, 311
sternum, 73
stirnorgan, 173
stomach contents, 71
strain, 266
striatal complex, 4
striated floors, 119
striatum, 15, 155, 161–163
stride length, 75
Struthiocephalus, 64
Styracocephalus, 92
subduction, 314
subequatorial regions, 128
suborbital vacuity, palate, 87, 96
substantia nigra, 162
substrate lick, 226
subtemporal region, skull, 91
subtropical environment, 125, 127, 136
success, 139
suckling habit, 11, 149, 230, 246, 247,
sulcal pattern, 150
sulcus pharyngis submandibularis, 259, 260, 288
summer, 114, 115, 118
superior colliculus, 162, 163
supinator process, 36
supra-acetabular process, 52, 55
supraoccipital, 27, 28, 32, 33, 87, 100, 175
supratemporal, 28, 32, 86
surangular, 72, 88, 90, 96, 99, 101, 103, 264, 267, 270, 277, 279, 285, 288
surface area in heat exchange, 186, 187
surface characteristics, global, 118
suspensorium, skull, 91, 286, 292
sustentaculum tali, 67, 68
sweat glands, 11, 190, 214, 230
symmetrodont mammal, 16, 279
symphysis, dentary, 272, 274, 277, 278, 280

symplesiomorphy, 83
synapomorphy, 84, 88, 90, 94, 95, 98, 101–103
synapsid reptile, 6, 25, 85, 88, 123, 128, 150, 151, 161, 164, 175, 181, 182, 195, 203, 220, 227, 228, 240, 243, 246, 261, 283–285, 287, 289, 290, 291, 309, 310
Synapsida, 1, 84, 285, 286
Syodon, 88, 90

tabular, 28, 32, 87
tail, 44, 62–64, 75, 186, 190, 299
Tanzania, 120, 121
Tapinocephalia, 90
tapinocephalian reptile, 52, 62–64, 66, 88, 90–92, 125, 137, 141
Tapinocephalidae, 88, 92
Tapinocephalus Zone, 9, 67
Tappenosaurus, 49, 50, 55
tarsus, 28, 37, 68, 299
teats, 247
technique, retrograde degeneration, 152, 153, 158
teeth, 9, 10, 16, 41, 49, 61, 86–88, 91, 94–96, 98–100, 139–141, 149, 245, 266, 267, 272, 273, 275–280, 296, 297, 299–303, 310
telencephalic projection, 161
telencephalon, 3, 150, 152, 154, 155, 159–161, 164
temperature differential, 188
temperature gradient 113, 118
temperature regulation, 195
temperature tolerance, 127
temporal fenestra, 6, 9, 16, 27, 28, 32, 33, 49, 72, 84, 86–88, 90, 100, 139, 141, 288
temporal region of skull, 51, 86–88, 91, 92, 96
tenrec, 13, 144, 272–276, 279, 280
Tenrec ecaudatus, 270, 272, 275
terrestrial communities, 57
terrestrial vertebrate, 134
territoriality, 221, 228
Tethys, 115, 118, 127
tetrapod, 27, 32, 120, 125, 134, 136, 138, 139, 143, 152, 155, 161, 175, 181, 182, 212, 220, 222, 241
Texas, 39, 41, 48, 57, 122, 181
thalamic nuclei, 158
thalamocingulate structures, 6
thalamus, 152, 154, 156, 159, 160, 162–165
  caudal, 153
  rostral ventral, 153
Thamnophis radix, 225
thecodont reptile, 127, 134, 138, 310
Thecodontia, 310
therapsid reptile, 6, 9–11, 14, 16, 28, 34, 39, 47, 54, 85, 86, 88, 89, 92, 94, 100, 110, 120, 123, 125, 127, 133, 134, 136–142, 144, 149–151, 161, 175, 176, 180–183, 185–187, 190, 203, 208–210, 212–215, 227, 228, 230, 240, 244, 246, 247, 255, 261, 265, 267, 273, 276, 279, 280, 285–291, 298, 307–311, 315
Therapsida, 2, 6, 61, 83, 84, 88, 120, 121, 136, 189, 207, 307, 310
Theria, 240, 244, 247
therian mammal, 103, 151, 155, 159,

208, 213, 214, 244, 254, 257, 258, 260, 272, 283, 292
theriodont reptile, 58, 61, 62, 71, 73, 74, 81, 86, 92, 94, 96, 98, 142, 211, 214, 285, 286, 308–311
Theriodontia, 6, 7, 84, 88, 92, 93, 95
Theriognathus, 87, 95, 96, 98, 100
thermal physiology, 186, 190, 191, 199, 213, 241
thermophily, 127
thermoregulation, 5, 10, 11, 81, 143, 174, 175, 181, 183, 186, 188, 191, 195, 196, 200, 202, 208–210, 212–215, 241, 246
Therocephalia, 61–63, 67, 68, 94, 96, 100, 120–123, 136, 191
therocephalian reptile, 9, 10, 39, 47, 62, 64, 66, 68, 69, 75, 81, 83, 86, 87, 93–96, 98, 125, 137–139, 141, 176, 180, 209, 210, 227, 246, 255, 256, 264, 285, 287, 288, 291
thoracic region, 139, 140
Thrinaxodon, 11, 101, 123, 185, 210, 211, 227, 229, 246, 253, 254, 267, 275, 276, 280, 287, 309
thrinaxodontid reptile, 99
Thrinaxodontidae, 101
Tibetan Plateau, 114, 115
tibia, 36, 62, 74
tibial condyle, 74
tibiale, 28
tillites, 110, 113, 119, 123
Titanophoneus, 62, 63, 66, 88, 90, 91
Titanosuchia, 88
titanosuchian reptile, 52, 62, 88, 90, 91, 137, 141, 209
Titanosuchidae, 90, 92
TMJ, 265, 266
tongue, 221, 226, 228
tooth row, movement of, 302, 303
torpidity, 213
torso, 186, 199
tract, lateral olfactory, 15
transition, evolutionary, 44, 102, 149, 151, 152, 157, 161, 163, 164, 222, 242, 246, 258
transverse process, 34, 37, 55
traversodont reptile, 99–102, 276
Traversodontidae, 99, 102
tree rings, 213
Triassic Period, 1, 6, 7, 26, 47, 54, 62, 74, 75, 80, 81, 95, 110, 113–115, 118, 119, 121, 123, 125, 127, 133, 134, 136–139, 141, 142, 144, 149, 150, 175, 180, 182, 183, 208, 213, 215, 246, 247, 267, 292, 295, 308–311, 315
Triassic faunas, 120
trichotomy, 90, 98
Triconodon, 150
triconodont mammal, 13, 16, 150, 151, 272, 292
Triconodontidae, 292
trigeminal foramen, 100
trigeminal nerve, 96, 257, 283
Trirachodon, 150, 267, 270, 285, 286
Trirhachodontidae, 99, 102
trithelodont reptile, 139, 265, 270, 285, 286
Trithelodontidae, 100, 120
Tritylodon, 296, 297, 299
tritylodont reptile, 9, 81, 99–103, 122, 127, 139–142, 209, 227, 265, 270,

276, 277, 285, 286, 288, 290, 295–297, 300
Tritylodontia, 185
Tritylodontidae, 99, 102, 295–297
Tritylodontoidea, 100, 102, 136, 200
Tritylodontoideus, 103, 299
trochanter, 64, 66, 67
trophic system, 57, 59
tropics, 125, 136, 202, 212
Tseajaia, 28
Tseajaiidae, 27
tuatara, 222
tubercle, olfactory, 3
Tuditanus, 28
Tunisia, 127
Tupinambis, 210, 255, 256
turbinal bones, 10, 208, 210, 211, 214
turtle, 26, 32, 40, 41, 43, 72, 84, 139, 150, 151, 155, 161, 164, 175, 189, 222, 311
tusk, dicynodont, 72, 76–79, 141, 308
tympanic annulus, 260, 264, 292
tympanic bone, 283, 284
tympanic cavity, 260
tympanic ear, 309
tympanic process of stapes, 287
tympanum, 28, 33, 43, 264, 270, 279, 284, 288–292, 309

Ulemosaurus, 123, 125
ulna, 74

upwelling current, 118
uricotely, 81
urodele, 222
USA, 47, 49, 57, 120, 122, 123, 127, 137
USSR, 110, 120–123, 125, 127, 139, 144
Utah, 308
uterus, 242

Vale Formation, 39
Varanosaurus, 5, 6
Varanus, 43, 197
vascularity, oviductal, 241, 242
vascularization, of bone, 10
velum, 257, 258, 260, 261
Venjukovia, 54, 55, 91, 92, 120
venjukovioid, 88, 91, 92
Venjukovioidea, 90, 92
ventilation, 140, 211, 245
vertebrae, 33, 34, 52, 54–56, 73, 139, 140, 297, 299
vibrissae, 10, 11, 16, 142, 210, 228
visual area, 160
visual sense, 143
viviparity, 11, 74, 149, 239, 240–242, 244, 246, 247
vocal amplification, 291, 292, 309
vocalization, 12, 309
volcanic activity, 314
vomer, 83, 86–88, 92, 94–96, 100, 254, 256, 260

vomeronasal organ, 221, 222, 224–228, 244

wallaby, 158
Watongia, 39, 48, 49, 52, 54, 56, 57, 59, 209
weather patterns, zonal, 113, 114
Westphalian Stage, 110
Whaitsia, 63, 98
whaitsiid reptile, 87, 94, 96, 98, 141
Whaitsiidae, 63, 95, 98
whale, 182
Wichita Group, 57
winds, 113, 118
Wingate Sandstone, 298
winter, 114, 115, 221
Wolfcampian Stage, 57, 144

Yunnan, 122
younginid reptile, 137, 138

Zambesi Valley, 120
Zambia, 121
Zones I–IV, Permian, USSR, 144
Zorillodontops, 62
zygapophysis, 28, 34, 73
zygomatic arch, 76, 77, 80, 86, 87, 90, 99, 100, 275, 287, 291